The Bothell Hell House:

Poltergeist of Washington State

2.0

By Keith Linder

In Memory of

Rhonda Lee Jimenez and Maria José Ferreira

Contents

Foreword

Imagine that your home is under attack. Improbable fires start spontaneously, utterly baffling the attending firemen. Doors are slammed; yanked off their hinges; broken in half. A cupboard weighing over 200 pounds is thrown around the hall. Personal items are stolen; Bibles set on fire. You are advised to improve your home monitoring and security. You do so. State of the art alarms, infrared trip beams, and numerous cameras enabling remote real-time monitoring are put in place. The attacks get worse. Not only that but before long it is clear that you, in particular, are being singled out. In old group photographs, your face is burned away. As you lie in bed trying to catch up on lost sleep, something dents the mattress. Completely invisible, but with definite weight, it comes padding towards you. The words "Die KL" are written in snow on your lawn; on your office walls; inside your car. Leaving the house one day, you find your shirt is open. Every button has disappeared.

All this and much more happened to Keith Linder and his girlfriend after they moved into a new, ordinary looking house in Bothell, Washington State. The police could not help. As you may have guessed, the attacker was not strictly human. The best guess is that it was a poltergeist or several poltergeists. I began studying these by chance in 2013 when researching a non-fiction book on vampire beliefs. I had managed to understand most of the strange things people said or did in vampire territory; but could not get my head around repeated claims (from the 1590s to the 1920s) that the vampire threw stones, furniture, beat people up, or hammered on their walls or roof. Enter the poltergeist.

I have spent the early part of my career, at two British universities, studying strange things: the search for the soul; the history of European medicinal cannibalism; the surprising uses of human fat, urine, blood, and excrement... Nothing has been stranger than the poltergeist. I actually heard my first poltergeist story almost thirty years ago. It was told by my old A-level Sociology teacher to our class. Mike was and is the most straightforward, no-nonsense person, and indeed agnostic about religion. And so, I had the strange experience of hearing something I could not believe, from someone I could not disbelieve. You may have that feeling yourself reading Keith's story. Poltergeists make your head hurt. They rip up and trample on many of the basic rules, laws, frameworks we have put in place to understand the world.

At the same time, they broadly obey their own laws and patterns. I know this, because I have collected hundreds of poltergeist cases spanning hundreds of years. The events in these stories are themselves bizarre. Yet in some ways they were not the strangest part of my journey through poltergeist country. In a way, the strangest thing about poltergeist country (a place which should lie right off ordinary maps of the known world) is that it is right beside you; all around you. Within days of reading up systematically on poltergeists, I started talking to my friends about them. Two of these were people I had known for seven and twelve years respectively. Both had suffered poltergeists. Until I raised the subject, they had never breathed a word of their experiences—even though in one case this was emphatically the worst thing they had ever known. Over following months and years, the same thing happened time and again. Friends, acquaintances, students, had all experienced poltergeists or ghosts. (In one case, purely by chance, I asked a group of just four students if they'd ever known this—immediately one woman put her hand up.)

There is, then, a pretty good chance that you know someone who has suffered a poltergeist haunting or seen a ghost. In many cases, they will not have told you. We now live in a world which values openness very highly. Only quite recently, victims of sexual abuse have started talking about things which traumatized them, sometimes after years of silence. Yet the ghost and the poltergeist have become new taboos. I sympathize with the incredulity (even anger) of people coming to this subject for the first time. But it really does happen. What it means is quite another question. I have no desire to push particular agendas about the afterlife or religion. I just want to know more about this, the strangest, most extraordinary topic I have encountered in decades of researching forgotten or marginal subjects.

If you also want to know, then read the full accounts of poltergeist cases. Listen to the people who were actually there. Go beyond the internet; beyond Wikipedia. Go beyond the false skepticism of people who say: 'There's got to be a rational explanation.' The poltergeist is a rational explanation. It just requires you to start thinking in different ways about what is possible or reasonable.

We should study poltergeists because they are extraordinary. They offer new ways to think about the powers of the human mind and body; about science; and about the history of the supernatural. And we should also study them for one other basic reason. When they happen, they can make someone's life hell. What if the worst thing that ever happens to you is something nobody will believe? Not only that, but you, the victim, will be attacked, ridiculed, derided by perhaps half the people who hear your story. You will have witnesses—perhaps including the police. You will have evidence—possibly sound recordings, photos, and video footage. But to the people who find your story somehow attacking their whole basic worldview, this will mean nothing. You must be denied, disproved, at all costs. So, the attacks will get personal; devious; nasty. Try to imagine, for comparison, these attacks being made on someone who had suffered ordinary criminal assaults.

When Keith Linder e-mailed me over a year ago, it was the briefest, most unremarkable few lines. He had heard that I was collecting poltergeist stories. Well, he had one I should hear. This was not the behavior of some crazy attention-seeker. As I learned over many Skype and email exchanges in coming weeks, it was in fact not even from someone who had ever experienced the supernatural at all until his early forties. All he did was move into the wrong house.

For almost thirty years it has been my vocation and my job to read—fiction, non-fiction; great plays, poetry, novels, and forgotten real-life histories. Keith's book is one of the most extraordinary books I have ever read. This is a real person telling you directly about something that was hell to live through, and very hard to relive, again, in the telling. It is a record of great honesty and great courage. It is worth bearing in mind that I only know this story because I decided to ignore the bewilderment of many academic colleagues and write publicly about ghosts and poltergeists. It is time to start talking seriously about this subject. If you read just one work of non-fiction this year, make it this one. When you have finished, tell your friends. You may be surprised by what you hear.

Richard Sugg
January 2018.
Author of "A Century of Ghost Stories"
rishardjsugg@yahoo.co.uk

Breath

Introduction

The German philosopher Friedrich Nietzsche once said, "That which does not kill us, makes us stronger." That proverb holds true for those who've lived in a haunted house. That's what my girlfriend and I did. We moved into a haunted house. From 2012 to 2016 is how long I stayed there. What we witnessed in my opinion exceeds the definition of what a haunted house is. Might even exceed the definition of what a malevolent haunting is. As you read this book, try to understand: no one knowingly moves into a haunted house. Not the kind of haunted house I'm about to talk about. The activity Tina and I experienced didn't begin right away. I mean things sort of percolated over time. Think gradual. 'Make yourselves comfortable, relax a little bit, unpack your stuff and oh by the way we're going to take a few things. 'You won't miss them right away but trust us you will miss them. Eventually.'

Think about it for a second: if a spirit doesn't want you in the house, why allow you to move into it in the first place? Why not throw something as the realtor is showing you around? Why not start a fire Why not drop a couch from the ceiling? Or any number of things which would cause the people to change their minds about taking the house? Someone reading this book right now might say *well spirits don't think like that, spirits are not intelligent. Not in that way.* To that I will say, I'm glad you bought this book. I have no doubt those with open minds will think differently upon the completion of this book. Allow me to share with you every activity we experienced while living in the Bothell home. Allow me to adopt the mindset I had on April 30th, 2012.

Odds are you bought this book it's because you already have some familiarity with this case. Your knowledge of it could have come from social media, or the internet. Maybe you saw an episode on Travel Channel's *Ghost Adventures* slot, titled "Demons in Seattle". Maybe that show left you with more questions than answers. *Was the couple telling the truth? Did it happen the way they say it happened?* Or maybe you found this book because you or someone you know is dealing with something similar or dealt with something similar in the past. If that's true, my thoughts and prayers are with you. Regardless of how you found this book, you, the reader, deserve a huge thank you.

This experience has taught me many things; one of the most important lessons it's taught me is to never get defensive about what you've gone through. Those that have seen something, have heard something, have felt something are not the ones who are crazy. The ones who are crazy are the people who give house occupants a tough time. The ones who are crazy are the ones who, after seeing the activity, make it their mission to now downplay them. The ones who are crazy are the paranormal teams who think that, if the activity doesn't reveal itself to them during the brief period they are conducting their investigation, then the activity being reported are not real. I can't tell how many teams came to me and Tina saying, "Nothing's paranormal until we say it's paranormal." Pray that type of arrogance never enters your home. If you're familiar with our story, the first question you probably want answered is: is everything we said that took place true? I can assure you that everything I've said is true. Everything my girlfriend has said and those close to us have said is completely true.

I'm still having trouble sleeping. You just can't tap me on my shoulder and say, "Keith, I have something to tell you." Not anymore. That freaks me out now. Every night before going to bed, I ask myself the question, 'is tonight the night they come back? Is tonight the night they come to yank the sheets off the bed in the middle of me sleeping? Will I ever hear a growl in my ear while taking a nap?' Those questions will make more sense to you by the time we reach the end of this book.

But we're going to go deeper than that kind of fear. Way deeper. My goal is to take you on a journey, a journey of uncertainty, a journey of isolation and frustration. You got questions? I have answers. One of the reasons for me writing this book is to answer those questions. To set the record straight on what might be out there about this case. Take comfort in knowing, I will not be pulling punches. Nor will I be exaggerating. It is what it is. No filter. No softening it up or dumbing it down. I'm not changing my story with the hopes of becoming more marketable. Some have asked me to—I've told them no.

One of the biggest obstacles Tina and I ran into when trying to get help was people thinking our claims were "It's too good to be true; no human being could survive what you've described." That response didn't come only from the paranormal community. It came from religious organizations. It came from friends and family. If you watched the "Demons in Seattle" *Ghost Adventures* episode, then you know it was pretty much implied that Tina and I were either making it up or exaggerating. In short, we were put on the defensive. Well, today is your lucky day. Today I'm on the offensive. Today I get to tell the true story.

So, you, the reader, are in good hands. You're getting the truth from the person who lived in the house. I will be one hundred percent honest in my account. I will describe everything we saw and everything that we heard. I'm going to share the emotions we had before, during, and after each activity. It's very important that I do that. What separates this story from previous accounts is that this case has been exceptionally well-documented. What other case do you know of where the evidence is easily accessible? I'm not talking about evidence sitting in the vaults of the SPR or some other paranormal organization, I'm talking about evidence made available to you the reader. Don't hurry to the back of the book. Trust me: it's better if you review the evidence in the order of when it occurred versus hurrying to the end. Let the evidence and statements from the previous tenant find you like it found us. It'll mean more, trust me.

I only have one request before we start this journey: Suspend for the duration of this book what you think you know about spirits. What you think you know about poltergeists. About ghosts. About demons. Most of what you know and believe will not make sense here. I sincerely mean that. We are on new ground where malevolent spirits are concerned. Are you ready? I hope not. We weren't. Let's go.

Chapter 1
May 1st, 2012

Everyone I've encountered since this ordeal began has tried to give Tina and me their definition of what we've experienced. Some have tried to school us. Others have tried to dumb it all down with the hopes of minimizing what took place. Those who have tried have failed miserably because they don't know what actually took place. How can you minimize something if you weren't there? I have spent most of my adult life going through the motion of reminding myself what it is I know and don't know. I thought I was doing OK balancing the two. I soon realized I wasn't doing OK. Not even close. I realized this within months of living in the Bothell home. Now try to understand for a second where Tina and I live. We live in Bothell, WA. What's a Bothell? Bothell is a quiet suburb outside of Seattle. As far as towns go, it's average. It's quaint. No matter what direction you look, everything, for the most part, looks the same. There are mountains, trees, and a little bit of water in and around the area. I'm not going to say we live in the woods, except to say that we have a town just south of us named Woodinville.

So, pretend you're me for a second. Pretend you're talking to a receptionist at a parish office or you're talking to the president of a local paranormal chapter. You tell them you're experiencing some loud bangs. You and your girlfriend have seen doors open and close by themselves. We hear pacing in the hallway. Items go missing. Scratching noises are happening and, oh, I almost forgot—our bar stool just rose and flew across the room. Their response? Silence. I'm pretty sure you (the person on the other end of the phone) have a lot of questions. So, I'm going to be quiet now. It's your turn to talk. Please ask me a question. Go!

Guess what their first question was after I told them all of that? "Sir: you probably have some raccoons in your house. I mean, it's possible you have a hole in your attic; that's probably how they got in." That's the response that we got when we began reaching out to people. That was at the beginning.

May 1st, 2012. I can remember that day as if it was yesterday. The sky was blue, the grass on the lawn we were about to walk past was green. The community was beautiful. I wasn't nervous at all about moving in with my girlfriend. Not that day. I was proud. I had accomplished something. Going from a one-bedroom apartment to a four-bedroom house was an accomplishment in my eyes. I was here to sign papers. I couldn't wait to see the room that would eventually be my office.

There we were, Tina and me, walking up the driveway. I think we even held hands as we made our way to the front door. That's how excited we were. I had found this house on Craigslist, a few months ago and contacted the landlord for a viewing. He told me he couldn't show it because a family was still in it. I thought to myself *why is it on Craigslist then*? He must really want someone to move within weeks of someone moving out. He would get his wish, because here we were—three months later, Tina and me. Since we're in the time of when Tina and I were moving I want to answer a question I often get from people. Did we experience anything similar when living elsewhere? Did we have activity in our previous homes? The answer is no, we did not. Neither of us had activity in the apartments we lived in before.

The house we were about to move in seemed like your normal vacant house. Nothing seemed unusual. The house was built in 2005, which I thought was cool—*that's the year I moved to the Pacific Northwest.* The landlord let us in when we got to the front door and walked us to the kitchen. That's where we signed the lease papers. After a few minutes of chit-chatting, the landlord handed us the keys, shook both our hands, congratulated us, and left. That's it. Just me and Tina and a bottle of wine that the landlord gave us. Time to tour the entire house again. Time to see where Tina and I would reside for the next few years. So, we walked upstairs and look around. Tina declared what rooms would be hers and what room would be mine. Ten minutes later we decided to head back downstairs and sat in the living room-the room closest to the front door. We were surveying the house from where we were sitting. I mean we were talking, laughing, and toying with each other. Hundred percent light-hearted conversation when... out of the blue, we heard a kid 'cough.'

Now, we all know sounds can resemble other sounds; a kid's cough is no exception. But this was different. I mean this really sounded like a kid's cough. I looked at Tina; she looked at me; and we both said at precisely the same time: Was that a kid cough? It sounded like it came from one of the rooms upstairs. I mean the sound was very distinct. I later learned that a kid's cough could have very easily come from within a few feet of Tina and me. It would seem spirits are masters at throwing their voice. Masters at deceiving. Something I was to learn more about much later. One thing is for certain, we both heard a kid 'cough.' I mean we talked about the cough for a few more minutes before finally disavowing it. It never dawned on us to go upstairs. Why would we? The thought never entered our mind that this was a ghost. We agreed it must have come from outside, without ever looking outside to see.

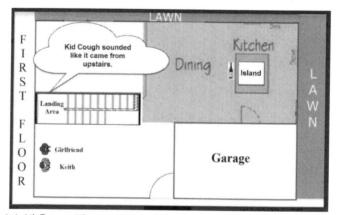

Fig 1.1 1st floor - Tina and I are sitting downstairs and hear a kid cough.

Two weeks after I moved in, I noticed my extra car key was missing. Now, these were not the keys I use every day. No, these were my spare set of car keys. There's no reason whatsoever as to why they were missing. I noticed a few days later that other items were missing: forks, spoons, cups, Tina's jewelry, and other easy to forget items. The funny thing about silverware is you only miss it when you need it.

I remember one day I turned from the dishwasher and asked Tina, 'Hey, I thought we had more forks than this? What's happening to our silverware?" We were still not yet connecting the dots. Why would we? The items that went missing were small. There had to be a logical explanation. Maybe Tina miscounted the amount of silverware we had? Maybe some got lost during the move? I had no clue as to why they were missing. All I knew was some were missing. The fact that we were having a conversation about missing forks and spoons meant they'd disappeared significantly. It wouldn't surprise me if there were items the ghost took that Tina and I to this day still don't know are missing. I mean these are little items that eventually add up over time. In retrospect, Tina and I were being sized up within minutes of walking into the house. I'm talking about May 1st. There was no logical culprit at the time other than ourselves. It's far too early to start finger-pointing—trust me, the finger pointing will happen soon enough. The spirits are going to make sure of that. In the meantime, where are my car keys?

Chapter 2
Banging

"Gentleman, you had my curiosity, now you have my attention."
(Django Unchained)

The first object to go flying in my house was an ivory plant located in our living room. It was your typical weeknight. I came home from work, still on cloud nine about qualifying for the house. I had been working in my office for a few hours and the idea hit me: I should watch a movie with my girlfriend. So, I went downstairs and asked Tina if she wanted to watch a movie with me. Fast forward to me holding Tina in my arms. We were about thirty minutes into the movie, when all of a sudden, the plant by the entertainment center rose. I mean literally—six inches off the ground, and very quickly too. It then done a complete spin and fell back on the floor. This happened in a matter of seconds. I looked at Tina and she looked at me. WTF? Our facial expressions said it all. Did that just happen? Did I just see a plant rise off the ground (no strings), do a spin, and fall over? Is that what I saw? It must be, because the plant was still laying there on the ground. It wasn't lying on the ground twenty seconds ago. At that moment in time, I thought this was the joke of all jokes. Somebody was having fun at our expense.

Tina and I leaped up from the couch and walked over to the plant. Tina stood it back up again. I immediately began looking for strings—a remote control device. I'm thinking to myself, *ok, this is somebody's joke. Someone figured out a way to make this plant float right in front of our eyes. Is someone trying to punk us?* Tina and I inspected the plant for several minutes, even re-enacting the part of it levitating, spinning, and falling over. I remember grabbing the plant by the pole, spinning it around with my hand, and then knocking it over. The only part we couldn't duplicate was the part where it levitated. As for trickery? Nothing was visible to the naked eye. No strings, no cords or wire. Nothing.

We gave up trying to duplicate what just happened. There were just two possibilities now. Either someone was playing a joke on us, which would be the joke of the century in my opinion, or we had a ghost on our hands. The only logical explanation was a spirit did this. I mean, let's use our God-given common sense. Plants can't fly. Plants can't levitate. Plants can't rise off the ground (on their own authority) and spin three hundred and sixty degrees. I don't need a paranormal investigator to tell me that. Neither does Tina. What are we left to think? Tina and me were left thinking we have a ghost on our hands.

Now, before you begin screaming at me, saying pack up, leave now! Understand something. This happened a few weeks after we moved in. We were still unpacking. I had a rental agreement on my hands and no clue whatsoever as to how to break it. We gave the landlord the first and last month's rent. We gave him a deposit, not to mention the moving expenses. If I go to my landlord now and say we want to move and here's why. How do you think he's going to react?

If I tell my landlord we can't stay here because we saw a plant rise off the ground (on its own), what do you think his response will be? I'm not going to lie to him. I can't lie to you and I can't lie to him. Our reason for moving would be we saw a plant float in the air—see ya and wouldn't wanna be ya. I can't do that and neither could Tina. We spent a lot of money to get into this house. Moving was not an option.

If we up and move now, that's six thousand dollars gone. Not to mention another six thousand to move elsewhere. We'd have to start this process all over again. How could we find another a place to live having just broken our lease? It took me four months to find this house. I'm not saying we were trapped. I'm just saying we knew very little right now. I wasn't scared and neither was Tina. If a spirit wanted to levitate Tina's plant, go for it. Do what you feel is right, Mr. Ghost. I mean we're not talking demon here. I'm thinking to myself, *oh, that's what the kid 'cough' was about. We have a kid spirit living with us. That's cute. I wonder where it came from? Why is it here?* The fact that the plant actually levitated sort of reminded me of the book "A Brief History of Time." I read Stephen Hawking's book when I was in the tenth grade. It blew my mind away. Seeing that plant levitate was like reading his book. Now I got a plant floating in mid-air. What the heck is going on?

I'm so glad I saw this with Tina. I mean how do you explain this to your significant other? Had Tina seen this by herself and told me afterward, I might not have believed her. It would take some serious convincing. Would I have called her a liar? No, I wouldn't do that. I would have thought she had misinterpreted what she saw. Tina would have been pissed at me for saying that. And rightfully so.

Now, if I had come to Tina with the same scenario? I know Tina. Tina would laugh in my face and say "whatever." She'd go on about her business. That's why I'm so glad we saw it together. Which raises a good question of why did the spirit do this in front of both of us?

There have been a few weird things happening as of late. I mean weird sounds. Weird knocking. Thuds and thumps were coming from behind the walls of the house. An occasional light flickering. We ignored all of it. Maybe the spirits were growing tired of us shrugging things off. Maybe they said 'let's do something they won't be able to shrug off. Let's do something that gets their attention. Let's take away their ambiguity.' So, we now have two inexplicable events taking place when Tina and I are together. A kid's 'cough' and a floating plant. I don't know about you, but it seems the seal had finally been broken. I mean, stuff really picked up after that night. Plants began flying just about every night. I'm not talking about levitation. I'm talking about plants being thrown.

There was a plant sitting on a pillar in the corner of the living room. I remember where I was the first time that plant got thrown. Tina was upstairs. I was sitting at the kitchen table working at my laptop when all of a sudden, I saw movement out the corner of my eye. A blur. Something hit the wall in the room next to me. Whatever hit the wall, broke on impact. I rose from my chair and walked over to where I heard the noise. It doesn't take long to realize what just happened. As soon as I turned the corner, I saw the plant resting on the floor. Debris was everywhere. Tina came from upstairs, once again we were both saying something to the effect of what the hell. I won't say that we were scared. I mean we were still caught between kid ghost and someone pranking us. *Someone's pranking us is pretty damn good.* If it's a kid ghost, then it must be throwing a temper tantrum. Or maybe Tina and I are being punked? I mean we live in that era now of people punking people. Maybe this was our initiation? I ask myself the question, "How is somebody able to do this from outside our house?" That's my brain at work, trying to rationalize what happened. My common-sense gene is telling me that it's impossible to do this from the outside. You couldn't even do this from inside the house. So many variables would have to be at play. I mean you would need Tina or myself to be in cahoots with you to make this prank work. And it would still be next to impossible to pull off.

I must admit during this phase of plants being thrown; I began to backtrack a little bit. Time to revisit the other events we witnessed. I told you about the lights flickering. That happened a lot. I remember asking myself the question, why is a house as young as this having electrical issues? What's up with the house noise? I know houses have to settle, new homes especially. This is the loudest house settling noise I've ever heard.

Another thing I ignored after we moved in which was very well apparent, was the knocking noise I heard coming from behind the wall. I'm talking about tapping sounds. Almost like Morse code. What's interesting about these tapping sounds is we could hear them throughout the house. I heard it in our bedroom closet. I heard it in my office. I heard it when I went downstairs in the morning and I heard it when I was leaving the house. Where is it coming from? It's coming from the walls. Correction: it's coming from behind the walls. But our first reaction was never ghost. Was never demon. All houses have their own characteristics. Minus the flying plants, everything else just might be house characteristics.

Another thing I'd noticed within weeks of moving in and this happens all the time—the scattering about i.e. pitter-patter footsteps. I mean you come home from work and walk into your house and all of sudden you hear something running away. Seriously! You open the front door and as soon as you do, you hear what sounds like someone running upstairs. It's like we interrupted a meeting or something. The sound is clear, it's very real. It feels like someone is home. I went room to room one day, looking for someone. I thought we had a burglar in the house. That's how real the noise was: pitter-patter, pitter-patter—the sound trails upstairs. Towards the direction of where we heard the kid 'cough'. So, I'm revaluating everything now. I mean I sort of have to after the levitating plant incident.

Then came the loud bangs. Without warning is the best way to describe them. No precursor: just loud, continuous banging. These were not bangs one would associate with house noise. (Or better yet mischaracterize as being raccoons in the attic.) These bangs sounded like someone hitting the wooden beams with a sledgehammer. Always in sets of three. Tina and I were in different parts of the house when we began hearing these bangs. I don't think there's ever been a time where we were side by side, and a bang erupted, except for the time we had company over. Yes, our friends have heard the bangs.

It took us awhile to locate where the bangs were coming from. I mean I could be in my office—*bang, bang, bang! I* swear it came from the hallway. Tina swears it came from downstairs—where she was. The house vibrates. The walls shake and still, you don't know where the noise came from. There have been instances where Tina and I were both upstairs and the bang occurred. Other times we were in our respective rooms. I would be working on something in my office and Tina watching TV in our bed. *Bang, bang, bang!* We rush out of whatever room we're in and try to locate where the bang came from. We agree it must have come from downstairs. But we're not sure. It's like it's happening everywhere at the same time if that makes any sense.

Can we all agree that this house is haunted? The activity, if I can call it that, has captured my attention. If this is a kid ghost, why is it upset? Why is it making loud noises? Why is it throwing stuff? I mean, what gives? This might sound weird, but each bang seemed to have its own vibration. I'm not talking about a tremor. Think ethereal. More localized. If I had to narrow it down to where I thought the bang was coming from, I would say the attic, or better yet the beams and boards behind the walls of the house; particularly the ceiling. It just felt that way.

But it would not be long before Tina and I would figure out where the noise was really coming from. A month or so after moving in we noticed an interesting groove in our bedroom doorway. A dip in the carpet. You'd roll your ankle there if you weren't careful. That's how deep the dip in the floor was. This dip wasn't there when we first moved in. I'm certain of that. Everyone knows when you move into a rental property you and the landlord do a complete walkthrough of the rooms. Remember that deposit I spoke about? Well, I want it back when I move out. The landlord wants his house back in the same condition of when he leased it. Therefore, we do a walkthrough. I call out imperfections and the landlords nods in agreement. That dip in the floor was not there. Tina and I would have noticed it the day the landlord gave us a tour of the house. The day we heard the kid cough.

I remember when we found this dip. We were downstairs: I was sitting on the couch and Tina was in the kitchen. The bangs started that night like normal, only this time lasting longer than usual. It was for that reason that I decided to go looking for the area of the house I felt the noise was coming from. The noise seemed to be loudest above our heads. Loudest around the hallway downstairs. This hallway I'm talking about sits between the kitchen and the garage. Tina saw me investigating and decided to join in. As I said before, the bangs came in sets of three. Three huge booming sounds. Silence. Then again—three more times. I looked at Tina and told her I thought the banging was coming from the upstairs hallway. I then ran upstairs and parked myself in the hallway. I was staring down at the carpet. Let me see if I can duplicate the sound we're hearing. I jumped up and down and yelled out to Tina, can you hear me? Does the noise sound the same? She said, "Yeah it kind of does." We then switched places. I went back downstairs and she went upstairs. I told her to jump up and down. The noise was a little different. I then joined her upstairs. Now we were in the hallway together, trying to duplicate what we think we hear. I walked back and forth, stomping as I go. Seeing if I can pinpoint where the noise is coming from. Something still feels out of place. I look at Tina and say, "I wonder if the stomping is coming from inside our bedroom?" We both look at each other and shrug. The best way to test that theory is to walk into the bedroom and begin stomping and that's exactly what I did. But something stopped me. As soon as I stepped into the doorway I felt the dent in the floor. That's it. This has to be where the noise is coming from.

I tell Tina to go back downstairs, stand where she was before. I start stomping like crazy. BINGO. The noise is almost identical. Not as loud as what we hear but damn close. I did my stomping inches from the dent of the carpet. I'm a big guy. I tried stomping as hard as I could. I could not get to the decibel level of what we were hearing. The loud banging had to be coming from here. I say that because the hallway has to be where the wood beams from all parts of the house come together. Now if I'm a ghost I might be thinking, this area might be ideal for me. The noise does sound like it's coming from every direction. But not anymore. I seriously believe Tina and I located the source of the noise or the area I should say. But now we have something we never had before. We now have damage to the house. The fact that this dent sits inside our bedroom doorway is kind of scary. The dip is technically in our bedroom. The fact that we know where the sound is coming from doesn't mean the loud banging is going to stop. Oh no, the banging doesn't stop. These bangs would go on for weeks. A bang usually meant something was about to go flying across the room.

Chapter 3
The Ceiling Fan

If you were to ask me what day of the week was the house most active, I couldn't really tell you. We'd had violent activity on just about every day of the week. I'm not sure the spirits coordinated their actions based on what day of the week it was. Now if you were to ask me, what day of the week did the house feel a little more uneasy? That day would be Sunday. Sunday, for reasons I can't explain, always felt denser. I always tell myself if Sunday was to have a theme song, that theme song would be "Wanna be Starting Something," by Michael Jackson.

What does that mean? It feels like something here wants to start trouble. Like, instigate something? Have you ever been somewhere where the mood went from light to heavy the second someone walked into the room? I mean it could be someone's energy. Someone's attitude, or someone's view on life. I mean they walk in looking for trouble. They're not leaving till they find it either. That's what Sunday felt like in our home. Not all-day Sunday. Far from it. Night time Sunday.

It's an accepted fact within the paranormal community that malevolent spirits tend to feed off negative energy. I can tell you from my three years of observation the spirits in my house not only feed off the negative energy, they also help create it. The hate, the status quo. They hate peace. The more restless the house, the more dangerous it feels—especially Sunday night. The first time I felt this energy change was on a few weeks after we moved in. Tina and I were getting ready for bed. I was flying out in the morning on a business trip.

Later that night the ceiling fan began making a weird squeaking noise. It had never made this noise before. The noise was loud—impossible to sleep through. Lying there, I asked myself what woke me up. The noise from the ceiling fan? Or the uneasy feeling I felt in and around me? So, there I was. I was looking dead at the ceiling fan, thinking to myself, *this noise is going to keep me up all night.* I leaned over and nudged Tina to let her know that the ceiling fan was on the fritz. She's looking at me with the expression of, why and the hell did you wake me up? My reply: I have to turn on the light and fix the ceiling, prep your eyes.

So, I'm tinkering with this ceiling fan; nothing's happening. The noise will not go away. I'm like *screw this; I'll worry about this when I'm back in town. I need to get some sleep.* Tina couldn't agree with me more. I look at Tina—I'm almost done. As soon as I say that, the bedroom door closes shut. It didn't slam shut. It just closes on its own. Just the way I would have closed a door. It wasn't like a wind draft came in and took control of the door. When the wind closes a door, it closes it abruptly; it slams the door shut. This door didn't do that. This door closed like you or I would close it. It was like someone reached in and closed the door by grabbing the doorknob.

What made it unnerving was how close Tina was to the door. Tina didn't see it close, but I did. Tina didn't turn toward the direction of the door until she heard it snap shut. She jumped as soon as it happened. Tina looked at the door and then turned back to me. We had the same facial expression we had when we saw the plant levitate. Did that just happen?

I remember climbing down from the bed and walking to the door. I opened it and stuck my head through the doorway. Just like they do in the movies. I looked back at Tina and said I have to inspect the house. Tina moved like Grease Lightning. No way was she staying in the room while I walked around the house looking for stuff. What was I looking for? I had no idea. I probably wouldn't know it if I saw it. It just felt like the right thing to do.

Common sense tells me no one is in the house. We were obviously the victim of a prank Tina and me? That's the question I'm asking myself. Who's behind this? Why are they messing with us? I never got the feeling from talking to neighbors that we were not welcomed here. I mean, I wasn't feeling bad vibes from anyone outside the home. The only bad vibes I'm getting are the ones inside the home. And I don't mean Tina. So, I just ruled out all the logical reasons as to why a door would close on its own. I've deduced it down to one simple fact: Our house is haunted.

The tell-tale signs were clear. The evidence, irrefutable. My brain was trying to make sense of it all. Common sense and denial were battling it out. It looked like common sense was going to win here. I mean seeing a door close on its own, that's a whole new can of worms. The entity for some reason or another wanted to close that door tonight. It wanted us to see that door close. And the ceiling fan was the trigger.

Let me be clear. The noise from the ceiling fan was caused by a build-up of energy. The ceiling fan was collateral in a sense. That uneasy feeling, I spoke about earlier? There's another way to describe it. It's called the feeling of being watched. It's when the forest goes silent all of a sudden. Trouble stepped into our room that night. How do I know this? Well, let's fast forward to a week or two. Tina and I were asleep. The ceiling fan was on and working fine. 3 am comes— SQUEAK, SQUEAK, SQUEAK! That damn squeaking noise wakes me up again.

As soon as my eyes opened, the bedroom door slammed. It jolted Tina awake to where she was now on my side of the bed. The room felt as dense as a neutron star. A few days later the same thing happens again. The activity is ramping up now. Instead of the door slamming, how about an ironing board flying across the room. Nothing flies while you're asleep. Not yet anyway. It seems like they want us to wake up first. And I can see the logic behind that. You will too by the time you reach the end of this book.

You see, objects would fly in our room within seconds of the fan making that noise. Lights that were on shut off. If the television is on, it won't be on for long. Imagine your TV channels changing by themselves. The remote control is sitting at the foot of the bed. You turn the TV off, and it turns back on. Those are just a few of the things we've seen when our ceiling fan is going crazy. And it doesn't go crazy every night. There have been lulls in between each unexplained incident.

But all of that pales in comparison to the feeling of being watched. I know some people have spoken about a sudden drop in temperature. We never experienced that. We never saw cold air in front of our mouths as we breathed or talked. The only thing to drop suddenly beside furniture was mood swings.

I remember one-night Tina and I were sleep. Something got knocked over. I think an iron board went flying across the room again or something. The room felt heavy, like always. We had stopped using the ceiling, due to it screaming all the time. We were hoping they would leave us alone. We were wrong. I knew then and there the house wasn't the one being haunted. We were. That realization prompted me to step out of the room. I grabbed my pillow and looked at Tina. "Come with me; we're sleeping downstairs." Tina didn't even hesitate. She grabbed our comforter, and we were out of there.

I remember the conversation I had with myself while lying on the den floor. *What have we moved into? What the hell is this?* It would appear the house had a secret it wanted Tina and me to know about. As my eyes closed, I'm thinking; we have a roommate. It would be two years before I realized how incorrect I was. We don't have a roommate; we have Satan.

The decision had been reached by the time we got up that morning. Tina would pack some clothing and stay with her friend Kim on days while I went out of town. That was one of the outputs from last night. Ground rules. We're going to have to create a few, until we get this sorted out.

Up until now, all I thought we had was a kid ghost. I mean, it makes sense, right? You hear a child's 'cough' that must mean kid ghost. Tina and I could be wrong though. Loud bangs, flying plants, items missing—doesn't strike me as kid-like. If I didn't know any better, I would say this thing was going out of its way to keep Tina and me on our toes.

I'm not sure what to do about all of this. There's no instruction manual on the subject. Everyone says "move." That's the knee-jerk, human response. "Run for the hills." And they're all telling the truth. I'd have that same reaction if it were me living on the outside looking in. No one knows what they would do until they've been put in that situation. Remember, we humans are capable of surviving impossible situations. Situations that on the surface appear hopeless and bleak. Tina and I were far from feeling hopeless and bleak. Nothing would please me more than nuking this house from orbit, should it come to that. But we're not there yet. Right now, my questions outnumber my need for eight hours sleep. I'm still riding on what I recently achieved. I'm a manager at a prestigious company. I have a beautiful girlfriend. I've acquired a beautiful house in the city of Bothell, Washington. I just want to relish for a moment. Enjoy my success and complete my lease agreement.

The desire to stay or leave is purely psychological. I mean the bad stuff hasn't even begun yet. This house is not going to turn into the Bot(hell) house for another two years. What you're reading now is just preliminary. The honeymoon phases. Think abusive relationship. There's the physical violence, and there's the psychological violence. You'll see both here. You'll discover later on how other people could hear noises that Tina and I couldn't. We couldn't because we'd grown immune to it. Violent acts like a giant armoire being thrown across to room that we now ignore it. We ignore it because we don't know how to deal with it. Moving it from room to room doesn't work. Nothing works.

Tina and I had no clue as to what was in store. Right now, I'm thinking, this ghost can't hurt me. It can scare us, but there are limits to scaring people? I mean, they say "there's nothing to fear but fear itself." That's the mentality I had. Tina has what I have. She's comfortable if I'm comfortable. The best way to deal with this is, in my opinion. Ask around. Ask co-workers. Ask the church. Ask whoever might be in a position to help us. It's time to get some information. It's time to use the internet.

We all know the internet can be a helpful tool when trying to figure out something. But there are risks associated with using the internet. There's so much bad information on it. I mean there's crazy stuff out there. A lot of noise. I couldn't find consensus on anything. Every website was giving me a different answer to the symptoms I was presenting. I accidentally uncovered a civil war taking place among paranormal teams during my search for answers. A lot of in-fighting among different organizations. No one trusts each other. I'm talking factions within factions. Everyone at odds with one another. Community versus community. Everyone's circled the wagon around their favorite TV personality. No consensus whatsoever in what's haunting people's homes. Here comes the demonic peddling, "You want to conduct your own exorcism? Take my class (there's a fee of course), upon completion you'll get a certificate that says you're a demonologist. I'm thinking *Jesus never said anything about needing a certificate. Let alone a credit card.* So, this might take a while. Finding true help that is. Oh God, please don't let me find the wrong type of help.

I'm reading all this crazy stuff about who can help us from 35,000 feet. Tina was working her end; I was working my end. One of the first websites I found gave me insight into the disappearing objects phenomenon. The website I was on said missing objects were a tell-tale sign of something malevolent. 'Malevolent': *having or showing a wish to do evil to others.* Objects disappearing were the early signs of something malevolent lurking around. And so too was the appearance of mysterious items. We began to experience that too. About the same time our silverware went missing, Tina and I began to find items neither one of us owned lain throughout the house. I'm talking about in plain view. Toys, children's jewelry, letters. Bill statements, correspondence from banks, loan offices, and IRS letters suddenly appearing out of the blue. Letters addressed to other people began appearing on the kitchen counter, on the staircase and landing area. Same address. Different people. These items had to once belonged to the people living here. The dates on the envelope showed these letters arrived here three years ago. Some were older than that. I remember one day I was in the kitchen looking for something. I opened one of the kitchen drawers to reach for something and instead found a whole bunch of letters. None of them were there before. It's like the letters had disappeared and all of a sudden reappeared again, only with our stuff in the drawer too. So now we have a drawer overflowing with our stuff and that of previous tenants. Go figure?

Chapter 4
The Gray Lady

How many of you are familiar with the movie *Predator*? Synopsis: A group of Special Forces descends deep into the South American jungle. Interesting things are happening in and around them. Things they can't explain. They have no idea what's haunting them. No clue at all. Not until Bill Duke's character see's something he can't explain. Something "weird." When his friends ask him to describe what it was that he saw, he's dumbfounded. His friends ask him again what it was he saw. His only reply was, "The eye's, they just ...they just... disappeared." The men all look at each other and think he's losing it; he's not making any sense. That's me, I'm Bill Duke's character. I had an almost identical reaction when I saw the Gray Lady.

Before I tell that story, let me answer a question I often get via email. Was I a believer in the paranormal before all of this happened? I was always fifty-fifty about the existence of ghosts. My father would tell us ghost stories when we were children growing up. He had some good ones too. The one that kept me up at night was the story about the Boogieman. According to my dad, the boogie man was the devil's son. He drags bad children into the woods and devours them.

That's the crux of what I believed. Then there's the afterlife. Is there a heaven? Is there a hell? Where do we go when we're done living on Earth? What happens to us after we die? Are we food for the worms? Or do we keep going? I like to think that we keep going. I certainly hope so. I mean the universe is an awfully big place. Our lifespan as humans, compared to what's around us is relatively small. I mean, it's minuscule.

Are ghosts real? Do houses occupied by ghost really exist? Will I see my dad again? My grandmother? I like to keep an open mind about stuff like that. I mean where do I get off trying to convince someone about who God is? Who am I to question another person's experience. Their account is their account. You weren't there. I wasn't there. Let them share what they experienced. What they've seen. If you have a mindset similar to one I just described, then you're going understand a lot of what I'm about to say.

August 2012—The banging was still taking place. Plants were still hopping around the house. Seriously, we had plants hoping around the kitchen and living room area. Tall plants. You'd pass one as you made your way into the kitchen, pass it again and it would be in a different spot. Or you'd hear a noise and turn around and there the plant is, gyrating around on the floor. All of these events were leading me up to seeing the Gray Lady. Probably the biggest lead of all was the activity when the lights went off and on.

There are two activities that I want to talk about that are sort of similar. They involve the light fixtures in the house. One I call lights on, lights off and the other one I call was ON, and now it's OFF. I'm using CAPS so you can tell which one I'm talking about. Try to follow me because this is very important. The ON and now it's OFF phenomenon can be described this way. You leave your room; the light is on. You come back the light is now off. Half the time you don't even notice it, you just turn the light back on and resume whatever it was you were doing before you left the room. This goes on for days to where you finally have to ask yourself the question: *I could have sworn I left the light on when I walked out of the room?* Maybe I did. Maybe I didn't. I'm not sure. *It's not important.* The best thing to do is turn the light back on and continue doing what it was you were doing. For me, that meant watching TV again or surfing the internet. The ON and now it's OFF phenomenon happens multiple times. I mean think about it. How many times do we walk out of a room? I lose count. And I'm sure you do as well. Now let's talk about the lights on, lights off phenomenon. The lights on, lights off phenomenon involves a light going off in an adjacent room. Usually the room closest to the one you're currently in. Example: I'm in my office. The room closest to me is the hallway. Odds are the light is on due to Tina or doing laundry or something. I'm watching TV or listening to music while in my office—all of a sudden, the hallway light goes off.

I first thought it was Tina. She was coming and going at times, due to her doing laundry. Then one day my common-sense gene slapped me and said— *Duffus, Tina's not even upstairs.* How do I know she's not upstairs? I know because I could hear her talking on the phone. Or I can hear her cooking in the kitchen. Just to be sure, I screamed, "Tina! Where are you? She yelled back "I'm the kitchen, shut up!" All of this within a few seconds of the hallway light turning off. Now I need for you to not laugh at me because I'm going to share with you what I did next. It might be funny to some. Its sort of is funny, now that I think about it. My first reaction to a light on, lights off moment involved me getting up from my chair and marching over to the light switch. I looked around high and low, thinking to myself the bulb must be going out or we must have a problem with the wiring. Those were my first thoughts. I was still clinging to the logical explanation despite everything we'd seen so far. I marched over to the light switch. I flicked the switch back on and return to the office.

Now let's go back to the other phenomenon, the one where I come back and the light in my room is off. You can see I'm not connecting the dots. It never occurred to me that I was being watched. I know how it feels when I'm in bed, *it's happening in the bedroom almost every night.* For some strange reason, I was not feeling it now. Whatever is watching me must have been thinking, 'wow this guy is not getting it. His clairvoyance is going to force me to turn off the light manually.' That must have been their thought process because that's how the spirit finally revealed itself. Whether it wanted to or not is a debate I'm still having with myself. Was it my clairvoyance, my naivety that the forced the spirit's hand (literally)?

There I was sitting in my office. I was downloading music from my computer. Tina was in our bathroom, taking a bubble bath. I was sitting at my desk, minding my own business, when all of a sudden, the light in my office go off. Now I was sitting in the dark. The only light I can see is the light that's in the hallway. Now we all know the sound a light switch makes when we turn it from the on to off position. You know what that sound, sounds like right? It goes "click." That's what I heard when the light went off. That noise made me turn towards the doorway. Instinctively towards the light switch.

So, I'm sitting at my desk, which means I'm sitting down. As soon as I heard the "click", I slid backward in my chair, hoping to catch Tina in the act. I honestly thought she was playing a joke on me. *Hahaha, very funny. Good one Tina right, now go back to whatever you were doing. Continue putting cucumber lotion on your face* (that's what she does after she takes a bath). But I was wrong! Tina's not standing at the door. Someone else is.

My eyes froze. It's a lady, but it's not Tina. This lady is gray. Small in stature. Smaller than Tina. She's not facing me though. She's turned sideways, or better yet I saw her turn sideways when I scooted my chair back. I can see her clear as day. As clear as the computer screen I'm looking at right now. This lady I'm looking at is very well defined. Shoulder length hair, petite, thin, frail looking. That's how I describe her. She has a dress on. Or a robe maybe? Did I mention she was well defined? That's how I knew she was a female ghost. Definitely a woman.

The thing I remember the most about her is she was gray. I mean completely gray. She looked confused. Whatever she just did, it would appear she didn't plan it well. She looked like she was stuck. Like she was confused on what to do next. I mean I'm taking all of this in within a second or two. The impression I got from watching her was she wanted to get the fuck out of my hallway. She wanted to disappear fast. But guess what? She couldn't. At least not the way she wanted. So that's a little bit of her scared side. Let me talk about her malicious side for a second. This lady wanted to turn my office light off with the hopes of getting my attention. What I can't understand is, why did she turn the light off manually? Think about it. I've been having lights repeatedly go off and on for the last few weeks. Coming back to rooms where the light is off when I'm a hundred percent positive I left them on. This is different. This woman turned off the light. She had to. I heard the click sound. My question to you is why a spirit would go out of its way to turn off my light manually when they easily could have done it the way in which I've already described? I have to believe her reason for turning off the light manually was for the simple fact of wanting to be seen.

I couldn't believe what I was seeing. My brain had just signaled to me that is not Tina. And you know the next question that came after that was, who and the hell is it? And then it happens. The object I'm looking at darts off. But hold up. Something's wrong? Fleeing was not her first course of action. Ducking into the washroom was. The lady I'm looking at is trying to disappear into the door in front of her. She can't though, and the look on her face makes me believe she's not entirely sure why.

Please understand, I'm still not sure what it is I saw. This all happened in a few seconds. Whatever this was has now concluded that it's not going to be able to go through the washroom door. The only thing it can do now is exit. And that's exactly what she done. I don't know if it was pure shock or pure disbelief. Something told me to get up and go after it. I can tell you honestly my reason for going after it most likely had to do with me still thinking it was Tina. Adrenaline in motion is what this is.

So, I'm hurrying into the hallway, and there's nothing. Whoever was standing at my door is gone. I saw them dart around the corridor. That's where I'm standing right now, in the corridor. Where did she go? I finish my pursuit, which I'm sad to say ends with me standing in my bedroom. There's Tina taking a bubble bath. I walked up to her with the dumbest look on my face, thinking to myself, *there's no way Tina turned off my office light, no way she took off running, Tina has never been the type that plays practical jokes.* Seeing Tina neck deep in bubble bath was confirmation that what I saw was real.

Tina saw the look on my face and asked, "What's wrong with you?" I looked at her and said I just saw a ghost. Her mouth dropped open. "No, you didn't, stop trying to trick me." Me trying to trick her. *The irony of that, I mean the reason I'm standing in the middle of the bathroom is that I'm trying to see if there's any way possible the Gray Lady I just saw could have been Tina.*

RECAP: the thing I saw standing in my doorway was a woman. She wasn't see through; she wasn't transparent or translucent. Just gray. Matte colored gray. Picture a gray egg carton. That's the exact color she was. She was about five feet-four inches tall, give or take an inch or two. Long hair. Very petite, very frail looking. Lots of thin hair. Her hair is what I remember the most about her. They went down to her shoulders. I'll never forget how much she had trouble getting into the washroom. Which still doesn't make any sense to me. Why would she manually turn the light off? I never would've seen her had she not did that. The noise is what gave it away. She had to have known, right? I mean where did she go?

This whole ordeal reminds me of the observer effect, which states—that simply observing a situation or phenomenon necessarily changes that phenomenon. It changes that phenomenon's outcome. That appears to be what happened. There's no way that gray lady was going to disappear into a wall with me looking straight at her. The observer effect prevents that from happening, her going through a wall while being watched. I mean think about it. She disappeared around the corner which suggests she didn't want me looking at her when she disappeared. I'm entertaining all theories, ladies and gentleman. I'm hoping someone out there has a similar tale. A similar experience where the image they saw could not move or negotiate through a wall and therefore took off pacing or running, only to disappear once they were no longer in view range of the observer.

If it's true that my seeing her is what prevented her from diving into the washroom, then it would it would resemble another phenomenon associated with poltergeist. That phenomenon involves the moving of objects. We're talking about plants, pottery, knives, ashtrays, plates, vases, bottles, lamps, iron, and iron boards. We've seen it all. The one thing we haven't seen is, and that in itself is what I want to call attention to. Tina and I have never seen an object go airborne. We've only seen objects already in flight.

There's a theory amongst theorists as to why that's the case. In my opinion, the reason the Gray Lady was not able to disappear in front of me or go through the door which was right next to her is the same reason why Tina and I never saw objects take off in our house (go flying that is). There might be a connection there.

Uncertainty principle—observer effect—observing an object changes the characteristics of the object—therefore, altering its course aka altering its outcome. The only contradiction would be the plant we saw levitate off the floor. So, there you have it. What the heck is going on here? Does the entity know about the laws I just talked about? Are they masters of it or are they just living in it like you and me?

I ask this question because of the sound I heard—that clicking sound indicates there was physical contact between the spirit and the light switch. WIKI defines sound as being—a vibration that propagates as a typically audible mechanical wave of pressure and displacement, through a medium such as air or water. In physiology and psychology, the sound is the reception of such waves and their perception of the brain. Did the spirit know I was going to look towards the doorway? I believe it did. The question I can't seem to answer. The one that's keeping me up at night is why. Why me? I mean what's preventing it from revealing itself again. Will I see her again? The answer is yes. The Gray Lady (that's her name now) has a role to play in what Tina and I are about to experience. She's coming back, and she's not alone.

Chapter 5
No Laughing Matter

"Let's give them something to talk about. A little mystery to figure out."
Bonnie Raitt

When Tina and I went to bed, we always made it a point to talk about the events of that day. Sort of a recap of what happened that day. We talk about a wide range of things. How each other's day was. Have you heard from such and such family? How is this person doing? Did you get the raise you wanted? In between those conversations were questions like, did you hear that? It sounds like a door just closed somewhere. "Can't believe that plant slid across the room like that? Is this happening?" That's slowly becoming the majority of our pillow talk conversations.

I was lying next to Tina, thinking—this house is only seven years old? How can it be haunted? I mean the house looks brand new. It feels brands new, that's why Tina and I wanted it. It's a lovely looking house. The fact that it was built in 2005 would serve as a detriment to Tina and I come the time to seek help. I mean a lot of paranormal teams didn't take us seriously based on how young the house was. It's very disheartening to hear someone tell you; your problem doesn't fit within the norms of being a true haunting. I mean I'm not a paranormal researcher. My background for the majority of my professional life has been in the information technology space. I like to think that this quote of "there's a first time for everything," applies to all disciplines—including the paranormal.

Allow me to go back a little. I need to explain the dream that led to me getting this house. By dream, I mean hard work. By hard work, I mean dedication. February 2012—I left Philips Healthcare to go to McKesson Healthcare. A friend of mine had told me about a new position opening up at her company. Long story short, I applied for it and soon after I got a phone call saying "the job was mine." It was a management position—Enterprise Support Manager. Can you imagine the high I'm feeling as a result of landing such a prestigious job? I mean, there was a sort of Keith has arrived feeling going through me as a result of moving into this house. But I could've gotten this house if it wasn't for me landing that job and it was a spectacular job. I would have fourteen people reporting to me. But the dream goes further back than that. I'm talking about going back to my youth days.

Did you know what city you wanted to live in when you were eleven years old? I did. Living in Seattle had always been a dream mine. Almost like an obsession. What kid obsesses about living in a certain city? I did. Very few people in my family know that. It's not something I openly shared for fear of my dream not been taken seriously. But I never lost sight of that fact. Never gave up on the dream of living in the Pacific Northwest. Why the Pacific Northwest? Why not stay in Texas? Well, Texas will always be Texas. I have no hatred whatsoever for the state I once lived in. But that's just it. I was born there. My dad (before his passing) had envisioned of all his sons residing elsewhere—creating new roots. That's what he did. It's my turn now. Time for me to set up shop.

When I told my family, I was finally going to move here, they looked at me as if I was nuts. No one, and I mean no one, thought I had the guts to do it. "Keith, you're crazy, Seattle is too far away, no one there knows you. There's no family up there." Trust me I heard it all when it came time for me to move.

It's so ironic to the point of almost being scary that the year this house was built, which was in 2005, was also the same year I moved here. I get goosebumps thinking about it sometimes. So, you see, the house was my gift to myself for a job well done. Now I want to talk about my girlfriend Tina and myself for a minute because this question gets asks a lot.

Keith and Tina FAQ:

Question	Answer
How long have we been together?	2 years (before moving in)
Did we live together elsewhere?	No, we had two separate apartments
Has either of you ever experienced anything paranormal elsewhere?	No
Ever played with an Ouija board?	No

Table 5.1

As the table above shows. Neither one of us has experienced remotely similar to what I'm about to tell you. No Ouija board parties while growing up and no Ouija board parties as a couple. It's so cliché how we met. I remember that day very well. It was Tax Day – April 15th, 2010. I was standing in line at a wine party inside the Columbia Tower building on the 76th floor. One of my friends was throwing a party as a means of celebrating Tax Day. *Any excuse will do.* So, I'm standing in line waiting for a wine refill. Tina is standing in front of me. She's with one of her girlfriends. The first thing I noticed about her was her height. I'm thinking to myself *wow, she's a tall glass of water, she's hot!* So, we started talking (I initiated) and here we are two years later.

Our relationship was not perfect though. Far from it. I mean we're nearing our two-year anniversary of when we officially became a couple which was July 5th, of that same year. I think it's safe to say that the honeymoon phase was over. I mean we carried it for as long as we could before we finally realized that's not sustainable long-term. I mean love is love regardless of what phase you're in. We are not your perfect couple. We're a modern couple. She has baggage. I have baggage. In between our baggage is a whole lot of fun. A whole lot of silliness. I call her booty-butt, and she calls me "black ass." Meaning whenever I make her laugh or call out something stupid she giggles and says "I can't stand your black ass." Terms of endearment of course.

So, how did we find this house? We found it sitting in bed one night. I was on my laptop and Tina was on hers (at her place). We were both searching Craigslist. I mean if you're going to move in together why not make a game out of it? The game we had was who could find a house first. Who has better taste where houses are concerned? Tina was trying to win me over with her selections, and I was trying to win her over with my selection. The decision had to be unanimous. If I showed Tina a house that she didn't like, she'd shoot the idea down. No way were we looking at that house. If she showed me a house I didn't like, I'd say no also.

We had to both love it. And we did—the house we found on Craigslist. So here we were lying in bed, recapping tonight's events, which included the Gray Lady I saw a few hours ago. We always do this, Tina and me. We always say, first things first—let's go down the list of what we've seen already. Tina and I done this ritual every night with the hopes of not forgetting anything.

You see, I might have forgotten something that Tina vividly remembers. She jogs my memory, or I jog hers. We want to limit that as much as possible. It's a great technique. You already know the first thing we're going to talk about is the kid 'cough.' We used to think it was a kid ghost that lived here. We might have to abandon that theory—new data has come in. Tina blurts out a question: "Where are all these toys coming from?" I've told you about the missing items. My car keys, a few of Tina's belongings. But what about the stuff that keeps appearing? Toys and jewelry. It's hard to ignore those instances because we don't have children. These items that appear don't belong to us.

One night, in particular, Tina and I decided to do something we hadn't done before. We decided to get deep and morbid with our questioning. We were bouncing ideas, theories, and innuendos off each other with the hopes of ascertaining what could be causing this. The questions become more twisted. We were asking ourselves, what happened before we both moved in? What went down here? Did somebody die? Did the Gray Lady die here? Was a crime committed? We were thinking out loud now. The realness of it all hit us. Here we are. It's well past midnight, and we're asking ourselves questions no other couple would dare ask themselves at this time of night. It becomes so surreal all of a sudden to where all we can do is laugh. I mean, we don't know what else to do. The Gray Lady turned off my light and took off running. It could be worse, right? Could she have come running in my room with a knife? I look at Tina, and she looks at me, and I guess we just got hit with the giggles all of a sudden because we started laughing. We could laugh, or we can cry. Which one should we do? We should run for the hills. That's what we should do. We should just leave right now. But we don't. Instead, we bust out laughing. I guess our questions got the best of us. So, we're laughing, loud mind you. Very loud.

All of a sudden, the bedroom door slammed shut. It shook the entire house. Imagine your bedroom slamming on its own in the middle of you laughing. If the loudness of it doesn't scare you, the proximity of the door does—it's less than three feet away. Something closed the door on us. Tina and I should be clinging to the ceiling right now. Had we been cats we would have been.

I'm not sure if whoever slammed our bedroom door did it because they felt we weren't taking them seriously. Or they slammed it because we were laughing (which is the same thing). Whatever they wanted to achieve they achieved it. We stopped laughing instantly. *Note to self:*

No more laughing in bed. It was as if they were trying to tell us something. Like they were saying '*listen, you two, you need to take us seriously. We're going to make your lives a living hell. This is not going to end well. For either of you. You think it's funny; we get it. No more laughter after tonight. We're serious about what it is we're about to do. You both need to be. You need to decide what you're going to do next. Let's have fun, on the mark, get set, go.*'

That's the message I got from the door being closed. The room was dead silent. Tina and I could have heard a pin drop in Tacoma. That's how silent we were. Up until now every activity we'd seen and heard had pretty much fallen into the wow category. As haunting as it is to see a plant rise from the floor while watching TV. It in itself is not scary, at least not for us. If the plant had started chasing us around the house, that would have been scary. Cabinet doors open, levitating plants, items missing and lights going off and on at will led us to believe this spirit was harmless. Creepy, but harmless. That's where our minds were at before the bedroom door slamming.

Even the door closing on its own the night before I flew out of town was beginning to feel harmless. You see, there's a cool component surrounding the paranormal, at least for me there is. One of the questions I have about what I'd seen so far was how do they make objects move like that? How is that possible? Where did my keys go once they disappeared? Where do spirits reside when they're not terrorizing Tina and me? Lastly, what's this fascination with kitchen cabinets?

The first thing that came to my mind after the door slam was we had an intruder in the house. *Hold that thought, Keith.* Intruders don't go around slamming doors. Second—*the ADT security downstairs is still on. No alert whatsoever about forced entry.* Third—I have to go open the door. I'm thinking, *please don't let someone be on the other the side of this door.* Especially the Gray Lady. *Where are we going to run if someone is on the other side?* I'd be lying if I said my heart wasn't pounding. My heart was pounding like a mother fucker. Heck, Tina was pretty much in my lap at this point. I'm going to have to peel her off me if I'm to open this door.

The only way we were going to know what's on the other side of that door was to just open it. Looking back on it our reaction is funny. There we were standing by the door. We were looking at it. I mean if the ghost wanted to open it now and kill us, it could. Just by opening the door right now would do the trick. I finally said fuck it lets get this over with. I reached towards the door and pulled it open. Nothing. *So far so good.*

I motioned to Tina that I was going to go downstairs. I had to see if the house was OK. Tina's shot back at me, "You're not leaving me here by myself, I'm coming with you." Here we go, venturing into the hallway. Going room to room, Tina and me. Nothing. Nothing. Nothing. That's been the theme of late. Nothing. Waking up and finding every cabinet door open, nothing. Plants flying across the living room hitting a wall, nothing. Lights are flickering off and on by themselves, nothing. No one's ever around. A gray woman turns off my office light-takes off running. I give chase and guess what I find? Nothing.

Tina and I walked back upstairs and went to bed after spending what felt like an eternity downstairs. I went through each room thoroughly. Each closet thoroughly. I knew we wouldn't find anything, but hey, you have to rule out the obvious, right? We now had something new to talk about. Except we didn't want to talk about it. So, we just laid there. Tina's wrapped around me like a pretzel, while I was staring up at the ceiling. The wheels in my head were turning. Why would the ghost slam our door? Have we offended it somehow? Are we trespassing on something?

Things were different moving forward. Imagine waking up in the morning and going downstairs and finding every kitchen cabinet door open. More than ever now. Every door downstairs was wide open. Our belongings were pulled out—all organized and neat. That happens every morning now.

When I get up in the morning, the first thing I do is iron my clothes. I shave. I shower. I marched into my office to get my work laptop. Tina is in the bathroom doing her hair. Neither of us had gone downstairs yet. We only head downstairs when it was time to leave. Or on occasion to grab something or throw something away. Someone could be waiting for us downstairs, and Tina and I would not even know. Someone or something.

The morning after the door slammed, I got up early and went downstairs to get a glass of water. I must have been on the next to the last step of the staircase when suddenly I saw all our kitchen cabinet doors were open. I mean you can't help but be impressed with the neatness of it all. Neither of us heard anything that night. We're talking fifty cabinet doors open? Not just cabinet doors. All three closet doors are open. How is this possible?

Every new wonder brings with it a new set of questions. How long were these cabinets like this? Why didn't the ADT security alarm go off? These doors if opened will trigger an alarm. They would if I opened them. But they don't. Why is that? Did the spirit open these doors while we were asleep? Or did it wait till we were awake? I honestly don't know, ladies and gentlemen. I remember what Tina said after I showed her the kitchen that day. She said "that's different." Different as in interesting. Neither of us has seen nothing yet.

Chapter 6
Housewarming Party

My grandmother advised me a long time ago too, "Always have your home blessed before you move in." I'm kicking myself now, saying why didn't I do that. And for the likes of me, I can't understand why. Why didn't I heed her advice? She gave it to me long, long time ago. She and my grandfather came over to my new apartment when I was living in Texas. Had to have been the mid-nineties. My grandmother whips out a white towel, olive oil, and a Bible. I asked her what she was doing. She told me she was "blessing the house." Here I think they were here to drop off some peach cobbler; no my grandmother came by to bless my house. I looked at my grandfather. "Let her do what she wants to do; she's protecting you." Protecting me from what? I asked, "Protecting you from evil spirits, she's telling the spirits here that they can't stay here." I should never have forgotten that conversation. So now you know. Tina and I didn't get our house blessed when we moved in. I forgot.

After that door-slam, Tina and I began our search for local churches in the area. Let's have our home blessed. Maybe that will calm these spirits down. In the meantime, the activity continues. We were now ninety days in. Every day was more of the same. Imagine you're loading up the dishwasher. Your partner is upstairs, maybe doing some laundry, sorting clothes, watching TV, etc. You're downstairs in the kitchen—loading up the dishwasher. Your back is turned to everything. That's me right now. I was cleaning the kitchen when all of a sudden, I heard a sound. *Must be my imagination,* I keep on doing what it is I'm doing. Ten minutes later I heard another sound. I had to turn around now. Something was happening. I spun around and oh my God. One of Tina's plants has come to life.

It was gyrating across the floor right in front of me. Not only was it grating across the floor but it was about to cross my path. If I didn't know better, I'd say it was attempting to intercept me. I stopped dead in my tracks. My eyes couldn't believe what they were seeing. When I stopped, the plant stopped. The plant is supposed to be on the wine rack. It's not supposed to be in the middle of the kitchen floor. This really happened, ladies and gentlemen. Honest to God it did. But let's not stop there. Let's rewind that situation a bit. Imagine the scenario— I'm in the kitchen cooking dinner. I turn around and scream, "Tina, dinner's almost ready!" No response. I begin making my way out of the kitchen. I went towards the staircase to scream, "Tina! Dinner's almost ready!"

I turned around and saw the kitchen closet door open. Weird, I don't remember going into it, let alone leaving it wide open. No biggie, I'll just close it. I do. I then make my way towards the den. The closet door by the staircase is wide open. As I'm walking up to it, my common-sense alarm begins going off. Two doors wide open is no coincidence. Remember, at this point Tina and I both have come downstairs in the morning and found every closet door open, every cabinet door open. As soon as I walked up to the den closet door, I saw that every remaining door downstairs was open, including the front door. This became a daily occurrence. Tina had similar experiences when she was in the kitchen. Whenever I heard a scream or a yelp come from downstairs, I knew something new had happened. "Keith, come here!" And there in plain sight was the front door. Wide open.

Imagine how frightening that was. Well, it gets worse. The entity can do way better than that. Imagine walking into your second-floor hallway in the morning, and upon doing so, you see that your front door is open. Wide open. Now, was that door like that all night? I hate to think that it was. The thought alone is terrifying. I doubt that it was. But we're not sure. It's the *not knowing* that drives you crazy. I have to believe the spirit opened the door within minutes of us waking up. It'll make more sense later in the book as to why I think that way. For now, try to imagine all of this from a couple's point of view. Try to imagine it within the time frame of four months. Then five months. Then six.

Plants moonwalking (sliding) across the floor and doors opening by themselves became common. Matter of fact too common, *if there's such a thing*. It got so bad that Tina and I finally, as a means of wanting to be notified whenever a door was open or closed. Took it upon ourselves to reprogram our ADT security system to say *front door open, garage door open, back door open*, whenever those doors were opened. That's what we did to mitigate the open-door problem. It worked. No more waking up to front doors being open. But the moving plants and us finding kitchen cabinets open would go on.

Finally, some good news. Tina was able to get in contact with a local church. A local ministry stepped forth. We were going to get our house blessed. I was so relieved when that news came.

I have to admit; I had a lot riding on the house blessing. I mean, there's a lot of things in the back of my mind now. Should we tell the minister about what's going on? We decided no, we would not. Let's just keep it simple. Let's just say to him that we're a new couple, that we moved into a neighborhood and we firmly believe in the notion of having your house blessed. That was it. Tina found a minister to bless our house, and he did. He did no more or no less than what my grandmother would have done had she been alive.

Obviously, it didn't work. If it did this would be the last page of this book. We still have a long way to go. In the meantime, summer was fleeting. Tina and I had unpacked everything by now. All the boxes we used to move in were gone. My man-cave was setup. Tina had her closet space. We've done just about everything a couple would be doing at this stage. Well, almost everything. We haven't shown our friends our new house. We haven't invited people over. I think it's time we did that. It's time to share the fruits of our labor.

Now, I know what you're thinking. Why have a party with this type of activity? Tina and I asked ourselves that question more than once. What would happen if our friends were over and all of a sudden, the lights went off? What do we do if a chair slides across the floor? What would everyone's reaction be? Short answer—make sure we have a lot of booze on hand. Lots and lots of alcohol. I wanted my friends tipsy should something go down. Let's give them a good time. I'm talking about our guests.

The day of the party Tina and I both woke up feeling anxious and nervous. Nervous about hosting our first party together. Worried about having enough food; enough alcohol; enough ice. And yes, nervous about what the spirit might do. We have to pray before our friends get here. We have to pray for an enjoyable evening. Let's give thanks for having great friends. Friends I regard as family. Let's give thanks for having a beautiful home. Albeit a little weird, it's still beautiful. Let's pray that our party goes off without a hitch. That we have enough food to feed everybody. Pray that Tina cooked enough side dishes. I hope everyone likes my music. I hope we have enough drinks; I hope we have enough ice. The most important prayer of all is the prayer of safety.

God, please watch over our friends. Please grant them safe passage to our house and safe passage back home. Tina and I even prayed for the spirits in the house. That the spirits find peace. Go into the light, spirits, go towards the truth and be at peace. The spirits living here need to understand something. Tina and I are not the enemy. We carry no ill will towards anyone. So yeah, we prayed for them too.

Hours later—the party was in full swing. Most of the guests had arrived. Everyone was mingling—talking, eating, drinking. But before too long, one of the peculiar things that Tina and I noticed together was regular exclamations from the guests. "Hey, something just touched me; something just bumped me," or most often: "feels like something just touched my hair." The ladies were reporting this in the middle of their conversations with Tina. None of the guys mentioned this.

And one of Tina's friends began to experience this more than any other woman in the house. I know, because Tina and I talked about it later that night when we were alone again. "Oh my God, something just touched me, something just combed my hair!" we would hear that throughout the night. Sometimes Tina was standing next to them when they get their hair touched; sometimes she's not. Where was I? I was on the other side of the room.

That wouldn't be the last time this happened either. Another friend of ours blurted out the same thing a few hours later. She described it as someone standing behind her, very close behind her; and then a feeling something brushing her hair. Every time one of our female friends did that I would look for Tina and she would look for me. We gave each other the 'what the fuck' expression whenever our eyes met. One lady saying something just bumped her is one thing. Three ladies saying somethings touched them; "something yanked my hair." What did we do? What could we do? We did nothing. Well, we did something. I took a big sip whatever I was drinking at the time as did Tina.

We both were thinking the same thing. Please don't show out, Mr. Ghost. Please don't do anything else. While the women were experiencing their level of word, I was experiencing something else entirely different. I had been making back and forth trips from the kitchen to the backyard patio for pretty much that entire evening. I started noticing how often I was getting locked out. Why is the sliding door locked? Why is the latch down (from the inside)? This happened multiple times. At first, I thought, *Wow, we must have a defective sliding door, why is it locking me out?* It finally got to a point where I had to leave the sliding door open. Well, I solved that problem, right? Not so fast. I still had another door to contend with—the front door.

31

We all know that one of the biggest goofs about hosting a party is not hearing the doorbell ring when guests arrive. To prevent that from happening, I decided to leave the front door unlocked. People could just walk on in when they get here. I even sent a mass text out to everyone coming over—door's open, all you have to do is walk in. Well so much for that effort because the entity began locking the door anyway. There were so many instances where I went outside to help people bring stuff in. The door for some reason or another is only locking me out. Mind you, I'm the one that manually unlocked it in the first place. No one's locking the front door as they come in. Everyone's hands were full, including mine. But I was getting locked out. That only happened when I was the last person walking in.

The wonders of me getting locked out both front and back happened so much that my one of my friends walked up to me laughing: "Dude, why do you keep locking yourself out?" I remember looking over Justin towards Tina. We had the same facial expression as before: what the fuck is going on? No answer. *Just drink, Keith. Just drink, Tina.* That's what we did. Big swigs of whatever it was we were drinking.

So how does an entity lock you out? I mean how does that work? I have no idea. They would have to be watching or something. Maybe even following you. I don't know.

Meanwhile, the night is still young. It would appear that the spirits weren't entirely done with Tina and me. I mean they're keeping us on our toes. Time to open some doors! Not me? Them. Throughout the night I found myself glancing at the front door—it was wide open. At first, I thought, maybe someone went outside and forgot to close the door? So, I went outside and see no-one. So why was the front door open? In one instance, Tina walked up to and asked, "What's wrong?" I look at her with the expression: "you know what's wrong." Now we had rules. Rules we agreed to prior to everyone arriving. If we needed to talk about the ghost, if something were important then we'd steal away from the party by going upstairs. And that's exactly what we did. We went upstairs to have a quick meeting. What the heck is going on?

Time to compare notes. Time to recap. Basically, we're just getting on the same page about everything that had happened so far. Is it going to get any worse? Is the spirit going to crank it up a notch? I mean we're talking about a house full of merry guests. Everyone was enjoying themselves. The last thing I need right now was for one of Tina's plants to go moon-walking across the kitchen floor? Our agreement was to keep an eye on everybody. Tina would watch the women. I would watch the men. If this is as bad as it gets, then I think we're OK. Let's just get through the remainder of the night.

Lucky for us things did begin to simmer down all of a sudden. The ladies stopped complaining about being touched. No more being locked out of my own house and no more front door opening on its own. Things were good. Activity notwithstanding, everyone, for the most part, had a good time. Our first house party was a success. But the night was not over.

One of my female friends walked up to me while the others are leaving and asks if she could have a cup of coffee. But of course! I'd be honored to make you a cup of coffee, and because you're a dear friend to me, you get to drink from the cup my mom gave me. Now, I've never drunk from this cup. That's how special this cup was. This cup and I traveled over three thousand miles together. It was a parting gift from my mom when I moved to Seattle. I remember telling my friend Claudia about how I got the cup. I told her it was a goodbye gift from my mom. When my mom handed me that cup, she told me two things. She said, "Take care of yourself. Seriously, son, take care of myself." The second thing she told me was "I love you." We hugged; she kissed me and out of nowhere came this green ceramic cup. I've had it for over seven years. It survived the move to Seattle, and it survived the move to my new house. I kept it on the top shelf in my kitchen. The kitchen in my apartment, and now the kitchen in my new home.

As soon as I handed it to Claudia, you could see she knew—there was something special about this cup. It's not a cup a man would ever buy for himself. It has flowers on it and stuff. I wanted Claudia to drink from it because of the role she played in helping me taking care of myself. I knew no one when I moved here. I'm talking when I moved to Washington. I was unemployed. I had left a perfectly good job back home to start a brand-new life here. I knew I could find a job but nothing's guaranteed. Talk about overcoming one's fears. The idea of living far scared the heck out of me. We're talking about a three-day drive into the unknown. Three thousand miles in a 1993 Toyota Corolla. All my friends that were here tonight played a role in me taking care of myself. If my sister were here, she would be drinking from that same cup. Claudia wasn't a friend. She's my sister.

It was just the four of us now: Tina's friend Kim, Kim's godmother, Tina, and I. The party ended pretty well. No one left coughing up pea soup, thank God. Minus the feeling of being touched and the issue with the doors, I think the evening went extremely well. I think we emptied out a half case of wine that night. I can depressurize now as can Tina. Screw the wine: I need a cocktail. Minutes later, we were all talking about how well the night went. Everyone was doing their recap of how the night went. Great music. Great food.

Kim, with a drink in hand, decided to stretch out on the couch (in the den). Reminder—this is the same couch Tina and I sat on weeks ago when the plant levitated. Where the couch is located, if you sit on it, your back is turned to everything behind you. If you want to see the people you're talking to, you have to prop your legs on the cushion of the couch and turn ninety degrees. And that's what Kim done.

Kim's godmother was sitting on a bar stool near the kitchen island. Tina was tiding up the kitchen, so she was walking back in forth from the refrigerator and kitchen sink. A few minutes into our talk I realized it was getting chilly in here, let me close the window behind Kim. As I was making my way towards the window, that's when I saw it. Something went flying across the room. Not the room we were sitting in. The room next to us—the room where the front door is (the living room). I saw out the corner of my eye one of Tina's plants hitting the wall.

Now Kim had the best view of all. She was already facing the direction of where the plant flew. As soon as the plant hit the wall, Kim leapt up from the couch and screamed, "What the hell was that?" Tina, who was loading up the dishwasher in the kitchen, couldn't see it; but she heard it. Kim's godmother (who flew in from LA) spun around on her bar stool and looked at Kim and me. It didn't take us long to get to the area where the plant landed. The reaction from all of us was pretty much the same. As many times as, Tina and I had seen objects fly and crash land, we were still in awe of it. It was so new to us. There was no rhyme or reason as to how it transpired. What's this thing with throwing plants? It would seem whatever was doing this was doing it because it wanted to. It wants our reaction. Well, guess what? It got it. Not only our reaction but our guests' as well.

There we were, standing over the broken pottery. I have no clue as to what to say. I mean, the cat's out the bag now. Tina's friends have just seen something very few people live to see. They've just seen a plant fly across the room. Where do I begin? Where do I start? While I struggle with what to say next, Tina blurts out, "Oh, I forgot to tell you, Kim, we have a ghost living with us!" That's it. That's all Tina said. She walked back into the kitchen and sat on one of the bar stools and took a huge sip from her wine glass. Kim and her godmother looked at Tina and me and then back at each other. I was thinking, *damn, I'm glad I made that cocktail.* Kim was still looking at Tina and me; I think she was shocked by our calm demeanor. She finally uttered the words to speak, "You guys have a ghost?" I looked at Tina; she looked at me. Together we say, "Yeah, we do." And that's when we began telling our story. Tina and I spent the next twenty minutes bringing Kim and her godmother up to speed on everything that had been happening.

Now, Kim is Tina's best friend. She's the one Tina stays with whenever I went out of town. So, Kim knows a little bit already. Now, I was never around to hear Tina mention stuff about the ghost, so I don't know everything she said. I'm willing to bet Tina mentioned everything over a glass of wine, or in the middle of one of their shopping sprees. In response to which, I'm sure Kim probably thought 'girl whatever.'

That cliché "seeing is believing" is nowhere truer than in the realm of the paranormal. Most people won't believe you until they see the wonder themselves. They believe everything else you tell them, except this. It's like suddenly you have a credibility problem. I've met a lot of people like that. They're that stubborn; my brother is one of them. He's not going to believe unless a ghost bites him on the ass. A part of me understands the level of cynicism one might get from hearing a story like this. I'm pretty sure Kim didn't think Tina was lying to her about our house being haunted. Best friends don't call best friends liars, let alone hoaxers. That's what internet trolls do. Kim probably just thought Tina was mistaking house noise for ghost noise. I mean, think about it, we've just moved into a house. There's got to be an obvious explanation. One Tina and I hadn't yet figured out. I'm pretty sure some of my friends have thought the same thing. And that's fine; I get it. Guess what? Plants can't fly. They can't move themselves. I know that. You know that. That's not even debatable. So, Kim has a decision to make. A realization. The same conclusion Tina and I made when we first saw a plant fly across the room. And that realization is you guys have a ghost living with you.

I think Tina and I were halfway through our story about what's been going, when all of a sudden, we hear a loud bang. *BOOM! BOOM! BOOM!* After the third *BOOM!* Silence. Kim looked at Tina and me and asked and waited for our answer. Kim, godmother looked at us too and said: "what was that?" Tina then stood and playfully looked at Kim and said, "Girl, I told you about the bangs weeks ago, that's what we hear at night." To which, Kim replied: "Girl, you didn't tell me it was that damn loud!"

"Well, now you know," replied Tina. The second round of bangs erupted. Three booms!

When I'm asked to describe the banging noises, I always begin by saying the noise sounds like something hitting the main structure of the house. Now I'm not a home builder; I'm not even sure a house has something called the main structure. I might be describing it wrong when I say the noise sounds and feels like it's coming from the main structure of the house, wherever that may be. But I'll share with you something I experienced in 2014.

There have been occasions where Tina and I have heard loud bangs, clapping sounds, popping sounds, piano crashing sounds, the sound of pottery being thrown when there is no pottery being thrown, and yes, even the sound of large furniture being thrown or dragged around. The sounds are random. The noise is so loud it forces you to stop what it is you're doing. You have no choice but to investigate. And I did. What did I find? Nothing? Not a shred of evidence as to what's causing it.

Minutes later, we discovered broken pottery, knocked over furniture, knocked over candles, cameras, and new dents on our walls. We find these items in the area where we heard the loud noise. The time frame between the sound and the debris we see is sometimes minutes, if not hours. What I'm telling you is very important. Especially if you're a researcher. These noises, although loud, violent, and troublesome, have an element to them I can't quite put my hands on. They sound close, but for some reason, sound dated. Imagine sitting a mason jar on the side of the world's busiest highway. Imagine if you could capture that sound within the jar itself. You pick the jar up twelve hours later and cover it with a lid. What do you do with the closed jar? You do nothing. The jar sits on your shelf for say, fifty years. On the fiftieth anniversary of that jar being put on the shelf you (if you're still alive) mail to it someone. Whoever receives that jar has clear instructions which states: open the jar when you and members of your family are watching TV, having dinner, getting ready for bed, etc. As soon as you open the jar, there appears the fifty-year sound. Traffic. Genuine traffic. But it's different from the traffic you know because fifty years have passed. Cars run quieter today than they did years ago. But it's still sound. That's what I mean when I say it sounds dated. Dated but real. If that makes sense? I had to deviate for a second. Because that's important. Might not be now but maybe somewhere in time, it will. My description of what we heard while living in the home.

It's quite possible the groove in our bedroom doorway appeared minutes, if not days, after the loud bang. After the so-called stomping frightening as all this, it's also intriguing. It's intriguing to me, and from the looks of it, it's become intriguing to Kim. In the middle of us telling our story, Kim done something Tina, and I couldn't predict. Kim raised her cell phone in the air and began asking, "What do you want? Why are you here? Where do you come from?"

Kim's godmother was shaking her head in disbelief. Kim was waving her iPhone in the direction of where the noise was coming from. She was asking questions. I looked at Tina with a look of 'what's she doing?'. Tina just shrugged and took a huge sip of her drink. Kim then looked at Tina and me and said, "You guys have to talk to them, you have to guide them to the light. They'll be peaceful and appreciative if you do that." My reply, "If you think that's going to work, go for it. By all means, do me a favor by getting these things out of here."

Kim went for it in more ways than one. In addition to the questions being asked, Kim turned on her video app. Now she was recording herself talking to the ceiling. I say ceiling because that's the direction she's aiming her phone. Within a few seconds of having her doing that, another *BOOM! BOOM! BOOM!* Now the bangs are corresponding with Kim's questions. Kim asked the same questions over and over. "Why are you here? What do you want? Why won't you go into the light?" *BOOM! BOOM! BOOM!* I looked at Tina and Kim's godmother. I think the bangs are getting louder; we should stop.

Nothing, and I do mean nothing, is leading me to believe that these spirits are friendly. That they have an interest in talking to us. I've tried talking to them, and the results have been the same as Kim's. *BOOM! BOOM! BOOM!* I have no idea what that means. Neither does Kim. Neither does Kim's godmother. The banging noise seems to increase with each question, so much that Kim finally decided to stop.

Time to try something else. That's when Kim's godmother decided to step forth. "Time to pray." Her suggestion was, "Let's stop what it is we're doing, enough with the guessing. Let's all go into the living room and pray."

When you have plants flying all over the place and phantom bangs, I think it's prudent to turn to God. Start praying, right? I mean, Tina and I have been praying since all this stuff began. I'll never say prayer doesn't work. It must have worked. Tina and I are still alive. We're still breathing. I looked at Tina, and she looked at me. Let's do this. Kim's godmother wanted us to pray in the living room, the room where the plant was thrown.

Kim's godmother had explained that her experience with spirits always involved praying. Your only option for dealing with them is remaining steadfast. Your best weapon is the word of God. Her advice right now was everybody, starting with me and Tina, would each say an open prayer. I went first. I can't remember what I said exactly, except to say that I began my prayer by thanking those around me. I prayed for those who left already. I prayed that each person who came to my house tonight got home safely. I prayed for both Kim and her godmother. I prayed for Tina. I then prayed for myself, and I prayed for the spirits. I asked them to see into their hearts, see deeply, recognize the fact that Tina and I are not here to hurt them, we carry no ill-will. I asked that the spirit understand that the only thing we wish to do is live our lives.

I informed the spirit that my goal was to take care of the house as if it was mine. I harbor no ill-will towards them. I told the spirit in my own words, to be at peace. Amen. Then came Tina's turn. Her prayer was very similar to mine. Now Tina's is shy, and she's very private. This was the first time I've seen her pray. I mean individually. Our prayers prior to tonight have consisted of me saying something or us praying in silence. Seeing her pray educated me about who she was. She's extremely shy when it comes to public speaking. Speaking, not talking. We all say our prayers out loud.

Then came the Lord's Prayer. Kim's godmother would be leading that. The way Kim's godmother said that prayer was really important. It put things in perspective. Here are Tina and me and our two remaining house guests. The activity thus far has not derailed what was, overall, a good night. It seemed the spirit waited for almost everybody to leave before doing what it's doing now.

Tina and I had twelve people in here tonight. Eight were now gone and looked at us. It was after midnight. Here we were reciting the Lord's Prayer while at the same time holding hands. After the prayer was over, we all looked at each other. I was relieved. Relieved by the fact that the night could have been worse. As I hugged and kissed Tina, pivot to shake hands with Kim and her godmother, I was thinking maybe the worst is finally behind us. Hopefully, this prayer will lessen the activity. Kim's godmother repeated: "remain steadfast". I thought about that as I made my way back towards the kitchen.

I was a few feet ahead of everyone when it came time to go back into the kitchen. As I walked past the stairs and into both kitchen and den my mouth dropped open. Uh oh! Behind me stood Tina, Kim and Kim's godmother. We all froze. I'm not a mind reader but I'm pretty sure we all thought the same thing. Wow! Every kitchen cabinet door was wide open. Every closet door. Heck, even the island cabinets were open. This is unbelievable. I don't know what's scarier, coming downstairs in the morning and finding every kitchen cabinet door open, or what we've just now experienced. I mean, we were just in the next room. Heads bowed in prayer. We heard nothing. Not one decibel whatsoever. No footsteps, no pacing, no hint of anything being in the kitchen.

I think we talked about what we just saw for about thirty more minutes before Kim's godmother said, "Just give it time. These spirits will grow tired and move on eventually. They want to test your resolve." Kim and her godmother would leave an hour or so after that. Now it was just Tina and me. There we were lying in bed. Back to that pillow talk I told you about earlier.

The next morning, I got up and went into the kitchen. I was going to make a pot of coffee when I suddenly noticed that the coffee cup was missing. The one I served to Claudia. I remember instinctively placing it in the kitchen sink prior to going to bed. Now, the only reason I can think of as to why a spirit would take something like that is because it heard me talk about it. It listened to me while I was talking to Claudia. It's essential that you remember this because other things are going to disappear as we get deeper into the book. This coffee cup was of no consequence to the spirit, but it was of value to me. My mom had given it to me years ago. The spirit knew that. How did it know that? It had to have been eavesdropping. Remember that word: eavesdropping. I never saw that cup again.

Chapter 7
Ad Hominem

Ad hominem is where an argument is rebutted by attacking the character, motive, or other attribute of the person making the argument, or persons associated with the argument, rather than attacking the substance of the argument itself ~ Webster's Dictionary

One of the first things Tina and I observed while dealing with this ghost thing, was people respond weirdly when you tell them you have a ghost living with you. Family members are no exception. The first conversation I had with my mom about the ghost in our house was when we were conversing about everyday stuff. How are you doing, Mom? How's everyone doing back home? Did my sister pass her physicians exam? Did so and so do what they said they were going do? Oh, and guess what? Tina and I have a ghost living with us. No matter who we tell the response is always the same. Silence.

"What gives you the idea that your house is haunted?" That's always the next question. Then I pause. I pause because I know whatever answer I give them they're not going to believe it right away. They're going to think Tina and I must be imagining things. They're going to think *uh oh, there's trouble in paradise, somethings wrong with the relationship.* They don't even have to say it. I know that's what they're thinking. The only answer I can give them is the truth—which is we saw a plant fly across the room. Either they're not paying attention, or they don't know how to respond. I can tell you from experience the latter is more correct. I know this because of the question they ask, "What makes you think you have a ghost?" I just told you, Tina and I saw a plant fly across the room. Second question, "What makes you think your house is haunted?" The second answer I give them is, "Tina and I saw a plant levitate. Tina and I saw a chair slide across the floor. Tina and I wake up in the morning and find every kitchen cabinet door open. We've seen it numerous times." Notice how I'm only mentioning the stuff Tina that I saw together. I'm doing this for a reason. I'm trying to let whomever I'm talking to know that I'm not the only one making this claim. Tina was having a similar conversation with her family. She was getting a similar reaction, which is avoidance.

So, I was telling my mom this, and finally, the genuine reaction emerged, which is "wow." And that was it. No drilling me with questions. No, are you doing something that you shouldn't be doing? Instead, my mom goes into her memory banks and begins recounting ghost stories she grew up with. I soon realized this kind of subject matter catches people off guard. I mean, what do you do? Your son just told you that his house is haunted. The plants have come alive at my son's house, oh my God what's going on at Keith and Tina's house? And that reaction is completely understandable. One of the things I noticed about the people after telling them about what Tina and I have seen is no one knows what to do with the information being told them. Everyone reacts differently.

Just the uttering of the word ghost can make some people very uncomfortable. To some, it's the ultimate buzzkill. To others, it's the root of their existence. They want to know more. "Tell me more, tell me more." Some pull up a chair and sit down right in front of me and say "tell me everything." Others take off running, with the parting words "I can't deal with that." It's a touchy subject to bring up. Even inside one's own family.

But now I have a ghost on my hands. My friends know this. My immediate friends, that is. My family? I'm not a hundred percent sure they know it. My mom's reaction was tepid. As were my siblings. They seemed to think something else was going on. The vibe I kept feeling was 'uh oh, there must be trouble in paradise, something's up.' And they're partially right. There is trouble in paradise, but it had nothing to do with Tina and me. That trouble is two years away.

So, what was going on Tina's end? How's her family reacting? They were asking similar questions; questions about me. Who am I? How well does she know me? Was it a good idea to move in with a man you've only known two years? What's his background? Where is he from? Are you sure he's not behind this? My brother asked me the same thing. Is Tina behind this? Is it her ex? Is it Keith's ex? These are the types of questions you get when informing family members about your ghost problem. No one wants to talk about the plants traveling through the air at miraculous speeds. No one wants to talk about the loud bangs. No one's acknowledging that the majority of the stuff taken place has happened when Tina and I have both been in the room. But the question still surfaces. "Are you sure it's not Tina doing this? Are you sure it's not Keith doing this?"

The advice given to me by my younger brother was, "Buy a video camera, get it on video. That's the only way you're going to get people to believe you, including your family members. Prove to me that it's not your girlfriend. I think she's pranking you." Siblings are notorious for their cynicism. My family is no exception.

A few weeks later a new wonder began to emerge. Lights were going off and on by themselves in several rooms in the house. One night I was in my office watching TV. I saw the hall light go off. I heard Tina downstairs, so I know it was not her. I know she was not upstairs. This was different than what I talked about earlier. The lights in the hallway were going off and on repeatedly. This went for a while, and it was beginning to happen every night.

It didn't take long for me to realize that this was something new. I came to that conclusion after inviting a few electricians over. "Nothing's wrong with the wiring," that's the conclusion of several electricians having visited the house.

We have two light switches in our hallway. One by the landing area, and right outside my office. Is the spirit doing this by flickering the light at the end of the hall or is it doing it by supernatural means? I can't see the other light switch. The only one I can see is the one right outside my door. I'm looking dead at it whenever the lights go off and on, off and on in the hallway. I'm going to take my brother's advice; I'm going to try to see if I can get this intermittent light thing on video. And I did. If you go to my YouTube channel (see back of this book), you'll see two of the oldest videos on their deal with the hallway light issue. I've perched a Sony Handycam on the hallway bookshelf. It's point towards the landing area. Titled: Haunted House October Hallway Light 2012 and Haunted House October 2012 Hallway Lights Off/On—they're the first videos captured inside the Bothell home.

I showed my brother the videos a few days later. He found it interesting, but it wasn't what he wanted. The video my brother wanted is the video that everybody wants—the footage no spirit is ever going to let you have. We'll discuss the reason for that later.

Something is interesting about the bookshelf in our hallway. The spirits seem to object when you sit books on it. Any book. The Bibles were not the first books to sit on that hallway bookshelf. No, the Bibles came much, much later. The first books I sat on that bookshelf were books I've acquired through my IT profession. Every night those books would get thrown off the shelf by an invisible force. The manner in which they were thrown reminds me of someone walking by and extending their arm to empty the shelf of its contents. Everything thrown to the floor in one full swing. This started happening every night—around the time of me setting up the camera.

So, every day when I go to work the first person I meet is my secretary. She's the only person I'm telling this story to on a daily basis. And let me tell you, she was enamored by it. Her suggestion to me was, "Try a Bible. Put a Bible on the bookshelf, open it to Psalms 91." That, ladies and gentleman, is how the Bible got introduced into all of this. The Bible was not the first book in our house to get thrown. Far from it.

Going back to what I said earlier about how my brother not believing nothings real unless it's captured on video. I mean he wanted to see what Kim and her godmother saw. He wanted to see objects thrown. Objects slide across the floor on their own accord. He wants the "wow factor." Who doesn't, right? I mean Tina and I get that request often. It's interesting how we get blamed for not being able to capture stuff like that—it's not for lack of trying. And that's just it. That's what people don't realize. You see, I started noticing something very peculiar within days of setting up the camera. I learned if you want to stop something from flying in our house, the easiest thing to do is put a camera on it. The object that's always flying around the house no longer flies around the house. It no longer gets thrown. You know what gets thrown now? The object that's not within peripheral view of the camera. I later found out that, that's the characteristic of a certain kind of spirit.

Chapter 8
Where's my Bible?

October 10, 2012, was the day Tina went out of town on business. If you told me her going out of town on a business trip would lead to one of the most profound events in paranormal history, I would never have believed you. But that's what ended up happening—here goes.

So far, we'd tried praying, candle lighting, house blessing, and the daily showcase of religious paraphernalia, e.g. my Bible. We're talking about a religious campaign that involved everything I've just mentioned. A campaign that went on for months. Nothing seemed to be working. All of that diligence, all of that steadfastness was leading up to one thing: The first Bible being stolen. Notice I said, *first* Bible. Three out of the five Bibles have gone missing. Three have caught fire—each one differently.

How did the Bible disappearance start? It started with the introduction of the Bibles. It started with me taking Bibles (one at a time) off my office bookshelf and placing them on the hallway bookshelf. The advice was given to me by my secretary. Those that got thrown off the shelf were neatly put back on the shelf.

The day the first Bible went missing was the day Tina went out of town. Instead of her driving me to the airport which she often did, it was now my turn. I went to work immediately after I dropped her off and sure enough had a conversation again with my secretary about what was going on at the house. Were any of the proactive steps working? Did the minister's house blessing calm things down? Was the Bible calming things down? I told her the Bible was getting thrown to the floor. So, I don't think things are calming down. That troubled her; the spirit, she felt, was showing definite signs of defiance. Neither one of us was thinking demon at the time.

Later that day my secretary walked into my office and asked, "Did you ever try smudging?" Honestly, I didn't know what she was talking about. She explained to me that smudging involves using a sage plant. It's supposed to ward off evil spirits. A light bulb went off in my head. Smudging? Yes, I've heard of it. Several of the paranormal websites spoke about cleansing or smudging, echoing what she said about ridding houses of unwanted spirits. The next question was: where can I find it? It turned out the best place to go would be the botanical store in Ballard, just a few miles from where I worked. Could this be it? Could this be the break we needed? Everything we read about sage that day led us to believe it would work. This felt like the closest thing to having a silver bullet. It sounded promising. There seemed to be no better time than the present to apply it. Tina was out of town. I would have total access to the home. I can buy this sage today and use it today. Maybe I'll be able to nip this problem in the bud before Tina gets back. Yes! Ladies and gentleman, this was problem-solving. This is what I do. I had a big smile on my face, for some reason or another this felt right.

It felt good. I gave a high five to my secretary for coming up with the idea, and I left work. Off to buy some sage.

The thing going through my mind while heading to the sage store was: I hope this works. I hope this releases the dark energy that's in our home. There were too many unknowns appearing before Tina and me. The question I began asking myself every night was, where is all of this going? Sometimes weekdays are worse. Sometimes weekends are worse. There was no pattern as to when things would occur. It wasn't stopping. And that was all we wanted. Stop with the loud bangs. Return everything you've stolen. Stop with the pacing back and forth. Stop running upstairs when Tina and I get home. Stop making those pitter-patter sounds. Stop with the intermittent cable, phone, and Wi-Fi interruptions. Stop locking me out of my own house. Stop turning off lights in rooms I'm coming back in. Stop slamming the bedroom door while we're sleeping. Stop slamming the bathroom door in the middle of Tina taking a bath. Stop opening all the cabinet doors in the kitchen. Stop throwing plants, and lastly, stop invading our personal space; especially while we're sleeping. If the smudging can solve half of these outbreaks, that will be a significant improvement.

So, I walked into the store in Ballard, and it looked like everything I would have expected. It looked like a place that might have the answer to our problem. When the store employee asked me what I was looking for I explained that I was in need of sage; I wanted to smudge my house. Matter of fact I said my new house. She was very helpful. She used sage herself at times when she felt negative energy settling around her. I almost felt compelled to explain to her the real problem. In the end, I held back. I mean, how do you tell a total stranger that you have ghost problems? To cleanse negative energy, she told me, the best type was white sage. I'll take it!

An hour later, I walked through my front door, and there went the hurrying footsteps. You'd think there was a party going on based on how it sounded. It was like I was interrupting something based on me walking through the front door. What's scarier than the sounds themselves is the direction you hear them going. What I hear are pitter-patter noises storming up the stairs to the landing area. Where they go from there is anybody's guess. Tina and I have talked about this several times. Occasionally she'll beat me home and hear the same thing. If you ask me how many of them there are, I would have to say (based on the sounds I hear) three to five. That's how precise the sound is. Maybe they know I brought sage home and now it's time to cleanse them out of here. But why are they running upstairs? As I'm asking that question, I'm also thinking about how to do this. Keep it simple, appears to be what the directions are saying. Thorough and simple.

So, I lit the sage stick in the kitchen and begin waving it in a roughly circular motion. As I do, I chanted, "In the name of God and His Christ, I command you to leave, you do not belong here; this is our house, I command that you go into the light." My chant ended with the words, "Get out of my house! I need for you to get out of my house." I tried to emphasize the word my as much as possible. That was the most important part; everyone said: declaring that this house belonged to Keith and Tina. I repeated this over and over while going in and around the kitchen, and in and around both den and living room area. I head upstairs soon after. The guest bedroom near the landing area would be first. I smudged the four corners of the room, starting high and ending low.

By now smoke was filling the house. So much so that it set off a few fire alarms. Heading into my bedroom, I was telling myself, *be super thorough here, Keith, this is where objects have been thrown.* I can't help but think: *Who terrorizes people while they're asleep? What do you gain from doing that?*

Before I leave the bedroom, I'm thinking, *I wonder if this is going to work?* As soon as I step onto the landing again, I saw something I was not expecting. The front door opened on its own. The ADT voice alert said *"front door open."* The front door opened wide and slammed shut. All by itself. I've never heard a door slam this loud before. There was no wind draft imaginable that can open a door the way my door just opened. No way could I duplicate what I had just seen and heard. I wouldn't even try for fear of knocking some of Tina's portraits off the wall. I could see the door perfectly from where I was standing.

The ADT alarm says *"front door open"* whenever we open the front door. As you'll recall, I programmed it that way, due to us finding our front door open some mornings, as well as some nights, while watching TV or doing dishes. Now, today, no one came in. No one went out. I was the only person here. But! Just to make sure I wasn't seeing things or just to confirm that no one was in the house, after seeing the door open and close on its own, I ran downstairs. I darted downstairs and opened my front door, hoping I'll see someone running from the house. I looked left and I look right. No one. I even walked further away from the house till I was halfway down the block. I could see one hundred yards in either direction. No one was outside. No one was walking their dog or jogging. No kids were playing. Had I seen someone outside walking, talking, or jogging along the sidewalk I would have kindly approached them and asked them if they'd seen someone, anyone walking, or better yet running from my house. But no one was outside. It was just me.

The only thing I could do was turn around and go back into the house. Back inside, the smell of sage was everywhere. The house did feel different. Only... all of a sudden, I was getting the "all eyes on me" feeling. It felt like someone was watching me. But how can that be? I mean, something just ran out of the house. That's what that door opening and closing meant. It meant something couldn't stand me smudging. Therefore it ran out of the house. Right?

Now, someone might ask why a spirit would open a door when they can just run through it. I don't know why a spirit with the capability of walking through walls chooses to open and shut a door when leaving the house. Maybe this spirit doesn't have the ability to walk through a wall. The Gray Lady tried to go through the washroom door and couldn't. Was that because I was watching her? The same thing could be said here. I'm six feet, five and a half inches tall. I can see the living room downstairs from my bedroom doorway. I can see the front door. No one was there. The door just opened wide and slammed shut.

When I saw the door open and slam on its own, I couldn't help but think that was because of my smudging. That's what I thought on the day it happened. I don't believe that's the case anymore. If there's one thing I've learned as a result of me living here, it's this: spirits can manipulate things. They can manipulate people. When that door opened and slammed, I could not help but think my smudging must be working. But several years have passed since that day. So many other things have happened in the house that forces me to alter that belief. This was not something fleeing the home. No, the door slamming was the sign of a spirit throwing a temper tantrum. A shot across the bow is what it was. It was for all practical purposes a statement of 'how could you?' I didn't know this at the time, no one ever told me. I had to learn the hard way. Some spirits react violently to smudging. Some view it as a challenge. A form of eviction, that's what we want, right? For them to leave? But wanting them to leave doesn't mean we shouldn't be careful. Think about it: who or what are we asking to leave? If we're not sure what it is we're asking to leave, maybe we shouldn't smudge so quickly and so nonchalantly. Which is exactly what I was doing when I saw my front door open. It was ludicrous for me to smudge by myself.

If the opening and slamming the front door was their way of getting me to stop smudging it worked. Wishful thinking led me to believe that the mission was accomplished. But that's not the absolute truth. What really happened was I lost my initiative. I lost the will to continue.

I walked back into the house and sat the remainder of the sage stick on the kitchen island and pulled out my cell phone to call Tina. I needed to let her know that I smudged the house, she replied, "You did what?" I smudged the house. I told her what happened as a result of smudging. I told her I saw the front door open and slam shut. I told her about the footsteps I heard when I came home. I ended the conversation with a light-hearted joke by telling her that the house smelled like sage now. I mean, it smells like sage. The conversation ended after that.

My friend Justin called me a few hours later to offer his advice on what to do about our ghost problem. Justin's a believer. He's been to the house numerous times. He was with me a few months back when the neighbor across the street decided to walk over and introduce himself. The neighbor said, "This house never keeps occupants." Justin was standing right next to when my neighbor said that. Justin and I thought nothing of it then. Why would we? He told me this within weeks of us moving in.

Justin and Tina's friend Kim have a lot of things in common. They've both seen things. Justin has seen chandeliers move by themselves when he's been over. He was the one that approached me about getting locked out of my own house during our housewarming party. He was worried though. He thought things might be escalating. Tonight, he was calling to offer more advice. The advice he gave was relatively simple. "Start praying over that Bible that you have laid out in the open. The one you put on the lamp table weeks back.

"Start reading from it every night, you and Tina. Read from it out loud: Psalms 91. Keep it where it is and keep it open to Psalms 91." That's the advice Justin gave me. When midnight came, I did exactly that. I opened up the Bible to Psalms 91, and I began reading out loud. I got done—I put the Bible back on the lamp table and made sure to leave it open instructed. Was I afraid to sleep in the house by myself? Not really. Tina and I had come to the agreement months back that she wouldn't be staying in the house alone whenever I go out of town. She's to stay with Kim.

I can't do that. I can't retreat or give ground to a spirit. That's exactly what I would be doing if I slept elsewhere. To sleep anywhere else would be me admitting to the spirits that I'm scared of them. That their tricks are more powerful than my God. I was scared and nervous right now. That's the human aspect to this thing. I have no idea what's about to happen. I have no idea what could happen as a result of me smudging. I have no idea is going to happen as a result of me sleeping here alone. So, yeah, I'm terrified. But I also determined. This might be a trial for Tina and me. For me especially. Who or what is testing us is anybody's guess. I mean no one could tell me with hundred percent sureties, what was going on. Everyone's guessing. As are we. So, I have to fall back on how I was raised. Tina is my girlfriend. I have to protect her. I can't do that if I'm away on business. Me? I'm a different story. I'm not spending a night with friends while my girlfriend is out of town. This is my house!

Before I went to bed that night, I made sure to turn on our ADT system. Check all the doors and windows—everything looked good. The last thing I looked at when I got upstairs to the landing area was the Bible. There it was sitting on Tina's lamp table (in the living room). The book was open to Psalm 91. *Good job, Keith, now go to bed.* It had been a long day; *maybe this sage thing will work. Who knows, maybe the spirits will get the message and leave.* I walked into our bedroom, closed the door, and went to sleep.

The next morning, I woke up and walked out of our bedroom. Something told me to look over the staircase wall while heading towards the guest bathroom. My eyes went immediately to the lamp table. *Oh, shit! The Bible is gone.* It wasn't on the table. Where did it go? *What the hell?* I darted downstairs and approached the table. Nothing was out of order. Everything was how I had left it prior to going to bed. The ADT security was armed.

The front door was locked; the bolt lock was as it was when I left it. Nothing had been changed. The only thing changed about this entire situation was the Bible. It was gone. I called Tina immediately. My heart was racing. They had to have taken the Bible either last night or early this morning. This was different from anything else that had gone missing. Car keys, coffee cups, silverware, jewelry, etc. We're talking about a religious item—a Christian book. The Bible was in a class by itself. I mean, I purposely looked at the Bible and the table it rested on last night as a means of telling the spirits, this Bible lying here means: *please leave this house. Leave this house now, tonight.*

Tina was shocked when I told her the Bible was now missing. She, like me, had big hopes for the sage. We were trying a lot of things, Tina and me. This, in my opinion, had the best chance of working. And maybe it will over time. We didn't know right now what will work and what won't. All we know was we had to keep trying. I went to work a little bit earlier than usual that day. I needed to tell my secretary what had happened with the smudging and what had happened with the Bible.

Her reaction was the same as Tina's. "Wow!" We agreed that the Bible was stolen as a means of defiance. As a means of ridicule. No need to go looking for it. It's gone. It wasn't like I misplaced the Bible. I was alone in the house. Me searching for something that I know is gone is not going to bring my Bible back.

I'm not giving the spirits the satisfaction of me going around looking for it. Not if I can help it.

From: Keith   [mailto:]
Sent: Thursday, October 11, 2012 9:21 AM
To: , Laura
Subject: Re: some more info

Hello Laura

Tina's out of town i in Vegas (work related). I bought some sage yesterday on the way home and lit and spread it through out the house: several times. Last night after I lit the sage my front door slammed open, and my ADT security monitor went off saying "front door open."

I went to bed around midnight and when I woke up this morning prior to leaving the house noticed in the den on the lamp table the Bible I placed there months a go is missing. This Bible was put there by me when the haunting started back in July. Its gone and would have had to disappear last night while I slept, because I saw it last night.

Is there anyway your deacon can tell me the significance of this? Or intervene on my behalf and get this looked at right away?

I welcome any man/woman of God into my home that can help resolve this issue.

Thanks

Fig 8.1 I emailed my friend Laura that morning about my missing Bible.

Chapter 9
2013

If I could name one subject that Tina and I began to disagree on, it would be the idea that something was still living in the house with us. By the time 2013 rolled around Tina's attitude was "let's not talk about it anymore. Things had quieted down tremendously, let's just leave it at that." And she was right. The activity spiked downward almost to the point of nonexistence by the time we got to January. The Bible went missing in October of last year. The other things I spoke about all began to lessen during the November and December months. But why?

I still can't point to one single thing that Tina and I did that may have caused the decrease in activity. Tina took it as a sign of the ghosts getting bored with us and therefore decided to move on. "We should let sleeping dogs lie," was the mindset she had. I understood why she thought like that. That's been the opinion of a lot of people I have talked to.

Up until now, the most horrible thing we'd seen or dealt with had been the door slams in the middle of Tina watching TV. That was Tina's most horrible event of 2012. My most horrible thing would be the kitchen bar stool being knocked over while Tina and I were trying to conduct a question and answer session—something the internet advised us to do.

That was my scariest moment in 2012. So, it's all about perspective. Tina's fear was the constant door slams which affected her more than it affected me. You might be thinking, what's so scary about a bar stool being slammed to the ground? The bar stools were right next to us.

Take every activity I've described and spread them out one by one. None of them would make the top one hundred list of the scariest things we've seen since living here. They all pale in comparison to what's about to happen. But not right away though. There was a lull period. It was called 2013. Not much happened in 2013. I have no clue as to why.

So yes, disagreement was setting in between Tina and me about what's still here and what's not here. Zero activity means zero ghosts, that was Tina's thinking. My thinking was the opposite. I still felt we're being watched. I kept saying to myself; *it doesn't feel over*. It feels like we're in the eye of the storm. Tina and I never had time to comprehend the things that were happening around us. That's how often things happened in the summer of 2012. We never had a chance to come up for air. Not till 2013. Now we're taking it all in. We're re-assessing everything that's happened.

One of the things Tina and I talked about and sometimes debated on was our missing belongings. Where are they? Why hasn't our stuff reappeared? If the spirits left, shouldn't our stuff reappear? No one knew the answer to that question.

I like to think out loud when I'm problem-solving. Share ideas sort of speak. Let's talk about this. If I can't share my premonitions with my girlfriend, who can I share it with? No one understands the missing item incidents better than Tina.

She lives here. She's seen it. But Tina's disinterested. In Tina's mind, our home was starting to settle down. It has settled down. It's starting to look like the home we saw on Craigslist. Maybe the objects that went missing are just gone; gone for good. Maybe the spirit took them with no intention of ever giving them back. Maybe our items are appearing in other people's homes the world over. Who knows? The opinions online, of spirits taking stuff and giving them back, was mixed. Some people have had their items returned. Others have not. Maybe Tina and I are a part of the group that doesn't get items returned. I mean, we're talking about the paranormal here: where's the official rulebook on what we should expect? There is no guide to read that says, do this, and we guarantee your stuff will come back. If you're wondering what items I specifically want back, it's the Bible; it's my car keys. I want my mom's coffee cup back. I want the earrings that I bought Tina back where the spirit found them. In the jewelry box.

Funny how the activity in the home sort of derailed one of our reasons for getting the house in the first place. Fixing our relationship. You see, the things that make this story compelling are not just the crazy events that happened in the course of four years. I mean, that's one component of it. What makes this story compelling is the fact that it happened inside a modern home. Pause and think about the house for a second. Think about Keith and Tina. Nothing sticks out when it comes to root cause. Nothing sticks out when it comes to what could be causing this. Why is it happening? Reminder: Tina and I did not have activity happening to us when we lived in our apartments. We'd been together two years. I like to think I would have noticed something at her place if that were true. Tina would have noticed something with me. One of the things I hope to accomplish by writing this book is calling attention to the paradigm within the paranormal community that new houses can't be haunted. Yes, they can.

I can't overstate the roadblocks we encountered based on the fact that this house was less than ten years old. No one wanted to take us seriously. Some churches thought our claims were "too hellish to be real." They did. I had a friend of mine reach out to the Seattle Catholic Church on our behalf—a member of the church. They gave her the run-around. Another friend of mine tried to do the same thing and got similar responses. Both friends have seen and heard weird noises in our house. How can a church member be given the run-around by their parish? If a church can't believe what its believers are saying, then they definitely can't believe what Tina and I are saying.

So, what happened in 2013? Well, I call these happenings, inconclusive events. Inconclusive because they weren't physical manifestations. An item appearing on the staircase that neither of us owned is a physical manifestation. So is a plant flying across the room. All of that and more began to lessen towards the end of 2012. Doesn't mean weird things weren't still happening. It just meant I no longer was sweeping up debris from a plant that once was resting on a bookshelf. Weird things were still afoot though. Exhibit A: I was asleep one night. It must have been after 3 am or so. I woke up and found myself sleeping on the top of my bed sheets (I never do that). I was lying flat on my back. It was like I was waiting to be operated on. I woke up gasping for air, and I mean seriously gasping for air. Not only was I gasping for air, but I was also shivering. Shivering like a puppy left on someone's doorstep. It felt like my body temperature had dropped so low that, had I not awakened, you probably wouldn't be reading this book right now. If I had to compare it to something I'd say the entire ordeal resembled having the air knocked out of you. My lungs felt empty, no air whatsoever. I never shared this experience with Tina; one reason being that, bizarrely, despite the noise of me gasping for air, Tina never woke up. Which is a mystery unto itself, because Tina is a light sleeper.

It took me twenty minutes or so to get myself together. The first thing I did after regaining composure was crawl back under the covers. I decided to just lay there and contemplate what caused all this. What was this about? I'd be lying if I said the idea of a spirit causing this didn't cross my mind. Of course, it crossed my mind. I'm in my mid-forties, and I'd never had an experience like this before.

A few weeks later, I got an email from a research company saying I'd qualified for their test study. This study involved the testing of the new Xbox game console. I almost forgot that I had applied for this study. How does it work? The project would involve me beta testing an Xbox and Kinect prototype simultaneously for three months. First off, the research team comes to my house to observe me playing the Xbox prototype. When they leave, the Xbox stays here with me. A virtual team would be monitoring me through the game console whenever I decided to play. Some nights they came over to watch me play, other nights they watch from afar (remotely). All they do is watch and take notes.

Mid-way through the project, in September 2013, the research turned from the Xbox console to the new Xbox Kinect. What non-gamers need to realize here is that the Xbox Kinect uses a complex system to monitor the game-players actual movements—in the room, in real time. This technology employed 'full-body 3D motion capture, facial recognition, and voice recognition capabilities'. In short: anything moving in the room, gets picked up.

With no activity to speak of through this year, I was starting to feel like Tina. Maybe the worst was behind us. But let's not speak too soon. The Microsoft research team came over one night to observe me on the Kinect. They came in like they always do, holding clipboards, tablets, and tons of video equipment. But then something happens that causes one of the remote technicians to call the team in my house. "Hold on, guys; we got an anomaly on our end of the screen; we can't tell where it's coming from." So, the project manager sitting next to me says, "Stop using the Xbox." Their engineers have picked something strange. With the Xbox now off and the Kinect still on, my TV began showing what appeared to be black masses on the TV screen. The masses were moving—the way wax moves inside a lava lamp, only throughout my TV screen. Now, given how the Kinect works, these masses or images cannot be coming from the Kinect itself. These floating black masses, perhaps five in all, and each about the size of a softball, were behind us.

Understand that the Kinect sits near your television. It has one specific job: distinguish animate objects from inanimate objects. The only thing of significance to the Kinect is a human being. Theoretically, the gamer when playing is the only thing in the living room capable of moving. Everything else is a stationary, e.g. couch, love seat, coffee table, etc. If something is moving, the Kinect is going to pick it up and interpret that as being human. The anomaly the Kinect kept running into was this: the objects it was detecting was not me. It was picking up something behind us. The objects were coming from the far end of the kitchen—behind the den, where I was sitting.

What the Kinect could not interpret or make sense of was the objects moving behind me. And when I say behind me, I mean floating in mid-air behind me. All of them. Some bigger than others. All appearing on the TV screen. The individuals at headquarters were asked to give their interpretation of what was going on. They were clueless as were the individuals in my house. The only person that wasn't clueless was me. Seeing those images on the TV screen as a result of the Kinect reaffirmed my hunch that something was still here.

When I asked the project manager what those images were, her response was: "I don't know." They've never seen this anomaly before. Those softball-sized black masses moving like the lava inside a lava lamp "are not supposed to be there." The engineers wrote what they saw on their clipboards. They couldn't explain it then. I doubt they ever came up with rationalization as to why this was happening. The engineering team would return to the house one more time a few weeks later, this time to conclude the study. I asked the project manager, the one who emailed three months ago, did they ever find out what those black orbs were. She replied, "Nope, we did not." Both Xbox One and Kinect were released publicly three months later. And that was the end of that.

Somewhere deep in the bowels of Microsoft, in some server or database room, might be the evidence the world seeks—grossly misunderstood and grossly ignored. In another sense, this was much, much bigger. As you might know, magicians from Harry Houdini through to James Randi have for a long time been offering prize money to anyone who can, under predefined experimental conditions, demonstrate a paranormal ability. In 1996 the so-called 'Randi Prize' was worth $1 million. So, shifting slightly from 'paranormal ability' to 'paranormal phenomenon,' we seem to have a pretty strong candidate here. First, the research teams, on-site and remote, have had no clue from me about the house's history. Second: their state of the art scientific technology is offering experimental confirmation of what we'd been suspecting since May 2012. There is something paranormal in this house. If the skeptics really want to know, then start here. If they don't want to know (and most don't), then they can do what they're doing now which is wave their hands and laugh. Well, fine: you do that. In the meantime, pay attention; let's see what we can learn. This in addition to what's coming towards the end of the book is worth debate and discussion among a lot of different channels.

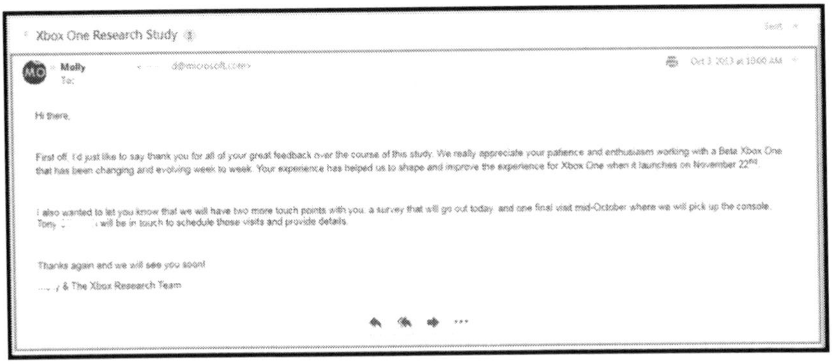
Xbox One Research Study

Molly d@microsoft.com>
To:
Oct 3 2013 at 10:00 AM

Hi there,

First off, I'd just like to say thank you for all of your great feedback over the course of this study. We really appreciate your patience and enthusiasm working with a Beta Xbox One that has been changing and evolving week to week. Your experience has helped us to shape and improve the experience for Xbox One when it launches on November 22nd.

I also wanted to let you know that we will have two more touch points with you: a survey that will go out today, and one final visit mid-October where we will pick up the console. Tony will be in touch to schedule those visits and provide details.

Thanks again and we will see you soon!

& The Xbox Research Team

Fig. 9.1 Email - the Xbox Research team and me.

[*Hi there,*

First off, I'd just like to say thank you for all of your great feedback over the course of this study. We really appreciate your patience and enthusiasm working with a Beta Xbox One that has been changing and evolving week to week. Your experience has helped us to shape and improve the experience for Xbox One when it launches on November 22nd.

*I also wanted to let you know that we will have two more touch points with you: a survey that will go out today, and one final visit mid-October where we will pick up the console. Tony ******* will be in touch to schedule those visits and provide details.*

Thanks again and we will see you soon!

****** & The Xbox Research Team*]

Chapter 10
Fat-Fingering

It had to have been the middle of 2013 when I began to notice my car trunk was always unlocked (not open, just unlocked) when I would leave for work in the morning. The first time I noticed my trunk was unlocked was when I got into the car, and before starting it up, I would see the trunk light is lit on my dashboard. That icon, if lit, means your trunk is open. *No biggie, I'll just get out of my car and raise the trunk, slam it down—problem solved.* Weird? *Why do I find myself doing this two to three times a week now?* I'm thinking somehow, some way, I'm fat-fingering my key fob. What does fat-fingering mean? Fat-fingering is when you inaccurately strike two keys at the same time with one finger.

It's not a huge inconvenience to get back out of your car, walk to car trunk, raise the trunk itself, and slam it shut. A few seconds is all it takes. Not a huge inconvenience if it happens now and then. Three times a week? What's up with that? That, and the weird images on the Kinect, our belongings never returning, and an occasional fire alarm going off in the middle of the night (no fire, mind you) were the only weird things I can remember happening in 2013. That and our TV channels changing by themselves are what I remember the most about 2013. Like I said: no physical manifestation, therefore, inconclusive.

It was now December of 2013. The house minus what I've mentioned feels normal as normal as can be. I'm feeling like a winner now. My decision to move to Seattle in 2003 and make it so in 2005 has paid off. I have a girlfriend, who despite our problems is fulfilling her half of the bargain. We're both equally invested in the home and equally invested in one another. So, what were some of our problems we had before moving in together? Allow me to give you a quick overview of what our relationship was like before moving May 1st, 2012. It comes down to two fundamentals. One of us had just ended a relationship, and the other has not been in one for quite some time. Reminder: we met standing in line at a fundraiser event. There we were standing in line at the bar—April 15th, 2010.

When we began dating, it never occurred to me that I should take heed of her being newly single. Here was a woman that recently became single, talking to a guy who had been single for at least eight years. It was love at first sight, at least for me it was. There was much to love about Tina that day. We had rapport, Tina and me. Now put aside our honeymoon phase for a second and you'll see a problem still remains. We both have baggage. One person is used to being married—that's all they know. Me? I've been single for quite some time. Our two worlds have just collided. Coming from a marriage that ended (for whatever reason) Tina's wants and needs were going to be different than my wants and needs. Neither one of us ever took the time to understand the world the other person was coming from. We never understood the other person's expectation. Or lack of expectation.

It was between those two realities that we clashed—I will be talking about more later on. Now, these clashes didn't happen every day. Far from it. But there happening regardless and when they did so they were pretty significant. I never knew till after we got together how inexperienced I was at arguing. I mean if you've lived with yourself for eighteen years who are you arguing with? I suddenly realized while arguing with Tina how much I hate being put on the defensive. Now Tina's not the scapegoat here, I'm pretty sure I would have had this feeling with anyone. But Tina was my first real deal relationship since moving to Seattle. I met her five years after I moved here.

So those gaps I mentioned were ignored and it's natural to ignore them. I mean you have a beautiful woman standing in line waiting for a drink. You strike up a conversation with her, and she's receptive. Of course, you're going to fall in love. That made me forget my baggage and Tina's baggage all in one swoop. But we're two years after-the-fact when it came to moving into the house in Bothell. Why quit now? Why try something unexpected. Like move in together. Maybe it'll help. We'll see.

December 2013. My employer, McKesson Healthcare announced they would be closing the Seattle office. All the managers, including me, were sent home immediately after the meeting with generous severance packages. The company that was instrumental in me living here was shutting down. Was I worried about being let go? Not in the slightest. The company had been telegraphing their decision for months. My boss was let go six months ago. *Oh well, life goes on.* My decision to move the Pacific Northwest and pursue an IT career had already taken into account the possibility of such McKesson closing this office. The fact that it happened in December, in the middle of the holiday season, didn't faze me. One thing you're going learn about me through the course of reading this book is, I don't freak out much.

Tina came home that day and found me playing on my Xbox versus drowning in a bottle of Jack Daniels. Me depressed? Not even close. I was relieved as relieved could be. No fear of being unemployed. No fear of wondering where my next job would be. Like I said. The handwriting had been on the wall for quite some time. I started seeking new places for employment months ago. Maybe I'm good at reading tea leaves; I don't know. It's not my fault the company chose to downsize.

The best thing I can do now is enjoy the break, focus on things in and around the house. Since I was no longer working, I pretty much had the entire house to myself. Instead of Tina kissing me goodbye each morning, I was now walking her to the front door and kissing her goodbye. That's what the last two weeks of 2013 were about. Me kissing my girlfriend goodbye when she left for work each morning.

January 2nd, 2014. An exciting time to be living in the Pacific Northwest. Everywhere you went in the state of Washington you saw and felt the spirit of the 12th man. The Seattle Seahawks were on fire right now. I mean pure 12th man mania had set in. GO HAWKS! That level of excitement was symbolic of the fireworks about to start. Everyone and I do mean everyone, was about to be caught unaware—especially me.

I was in my office applying for jobs online when the urge hit me to go downstairs. *Time for a drink*, I thought. I can smell the food from downstairs, whatever Tina was cooking smells great. Perfect time to go downstairs to see what's up.

I reached the stairway at the end of my hall, which I guess is called the landing area. Coming from my office that's the first landing you see and travel over when heading downstairs. You then take about eleven steps on the stairway, going down to reach what is called the halfway landing. When you reach the half-way landing, you turn left and are met with the remaining steps that lead to the first floor.

If you're like me walking up and down your house stairs each day, pretty much becomes second nature. We've done it so much we probably don't even remember how many times a day we've gone back in forth. That's how second nature it becomes. That night I wanted a refill, and the only way to get my refill was leave my office and head downstairs. There's absolutely nothing spectacular about that except the fall that's about to happen. When I got to the halfway landing, I did what I always do. I put my foot on the step and began my journey downstairs. I was at the midway landing now when all of a sudden, I went flying downstairs.

By the time I realized I was falling and falling hard, it was over. I was now lying on my back at the bottom of the stairs. My right leg was extended. Talk about a lot of noise. I'm six feet, five inches tall and weigh 250 pounds. That's a lot of weight to be falling down stairs.

I can't remember touching any other step except that first step on the way down. My body didn't have time to react. My arms didn't have time to react. No time to catch myself in any way. I've just completed one of the deadliest home accidents imaginable. I've fallen down a flight of stairs.

This was a bad fall. I knew it was bad. There was no way a guy my size falls down a flight of stairs like this and gets up and walks away. I'm thinking that while lying on my back. I'm waiting for the pain to confirm my suspicions. *Come on nerves, do the math—send pain signals to my brain so I can begin screaming my ass off.* Nothing, not yet anyway. Tina had heard the fall, but she didn't respond. Not right away she didn't. She thought I was faking based on the pranks I've done with her before. So, she heard me fall; she just didn't think it was real, not until I began screaming at her that it was real. When I screamed "Tina!" the third time that's when she decided to walk out of the kitchen and see what commotion I was making. Her response was "are you playing with me?"

I guess seeing is believing because Tina after seeing my legs in the pretzel position began screaming "oh my God, did you just fall down?" I'm like yeah, and it's pretty bad. The first thing I did after the fall was wiggle parts of myself to see what of me was still attached. What part of me was hurting? My arms and hands reported in as being OK. I can wiggle my toes, cool. I can wiggle my fingers, cool. I'm not feeling in pain. No tingly feeling in my spine or back area. That was good.

My head's OK, that's good. All my limbs were reporting to my brain that everything was OK. Everything was normal. *Let's see how my legs feel, can I move them?* Uh oh, right leg feels funny. My right knee feels tingly. With Tina standing over me I decided to do something that sort of puts this whole evening in perspective. I decided to pull my right pants leg up. With my pant leg up, I could now see my knee. It was the size of a grapefruit. *There's no walking away from a fall like this.* That's what I said to myself. This was bad. Very bad. I asked Tina to help me up. The pain intensified the moment I stood. Tina and I did something that we probably shouldn't have done. Which is, we went back upstairs. I should have stayed my butt downstairs because the kind of injury I got was going to get worse in the next few minutes. The only thing on my mind was my office chair. Let me get back to my office—I'll know what to do once I get back there.

My knee was pulsating, it felt weird, and my right thigh was now feeling tingly. A few seconds after I was in my chair. Tina returned with a bag of ice. We were both in wait in see mode. There was swelling, but that's it. I was thinking *let's let the ice pack do its thing. I'll go back to looking for jobs online, and this will resolve itself. We'll see what happens as the night progresses.*

I took the ice bag off my knee thirty minutes later. My knee was now the size of a beach ball. Tina was in the room at the time. She looked at me and said, "This is not good." I'm thinking the only way to find out how bad it is, is to stand. And that's when the pain hit. And wow did it ever. I looked down and saw my knee and thigh in full spasm. I couldn't help but fall back into my chair. That's how bad the pain was. Sitting down made the pain worse, so I leaped back up. Standing made the pain worse, so I sat back down. Everything I did made the pain feel worse.

Outside of my thigh contracting, I really couldn't tell what was wrong with my knee. A knee shouldn't be the size of a beach ball. I don't care what planet you live on that's not supposed to happen. The only thing I could do now was look at Tina and say call 911.

After 911 was called Tina then helped me limp to our bedroom. I can't say if my moving around was making the pain worse, the pain felt pretty much the same whether I was moving or if I was still. This is the worst kind of cramp ever. Imagine your thigh muscles contracting, and going into spasm mode, all at the same time. That's how it felt. My knee was pretty numb at this point. It didn't appear to be working. I could hear the sirens as they drew near—the Bothell fire department was pulling up to my driveway. This is how 2014 began for Keith and Tina.

As painful as it was it was also embarrassing. Here I am these six feet five inches two hundred fifty plus pound man lying spread eagle on the bed with immense pain. I was lying in bed in my t-shirt and boxers; my right knee is getting bigger by the minute. The fireman walked to my side of the bed. Everyone in the room could see the knee was in spasm. The captain leaned over me and asks me if I could wiggle my toes. I could. "Great," he said. He then asked me if I could lift my leg up. My right leg. I tried. I couldn't. He then asked me if I could bend my right knee. I tried. I couldn't. And that's when he said; you've torn your patella tendon.

What the heck is a patella tendon? In short, the patella tendon is the rubber band that connects the kneecap to the thigh muscles. It what gives you the ability to raise your leg when walking. I never thought about the importance of this tendon, this muscle till I was lying flat on my back with five or six firemen looking

55

over me. The captain informed me he had the same injury a few years ago. The determining factor of a torn patella tendon is the inability to bend and raise one's leg when lying down. This was not going to be solved tonight. This was not going to be solved tomorrow. To repair a tear likes this requires surgery. *Tag 'em and bag 'em, boys, Keith Linder, is going to the hospital.*

Two hours in the ER is what it took for them to come back with what I sort of already knew. The x-rays confirmed what the fireman had said, my right patella tendon was torn and would require surgery to repair. With surgery and all, you're looking about ninety days of rehabilitation. Talk about a buzzkill.

To get through something like this, one has to be considerably blessed—in more ways than one, mind you. How in the world did Tina and I survive something like this? The only answer I can come up with is we're blessed; we had to have been. I've just sustained a serious injury while unemployed. Remember, I was let go from my job just a few weeks ago. I was given several months' severance, which included keeping my current health insurance. Great news—the ER visit and knee surgery were hundred percent covered. I owe nothing. I think I entertained the thought of how I was going to pay for this for about a second or so. That's how long I anguished. That's how long my anxiety lasted. A few seconds, nothing more. Yes, my job let me go. Yes, I'm unemployed but not technically. I'm still receiving a paycheck from my former employer which means I have insurance. I'm a hundred percent covered. That's being blessed.

So, the hospital sent me home after my knee diagnosis. No surgery that night. I remember the physician on duty asking me, while holding a tablet, what time could I come in tomorrow to have patella reattachment surgery. I looked at Tina, and then looked at the doctor and said, can I have it a week from now? The doctor looked up from his tablet and said "huh?" No one knew except Tina and me about the job interview I had scheduled. A job interview with a very important IT company.

Rewind—a day before my fall I got an email from a recruiter about a possible job interview. The employer wanted me to come in after acing the phone screen. This job if I get it would be a huge win. We're talking huge win! Surgery now means postponing my job interview. If I postpone this interview, odds are there going to give it to somebody else. I can't risk that. Not with this company. "Doctor, this is an opportunity of a lifetime—I need to get this interview behind me and then have surgery." The doctor while understanding my predicament said, "You know you're going to be in a considerable amount of pain till you have surgery? Your kneecap is not attached to your leg." I reiterated to him and Tina, the recruiter and I have been playing phone tag for months. I can't postpone the interview, operate on me next week.

You heard it, right ladies and gentleman, a week from today. My knee cap would have to remain in my thigh for another seven days. And that's exactly what happened. I postponed the surgery for a week, thinking I could probably lose the job I'm currently seeking if I rescheduled this job interview. Living with a ghost was the furthest thing on my mind that night. Up until now the question inside had been: Will the Gray Lady show up again? Will my Bible reappear on the lamp table? I can't stop thinking about the stuff we've seen. Except tonight. I now had new problems to deal with. I was in need of surgery.

Yes, my insurance provider is going to cover tonight's visit and next week's surgery. That's one less thing to worry about. I'm still crippled; I'm looking at least two months of being incapacitated. No matter how routine the doctor made it out to be surgery is still surgery. I'm going under a knife. On the ride home I'm thinking, good job, Keith, way to bring in 2014.

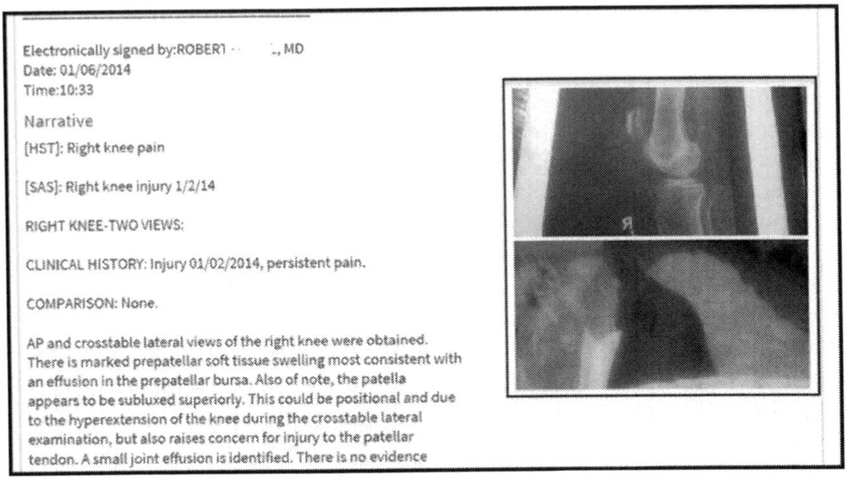

Electronically signed by:ROBER1 ··   ., MD
Date: 01/06/2014
Time:10:33

Narrative
[HST]: Right knee pain

[SAS]: Right knee injury 1/2/14

RIGHT KNEE-TWO VIEWS:

CLINICAL HISTORY: Injury 01/02/2014, persistent pain.

COMPARISON: None.

AP and crosstable lateral views of the right knee were obtained. There is marked prepatellar soft tissue swelling most consistent with an effusion in the prepatellar bursa. Also of note, the patella appears to be subluxed superiorly. This could be positional and due to the hyperextension of the knee during the crosstable lateral examination, but also raises concern for injury to the patellar tendon. A small joint effusion is identified. There is no evidence

Fig 10.1 Knee exam

Chapter 11
Home Alone

A dark cloud was slowly forming above the house in Bothell. Tina and I couldn't see, we couldn't even feel it, but it was there though. In more ways than one, it was there. I can't quite put my finger on it except to say the mood had changed. Mine and Tina's. The question you might have right now is: Did the entity push me downstairs? Truth be told it all happened so fast I can't remember. All I remember from that day was my feet just seemed to slip. I have carpet stairs, and I was wearing socks. I could've slipped. I really don't know. I'm pretty sure there are others who were pushed down stairs by a ghost and remember the force and gravity of it all. Not me.

Since I have no clear memory or feeling of being shoved off the midway landing area, I have to honestly give you the answer I gave myself at the time. I don't know. I was not attributing this fall to being ghost related. I'm just clumsy pure and simple. It happened so fast. Was it a deliberate accident? You'll have to decide that when I provide more information (at the end of the book.) For now? Good news. I got the job. In keeping with that blessing idea, I had earlier, it would seem I was right. Not only did I get the job, the recruiter asked (in a somewhat sheepish way) if I could start in mid-February versus the end of January. Who gets hired and is then asked can they start a month later? No better yet five weeks later? Being asked that question was a dream come true for me. Instead of starting in one week or two, I was being asked to start in five weeks. Five weeks is a lifetime when undergoing physical therapy. Instead of showing up to work with two crunches, I would be showing up with just one.

There seemed to be an atmospheric change in our home after the surgery. Something wasn't right. Me, unemployed, looking for jobs online all day, while watching reruns of *Supernatural*, is different than we sitting at home with one knee in a brace and cast doped up on pain meds. Everything I do now involves carefully coordinated steps. That's what happens when you have patella tendon surgery. Everything I do now is labor intensive. I'm restricted to the upstairs. That sucks.

It didn't take long for me to ask myself the question: Is my house alive? I was in my bed doped up on pain meds, in and out of sleep when suddenly I heard noises coming from the hallway. It sounded like someone was rummaging through something downstairs. I wanted to investigate, but I couldn't. I was crippled.

There I was sitting in the middle of the bed; TVs on. I had a cup of orange juice at my side and to the right of me was my bedroom door. I heard pacing downstairs. It sounded like someone was in the house with me. Maybe it was Tina returning home; maybe she forgot something. There came the point where I had to get up, I mean painfully get up. There I am limping in the hallway, looking for someone. God knows who. By the time I got to the landing area, the noise was gone. The sound from the kitchen had stopped. Everything had stopped including the noise I heard coming from the office. "Tina is that you?" Nothing.

One morning after Tina left for work I sat on our bed watching TV. Once again keeping my leg mobilized. I would be returning to the Orthopedic in a few days to have the cast and brace taken off. Until then it was stay off the leg and wait. This morning, in particular, I was sitting in bed longer than usual. Instead of getting up and limping into the office, which I normally did to avoid sleeping all the time, I decided to turn on my side. My back was facing the door. Rarely do I sleep with my back faced to the door, activity or no activity. The events of 2012 are still engrained in my psyche. Thanks to all that, I try not to sleep with my back turned towards the door.

But the pain in my right knee was immense. The only way to relieve the pain was to sleep on my left side. Everyone knows how our eyelids get heavy right before we sleep right? Well, I'm the type of person that lies very still until my eyes just can't stay open anymore. I'm lying there staring at the wall and the dresser in front of me; I feel my eyes getting heavy. They begin to close. I open them. They get heavy again. I open them. They get heavy, over and over again, until right when I'm about to nod off.

Then I feel something jump in bed with me.

The hamster in my head that was this close to falling asleep suddenly froze— my eyes darted open. *Keith don't go to sleep yet. Something just hopped on the bed with you.* Now I need for you to listen very closely because if I explain it accurately most of you who've grown up with pets as a kid or have pets now, especially a cat, are going to know exactly what I'm talking about. Right before my eyes were about to close for a nap, I felt an indention in the bed. Not an indention you feel when your partner gets in bed with you. No, I felt the indention in the mattress as if a small cat or small dog had just leaped into the bed with me. Now dogs and cats walk differently. Dogs approach you with a sense of urgency. They want to be rewarded right away. There are ready to play. Cats are different. They approach you more so in a stealth mode. They sort of ease their way towards you. Sort of like that scene in the Stephen King movie *Cat Eye.* The little girl is asleep. The cat leaps into bed and slowly but surely makes its way to her when it reaches her it begins licking her. I just dated myself I know, forgive me.

The indention in the bed that I felt right as I was about to fall sleep is similar to a cat approaching you while you sleep. I'm not saying a cat got into bed with me. No, I'm not saying that at all—we don't have pets. I'm saying whatever hopped in bed reminds me of how a cat would have approached you if you were lying in bed. I grew up with cats. I'm very familiar with how they leap in the bed, very familiar how they approach you, or sometimes they don't. Sometimes they just leap into the bed to snoop around. That's how the bed felt right now. The indention was felt. As soon as it happened my eyes opened wide, and that's when I felt the approach. The approach is what I mentioned earlier. Something leaped onto the bed with me and was slowly making its way towards me. Remember, though my eyes were open, my back was still turned.

I now have less than a few seconds to react. If I don't turn around and turn around soon, logic tells me something is going to happen that I might not approve of. Logic also tells me I might not like what I see once I turn around. Is this what death feels like? Is this the Grim Reaper coming to get me? If this was death coming to get me why am I awake? As I asked that question, I then realized I am awake. And with that in mind, I spun around. *If this was death coming for me, then let me face it. Don't let me die with my back turned.* Whatever it was, it was getting closer. I spun around and soon as I did, it was gone. Nothing was there. It was like it had evaporated.

I never told Tina about what I felt that day. I didn't want to alarm her. Maybe it was the medicine I was taking? Doubt it. But I have to say that, don't I? I mean, that's what a paranormal researcher would say, 'it was your pain meds'. They never qualify stuff, why is that? I know what I felt. I grew up with animals in the house. Cats and dogs. What I felt was real. Something got in bed with me. How do I explain this to Tina? We had been debating all year long about the spirit still being here or not being here. Tina believed, or maybe I should say hoped and felt that it was gone. I felt differently. When I feel something strongly, I stick to it.

I became adamant. My gut instincts were telling me something is still here. Tina thinks there isn't. I think there is. For the first time, I wanted Tina to be right and me to be wrong. I can't make sense of what went down that morning. Was it the meds? Was it the knee pain? No, it was not. I know what I felt. The question now is, what now?

Thirty days later, the doctors removed the bandages to inspect my knee. *Wow, my right leg has atrophied. Let the physical therapy begin.* No more being confined to just the upstairs area. It was time to begin bending the right knee. That's not going to easy. This knee has been purposely straight for over a month. A key factor to my success is increasing my movement throughout the house. Cabin fever was getting the best of me, so was me being overly dependent on Tina. We were constantly in each other's face right now, her waiting on me hand in foot and me yelling Tina come here! Whenever I needed something.

They say physical therapy can be painful. I never knew it would be this painful. The muscles surrounding my knee had for all practical purposes receded elsewhere. My knee had become accustomed to being straight all-the-time; therefore, getting it to bend was going to be a challenge. On the positive side, I could go downstairs now. The last time I was down here was the day before the knee surgery. Talk about returning to the scene of the crime. The prescription from my orthopedic doctor was straightforward: do the leg rehab regiment three to four times a day, thirty minutes each time. The den was the only room in the house big enough for me. I could lie down, spread out, and do what the doctor prescribed in the den. In the area where I fell. Weird.

Physical therapy day 1—I was sitting on the couch in the den, resting after doing my exercises. That's where I was when the noise happened. It sounded like someone was walking from one of the room upstairs. The sound of doors opening and closing. My right knee hampered my will to investigate. I was not ready to walk upstairs, at least not quickly. My knee was not ready. This went on for several days. So much so that I finally had to accept the fact that no matter how fast I try to respond, the noise was going to inexplicably subside by the time I get halfway up the stairs. There was no one home but me.

The next time it happened I did nothing. I suspended my PT for a second; I just laid back and listened from the den. The sound was right above my head. Pacing back in forth. How long does it last? A few minutes. Sometimes a few hours. It was so real that had I been asleep and woke up to it, I would have bet my life Tina had come home.

Now the only time I chose to stay in bed late was when I was in immense pain. It was during those times that I began to hear tapping sounds and sometimes outright banging noises. The noises I've just described were not coming from outside my room. It was coming from behind my headboard. What's interesting about these bangs compared to the other bangs we heard in 2012? These taps and bangs came minutes of me falling asleep. It's almost like someone is sending you Morse code from behind your bed. Tap, tap, tap, tap, tap, tap, ping, ping, ping, tap, tap, ping, tap, tap, tap, and tap. Occasional loud tap. Occasional bang. These sounds are coming from the bed I'm lying in.

The noises I heard as a result of being home during the day included: footsteps, pacing back and forth, the sound of someone in one room walking to another room, the sound of a bedroom door opening and closing. All these sounds seemed to resemble the noises we sometimes heard when we first arrived home. I shared with you earlier the times where Tina and I came home and upon opening the front door we would hear the sound of someone running upstairs.

I'd been home by myself for about a month now. I wasn't hearing these noises before my fall. Remember the day I fell down the stairs I was unemployed. I was home all day then like I'm home all day now. The only difference now is I'm wounded. I'm now hearing noises when I'm upstairs and when I downstairs. I hear noises from behind the headboard—all of this happened after my fall. I note that in my diary. *"Noises in the house seem to have returned after I took my fall."*

What I'm hearing is fueling my theory of something still being here. Time to share my hunch with my friends. It's time for me to tell somebody; you see the fall I had was not only on my mind. It was my friend's mind. The question floating around was, was this fall an accident? Was it deliberate? The second question from friends was, "Are we OK? How is Tina and I holding up?" Tina's friends asked her that. My friends asked me that. The question that got asked the most was, "Did the activity subside and if it did why?" My answer back then was I don't know. If you asked Tina and me together, the answer would be mixed. Tina felt it was gone or more importantly felt it was not worth discussing. I felt differently and maybe that's because of what I'd seen. Tina never saw the black shadows when Microsoft was here. She never saw how stumped the Microsoft engineers were. I mean these were Microsoft developers. Microsoft engineers— some of the brightest minds on earth where technology is concerned. They were stumped.

All these sounds I'm hearing could be the result of me being home. I mean, a tree makes a sound whether someone's nearby to hear or not. It's possible the noise I'm hearing has always been here. There's no way to test that theory. Dammit, I'm out of time. Four weeks had now come and gone. I started my new job a week or so later. Several weeks of physical therapy had finally paid off. It was now the end of February; the new year had pretty much taken off for everyone else except me. Me going to work would be one of the first few times I'd stepped out of the house. I think I was more excited about riding in a car, albeit the back seat of Tina's SUV than actually having a new job. It felt good to be out and about. I could see the city again. I could see people walking their dogs. I could see people standing in line at Starbucks. Heck, I'm sitting in traffic. This felt great.

Two weeks later, my life was slowly coming back to me. The ability to drive myself to work versus Tina taking me sort of lessened the tension between Tina and me. I never knew how cumbersome it was to take care of someone full-time till after I fell down. It's extremely hard. Add on to that, Tina dropping me off at work and picking me up afterward and you realize the stress involved. I worked downtown Seattle. Tina worked in Issaquah. It takes an hour to get to my job. Another hour for Tina to get her job after dropping me off. We'd been doing this two times a day for the last three weeks. Remember I took my fall January 2nd, 2014. Tina drove me to the hospital. She drove me to my job interview. Tina drove me to my check-ups. To my physical therapy. She drove me to work. She picked me up from work. That takes a toll on you. Takes a toll on both of us. Maybe more so because of who we live with. You can't help but become irritable when you're constantly around someone.

Bad day at work or no bad day at work, Tina still has to come home and care for me. That need for mental separation doesn't take place. That need of missing someone. That creates tension. Something in this house was watching us. It was taking notes. If it's not causing the irritability, it definitely is learning from it. Something's about to happen. The day I chose to drive myself to work was the weekend Tina, and I had a heated argument. I decided to do a test run to the corner store—just to see how my knee would respond. I seemed OK. How would my leg respond to me driving myself to work? I lived thirty minutes north of Seattle. My commute to work on a good day was about an hour. An hour and a half on a bad day. Seattle has more bad days than good days when it comes to morning traffic.

Driving myself to work was premature on my part. My right knee was not yet ready to spend an hour in Seattle traffic. My knee let me know within twenty minutes of me driving that it did not approve of the decision. I was in excruciating pain. Being a passenger is one thing. Driving yourself to work two months after a patella tear is another. But that's what arguments do; it gets you doing something you ordinarily wouldn't do had things been hunky dory. But things weren't. Fatigue was wearing on both us. I was sitting in bumper to bumper traffic, and I realized something. This was the first time I've driven my car in over three months.

The next morning, I walked out of the house and after getting into the car, notice that my trunk light is on. I'd just loaded my laptop bag and my crutches into the back seat of the car. Why is my trunk light on? *I for the life of me could not understand how I was fat-fingering my key fob when unlocking the door remotely.*

Chapter 12
The Calm before the Storm

This change in mood all of sudden created a passive-aggressive campaign between Tina and me. The inability to resolve disagreements peacefully seemed to be diminishing. I was now driving myself to work three weeks ahead of schedule. Against doctor's orders. Knee pain had become more preferable than resolving whatever disagreement I had with Tina. I can't for the life of me remember what our last argument was about except to say it was huge. Huge and childish. Guess what appeared during our self-imposed silent treatment? Inexplicable rappings.

These bangs were different from the previous bangs we experienced. It was weird that there coming from the headboard versus from the wall or ceiling. To the skeptics reading this, I'm sure you will agree, that there is nothing written in the annals of history about beds making banging noises. I'm talking about a loud thunderous noise. The closest thing I can compare it to is two four by four wood planks being slapped together. That's what woke me up one morning. I rose from my pillow and looked around. I saw nothing. Right when I was about to close my eyes, another bang. My eyes popped open again. I know that noise all too well. These were the sounds I heard during my knee recovery.

I'll never forget the loud bang that happened one night when Tina and I were sound asleep. The noise sounded like it was coming from the guest room behind us. I'm talking about a thunderous clap. My heart began to race because I was beginning to feel what I hadn't felt in over a year. I felt like we were being watched. The room had turned dense all of a sudden. To confirm my hunch, I did something I hadn't done in a while; I reached up and pulled the string that turns the ceiling fan on. If it's screeching, that means we're not alone. *Dammit, I hate when I'm right*. The ceiling is screeching all right. It's screaming like it was in 2012 (hasn't made that noise in almost two years). I looked down at Tina to see if she was moving. Nothing. She was sound asleep.

Time to get up and walk around. I began surveying the hallway from our bedroom entrance before stepping out of the room. Nothing felt out of place. The dense feeling that I was feeling seemed confined to our bedroom. That dense feeling, I often refer to in this book is almost identical to that uneasy feeling we all get when someone invades our personal space. Imagine your worst personal space invasion ever and multiply it by a hundred. That's what I was feeling.

The downstairs looked OK. Here comes the feeling I felt earlier. That personal space invasion feeling. *Why am I all of a sudden feeling claustrophobic?* Now I can do two things. I can go back upstairs; crawl back into bed and ignore everything I'm feeling right now. That's what I should do. Second option? Smudge the house right now!

Minutes later, I walked into the kitchen and opened up the refrigerator. We had no dry sage in the house; I knew that as I made my way towards the kitchen.

Maybe Tina has some sage for cooking purposes. Lucky for me she did. Now, the sage you cook with is different than the sage you smudge with. The sage in our refrigerator was green, not dried out like the stuff I bought from the botanical store. But sage is sage, so with that in mind I placed the sage leaves on a cookie sheet and turned the oven on. Within minutes the sage began looking like the stuff I had bought two years ago. The only thing to do now was place the sage leaves on a hard surface and commence to smudging. I think I made two motions around our bed before thinking, *what the hell. I might as well smudge the hallway too.*

Instead of just waving the saucer that the sage was sitting on around the hallway I decided just to set it on the bookshelf. Let it smolder itself out. That's what I did before going back to bed. I don't know how many minutes passed before the next bang erupted, but a bang did erupt, and it was loud. This time the noise came from the hallway. Tina rose from the bed at the same time I did. We both heard it together. Something was thrown. There's no ignoring a disturbance like this. We had to investigate it. Tina and I both looked at each other, and our expression said it all. *We'll go together.*

So, we stepped out of the bedroom and into the hallway. There on the floor was the shattered saucer. The saucer was in bits as was the sage leaves. Tina, upon seeing this, put both her hands over her mouth and began crying. Why was Tina crying? She knows as well as me, that this is not the end of something, no this is the beginning. If 2012, is anything to go by, we're about to get bombarded for weeks and months. Some of the websites I went to for information didn't pull any punches when describing what would happen should the activity return. When the activity comes back, it's usually worse than before. Way worse. There's no way I'm going to tell Tina that. From the way she was sobbing it looked like she already knows. The only thing I could do right now was walk my girlfriend back to the bed we slept in, sit her down and say we have to be vigilant. We have to maintain.

One thing that stood out and I recognized it almost immediately: The spirits in this house seem to object to smudging. Remember the front door open and close by itself when I first smudged the house back in 2012? This response was worse than that in my opinion. Throwing something in the hallway while we were asleep had never happened before. We're talking about an immense amount of force. The saucer was in a thousand pieces. The sage leaves have been reduced to the size of particles.

Does this mean I should give up smudging? Nope, not even close. I went to work the next day more determined than I was the night before. I was right, these bastards never left. If anything, they'd been lying dormant. Or bidding their time or something. Now, there's a lot of theories out there about spirits coming back. I don't think they come back. Is it possible they just hang around you, loiter a bit until something worthwhile happens? Something like an illness, a disease, financial strife, or a relationship in turmoil? In short, they go dormant.

It's impossible to know why the activity returned but I think it's more plausible them having never left versus them leaving and coming back. The black masses the Microsoft engineers caught while here kept feeding my idea of something being here. I think we all can agree. Saucers can't fly by themselves. Someone has to throw them.

The loud bangs have officially returned. What made these rappings different from before was the time day of which they occurred. More at night versus during the day. The bang, the thud noise, and the pacing back and forth all seemed to be happening right above our heads. It's like they were in the attic or something.

NOTE: houses in the Pacific Northwest didn't have attics. More like ventilation spaces, roof crawl spaces are how I would describe it.

So, it's door slams and rapping's 2.0 now. Both door slam and rapping happen in the middle of the night. Time to start prodding our bedroom door with pillows again. That takes care of that for now.

Then came the flying objects. Or objects going airborne I should say. The interesting thing about an iron board being thrown or a plant being thrown (yeah, that's back too) is the atmospheric change you feel inside the house. Lights flicker off and on—minutes later an object goes flying. Ceiling fan (if on) begins squeaking in the middle of the night—minutes later the iron board that's standing in the room with us goes flying across the room.

It took me awhile to figure this out. The atmospheric change I mean, e.g. snapping and popping sounds. I'm talking about every wall in the house suddenly acts as if they are alive. I mean, seriously, your walls are acting as if someone put them in a microwave. They're popping, snapping, and pinging. It's like the house is contracting or something. Then comes a flying object.

Now, if I sound like a broken record, it's because the premise of these nightly events is mainly the same. We're asleep, something happens. We're awake, something happens. We've been awakened by our fire alarm going off. We've been awakened by another plate being thrown. The Sunday night our armoire went flying from one side of the hallway to the other was the week after the saucer and sage incident. What does a flying armoire sound like at 2 am? It sounds like a bowling ball ping-ponging throughout the house. There, leaning like the leaning tower of Pisa, was our armoire. Whatever happened resulted in a tennis ball sized hole in the wall. So, began the damage to our hallway and bedroom walls. I told my brother about what happened to the armoire. His reaction was who's going to believe this, he thought. I mean, we're talking about a very heavy object here. A giant armoire, made out of solid wood. There was no more thinking Tina was behind this, at least not from him. Humans can't throw armoires around. The fact that Tina was sleeping next to me when it flew cemented my brother's belief that something nefarious was going on.

Wait a minute. I still have a video camera. Should I try to get something on video? Why not? It's worth a try: I mean, what can possibly go wrong? My brother wants to see the wonder on video. Research teams I'm going to reach out to in the future are going to want to see the wonder on video as well. The idea then hit me. Let's go to bed with the door open. Let's remove the pillow. We know whenever we do that, the door slams by itself. I'll put a video camera in the hallway. Now, we tried this for a couple of nights, and nothing happened. The only time the door would slam violently on its own was when there was no video camera trained on it. Time to try something else? Let's just see what happens if we sleep with our bedroom closed. *Mr. Ghost, do something, please.* Uh of, it did. It finally did.

The night I caught something on video was March 27th, 2014. Tina and I decided to sleep with the door closed. I don't know how long we were asleep before we heard the loud bang on our bedroom door—it scared the crap out of both of us. If you watch the video, you'll hear the talk Tina, and I are having prior to me opening the door. We're debating what to do. It sounds like someone walked by and hit the door extremely hard. Tina and I might be crazy for still being here. That doesn't mean we aren't practical. Despite everything we've seen and heard in these two years, our brains were still going to default to the horrible conclusion of someone has entered our home. Is it a burglar? Maybe a thief? Should I call 911? Should I look for a baseball bat? Should I hide Tina under the bed just in case an intruder is really in the house? All these things are running through your head within seconds of hearing something this loud. The only thing left to do is open the bedroom door.

Talking about a level of satisfaction. The video camera I placed in the hallway was still running. It was facing the bookshelf; it had to have captured the banging on the door. What I was hoping for was not there. *Dammit!* I was hoping the video would show me the Gray Lady banging on our door. She's the one I want to capture. That's what I was hoping for. I've learned something in my four years of dealing with this. I learned you have to be grateful for the evidence given. I must have watched it several times at work before sending Tina the link. This was better than the two previous videos. This video shows Tina and me sleeping. If you listen carefully, you can hear me snoring. When out of the blue comes this loud bang. WARNING.

https://youtu.be/-BmKV6jOPxQ

Fig 12.1 Noise

https://www.youtube.com/watch?v=-BmKV6jOPxQ
Loud banging on the door at 3:03 AM 3/27/14 Time stamp 4:58.

Tina and I had a lot of electrical problems while living in the home. I'm talking about problems with our telecommunications, cable, and electrical systems. Comcast had to make multiple trips to the house fixing problems they couldn't even describe. The same with the power company. Weird spikes in electricity use. Unexplained power surges. Unexplained outages in nearly every room in the house. Hard to explain, said the power company. Our ADT security system on occasion would say 'garage door open' or 'front door open,' when neither of those doors was open. Then came the lights off and on over and over again, constantly. We're talking about a hundred times a minute. Just off and on, nothing else.

Then came the appliances. Oh yeah, those two. How about the microwave turning on by itself? Imagine your microwave only working when your back is turned. Imagine putting food in it and pressing *defrost* or *cook*. Nothing happens. You try over and over again, to the point of giving up. You walk away, and as you do the microwave comes on. It comes back on to the setting you last gave it. If you said cook for three minutes, that's what it comes back on to. Always when your back is turned. Or even weirder, when you re-enter the kitchen hours later. You've placed the item you wanted to cook back in the refrigerator. You've given up. It seems the microwave hasn't, though. It comes on, but there's nothing in it. You put your food item back in it; it goes off. Take your food item out (in frustration) it comes back on.

The microwave isn't the only kitchen appliance that had a life of its own. Tina and I had constant issues with the dishwasher. Constant electrical issues with the garbage disposal. Of course, we contacted the landlord. His recommendation: call the designated repairman. The repairmen would come, and sure enough, there would be nothing wrong. Each room had its own set of issues with the power outlets. Trying to figure out which outlet was working was like playing a game of whack-a-mole. You never knew which outlet would be working when it came time to iron your clothes in the morning. Weird and very inconvenient to have outlets in the kitchen go out when trying to cook dinner. It's hard to explain your garage door going up and down on its own. Each one of these things by itself is perhaps nothing. Combine what I've just mentioned with objects flying, loud bangs, previous tenants moving in and out of the house, missing Bibles, and a whole list of other things, and then you have to believe that none of what I just mentioned is a coincidence. Hiring an electrician costs money. Hiring a repairman to fix the dishwasher costs money. Having the electric company and Comcast over multiple times costs me time off work. It costs me money. It's an inconvenience to do these things but you have to do them. You have to rule out the obvious.

You think it's hard explaining that objects move and levitate in your house. Try explaining the unexplained wonders with your cameras. The house didn't come with cameras. I had to buy them. Each camera I bought would get manipulated in one way or another. I'm talking immediate battery loss, cameras unplugged, turned around or turned upside down. Which reminds me, I want to talk about the cameras that the *Ghost Adventures* crew brought in.

Many people had gone out their way to inform me how out of character Zak and crew were when they chose to ignore the multiple battery drainage instances they experienced while in the home. Tina and I were knee deep in camera malfunctions by the time *Ghost Adventures* arrived. We were used to that kind of thing. What shocked people, myself included was their dismissive attitude to three identical events. I mean let's be honest; *Ghost Adventures* have latched onto lesser things when investigating.

You'll discover later in this book that the activity taking place around Tina and me, and around everyone who brought electronic equipment here, points to a culprit *Ghost Adventures* should have been better prepared for.

Chapter 13
Spring 2014

If there are two months in 2014 that deserve their own book, it would have to be March and April. We're talking about the most active month and the deadliest month side by side. I believe March was the prepping month. Prepping, as in, shit was about to intensify. Remember that night in 2012, when Tina and I were lying in bed reliving how the day went? Remember how the bedroom door shut on Tina and me while we were laughing? Remember what I said about the spirits wanting us to take them seriously? Well, they were telling the truth. We should have taken them seriously.

Tina and I began noticing new noises in the house by the time March rolled around. We were both familiar with the pacing. Tina and I had that noise down pat. We heard it when we go to bed, and we heard when we came home from work. We got stomping. I mean actual stomping coming from the hallway. It's so reoccurring that Tina and I at times have to stand up from wherever we're sitting and scream, "Cut that crap out! Cut that shit out." And that works for a few hours, or a few days. Guess what? It comes back. Louder than the previous time of course.

Imagine having dinner with your significant other. All of a sudden you hear the sound of someone running upstairs. It sounds like someone is going room to room—pacing back and forth. I was thinking to myself that has to be the Gray Lady. Who else would be going room to room like that? Our friends have heard what I've just described. They always say, "Wow, you got some serious house noise going on." Or, "What's that noise coming from your hallway?" Mind you, Tina and I are trying to have dinner. The noise we hear interrupts that. It interrupts conversations. It interrupts us watching TV.

The armoire got thrown in March again. Thank God we were awake this time. Let's see how many times has it been thrown? 1-2-3, it's been thrown three times. This time it left a sizable hole in the wall. Tina and I ran upstairs in response to the noise; there it was leaning on the wall. Now we got a third dent. Now I was frustrated, so frustrated that I asked Tina to help me move the armoire. *Let's get it out the hallway, let's put it in the guest room. How you like me now Mr. Ghost I took your toy away from you.* Tina and I took the armoire out of the hallway.

The next morning, I woke up tired and irritable. Constant tapping on our headboard throughout the night. It's like someone was living inside the wall of our bedroom. I more tired now than I was before going to bed. Then came the trunk incident. I got into my car that morning and saw my trunk indicator light on again. Dammit, I've fat-fingered my key fob again. I am so clumsy when it comes to unlocking my car.

I called Tina later that day to see what progress she was making with trying to reach certain churches. You guessed it? We were reaching out to churches again. That armoire that got thrown weighs over three-hundred pounds. That's not a good sign; seeing it get tossed around like that. Hopefully, someone can tell us. Or better yet. Help us. The sigh in Tina's voice told me everything I needed to know. The Catholic Church in Seattle was telling her to call the parish in Bothell. The parish in Bothell was telling her to call the parish in Seattle. Those were our roadblocks. Tina was calling churches. I was calling paranormal teams. The response I was getting from local teams was "we want to see the evidence. Send us pictures and videos of what's happening. We'll contact you after we've reviewed them." This nonchalant response prevented me from sending them anything. I'm not the paranormal investigator, you are. You want evidence come and get it.

At the tail end of March, Tina and I had another one of our arguments. And just so you know these arguments are always frivolous. I mean half the time we forget what we're arguing about. The only thing I can remember is they tend to lead to miscommunication. Not properly talking to one another or not talking to each other at all is what I mean by miscommunication. When my girlfriend and I can't agree on something, that's usually because of both being stubborn. We separate mentally, emotionally, physically and you guessed it, socially. Tina and I might not have invented the phrase "cold shoulder." I'm pretty sure we had perfected it though.

I left the house that night at 6 pm to meet a friend for drinks and conversation. I must have been gone four hours at the most. I walked into an entirely different house when I returned home – that's what it felt like. I entered the house through the front door like I always do. I was expecting to hear a TV on or something. Instead, I heard silence. Every light in the house was on. It would appear that Tina had gone to bed already. But not in our bedroom. Instead, she chose a guestroom. I found that behavior odd because in the history our arguing we've never opted to sleep in different rooms. Even in our most heated exchanges, we've never chosen a cold bed over a warm one. I can hug the far end of the mattress better than anyone. Tina can too, which is why I was shocked to see her sleeping in one of the guest bedrooms. With the door closed of all things. She must have forgotten the house she was living in.

I closed the bedroom door on Tina and walked into our master bedroom and went to bed. It wasn't long before the banging started. Right above my head. Then came the sound of a door closing. Where is that sound coming from? I have no idea. All the doors upstairs were closed. The sound I heard kept repeating itself. This went on for a considerable amount of time. Nothing else for me to do except turn on the TV. That's the only solution to the noise above my head, is watching television. But that got old quick. What do I do? I rose from our bed and walked back towards the room Tina was in—silent treatment or no silent treatment, Tina and I need to be in the same room. I doubt Tina was hearing what I was hearing because she used to sleep through my snoring—so I'm just going to crawl in bed beside her and try to go to sleep as soon as possible. No sense in waking her up.

Tina never knew this, but I slept with her that night and in doing so heard all kinds of strange sounds. Sounds that originated out of our room (the room I just left). If I didn't know any better I would think someone was looking for us. I'm talking about the sounds of someone pacing back and forth. I'm talking about knocking and tapping sounds from the ceiling in the master bedroom. That and the feeling of being watched were what took place that night. Suffice to say I got little sleep that night. When I woke up around 10 am—Tina was gone. I could hear the TV on downstairs. That must be where Tina is. Allow me to describe to you what's about to happen next. Tina and I are about to be attacked. We have no idea what's to unfold. It's almost like an army invasion except you can't see it because of the foggy horizon. But there's no foggy horizon in this house. It's just us. Tina was downstairs doing what she usually does on a Sunday morning. I'm pretty sure she had a glass of orange juice in one hand and the remote control in another. Usually, when I wake up on Sunday, Tina has already got breakfast fixed. There's a smell of bacon in the air. I did not smell bacon which means Tina is just going to chill for now.

From my horizontal down position, I can sense that the house feels worse now than it did last night. My spider-senses were going the fuck off. Something's not right. Something huge is about to descend on this house. It's almost indescribable. The only thing I can compare it to is a concussion. A force is present. It's everywhere. It's looking at me. It's looking at Tina. It's looking at the hallway. It's looking at the bedrooms. It's looking at everything. This force is the sole proprietor of this dense feeling I keep having. Both are standing side by side right now, and that's not a good thing. Dear reader, hell is about to explode in Keith and Tina's home. The devil has sent one of his minions out to play with us.

Minutes later, I get out of the shower and what I just described is still weighing heavy on me. I know Tina and I are not talking right now. Things have been on the decline relationship wise since the tail end of my knee injury. She's mad at me, and I'm mad at her. If you were to ask her why she was mad at me right now, I'm pretty sure she couldn't tell you. And I'm the same way. I can't tell you why I'm mad at Tina. And maybe mad is the wrong word to use. I'm not mad at Tina. I'm upset at Tina. I can't remember what we argued about that Saturday except to say it had to have been heated; only our heated arguments result in us not talking to one another. This argument felt different. It feels contrived, and I don't know why.

I need to talk to Tina. She needs to know what the heck it I'm is sensing. Whatever it is, it's fast approaching. I leave my office and head downstairs. Tina was still sitting on the couch, watching TV. I walked up to her with full determination and said, "Hey, something's about to jump off. I don't know what it is, but whatever it is we need to be ready for it."

Tina looked at me and asked, "What do you mean? Something's about to jump off?"

"I don't know; you don't feel it?"

"Feel what?" she said. The tension in the air, we're being watched, something's about to happen. Tina looks at me mystified. "What the heck are you talking about?" And that's when I said, "Just be ready, we're about to be attacked." Tina stares at me for a second and then turns back to her TV show. I walked back to my office and sat down. Tina was doing her thing and was doing mine. There must be enough negative energy between us to fill a football field. That's how disconnected we were right now. I'm talking about tension city.

12 noon that same day—a loud explosion came from in the hallway. This noise was different to the other noises we'd heard. It sounded like something had just crashed into our house. It's amazing how our instinct at times does things that surprise even us. I ran towards the noise instead of running from it. I was in my office when the explosion came—so I ran out my office and stood dead in the hallway. There on the floor was our bedroom door. It had been ripped off the hinges. Half of it on the floor and the other half just dangling. Who could rip a door off its hinges like this, in an instant?

I saw Tina coming up the stairs with the same expression as me. We both stood there motionless. Not one word was said. Then *BOOM! BOOM! BOOM!* Tina and I looked at each other again. Our faces said it best—where in the hell did that come from? I think I tried lifting up the door; thinking can I fix this? Then came the second round of *BOOM! BOOM! BOOM!* Tina took off downstairs. I hurried back to my office.

Something told me this wasn't over. Oh, the spirits here were just getting started. We need somebody here right now! Who's going to come to our house on a Sunday? Who out there responds to situations like this? I was hoping the internet would tell me. Time to mass search: paranormal teams, Catholic church, whatever—somebody's got to get here.

Now I'm combing through websites, and I'm getting angry. Most of the websites are defunct. I'm calling the phone numbers listed, and most of them are saying 'you've reached a phone number that's been disconnected'. The emails I'm sending are coming back to me with the message your email was undeliverable. This is getting nowhere. Another explosion!

This noise was different from what we just heard. Sounds like something breaking. It sounds like something had exploded into a million pieces. And that's pretty much what happened. I ran out of my office to locate what I had just heard and soon as I stepped into the hallway I, saw what it was. The light fixture that hung over the midway landing area was gone. The porcelain had been obliterated. Debris was everywhere from the hallway to the front door. Hell, we had broken glass under couches and love-seats. You see, the porcelain glass fixture that dangles from the house ceiling above the middle staircase had exploded. The remains were mostly dust now. Do you understand what I'm saying when I say dust? This object that hung over the midway landing was about the size of a mini-lamp shade. It was gone now. What remained were dust particles. Dust particles mixed in with two to three inches of broken glass.

I remember saying to Tina as she came back upstairs, "We're under attack!" Things we could never imagine being destroyed were all of a sudden being destroyed. I couldn't tell if the worst was behind us or if it was still on its way. Tina and I are both chasing explosions at this point. We could be standing in the kitchen, responding to cabinet doors being slammed and all of a sudden you hear a loud bang come from upstairs. You go upstairs to investigate and there on the floor is a new mess. Iron board, lamps, lamp shades, books, pottery, dresser drawers and coat hangers. Everything's on the floor.

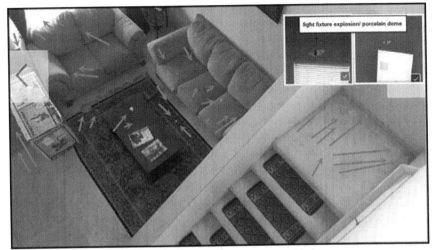

Fig 13.1 March 30th. Arrows = Debris.

We're going to have a horrible story to tell the landlord if we can't get a handle on what's happening. The only thing I can think of at the time was, let's open the front door. Let's open the windows. Every window. We have to get this energy out of here. Doing that seemed to calm things down a little, but just a little. A short fix is just that: it's a short fix.

We needed something longer, something lasting. That was our motivation for dialing local churches. That's what kept my fingers on the keyboard. We needed help, and we needed help right away. I must have emailed a hundred paranormal teams that day, all within a few hours. Tina was getting voicemails, and I was getting undeliverable email messages, until I finally found a website called No Bull Paranormal. Yes! They have a phone number; now we're getting somewhere. I grabbed my phone and called the number listed. A woman named Jennifer answered. Now Jennifer can hear the destruction in the background. She can hear the loud bangs and the sound of objects being thrown. She can hear the stress in my voice, my plea for help.

We talked for a brief moment before she put me on hold. After a few seconds, she came back to the phone and said the words I wanted to hear: "we're on our way." Luckily for us, her team was close by. Getting their gear together and driving over would be about two hours. Fine by me. Let this be an example of how terrified Tina and I were. How frantic we became within seconds of the first explosion.

No Bull Paranormal would be the first paranormal team to into our house. Her team has seen the most devastation out of every team that's come here. That's probably because of how quick they responded. It's important that I mention this because every paranormal website that listed itself as being available was in fact not. You don't know how aggravating it is to seek help and instead get disconnected phone numbers. That and defunct email aliases were some of the problems we encountered when seeking help. Those who did respond couldn't come right away. I've heard every excuse imaginable as to why they can't respond right now. Too many to list here but trust me they're all silly reasons.

Jennifer called me back minutes later to let me know that they would be leaving soon. By 3 pm they were here. Talk about a sigh of relief. New eyes, new ears, new everything. Tina and I stood in our doorway and watched them pull up to the house. The first thing Jennifer did when she walked in was hug Tina. It never hit to me as to how traumatized we were until I saw Tina cave into Jennifer's arms and begin crying. I was stunned. Jennifer then said, "Don't worry, baby, it's going to be OK." I can tell you right now, no one in the *Ghost Adventures* organization told us it was going to be alright. We never heard that from Zak, or Dave or anyone else for that matter. Jennifer reached for Tina the second she walked in. Interesting how some teams can come into our house and offer no empathy whatsoever. They're totally void of it. Which to me doesn't make sense. Why in the hell would you be colder than the spirit you're so-called investigating? My advice to paranormal teams is to let your clients know they're not alone in dealing with this. Anything's better than just saying "show me were the ghost is at?"

No longer was this a Keith and Tina problem. No longer were the events in our house restricted to just family and friends. The first thing Jennifer said after coming inside was, "Your house is humming, son!" I looked at her. Humming? "Yeah, I can hear it, I can feel it, there's is so much negative energy here. And my phone just died." Everybody's cell phone suddenly died. As do their equipment. We all acknowledge the abrupt lost in battery power in everyone's device when Jennifer points to Tina and me.

"Please step outside for a second, and then step back into the house," she asked. We obliged, and sure enough, there it was: a humming sound. The house was making a noise so low in pitch that you had to leave and come back in order to hear it. What does that mean? I have no clue, but the look on Jennifer's face told me something wasn't right.

Now, there were all kinds of humming noises. Machines make humming sounds. Engines make humming noises. The sound we were hearing resembled a beehive. If you've ever been to a bee farm or know someone who's into bee husbandry, you know the faint humming sound. That's what our house sounded like.

The only reason I can think of as to why Tina and I couldn't hear it was because we were focused on what was happening at the time. The noise seemed to coincide with the uneasy feeling I had. Tension, strife, anxiety, uncertainty, anger, depression, and outright fear had been running amok that entire morning. Jennifer was right; there was a negative vibe about the house. It's debatable as to when that began, impossible to know for sure. I'm willing to bet, though, that whatever lived here with Tina and I took it upon itself to exploit our tension. However short-lived that tension was, the entity finally had the fuel it needed to escalate things. We're dealing with that escalation right now. The question now is, how do we put the genie back in the bottle?

Tina and I spent the next twenty minutes or so showing Jennifer and her team all of the destruction that had happened that day. I'm always fascinated by the different reactions Tina and I get when giving people a tour of the damage.

Sometimes peoples' mouths would drop open. Sometimes they say "wow," or "oh my." Sometimes they respond nonchalantly; it's hard to read what it is they're thinking. A nonchalant response sort of put me at ease. I would later learn that the opposite reaction is the most genuine. Too cavalier meant you were arrogant, or perhaps a thrill seeker. Shocked and surprised meant you had respect and appreciation for what had unfolded.

Jennifer and her team were in awe of what was happening. I mean, we showed them everything. I led them upstairs to the guest bedroom. Jennifer's team was just amazed at the destruction; amazed at the amount of force it would take to hurl an object like that. And the debate Tina and I had had about something still being here would finally be settled. Jennifer settled it when she said, "This thing has never left the house. Just because the house was quiet in 2013, doesn't mean the spirits left. Spirits can lie dormant for days, weeks, months, even years, and all of a sudden re-appear…"

Tina looked at me, and I looked at her, and we're both thinking the same thing. How do you get rid of it? How can you make it leave for good? The response from Jennifer was "we'll do our best; we're here now, the best thing for you to know now is you're not alone anymore. God bless both of you for dealing with something like this." It was time to let No Bull Paranormal do what they came here to do. It was time for them to investigate. Only, how can you examine something when all your battery-operated devices are dead? Talk about a speed bump,

It would take an hour or two before everything was recharged and back working again. Was it a coincidence that everyone's equipment died within seconds of them arriving? Knowing what I know now, no it was not. In the meanwhile, the team had something else to do. They questioned the neighbors— to see what neighbors knew about the house, about the land, and about the previous tenants. Tina was taken aback as was I. This was all happening very fast, and it was all very real. There was a black van parked in front of our house, and it read: No Bull Paranormal Team. It doesn't say, Pizza Hut; it doesn't say Domino's Pizza (that would be OK) instead it says, paranormal team. Our neighbors must think we're nuts.

Until now, no one in our neighborhood was aware we were having ghost problems. That's not something you volunteer when making small talk. I'd spoken to three of my neighbors. I never mentioned to them the stuff we were experiencing.

It was a bright a sunny day. People were out and about. Dogs were being walked. Grass being mowed. Kids playing hopscotch on the sidewalk. And here comes a stranger with a clipboard asking whoever is outside, whoever is inclined to talk to him, about the history of the neighborhood. The history of the house in question. It comes with the job, right? You have to interview people. You have to get a sense of the neighborhood you're investigating. What Jennifer and her team were doing made sense. I better make a pot of coffee.

It didn't take me long to realize that waiting is a requirement when it comes to paranormal investigations. You're waiting for something to happen. You wait for something to talk into your voice recorder. You wait for something to crawl across the screen. You wait for a spike in EMF. For a light to turn red or green or orange. You wait. You wait, and when you're tired of waiting, you wait some more. It's nothing like what you see on TV. It's like a stakeout. You wait for the activity to take place. But you don't know when and where it will to present itself. Who says it will? You just don't know. But waiting is not my biggest problem. I'm used to waiting. I'm a fisherman. Waiting is ninety-nine percent of fishing. I'm also in the information technology field. I've worked countless graveyard shifts where waiting is required. Countless maintenance windows were waiting is all you do. That's all the project manager does while his or her engineers do the change management. We wait.

Jennifer's team had laced the entire upstairs with some awesome camera equipment. There was a camera in every room. I'm talking about tripods and everything. There we were in the kitchen, watching on the dual monitor. Guess what we were doing? We were waiting. Now and then an occasional thud would be heard. The screen goes blank. Tina and I look at Jennifer's team and ask, is that supposed to happen? What does that mean? No one knows for sure. All they know is "it's interesting." The phrase I kept hearing was "that's never happened before, are you sure we bought the right cameras?" Tina and I would look at each other and shrug.

4 pm. Mist was seen coming off the floor, near the doorway my office. Weird. Even I know that's not supposed to be there. I asked, "What is that?" Jennifer's brother points to the computer screen where the white mist is. I found out a few years later that white mist coming from the floor speaks to a strong "Geist" presence. Jennifer's brother went upstairs to confirm that the white mist was only visible through the infrared. We're watching him on the computer screen downstairs. He's walking in and out of the mist. He, of course, can't see anything. That blew everyone away.

After about five hours of monitoring all the rooms, it was now time to cleanse the house. Everyone agreed that the upstairs hallway seems to be an active area. Trouble seemed to reside there and near my office. So, what did Jennifer and her team experience? Well, the power loss of everyone's cell phone was weird. You can explain one cell phone dying, but three cell phones dying at the same time? That's hard to ignore. Not only did their cell phones die, but their equipment died also. Everything they arrived with that ran off battery was dead.

And then there was the humming noise. That was weird. I'm not sure what to make of that. I'm trying hard not to go super dark with what that could mean. I'm trying to stay positive. But these revelations were not making it easy for Tina or me. I mean, humming noises? Mist was coming from the carpet upstairs (only visible through the infrared camera) that they bought? The only thing left to do now was to cleanse the house; cleanse it thoroughly. That was Jennifer's primary role and responsibility. It was time to call upon her Native American background.

The cleanse she did last about thirty minutes. Was she thorough? Absolutely. Way more thorough than what I did two years ago. Jennifer told everyone to stay downstairs. She needed to talk to these spirits alone. Jennifer was going to try to ask the spirits to leave—to walk on out of here. Since upstairs was where all the hell was, that's where she used a majority of her sage stick. And yes, her sage stick did light itself prior to her beginning her ceremony. *Ghost Adventures* mentioned that briefly during the "Demons in Seattle" episode. Tina and I were in the downstairs when it happened. No one (team included) had ever seen anything like this. Anything like what? Humming noise, walls and ceiling contracting, mist coming from the floor and Jennifer screaming from the hallway landing "my sage stick just lit itself."

Hour later. No Bull Paranormal is done. Now for the homework. The team began dishing out papers: Christian prayers and Native American chants. Our assignment? Recite what's written down whenever you feel angst set in. Stay positive. You have to be strong, and you have to reclaim your home. These spirits will leave once they know they can't rule a house the way they want to.

Everyone agreed that the humming sound was now gone. No way was the team going to leave a house still humming. The atmosphere was way lighter than before. Compared to this morning, the house felt normal. Tina and I were relieved; we were both feeling good about how the day had unfolded. "You're not alone," Jennifer told us. "Tina, you have to be strong; call on Jesus, he'll protect you." Those were Jennifer's words to my girlfriend and me. The last thing I remember about that night was what Jennifer told me. "If something happens, call us right away." We all hugged each other—, gave thanks, and that was it. They spent eight hours with us that day. Now it's just Tina.

I went upstairs after saying my goodbye. Time to shut everything down, time to go to bed. Only what are we going to do about our bedroom door? Half of it was hanging off the hinges. No way was I sleeping with the door open. Nope, I had to fix this door before we went to bed. Let me see if I can just piece it together for the time being. Surprisingly I did just that. That was my contribution for the day. Our bedroom door is working again. Tina walked into the room a few minutes after me. We tidied up a bit and went to bed.

☛ *Summer 2012. I placed one of my favorite Bibles on the lamp table in our living room. It was gone the next day. It never re-appeared until 2014.*

Chapter 14
The Burning Bibles

Tina and were eager to go to bed that night. That's how exhausted we were. Talk about a day with exploding light fixtures and doors being yanked off the hinges. All of that horrible was nothing compared to what we were about to experience. Our pillows ended up being the most valuable item that night. No need to recount of anything—let's just go to bed. That's how tired we were. No more arguing. No giving each other the cold shoulder. I'm spent. Tina's spent. Let's just go to sleep.

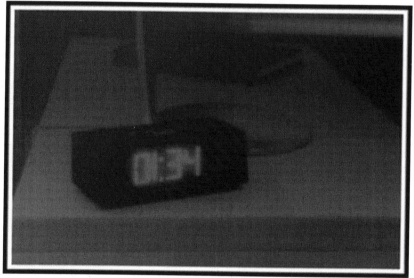

Fig: 14.1 Fire alarm goes off.

Reenactment Video to hearing fire alarms going off
https://youtu.be/Ni1ywTi_Wl8

March 31st, 2014 - 1:34 am. The fire alarm goes off. Hallway first then the rest of the house (that's how these alarms work). Didn't take much to jolt us awake. I was practically sleeping with one eye open to begin with; I'm sure Tina was too. As soon as I heard the alarm go off, I thought about the mysterious fire alarm we had in 2013. Fire alarm, but no fire. Somehow this felt different. Something new had just happened. The first thing I did was leap out of bed, thinking there has to be fire this time. Somewhere in the house, there's a fire. Where is it?

When I yanked opened the bedroom door there it was a bright orange light. There on the floor, lying inches from our doorway was a book. It was on fire. The light from the flames had illuminated the hallway, talk about an eerie feeling. Instinct alone forced me to lean down and close the book. That put the fire out. All we have left is a hallway filled with smoke and soot. Pages of ash are floating in the air all around me. Wait a minute? I know this book. This is my book. It's the Bible that went missing on October 10th, 2012. The one I left on the lamp table before going to bed.

I leaned down to pick up the Bible, and I'm thinking to myself, oh my God, *it's come back.* And that's when I felt the bulge. Something was inside. I opened it up, and there within the burnt pages was a wooden cross. *I know this cross.* This was the cross that I bought from Amazon (see page 415). I couldn't tell what more was frightening: The Bible returning on fire, or the cross inside, which was almost unrecognizable. This cross was not resting in the Bible on the night that it went missing. Hell no. I bought this cross online a few weeks ago. We hung it above our bed as a means of protection.

Talk about a sure sign of defiance. That's exactly what a burning Bible is; it's an act of defiance. A slap in the face for Tina and me; mockery of our religious beliefs; or a sign of mockery for contacting Jennifer.

Tina was in the hallway with me now, in equal shock. The fire alarm was still shrilling above our heads, due to the amount of smoke present. I decided to call Jennifer right then and there. She said if anything should happen after they left to call her. I did; no answer. The only thing I could do was leave a voicemail. The edges around the cross were singed. The Bible was destroyed. Ash was everywhere. I shook my head, looking at Tina. What should be your reaction when you experience something like this? What should the response be? Do we pray? Certainly. We did. And then what? Do we move out of the house? Do we bunker down? Do we call in the big guns? What big guns?

Jennifer nearly dropped the phone after hearing about what had happened that night. She'd never heard of anything like this. A spirit that can set fires, the ability to teleport or apport objects at will is a spirit you don't want to fuck with. They are deadly and unrelenting. No need to get between these types of spirits crosshairs if you can avoid it. Jennifer's advice to me was: "Move out of the house; it's best to cut your losses now, versus becoming too entangled with whatever this was." That was her honest assessment. I was taken aback at first. I mean others have told us, No Bull Paranormal included, it's important that we stand our ground. It's important to be firm, to be steadfast. Kim's godmother said the same thing.

I told Tina about my conversation with Jennifer over dinner that night. I told her that Jennifer's recommendation was "we should move." In Jennifer's twenty years of investigating she'd never seen anything close to this. The theory floating around was this has to be linked to the land. Something terrible happened to the land, or something terrible happened inside the house. Her recommendation, should we decide to stay, was "do research on both the land and the property." Try to find out who the previous tenants were. There's a risk attached to that recommendation; it's called time. It's doubtful the spirits are going to lay off their attacks while Tina and I conduct research on the home. Research takes time.

Jennifer's not sure if we have that. Tina looked at me and asked, "what do you want to do?"

My decision was to try to get some help. I was never cool with the idea of moving. Moving out means quitting. This is my house. Why would we move if God is all-powerful and all-protecting?

Of course, I had no idea what's about to happen next. Who knows what else these spirits have in store—there are two more Bibles upstairs that have yet to catch fire. And that's not even the worse of it.

But now I'm thinking: someone somewhere understands this stuff. Someone has to know how to deal with it. It's 2014—you're telling me there's no one out there in the world with the skills and expertise to go after such phenomenon? I find that hard to believe, embarrassing if you think about. You mean to tell me there's no organization on earth with the wherewithal to immediately investigate something like this? We're in the twenty-first century, ladies and gentleman, that's unacceptable.

The decision Tina and I made that night was we would remain steadfast. We'll continue doing what we've been instructed to do. We'll pray, we'll smudge, we'll recite chants, we'll light candles, we'll continue reaching out to religious houses and organizations. We'll do our part. Hopefully, someone out there will do their part. The remainder of the week would be quiet, minus a few phantom footsteps here and there, things just stopped. Then came April 4th.

I was touring internet sites for solutions to our problem. Maybe I'll find some answers. And guess what? I did. A member of one of the paranormal message boards I found said a word I had not heard in a long time. They said "sounds like you have a poltergeist living with you. The first thing that came to my mind when I read the word poltergeist was that Stephen Spielberg movie titled *Poltergeist*. Hollywood or not, please don't tell me that's what we have. Screw that. I'll pack up my things right now. That being said, the word 'poltergeist' ended up being a good lead. What's a poltergeist? In short, a "noisy ghost," or better yet, a "noisy spirit." These spirits in our home are definitely noisy, I'll give them that.

If this is a poltergeist, then the next question is: how do you get rid of it? That's where my brain was at when, all of a sudden, the TV in our bedroom switched on. Now, wait a minute. Tina was downstairs. Why is the TV suddenly coming on in the bedroom? I got up from my chair and walked out of my office and into our bedroom and saw that the TV was on. It was on the music channel. No sign of Tina whatsoever.

Here she comes though, marching upstairs. I was looking at the TV with the remote control in my hand, trying to turn the volume down. I told Tina the TV just came on by itself and it was playing music. She looked at me and says, "Oh—I thought that was you." I told her, "No, it's not me; I was in my office; why would I be blasting loud music from our bedroom?" We both looked at each other and shrugged. Tina looked at the TV and said "that's different."

I then switched the TV channel to a regular programming channel and turned it off. Tina went downstairs. I went back to my office. Five minutes later the TV switched on again. Loud music as before. I darted out of my office and headed back into the bedroom, and sure enough, it was on again. Now, I turned the TV off five minutes ago. Not only is it on again, but it's playing the same song. From the same music station. Tina comes back upstairs and looks at me. The TVs on, and it's on this music channel that neither Tina nor myself ever use. Why is the TV on the music channel? Why is the same song playing? I suddenly realized something. We're being haunted. At this very moment, Tina and I are being haunted.

I looked at Tina, and she looked at me. I said: this is the same song that was playing five minutes ago. Tina said, "What the fuck?"

I said, "Yeah: this is a music channel; songs don't play in repeat mode. We should be hearing a different song by now." And that's when a light bulb went off inside my head—what's the name of the song? The name of the song is "Dark Horse" by Katie Perry. Now, this is where it gets weird and dark. The part of the song that we heard, over and over were the words — *"are you ready for, ready for a perfect storm, a perfect storm, cause once you're mine, once you're mine, there's no going back."* Mind you, Tina and I are hearing the entire song. The verses above are playing through our TV as we enter the bedroom. You have got to be kidding me? How is a spirit able to do this? I turned off the TV again with the remote control I was holding and decided to one step further by unplugging it entirely. There. All done. That should settle it right? Not quite.

The TV came on again five minutes later. I was in my office, googling 'Katie Perry' with hopes of finding that song. I found the lyrics, and I found the video for it. I was four minutes into my search when the TV came on again. Came on with no plug; no cord sticking in the outlet whatsoever. The same Katie Perry song was playing. When it comes on it's always on that verse—the verse about *"...are you ready for a perfect storm, a perfect storm..."* That's what's blasting out the bedroom now. Then the remainder of the songs plays.

Instead of turning the TV off, we decided to leave it on. But not on the music channel. I think I put it on an R&B channel, which for no apparent reason seemed to work.

Only now, as I write this, does the question hit me: what song other Comcast customers are hearing if their TV was tuned to this channel at the same time Tina and I were hearing "Dark Horse?" The channel is real. It's not fabricated. The song is real too. It's been playing in our house for the last fifteen minutes. I wish I could go back in time (back to that day) and run to one of our other TVs. I wish I could go put those TVs on the same channel the bedroom TV was on when it was playing "Dark Horse." Would "Dark Horse" be playing on those TVs? It's probably best not knowing. Tina and I call that weekend The Katie Perry Weekend. It's trippy. It's crazy. It's what Tina meant by "different." Different from anything we've seen before. Different from anything we heard before. It's in its own category because it never happened again. No other TV (whether it was plugged in or not) has ever come on by itself blasting music. Not like that they haven't.

It's debatable; but I kind of feel this song, these lyrics which we heard three times, were a precursor to what was coming. Keep in mind; it's now April. The weekend was about to get started. *"Are we ready for the perfect storm?"* The message the spirits was sending was: Are we ready for the perfect storm? Here it comes.

Nothing else happened that Friday; no more music coming from unplugged TVs. Up until now a majority of the events happening in the home were witnessed by Tina and myself. Things flew in front of us. Things flew behind us. We'd hear banging noises while having dinner or while watching TV. One of the most relentless banging events we'd ever experienced happened during the middle of the night or the early morning hours. Saturday would be no exception. Most weekend mornings, Tina and I slept in. Or we tried to. This Saturday morning, we both were awakened to three loud bangs. They were not the normal rapping noises we'd grown accustomed to hearing. These bangs were more like loud taps. I swear to God the noises were nearby.

One of the things Tina and I were instructed to do when activity emerged, was scream the words "get out of my house!" Inform the spirits that this is not their house. It's Keith and Tina's house. You're not welcomed here. Get out of our house and get out of it right now. That would quiet stuff down sometimes. If that didn't work, we'd grab one of my other Bibles, now sitting on the hallway bookshelf. Open it up to Psalms or Proverbs and recite. None of that seemed to be working this particular morning, so the only thing we could do was get up. No sleeping in that morning.

I went back into our bedroom an hour later and see something that wasn't there when we woke up. Three holes in the wall on Tina's side of the bed. I called Tina upstairs to confirm when these markings appeared. I was right. These markings weren't here when we woke up. But the sound was. What woke us up in the first place were three distinct banging noises. Very loud wall taps. Tina and I couldn't pinpoint where it was coming from, but it felt nearby. I have no doubt these are the noises we heard some few hours ago. It would seem the noise came first and the markings later.

I decided to take photos of the holes (recording keeping purposes). Time to research that event and a list of others on the internet. Everywhere I looked online about malevolent hauntings, said we were dealing with a very nasty poltergeist. But something didn't make sense. Poltergeists feed off a human agent. No way are Tina or me an agent?

That aside, it's beginning to look like that's what we have. The outdated definition of a poltergeist once again is a "noisy ghost." Our ghost definitely was noisy. Case solved, right? Not quite. If this was a poltergeist, then the next question was: how do you get rid of it? The answers to that question were almost as elusive as the spirits plaguing our home. It seems one cannot get rid of or remove a poltergeist; they for all practical purposes have to remove themselves. "Geist" activity can last several weeks, several months; or several years.

Saturday night. I left the house to go have Happy Hour with some former co-workers. I anticipated that I would be gone for a few hours. It never occurred to me the house would be attacked with me not in it. I guess I didn't take the Katie Perry song seriously (which happened the night before). Up until now I've been basing my knowledge on what poltergeist can do by what we've experienced, not by what we haven't experienced. That was a huge mistake. That night I realized the only thing predictable about this haunting is that it's unpredictable. All theories go out the window. The entity is the one holding all the cards.

I told Tina where I was going when I left. I told her what I was doing. She mentioned to me that she may or may not go out; depends if she hears from Kim. That was the last conversation we had. The last conversation before I got to my car. Oh, and *I must be fat-fingering my key fob again because sure enough, the trunk light is on.*

It was a little bit after 9 pm when I got home. As soon as I pulled up to the house, I noticed that Tina's SUV was gone. I thought nothing of it. She probably got done with whatever it was she was doing and decided to go have dinner with Kim or something. I looked at my phone: no texts from her. No missed phone calls. No nothing. Oh well, I'll just go in and pretend I have the house to myself. Notice I said, pretend.

As soon as I opened the front door that feeling hit me. That feeling I had a week ago. That concussion-like feeling that proceeded last week's house attack. Something was wrong. I walked in and saw debris everywhere. Shards of glass littered everywhere. What the hell happened? Then I heard something. It sounded like a faucet was left running. As soon as I stepped into the kitchen I saw that the faucet was running. I ran upstairs screaming, "Tina! Tina!" No response. I reached the midway landing point. That where I was when I saw it, all the light fixtures and light bulbs in the hallway and guest bedroom were busted and broken. Wires were hanging from the hallway ceiling. The porcelain dome that covered the lights in the upstairs hallway was missing. Just little pieces of glass now. Wiring was hanging from the ceiling like Louisiana moss. The bedroom door I had jimmy-rigged last week was folded on the floor. Now my blood pressure's up. The house looked like a bomb had gone off in it. And where the fuck was Tina? *Tina! Tina!* Nothing. What the hell was going on?

I called Tina's cell phone. Nothing. No answer. I then texted: *where are you? What happened? Call me.* Still no answer. Then I thought, if the house blew up while Tina was here, the first person she was going to go to is Kim. Lucky for me I had Kim's number. But when I called Kim, I got voicemail. All I could do now was wait. I roamed through the house looking at the destruction. The upstairs looked as if a tornado had run through every room.

This was starting to resemble a Hollywood movie. Man leaves girlfriend alone for a few hours. Comes back, and finds girlfriend gone. House is turned upside down. Had this been a movie, Tina would have eventually come back and as soon as she walked in the door she would have ran to me, we would have embraced. We're both frantic. We're OK, though. No broken bones. Had this been a movie Tina would have cried on my shoulder. Had this been a movie I would have wrapped her in a blanket, made her some tea, and asked her very gently, what happened? Honey, tell me what happened? But this is not Hollywood. Damn sure isn't a movie. This is real life.

When Tina came back she didn't come back hysterical. She didn't come back frantic. She came back pissed. She wasn't pissed at me for leaving her there alone. We've left each other alone hundreds of times. Tina was pissed because she couldn't get a hold of me. Every call she made to me went straight to voicemail. I'm like, what are you talking about? I have no phone calls from you. I pulled out my phone and showed her I had no missed calls. And that's when the argument started. The accusations. In Tina's mind my phone was off for nefarious reasons.

There are only two ways one can miss a phone call. Either your phone is off purposely or the battery has died. My battery hadn't died. And my phone wasn't off. Maybe I was in a dead-zone. But that didn't make sense. I had coverage where I was at. I had missed calls from other people. Now I was trying to get information from Tina about what happened. Her voice was raised, which meant my voice was raised. I was trying to find out why our house looks like tornado alley, while at the same time she was yelling at me for not having my phone handy. Neither one of us was getting a word in edgeways. I was trying to tell her I had my phone with me at all times. I even hand my phone to her so she can look and see: zero calls from Tina during the time frame in which this happened. Tina's not buying it, she's pissed. So now I'm mad, because I'm being falsely accused. Do you see what's happening here?

I can understand Tina's anger. Most of what she's giving me can be summarized to her being afraid. I get that, the house was attacked and I couldn't be reached. (If I didn't understand then. I certainly was going to in a few days. My own personal house attack was coming; oh yes, it's coming). I can't even begin to imagine how all this turmoil unfolded. From what Tina told me, it happened like this: She was loading up the dishwasher when suddenly, the lights in the house go off and on. She then hears a noise, a loud crash—which sounded like it came from upstairs. She went upstairs to investigate. According to Tina, she witnessed the lights in the hall going off and on. Literally flickering off and on. Tina was now standing underneath one of the porcelain light domes. She was staring at it directly (waiting for the light to go off again) all of a sudden, the porcelain dome explodes. Debris goes everywhere. She grabs her keys and her cell phone and darts out of the house.

The question I'm left asking is, did the spirit purposely wait for me to leave? Did it want Tina by herself? What's up with me not receiving any phone calls? How convenient was that? There seems to be some forethought going on with Tina and my everyday actions. This suggests the spirits were watching us for the purpose of using our words and actions against us.

Tina never talked about that night again. Total silence on what happened that night. She remained upset with me for the rest of the night, for a majority of the weekend. I was shocked too—I was not lying to her. Her call to me never arrived. Tina wasn't having it. In her mind, I was doing something I shouldn't be doing. The tension between us seemed to be getting worse and worse. We were back to giving each other the silent treatment which is the wrong thing to do where malevolent spirits are concerned. Neither of us knew at the time that we were being manipulated.

Sunday morning came. I was upstairs repairing the light fixtures. Tina was downstairs cleaning up the kitchen. I couldn't help but think about the Katie Perry song we heard on Friday. 'Are we ready for the perfect storm? The perfect storm?' Hell, no we weren't.

If last night was to be a sign of one of us being targeted, then something had to be done. I had to dig deeper. Not only did I have to call Jennifer back. I had to find someone, somebody out there knew what to do. How do we lessen what's going on? Here I am, tip-toeing over the remaining broken glass in the hallway. Tension and silent treatment, that's what's for breakfast. Now, when I get up in the morning, Sunday especially—the first thing I want is coffee. Coffee and my television show *Meet the Press*.

I went straight to my office after getting up. I went in there to turn on both TV and computer. The hallway bookshelf sits in the corner of the hallway. I saw my Bible sitting on the bookshelf when I passed it the first time—it's impossible to miss. This was my second Bible. The one that was burnt last week was now sitting in my closet.

Three minutes later, I was coming back upstairs, heading back to my office. As soon as I hit the top staircase, I saw the bookshelf. The Bible was gone. The candles were still there. The sage was still there. The ashtray the sage stick sits in is still there. Everything's there, except the Bible. Tina! (I'm starting to get good at this). Calling for Tina whenever trouble breaks out. It didn't take Tina long for to come up the stairs. I asked her, "Did you move the Bible?" She says, "No." I'm puzzled; she's puzzled. Now my heart didn't have a pitter-patter moment like it did when the first Bible went missing. The book was sitting here a few minutes ago. Now it's gone. Not once did Tina and I say "we should go look for it." That would be pointless.

I mean, there's no reason to go looking for it. What would we gain? We know who took it. Searching for it would amuse them, not us. That's where my head was at right now. Let's just accept that it's gone. Let's pretend this is a normal Sunday, and that's precisely what we did. Now don't get me wrong, it was never truly business as usual once an event took place. We smudged that morning. We prayed. I'm opening the blinds throughout the house with the hopes of preventing another attack. The Bible's gone. Could an attack be imminent? We do this for several minutes: smudging, cleaning up, spraying air fresher, and opening up doors and windows before finally returning to our normal Sunday routine. Me upstairs in my office and Tina downstairs watching TV. I depart my office again that morning for a coffee refill. I enter the kitchen, and the first thing I see is the missing Bible. The Bible that rested on our hallway bookshelf was now sitting on the island counter. Significantly altered, however. It was burnt. This Bible was more singed than the first Bible. How is that possible?

I saw the first Bible; it was on fire. It had flames on top of the pages. Not this Bible. This Bible was a pile of ash. A shriveled mess of Bible passages. I screamed, "Tina! Come here, Tina!" I stepped aside so Tina can get a good look at the Bible, the minute she reaches the kitchen. Her first response was, "What the heck?"

We were both standing shoulder-to-shoulder; both of us dumbfounded. I remember grabbing my video camera, something I forgot to do the night the first Bible returned. It's been said that "history is the most qualified to reward all research." There are documented cases of inexplicable Bible burnings. Some of those cases are sitting on the bookshelf at your local library. Some are sitting in the warehouse at Amazon in spectacular books about poltergeist. Some are documented online. This was the second Bible in our home to go missing. It's burned, but it's burned differently from the first. It seems to have undergone some immense heat. The pages are singed. It looked like shriveled-up wood chips or notebook paper. The burnt pages are folded up unto themselves. Folded inward.

I'm inspecting this as is Tina. Where do these items go when they're taken? It could've been burned here. That much is certain. But where did it burn?

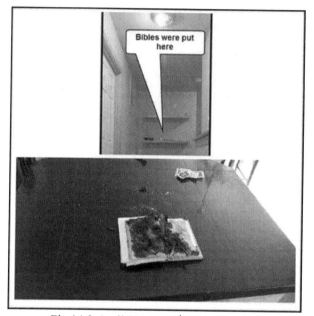

Fig 14.2 April 2014 – 2nd Bible Burning

The other difference: it's only been gone a few minutes. The 2012 Bible was sitting on the lampstand on the first floor when it went missing. It reappeared on the second floor over a year later. The second Bible was on the second floor when it went missing. It re-appeared on the first floor. What does it mean? I'm not sure. I'm hoping someone reading this can tell me. Will the scientists of the world please answer Keith Linder's question?

The only thing I can say that's similar about these books is they're Bibles. Both books have been in my possession for over fifteen years. I bought them brand new. It seems the spirits in this house were making a statement. That statement being *'your Bibles are, for all intent and purposes, useless. Planting them in various parts of the house is useless. Reading from them is pointless, borderline laughable. They have no ill effect on us; we're taking them with the hopes of proving to you how useless they are. Some we take for long periods of time, others we take for short periods of time. We're setting them on fire right before checking them back in. Remember you just got here; we've been here for millennia.'* Tina picks up her cell phone and began calling the local Bothell parish. Voicemail after voicemail, that's all she got. The Seattle parish told Tina to call the local parish in Bothell. She tried. Nothing but voicemail. I know priests are busy but, wow, are they this damn busy? You don't have to answer the phone when we call but you should at least return our phone call.

I'm not trying to indict the Catholic priesthood. But shouldn't there be a better way to inform the church of such happenings? I can't understand why we're getting the run around between the Seattle parish—who Tina called first and the local parish who Tina was referred to. Why are you passing us around? Why are you forcing us to deal with this ourselves? Why are we alone?

2nd Bible Burning April 6th 2014
https://youtu.be/uVZVtcjZzgo

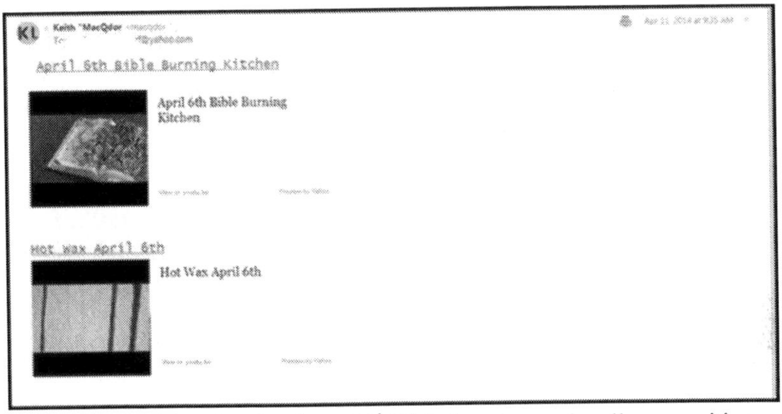

Fig 14.3 Email to family about 2nd Bible burning and wall wax writing.

Chapter 15
Courage under Fire

May 2014, without a shadow of a doubt, was one the deadliest month for Tina and me. When you think about the activity we're experiencing theory suddenly becomes fact. Things are escalating. Each activity that we've experienced is a precursor to something else about to happen. The house occupant (that's us) knows nothing. A good example of that was me not knowing in advance that Tina could be attacked while being at home by herself. My assumption then was she couldn't. Well we know that's not the case anymore.

Tina, bless her heart, was still trying to reach local parishes in and around Bothell. She was a victim of what I call the game of playing hot potatoes. No one in their right mind believes this could be happening. Let's recap what Tina and I have seen and heard so far.

Activity	March / April
Armoire thrown – 3X	Both
Loud bangs	Both
Knockings	Both
Wall tapping sounds	Both
Pacing back in forth	Both
Exploding light fixtures	Both
Bedroom door torn off hinges	March
1st Bible burning	March
TV turns on by itself – 3X	April
House attack	Both
House attack (Tina's home)	April
2nd Bible burning	April
Wax wall writing	April

Table 15.1 Activity List

Jennifer had concluded that Tina and I wish to stand our ground. We're not leaving. Don't call us stubborn. Call us naive. We have no idea what staying means. No clue whatsoever. No one's written a book on how to do deal with malevolent spirits effectively. Remember, poltergeist activity is supposed to subside eventually; that's what many people say. "Give it time; the activity will pass." So, I guess that's why we're staying.

Early May. Other things are happening in and around Tina and me that are less attention-getting but equally important. I'm talking about the intermittent issues we were having with our electronic devices in the house. Televisions weren't coming on by themselves anymore, but TV channels did change by themselves. Our VOIP landline can't seem to make up its mind on whether it wants to work or not. The cameras I'd installed in the hallway and the living room were being found turned around. Some are being found unplugged or, get this, upside down. That's what May looks like right now.

May 18th. I got an email at work alerting me that all the cameras in the home were offline. There has to be a logical explanation as to why that's the case. I mean we're only talking about two cameras at this point. There was no reason for me to rush home. No reason for me to think something was up. I was wrong. Something was up.

When I walked through the front door of my house I heard no phantom footsteps. I kind of wish I had. That would've been way better than the utter destruction I saw within seconds of walking into both den and living room. The couch and love seat had all been moved. They were upside down. The coffee table in the den had been moved as well. Everything that was on it is now on the floor. Tina's plants have been thrown around. Items are knocked over in a such to suggest a vandalism. It looks like we've been burglarized except for one crucial fact. We haven't. The ADT security system was still on when I got home. Which raises another question, how was all this movement done without tripping the ADT?

Fig 15.1 The month of May involved a series of house attacks.

1.) Every kitchen cabinet door is wide open. 2.) Furniture in the master bedroom has been ransacked. 3.) TV stand in master bedroom has been knocked over, including items that sat on it. 4.) Den area has been ransacked Ex. Couch, love seat, coffee, table, plants, etc. all knocked over. 5.) Bottles of wine emptied out of the wine rack. Wine rack door open. Kitchen chairs pulled out.

I venture deeper into the kitchen and see that every kitchen cabinet door is open. We're talking a total of sixty cabinet doors, ladies and gentlemen Even the closet door is open. The wine rack is open. The contents of the kitchen table are all over the kitchen floor. Understand me when I say this. You can always tell when the activity is escalating by the new stuff happening around you. Or, in this case, happening while we were gone. That was it. No destruction whatsoever upstairs. Not that day there wasn't.

Tina and I would come home and find our house like this for the next few days. So much destruction, so much upside-down turmoil that I had to follow people's advice. I went out and bought more cameras. Not video cameras. CCTV cameras; motion detection, email alert cameras. My brother told me, as did other people: no one's going to believe you unless you capture it on video. People are going to think Tina did it. People are going to think you did it. So, I went out and bought a few more motion detection cameras. Cameras built to detect motion. Not cameras built to detect a poltergeist. Just so we're clear, that camera doesn't exist.

One of the most horrendous house attacks to ever happen took place a few days after the first incident. I came home and discovered the house in disarray. The couch and love seat were turned upside down. Kitchen cabinet doors were wide open. Everything had been ransacked like before; except now I had cameras. Now, these cameras are configured to send me email alerts whenever they detect motion or sound. They come on thirty minutes after Tina and I leave the house.

I could feel something—that dense energy feeling. The humming sound had returned. All this told me that whatever had happened, happened recently. I looked down at my phone and saw just a few emails. A few snapshots had come in, the majority of them taken after the attack had occurred. The subject line of the email read: Sound detected. The first camera I went to inspect was in the kitchen. Was it still on? I looked at it; it was facing up. The lens was aiming at the ceiling. That wasn't how I left it. Time to go upstairs to see what the hall camera is doing. When I got to the upstairs hallway, I saw something I was not prepared to see: broken glass all over the floor. Our bedroom door was smashed again. The armoire in the guest room was lying face down on the floor (again). The room was in shambles. Our bedroom had been ransacked. Two of Tina's dresser tables had been knocked over (See fig 15.1). The contents of both dressers were all over the floor. The lamps which sit each side of our bed were on the floor—iron and ironing board too.

As I've said, in this house it's impossible to make your way upstairs and not see the bookshelf some twenty-odd feet away. It's dead ahead. It's the first thing I see when I come upstairs, especially nowadays. And the minute I see it I notice something very different. I notice I can't see the Bible. Bible? Yes, the third Bible I owned. Tina and I placed it on the bookshelf after the second one was burned. I'm no longer looking for a Bible, ladies and gentlemen. There's hardly any Bible left. More like a pile of ash.

My Foscam sits on the second bookshelf, right above the first. The camera's facing upward. Just like the camera in the kitchen. What does that mean? That means the spirit behind all of this is smart as fuck. It's smarter than me. It's smarter than my brother. It's smarter than the people giving me advice. It's smarter than skeptics and cynics. In the event of a power loss (for whatever reason) the cameras go to the default position. They point upward after rebooting, in the event of abrupt loss of power.

That means sometime during the attack the power in the house went out. Good move by them. They obviously read the manual better than I did because there's a chapter in the manual that says if the event of a camera reboot—cameras will go back to the factory set position of facing upward. In fact, several power outages happened between the time I went to work and the time I got home. The ADT security system was not impacted by the power outage. It stayed on.

Third Bible Video
https://youtu.be/CjkYw2kleBU

Fig 15.2 3rd Burnt Bible / House Attack

So, the house wasn't vulnerable to an outside attack. What's the best way to confirm a power outage? Check your printer tray. Most printers do a reconfiguration, which includes printing out test pages when they lose power. I had several blank sheets of paper in my printer tray when I got home, which confirmed a power loss did take place. I'm talking about five to eight instances where power was cut to the upstairs area.

Tina had just arrived home. She didn't know the upstairs looks exactly like the downstairs. She didn't know our bedroom is a mess. All our belongings were thrown about. The destruction of our bedroom totally caught Tina off guard. It floored her. And I understand why. The brain can't interpret an armoire lying on the floor face down. The brain can't interpret dressers and drawers turned upside down. It can't interpret your clothes spread everywhere. It tries to make sense of it all. That's all it can do, is try. What about the human heart? There's not a human heart on earth that can make sense of what was done to our bedroom. I know this because Tina broke down. My girlfriend walked into the bedroom; there I am standing at the foot of the bed. She does what I do. She surveys the destruction, picks up a candle here and there, tries to avoid stepping on broken glass. She sits down, with cloth in hand and begins sobbing.

My girlfriend didn't have to tell me why. I know why. She was crying because our room had been violated. The emotion that overtook Tina was the feeling of being violated. The spirit had violated our room in such a way to the point of Tina and me feeling helpless. Your bedroom is where you go to sleep. It's where you have your dreams. It's where you and your partner have conversations. Conversations on just about anything—including paranormal activity. The bedroom is where you make love. The bedroom is a lot of things. The spirit who did this knew what they were doing. They knew by attacking the bedroom what that would do to Tina and me. Our resolve had taken a direct hit.

Now, people have emailed me from all over the world. Many are sincere as sincere can be. I write back to those people immediately—guess I'm just a sucker for intellectual curiosity. That and empathy are what move me. There's one group of people I hate writing back to. Those that say "I wish this were happening to me. I wish I could live through something like this." No, you don't. TV and Hollywood have painted you a poor perception of what the paranormal is. I'm speaking about malevolent hauntings. I never thought in the history of my existence that I would see an object levitate. The idea of an object flying through a wall; through a ceiling never crossed my mind. Those thoughts don't enter your head when looking for a home on Craigslist. Let me tell you what crossed my mind: I wanted to find a home that would impress my girlfriend. I wanted to find a home that would make my mom proud. Make my dad proud (had he still been alive).

You don't understand what's going on here. Let me tell you what's going on. It's called a beat down. An unequivocal beat down. No one volunteers for it. A beat down is a set of circumstances one finds themselves in through a variety of reasons. Preventing us from sleeping in is a form of beat down. Slamming the bathroom door while one of us taking a shower is a form of beat down. Trashing the kitchen while we're both at work is a form of beat down. It's tormenting basically. Plain and simple torment. And that's my reply to people who say they want to "experience something like this."

The only thing I remember doing while sitting next to Tina was telling her, it'll be alright, we'll get through this, we must be strong. Did I believe what I was saying? I like to think I did. But I wasn't sure. I'm still not.

The advice still being given was: smudge the house. Make sure you're always thorough. Make sure you are vigilant; make sure you're doing it together, versus doing it by yourself. That's the advice we followed. I think we might have followed the advice a little too correctly one particular night. I'm talking about the night where I asked Tina if she would smudge the house before we went to bed. She said, "OK."

The house was quiet after that. Nothing jumped off. We woke up the next morning to the smell of sage everywhere. That's how thorough Tina was the night before. I mean, our definition of a good smudging was a house filled with smoke. We thought we weren't doing a decent job until we set a few fire alarms off. That's our definition of smudging. Tina left the house before me that morning. I remember walking her to the door and kissing her goodbye. I marched upstairs and got into the shower.

Five minutes later, the fire alarm went off. *Shit! Seriously, is this going down now? Right when I'm trying to dry off.* I run out of the bedroom and into the hallway. That's when it happened. Something ran past me within seconds of me hitting the hallway landing—an invisible force. The front door of the house opened wide, and I mean wide. So wide I can see into the street. Then *SLAM!* The front door has just opened and closed on its own. I'm thinking; there's an intruder in the house, someone is in the house. *What do I do*? I run downstairs with the hope of giving chase. I was at the front door; the fire alarm was still ringing throughout the house. I twisted the doorknob. The door doesn't open. *Uh-oh, I've seen this movie before*, I remember a similar incident happening a few weeks ago. The door won't open because they don't want it to open. And that's when it hit me, *Mr. Linder; your house is on fire, remember you have a fire alarm going off. Find the fire, Mr. Linder, find the fire!*

I turn my back to the door and begin looking for the fire. There's no smoke downstairs. The kitchen looks fine. The coffee maker's fine. Toaster and oven are fine. *Where in the fuck is this fire?* I run upstairs, thinking *the fire must be upstairs. I'm not losing sight of something running past me just a few seconds ago, what the fuck was that that ran past me?* As soon as I get to the landing, I can see dead ahead that there's smoke coming from my office. The hallway's filling up with smoke because my office is on fire.

I get to my office and there above my computer station is my Final Fantasy poster. The sci-fi poster was shooting fire similar to the Bible a few weeks ago. I mean seriously it's on fire. There's no time for buckets of water. No time for fire extinguishers. Use what you got on you to put the fire out, a voice tells me. I have a damp towel; I can use that to extinguish the fire. And that's exactly what I did. I extinguished the fire, but the alarms were still ringing. Now keep in mind, only a few seconds have passed since the first alarm went off and me now extinguishing it. Tina's been gone five minutes at the most.

I probably should be urinating my pants by now because whatever ran past me in the hallway was extremely big. What can be my size and move that fast? All I could feel was pure evil as it ran past me. It's hard to think straight, because of the alarms still going off. Final analysis: the house is under attack. *Get out of the house, Keith; get out of the house, Keith.* That's what the voice in my head was telling me. So, I'm back downstairs now; smoke has now reached every room in the house. The burnt plastic stench is taking over. They say *it's not the fire that kills's you; it's the smoke inhalation. Get out of the house, Mr. Linder.* So, I pull the front door, and nothing happens. It feels like it's been sealed shut. It's not budging one bit. That's when the realization came; *the house is not under attack, idiot, you are. Call 911. 9+1+1.* Ringing.

The first thing they ask me is, "What is your emergency?"

"Yes, operator, I have a house fire taking place, and I need fire department assistance!"

"What's your address?" Static breaks out over the phone the second I begin giving my address. "Sir, can you repeat that? You're breaking up." I try again, nothing. I try a third time, still nothing. At this point I'm pissed off and because the operator can't hear me through the phone. Six alarms are ringing simultaneously, and the lady on the other end can't hear me. She finally, does after the fourth try. I hang up with her and call Tina. Thank God Tina answered!

Come back to the house; the house is under attack, come back to the house. I didn't even wait for her to acknowledge me. I quickly hung up and ran to the garage door, touched the door opener so the garage door could open. I now have a way to get out of the house.

Here comes the Bothell fire department. Here comes Tina, thirty seconds after them. I point the first responders to the upstairs room where the fire was. In walks Tina, hysterical and full of terror. I have no clue how I look. I think I'm in t-shirt and boxers. I must be half naked or something because Tina walks in and begins throwing blankets over me. I'm shaking like a leaf. Tina's crying, and so am I. The house is a mess. Smoke is everywhere. The fireman does something; I'm not sure what, but the alarms finally stop ringing.

What just happened? Spontaneous combustion, that's what happened. A poster caught fire on its own. But not really on its own. A poltergeist started it. Five firemen are standing in my office. Nothing looks out of order except the poster on the wall. No heat source whatsoever. Three other firemen are in the garage inspecting the fuse box; nothing there either. Everyone was scratching their heads except Tina and me. The question they were asking was, "How does a poster catch fire?" I wanted to tell them so bad how a poster catches fire. I wanted to say: it catches fire because we have a poltergeist living with us. It's trying to beat us down. It's been outsmarting us; around everyone who's helped us for the past two years.

I wanted to go into my closet and pull out one the three Bibles and show the captain the condition it was in so bad but *wait a minute, he might not believe me.* I couldn't. Instead, I just sat there wrapped in a wet blanket next to Tina. We must have been a sight to see. We looked horrible sitting together. The house didn't smell like sage anymore. Instead, it smelt like burnt polyester. I think that's what my poster was made from.

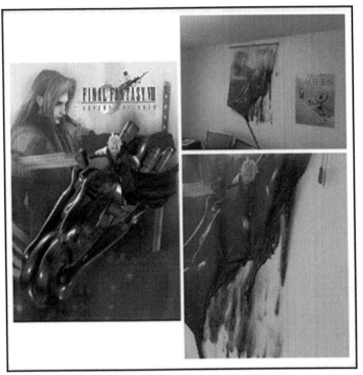

Fig 15.3 Office Attack – *Final Fantasy* Poster Fire

Now here comes the part you couldn't make up. Well, none of this you can make up, it all happened as I described it, but here comes the kicker. The fire captain walks up to me and says, "I remember you; you're the guy who fell down the stairs. We were here back in January; I see your knee has healed." Tina tries to smile, as do I. Yeah, I'm that guy. I immediately knew what he was talking about. These guys have been here before. They're the ones that carried me downstairs after I tore my patella tendon. Today, the last thing that captain said before leaving, after making sure everything was alright, was: "Remind me to take you with me when I go to Vegas; you're a lucky man; on both counts, you are a lucky man." An hour later they were gone. Thank you, Bothell Fire department.

We've all had moments where we ask ourselves: did that just happen? Is this "real life?" Tina was asking herself the same question as was I: is this really happening to us? Look how far we've come from the kid 'cough.' How far we've come from having a bedroom door slam shut on us in the middle of us laughing. Tina and I went back upstairs to review what we had seen earlier.

The burnt poster was still dangling from the wall. Lopsided now due to the fire. Thank God, the office table stood between the poster and the floor. The damage would have been a lot worse. The picture above (Fig 15.3) of how nothing else was near it. Nothing could have started that fire except a mean-spirited poltergeist.

95

Sometime during this ordeal, I can't remember exactly when I picked up the phone and called my boss. I'm taking the day off. I'm beaten. Tina and I left my office and headed back to our bedroom. What are our next steps? Who have we not called? Who was not returning our calls? We had already had three Bibles catch fire. Now we have posters catching fire. We are in desperate need of help. I'm not talking about short-term help. I mean we'd tell this story to paranormal teams, to clergy, to churches, and the best they could do is come by and bless the house. Then they're gone. You email or call them back to give them an update, and they don't respond. No one's returning our calls. This is what my brain is thinking as I sit on my bed. Tina then blurts out, "We're going to the Bothell parish office; we're going to demand that the priest sees us." The look on Tina's face told me everything. She was fed up. She was tired of the bullshit. The bullshit people are giving us. Fed up with the run-around. It was time for the Catholic Church to put its belief where its mouth is. If battling demons in the form of performing an exorcism is what they do, then dammit they're going to do it. It's time Tina, and I visit the Catholic Church.

Chapter 16
Parish Visit

Tina and I had made up our mind before arriving at the parish that we were not going to leave until the priest saw us. Both of us were determined, upset, and resolved. Resolved that it was time for someone to take us seriously. It was time for someone to help us long term. If you can't help long term, please refer us to someone who can. And if you can't help us, then tell us you can't help us. Don't give us the run-around. The only thing worse than no help is someone giving you the run-around.

There seemed to be a passive-aggressive theme among the churches that we reached out to: ignore them, and they eventually go away. Ignore them till they get the idea of just moving out. Tina and I are not defeatist. At least I like to think we aren't. As scary as a bump in the night is, it's not nearly as scary as cutting and running. Understand me fully. This is my house. It's our home. We deserve it. I'm not going to just up and leave over something I don't understand. Not without first trying every option imaginable. This case has challenged my belief system. It's got me asking serious questions about life, humanity, and people overall. I'd be leaving with so many unanswered questions if we just cut in run now. That's my thinking as we head to the local parish. *God, please give us some help today.*

As upset as Tina and I were about what happened a few hours ago, it's important that we don't give the people here a reason to not help us. Walking in screaming and yelling will only confirm their perception of us. Tina and I are not crazy. Far from it. We are civil human beings. We have a right to ask questions. Our goal is to be heard. That's all we want. Tina and I looked at each other after we got out of her SUV—we had the same mindset. We're not leaving till after we've seen the priest.

Tina and I were met by an elderly lady sitting behind a glass wall and wooden desk within seconds of walking in. She looked at Tina and me and asked, "What can I do for you?" Tina replied, "We'd like to see the priest."

The lady asked us if we had an appointment. We said no. The lady looked at the clipboard and confirmed what we said. Then came the news we knew already. The lady told us that the priest had back to back appointments today and that we could schedule an appointment and come back later. Tina then asked: "Could we just wait?" The lady glanced at the clipboard again and said, "Well, he's in a meeting now, it just started, so you're looking at about a two to four-hour wait." And that's when Tina and I said together, "We'll wait."

She then took our names down and asked us for the nature of our visit. Tina told her she had been referred to this office by the Seattle parish. She'd left multiple voicemails and emails for the priest here, messages asking him to call her back. The lady then chuckled and said, "Oh, your name does ring a bell, Father is not as organized as he should be, and I think I spoke to you a few times. I gave him your messages." As the lady was writing down Tina's info, I was doing a quick survey and glanced over the reception area and parish itself. We were in the administration portion of the building. Everything I see was pretty much what I would expect inside a Catholic Church. Catholicism is everywhere. The lady taking down Tina's info was elderly. She was about eighty years old. I saw no computer behind her. I'm thinking to myself; *they could use an upgrade in here. An upgrade of everything.* So, after three minutes of getting our info, Tina and I are instructed to sit down. Now the waiting begins. One learns a lot by waiting in the lobby of a parish. The activities happening around Tina and I seem basic and mundane. Now and then the elderly lady would rise from her desk and walk into the break room to check on Tina and me. I was on my third cup of coffee when all of a sudden Tina blurts out: "I don't think your fall was an accident." I was taken aback. Tina's has never initiated a conversation about the January 2nd fall. We've rarely talked about it. I've talked about with other people. Oh, hell yeah. My male and female friends ask me all the time, "Do you think the ghost pushed you?" My answer then was I don't know.

What shocked me about Tina was not the statement itself, it was the agreement. Tina was agreeing with what I knew already. Agreeing with what my friends knew. I was so relieved. So relieved to talk to my girlfriend about something that wouldn't result in an argument. So: was I pushed? I don't know. How can you tell if a spirit pushes you? Did I slip down the stairs? Or was I pushed down the stairs? By the time I realized I was falling, it was over. Tina then says your fall was intentional. I asked her, "What makes you think it was intentional." Her reply: "It locked the door on you today so that you couldn't get out of the house. You had to fight to get out of the house; it's like it was trying to trap you." We both looked at each other. Her facial expression said it all. *They pushed you.*

Can a spirit kill you? I don't know, can they? There have been cases in the past, famous cases, in fact, where people have succumbed or died while being pursued by malevolent spirits. One case in particular: The Bell Witch Poltergeist.

If you've never heard of it, I suggest you read up on it. If I had to compare what we faced to any other case, I'd have to go with the Bell Witch Poltergeist. Not so much for the activity taking place in that home, more so for the isolation aspect. The one man who was singled out. John Bell seemed to be the primary target of that incident. We're talking about 1817. The story if true says he succumbed to the constant bombardment of attacks. Poltergeists attacks which were demonic. Like ours. Bell was simply beaten down, mentally and physically. His will to live was taken away from him after so much torment. That to me is the only way a demon or poltergeist can kill you. They beat you down so much to where death feels better. I'm starting to understand that sentiment—death feeling better than a malevolent attack.

I have to believe the spirit that set fire to my house did so with the intentions of scaring the crap out of me. It worked. It blew up all the light fixtures in the hallway when Tina was by herself as means of scaring her.

We've all pulled fruit off the bottom of the pile when shopping in a grocery store. We've seen what happens. All the fruit on top comes tumbling down. My fall was a precursor to everything that had happened since then. They say house attacks should they taper off, always come back worse than when they left off.

Man, that's so true. But that begs the question: what sparked the second wave? I was asking myself a thousand questions while we waited for the priest. Suddenly his secretary appeared. "The priest can see you now."

I never met a priest before. Time to get ready, because here he comes. He walks out, says "hello" to Tina and me; we all shake hands. Tina and I follow him back to his office; he immediately disarms our worries by being openly friendly and cordial. His office seemed to fit the clichés I had heard about parishes. Tina and I sat in the two chairs in front of the wooden desk. Between him and us was an inordinate amount of paperwork. One stack of paperwork that caught Tina's eye immediately was a series of post-it notes all piled up on each other. They were stacked about six inches high. Tina nudged me with her shoe. I looked at her, and immediately her eyes led me to the stack of phone messages. A majority of them were from us. Two months' worth.

The priest saw that we saw our messages stacked six inches high off his desk. He immediately apologized for not returning our calls. The priest was very apologetic, very honest about how disorganized he was. *He would not be the last person to tell us that.* My hopes of us coming to the right place were slowly fleeting. That said, what other option did we have? This is who the Seattle Catholic Church referred us to. We're all looking at each other. So: where do we start? We start from the beginning. Let's start with the events of today first, since it was the fire, the last straw if you will, that brought us here. Tina talked. The priest took notes.

When it came time for me to talk, I did. The priest kept at it; he kept taking notes. Not once did he interrupt Tina and me. Only when we had to come up for air metaphorically, did he interject with a call for prayer. There was a lot of prayer going on in that office that day. If you want to get me believing in you, talk about the power of prayer. Tina and I needed lots and lots of prayer. The priest was giving us that. He was slowly but surely taking the load off our backs. A load we carried for two years.

I was relieved to learn that nothing Tina and I shared was of shock value to him. I mean, we told him some tripped out stuff. He then began sharing stories of his own. Some that made our mouths drop open. I know Tina, and I was not the first people to live in an infested house. That's not what shocked me. What shocked me was how recent some of his stories were. How close to Bothell some of these demonic hauntings were. We're talking just a few miles up the highway.

The gist of our conversation centered on what Tina and I were going through. The priest once again reiterated the fact that we had come to the right place. How he felt bad about not calling us sooner. Everyone was playing hot potato with us. No one wants to own this, not even the Catholic Church. The priest as good as admitted to us that the church, by and large, viewed such events as taboo, even though history says differently. I was starting to understand why people simply move. Who's going to believe you? Who's going to stand by you? His church in this part of the country, in this part of the world, views hauntings like this very differently. People are scared. The paranormal frightens them. I knew the priest wasn't lying because I've seen it on people's faces. I've seen people's reaction when we tell them our story. Their faces turn pale. My family goes quiet. As does Tina's. Our friends? Some of them go quiet too. Paranormal organizations? Some of them go quiet too. Houses of God? A lot of them go quiet. And by quiet, I mean scared shitless.

Tina and I learn two things after being in the priest's office. One: The priest has a fondness for roller coasters. He has a fascination with them. That's his release from it all: riding roller coasters. The second thing we learned was that the priest is extremely disorganized. *That's going to become a problem in the long-run.* A problem we all should have mitigated while in his office that day.

Overall, he passed the test, the ultimate test of all. He believed us. The fact that he ignored so many of Tina's phone messages proved he wasn't a thrill seeker. Tina and I were satisfied. We would forget the fact that he ignored two months of emails. We would give him the benefit of the doubt. The priest asked us to stand up. "Let's pray." We stood. We prayed again. We laughed again. "As of today, we fight this thing together." That's what we were told. We're not leaving empty handed either. The priest had homework for us. In his hand were Saint Michael the Archangel Prayer sheets. We must say these prayers together, say them as one. It's very important that Tina and I do this together, the priest said. "Time to put on God's armor; time to take your house back."

The priest felt these were low-level demons, doing what demons typically do: create havoc. Advice number one, "Be mindful of everything around us." Stay strong. Stay firm. Watch each other's back and remember to call on God." That made Tina and I feel good. Maybe this house can be made livable after all. Call me naive, but shouldn't good always conquer evil? We'll see, we will see what happens next. The meeting was adjourned; after a few more prayers. The priest said he would contact his bishop to let him know that he was going to help us. That, ladies and gentlemen, was how we ended our meeting.

The house remained quiet for that day and the next couple of days. Which is was what usually happens after a house attack. Things go quiet for a while. Not dormant, but quiet. I don't know if it was because of the spirits expended a large amount of energy, or because they just wanted to wait and see. Wait and see what Tina and I were going to do. They knew we went to the Catholic Church, I believe that wholeheartedly. What else do the spirits know? Do they know the priest said yes? Do they know he's coming? Did they feel threatened? Who knows?

Two weeks later, the priest did come over. He kept his promise; he received his bishop's blessing. He brought with him his assistant, an observer if you will. Wow, a priest was stepping foot in the Linder home. Who would have thought? If you asked me if I ever thought I would have a priest in my home, I would have looked at you like you was crazy.

Tina had prepared dinner for both the priest and his assistant. No way was a man of God going to enter our house and we not cook him a meal. My grandmother would turn over in her grave if that were the case. No, today's visit was simply an introduction to both the house and the activity taking place. Several rooms had been damaged significantly, the hallway especially. Pictures can only do so much. You really must see it first hand, to get a full understanding of what Tina and I are reporting. It's easy to say those holes in the walls look man-made, any troll can say that from the comfort of his mom's basement. An intelligent person knows better. Seeing is believing. That's why he came today. He was here to see and learn things. I invited two of my friends over as well—two of my

Catholic friends. I wanted the priest to hear what they had to say. I wanted him to hear the difficulties they faced when they contacted the Seattle parish. We all talked at the table for at least two hours before the priest rose to begin his ceremony. It was time to bless the house.

I wish I could say that the second he began performing the house blessing, cabinet doors swung open. I wish I could say that. But I can't. I wish I could say that while the priest was going room to room, blessing every nook and cranny, whispers of "why are you casting us out before our time?" could be heard. I wish I could say that. But I can't. I wish I could say that each time holy water was thrown on the wall, that wall responded by releasing steam and foul language. I wish I could say that. But I can't. Nothing moved. And that's not a shot against the priest. The priest knows like me that this isn't Hollywood. The way Hollywood describes it: The priest walks in, the house trembles because of his arrival. The priest is viewed as being Superman at this point. He whips out his Bible, his cross, his cloak, and goes to town. The unclean spirits beat him up a bit but, in the end, he wins. All in within fifteen minutes. That's Hollywood. It doesn't work like that in real life. The priest said this would be a long drawn out process. Ecclesiastes 9:11 reads, "Battles are always won due to time and endurance."

Satan, demon or Lucifer for that matter will not be defeated in a day. Tina and I knew that. The priest blessed every crook and cranny of the upstairs area. All the bedrooms. He sprinkled holy water on the burnt markings on the wall; he blessed the windows, the window seals, and the doorways. He put a lot of emphasis on the doorways of each room. Especially our bedroom. The priest was as thorough with the downstairs area as he was in the upstairs area. Overall the ceremony ended up lasting about an hour and a half. Time for levity. Time for dinner and conversation.

Amazing how much you get to know somebody by breaking bread with them. I was astounded by the priest's knowledge of the Church. I'm not talking about his church; I'm talking about all churches. He told us how excited he was that the Church he belonged to was going through a transformation. A new Pope had been recently elected, which hopefully meant a new paradigm shift in how church business is conducted.

And here in Bothell, the mood had become way lighter than before. The house felt different. Zero tension in the air. When I went to bed that night, I remember thinking to myself; *this was a meeting that needed to happen. I'm proud of Tina and me. Proud that we stood our ground. Proud that we waited in his office.* There was no way I was going to turn this house over to new tenants, *new tenants with children.* Not without exhausting all options.

Screw that. No way I'm going just to cut and run. That's been the problem up until now. People have just been moving: 'screw the landlord, we're out of here.' What does that solve? Nothing. The spirit is still here. It's just going to haunt somebody else. Tomorrow I'm going to tell Tina that I'm here to the very end. If there is a lease underneath me, I'm staying. Hear that, poltergeist? Keith Linder is staying.

Chapter 17
Email Alerts

The priest couldn't overstate how important it was for Tina and me to recite the Michael the Archangel prayer every night. "Recite it together." Take turns reciting it. Feel free to incorporate your prayers, your religious beliefs. Consistency is important. The only thing more important than consistency is unity. Both of you must do this. If the demon senses any hesitation from either one of you, it'll exploit it. Remember: regardless of what type of demon it is, their goal is the same: divide and conquer."

So, there we were, doing what the priest requested. Praying and reciting Biblical passages together. That night while lying in bed seemed like the perfect opportunity to tell Tina about my plans for the house: I intend to stay here. I can't subscribe to the "cut and run" philosophy—not after what I've seen. I'm probably not the right person to do it, but this house needs to be made whole again. Something very wrong happened here before we moved in. We may never know what that was. If we leave, now we're telling ourselves: this is someone else's problem. That doesn't feel godly. It doesn't feel Christian. If Psalms 23 is correct (and I believe it is), then Tina and I should be OK.

That's what I told Tina that night. I'm going to stay. I'm going see it through. At the same I'm telling Tina this I'm thinking to myself, *I must be an idiot.* For all I know, I could be pushed down the stairs again. Who knows at this point? I don't know what seeing this through really means. It probably means I don't like being kicked out of my own house. The fact that I'm leasing it is irrelevant. People have moved out of houses they've owned for years. I'm not one of them. I'm going to move out when I'm ready to move out. Not when the demon tells me to. Are you going to stay with me? That's the question I gave Tina. It didn't take her long to answer. Her answer was "yes."

The next day I woke up and did what I normally do. I walked around the house. Not so much looking for paranormal activity, actually the opposite. I was looking for ways to increase mine and Tina's house presence. How do I show the spirits living here that this is our house more than it is theirs? I'm greeted by new Catholic paraphernalia. Parting gifts from the priest.

The items I'm looking at include a Saint Benedict cross, now hanging over the front door. Three wooden crosses, now sitting in the hallway. Three white candles, now sitting in our bedroom. A bottle of holy water, and the best gift of all: a wooden statue of the Virgin Mary. The priest handed the wooden sculpture to Tina and said, "Put this by your bedside; it'll protect you and Keith."

So, I'm strolling through the house; making my rounds when, suddenly, I step on something *Ouch, what the fuck!* I look down and see three shards of glass on the floor. There in the doorway of our bedroom—in plain sight. I'm thinking to myself, *where did these come from?* Tina and I had been very thorough with our clean-up effort. We've had countless glass explosions. Porcelain, ceramic, you name it—things blow up. And for the record what I've just stepped on is that: porcelain, three shards of it. Each shard is about the size of a Tic Tac. Why would three shards of glass be sitting in our doorway? It's almost like they were put there on purpose.

Lucky for me I was wearing socks. Now, the first time I stepped on these three shards I thought nothing of it. My mind wasn't even close to connecting the dots. But come the third time, I realized these pieces of porcelain I was stepping on, were being put in my path purposely. How do I know that? *Try this*. I was watching downstairs watching TV. Tina was upstairs in our bedroom. When it came time for me to turn the TV off, shut the kitchen down, and go to bed, I stood and as soon as I did, I got pricked. I looked down to see what it was and sure enough: three shards of porcelain. You're probably saying to yourself: I don't get it; what does that prove? It proves a lot—here goes.

That morning the carpet cleaner guy came by. He vacuumed, and carpet cleaned the entire house. The entire house! By the time he got done, there was nothing on the floor. The carpet was brand spanking new. There was no way he could have missed three pieces of porcelain on the den floor. No way, no how—and just in case a skeptic is reading this, even the location alone makes it impossible on that night. You see, glass or porcelain for that matter, has never exploded in the room I'm standing in. All the explosions have taken place in the hallway, office, and corner landing area. Light fixtures that explode upstairs can't under any circumstances whatsoever get to where I'm standing. One of the most often repeated chores in our house is vacuuming.

Tina vacuums a lot as do I. You want to know why? We vacuum a lot because things get thrown a lot. Now the shards of glass that I just picked up are obliterated porcelain. Leftovers from the previous light fixture explosions. I've been stepping on a few of these the last couple of days. They've appeared in odd places of the house. I throw away everyone I step on. The only reason why I'm telling you this is because of the multiple carpet cleaners we 've had in our house over the last few months.

So, the priest did his first house blessing a few days ago. These shards aside, the house is virtually quiet. But, as we learned, quiet does not equate to zero activity. Something's always happening; we just don't know it. Just now, we were in for something new: and that was the appearance of items which neither of us owned. Sure, this had happened before. Only not with this new level of cunning. Not with this new level of malice.

Let me tell you; there are a lot of embarrassing things about living in a haunted house. One of them involves leaving your house thinking you have money in your pocket, only to discover at the Starbucks counter that you don't. You could have sworn you had ten dollars. But you don't. Imagine you're having lunch with your friends at work. The time has come for everyone to pay their bill. You reach into your wallet for cash, and learn you only have five dollars instead of ten dollars. You vaguely recall having had two fives in your wallet the night before. What happened to the other five-dollar bill? If it weren't for the fact this was happening quite often, like every other day, I wouldn't even be mentioning it you. But it did happen, and it happened enough to where I began to take notice.

So much so that I stopped carrying cash on me. Then I realized something. The entities were taking dollar bills from my wallet with the hope that I would falsely accuse Tina. If you think I'm hallucinating—well, just keep reading. Because here comes the malice. I return from a business trip one day. I think I was gone for a week. Tina and I had worked out a process of her staying with friends whenever I was out of town. We've reactivated 2012's protocol of no one being in the house while I was away on business. A few days after I'd come back from my business trip, I noticed something. I saw what looked to be female jewelry sitting on the staircase. I came in for a closer look, and sure enough, it's a female earring. Finding your girlfriend's earrings on the bathroom counter is one thing. But this wasn't normal. The second I saw the earrings I did what any guy would do. I picked them up and walked them over to Tina. I asked her straight out, "Did you lose any earrings?" Tina looked up and said, "No." Now I'm scratching my head; if these are not Tina's earrings, whose are they? Then it hit me: must belong to one of Tina's friends. You see, instead of going to a friend's house while I was out of town, Tina decided to have a friend come stay with her. Maybe these earrings belong to her? That was my second question to Tina, and her reply was a quick and firm "no." So, I'm hovering over my girlfriend with some earrings in my hand, earrings that Tina barely looks at; and I'm thinking: how do you know for sure they're not Kim's earrings? You barely even looked at them. I wanted to ask Tina that question, but I didn't. I turned around and walked away.

Despite what I just mentioned, the house is quiet. I'm thinking to myself: is that a good thing or a bad thing? You know the house must be quiet if I'm thinking about taking down the two cameras I have up.

I was just about to do that one night when suddenly something happened that hadn't happened in a while. Tina and I get into an argument. A huge argument. And guess what the argument was about? It was about a piece of jewelry she found in the living room. Not under a couch cushion, no that would be too explainable. The couch and love seat are Tina's; they arrived when she arrived. A "Geist" is not going to put a piece of female jewelry underneath a couch or a seat cushion. Hell, no, odds are we'd never see it. The best place to put a piece of jewelry that's not yours is out in the open. That's where all items appear that Tina and I don't own. This night was no exception.

That day I had worked from home. I was sitting at the kitchen table after dinner, and Tina comes storming towards me with an object in her hand—a gold earring that I can barely see. Before I can accurately make out what it was that was in her hand, she blurted out, "You had another woman in the house." She says that and sticks the piece of jewelry dead in my face. A gold earring. My reaction? What are you talking about? Who's been in the house? "Another woman, you had someone here today!"

I'm like, no, I didn't. I don't know what you're talking about. At this point, I had completely forgotten that just a few days ago I walked up to Tina and showed her an earring that I thought was hers. At this point, we'd lived in this house a little over two years. Weird stuff pops up all the time. It's almost like you're living in a house with no ceiling. Objects appear to be falling out of the sky that neither of us owns. Tina knows this. I know this. So why is Tina waving a woman's earring in my face? And that's how arguments begin. Tina believes she has right on her side. She's loud. She's angry. Me? I'm playing catch up. I deny the accusation. No woman has been in the house: period.

So, I looked at Tina, and I asked, "Where did you find that piece of jewelry?" Tina pointed towards the middle of the den floor and began screaming again, "How could you? What was a woman doing here while I was gone? You're lying", and more. Oh, when Tina gets mad, she gets mad. Good luck getting a word in edgewise. And that's where we were at right now; she was shouting a bunch of "how could you?" I'm shouting a bunch of no woman was here, you're tripping. Why would I have a woman in here? Who would I have in here?

And our peaceful night was over. The one thing I can't stand is being falsely accused. This looked and felt like I was being accused of something I didn't do. The reality of it didn't make sense. There are a trillion reasons as to why I would not have a woman in this house if Tina were not home. One of those reasons was, we just had a priest sanctify our home. Why would I sabotage what he did? The whole other women thing didn't make sense. The only thing I could do now was fold up my laptop and retreat back upstairs—the room where the poster caught fire. Tina can have the downstairs for all I care. I stormed off, and that was that.

We said nothing else to each other that night. Not a word spoken before bed and not a word spoken after we woke up. Tina went to work the next day earlier than usual. That's how mad she was. She normally leaves after me. I arrived at my job tired and confused. I couldn't sleep a wink last night. My biggest fear was the argument we had. Were there going to be repercussions for Tina and me arguing? There usually is.

It must have been 10 AM when I began receiving motion and sound detection emails. Now, my two cameras have been set up in the house for a while now. Up till now, the only emails I've gotten have been *sound detected*; and when I log in to see what the sounds are, all I hear is my landscapers mowing the lawn, or the city garbage team stopping by to get our trash. But today my inbox was filling up, and I mean fast. Something was going on at my house. I'm thinking Tina must have forgotten something; she must have come back home; maybe she had a doctor's appointment or something. Let me open one of my emails and see. My cameras will take five snapshot pics when they detect motion or sound. Two snapshots before the motion or sound were detected, and three snapshots afterward. I have over thirty emails in my inbox—more are coming in. What do I see? Each attachment I opened showed my house in turmoil. Still images of every cabinet door open. Images of couch and love seat turned upside down. Images of coffee tables and lamp tables knocked over.

More emails were coming in while I was looking at the still photos. Not a ghost or apparition in any of them. Instead, I got a house that was upside down. The fact that the emails were still coming to my inbox while I was reviewing other emails meant that the house was still be attacked. Then it hit me. I can log into my camera remotely and watch my house live.

The first camera I tried to log into was the den camera—the one that was sending me emails. *Time Out,* that's the message I got when I tried to log in. I was not getting invalid password. Instead, I'm getting *your browser has timed out, try again.* This could only mean one thing. The cameras were offline. But how can they be offline if I'm still getting email alerts? It didn't make sense. Then I remembered. I put a video camera in the den before I left this morning. I left it sitting above the fireplace? Dead center in the den room. It was running when I left.

I had no choice but to go home if my cameras were not allowing me to log in. I have to retrieve that camera. My house is under attack. Two things were motivating me. Protect the home Tina and I live in. For all I know, the spirit could be setting fire to the house. Maybe it's trying to finish what it started a few weeks ago. Second motivation: secure the Sony minicam. Thank God for SD cards, and thank God for battery-operated cameras. Even if the entity cut power to the house, this would not stop a video camera from recording. The battery pack attached to the video camera would kick in.

So, I was driving home now and let me tell you; it was the longest drive ever. It felt like time had stood still. The question I was asking while sitting behind a steering wheel was, what will I find? So much for moving forward versus moving backward. The last email I'd opened showed every kitchen cabinet door open. I saw a lot of things resting on their heads. What kind of force takes it upon itself to lift couches and love seats? How do you turn a couch upside down? What can do that? The only thing I had to go on now was the Gray Lady. I wasn't even sure she was still in the house. Odds are she was. But the house felt like it was being occupied by more than just one spirit. It felt like several spirits were in cahoots together. And then it dawned on me: Why am I doing this? Why am I going to the house alone? Why haven't I called Tina? Why haven't I asked any of my friends to meet me at the house?

What I'm doing right now is crazy. I've told no one where I was going. As of right now, only me and the spirits in my home are aware of what I'm doing. I'm in my neighborhood now; I'm getting close. When I turned to the street, I lived on I was relieved to see that no emergency responders were present. No fire trucks. No police. The neighborhood was dead silent. I decided to park in front of my house like I always do. I pulled up the curb and stopped. The neighborhood looked OK. A crowd hadn't formed around my house. No one was asking themselves: what's that noise coming from inside his house. I pulled my key from my pocket and stuck it into the lock of my front door. I probably don't have to say it, but my heart was beating rapidly right now. If I could turn back around, get back into my car, and drive to eastern Washington, I would. That's how scared I was.

If I'm going to die Hollywood-style this would be the moment where it happens. I could see it now. *Tina arrives home a few hours later and finds me lying dead on our front porch. She goes into hysterics and takes off running down the street. A neighbor driving up the street sees her running in the middle of the road. Driver stops his car, gets out and chases Tina down. He asks her if she's OK. She tells him her boyfriend is dead and begins going into hysterics even more. Minutes later, police, EMT, and fire trucks arrive. The same firemen as before, matter of fact. Everyone's looking at me slumped over on the patio. My key is still stuck in the door. The EMT people try to revive me but can't. I'm pronounced dead at the scene, and no one knows why. Finally, someone realizes Tina is distraught; she should sit down. The police sergeant finishes what I started. He*

106

opens the door and steps into the home. Everyone walks in after him. No one sees what I'd seen. Oops, I'm dead now. No one sees or knows what I saw. The house is in pristine shape. Both couch and love seat are turned up straight. All the cabinet doors are closed. Nothing's out of place. The house looks brand new. No one's the wiser. Tina's shaking like a leaf. The EMT has put in a call for the coroner to come pick my body up. The neighbors are all outside scratching their heads.

Someone finally asks the sixty-four-thousand-dollar question: What was Keith doing home? Did he forget something? Everyone looks at Tina, but Tina can't provide any answers because Tina never got the call that I was returning home. The logical theory is, he must have forgotten something: but what? His key, his cell phone, and his wallet are all on his person. What brought him back to the house? Everyone's clueless. Those pictures that came to my work inbox just sit there. They never get looked at. My employer confiscates my laptop after learning of my untimely death. My hard drive is erased. It's as if none of this ever happened. No one knows what brought me home except the spirits, and they're not talking. That's the Hollywood way.

So, there I was, standing at my front door with the key in the door. I turned the doorknob and walked into my house. What do I see? I see the same thing that my emails sent me. The same destruction. I see the couch and love seat turned upside down. I see marbles that sat on a tray on a coffee table scattered throughout the house. I see the kitchen cabinet doors open. I see how perfectly aligned they are to the cabinet doors next to them. I see every closet door open. I see objects thrown about. Objects broken. I see kitchen chairs moved about. I see it all. I see the aftermath of an F1 tornado. I see destruction.

What I don't see is my video camera. The video camera I placed above the fireplace a few hours ago. It and the power cord are gone. That's when I knew: you've been played Keith Linder; they played you big time. Here I am, just left work. I drove thirty minutes or so to get here. I arrived to discover the downstairs area is in fact a mess. My snapshots weren't lying. And that wasn't all they showed. A picture from the kitchen Foscam showed the Sony minicam sitting above the fireplace. The Foscam (motion camera) took that picture thirty minutes ago. The spirits must have taken the minicam while I was driving to the house. Dammit! *I never saw that camera again.* The clocks on my stove and microwave were blinking, indicating that somewhere during the drive here the power to this room or to the home had been cut. The Foscams are useless if the power to them is cut. I'd be lying if I said I wasn't pissed. I was beyond pissed. I was mad as hell. Even in the midst of this, I realized something. These spirits are not only malicious. They're calculating. They're freaking intelligent.

I wonder how many eyes were on me as I came to that realization. I wonder how many spirits were in the house when I arrived. How many were in the den? In the living room? In the hallway? In the doorway? How many were maybe in the car with me as I drove home? I wonder how close they are to me right now. I doubt very seriously they're hiding. They're probably looking, laughing, and snickering at me right now. I read a few physics and astrophysics books during my days in college. I understood enough to know that it was quite possible that both spirit and video camera, my video camera, mind you, were still in the same room with me. I just can't see them. It's possible my video camera is where the first Bible was when it was taken. Either way, I was left standing here with a house turned upside down.

But I'm not laughing. There would be a payback. At this stage of the game, the video camera was the most expensive object ever taken. That video camera was useful. It was the one that captured the objects flying off the hall bookshelf. It was the video camera that witnessed the ironing board go flying across the room. It was the camera that saw Bible and sage trays go flying across the hallway. If the minicam was live and going when the attack happened, then I have no doubt that, somewhere in our dimension or elsewhere, exists the paranormal event of a lifetime. Somewhere in this universe is the SD card that shows couch and love seats being turned upside-down while no one's home. That to me is the only reason why they took it. That, plus the need to piss me off.

I remember tidying up the house a little bit before heading back out the door. I needed to head back to work. I needed to shake this off. I can't afford to get depressed. Not about a video camera; nope, let's go back to work and orchestrate a Plan B. When I got home the second time, I found the house pretty much the way I left it. Tina walked in and found me tidying up. She had the reaction I'd had five hours ago. No use in telling her what happened, she could see it.

Can you imagine walking into your house and seeing destruction such as this? Imagine seeing this every day for weeks and months. Cabinet doors being open was nothing new. It happened so many times that whenever we come home now, we'd pretty much walk in, march to the kitchen and immediately begin closing cabinet doors. We know doors are open because of the emails I'm getting. But the cabinet doors were just one piece of the mess. Each attack gets outdone by the one after it.

This was the first house attack we had since the priest came over. The tension between Tina and me had come back. The silent treatment was in effect. There we were cleaning up the house, sometimes side by side. Not a word being spoken. Later that night, I decided to break protocol. I decided to engage Tina. I walked into our bedroom and asked her if she could call the priest. Call him and let him know what happened. He asked that we keep him up to date. Let's at least do that. Tina nodded, and that was that. That's how the night ended.

Fig 17.1 Coming home and finding kitchen cabinets opened house torn upside-down became a daily occurrence in summer 2014.

Chapter 18
Wall Writings

They say your first reaction to any given situation is usually the correct one. Do yourself a huge favor; try not to think that way when responding to a malevolent attack. It never occurred to me (at least not early on) that I was doing exactly what the spirits wanted me to do. They wanted me to buy more cameras. You see, spirits love attention, malevolent spirits especially. Nothing excites a spirit more than a house occupant setting up a home monitoring system. Not that this attention-seeking was exactly straightforward. It's not. The spirits are very clandestine when it comes to seeking attention. The bad advice I've been given combined with my driven ego is a dream come true for spirits.

There's a theory within the paranormal community that states entities can and will feed off of electronic devices. Recall Jennifer and the No Bull Paranormal team. Their equipment died the second they entered the house. Batteries sucked completely dry. That's just one example of a spirit's manipulation of electronic equipment. Hang tight, here comes some more.

In the next few weeks and months, every camera I bought would either go missing or be found broken. I began finding my cameras unplugged. Especially the cameras in the hallway. I remember asking Tina if she'd unplugged one of my cameras; she replied with a quick "no." For the record, Tina was never a fan of the cameras. She understood my reasons for doing it, but she didn't like it. It's sort of like an invasion of privacy. People typically set up motion devices on the outside of their house. You do that with the hopes of deterring break-ins. We had five to six cameras, all with motion and sound detection. Every room had one. No woman is going to like cameras being set up in her house, let alone in every bedroom. So, who told me to install cameras? The question should be who didn't tell me. My brother told me because he wanted to see objects thrown in high-definition. Other people did too. I'm talking about paranormal teams, skeptics, cynics, places of worship, and disbelievers.

The question I couldn't answer (or understand) Why didn't the spirits like the cameras? Why were they going around unplugging everything? I believe this was a warning tactic, a shot across the bow. *We see what you're doing; you'd better stop it.* Did I? Of course not, full steam ahead. Every adapter I found unplugged, I plugged back in.

Imagine coming home and seeing the house in disarray: furniture upside down, kitchen cabinets wide open, closet doors wide open, and stuff scattered all over. And in the corner, turned upside-down or unplugged, is your motion detection camera. Those that are unplugged are plugged back in. Those that are facing the wall are turned back around. Do you see what's going on now? It's becoming a cat and mouse game now. Reminds me of that Aretha Franklin song, titled "Who's Zooming Who?" I was becoming angry and frustrated. Frustrated due to the cameras being turned around. Angry because of the amount of money

I was spending and getting nothing in return. I don't want aftermath. I want real-time stuff.

A few days later I pass those same motion detect cameras in the hallway. The one I plugged back in, and the one I turned back around. They're gone. Even the power cord is gone. This angers me even more, and guess what I do? I go out and buy more cameras. What's feeding my idiocy, you might ask? Several things. I'm thinking; I can outsmart these spirits. Who are they? I'm Keith Linder. They're dead; I'm alive, of course, I can outsmart them. Try to understand this. I've never encountered a poltergeist before. I've never encountered a malevolent spirit before. They don't teach you "How to Deal with a Poltergeist" in grade school, not even in high school; heck, not even in college. I'm more than naive. I'm ignorant. *Geist are not known to suffer fools—remember that.*

No one is saying: stop with the cameras! I never heard that from anyone. Not until it was too late. So, what do I do? I continued. And meanwhile, the one thing I forgot was this: these spirits never sleep. They never rest. They're always watching. I know that now. Too bad I didn't know it then. There's an old proverb that says: when the cat begins chasing its tail, that's usually how the mouse gets away.

A word or two more about cameras and evidence. In their strange way, played a big part in making this controversial. Yeah, the Bibles did too, yeah, the wall writings did; and so, did the sheer level of activity. Only, take note here: the second and third Bible catching fire and the wall writings came after the cameras were set up. To be fair, they also came after the smudging and the open display of religious objects.

But I think the cameras edge out those things. Why? Because we've become a world consumed by film cameras. Think about it. Did you ever think you would live to see the day where people take pictures of the food they're about to eat? Or the dress they're about to put on? Vanity is now photographed. Poltergeist like that very much. Our case is the perfect example of that. A lot of people (I have their emails to prove it) told Tina and me that they couldn't help us till we show them something on video. Show the plant flying across the room. Show us the Bible catching fire. Show a cabinet door opening by itself. I can't think of any other profession that (in the event of an emergency) requires the one needing help to prove they, in fact, need help. Can you imagine a doctor telling a patient over the phone, 'show me your tumor?' Can you imagine an attorney telling his or her client 'show me how innocent you are'? The 911 operator that I called a few weeks ago never asked me to hold my phone up to the fire? She never put me on the defensive. I wish I could say the same about the paranormal community (*parapsychology included*) overall.

In the paranormal community, the mindset is increasing: nothing is real unless it's captured on film. How do I know? I was told this. You can't tell someone today that you just had a pot plant go flying across the room. Their first response is, "Where's the video?" That's what skeptics, cynics, paranormal enthusiasts, thrill-seekers, and priests all have in common. They ask the same question. Or they'd say: "it's always happening off camera. Why can't you get the activity on video? If it's real, get it on video; stop wasting our time."

Instead of saying "it's always happening off camera" (meaning that you think this is being faked), the real question should be: why does the activity always happen off camera? The spirit is televising its characteristic, and you're purposely ignoring it. What did I say about the Gray Lady when I saw her? I said she couldn't disappear into the washroom. Believe me, she tried. I believe she couldn't because I was watching her. When she darted away, I gave chase. When I got to the center of the hallway, she was gone.

So: here's the big question. Does observation (by humans or cameras) disrupt the spirits' abilities? Or do they simply dislike being watched? The answer might be both. The spirits in our home certainly seemed to understand our human fascination with cameras and objective verification. It became humorous to them. It might have even angered them. It ratcheted up the activity. I'm not yet comfortable saying that they took me adding cameras to the house as an insult. I don't have enough data to say that yet. But it interests me to know that some of the most violent acts we witnessed, the most violent acts against me, centered on the cameras. I'm being encouraged, and in some cases bullied (by people online), to add more cameras to the home.

Even after I said the spirit just unplugged a camera. A spirit just stole a camera. The ill advice I got from inside the paranormal community was to put a camera on the camera that's watching the living room. Put a camera on the camera that's watching the camera that's watching the bookshelf—and so on.

Then July 1st of 2014 came. Around 10 a.m, an email came to my inbox saying *motion detected*. The still pictures that came with that email showed the house looking normal. Why a *motion detected* email, then? I don't know. Let me log into the camera and see what's going on. Nothing's happening. I can't log in. Every attempt I made to log in resulted in a connection error. *Are my cameras offline? Are they missing? Has the spirit taken them? Has it pulverized them?* It has before. I tried logging on every camera three times. Nothing. I finally gave up. Maybe that email was a false alarm? A few hours passed. No more emails come in. I was sitting at my desk, done with all my work meetings, thinking, *let me try logging in again*. This time I had success. My cameras were back online, and I could see everything. Or could I?

The house looked to be in order. The hallway was in order. The den was in order. The kitchen was in order. Nothing was moved. So, yeah, it was a false alarm; either that or the spirits were fucking with me. They've done something, and they're hiding it from me. I get home hours later, and I'm not even thinking about paranormal activity. Just one email came in today, and nothing was on it.

I remember walking into my kitchen for a glass of water. I'm going to rest myself on this couch and enjoy some TV. At this moment in time, I had no reason to believe something was wrong. Gravely wrong. Time passes; it's been thirty minutes or so since I've been home. Tina should be home soon. *I'll go up to my office and watch TV up there.* So, I walked upstairs, and everything looked OK. The hall camera was exactly where I left it. I was getting emails again—only because the camera was detecting me as I walked past it. I walked past it and entered my office. That's where the horror was. I see something that would suggest this has been torn out of the pages of a Stephen King novel. I see "666" written on my wall. All my office belongings are thrown on the floor. My printer.

My stereo speakers. My computer mouse, my keyboard, my pen holder, my magazine—everything's on the ground. Oh, and did I mention that my office chair is split in half—my metal office chair?

And that's not all. Now I see something else; something more horrible than the 666 wall-writing. I see one of my crosses stabbed into the wall near the 666—it's embedded horizontally, bottom end in. Something then tells me to look down. And, sure enough, there on the carpet similar to the wall was an upside-down cross. An upside-down cross has been drawn on our carpet. But let's not stop there. I'm completely in the room now. My eyes have only seen what's in front of me. I should turn around and see what's behind me and I do. There drawn on the wall behind me is another upside-down cross. There drawn on the door is another upside-down cross. A total of three upside-down crosses in my room. Three inverted crosses.

I soon learn from looking more closely that the markings have not been written in paint, but ash. That's right. It's ash. Ash from where? If I had to guess, I would say it was ash from the sage stick. The ash smells like burnt sage. Now we've been smudging the house off and on. The sage stick was always left on the hallway bookshelf. It was still sitting there—except now it was much smaller than it was when we left for work this morning. It was almost gone; that's how much of it was used. Was it hot? No. Was it warm? No. All of this was scary and interesting, but I had bigger problems than both the sage stick and the upside-down cross on the wall. My concern was Tina. She was going to be home soon. I have no clue as to how I'm going to tell her.

Skeptics leap to the conclusion (premature of course) that the markings on the wall are fake. They think Tina and I drew them to get attention. That's their main argument for all of this being staged or faked. What they don't understand is that it's not the 666 that's terrifying. It's not the upside-down crosses that keeps me and Tina up at night. Not even close.

What keeps me up at night is the implicit level of intelligence, the level of preparedness, the trickery involved. What I mean is this. It writes 666 not just because this is what demons do. No. It's way simpler than that. I can't believe a lot of people didn't figure this out. Tina and I did, and we're not paranormal researchers. The spirits wrote 666 because that is what outsiders would expect us to do if we were faking. If it can do all of this, plus everything else I've mentioned, what can it not do? If it can cajole the *Ghost Adventures* team and their fan base, plus the skeptic community, into thinking these markings are fake (based on the simple fact that it's 666) what else can it do? How does this problem get solved when the people who claim to be experts are so easily fooled?

True enough, there may have been another reason for the 666. The spirit may have hoped that our religious upbringing might lead us to see this as demonic in nature. It thought it could raise our emotional level. Well, our emotional level did get raised; only it got raised by the negative response we got from people who accused of us doing this ourselves. Well, while we're on the subject, let me be clear: I could not duplicate what the spirit had done. I tried writing similar things using the edge of my burnt sage stick, and my results were completely different.

So: the "Geist" is trying to use our religious belief against us. Think about it, for the past few months we have been putting out Bibles, putting out crosses.

We've been smudging. The "Geist" sees this; it's looking dead at us. What better way to create fear and uncertainty than by disrespecting our biggest means of protection? What better way to display mockery and humor than to take a sage stick we've been using for months, and write and draw on our wall? That, ladies and gentlemen, is very interesting. This spirit wants Tina and me to believe that it's immune to our proactive measures. It's trying to let Tina and I know all of our proactive measures, most of them religiously based, are not going to work. In addition to it not working, people who see it are going to think me and Tina did it. It's a win-win situation for the spirits involved. They cajole a lot of so-called professionals, and we get the angst because of it. It's brilliant tactic taking on by the spirits to ridicule Tina and me while at the same time create the belief among skeptics and purists that this is all a hoax.

I'm trying hard not to appreciate the level of the spirit of intelligence while at the same time ridicule, i.e., call into the question the intelligence of the paranormal community. One is showing how smart it is; the other is not. Embarrassing. The spirit has gone out of its way to reveal how much it knows about Tina and me. How much it knows about our society. How much it knows about the artificial fears of men. Hollywood and religion have done wonders with the number 666. How many horror movies have used this supposedly demonic "666"—whether on a wall, a person's forehead, or book? The 666 never frightened Tina and me. There are idiots in this world on both sides of the same coin that believe Tina and I wrote on our walls for attention-seeking purposes. They're dead wrong.

From a historical point of view, from a Biblical point of view, the number doesn't even deserve to be mentioned in the same sentence as a demon or devil. Hollywood has given that term an incorrect meaning by the multiple movies that show it. The spirit knows that.

But the spirit knew what it was doing here. It did it because it wanted to cut us off from outside help. It wanted to prevent us from being taken seriously. And it worked; tremendously well. The more writings and attacks we report, the more our claims appear to be "too good to be true."

Can you imagine that? Can you imagine our reaction to hearing "the activity you're reporting sounds too good to be true?" I'm thinking wait a minute. We're talking about the paranormal here?

My advice to the investigator? Always remember to hit the reset button (inside your head) whenever you take on a new case. All paradigms should start back at zero the minute you get an email from a stranger showing inverted crosses, 666, and worse. Oh, the wall writings in our home are going to get worse. They have to. The spirit has to isolate us. Isolation throughout history has always come before the kill.

So, where did the cross (that got stabbed in the wall) come from? It came from a Spokane, Washington business trip I'd taken a few weeks back. I bought the cross at the gift shop in the Davenport Hotel. I went to the store looking for a new Bible and left with a bronze cross. The cross reminded me of something my grandmother would've owned had she still been alive. That's why I bought it. It was originally hanging on the wall, between the first and second bookshelf. Not anymore. Now it's in my office—protruding from the wall behind my desk.

114

Now, new as it is, this cross also has a bit of domestic history. Let me explain. Tina was never a fan of the bronze cross. A few days after I hung it up, she approached me and asked me point blank: "Where did you get it from?" I told her I got it from the gift shop inside the Davenport Hotel. She nodded and said, "Uh huh," and walked away. I think *she must think I got the cross somewhere else.* She seemed to imply that another woman gave it to me. That's just it. Another woman didn't give it to me. But bear in mind, this all happened during the time when we had female jewelry appearing in the house. The same time period where Tina thought there was a woman in the house. An argument about where the cross came from doesn't do me any good, doesn't do Tina any good. Tina knew that the day she asked me. The spirit knew it too; it had heard that entire conversation. You best believe it was taking notes. This was the first time we had wall markings. The first time my office had been attacked in this manner. Tina's reaction after seeing the attack was "that's different."

Time to update the priest and Jennifer on what took place. Once again Jennifer reiterated the need to "be careful." She said, "Get out while the getting is good," Failing that, the next best thing was to be vigilant. "Be vigilant and strong," she said, and "watch each other's back." Jennifer liked the idea of a priest being involved.

The priest's response was a little different. It didn't shock him to know that activity might resurface. Activities like this rarely get resolved in one swoop. Our homework was the same: pray, stay firm, stay vigilant, and update him on the action when it erupts.

The priest said he would talk to his bishop about what to do next. Meanwhile, I was sending him and Jennifer videos and pictures of all the destruction taking place. What I'm about to share with you next is something I put in the manipulation category. Every few days, Tina would ask me about the mysterious earring she'd found in the house. That topic would always come up whenever we disagreed about something else. Today would be that day. I'm not sure what the argument was on this particular day, except to say two things were verbally mentioned, the earring and the cross on the wall. Where did the earring come from? And where did the cross come from? First: I don't know. Second: I bought it in a gift shop. Neither answer was satisfactory to Tina. To end our stalemate, I did what I always do; I went upstairs. I needed to run errands, so let me take a shower, run my errands and hopefully cooler heads will prevail.

So, I'm done with my shower now. I'm all dressed and ready to leave. Where is Tina? She's in the kitchen cooking and cleaning. I'm off to run my errands. Tension has set in again, so no goodbye kiss, no goodbye period. Soon as I get to my car, I see something I know shouldn't be there. I see scratches on the side of my car—bumper to bumper. I became immediately upset. What shocked me about these scratches was how fresh they looked. I could tell by the tiny dust residue alongside each scratch that the marks were made recently.

Did Tina come outside and key my car? The more I ask myself the same question (did Tina do this?), the angrier I'm getting. The scratches I'm talking about are sizable, so noticeable my friends and co-workers began asking me days and weeks later: who keyed your car? My answer to them was I don't know. Well, I lied. I did know and let me tell you how I came to that conclusion. The first person I suspected was Tina. We had just had a very heated argument. An argument over infidelity, which is a dangerous argument to have.

She was playing offense; I was playing defense. This argument ended in a stalemate. She went to do her thing. I went to do my thing, which was to take a shower. *Did Tina go outside and scratch my car while I was in the shower?* I asked myself the question as I surveyed the damage. Did she deliberately do this?

The first thing I wanted to do after surveying the damage was to march back into the house, find Tina, and let her know how furious I am that she would do such a thing. Everyone has a right to be mad sometimes. If Tina wants to think that the earring came from a woman that was in the house, so be it. Get mad then. If she wants to believe the cross was given to me by a woman, so be it. Get mad then. She has a right to get mad. She doesn't, however, have the right to scratch up my car. Now I'm mad. I'm getting hot under the collar because I know I'm within my rights to challenge her about why she did this. Why did you scratch my car? Who does that?

So, I have two options now. I can go back inside the house and resume our argument. I can pick up where we left off, except now I have ammunition: my car has been recently keyed. I know Tina's upset with me right now. I was upset when I got in the shower. I was upset when I got out the shower. Not mad, just upset. But now I'm pissed. I'm pissed at the idea that my girlfriend might have keyed my car while I was in the shower. So now I've got two competing options. Should I go inside and confront Tina about the condition of my car? I know me: it's going to make me very upset if she denies it. Pause. Think now. *What can a poltergeist do with this level of anger?* Let me tell you what it can do. It can toss a giant armoire across the room. It can lift up a kitchen table and hurl it across the room. How about a sixty-inch high-definition TV? Oh yeah, it can toss that too. It can blow up every mirror and light fixture in the house—at the same time. If I go back into the house right now, it would be like bringing gasoline to a bonfire.

OK, Keith, let's not go in. Try to think this through. I obviously don't have the time now, and I need to run my errands. One thing is for certain: those scratches are not going anywhere anytime soon. Then I get it. I know what I'll do. I'll pull the ADT monitoring logs. The logs will have a time-stamp, showing every time that the front door was opened. It's only been ten minutes or so since I stepped out of the shower. The security system time-stamps every window and door inside our house when they're closed or opened. Any door you open downstairs, the system knows about it. It's why I got it.

Tina doesn't even know the system has this capability. She wasn't even home when the technician came to set it up. Heck, she didn't even have access to the cloud account. The logs were stored in the ADT cloud-system, which meant I could access it, review it, save it, and print it. I can do whatever I want with the logs except edit them. There's no doctoring the data. If Tina scratched my car while I was in the shower, the ADT system would know about it. It would have time-stamped her opening the front door, or the garage door. That sounded like a better plan. I'll let the data convict Tina, not my innuendo. I won't create an accusation based on guesswork. I have to give her the benefit of the doubt. She's my woman, I love her, and I care for her. I'd be very disappointed if the data tells me she did this. Doesn't sound like something she would do, but the marks on my car are visibly there. They're fresh marks.

When I got to work the next Monday, one of the first things I did was log into my ADT account. It didn't take me long to find what it was I was looking for—there in black and white was the time-stamp of when I left the house the other day. No record whatsoever of the door being opened while I was in the shower. The earliest time-stamp before mine was from the previous night when we both came home.

Son of a bitch! The poltergeist tried to set me up. It tried to set Tina up. I was this close to falsely accusing my girlfriend of keying my car. Tina would not have taken the accusation well. I know her. Her opinion would have been: you have the nerve to accuse *me* of scratching your door after I've accused you of cheating? It would have been World War Three in that house. That's what the poltergeist wanted. It wanted us at each other's throats—and it very nearly got it. I can only imagine what would have happened had I gone back into the house. But I didn't, and that's the point I'm trying to make. Had I gone back in and an argument ensued there's no telling what kind of paranormal activity would have taken place. So, just to be clear, Tina was not responsible for the scratches on my car. Nor was anyone else for that matter.

I never told Tina about the car scratches. I mean, she saw them a few days later. She even asked me how the scratches got there. I believe I gave her some lame excuse about parking close to a car in a Bellevue parking garage. She never asked me again how it happened. I think I didn't tell her because I knew what her reaction would be. She wouldn't believe me. Even with everything we'd seen, everything we'd heard, a gap still existed between us about what was normal and what was paranormal. Things Tina saw and heard that she couldn't explain fell into the paranormal bucket. Those things were not debatable. But there's an inner realm, a realm Tina didn't want to explore, that realm being the activity we can't see, the activity we can't hear. My gut instincts, my so-called spider-senses, are telling me that's where our focus should be. That's where we can't afford to be caught flat-footed—or we'd fall for stuff like this: the car scratch frame-up attempt on Tina; and the earring frame-up attempt on me.

Everything I said to Tina or tried to say fell on deaf ears. It was like she wasn't interested. Even if she wasn't, I was. *Only two of us live here. We're all we've got.*

No one understands the television coming on by itself better than Tina. No one understands waking up and finding three Bibles burned better than Tina. She's who I want to confide in the most—unfortunately, that wasn't always possible. But there are people that I can confide in; they're called friends. Some of my friends are looking for a positive outcome to this thing. They're like me—they love problem-solving. There are things I can tell them that I can't tell Tina. I wish I could, but I can't.

For now, as mad as Tina was at me, and as mad as I was at her for being mad at me, I couldn't let our anger interfere with what I had planned for our four-year anniversary. It's time for us to get out of the house. Time to take a vacation, and maybe (and this is wishful thinking), just maybe the activity will be gone when we get back. Let's let the house stay vacant for three days, let's see what happens then. Where are we celebrating our four-year anniversary? San Juan, WA. If you've never been to this part of Washington State, I strongly suggest you go. Do what we did, go in the summertime, and visit Orca or San Juan specifically. That's what we've been doing for the last two years. I try to think of it as hitting the reset button. Stay-cation, vacation, whatever—if anybody is in need of one, it's us. We're going!

One thing Tina did before we headed out of town was call the priest. She wanted to reconfirm with him what the next steps were. The priest knew about the cross being stabbed in the wall. He knew about the upside-down cross and the 666 wall writings. The last thing he told us was that he was going to contact his bishop and confirm with him what the next steps looked like. We were still waiting.

The trip Tina and I took to San Juan Island, WA, we did what most couples do. We hiked up a few mountains. Went to a few lookout points. Ventured into the local towns; drank some exceptional wine. Tasted some great food. We even agreed that the best eggs benedict resides on San Juan Island. Tina bought some clothes; I bought some postcards for my mom, aunt, and sister. We never mentioned the house or the activity that was taking place. It was pretty much understood that this was a staycation. Our chance to get away. We're not going to talk about the house. Tina and I decided to cook dinner together—our last night on the island. We stood side by side on our deck. It ended up being one of the best weekends ever. Dinner, a Puget Sound sunset, and Washington Cabernet. The conversation we had while heading home was great. We needed this. We deserved this. It would be our last vacation together.

Chapter 19
A Letter Arrives

July 14th, 2014. We had hoped that our three days visit to San Juan would have tricked the spirits into leaving our house. We were wrong. A few nights after we got back from our trip, Tina and I were watching TV. We were talking, when suddenly I looked down and noticed that Tina's giant throw rug was folded in half. Tina looked at me and asked, "How did the carpet get like that?" There's no way this rug could have been folded without us noticing it. The rug was not this way seconds ago. Somehow, we missed seeing it fold. How in the hell did we miss that? We're talking about a giant Persian rug, ladies and gentlemen. We could not have gotten to the couch earlier had this rug been folded this way. Tina said, "That's different."

Another phenomenon taking place in the house while we waited for the priest to get back to us was an instance that involved coins. I accidentally dropped my piggy bank jar while adding more dimes to it one day. I cursed myself out loud for being so clumsy—coins went everywhere. A few days after that happened I began finding a dime in various parts of the house. Not several dimes. One dime, that's it. As with the other objects appearing out of nowhere, these dimes began appearing in open places throughout the house. The only difference now is this: these dimes are always right on my immediate path. I could be taking a shower and upon stepping out of the stall, *bam*! There on the floor, is a dime. There were no dimes here earlier. I soon began seeing dimes just about everywhere I went— on the staircase, on the driveway, on the seat of the car, driver and passenger side: one dime. It took a while for me to notice how often this was occurring. What got my attention was a day I decided to work from home.

I had set up my workstation in the kitchen. I needed a break, so I got up and went upstairs. There at the base of the landing was this dime. Since I was heading to my office, I thought *I might as well pick this dime up and put it in the piggy-bank.* I remember looking at the dime and reading what year it was made in before dumping it into my glass jar. It read: nineteen sixty-nine. *Hmmm, that's the year I was born.* A few minutes later I was leaving my office and heading back downstairs. There at the base of the landing, again, was another dime. Dear reader, I just walked by here minutes ago. There was no dime here. The only dime that was here was the dime that I picked up. That dime now resides in my piggy-bank. Where did this second dime come from? I pick it up, and I'm thinking to myself, please don't read nineteen sixty-nine. Sure, enough that's exactly what it read— nineteen sixty-nine. I said to myself, holy crap! *These bitches are playing with me.*

I then turned around to face the direction of the hallway. Before I could stop myself, I blurted out: "are you responsible for these dimes around the house? Are you watching me when I pick up these dimes? If you're watching me right now, can you make a dime appear?" Silence. I circled the floor with my eyes in the hope of a new dime appearing. Let me try one last time. "If you're watching me, if you're the one responsible for me finding these dimes on the floor, I want you to make one appear right now. I dare you to make a dime appear right now. "

In less than the time it takes for the human eye to blink a series of dimes fell from the direction of the ceiling, I say that because I saw them fall from above my head. From above my upper peripheral vision. About three dollars' worth of dimes falls from the direction of the ceiling. All at the same time. They all hit the carpet simultaneously. Nothing else afterward, just a hallway littered with dimes. I don't remember inspecting each dime to see if it read nineteen sixty-nine, all I remember is how trippy the experience was. The inexplicable appearance of dimes never happened again. *It's weird how certain wonders only happen once.* Tina's Persian rug and the dime event are perfect examples of that.

I'm forced to go back to the missing money in my wallet. That was trippy and interesting. I mean, why take dollar bills out of my wallet? Then I thought, *you did that hoping I'd accuse Tina.* I mean, the house was quiet during that time frame; maybe the entities living here require a certain level of turmoil. Did this level of manipulation work on the previous tenants? Speaking of previous tenants, I remember asking our landlord in 2012 if he had the contact info of the previous tenants. He said he did, but he can't divulge it. The reason I gave for needing their contact info was that Tina and I were receiving mail that belonged to the tenants living in the house before us. Which was true, we did get mail coming to us that belonged to other people. In the mailbox outside and sometimes inside the house. The difference between the outside mail and inside was the dates on the stamps. We're talking about four to five years difference. The landlord advised us to forward him the letters to him. He'll make sure they get to the previous tenants.

Mid – July 2014, Tina and I received another letter in our mailbox that didn't belong to us. Instead of going to the landlord with the hopes of him telling me where this person is, let me try another alternative. That alternative being Facebook. What do I have to lose? So, I tried right then and there. One quick search of this woman's name on Facebook brought me straight to her profile page. I was holding this white envelope in my hand while looking at this person's profile and trust me when I say this, I knew I had come to the right place. I could see her entire profile, and we're not even Facebook friends. *Alas, I've finally found a previous tenant.*

It must have taken me two days to come up with the question I wanted to ask her. I need to email her—the only way to be sure if she gets my email is to send her a friend request. So, I did. And guess what? She accepted. *Very quickly I might add.* I go silent again. I mean, I'm a stranger; granted she accepted my friend requests but that doesn't mean she's going to respond to me, especially given the questions I want to ask her. Everything inside me is saying, *Keith, she used to live in the house you now live in. You have to introduce yourself; you have to ask her the ultimate question.* Everybody Tina and I have talked to when seeking help have all asked us the same three questions. They are: have you and your girlfriend had any type of before moving in? Has either of you ever played with an Ouija board? Lastly, have you gotten a hold of any previous tenant? I wish you could see the look of disappointment on our face when we tell these people no.

Tina and I were disappointed because we wanted to be a part of the solution and not part of the problem. We're honest you see. We know a no from us means we've hit a dead end. But that's about to change. Instead of three, no's, it's about to be two no's and one yes. I've found a woman who used to live in the house. Now I have to figure out how to ask her the question others have asked Tina and me. I decided to keep it short and simple. Don't freak her out. The question in my email went like this. *Hi: my name is Keith Linder. I found your name on Facebook after receiving a letter in the mail. I believe you were once the tenant of the house my girlfriend and I now live in, a house in Bothell. We've been experiencing some weird things.* (I didn't tell her what our weird things were exactly). I then asked her if she and her family had experienced anything unusual, anything bizarre.

It took her two days to respond, an interesting response it was. Her reply was three emoticon eye winks ";-) ;-) ;-)" That's right: a total of three smiley wink faces. My reply to her was, "Can you please elaborate?" and that's when she typed: "I need to get my thoughts together before I can respond; I need to confirm if it's OK with my husband, we just got back together." Now I was sitting at my computer desk upstairs. I was reading her response over and over, and thinking, *BINGO, we nailed it Keith, hot damn! We nailed it.* Now, don't spook her, don't start sending her mass emails and mass text messages via Facebook. If she needs time to think it over, let her think it over. If she needs to clear it with her husband, let her clear it with her husband. She's told you enough already. My only reply needs to be, take your time. She knew something. I need to know what that something is. If I want to know what that something is, then I need to wait. She'll block me or vanish completely if I spook her too much.

Of course, when she told me she needed time to gather her thoughts I had no idea it would take two months. But if that's what she needs, so be it. I've waited this long. I can wait a little longer. In the meantime, our house was showing signs of heating up again. There was a new level of haunting that was about to be introduced. The activity has put itself in the driver's seat in reshaping my opinions about the Church and those we are reaching out to.

While I waited for the previous tenant to respond to me in detail about what she and her family had experienced, Tina and I had to do what we normally do. We had to maintain the status quo. One has to go to work to the pay the bills, right? Only now, one part of maintaining the status quo meant me lacing the house with more cameras. I'm talking about a camera in every room. Some rooms had two cameras in them. Yes, that's right, two cameras now. The most active rooms in the house need two cameras because the spirits are doing donuts around me with one. Maybe I can even the score.

And a new room would be coming into the fold as far home monitoring goes. That room was my office. What are the odds of me capturing wall-writings on my office walls? Zero, of course, I didn't know that at the time, neither did my brother, and it's safe to say neither did the so-called experts who encouraged me to try.

It must have amused the spirits a great deal to see me walk into my house with a box full of CCTV cameras. Built-in infrared, built-in Wi-Fi, email alerts, alarm and clock synchronization, everything. I'm at the point now where I'm programming each camera to begin and stop at certain times. The cameras automatically go offline when Tina and I are home. The motion alert comes on automatically now. It comes on when we go to bed, and it comes on when we leave the house in the morning. No longer am I restricted to the computer at home or my computer at work.

I've upgraded my cameras to the point of having apps installed on my phone. I can now view my house from the palm of my hand. So, yeah, I think the spirits might be amused right now. How do I know? I know because I got mass email alerts a few days after installing new cameras. Emails with pictures—showing our house under attack.

Tina and I have come home and found our bedrooms, our hallway, and (one time) my office in chaos. We've seen what these spirits can do while we tried to earn a living. I've come home and found burnt Bibles. I've come home and found heavy objects knocked over. I've come home and found upside-down crosses drawn on my office floor, my office door, and my office wall. I've come home and found a pair of scissors (ones I'd just used to trim my mustache that morning), stabbed into a wall. I found all of that and more.

Today, I found something new. I found all the contents of my closet spilled onto the office floor. Speakers knocked over. My chair disassembled again. My printer was knocked over. The scissors and the cross (the bronze one that Tina had questions about) were both stabbed into the wall—same as before. Today's what-the-fuck award goes to the 666-wall writing. It's been written on three walls now. Not written in ash like before; more like paint. But paint from where? The substance was eerie looking. No way is soap and water going to do the trick. Make no mistake about it. The damage done now, especially to the wall itself, would require a complete paint-over.

Tina got home after me and saw the 666 wall markings. She saw the cross and scissors embedded in my office wall; she saw the room turned upside down. She left the room and called the priest. She ended up leaving three voicemails that night. It seemed obvious that the spirit was trying to scare us. The violence of it all scared both of us. The cameras at the time were not doing the trick. I need more cameras, more than I had now. Can you see how flawed my logic is? I mean, it's moronic. Cameras perform when the conditions are ripe for them to perform. They can't perform when there's no power. It's hard to take photos if you're unplugged. And let's not think for a second that, had they not been unplugged, had the power not been cut they would have captured something.

Cameras in a poltergeist-infested home only capture what the poltergeist wants them to capture. Today, that was nothing. I captured nothing. *As a parting gift, we leave you with a room to clean up, a carpet to vacuum, furniture to pick up including the armoire that moved from the hallway to the guest bedroom as if doing that was going to prevent us from knocking it over again. Feel free to put the pictures back on the wall, stand up the cameras we knocked down, stand your speakers back up. BTW your coffee table is upside down, and you might want to close your kitchen cabinets; oh, and we left you with three cameras instead of the five you had when you left for work this morning. And lastly, enjoy painting over the new 666 wall-writing we left you. We used black paint this time. Or, better yet, what you think is black paint.*

As you can see, my ineptness and ego were fueling me to buy more cameras. I went out and bought a digital video recorder system—a four channel DVR terabyte hard drive was now running twenty-four seven in my den and kitchen area. I've not solved the power-loss issue. Instead, I went out and bought a two-hundred-and-fifty-dollar DVR system. I'm pretty sure the manufacturer of every device I bought never thought their camera would be used to record some of the most compelling paranormal events on record.

Every motion sensor camera I have allows me to remote in anytime I want to. And that's what I'm going to do today. Instead of listening to music while I'm working at work, I'm *going to remote into my cameras at home, earphones tuned to the house.* I'm going to listen in. By this stage I was thinking, maybe I was doing this wrong. Instead of waiting for the email alerts to come in, let's switch to a more proactive approach. Enough with being reactive, which up till now is all I've been doing. The email alerts come in; they show me still images of a house in chaos; all I do is come home and clean up. The spirits here are insulting me that's what they're doing. They're terrorizing and insulting me at the same time.

If I listen in from work, beginning first thing in the morning maybe that'll eliminate the power to the house being cut. If I can eliminate the power being cut, I can keep the cameras going. I'm bound to get something if the power keeps going. All I have to do if I hear a sound, after already being logged in, is maximize my computer screen. That's real-time monitoring, ladies and gentleman. That's what I'm going to do.

So, I was at my desk working. Earphones in my ear. I had the dashboard which shows the inside of my house minimized on my toolbar. I'd been doing this for some days now. So far not much was happening. Day three, something does—a loud bang. This bang was different from the previous bangs I'd heard. This bang came from the hallway. It sounded like one of those wooden spring ladders that lower from the ceiling. My house doesn't have a ladder; we don't even have an attic. Whatever that sound was it sounded like it came from nearby, sounded like it came right above the camera—the one I'm logged into.

Then came a pause. It built up to a crescendo of sorts. The noise then switched from sounding like a wooden attic ladder being lowered to the sound of an old-fashioned chest of drawers being dragged around. You know the old-fashioned chest your mom or grandmother owned that sat at the foot of the bed in the guest bedroom. These chests or dresser drawers had those hinge handles that rattled when moved or when dragged. That's exactly what it sounded like. There would be a loud crash, a loud thud, and then the dragging sound, then a pause. After the pause, the sound would begin again with another loud thud or crash. It's very repetitive.

I thought to myself: *what the heck is going on? Is someone breaking into my house? Is something crashing through the roof of my house?* That's how it sounds, ladies and gentlemen; very loud and unexpected. This went on for about thirty to forty minutes. It began abruptly and ended abruptly. I took to Google with the hopes of finding out what this was and sure enough, there it was the perfect description. The dragging furniture phenomenon heard in the rarest of both demonic and poltergeist cases. I'm thinking to myself: *demonic* and *poltergeists?* Everywhere I go for information, every turn I take leads me back to those two words. The priest says we have demons living in the house. Jennifer says the same thing. No one knows what the silver bullet is for getting rid of these things. I guess you could say time is what gets rid of poltergeists. And the true word of God is what get rids of demons.

Demon or "Geist" aside, this video is a huge accomplishment. Who can I give this to? Who can I call or email and say: can you listen to this? I sent the file to the priest: no response. I shared the video with Jennifer, and she was like "wow." I shared it with Tina, and she so impressed about it that I created an account for her. She could now log in and listen to the house while at work herself. And she did. We did.

One day the noise got so loud, or better yet became so frequent, that I began getting mass emails saying *sound detected*. Sound detected meant only one thing: the furniture dragging campaign was about to start. So here we were listening in together, Tina and me. No way should we be hearing furniture being dragged on what sounds to like a wooden surface. Our house is primarily carpet; the only wood surface we have is in the kitchen. The noise was not coming from the kitchen. If you combine the large furniture sound with the wooden floor sound, you come to the quick conclusion that neither element existed in our house. Tina and I came home from work thinking we're sure to find something has moved or been shifted. There was nothing.

Neither of us owned anything resembling the sounds we heard. There's no ladder to the attic. Hell, we don't even have an attic, *not one we would ever get to.* So, where was that noise coming from? No one knew. Not Jennifer, not Tina, and not the researchers I gave the file to later. *Definitely not them.* So that's one interesting piece of evidence my cameras were able to pick up after several days of back-to-back surveillance. Let me tell you about the most compelling piece of evidence of summer 2014, which would be the night the camera downstairs picked up something.

House Attack - July 2014
https://www.youtube.com/watch?v=AQpnnsvU5ws

Fig 19.1 July House Attack – Upside-down cross writings, cross, and scissor stabbed into wall.

Chapter 20
The Gray Lady Again?

I have to say when it came to reviewing video footage I was horrible (at first). The discipline it takes to sit down, block out everything, and try to look for something abnormal. I mean, we're talking about six, eight, sometimes twelve hours of video footage. Who has time for that? I know I didn't, not at first. Not until my friend Justin one day emailed me, saying: "I think you should look at something."

"Look at what?" I replied.

"You need to look at this video you sent me. There's something about it." My friend never told me what the something was. He just said, "Look at the video, and when you do, go to this time stamp." I did. I was blown away. My email back to him was: that's the Gray Lady. I think? I mean, it's gray, but the whole video is gray; the video my friend sent me was originally filmed at night when the infra-red was on. In further email exchanges, Justin and I agreed that what we were seeing was well defined: human torso; guitar-shaped. A well-defined woman.

This video my friend is referring to if from an April party Tina and I had at the house. It's been sitting on my hard drive all summer—just waiting to be looked at. Tina and I had heard considerable noises the night before which is one of the reasons why the camera is where it is (see Fig 20.1). *During the period where all the kitchen cabinets were opened in the middle of the night.* So, I turned the camera on after my friends had left.

So, we were chatting, my friend and me, and he was pointing out stuff that I never thought for a second would be interesting. I guess I had become what I was critiquing. Which is if it's not an object being thrown or a book catching fire then I'm not interested. That's what people told us when we sought help. "Show is a Bible bursting into flames." I'm glad Justin reviewed multiple video files on behalf because our conversation was immense that night. My friend pointed out multiple things happening in the living room while Tina and I were asleep.

The female torso at 4:58 is one of the main highlights.
https://youtu.be/-F9K0bvVa2s

Fig 20.1 Something materializes 4:58 through 5:07 (don't blink) please
maximize your screen

Fig 20.2 Foscam Kitchen

I congratulated my friend for pointing this out to me. I probably never would
have noticed, because my mind at that time was focused on capturing movement.
That's the only reason I had for buying the cameras. Justin finding that apparition
helped me realized something. If you're going to go out and buy video equipment,
you best be prepared to review everything on it. Reviewing sucks up until the
time you find something. Contrary to what's on TV—finding something of value
is extremely rare. This apparition (if you watch the video closely) manifests over
a period of a few seconds. Then it's gone.

Fig 20.3

Tina's reaction to the apparition was identical to mine. Unbelievable. Unbelievable in the sense of: here we are living through this. Here we are trying to fight off something that's not friendly. And now we have this. We have a symbol of what we're going through. It might not be the best symbol in the world, but it's a symbol nonetheless. It's something. Tina started showing her family the video as did I; the conclusion was the same: that it's a female apparition. Of course, family members don't use the word apparition, they use the word "ghosts," or they ask, "What the fuck is that?"

The question I'm asking was this the thing that's setting fires off. We don't know. Did she push me down the stairs? We don't know. We don't know a lot of things, but this is good. Tina can show the priest this when she calls him. He'll look at the video himself, and hopefully after looking at, update his course of action. Tina's left several voicemails, sent several emails. No response.

She finally gets to speak to the priest after countless call-backs—finally gives him an updated (his request remember?) She told him that the events in the home had escalated. Everyone's in agreement that the spirit is throwing tantrums at Keith and Tina. I'm aware of it, Tina's aware of it, and the priest seems to be aware of it. That night when we went to bed, I decided to stay up a little bit. I needed to think some things through. One question I had while I was lying there was, do we have the church's backing, the church's blessing?

The first time the priest came over, which was two weeks after the poster fire incident, the answer was, "Yes. We're all in this thing together. There's no need to move; you and Tina don't move." These "tantrums" the spirit is throwing at Tina and me, the priest told us, were meant to break our will. I don't think the spirit has broken our will yet. What worried Tina and I was the trashing of my office. You can't help but be nervous about the violent nature of it. 666 wall-writings, that's not violent. Upside-down cross, that's not violent. Cross and scissor stabbed into the wall? That's violent, that's unsettling. It's unsettling because you don't want that knife stabbing you. I don't want to be stabbed; nor does Tina.

What Tina wanted to know from the priest was, "Should we be worried that the spirit is now picking up sharp objects?" As we say in the south "is the spirit selling wolf tickets?" *Is it bluffing?* If it isn't, what should we do? The priest's answer was: "Continue doing what you're doing. Remain vigilant, remain steadfast, and keep giving me updates." Now, I think we're doing all those things. But I also think that I'm more aggressive than Tina when it comes to homework. I'm leading most of the prayers; I'm leading most of the chants, most of the recitals. That can't happen. We both have to be fifty-fifty in this. If the spirits should even get a suspicion that it's me leading all the efforts for its removal, it might start focusing on me more. We can't let that happen.

Another thing that seemed to bother Tina was the cross. The cross I bought when I was in Spokane. Seeing it on my wall, like a knife sticking out of a stabbing victim, sparked some odd dialogues between Tina and me. She would always ask me where I got that cross from. My answer was always the same. I bought that cross from a gift shop in the Davenport Luxury Hotel. Why are you having a hard time with that being the case? That was my response. Her answer? Nothing, absolutely nothing. Tina just walked away. You can tell when someone doesn't believe you; they keep asking the same questions over and over. I'd told Tina three times already that I bought this cross while traveling on business. If there's one thing I hate more than being put on the defensive, it's repeating myself. In court, they call that 'asked and answered.'

The priest had mentioned to Tina when she finally caught up with him that the church has protocols, ceremonial formalities, red tape, and bureaucracy it goes through when dealing with these kinds of manifestations. It's a lengthy process. "No one should be thinking house exorcism." Tina and I thought why the hell not? I'm not the expert here, but I think they are multiple spirits haunting this house. Tina got an email from the priest the next day informing her that his bishop approved of his next steps. "Phase two" is what he called it. What's phase two?

Phase two is holding communion at the house. I have no idea what communion is or what communion does. Neither does Tina. But we were grateful for the fact that the local priest came back, and even more grateful that he held communion. Now, you have to remember, the last time the priest visited our house, my office was not in the shape it was in now. Nor was the hallway. I purposely delayed painting over all the 666 wall markings because I wanted the priest to see them.

Tina showed them the giant armoire in our guest bedroom again. It had been thrown a few more times since the last time they were here. It was showing signs of wear and tear. No one's writing anything down. No one's taking pictures which Tina and I thought was odd. We want to ask them the question, should you be documenting this? But we don't. We're trying to be grateful, and we're trying to be respectful. But in the back of my mind, I'm thinking why aren't you taking pictures of the wall scratches? Of the 666 and upside-down cross symbols? Tina and I looked at each other and shrugged.

So, we all went back downstairs and began the communion ceremony. Laura and her husband were back again; to assist with the service. Lots and lots of prayer going on. No thuds, no booms, no door slams whatsoever. The priest then went upstairs and began dousing every room with holy water. Everything was doused—the 666, the upside-down cross, the new holes in the wall, the new scratches on the wall, the sage stick, the Christian paraphernalia, everything. And he was done. We all went back downstairs, and that's when the question came. The question about praying.

"Are we being punctual with our prayers? Are we consistent?" I hesitated and said yes. I knew his definition of being consistent was different from ours. If I had to give us a grade on how consistent we were I have to say we were about a solid B. Even I knew a B grade was not going to cut it with the entities occupying this house. I knew that for a fact. Consistency is one of the pillars for being successful, and we had some little ways to go. The priest then asked Tina and me: "were we carrying out the prayers and rituals equally? Were we sharing the workload when it came to praying? Sharing the workload when it came time to smudging the house? And most importantly, are we both including in our prayers the words "leave", "get out", and "seek our Lord Jesus Christ."

If one person is doing more of the reminding, we got trouble. If one person reads more from the Bible than the other, if they pray less than the other, if they're thinking in their heart that this is all over-kill, then we got trouble.

I hoped that Tina was paying attention right then and there as to what the priest was saying. We had to have a united front. We had to share the workload. It can't be me smudging all the time. It can't be me calling us to prayer all the time. It has to be fifty-fifty. Right now, it wasn't. It was more like sixty-forty. On nights where we argued it was seventy-thirty or eighty-twenty. I was doing a majority of the homework, and it's not a coincidence that the majority of the homework I'm doing coincides with the increased office attacks. Tina even noticed that the attacks on me have increased. I'm not sure if she knows why though.

Please don't take what I've just said and extrapolated it to mean, "Ah ha! Something must be wrong with Tina". You'd be making a big mistake if you did that. The same mistake *Ghost Adventures* made when they suggested, through well-crafted editing, that Tina might be cause for all of this.

Let me be clear: Tina and I are very different. Tina is more introverted than me. She's reticent about certain things. That's been her character trait ever since I met her. She initiates only when you force her hand. And you really have to force her hand. Let's go back to the housewarming party of 2012. The night the first plant got thrown, the night Tina's friend Kim and godmother were at the house.

Kim's godmother requested that we all recited the Lord's Prayer and she requested that we all said an individual prayer. It was then that I saw something I'd never seen before. I saw Tina's reluctance of praying openly. I saw nervousness. I saw shyness. I saw meekness. I came to discover that Tina, no matter what she's being asked to do, will default to the introvert inside her when asked to do certain things. Her defense mechanism is to agree right then and there, and then, when everyone's back is turned, pass the baton to someone else or just change the subject. Unfortunately for Tina, in this situation that isn't going to help. This circumstance we find ourselves in right now has called to attention our individual weaknesses. Tina's weakness (for lack of a better word) is shyness. Shyness won't cut it here. My girlfriend hates speaking in front of people. She hates being vulnerable. If I can see that, then so can the spirits. The difference between them and me is I'm not going to exploit it. I'm not going to use her fear against her. The spirits are a different story. They will use your fear against you.

What are my weaknesses? One of my biggest weaknesses is pride. That's a big weakness to have. Demons can have a fill day with pride, ladies and gentlemen. What can I say? I'm my father's son. Linder men are proud men. We're not perfect men. We're proud men. I make it a point in life of not trying to offend people. I try not to wrong anyone, and I don't want anyone to wrong me. Sometimes my pride gets in the way of me asking for help. Sometimes my pride gets in the way of seeing things clearly. I have to remember that while living in this house. I have to keep pride checked. The spirits know more about Tina and me than we know about ourselves. It's a scary thought, but it's true.

One of the questions the priest forgot to answer while here was what sort of penalty do Tina and I get for not being united? What are the repercussions? The repercussions are endless. One fallout for not having a united front is resentment. A certain level of resentment would begin to surface as result of me doing most of the spirit-removal ceremonies. And it was beginning to show itself whenever I said Tina; it's time for us to pray, hey it's your turn to read from the Bible; hey, your turn to smudge; your turn to place the pillow, so the door doesn't slam on us in the middle of the night. It would become, hey, it's your turn over and over again for the next few days. To the point where you just get tired of asking. A communication gap was slowing forming between Tina and me. In a funny kind of way, it reminds me of a big event from back in childhood.

I can't remember what year it was when me and my twin brother got an Atari for Christmas. Model 2600. It was a big deal at the time. I think we were the only kids on the block to have one. My twin and I loved that Atari system to death. That Atari system had changed the entire dynamics of the house by the time March rolled around. I mean, the attitude among us four siblings had changed as a result of that Atari system. I'm pretty sure when my parents bought the gift for my brother and me, the furthest thing on their mind was it creating more problems than it solved. But that was what happened. All the siblings were at odds with each other, as a result of this new gaming system.

It didn't take long before fights would break out between my twin, myself, and our younger brother; fights over who got to play with the Atari first. It never occurred to us that the more we fought over this device; the more we risked losing it. And that's exactly what happened. We lost it. It was gone within four months. Only after it was gone did the house turn back to normal. We found ourselves loving each other again. I guess you can say we were not ready for an Atari system. I guess you can say we were not appreciative. Now the Atari has no power. It can only control us if we let it. I share that story because I want you, the reader, to understand something. I want to help the next person who, through no fault of their own, happens to enter a house occupied by malevolent spirits. Tina and I can't see the spirits that live here. I wish we could see them like we saw that Atari 2600. It would help me deal with them like that Atari helped my parents deal with us. The spirits know Tina and me. They know we have different character traits. There are enough character flaws between Tina and me to keep a "Geist" busy for quite some time. There's so much to exploit. Tina and I have to be mindful of that.

Throw in the insecurity, the innuendos, the ego, the pride, and the ignorance, and you see a wall is about to be put in place between us both. The spirits are about to pivot from haunting Keith and Tina to just too haunting Keith. This level of horror is going to create more division, more strife, more angst, more finger pointing and more uncertainty. It's the gift spirits keep giving themselves when it comes to haunting a household. It was during this phase that I begin coining an interesting new phrase. Instead of looking at what the spirit is doing, or has done, maybe we should look at what the spirit has yet to do?

Up until now, nothing has been damaged to the extinct of being utterly destroyed. I mean things are broken; the armoire is a good example of that. We have the burnt Bibles; my cross from Spokane is bent. My scissors are bent. We have holes in the hallway now. Dents on the floor from "Geist" stomping, holes in our bedroom, and holes in the wall in my office.

But even through all of that (and I left out a lot of stuff), there are still things the spirit hasn't yet done. Why hasn't it destroyed our most expensive items? Why hasn't it tossed a high definition TV? Why hasn't it tossed one of Tina's mirrors? I mean, it's emptied my wine rack sometimes without so much as breaking one bottle. If you think painting over 666 repeatedly is expensive, imagine how much it would cost to get red wine out of a carpet. I mean, I have over two cases of wine in my wine rack. One bottle gets tossed on Tina's Persian rug, and that rug is ruined.

If want to see a grown man cry, break a few of my expensive bottles of wine. Empty my wine collection on the carpet. That'll get me upset. The spirit never did that. Why not? Let's not forget the kitchen cabinets. I've read of cases where the contents of people's kitchen cabinets get flung out all over the floor. I can't even fathom what that feels like. Tina has hundreds of dishes, masses of China, hundreds of porcelain plates and bowls. The spirit never touched them. The only thing they've touched was my mom's coffee cup.

I soon found myself logging into what I thought was the kitchen camera— only to realize that I'm looking at my bedroom now. What the hell is going on? Hold up, don't drop the book just yet; it's about to get even weirder. The first time I experienced this I did what most people would do: I logged out and logged back in. Maybe I clicked the wrong camera upon logging in. But the same thing happens again. I'm looking at the bedroom when I should be looking at the kitchen. My dashboard says kitchen camera. I've remoted into the kitchen camera. I know I am. It has its own MAC address. Why do I see my bedroom? OK. Let me try my bedroom camera. What is my bedroom going to show me? Nothing, it's showing me nothing. I'm getting connection errors; my bedroom camera is offline. Something is going on.

Just to be clear on the tech side. All the cameras in my home go through my wireless router. Each camera has its own MAC address. What's a MAC address? MAC stands for media access control; it's the numerical address of a computer. In layman's terms, the MAC address for each camera is kind of like your house address. The information is sent via Wi-Fi or via Ethernet comes in the form of packets. In those packets are headers that say: send this information here, don't send it here, send it to this specific address, i.e., MAC address.

Well, MAC addresses can be altered; after all, we're talking about a series of numbers. If a MAC address is altered (i.e., the header changed) then that information is going to be rerouted. In my case, the information being re-routed is the images my camera is sending me, still in the form of packets. Instead of seeing my living room, which is what I should be seeing, I see my bedroom. As an IT professional I can assure you, ladies and gentlemen, this is outstanding. Machines do not reconfigure themselves. I'm not reconfiguring anything. I'm at work being bombarded by emails that say: motion detected, sound detected. It's not Tina. So: who is it? What is it?

A cynic or skeptic might say, someone's hacked into your cameras and is playing a bad joke on you. You could say that. You'd be wrong, but you could say that. The odds of that happening are next to zero. Let's start inwards and work our way outwards. You may be able to hack my cameras, maybe even my network but you can't program my camera to send out a motion or sound alert. Not unless you're inside my house. I checked my ADT system, and nothing's been tripped. It's all working as it should be.

Maybe the breach could come within the Comcast network itself. It's possible but highly unlikely. Companies like Comcast make their bread and butter out of providing internet service that's secure. The security aspect is important. That's where the money is spent. A company would not be in business long had their network service been so questionable. No, if there's hacking going on then, it would most likely happen within my own setup. An internet hacker is mostly going to seek out the vulnerability of the home user. Most people's home networks are set up incorrectly. They're vulnerable to a breach because they're not encrypted, or they have a soft password. My home network is not set up that way. I have a pretty strong firewall set-up, as does Comcast. To top it off my routers are WPA2 enabled. As you'd expect from an IT pro, my home network is pretty damn secure. No one's hacking my network. Let alone for a year or more. Too many coincidences are happening for that to be true. It would appear the spirits in the home finally figured out how the network works; finally figured how to re-route things.

It would seem these spirits had a sense of humor or were up to something. Or both. I couldn't see the room I wanted to see (the one that's sending me email alerts) but was forced to see the room *they* wanted me to see, where nothing was happening. Being locked out like this was driving me insane. I began receiving mass email alerts a few weeks after the priest conducted the communion. They began arriving after 10 am for days. The headache you get as a result of these emails is not knowing what is taking place at the house. You can't access the camera that's sending the email. I finally decided that I needed to call Tina. She needs to know the house might be under attack. She tries to log in with her account and also gets nothing. For about six hours or more we knew nothing. When I got home, the first room I went to was the one that I couldn't see. When I got to that room, nothing. Nothing was out of place.

This went on for several days. It was like they were toying with me. If your inbox fills up with hundreds of motion-sound detected emails, odds are you're going to stop what it is you're doing to see what's going on. The spirits know this. They'd been studying me for months now. Sometimes they let me in, and what do I see when I'm let in? I see the room I don't want to see. Sometimes they don't let me in. Sometimes they make me wait. I don't know what I'm going to see till I get home. And when I get home, what do I see? Well, this depends on what happened the day or night before between Tina and me. That is: how is the energy in the house? I might see the love-seat upside down; I might see the coffee table upside-down—all the contents spread throughout the house. I might see the hallway in shambles. I'm guaranteed to see something if Tina and I argued that day.

I soon realized why the spirits were doing this. Inconvenience. For me to correct what the spirits have done, I now have to take the cameras offline; I must reset them, reconfigure them, and then place them back where they were. It takes me thirty minutes to fix one camera; and by the time I've reconfigured them all, the chances are that the first one has gone back offline again. It returns to showing another room in the house.

It becomes a test of wills. Theirs and mine. I remember one-time Tina came home and I called down to her from the office to see some evidence I had captured on one of the Foscams. She walked in and started watching a video with me. I showed her video of the furniture in the kitchen being rearranged. She was looking over my shoulder when suddenly one of the Foscams got thrown to the floor. We heard the thud. We spun around at the same time. There on the floor was the Foscam. Facing down, of course. I looked at Tina, and she looked at me. I then picked up the camera and placed it back on the entertainment center. We commented on it and soon turned back to watching the video. We heard another thud. We turned around again and once more the Foscam was lying on the floor. Tina backed away from me and began circling the room with her eyes.

I picked up the camera and placed it back on the entertainment center. We turned our backs to it one more time. We' were a few seconds into the video when suddenly the TV volume goes from off to on. Scared the heebie-jeebies out of both Tina and me. There's nothing scarier than watching a ghost video and being scared by a ghost while you're watching a ghost video. I almost shit my pants, that's how loud my stereo was. Tina had enough. She ran out of the room saying, "Screw that video, and screw your office!"

Chapter 21
"The Day of the Dove"

August 2014. I'm about to share with you another haunting story. There have been a few already, I realize. But there are levels, even within the impossible. Here comes a new level. This night, Tina and I had our light-hearted pillow talk—we could feel the mood changing during the middle of our discussion. Our mood was not changing. The mood in the room was. We know we're right because the ceiling fan which was silent when we lay down was now squeaking again. Just out of the blue, it begins wailing.

Both of us were gazing up at the ceiling. I mean we're having a conversation in bed, which was rare at this stage. The activity we'd witnessed for two years or more had pretty much killed the idea of having pillow talk. Not tonight, though. I guess we had a good dinner or something because Tina and I were having a light-hearted conversation, when suddenly, we just stopped at the same moment.

We both realized: we weren't alone in the room anymore. Both of our personal space had been invaded. The room shrunk all of a sudden. Tina felt it, and I felt it. *Goodbye pillow talk*. Grim reality slams back in. Tina and I have got to be the stupidest people in the world even to be laying here. We sort of say that out loud together when suddenly the bedroom door slams shut. Tina sits up, and I sit up.

The light from the hallway pierced through the cracks underneath the door, casting light on the floor and wall in front of us. Then the shadows began emerging. Not in our room, but in the hallway. Tina and I could see the shadows coming through the bottom of the door. It was like we had human traffic in our hallway; it's as if we had people staying with us and all of a sudden one of them decides to get up and use the bathroom.

The light from the hallway was giving us multiple shadows—someone's going right to the left and left to right. That's what we see right now. I'm talking about movement right outside the door. No noise, though. No door being closed. No human footsteps. No movement noise whatsoever. Only shadows, about seven in all.

I think this calls for the Saint Michael prayer. And that's exactly what we did. We recited the Saint Michael prayer, the Lord's Prayer, and a few others. All from inside our bedroom. What made this real to Tina and I was the door slam. We forgot to prop open the door with a pillow that night, and this is what happened. Your typical poltergeist door slam. The uneasy feeling and the shadows traversing through the hallway lasted a few hours before finally subsiding.

The next morning, I woke up grumpy and pissed. I may have gotten about two hours sleep; Tina maybe four. And now we got to go to work and do whatever it is we do to earn a living. Now I don't normally let things get the better of me. Anybody who knows me will tell you; it takes a lot to make me mad, a lot to make me want to do something that I know I will regret the minute my anger subsides.

But today was that day. I got up out of bed that morning after both our alarms went off and said: "I'm tired of these damn spirits. Fuck this shit; fuck them and whatever demon they report to. Fuck the poltergeist that lives here, fuck the Gray Lady. Fuck all of them!"

Tina just gets up and gets ready for work. I should have done what she did. I didn't. I was pissed. I'd been sleep deprived, and now I was angry. I went into my office, yanked several sheets of paper from the printer tray, located a blue sharpie, and began writing. Frustration was writing, not me. *It's on now bitches, it's war now bitches*; *my God and I are going to defeat you*; *leave now or else*; and last but not least, *look at me, look at me—I'm the captain now.* I wrote this and taped it to the walls in my office. Tina walked by and saw what I was doing and shook her head in disbelief. I was upset. I mean: what was their end game? What was their motive? Their rationale? Besides just being assholes.

I should have stuck with praying. You never, ever, give a spirit a reason for engaging you personally. My calling them out on sheets of paper was the ultimate gift to them. I gave them wrath. I gave them attention. I just acknowledged how pissed off I was; I just told them everything they were doing was working. I'm pretty sure I would've heard a faint whisper saying *thank you* had it not been for the TV being on. Oh yeah, the spirits were saying 'thank you' alright. *'Thank you for doing what you did, Keith, we're coming, we're coming, baby.'*

Now one of the first things I did when I got to work after experiencing a horrible night like last night is get online. I was looking for similar cases elsewhere. I can't find any. The second thing I was looking for is a solution: a silver-bullet. What, if anything, is out there can fix this situation in one fell swoop. I'm finding nothing; nothing remotely close to solving this problem right away. The priest told us this was going to take a while. I believed him, it is going to take a while, but I had to try, right? I have to see if there's anything out there that can end this right away. There isn't.

When I get home, some eight hours later, I walked in and picked up the paperwork the priest left us. I marched up to the landing area and begin reciting some of the prayers. There I was standing at the top of the stairway, calling for Michael the Archangel. There I was, calling for the Holy Spirit. Tina was not even home yet, no telling when she was going to get here. I felt an urgency to not wait for her; an urgency to do something. That's how tired I was.

Later that night, I saw a book sitting on Tina's side of the bed. A new Bible. *Tina bought a Bible?* I said to myself as I walked over to her side of the bed. Now, Tina and I have been together for four years. I've never known her to own a Bible. She's never introduced one during our two-year dealings with malevolent spirits. My reaction to seeing a Bible on her side of the bed was interesting. The first question I asked her when picking up the Bible was, where did you get it from? It turned out it came from Kim. It'd been blessed at the church that Kim went to. As far as Bible's go, this one looked pretty good. It reminded me of the Bible my grandmother had, the one she took to church on Sunday. My grandmother had her own personal Bible. No one read from it but her. That would be the case for this Bible. Tina wanted this Bible to stay by her side. Makes sense. I get it. If this Bible's been blessed, if its Kim's personal Bible, and Kim gave it to you then, yes, keep this Bible by your bed.

136

Tina walks back into the room a few minutes later. She has something in her hand; it's another Bible. This Bible is brand new. It's way thinner than the Bible we just looked at. Tina tells me she bought this Bible specifically for the hallway. In my mind I'm thinking, but we have a Bible in the hallway already, we have a Bible that I bought from Spokane.

NOTE: Everything I've brought back from Spokane—be it a bronze cross or a new King James Bible—Tina's never been fond of.

Tonight, she was holding a brand-new Bible. She asked me if we could remove my Bible and replace it with this one. Of course, I said yes. The last thing we needed to argue about is whose Bible was going to sit in the hallway. The spirits had already burned three of my Bibles. If this was Tina's attempt at contributing spiritually to the removal of negative spirits, then I needed to support her. So, I did. We recited a few prayers before setting her new Bible on the bookshelf and taking mine down. And that was it. As far as I can know, nothing major happened that night. It was a quiet night.

One week later—Tina was going out of town for a few days. And this, as it turned out, was an opportunity too good to pass up for the spirits living with us. I mean, it should be an accepted fact to both Tina and me that manipulation is their preferred method for escalating the activity within the home. Jennifer and the priest advised us to stay on our guard. They advised us to stay firm, stay vigilant, and to watch each other's backs. And that's what we did ninety percent of the time. But guess what? Ninety percent is not good enough. You'll be shocked to see what a malevolent spirit can make do with. That ten percent of innuendo, of doubt, false accusation, finger-pointing, and lack of trust creates lots of anxiety. It creates contempt. It creates turmoil. And turmoil is a demon's specialty.

The house had been quiet in the two days before Tina's departure. It remained quiet for a few days after she returned. But as you now know, when the house is quiet, that means trouble is on its way.

I was downstairs watching TV that night when suddenly I heard major stomping upstairs. It wasn't the ghost. It was Tina. By the time she reached the bottom stair, I had thought, *sigh, I wish it was the ghost.* Tina had just stormed down the stairs and was now standing between me and the TV. In her hand was an earring. She'd been upstairs making up the bed, and in doing so found a female earring. If you're a woman reading this, you know this is not good. You're probably wondering: why am I still alive? Why am I still breathing? My problems have just multiplied by a factor of a hundred. Not only is Tina holding an earring. She was holding an earring that she found in our bed. The bed we sleep in. Now I'm not stupid. I recognize the situation I'm in. I realize I need to be very careful in what I say next. I'm cognizant of the fact that we have a spirit listening in. I'm cognizant of the fact that the house was quiet for several days. I'm cognizant of the fact that the spirit has now shown its hand. I'm cognizant of a lot of things, the main one being if I respond back to Tina with anger, this house might blow up.

To say Tina was on the rampage would be putting it lightly. Tina was all of that and then some. To say she felt like slicing my throat, would be putting it lightly. Tina was all of these things and then some. She was within her rights to be angry, if what she was holding meant what she thinks it does. But, it does not. Not even close. Somehow, I have to convince her of that. But how? Where do I begin? In my mind, I was being framed. In Tina's mind, I was cheating, the worst kind of cheating—having a woman in our bed while she was gone. Does anything hurt more than that? I doubt anything else does. The optics weren't good at all. I mean, an earring has been found in our bed. The bed of all places. Kind of a coincidence, looking back on it. But who's thinking rationally when you're holding what you believe is another woman's earring?

In one sense I could understand her anger. I totally get it. But in another sense, it just didn't add up. It's too convenient. I mean, we've seen this movie before. Tina and I have found jewelry before; we're always finding jewelry. That's not unusual. What's unusual now is where Tina found this earring. The last major argument we had was about an item found on the stairway, a piece of jewelry that could have only belonged to a woman. That woman was not Tina. In Tina's mind, I was guilty as sin then, and I'm guilty as sin now. Matter of fact, I'm guiltier now, based on where she found the earring. "How could you do this to me?"

"How could I do what? What did I do? I did not have a woman in the house. There was never a woman in the house while you were gone." I kept saying that over and over. "I don't know where that piece of jewelry came from?" And that's not a lie. Neither of us knew where that piece of jewelry came from. The only thing we knew is that it's here now.

Now, when it comes to arguing I can dish it out as well as I can take it in. Tina is sort of the same way. She can dish it out and she can take it in—that's one thing I hate about our relationship, our ability to argue till sunrise. This seemed like one of those events. And no way can I let that happen. My reply to Tina was this: "I don't know where that earring that came from, I bet the ghost put it there!"

Tina never stopped to think about that. Not for one second did she pause to think that all of this was just a little too convenient, too circumstantial. Remember the house we live in? Remember what we've seen so far. Remember what the priest told us, and lastly, remember what you learned in Sunday school. None of that was important now. The only thing I could do was resent the accusation. My father once said, "It takes two to tango; if you walk away the argument should subside." Well, that's exactly what I did. The mood of the house was changing with each pointed accusation, and with that in mind, I decided to head upstairs. I went straight to my office—a place I know Tina hated walking into.

Not today though, Tina followed me into my office, and the argument went right on. Now she's bringing up all kinds of things: the jewelry on the staircase, the cross and Bible I bought while in Spokane... that and more is coming out today. This goes on for hours. I can't remember how it ended, except to say I must have denied it over and over, till I was blue in the face; until there came a time when I said: "If you think I did it, then why be here with me?" To which she responded by saying: "I don't know why I'm here either!" Then the stalemate. I will not admit to something I didn't do.

And that's the only thing that will satisfy Tina at this point. Me admitting to having another woman in the home. A woman in the home while she was gone, which makes this situation worse. Tina finally realized that the argument wasn't going anywhere, as did I. Time to take this to the next level, that is sleeping in separate rooms. Tina chose to sleep in a different room that night. I don't think we'll be reciting prayers together for the next few days. No more anything. It's back to what we know best—the silent treatment.

I was demoralized the minute Tina stormed out of my office. There was no reaching her. No way of making her see that it was the spirit that put that earring in our bed and not me. What upset me more than anything was the fact the spirits were listening. You have to believe they're listening. It's obvious these spirits are trying to get Tina and me to argue to the point of being at each other's throats.

They keyed my car a few weeks ago with the hopes that I would restart an argument with my Tina. I could have gone off the deep end then, but I didn't. I let my ADT security logs make my decision for me. I'm glad I did.

If you want to get an idea of what a troublemaker spirit is, watch the Star Trek episode titled "Day of the Dove." That episode describes what Tina and are up against—a troublemaker spirit. *A minion.* Things are about to go dark in this house. I'm talking real dark. Keep in mind Tina, and I knew none of this in the beginning. How could we?

Chapter 22
Upside-Down Man

A few things began to happen as a result of Tina and me now sleeping in separate rooms. One of the scariest would be the stomping noises coming from the upstairs hallway. Tina was sleeping in the guest room next to my office. I was lying in our bed, listening to the pacing noise coming from outside my door. Occasionally I'd hear a door slam. Not my door. Not Tina's door. Just a door slam. I came to accept the fact that no doors were being slammed. I learned after hearing the sounds of furniture being dragged around the hallway when in fact we have no furniture in the hallway. The noises are artificial—they're conjured up in a way that scientists have yet to explain.

The same thing applied to our kitchen cabinets. Now I could see my kitchen from the Foscam app I had installed on my phone. No kitchen cabinets were being slammed, not based on what I'm seeing; there aren't. Where is that noise coming from? Bangs, thuds pings, pops, slaps, and clapping were coming from all over the house, except there's no corresponding visible manifestation. Imagine a piano dropping from a four-story building and landing right outside your window. You heard the noise. It's very distinct and obvious. You look out your window and see nothing. No broken-up piano or anything. No commotion. No assembly of startled onlookers. Not one thing supports what you just heard. That was our house, days and weeks after an argument. How Tina slept through that is beyond me.

Now, the purpose of me installing cameras was to catch something. I was trying to catch the action in real-time and failing miserably. This day, in particular, I was sitting at my desk at work, working, chatting, etc. Then it happened—my inbox begins filling up with motion and sound detection email alerts. *Uh-oh, something's going on at the house again!* Each email alert coming in has five snapshots attached to it, i.e., five JPEG pictures. I open one and see the kitchen. Everything looks fine. Why was this email sent to me? I look in the subject line, and it says motion detected. Something happened in the house that triggered the motion alert. But I can't see what it is.

From what I was looking at, everything looks to be in order. All the cabinet doors were closed. The couch and love seat were the right side up. The coffee table was the right-side up. The wine rack door was closed. But more emails are coming, more motion and sound detected notifications. Something must be going on—let me log in and see what it is. *Unable to connect.* That's the error message I'm getting; that and *your browser has timed-out, please try again.* Now I know something's going on.

As strange as it may seem the emails kept coming in. I can't log into any of my five cameras, but emails were coming in from about three of them. Since I couldn't remote in and view my house live, I decided to look at the snapshot pictures again. It's funny what you miss when you're in a hurry, or when you're multi-tasking. A closer look at one of my email attachments revealed a kitchen chair was missing. There should be six chairs at our kitchen table, and now there were only five. The first thing I thought was Tina must have done something with the missing chair. Maybe the chair was moved this morning after I left for work. Maybe Tina needed to reach something and, therefore, pulled one the chairs away from the table. Maybe that's why this chair is gone.

The quickest way to debunk that idea was to revert to the earlier pictures. And by early, I mean just a few minutes earlier. I don't know what scared me the most: an earlier picture showing just five chairs or an earlier picture showing six chairs. The picture showing six chairs was taken well after Tina, and I had left. Ladies and gentlemen, we have a chair missing from the house! Which chair is missing? The chair that I sit in when eating dinner is gone. Where's my chair?

Fig 22.1 Morning August 2014. 1.) Snapshot of the kitchen/den before house attack. 2.) Snapshot—missing kitchen chair. 3.) Six hours later email alerts begin sounding off in the office. Cameras come back online and my kitchen chasing a camera.

I wanted to call Tina so bad. I can't remember if I did. What I remember is getting up from my desk and heading to one of my work meetings. Thank God for smartphones and mobile apps. The mobile app that accompanied the motion cameras was spot on. I remember leaving my desk and while in a meeting glancing down at my phone whenever a new email alert came in. This must have gone on for the majority of the day. Now and then I would try to remote access my cameras. Each attempt brought about the connection error message. Strange how it let me reboot my cameras, but it won't let me log in to where I can see what's going on. It was almost as if it was toying with me. I later realized that there was one room the spirits didn't me looking into: my office.

The cameras started coming back online towards the end of the workday. One by one I began accessing them. Everyone except the office camera. Why is it preventing me from accessing the office camera? And that's when the notion hit me. Something was going on in my office; they were doing something they don't want me to see. I was still receiving email alerts from the kitchen. I have not gotten any emails yet from the office camera. The hallway, yes. The office, no.

I don't understand the significance of a missing chair. I can sort of understand why a "Geist" would take a Bible. I can understand objects being thrown. I can understand cabinet doors being left open. I can sort of understand a lot of things. A missing chair I can't understand. What's the significance behind that? As much as I've seen (and I've seen a lot) I'm not ready to see my chair hanging upside-down from a ceiling. I'm not ready to see it fall from the ceiling of my house the minute I walk through the door.

Let me try to log in one more time before heading out. Let me see if I can get in. I wasn't expecting to get in. I've been locked out my cameras for hours. Usually, when I'm locked out this long, I get angry. I'm frustrated. I'm frustrated because hours and hours of being locked out of one's camera system means I have to reset the cameras; I have to reconfigure them. It's very time-consuming. And even configuring them is not a guarantee that they'll work soon after. But so far, so good. The kitchen camera took my password, authenticated and, *voila*! I was in.

God save us! The kitchen chairs have all been rearranged. Three chairs had been separated from the other two to form a triangle. Keep in mind; I had an inbox full of emails showing these same chairs sitting correctly at the table, some few hours ago (See Fig 22.1). Now they're rearranged? Why are three chairs sitting in a triangular position? What does that mean? And the question remains, where is my kitchen chair? The chair that I sit in when having dinner with Tina is missing.

I spent about five minutes looking at both den and kitchen through the lens of my Foscam camera. If the kitchen camera was working again, then maybe that meant the office was working again? Let me try it. *I'll be damned... it's working.* As soon as I logged into the office, I immediately came face to face with what I was looking for. The kitchen chair had been moved alright. It had been moved to my office. Not only that. It was sitting within inches of the CCTV camera.

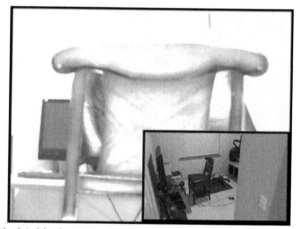

Fig. 22.2 Black/white is a snapshot from the motion cam. That's exactly what I saw when I logged in. Split chair in the background

I mean, the chair was positioned so close to the camera it literally blocked out everything else in the room. Which means I can't see anything beyond the chair. That tells me there's something they don't want me to see. Out the door I go. Time to head home.

Fig. 22.3 Late summer 2014. Pic on the left is from a motion camera. Picture on the right is from my cell phone upon arriving home.

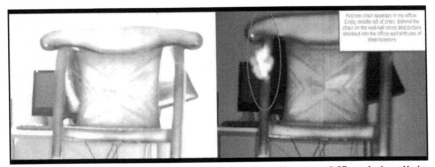

Fig. 22.4 Late summer 2014: Snapshots taken from Foscam. Office chair split in half. Wall writings a) Upside-down man b) Upside-down cross and c) 666.

They say, "The longest ride is always to the destination you're most anxious to reach." I've never been more anxious to get home in my life. My gut tells me what I'm about to see is something new. Not only new to me but new to the paranormal community. I already know that the chair I sit in when eating dinner when working from home is now sitting in my office. According to my ADT security no one has entered the house or left the house since Tina, and I left this morning. Nothing's been tripped. Zero entry whatsoever. So, no, it's not Tina.

Hour later, I came in through the front door as I always do. No pitter-patter footsteps today. I heard nothing while making my way into the house. The downstairs looked exactly how the pics showed it, exactly how it looked when I viewed it from the camera—an unholy mess. I glossed the room over quick and then ran upstairs. The first room I ran into was my office. There it was. My kitchen chair. Not just any chair. My chair. The chair I sat in when having dinner with Tina. The chair I sit in when I work from home. One of the interesting things about the chair being in my office was the direction it was facing. It was facing the television. I mean it was positioned within inches of my entertainment center. The only thing that sat between it and my TV was the CCTV camera.

Underneath my chair, I saw a familiar floor writing. There it was again: a new upside-down cross written into the carpet. It looks to be ash again, most likely sage ash. I'm thinking to myself, *that's easy to clean up, no harm done.* My sigh

143

of relief would be short-lived, super short-lived. My focus up until now had been the chair and the chair alone. I completely forgot about surveying the entire room when I walked in. Now I step in from the doorway and look closer. And there it was: a new wall writing. Wait a minute; it's not writing it's a symbol. Above my computer monitor was a stick symbol. A stick symbol of a man upside down. It wasn't drawn with sage ash like the 666 and the upside-down crosses had been. This was different. This was a paint-like substance. I'm thinking to myself; *I'm going to have to get a professional painter to paint over this.*

As I pan right, I begin to see that nearly every wall has some writing on it. Even the closet door has writings on it. The 666-wall marking has been written on the closet and office doors. But hold up, let's look closer one more time. I now see that something else has been added to the wall—something I over-looked when I first looked in. A small photograph of me. That's right, a picture of me was stuck to the wall, one of my old wallet size J.C. Penny portraits. It was stabbed into the wall with my scissors. The sharp end of the scissors goes through my torso (picture) and into the wall. *The scissors I use each morning when I shave.* The last time I saw those scissors they were in the bathroom. They've now been used as a nail to hold my picture up. What sort of power are we dealing with here?

I had seen enough for now. It was time to survey the other rooms. Time to see what condition our bedroom was in. It was a mess. Time to see how the guest bedroom was—the one with the armoire in it. Another mess. The armoire was face down again. It had been thrown, who knows, several feet.

I was looking at this and thinking: it took myself and two other guys to move that armoire upstairs. The condition it's in now won't require three men to move it downstairs. It's so beat up now, barely holding together as it is, I'm going to be able to move it downstairs by myself—in pieces.

Just then I heard a noise out of my left ear—Tina must have just come home. Time to make up again. Time to squash whatever it is we were arguing about. Time to come together. Time to call the priest again. Tina did.

That night we ate dinner together, and Tina told me how she'd been reaching out to the priest just about every day. She'd left voicemails and emails. The secretary on the other end calmly said the priest will call her back as soon as possible. So far, he hasn't. The priest, if you recall, wanted to be kept up to date on the house activity. And we now have plenty more to tell him. The upside-down man was a new development. That's never happened before. My face stuck into a wall with a pair of scissors, that's never happened before. The wooden statue of the Virgin Mary (a gift from the priest) had been thrown across the bedroom.

These events seem to be acts of defiance. They seem to suggest anger and mockery of our religious belief. One question we wanted to ask the priest that night was: do we intensify what we're doing, or do we ease off it? We'd feel more at ease if you were here when we intensified some of these removal activities. Tina had that concern, as did I. What does the upside-down man stick figure mean? Why was my kitchen chair taken upstairs and not Tina's? Why is my wall the only wall in the house suffering from wall writings? Why was the scissor stabbed through a picture of me? Should I be worried?

Every night before I went to bed I made a point of reciting the Lord's Prayer. That and Psalm 23:4 *'even though I walk through the darkest valley, I will fear no evil, for you are with me; your rod and your staff, they comfort me.'* It's the last prayer I say before going to sleep. Do I believe it? I most certainly do. Am I terrified? You're damn right I'm terrified. But I'm also comforted. I'm comforted by the fact that we're still here. I'm comforted by the fact that we didn't turn tail and run.

Why do two people need a 2,300-square foot, four-bedroom house? We got this house because we wanted to invite our family members over. We wanted to invite our friends over. We wanted to be host and hostess to those we love. I'm pretty sure the spirits living here know that. *They seem to know everything else.*

That picture the spirit destroyed by stabbing it with a pair of scissors was eight years old. It was tucked away in one of my boxes. How did they find it? It's not like it was sitting out in the open. It's too small to frame. When did it find it? Most of all why did it find it? These are the questions I had for the local priest. If he would only return our voicemails, maybe, just maybe, I'll get some answers.

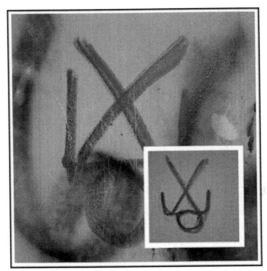

Fig 22.5 Aug – October 2014. Multiple upside-down
wall writings. Keith Linder's office

Chapter 23
Plan B

Tina was waiting for the local priest to respond. I was waiting for whoever I've emailed or called to respond. But the spirit behind all of these horrors is waiting for no one. It was full steam ahead where it was concerned. *Let's crank this thing up some more.* Time to increase my search radius. Who else out there might be able to help us?

Mid-August, 2014. An accumulation of emails began filling up my inbox while I was at work one morning. Emails saying: sound and motion detected. This time the emails were coming from every room that had a camera in it. I mean, my dashboard was lighting up. That's how fast they were coming in. As always, the photos coming from the CCTV cameras at first show nothing out of the ordinary. The house appears to be baselined. I thought. *Let me see if I can remote in and view one of these rooms, any room that'll let me in.* I couldn't. Not one single room. 'Connection error.' Connection error could mean a lot of things. It could mean power has been cut to that camera. It could mean power has been cut to that room or cut to the house entirely. It could also mean that that camera is now gone; they've taken it or destroyed it. It could also mean the camera is rebooting, which means it's going to be pointing upwards towards the ceiling when its reboot is complete.

Now, our power company has made repeated visits to our house. They've yet to find a reason for the abrupt power loss. Comcast has made repeated visits to our house, and they have yet to find any reason for the strange disruption of our cable, phone and internet service. Both companies have replaced parts, have replaced wires, and have swapped out stuff they've already replaced. Everyone leaves scratching their head. I can't explain it. Tina can't explain it. The electrician can't explain it, and the landlord can't explain it. It makes no sense. These people who inspect and service our house are professionals. We're talking about certified electricians. Certified cable installers and more. They would not be doing their job well or doing it long if they were somehow incompetent. None of them can explain the intermittent service or power loss. I've invited several independent contractors to our home with the hope of finding the source. None can. Who pays for their time? I do.

Meanwhile, every camera in the house was sending me emails. Each one with a time stamp of December 31st, 1969. That's nuts, right? I didn't dart out of the door as I had done before. I'd learned from that mistake: leaving work early doesn't stop the activity. But the emails were still coming in, and they'd been coming in for a while. So much that so I decided to call Tina. She needed to know what's happening. I told her that the house is active again. I've gotten over two hundred motion, and sound detected emails. Every room is saying the same thing: motion detected, sound detected. Her reply was: "I just called the priest and left another voicemail." We both sighed on the phone together. The last thing I told her before hanging up the phone was: if you get home before me, don't go inside. Wait in the car.

That would become our new protocol. Sometimes traffic on Tina's side of town was better than mine. Sometimes she got home before I did. She would wait for me to arrive before she ever entered the house, especially on a day like today.

It's almost moviesque to see me arrive in my neighborhood on a day like today. The only two people who know what's happening inside my house right now are Tina and me. My friends don't even know. My mom doesn't even know. Tina's family doesn't even know. We haven't had time to tell them. My inbox was still filling up with emails as I'm turning the corner into my neighborhood. Kids were riding their bicycles. Some were playing hop-scotch on the sidewalk. I looked out my left car window and saw a woman walking her dog. I looked out my right car window and saw a man jogging up and down the street. Neighbors are watering their lawns. My neighbor across the street—the one who introduced himself to me two years ago—was working on one of his antique motorcycles. He sees me coming up the street and waves. No one knows my cell phone is vibrating like crazy in my pocket. Why is it vibrating? It's vibrating because our house is a house from hell. It's vibrating because of the three hundred or so emails coming in. Emails that indicate something is going on inside.

I finally pull up to my house. There she sits—our house. It looks peaceful and quiet from the outside. My office window faces the street. I was looking dead at it as I pull up. Lucky for me there was no plume of smoke coming from it. Lucky for me there was no fire department or EMT here. Lucky for me there's no armoire sitting in the middle of the street. I have to go inside now. I have to see what the hoopla is about. They've done something. That much I know. Something new has happened. Something they want me and Tina to see.

It's like coming home to an adolescent dog. You know they've torn your house up. You just don't know how bad. That's what I think as I walk in the front door.

What the hell? The downstairs looked fine. It was exactly how we left it. The couch and love seat were not sitting upside down. My wine rack was still closed. None of my wine bottles had been teleported elsewhere. Good news? I don't think so. This means they've really done something. Let me run upstairs and see. The first room I passed by was the guest bedroom. The giant armoire had been knocked over again. The camera in that room is gone. The hallway and landing area are a mess. I've got to tell Tina that we need to start wearing steel-toe boots when we come home; that's how much destruction was in the hallway. The glass dome that covered the hallway light was shattered again. We're talking about shards and shards of obliterated glass on the hallway floor. Everything that sat on the hallway bookshelf now rested on the floor.

One camera was broken. Another one was missing. Now, allow me to describe to you how an entity breaks a camera. They don't break it in the way you and I would break a camera—which would probably be in a few pieces. No, they break a camera into a hundred pieces. Parts I didn't even know existed on a camera are broken into almost powder form. I'll never be able to prove it, but I bet those cameras exploded. That's how broken up they cameras are. But I can't focus on the cameras too long because there's also paper everywhere. I mean confetti

147

everywhere. That's what Tina's Bible has been turned into. It's been shredded into confetti. This was the Bible that Tina asked to be placed on the bookshelf.

Next thing I'm wondering is: why is the bulk of the confetti coming from my office? Between the confetti and the door are our sage tray and sage stick. The sage stick is broken in half. More glass on the floor implies another light fixture had exploded; and turns out one had, the one inside my office. Wires are dangling from the ceiling. Our bedroom double door was yanked off the hinges again! *Let's go into our bedroom.*

The chest of drawers had been knocked over. Everything that had been on it was now on the floor. The wooden statue of the Virgin Mary was on the floor again. Tina's candles were on the floor. Some broken into pieces. All of Tina's artificial plants were on the floor. My lampstand was a mess. Our bedroom clock was now lying on the floor. Tina's lamp was leaning on the floor. It had been severely damaged. The wooden entertainment center that our TV rested on was had fallen to the floor. TV and the components thereof were all lying on the floor. Cable wire, component wire, speaker wire all looking like a bowl of spaghetti had exploded.

The drawers within the entertainment stand had all been yanked out. Everything inside it was on the floor. The closet was untouched. The bathroom was untouched.

I saw a shadow dart my shoulder. I turned around, and there was Tina. I didn't even hear her come in. That's how immersed I was in the destruction. She was taking it all in. So was I. We haven't seen this type of destruction since the Katie Perry weekend. Tina's mouth dropped open upon seeing the condition of her Bible. A Bible sitting on a bookshelf is not going to remove these things. Only our love, unity, and commitment will do that. If we had put a phone book up there, it would have had the same reaction. Her Bible, my Bible makes no difference to the spirits. It's all a joke to them. I looked at Tina, and she looked at me. It was time we went into my office. Something told me that's where the major hell was. Something told me that's where my knees might buckle. I said to myself: *let's get this over with it. Let's see what they've done to my office.*

I wished my office had new wall markings, as opposed to what Tina and I saw when we walked in. There stabbed into the wall again were new pictures of me. Pictures of me with my family. Pictures of me with my mom, my dad, my brother, and my sister. On the computer desk were more pictures of me. Laid out so that they were impossible to miss. About seven pictures in all. Each picture included a family member. Sister's college graduation. Brother's graduation. Vacation pictures, some group family pictures. My face had been burned out of everyone. I heard Tina gasp and "oh my God." None of the pictures felt warm or hot. How they did this is beyond me. The surface or wall beneath them was not burned or scorched. Yet the heat must have been significant enough, because the pictures were curved, almost shriveled up, rather than flat. The burn marks appeared localized. A level of focus and intent. There was no trace of my face. Let me be clear. You could get a black Sharpie and go to town blotting out my face on a picture of me; but when you were done, there'd still have been more of my face left than what these pictures had. My face was gone. No other family member was touched. Not so much as a blemish on my family members' faces.

Where did they get all of these photos from? They were packed in boxes that were packed in other boxes. Some of the pictures I haven't seen in years. We're talking about fifteen-year-old photos.

Today's activity took place days after the upside-down man marking. It makes no sense painting over that till after a priest or paranormal team has come in to investigate. We've now had multiple instances taking place since the priest was last here. No returned phone call whatsoever. I was forced to ask myself the question: does the Catholic Church want to know about this stuff? Do they care? I'm not trying to make this personal, but do they care? Does the local priest care about what's happening? I mean, Tina's calling the local parish every day. She's leaving voicemails. She made a few surprise visits. Nothing happens. I've sent over a few pictures and still: nothing happens. If there ever was a doubt about me being pushed down the stairs, that doubt was now gone. These pictures of me with my face burned out made me believe one hundred percent that my fall back in January was not an accident. The spirits were sending a message, and that message was loud and clear: 'we're narrowing our focus. We've decided to make you our project. Those notes you taped on your wall, those condemnations are what sealed the deal.' That's the vibe I got while standing in that office.

The Foscam in the bedroom was now missing. Tina's iPad was now missing. I lost five cameras that day. That's not counting the ones that were destroyed. My mind immediately snapped out of disbelief upon witnessing what Tina did next. She picked up all my scorched-out photos, picked up the cross I bought from Spokane, and headed downstairs. I heard the ADT say *garage door open*. It says *garage door open* again a few seconds later. She came back into the office and looked at me, tears in her eyes. I didn't even have to ask what she did. I knew what she did. Tina had just made her own executive decision of destroying the photos and removing the cross. I could understand her knee-jerk reaction to the photos. Someone's face burnt out of a photo conjures negative connotations— some unimaginable. Here we have an upside-down man stick figure, and every picture of me in this house burned. That can't be good. So, I get why Tina did that.

She did that to protect me. That was her way of saying: I love this guy, he pisses me off, I think he's cheating on me, but damn, I still love him. If anyone's going to cut off his balls, it's me. That's the Tina I love and respect. That level of spiritual defiance. Now if she would only pray with me at night. And by pray, I mean lead some of it. That might help us. I'm not going to lie: I was upset when she took the cross, and not because of it being a cross. I was upset because of why I thought she took it. Tina never admitted to me openly, but I knew from her countless accusations that she thought another woman had given me that cross. Which is not true. I could have gone downstairs and gotten it out of the trash receptacle. Yeah, I could have done that. Only the moment didn't call for that. The moment called for unity. We could go out and buy a hundred crosses. They're not going to solve our problem. This was spiritual warfare, not retail warfare. Which brings us back to what I talked about before. My cameras.

Losing this many cameras all at once was a big loss. I mean, it's demoralizing to see something you've invested time and effort in just utterly vanish. Of course, I'm going to go out buy some more. I have to do that, right? I mean, that's what my brother says I must do. That's what certain clergy are telling me to do. That's what some paranormal teams are telling me to do. No one wants to believe the activity being reported by Tina and I are real until they can see it for themselves. Everyone, even a few that helped us, are reluctant to go on record and say, "Yeah, Bibles did burn on their own. Objects did get thrown. Plants did fly. Cabinet doors opened on their own, and 666 was written several times." People seemed to be more in fear of what their so-called colleagues think about them than in providing good help. Which is sort of a contradiction? I mean, it begs the question. How can you say you want to help someone and at the same time worry about the opinion of others? If you're going to help someone, help them. There's no such thing as halfway help. Either help all the way or don't help at all.

That trend was beginning to emerge with the local priest, as well as with local teams in the area. And eventually paranormal teams abroad. I do not doubt the local priest's involvement with similar cases. I mean he told us stories about events taking place in and around Puget Sound. The Seattle parish referred us to him; they said he was "our guy." His testimony about the people he's helped solidifies that belief. He is our guy. If that's the case, then why are we having such a hard time getting a hold of him? I've probably sent him more pictures than all the people he's ever helped combined, and Tina still can't contact him on his office phone. If you sit across from Tina and me and tell us point blank you believe us, I have to believe that you do. Thank you for believing us. Thank you for not viewing us as attention seekers, as fakers, as hoaxers. But I soon learned that it doesn't stop there. The local priest might be onboard with our claims, but is the Church? Does the Church believe it? If they don't, why not? That revelation was about to emerge in the coming days as Tina and I attempted to deal with this thing. She would be as shocked as I was.

The chair relocation was something new. It becomes an everyday thing after it's happened once. What you have to understand about this is just how strange it was—the actual process of putting it up there. There's no way to explain it, except to say it suggests some form of apporting. You see, on my wall in the living room at the bottom of my stairway is the ADT dashboard. Above that dashboard is a sensor. That sensor was put there purposely by an ADT technician when they visited my home. It was positioned in this precise area to detect intruders coming through both front doors, garage door and den living room window. The reason for the sensor being there versus anywhere else downstairs was to catch a burglar before they hit the staircase. An intruder has an insurmountable number of beams to bypass if they want to evade detection. One of the hardest beams to evade is the one that's pointing directly at the staircase. Which begs the question: how did the spirit get my kitchen chair upstairs without setting off my ADT security system? The sensors are set to pick up anything bigger than a cat. I'm sure you will agree our kitchen chairs are way bigger than a cat.

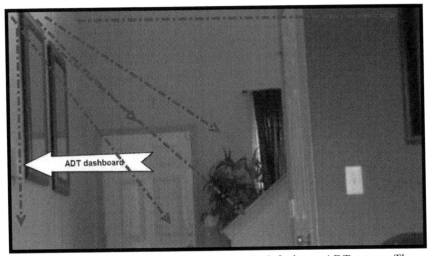

Fig. 23.1 A few inches above the mirror on the left sits an ADT sensor. The bottom staircase is one area of its concentration. How did a chair get past it without setting off the ADT security system? It's powered by the phone system.

Tina and I would come home and find my kitchen chair in my office for the next couple of weeks. It would happen at least three to four times a week—all the way to the end of October. Not once did the ADT alarm go off. Not once was another chair ever chosen. Always my chair. Always my office. If you don't believe that they're beginning to pick on me and pick on me alone, then read what I'm about to say next. Something more troubling than my kitchen chair being found in my office.

Given that this next thing involved us back in bed together, allow me to catch you up briefly on the domestic situation at this time. Tina and I had still been arguing off and on about the earring being found in the bed. She held strongly to the idea of a woman being in the house while she'd been gone. No matter how many times I offered up suggestions to the contrary, she still held to her belief. So, the question you might be asking yourself right now is: why is she still with me? The simple answer is love. Tina is a strong woman. You have to be a strong woman to put up with what we are experiencing. But what about the infidelity? I have to believe that, deep down somewhere, Tina doesn't really believe I've been unfaithful to her. She was in turmoil right now, we both were. I have to believe a percentage of Tina believes I'm telling the truth. I mean rings appearing convenient places, seems a little bit contrived. Contrived as it may be, the pain is still real. No one including me wants to find a stranger's belongings in one of the most sacred rooms in the house—the master bedroom. That's what I mean by turmoil.

Tina and I both love each other. Whether we make it or not, one thing is for certain. We will both know what we're made out of at the end of this. So, was the jewelry thing resolved? Heck, no. I would use the word "fermenting." That's exactly where we stood right now. The office attacks took precedence over our disagreements. I was still doing a majority of the prayers, a majority of the chants, and a majority of the smudging. Did it create tension between us, me doing a majority of the stuff the priest asked us to do? Sometimes it did. Sometimes it didn't. Tonight, it didn't, because here we were lying in bed together—watching TV.

I remember lying on my back, with my book in hand when all of a sudden, I felt something poke me. To be exact: something jabbed me in the back. Whatever jabbed me, hit me right below my rib cage, right in my kidney area. It was a strong poke. I can account for Tina's whereabouts, and in particular her arms and hands. I then think to myself: *did something just poke me?* I must have laid there frozen for a few seconds. Just when I was about to shrug it off as probably being my imagination, or something being loose from within our mattress, I got poked again. This time the poke was more noticeable.

I thought to myself: *do I tell Tina? Or do I keep this to myself?* I reluctantly kept it to myself. I hope this was a fluke. I mean, the jab felt like a finger was coming through the mattress. That's how distinct it was. I looked towards Tina again to see if she could sense my anxiety. She couldn't. She just sat there watching TV. I continued talking to Tina up until the time we went to sleep. Nothing else happened that night. We both slept fine. The next day we woke up and went to work. And we completed the week without a new incident taking place.

Then came Saturday. I was lying in bed; my back turned to the bedroom door. I could hear the TV on downstairs, and some occasional rummaging through the kitchen, which I assumed was Tina. *Please cook pancakes and bacon, Tina, that's what I'm saying while attempting to fall back to sleep.* I'll be up the minute. *I must.* I smell pancakes and bacon. I'm close to drifting back off, when suddenly I feel an indentation in the bed. The last time I felt an indentation like this I was recovering from knee surgery.

Something had just jumped in the bed with me. It wasn't long before I began feeling another one, and another one, and another one. The indentation I'm describing, ladies and gentlemen, reminded me of a cat or dog jumping in bed with you. That's how it feels. Which would be OK if Tina and I were pet owners, we're not. This indentation would also be OK if it were, in fact, Tina coming back to bed. Nor was it her. The indentation felt just like something jumping on the bed and making its way towards me. How do I know that? I know that because of the series of smaller indentations, smaller vibrations coming right after it. The indentations didn't stop. Something was making its way towards me. Any pet owners reading this must know the feeling I'm describing. Especially cat owners. I say cat because the thing heading towards me is very slow. It appears stealthy. Whatever was making its way towards me seemed to have calculated (through observation) that I was about to doze off. No way was that going to happen. Not this time anyway. By the time I noticed the third or fourth indentation I spun around. I was hoping I'd find Tina trying to play a trick on me. I knew that would not be the case. When I turned around (and mind you I turned around quickly), I found nothing. The feeling within the mattress was gone. There I was sitting up in my bed, thinking to myself: what just happened? What's going on? Tina's downstairs cooking and I'm upstairs experiencing some weird stuff. Time to get up.

Chapter 24
The Previous Tenant

I mentioned to you a few chapters back that I had finally come face to face (via Facebook) with one of the previous tenants. I had asked her if she and her family had experienced anything unusual in the house. Her response was a cryptic yes, followed by three wink smiley faces. 😉 😉 😉 I asked if she could go into detail and her response she needed time to "get her thoughts together."

I guess today was the day she got her thoughts together because an early morning of October, 2014 I got an email from her. She told me that the house (I'm now living in) was a "living hell." She said her families had been awakened to loud bangs, footsteps, and pacing noises. They'd experienced the kitchen cabinet door phenomenon. To hear her say the house was a "living hell" sent chills down my spine. I mean, that's how it's been so far with us. A pure living hell. The Bothell Hell House, ladies and gentlemen. There's no better way to describe what goes on here.

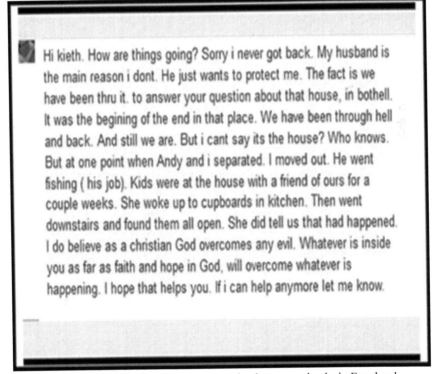

Fig 24.1 Previous tenant contacts me back as promised via Facebook

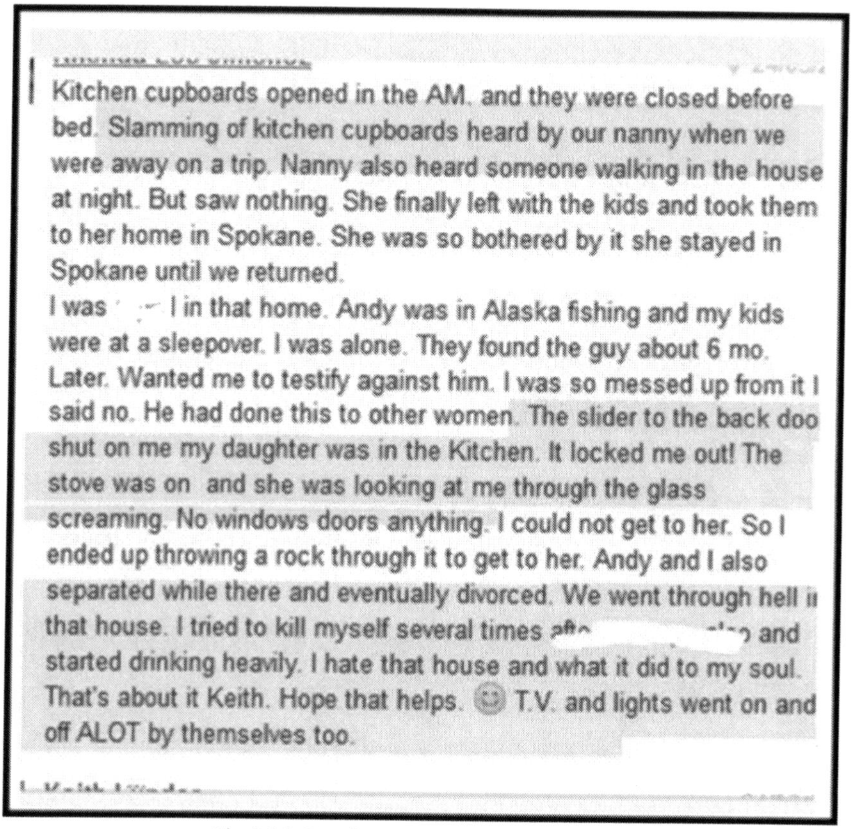

> Kitchen cupboards opened in the AM. and they were closed before bed. Slamming of kitchen cupboards heard by our nanny when we were away on a trip. Nanny also heard someone walking in the house at night. But saw nothing. She finally left with the kids and took them to her home in Spokane. She was so bothered by it she stayed in Spokane until we returned.
> I was ⸺ I in that home. Andy was in Alaska fishing and my kids were at a sleepover. I was alone. They found the guy about 6 mo. Later. Wanted me to testify against him. I was so messed up from it I said no. He had done this to other women. The slider to the back doo shut on me my daughter was in the Kitchen. It locked me out! The stove was on and she was looking at me through the glass screaming. No windows doors anything. I could not get to her. So I ended up throwing a rock through it to get to her. Andy and I also separated while there and eventually divorced. We went through hell in that house. I tried to kill myself several times ⸺ ⸺ and started drinking heavily. I hate that house and what it did to my soul. That's about it Keith. Hope that helps. ☺ T.V. and lights went on and off ALOT by themselves too.

Fig 24.2 Previous tenant Facebook chat.

Jane Doe (withholding her real name) said her husband was reluctant for her to contact me. Evidently, the two had a lengthy conversation about the need to contact me. He was against it, out of obligation, she was for it. In her mind, it was the Christian thing to do. Her son at the time of them living in the home spoke of seeing shadows. He still sees them to this day, she said. The first time her son began seeing shadows was when he had meningitis. The physicians tending to him told her it was "a rare form of meningitis, the kind they rarely see." I'm not sure what that means, but it sounds serious. Jane Doe said her son almost died. That's how sick he was. I knew about his illness already, from reading her Facebook posts during the period she lived in the house. I won't go deeper into his illness, except to say he was at death's door a few times (while living in the house). Other things they experienced while in the home included power fluctuations. Off and on light and TV incidents.

The thing that startled me the most was the level of activity they faced compared to Tina and me. You're talking about a family of five (live in nanny), therefore, every room had to have been occupied. More people should have meant more activity. *So, I thought?* It was only after she confessed to me what their heightened activity had consisted of, that I felt comfortable telling her what we were going through. She was shocked.

Jane Doe said they've had never experienced fires. They'd never experienced objects being thrown or objects moving. They'd never seen wall writings. No 666, no cryptic messages of whatsoever. Thank God!

Then came the second shock. She and her husband had just gotten back together. That threw me. Timing be it as it may, this revelation meant more to me than the activities she'd described. It was like she had just foreshadowed my and Tina's relationship. Jane Doe and her family had been out of the house for some years. It must have been hell living here if the two have "just reconciled." When Jane Doe uttered the words "a living hell" it was almost like she was saying the house was alive. It was like she was blaming the house for breaking up their marriage. I asked Jane Doe to define the words "living hell" Her reply, "When we moved into that house, that's when things started going south."

The US economy had tanked significantly during the time they were living there. Her own home business had tanked. Her son's illness manifested and got worse. Her husband worked out of state as an Alaskan fisherman. It doesn't take a rocket scientist to see how a home stricken with both financial difficulty, a father's absence, and the ill-health of a son could put a family in turmoil, mentally and emotionally. This creates unimaginable amounts of stress, uncertainty, angst, and anger. Sound familiar? She and I were chatting via Facebook. I had to respond with a question or two. The main one being: what else do you remember about the house? What other weird stuff? Her reply was, "A lot of weird stuff happened." Some she can't quite remember, other things she purposely tried to forget. The more she tells me, the more my mouth drops open.

I shared a story with you at the beginning of this book: those instances where I was inexplicably locked out of the house. Jane Doe told me she experienced that a few times. One, in particular, was a horrific story. Bear in mind—she was telling me this without knowing I had already experienced something similar. One day Jane was outside smoking on the patio. She had put baby formula or something on the stove. Her infant was in the house while the pan was heating. When it came time for her to re-enter the house, the sliding door was locked. The same door which had locked on me during the housewarming party. Any mother reading this knows the level of panic that's about to erupt. Jane's baby was locked in the house, with a pan on the range, ready to catch fire. She had to break sliding door (by shattering the glass) to get back into the house. That's a textbook description of what malevolent spirits do. But what kind of malevolent spirit? Demon? Poltergeist? Both?

Jane Doe's revelation was huge. She described their time in the house as "hellish." Their level of activity meant neither Tina nor I had brought this thing with us when we moved into the house. Who knows? The kid 'cough' we heard on that first day could have been a demon mimicking her son. Maybe some sort of residual type phenomenon where events are played back. If you ask me if Tina and I had ever thought that we were the ones responsible for the activity taking place, my answer would be no. We must have answered tons of questionnaires given to us by paranormal teams. "Did we ever play with a Ouija board?" That answer was no. I shared what Jane Doe told me with Jennifer of No Bull

Paranormal. She's was blown away by the news. I called the local priest to let him know and got nowhere.

There was a lot to decipher here. A lot to unpack. Tina had the same reaction as Jennifer—interesting, especially the son's illness. Kitchen cabinets were opening by themselves when they lived here. Combine that with the door slams and the loud banging. It's safe to say this activity started way before Tina and me. I'm not so sure we can even call it a poltergeist anymore, based on my current understanding of the term. Poltergeists are described as being "noisy ghosts." They usually surface around adolescent children—especially young teenage girls. That's the twentieth-century understanding of them. As for cause? Nothing I've learned or mentioned suggests that's what's taken place here. This is a new type of poltergeists. Poltergeist gone rogue as to not resembling what's currently written about Poltergeist. Poltergeist 2.0?

I'm not able to share everything that Jane Doe told me. Not even with me using Jane Doe as a placeholder for her real name. But I'll say this. I couldn't even imagine what Tina and I would do under similar circumstances. Had Tina and I had children I know for a fact we'd be gone already. My heart can't even entertain the thought that a child of mine would develop an illness doctors to this day are still scratching their heads on. Treatment after treatment—nothing working. Imagine having a son or daughter walk up to you and tell you they see shadows out the corner of their eye. Not only in this house, but in Yakima where they now live. It's important you understand that Jane Doe's family lived in the house years before Tina and me. Several families have lived here since then. I've not found them yet. How many years exist between Jane Doe and Tina and me? According to the landlord, six years.

The thing that stuck in my head the most was the "living hell." My brain keeps coming back to that. Jane Doe said the house was "a living hell" for her family. Everything seemed to go wrong within weeks of living in the house. Then it hit me, Rollo Tomasi? Remember him? He's the reason for Ed Exley becoming a cop in the movie *LA Confidential.* Ed describes him as the man who always gets away with crimes—the unknown assailant. Understand what Ed is saying when he says the reason for him becoming a cop is because of an unknown assailant he's coined, Rollo Tomasi. Rollo Tomasi never appears in the movie—we never get to see him. Whatever devious work Tomasi did in the past end up leaving a lasting impression on Ed Exley. That's exactly what a poltergeist is; it's an unknown assailant that lives in a home—creating havoc whenever possible.

After chatting with Jane Doe several times via Facebook, we felt it was time to migrate to the phone. I mean, you can't help but bond with someone who's been through what you've been through, right? I'm talking to somebody who once lived in my house. I'm talking to somebody who's experienced some of what we've experienced. Pardon me for saying this but that's got to be the best collaborative evidence in paranormal history. Combining what they've been through with what we'd been through sort of re-ignited my reason for staying. Look at everything that's happened. This demon is a home wrecker. Look what happened to Jane Doe's family. Look what's happening to Tina and me. If we leave this house, only one thing is certain: someone else will move in. Our leaving doesn't solve the problem. Jane Doe's testimony is proof of that.

Trust me, I understand those who say "why be there? Why deal with it?" It's a question I ask myself every day. Matter of fact several times a day. Our friends asked us the same question. The answer varies depending on what day of the week it is. I can't even count the number of times I've asked myself the question: why stay here? *This is not your problem. It's not even your house. Just walk away.* If Tina and I leave now, the only thing the landlord is going to do is put the house back up for rent. Putting the house up for rent means another family will move in. The odds are that family will have children is extremely high. Possibly newborns.

This was not my attempt at being a hero. Nor was it Tina's. Far from it. Tina's here because she loves me. She's standing by the man she loves. Most girlfriends would be gone by now. Not, Tina, it didn't take much convincing for Tina to stay. The decision to stay is constantly being reevaluated. It has to, look at everything that's happened so far. What people fail to realize is the decision to stay was much harder than the decision to leave. Leaving is easy. To leave just requires an email to the landlord. Bad rental history or no bad rental history Tina and I are gone. Of course, he's going to ask why. You signed a lease agreement. A renewal in fact. What gives? Fair questions to which I reply, your house is haunted, dude. And I mean extremely haunted. The easiest decision to make felt like the wrong decision to execute. I decided before. I decided again. I'm staying.

Do I have regrets about staying? Of course, I do. I wish to God I'd never found this house. But you see, that's the irony of it. Two years ago, I was thanking God for blessing me with this house. Tina and I sat on the living room floor, surveying the house as we held hands. The house was a dream come true. Here I am, a successful manager working for one of the largest healthcare companies in the world. This Texas native decided to move to a part of the country where his family had never been. I found the house of my dreams, or so I thought.

This house must become livable. The spirits creating havoc have to be evicted. Not Tina and me, not future occupants. Who's going to help us? Is it Jennifer? Is it the priest? Is it someone I don't know yet? All I know right now is that I can't leave the house the way I found it. I can't let someone else come in, totally unaware of what's happened. Do I want to leave? Of course, I want to leave. Should I leave? Probably? Why stay then?

Hopefully, I'll be able to give you a definite answer by the end of this book. Take this answer for now—the entities have plagued and hurt a lot of people. They're responsible for a lot of things. They turned Jane Doe's home into a living hell. They're attempting to do the same to Tina and me. I have to believe the activity would not evaporate based on us leaving. I have to believe we might be followed as a result of leaving. I have to believe another family moving in would experience something similar or worse. I have to believe it's most likely going to be family that moves in here after Tina and me.

The priest ended up arriving at our house a few days after my chat with Jane Doe. A lot has happened since the last time he was here. My kitchen chair being found in the office, 666 wall writings, upside-down man wall writings, the trashing of religious objects, some of which he gave us. Today's visit consisted of blessing the house. *Again!* My question to the priest now was: what are the next steps? What happens if the spirits don't want to leave? The priest would have to

157

take these developments back to the church. Back to his bishop, though once again he never asked for the burned picture of me with my family. He never acknowledged Jane Doe's testimony. His assistant never took photos of the house damage. Not one. Tina and I would go to bed that night asking ourselves the question: what just happened? What got accomplished? One thing Tina did do that I was sort of proud of was: she admonished him on his communication skills.

As appreciative as we were for them being here, we had to come clean and express our displeasure about their delay. Some of the most horrendous attacks happened a few weeks ago. Unreturned phone calls and unreturned emails, lead us to assume we were not being taken seriously. If you're not returning our calls, if you're not collecting evidence, you must not want to help us. I think we're within our rights to feel this way. Keep in mind that the doubt, the angst, and the uncertainty we're left with becomes food for the spirits living here. Tina's pointed question to the priest that night was: "can we depend on you? Can we rely on you?" Tina was honest, as was I. We don't feel the church was giving this case the attention it deserves. And we couldn't figure out why.

The priest apologized and turned toward his assistant. They both nodded and agreed: they would do a better job in responding to us in future. The church would do a better job. The last guidance question I had, and I was very frank when I asked it, was: do you think we should leave? Should Tina and I move out? If you believe that, then tell us. Tina and I are not religious people. We don't go to church regularly. I was baptized at an early age, as was Tina. I believe in God. As does Tina. We've based our lives and our success on following to the best of our ability God's principles. So, if you tell me we need to be in church every day to beat this thing, then that's what we'll do. Tell us what to do, and we'll do it. The priest then said, "Moving from this house is not required." He admired Tina and me for staying, for remaining steadfast. We all agreed that God is more powerful than the demons that live here. If we're all in agreement about how light defeats darkness, then let's pray together, let's understand the task at hand and defeat this thing. Let's conclude tonight with a big hug. After dessert, we all rose from the table, shook hands, and kissed each other. It turned out to be an emotional night.

Tina and I wanted our hearts to be heard. Forget about the events taking place. Ignore the fact the spirits were listening to us at this very moment. Forget the notion that things were about to get unbelievably worse. Let me be clear about this now. Our house is not a fun-fair. If you say you can help, you need to do that.

One of the things I learned while living here is: almost everyone who's come through our door screaming the words "we're here to help" was way in over their head. Talk about being incompetent. I'm speaking about the teams who came in 2014. Most just came for a look. Tina and I both have found ourselves dumbfounded on a few occasions watching individuals walk into our home and not have a clue as to what they're supposed to be doing. So please, if you are able to truly help someone, understand that your cavalier response, cavalier attitude can in fact be fuel for the spirit. Same thing for bad communication and poor record keeping. You're doing more harm than good. Tina and I never saw the local priest again after that day.

The precursor for the activity returning was something relatively subtle. If you don't have a keen eye or a keen sense of self, you're guaranteed to miss it.

My curse is I don't miss anything. I remember one night I was in my office, surfing the internet. Behind my dual monitors is a wall. The wall with the 666 writings on it. I began hearing taps, almost like Morse code, coming from behind the wall. Occasionally I'd hear thuds, pops, pings, snaps, and crackling. If I had to guess, I would say the entity was maybe a foot or so from me. The room would turn from light to heavy. A feeling of being watched would set in. Then, out of nowhere, a loud bang. Or worse than that, an object would get hurled down the hall. A force so powerful it gets lodged in the wall.

Tina and I call this subtle activity... a level one compared to what happens next. Somewhere in this horror of a tale lurks a theory that maybe, just maybe, spirits are required to adhere to a code of warning before seriously alarming you. Had no warning come most people, myself included, probably would just keel over and die. That's one way to look at it. Do these precursors, these subtle wonders, somehow telegraph what's about to happen next? Another question Tina and I raised amongst ourselves: it seems that daytime activity purposely differs from night-time activity. And night-time activity (while we're home watching TV) differs from bedtime activity (i.e., in bed before sleeping). The patterns are as follows.

Activity Type	Phenomenon
Day Time Activity (Home or Not at Home)	Bible catching fire, Wall writings, Objects thrown, Loud bangs, Footsteps pacing back and forth, Wall snaps, Cabinet door open, Objects appearing, Objects disappearing, Fires, sound of furniture being dragged
Nighttime Activity (events happening prior to us going to sleep).	Door slams, Lights going off and on, TV turning off and on by itself, floating rugs, throwing rugs, Smaller objects thrown, pacing back and forth, Lights being switched off manually, Loud bangs.
Bedtime Activity (events happening before and during sleep. We're in bed now.	Bible catching fire, Door slams, ceiling fan noise, pacing back and forth, smaller objects thrown, shadowy figures, Fires, Poking and prodding, sheets yanked off bed. Shredded sheets. Flying carpets.
Morning Activity (Week Day)	Objects missing: toothbrush, toothpaste, razor. Moving plants, lights going off and on. Fires, Clock malfunction, car malfunction
Morning Activity (Weekend)	Objects appearing, Objects thrown, TV turning off and on. Loud bangs, door slams, pacing back and forth.

159

Table 24.1 Activity Chart (previous page)

Which activity type would you like to experience? Which one did *Ghost Adventures* try to take advantage of? If you're familiar with the show, you know that answer right off the top of your head. *Ghost Adventures*, when at our house, opted to conduct what they call "The Lock Down" investigation after midnight. *Suggestion: If you're going to conduct a majority of your investigation at night, then you should put a camera in each room and climb into bed. Go to sleep, why don't you.* The activity at night, i.e., bedtime activity is, for lack of a better word, more intimate, more personal than the day-time and night-time activity. Everything in the day-time column happened while Tina and me where at work— most of it did. That's the column critics and skeptics cling to. I swear they all must live in Missouri. Because that's where Tina and I always heard "show me. Show me a wall writing, show me a cabinet door opening itself, show me objects being thrown, show me your house being attacked."

The nighttime activity begins the second we come home from work. The activity could be close by or far away. The plant levitating in front of us is close by. The TV turning on by itself upstairs is far away activity. We respond to what we hear; there's no telling what we find when we get there.

The bed-time activity (was the time-period *Ghost Adventures* investigated in) Tina and I are usually in bed at this time. The activity was within a few feet of us. Now if you ask us to stay in a hotel while you conduct your lockdown don't get mad at us if leave empty-handed. Conducting your investigation at night (in our house) is not going to yield you impressive results. Why blame us?

I would say the activity Tina and I experienced while sleeping (or trying to sleep) I should say was without a doubt the most intentional and deliberate activity we faced. Where it lacks in quantity, it makes us up for in quality. Just about every activity I have listed in the Bedtime Activity column happened in nearby— meaning it took place in our room—I'm talking within inches of us.

Chapter 25
Second Office Fire

The office might not be the most active room in the house, but it gives the hallway a run for its money as being the most dangerous. In case you didn't notice, my office has been experiencing some heinous activity as of late. We're talking spontaneous combustions, growling noises, wall writings, knocks, bangs, rapping's, power loss, and other electrical issues. But none of what I've just mentioned prepares me for what I'm about to see next—something which would make me feel that what we had living in our home was demonic. Not till now.

One night I was watching TV in my office when all of a sudden, I saw something zip past my office door. It wasn't Tina. It wasn't the Gray Lady. Way too short to be the Gray Lady. (I wonder where she is, by the way.) Whatever zipped by my office door was small. About a foot tall. A few nights later I saw it again. Only this time, it didn't zoom by. This time it just sort of hung around. Like it was checking me out or something. I was thinking to myself: *is this what Jane Doe's son saw?* What I saw had arms and legs. Have you ever seen those old Sinbad movies? A special effects technique known as Stop Clay Animation? What I saw walks like that. It walks like the 1930s *King Kong,* the 1930s T-Rex in those old-fashioned monster movies. I see this with my naked eye, and I'm asking myself: *is this for real? Did I just see that?*

That began to happen a lot as we entered into the fall months. I tried not to focus on these things, but I sort of had no choice. Shadows were now forming outside of my office. I still remember the poke in my rib cage. I remember the indentions in the mattress. None of those are coincidences.

A majority of what I do, I do in my office. That might explain why I see them. Why I feel them more than Tina. I'm starting to feel picked on. I'm starting to feel isolated. It bugs me to know that I saw the Gray Lady and Tina didn't. It bugs me to know I was possibly pushed downstairs. It bugs me to know the dimes I pick up throughout the house all read nineteen sixty-nine, the year I was born.

It bugs me to know when my cameras get mysteriously reset; they're set to the year nineteen sixty-nine. The year I was born. It bugs me not knowing what poked me while I was lying in bed.

But that's nothing when you think about the other events taking place. The poster catching on fire. The 666 wall-writings; the upside-down man; the scissors stabbed into the wall. And the cross. We can't forget about the upside-down cross being drawn on the floor with ash from the sage stick. We can't forget about the upside-down cross being drawn on the wall with an unknown substance. How much force does it take to split an office chair? Why would you split an office chair? Why would you set one end of the office chair on top of the Bible? What's the purpose behind that? And we can't forget about my photos. How did they *find* those photos? It's not like those photos were laid out in the open. It's not like they were framed or hanging on a wall. No, these photos were tucked away in boxes. But the entity found them. How did it even know that those photos existed? These questions I'm asking are not rhetorical. They each deserve an answer. Unfortunately, I don't have the answer.

But each question provides the reader a glimpse of what took place. There's no ambiguity about one face being burned out of a picture. Not just one picture, all pictures—all pictures of me. I'm having a hard time deciding which is more heinous: my face being burned out in every picture that I own, or the fact they found them in the first place. How can you find something that I through the course of living my life, forgot even existed? And lastly: how long did they have these pictures? What's their thought process before taking them? They achieved one thing, though: fear. Seeing your face burned out of a picture forces you to put things in a new perspective. The perspective I have now is these events are proving themselves to be supernatural in nature.

These shadowy figures? They're all over the place. Let's go back to when Microsoft was at my house. The engineers in my home picked up and saw with their own eyes strange formations on the TV screen. Strange images. Dark anomalies they couldn't explain. One of them even said, "That's not supposed to be there. Everyone take a ten-minute break, we got to get this defect sorted out." There I was sitting on the couch, about six people observing me play, all holding clipboards, microphones, video cameras, and other remote monitoring equipment. These shadowy blobs were not stationary. They moved. Almost identical to what I saw moving outside my office door. They were hanging and dangling on the kitchen ceiling—behind all of us. The Kinect device picked them up when it shouldn't.

Microsoft was very bothered about what was happening. They couldn't explain it. Headquarters couldn't explain it. I now know what those shadowy figures were. They were the figures poking me in my sleep. They are the figures hovering around my office. They are the figures listening to me, and Tina argue. They are the figures dropping earrings in our bedroom and staircase for Tina to see. So why are they trying to frame me, and not Tina? Why got me in trouble? If I had to guess I would say my office did.

My office is the command center. The center for monitoring, reviewing, messaging, and storing evidence. It became that when the activity returned earlier this year. It's the hub for just about everything. If you got an email from me, odds are I wrote it from my office. The office is where I do my online research. I configure the cameras in this room. I monitor the DVR system in this room. I have two computers in here—two monitors. All my videos and pictures that I take are kept on my portable hard drive. What I don't keep on there I keep on my laptop. What I don't keep on my laptop I store on the internet. The WIFI router is in here. The cable modem is in here. The LAN phone system is in here. The ADT system is monitored from in here. Everything I do, be it work-related or personal, stems from the office. This much equipment is bound to catch attention. Good and bad. Mainly bad. You see, the office is the only room in the house that's ever had a fire. Two fires, as a matter of fact.

The first office fire you know about. The second office fire is but a few pages away. Now, when the landlord handed me the keys to the house, he said, "Feel free to make yourself at home. Decorate it as you see fit." Only, that didn't include vandalism. That didn't include writing 666 and other horrible things on a wall. No landlord would tolerate that being done to his home. Sceptics might want to bear that in mind if they're peddling the line that we hoaxed all of this. They might also want to bear in mind the work involved here. The first wall writings were done with ash, presumably from a sage stick. That happened a few times. It's easy to clean. All we used was a warm soapy towel. A few days later we had new wall writings. On more walls than before. Soap won't do the trick this time. Time to buy some paint and paint over it. Now, when I paint over these wall markings, I have to cover up everything else in the room so as to not spill paint on it. I have to cover up my entertainment center, cover up my computer monitors, cover up my computer desk, and cover up the carpet. That's very time-consuming.

Even after all that prep work I still manage to get paint or primer on something. I always find a drop here and there in an area of the room that I failed to cover correctly. By contrast, the entity does what it does in a matter of minutes. It doesn't cover up anything. Not so much as a drop of ash is spilled. Ash in one place only—the place where it's writing. Guess what happens when I paint over the wall writings the spirits did? I get new wall writings. The spirits started out with ash and now have upgraded to an unknown substance. Some of it looks like paint but where and the hell did it come from? Study my photos and videos. You'll see a new a substance was used. Why is that? Inconvenience. The entity learned something when it saw me clean up the first wall writing. It saw me use a warm soapy towel to remove the 666 written in sage ash. So now, not only does it write on more walls each time, but it also makes the markings harder to remove. I'm now buying two buckets of paint where I was buying one. I'm buying buckets of paint to paint over the wall markings.

And even then, I can't paint over the markings just yet. I have to figure out what they mean. We all know what the entity wants us to think when it wrote 666 on the wall. We all know what fear it wanted to convey when it drew an upside-down cross. It wanted to spark fear and insecurity. But what message is it trying to send by drawing an upside-down man? *I finally found out.*

The night I realized what that symbol meant was the night I decided to sit in my office and just stare at the symbol. That's all I'm going to do. I'm just going to stare at it. I'm going to stare at it until it tells me what it means. How many of them are staring at *me* right now, I wonder?

Here I am, forty minutes in asking myself the question. What do they mean? What do the markings look like to me? The answer I kept coming up with was: It looks like an upside-down stick figure. It looks very simplistic. An upside-down stick figure of a man. Since that's what it looks like, that's what I'll Google search on.

Several Native American websites came up within seconds of me typing "upside-down man symbol." Each one had a picture of what I had on my wall. Two meanings came up. "A man has died," and a "man is about to die." The website I was on described these things as being pictograms. A Native American pictogram that meant a man has died nearby or is about to die. *Gulp.* I swallowed real hard after reading that. A man is about to die? What man? *Are they talking about me?*

Now the definition doesn't necessarily say the upside-down man is a symbol to be feared. Not conclusively. It is what it is. Are the spirits trying to tell me something else? Is this a clue about the land underneath the house? Is it that, or are they just fucking with me? Are they saying, "You are about to die, Keith Linder"? Once again, more questions instead of answers. I'm beginning to feel every step forward means two steps backward. Which leads to my next story. The activity is known as apporting.

What is apporting? Apporting, as defined online, is "… the vanishing or removal of objects (by a spirit) and the subsequent reappearance in another location." Demons and poltergeists both have this power and they execute it brilliantly. I bring the mail in for Tina and me every day when I get home. This day, in particular, I remember walking into my office and doing what I always do with my mail. I set it next to my keyboard. I turned around and walked out. I was in and out of my office in less than ten seconds. I was now in the hallway heading downstairs. As I approached the staircase landing area, I saw something. There on the midway portion of the staircase were a series of envelopes. I walked closer and said, "What the fuck?" There on the staircase were the letters I left on the keyboard. I knelt and picked them up and headed back to my office. I walked into my office and saw that the letters I sat on my keyboard were gone.

That's just one ability out of many these spirits possess. I'm reminded once again of their level of observation. This happened within ten minutes of me being home. To my knowledge never has a wonder like this taken place within minutes of us being home. (I won't count the pitter patter footsteps Tina and I have heard when arriving home.) This in itself was new. Very new. We usually have to be home for a few hours before something inexplicable takes place.

How do letters go from being on my keyboard to being on the staircase *in less than ten seconds? Answer that question for me, Neil deGrasse Tyson.* What was my reaction to seeing this? I was taken aback; I was shocked. I wasn't terrified. Normally I would be, normally I'd be looking over my shoulder for an object to fly by or a loud bang to erupt. I didn't do that this time. I remember picking up the envelopes and walking downstairs. I'm pretty sure I told Tina about it once I saw her. Her reply was, "That's different."

A week later I came home and found the office in disarray again. If you think these are identical house attacks remember, the "Geist" left something new for us to find after every attack. Today we had scratches on the computer desk and office. These razor-thin scratches formed the shape of an X on the wall behind my computer monitor. The scratches have cut well into the drywall. It's going to take more than just paint to fix what the "Geist" had just done. I'm thinking to myself, *damn, I just painted over these walls a few days ago.* What gives?

The office chair had been split in half again. Not sure what that's about. And my kitchen chair was in my office again. My entertainment center was on the floor. All the contents of my closet were on the floor. Now I'm used to this. I mean, we're talking about the fifth or sixth time this has happened. But I'm now getting a little bit nervous about how often this is happening. Attacks are happening two to three times a week now. At this point, I'm sort of in a bind. If I don't paint over the wall writings, my office gets attacked. If I do paint over the wall writings, my office gets attacked, albeit more frequently. As crazy as that sounds, you still sort of have to get used to it. But how can you be used to something like this? I mean, you sort of prepare your mind for the what-the-fuck moment. Well, today's what-the-fuck-moment end up being my portable hard drive. It's missing.

This hard drive has everything on it. It receives video and photo from every motion camera in the house. I chained that hard drive to my computer desk. To separate the hard drive from the computer, you need a key. How was the spirit able to remove my hard drive, minus a key? I keep both keys at my job as an effort to rule out human tampering.

Just to add insult to injury, there underneath my computer desk is the chain I bought from Best Buy. It was still tethered to the desk. It hasn't been moved at all, let alone unlocked. The only thing that's been moved is my hard drive. It's gone.

August and September, 2014 seemed to be the months for running up the scoreboard. Incident after incident, and by incident, I mean violent activity. And that's just the visible stuff. It's easy to forget about the stuff we can't see. You see, as horrible as the events are that I'm about to describe, you have to remember what Tina and I can't see is actually more horrible. In my opinion, putting an earring where Tina and I sleep is more frightening than a poster catching fire. It's impossible to predict both instances but tell me which one has the longer lasting effect? The earring in the bed is like cancer; it's slowly but surely eating away at our relationship. Without trust you have nothing. There are two types of eggshells I'm walking on now. One involves spirits, and one involves Tina's reaction to what the spirits might do. Neither are predictable.

So, we're now to the point of having good days and bad days. The definition of a good day is any day devoid of drama. Any day devoid of arguments is by definition a good day. No false accusation? That's a good day. No crazy innuendos? That's a good day.

Tina's family was not griping at her. My siblings were not griping at me. No one's armchair quarterbacking. Those are good days. No paranormal activity, definitely a good day. If Tina forgot to smudge (and it's her turn to smudge the house), that's a potentially bad day. If neither of us wants to pray with the other person, that's a potentially bad day. Any disagreement whatsoever (and I mean the slightest disagreement) meant the house is most likely going to be attacked. What do I mean when I say the house is going to be attacked? It's becoming more localized. More focused. More close proximity.

The house was no longer being attacked like it was in March, April, and May. The house wasn't being attacked like it was in June and July. There are two areas in the house where the entity now seems to be sharply focused. Those two areas are the office and the hallway.

I want to be very clear about something. From here on out the majority of the destruction Tina and I are going to witness is going to come from disagreements that we have inside and outside the house. I put these disagreements in the small, medium, and large categories. Some are universal, meaning every couple has argued about this from time to time, e.g., *you spend more time in your office than you do with me or I don't want to drive my car to the movies, let's take your car. Your car has more leg room. No, I don't want to drive my car, it has no gas in it, it drinks too much gas, we're taking your car. But we took my car last time?* So yes, some of these arguments are frivolous. Frivolous and basic. But a "Geist" doesn't care about basic. A demon doesn't necessarily care about how an argument ends. It cares about how an argument starts; and it starts quite a few of them. Its game on the second you reach that disagreement threshold. That's when the level two through level five activity begins. That's when my office gets torn up.

As time goes on, we're arguing about prayers. I ask Tina if she feels like leading the prayer tonight. If she doesn't respond to me, tension builds and when tension builds shit starts happening. Just to be fair, I can say no to a lot of things. I can give Tina the cold shoulder when I'm upset with her. You know that saying about "waking up on the wrong side of the bed?" That happens a lot in a house infested with malevolent spirits. It comes with the territory. I want to give you another example of how an argument unfolds.

The priest advised Tina and me to always pray before going to bed. Recite several prayers, especially the Saint Benedict prayer. Do this every night. I leave my office around 11 pm, to fetch Tina. It's near bedtime, so we best get this prayer stuff out the way.

"Tina, it's time to do the prayers, do you want to come upstairs and pray with me?"

"No, I'm too tired." My response to her "no" was usually something like, but the priest said we must. We have to do this together or else. Her response would then be, "What's the point?" My reply was we already know what the point is; the point is very clear. We have an entity living with us, and if we're going to get it out, make our house whole again, then we have to do what we've been asked to do.

Her response? "What's the point? You're just going to have another woman in here." And that's how the argument would start. A heated back and forth begins about the need to pray. It's hard to join someone in prayer if you're mad at them. It's hard to join someone in prayer when you pull an earring out of you and your partner's bed (after coming back from visiting family). Tina was upset about the earring (the topic comes up every once in a while), therefore, she's not eager to pray alongside me. She's not eager to smudge when it's her time to smudge or lead the prayer service when it's her time to lead the prayer service.

Now the earring thing wasn't the only sneakiness taking place in our house. There were a lot more. Some Tina and I don't even know about. The scratches on my car was a manipulation attempt. The fall down the stairs was a big one. Look what it did? It brought back the activity. I call attention to these things because I want the reader to understand something about Tina and me as it relates to evil spirits. Our relationship is not perfect. Far from it. We're just average human beings. The stuff we're going through could happen to anyone. Heck, it might even happen to you one day, God forbid. That dark cloud that's forming over our house is changing her mood and mine. It's laying the ground works for some serious isolation. Isolation between Tina and me. We have no idea we're being controlled. The spirits got Tina thinking one thing, and they got me thinking another. They got me thinking, I can get them on video if I just apply myself. They got me believing if I just listened to the advice given to me by other people (paranormal teams, clergy, so-called priests, family) that I will eventually get something on video. Little did I know (at the time), most of those people giving Tina and me advice didn't have our best interests at heart. That and the sudden convenient appearance of female jewelry was ratcheting up the activity in the house.

I had come home from work one day and discovered several of my collector items were gone. We're talking about baseball cards, video game paraphernalia, coin collection, foreign CDs, and cash. I was pissed. Pissed to the point of buying two new safes. One was a combination safe. The other a key safe. That was my game plan, everyone. Cast iron safes. Why was I buying a safe? I'm stupid, that's why. How stupid am I? Stupid enough to buy additional CCTV cameras in conjunction with my safe purchase. If you have safes, you got to have cameras watching them, right?

The office and the upstairs hallway had two cameras now. I put the two safes in the office closet and my new portable hard drive on my computer desk. Everything was back to how it was before the last office attack. I know what you're thinking. Why am I buying all this stuff when I know the spirit can simply steal these items as it did the first items? One word: Pride. That's what was fueling me right now. Pride and determination.

I'll close this chapter with some of the most horrendous attacks Tina and I ever faced while living in this house. The first story involves a chef knife. Tina and I had just had a major spat about who's turn it was to pray. We ended the argument in a stalemate, which means she returned to doing what she was doing which was watching TV and I returned to what I was doing which was sitting in my office. I almost feel embarrassed sharing this story because it raises an important question. If a couple has to argue about whose turn it is to pray, whose turn it is to smudge, then we have a serious problem. Even if one of us changes our mind and decides to kick start the prayer, after a heated debate, how effective are we now? Tension was in the air now. It didn't take long for stuff to happen when Tina and I have even the slightest disagreement.

I'd been in my office now for thirty minutes or so when all of a sudden, I heard a loud sound. The noise came from outside of my office door. I knew right then and there that something was thrown. I couldn't see it yet because I was sitting down. So, I get up, and sure enough, something was thrown. A freaking chef's knife. Can you believe it? There in the upstairs hallway, few feet from my office doorway was a broken-up chef's knife. I stepped into the hallway and began looking for whatever it hit. The knife hit something; I heard the impact. Seconds later, there it was—a nick on the frame of my doorway. It looked like whoever threw the knife threw it with the intention of landing it in my office. The knife stopped short of that. Instead of landing in my office, it ricocheted back into the hallway. I know this knife. I've used it many times when cooking. It was one of Tina's knifes from her knife set. To confirm my suspicion about where this knife came from, I decided to go downstairs, inspect the holder. My suspicion was correct. The chef knife was missing. Of course, it was. I wish I could say that was the only time I had a knife thrown at me. More knives are going to be thrown at me in the coming months. We're in September now. By the time January rolls around, I will have confiscated all the sharp knives in the kitchen.

Now the knife landing outside my door allows me to introduce a word that speaks to things escalating. That word is projectile. Tina and I have seen many items thrown around the house. These objects are thrown far away from us. Never in our vicinity. Just within our peripheral view do they go flying by. Not this time though. This knife landed deliberately outside my office door. It should be in the kitchen, in its sheath. Not in my hallway: not outside my door.

Fig 25.1 - Objects thrown at me a.) Candles b.) Cameras c.) Cologne bottle d.) Knives e.) Bible f.) Beer bottles

Second office fire. The night before the office fire I came home and found Tina sleeping in one of the guest bedrooms. The falling out over whose turn it is to smudge or pray had survived one more day. If one ever needs an example of activity being spawned from two people giving each other the silent treatment, then here it is. I just had just come from having dinner with friends about the next steps for the house. The hour was late.

I marched upstairs and was immediately hit with that feeling of being watched. The upstairs hallway felt like it did when the Bible caught fire. I was standing outside the room Tina was sleeping in. Under no circumstances should we be sleeping in different rooms. No circumstances whatsoever. Let me try to convince her to come to bed with me. People have a right to be mad. But Tina's upset I couldn't quite understand. I mean, by all means be mad at me. But don't let your anger for me push you into another, especially when you know firsthand what goes on here. I knew Tina was not going to come to bed with me, but I had to ask, and I did.

Tina's response was "no." I gave up after the second nudge and went to our room and crawled into the bed. I'm not going to sleep too though. It's impossible to sleep based on how the house feels right now. Here comes the rapping. Here come the wall taps. Fuck it, here comes whatever it is that does the poking and prodding. Bed indention, after bed indention, after bed indention. Stay awake, Keith, the demons won't throw things if you're awake. They won't walk by and slam your door shut if you're awake.

The only thing that can keep me awake this late at night is a good western movie. Please let there be a western movie on TV tonight. *Yes! I found one—Wyatt Earp*, starring Kevin Costner.

I must have gotten halfway through the Wyatt Earp movie before I dozed off. But not all the way. I woke up a few times and looked around. The house still felt the way it did when I came home earlier. It felt evil. I was lying in bed, when I heard what I know are bangs and tapping noises. The noise was coming from behind the headboard of my bed. I get up from the bed and walked into the hallway. I looked around and saw nothing. I then opened the door where Tina was sleeping and saw that she was still asleep. I looked out her window and saw the sun piercing through the blinds. *Ah, morning has arrived, the sun has finally come up. I can finally get some sleep.* I checked on Tina one more time before closing the door. *Get some sleep, Keith Linder, get some freaking sleep.* I took my mind's advice. I crawled back into our California king bed and threw the covers over me. I was asleep before my head hit the pillow.

The house fire alarms began ringing within two hours of me being asleep. *Oh shit, what the heck is going on?* I leaped out of bed. My heart was racing. *God help us,* I thought. *God, please don't let this house burn down. God, please protect Keith and Tina.* I thought this and more as I ran out of the bedroom and into the hallway, yelling, *Tina! Tina!* All of sudden the guest bedroom door swung open and Tina burst out. I thought to myself, *crap, she was still asleep, that's not good.* Normally she's up by now. I was so hoping she was burning bacon in the kitchen. There goes that idea.

And here comes the smoke from my office, *dammit, why couldn't Tina be burning bacon instead of this.* I ran towards my office. I was floored within seconds of reaching my doorway. That's how bad the smoke was. *Burnt plastic?* This wasn't a poster on fire. No, this was worse. My two computer monitors were on fire. Flames literary dancing off both computer screens. *Shit, my desk and keyboard are on fire too.* The smoke was horrendous; but nowhere near as horrendous as the smell. I knew right then and there that smoke in a home is typically deadlier than fire.

Add burnt plastic to the mix, and you got chemicals going into your lungs within seconds. My monitors were fried right now. *If I don't get this fire extinguished quickly this room is going to be gone.* I was now faced with the same scenario as before. Don't let the flames touch the wall or ceiling. Don't let the flames touch anything.

I darted from the office to the guest bedroom. *Get some towels, Keith, get some freaking towels.* When I ran back into the office, Tina was with me. In her hands were bed sheets. I threw the towels over the monitors, and Tina threw her set of bed sheets over my towels. I reached down and unplugged the monitors from the surge protector—*something I should've already done.* The fight with the demon wasn't over. After ten seconds of us dousing the flames, here they come again. This time the sheets caught on fire. Now maybe the sheets caught on fire due to the monitor being hot, that's possible. Or maybe we just witnessed the sheets catching fire all by themselves. Either way, we had a second fire on our hands.

The flames were devouring the towels and sheets to the point of us seeing the two monitors again. Now they're on fire. Again! *OK, the monitors are unplugged now, now we can use water. If water doesn't work, we're going to have call 911. We cannot let these flames touch the wall or ceiling. Keep the fire on the desk,* I thought, *keep the fire on the desk.* I ran back into the bathroom and grabbed the trash can. I threw it in the sink and began filling it with water. As we were doing this, the fire was building back up. Fire alarms still ringing like hell. We've got nothing but snap, crackle, and pop sounds coming from the melting monitors. I ran back into the office and right when I was about to dump a half a gallon of water on the monitors, Tina ran in and pushed me aside. In her hand was the shower curtain from the bathroom. She threw it on top of monitor and desk, followed by some wet towels, which seemed to do the trick. The fire was extinguished. Now for the fire alarms, *how and in the world, are we going to get them to stop ringing? There's so much smoke in here.*

Ten minutes later, there we were walking around in circles, Tina and I, thinking: what the hell just happened? For a couple who had just woken up, we looked like we haven't slept in weeks. I would occasionally look at Tina, and she would occasionally look at me. Neither one of us could speak. I was physically and emotionally drained.

A house fire is one of the most horrendous things you can experience. It doesn't matter the size of it. Fire can kill you. The smoke from a fire can kill you. If there are any awards to be given, it has to be given to the fire alarms. They saved our lives big time. They saved this house. Tina and I have now experienced two house fires—from inside my office.

The most horrific thing about this last one was how well timed it was. I had an uneasy feeling following me ever since I stepped into the house last night. There's a certain kind of mood the house has to be for something like this to jump off. I've sensed it many times before. I like to think that I have some sort of control over it, but I don't. Knowing something is going to happen doesn't mean you know what's going to happen. You can't predict this stuff. Let alone imagining it will happen.

Fuck what the skeptics say. Fuck what the cynics say. You can't make this stuff up. Who can I tell this story to? Who can relate to something like this? Leave? Move out? Doing that doesn't solve the problem. You think it does, but it doesn't. What if it follows us? What if it follows me? What if it follows Tina? And let's say that it doesn't, who in their right mind is going to be safe living here? What room in my house would you turn into a baby's room? Which room would you make into a nursery? My office? That's the room with the wall writings? The room with the animal scratches? How about the guest bedroom by the landing? Would you turn that room into a kid's room? Would you? That's where the armoire sits. It's been thrown over five times already. It'll be thrown again before the week's out. How is that room safe for someone to live in? How about the room next to my office? That's the room Tina and I sleep in when the bedroom is being noisy.

The doorway to my office and that room are but inches apart. Who sleeps in there once we leave? Some of you reading this might be thinking: "that's not your problem, Keith, that's the landlord's problem. It's his responsibility to tell them, not yours." Well, he didn't tell us. He didn't tell Jane Doe. Jane Doe didn't tell the landlord, they just up and moved. Can't you see? No one's telling anyone anything. The problems have been passed on or better yet ignored. Well, that ends with Tina and me. I keep imagining this scenario in my head of new family moving in. It's a family of four. Husband, wife, young girl, and toddler son. The toddler's name is Johnny. I keep imagining little Johnny walking into his parents' room late at night and saying, 'something keeps touching him while he sleeps,' mom and dad take turns tucking him in, but that's it. That's all they do. But Johnny isn't imagining things. The difficulty he's having is similar to the difficulty Tina and I are having. There seems to be a lack of response within the paranormal and religious communities about malevolent outbreaks.

Do you see the point I'm trying to make here? We're trapped. Tina and I are trapped. This merry go round seems to provide us with no clear solution. My girlfriend thinks I'm a cheater. She thinks I've had women in the house while she was out of town. It's a miracle she hasn't killed me in my sleep. What woman wouldn't hate the man they live with if they knew he brought another woman into their bedroom? I can think of no worse betrayal than that. And obviously, the demon behind all of this can't either. If it could, it would have chosen that frame up over the one it executed. The demon is using Tina's insecurities against her. The minions are hard at work, ladies and gentlemen—there's no let-up. Tina told me what a cheat her previous husband was during their two attempts at marriage. She spelled it out to in big bold letters. The guy was an idiot. Here we are four years later dealing with that conversation. The demons in this house know each of our insecurities. They have their marching orders—minions often do.

Hour later, I was sitting outside the door of my office—shell-shocked. Tina was hovering nearby, equally shell-shocked. We'd just had our asses handed back to us in the worse way possible. The damage done to my office pales in comparison to the mental damage being done right now. I leaned over and looked at my office from where I was sitting and thought to myself: *we're losing this war.* Tina and I evidently do not have what it takes to beat this thing. How did we go from sitting on the living room floor May 1st, 2012 to putting out fires? I remember the housewarming party like it was yesterday. I remember Tina and I were showing our friends the upstairs bedrooms. We were giving friends we regard as a family a tour of the house. We finally got to our bedroom, and I paused; the door was closed. I looked at Tina, and I waited for the acknowledgment. She knew I was asking her for permission to show our friends the master bedroom. The huge master bedroom. Everyone has a drink in their hand. Everyone's laughing and lollygagging. Tina looks back at me and says yes, it's OK to show them our room. Why did I wait for permission? I waited because Tina is my woman. She's my girl. The room is Tina's—all I do is sleep there. A couple's room is a sacred place.

If Tina wasn't comfortable showing that room, then guess what? I'm not showing it. As ironic as it is one my best friends blurt out in a joking manner, "So this is where the magic happens?" The girls all huddle together and start high fiving each other. The men slap me on the back and yell "Big Keith!" My friend didn't know it at the time, but yeah this is where the magic happens alright, it's called paranormal activity. Then it hit me. As I'm sitting there, it truly hits me. *This is not going to end well.* The doctors must have removed both tear ducts from me when I was born. I wanted to cry, but I couldn't. I mean, I wanted to cry my eyes out right then and there. Not because my computer was gone. I wanted to cry because I know me. I'm incapable of quitting. I'm incapable of throwing in the towel—without first attempting all options. I wanted to cry because I knew this would not end well for Tina and me. As far as relationships go, our days seemed numbered now. I don't know how it's going to end. I don't even know when it's going to end. I only know what Jane Doe told me. The house "was a living hell" for them. It's clear; the demons have the upper hand on Tina and me. They know our faults better than we know them.

Cameras increase the activity. Arguments increase the activity. Silent treatment increases the activity. False accusations increase the activity. Fixation increases the activity. Fascination with what's taken place increases the activity. Praying increases the activity. Forgetting to pray increases the activity. Smudging increases the activity. Forgetting to smudge increases the activity. Having a light-hearted conversation with my girlfriend over dinner (which in the spirit's eye appears to suggest we resolved our differences) triggers the appearance of circumstantial evidence, which then increases the activity. Not hearing from the priest increases the activity. Churches and paranormal teams asking us to provide better evidence increases the activity. Tina's friends and family thinking it's me that behind all of this increases the activity. My family thinks it's Tina that's behind this increases the activity. My woman being upset because I haven't made love to her in two years. Therefore, I must be getting it from someone else, increases the activity.

As I was sitting in my hallway, sleep deprived and emotionally drained; I asked myself the question. What doesn't increase the activity? What would Tina and I have to do to put a stop to the supernatural that's unfolding right before us?

I was circling the office and hallway when suddenly my eye went back to Tina. The word "death" came to mind. To stop this activity one of us was going to have to die. Death by suicide, something Jane Doe told me she tried to do several times while living in the home. That's right, the lady I refer to as Jane Doe told me she "tried to kill herself multiple times in this house." That's how dark it got. I'm beginning to see how one would contemplate suicide living in this house. Hopelessness and despair make perfect bedfellows. A son with an unknown illness and a couple in dire straits financially are but one of the few ingredients needed for a suicide attempt. That in addition to the other stuff she told me. The secret ingredient would be the minions themselves. Well, no way am I killing myself. No way is Tina killing herself.

We know that, and the demon knows that. We're in full agreement there. The only things left are accidental death and murder. You've already read about the accidental death moments. *Oh yes, you have, way more than you realize.* That's not going to stop either. More accidental death moments are on the way. Hell, the spirits are probably putting some in motion right now.

Could the spirit cajole Tina into killing me? Hmmm, let me put it like this. All bets are off should Tina find another piece of woman jewelry in our bed. The demon is not going to put a pair of man's shoes next to my bedside in the hope of me thinking another man was in the house. It could. But I wouldn't fall into that trap. The demon knows that. Insecurity is not my weakness. Not when it comes to Tina it isn't. My weakness is the technology around me. That's my blind spot. What gets me, in the end, is the technology I brought into the house. The cameras. The super speed internet. The mass network I've assembled with the hopes of catching this thing. I want to catch it in the act. I know good and well I can't. But I'm going to try anyway. I'm going to try because that's what IT professionals do. We problem solve. I've been a problem solver my entire adult life. My dad was a problem solver. There's no such thing as an unsolvable problem. There's a solution somewhere; we just haven't figured it out. The right minds haven't been brought in yet. *Until then, all we got is each other.*

It's weird how an office fire can bring a couple back together again. There's no makeup sex going on, but there is communication. We have bigger fish to fry now. My office is in shambles. The bathroom where Tina yanked off the shower curtain is in shambles. The entire house smells like a plastic factory. We had black smoke billowing out my office window for twenty minutes after the fire. That's how thick and toxic it was. I never knew computer monitors could smell so bad, but dammit they do. They and the keyboard are gone. My computer mouse is gone. Thank God, the fire never reached the floor. Thank God, the fire never reached the ceiling or the closet for that matter. The entity knew exactly what it was doing when it decided to hit us. I mean, we got hit at the crack of dawn.

I'm out a hard drive, a keyboard, two monitors, and a computer mouse. The room reeks of Satan and destruction. It's impossible to go in and begin cleaning up the office—the stench is too heavy. All I can do is sit on my hallway floor, inches from the possessed bookshelf, and look at Tina. We both look like we just came from a chimney sweep convention gone bad. Tina's shaking like an aspen leaf. She's crying her eyes out. When she looks up at me, I see the confusion in her eyes. I see disbelief. I see her asking herself the question: what the fuck just happened?

She's thinking the same thing I'm thinking which is: I must love you an awful lot to be here. My girlfriends think I'm crazy; they think I'm insane. Her friends tell her that, and my friends tell me that. No one knows what we've just experienced because no one was here. Over seven billion people live on this planet, and not one of them knows what just happened. Tina and I saw a fire restart itself. We saw flames dancing on top of my monitor. It took me two days to get the smoke and soot out of my nostrils. The back of throat ached due to so much smoke inhalation. I can't think of anything more enjoyable to a malevolent spirit right now than to observe two emotionally drained house occupants. I know we're being watched right now. I want to shoot the middle the finger so bad. But I don't. I can't. I'm too damn tired.

Chapter 26
Night Terrors

Between the priest and Jennifer, guess who returned our phone call first once they got news of the office fire? I hope you said Jennifer; you'd be right if you did. I called and left a voicemail with Jennifer about the office catching fire again, day after it happened. Tina did the same with the priest. Jennifer returned my call in less than twelve hours. The priest we were still waiting on.

Now, let me tell you what Jennifer suggested, while we waited on the local priest. She thought maybe it was time we got another priest involved. Maybe it was time we contacted other parishes—the one she had in mind existed on an Indian reservation. It was a worth a shot. We were getting nowhere fast with the priest we know. If a priest on a reservation wants to help us, that would be good, especially given the recent upside-down man Native American symbols. Maybe that priest will see a deeper meaning behind it. Maybe he'll be able to talk to the spirits and get them out of here. I told Jennifer to go for it. So that's what I accomplished at work that day. It always feels like a lot, when it isn't. I mean, Jennifer was great for suggesting what she did. When dealing with a spirit such as this, you must upend every rock with the hope of finding someone.

When Tina got home from work that day she had bad news to report. The sort of the news you always suspected was true but dare not look for it, for fear of it being true. Well, that day had finally come. Tina can be relentless when she wants to be—trust me, I know. Today she called the regional Catholic Church. She got bounced around a few times before finally reaching the bishop who presided over our beloved priest. She reached him, and she talked to him, and boy did she get an earful.

The bishop she spoke to knew nothing about our case. I mean zero. He'd never heard of us. He knew of the priest she was referring to, but that was it. That was all he knew. I'm not going to pretend I know the inner workings of the Catholic Church. Nor am I going to guess about the levels of communication between a bishop and his priest. I think it's safe to say that over the course of four months, a priest is going to have some conversation with his bishop. I mean conversations about parish stuff. I have to believe that somewhere during that time our house was going to come up. I mean, the priest told us he had gotten approval from his bishop to get involved. He told us he was updating his bishop regularly. Well, Tina had just spoken to his bishop, and he'd never heard of us. He'd never heard of this house, and he'd never heard of the issues we'd been having. We held communion in the house. I have to think the bishop would know that. He didn't.

The bishop got an earful after talking to Tina. Tina told him everything the local priest had done and not done. His response was, "I didn't know that." Well, guess what? He does now. The question now is: what is he going to do next? The bishop told her that he was going to call the priest and get more information. He too was confused about why he was left in the dark. That's what he told Tina.

Guess what Tina and I had to do while he verified what she just said? Nothing, there was nothing for Tina and me to do. Which brings me back to Jennifer—my reason keeping her updated was obvious. Little help is better than no help. Jennifer's latest recommendation was to leave the stereo on when we leave the house. Fill the house with gospel music and Native American chants. She even provided a few. Hopefully, that will irritate them and make them leave. Her thinking was that we had a vengeful Native American spirit living with us.

A spirit who thinks he's obligated to protect the land the house is sitting on. The upside-down man spoke volumes to Jennifer and the people she was speaking to. Only a Native American spirit would write something like that. Tina and I discussed what Jennifer recommended over dinner. We both agreed, it was worth a try. Did it work? Of course not. Did it increase the activity? It most certainly did. It gave us something to argue about in the coming days.

It didn't take long before it was just me walking out the door with music playing in the background. Some days Tina forgot. She didn't forget on purpose; of course, she didn't. She's just wired differently to me is all. Knowing that doesn't eliminate the verbal exchange we had whenever she forgot. That conversation consisted of me coming home and noticing the music not on. Of course, the entity could have turned off the music when we left; and it did turn our music off a few times.

But I asked Tina, just to be sure. Some days the spirit turned off the stereo. Some days it didn't. Jennifer advised both of us to leave music on whenever we left the house. The last thing I do when I leave the house is turn the TV station to Comcast Gospel station. The music must be having some effect because the TV is off when I get home. If I'm lucky, that's all they'll be. If I'm not lucky, it's more wall-writings, more office destruction.

That could be the den; could be my office, or could be our bedroom. As I said, we were advised to do this, and we did. I was having a tough time understanding if it was me they object to or the music we left playing. I remember one time I put on a Native American song on in my office and left for work. By the time I got to the front door, the music channel had changed. I mean it switched channels before I got to the front door.

Sometimes the channel changed as I was making my way to the car. I'd get to my car and see the trunk light open, indicating my trunk was unlocked. *You know me, always fat-fingering my car fob.* I got out of my car to close the trunk and upon doing so heard the music station switch from gospel to 80's greatest hits, right then and there. Did I go back in and readjust the channel? Sometimes I did. Sometimes I didn't. It all depended on how late for work I wanted to be. I can't tell you how many times I'd marched back into the house, to turn the music channel back to the gospel station or Native American YouTube station only to come home eight hours later and see the house upside down—mainly my office.

This speaks to their level of observation. Their level of torment. Let's set aside their ability to change music channels for a second. We know they can do that. Remember the Katie Perry incident? We know they can manipulate our electronic equipment. Allow me to address their level of focus; that is, their level of intent. If we are to judge an individual by their actions, then malevolent spirits are no exception.

Saturday morning. Tina got up early and began running her errands for the day. She walked over to my side of the bed and kissed me goodbye. *That lets you know we've made up.* The house was dead silent—*that in itself should have been my first warning to get up.* Our house is never silent. I fell back asleep within minutes of Tina leaving. I must have been in and out of sleep that entire morning. I remember hearing a car with a bad exhaust pipe go up and down the street that morning. *I wish they would cut it out; I'm trying to sleep. Kid on a bicycle I can deal with.* A neighbor walking his dog, I can deal with. A car zooming up and down my street every thirty minutes is just keeping me awake. And suddenly I felt it. Something jumps onto bed with me. Always when I'm about to nod off.

The leap came from Tina's side of the bed; that's how it always starts. Always from the side closest to the door. Evidently, these things can't climb into the bed. I would feel something different if that were true. What I feel resembles someone leaping in the bed, or someone falling from the ceiling into the bed. The feeling is the same. The mattress indents, the pressure shifts. My eyes shoot open because my brain is telling me this shouldn't be happening. Tina's not home. No one's home. Nothing should be jumping on the bed with me. Not even an animal from outside. (And yes: a skeptic once suggested that.)

Whatever leaped into bed with me was slowly making its way towards me. Just like before. Just like when I was healing from my knee injury. Just like several weeks ago. Each time this happened I spun around. There was nothing to see, only feelings. It was like they vamoosed. Nothing was there. Not even an indentation or vibration moving in the opposite direction. Which made me think maybe, just maybe, I imagined this. Maybe my mind was playing tricks. The only thing to do was to let whatever was about to happen run its course. This couldn't be death coming to get me. I doubt it. I mean, if death wanted me, it had had plenty of opportunities before. Why wait, why try a third time? The same level of deduction I gave to the angel of death I gave to the possibility of this being a demon. Is this how possession occurs? Is this how it goes down? I'm not sure. I didn't know. All I knew at the time was, I was tired. Whatever did this woke me from a deep sleep. My thought while this was happening, was: *OK, whatever this is, let's see what they do when they get right up on me. What are they going to do, dropkick me? Am I about to go flying out of my bed? Is this the Gray Lady? Whatever it is, it's obviously making its way towards me. It obviously prefers me being semi-awake. Obviously needs my back turned. I'm thinking this while half-awake. While half-fatigued. Eyes slightly open. The indentations are getting near. It's getting closer.*

I remember thinking, *do whatever you're going to do and get it over with.* As soon as my brain said that I felt a rush. Whatever it was it zoomed right through me. I felt a rush, as in charge of energy. I felt a sense of euphoria. A numbness. The only thing I could do was quiver and gasp for air. I was shivering for a few seconds. Such euphoria. Then it was over. Did something go through me or in me? Either something touched me, or something ran through me. I rose from the bed and looked around. Nothing. The house was silent. I must have sat up in bed for a few seconds. What's my next course of action? Did something leap into my body? It seemed too simple to be a form of possession. I mean, I've been asleep countless times, as has Tina.

It didn't make sense. What did make sense was the level of energy, the level of rush I felt when whatever it was, it finally touched me. Something touched me. How did it feel? Honestly? There's no tangible way to describe it. No word comes to mind except a feeling of euphoria. Had it been a sword it never would have come through the other side. No way was I ran through.

How long did it last? About a second. I remember an internal tug of war. My body, or for a lack of a better word, my aura defense system, simply kicked in. My soul or spirit went to Defcon one because of being touched. Did I win is the question? Did my aura fight it off? I don't know. Something went down, and I have no clue what it was or no clue as to what it meant. All I can say is the poking and prodding began to increase after today, as did the night-terrors.

I never told Tina about the experience I had that morning. Since I couldn't explain it to myself, how in the world can I explain it to her? I'll just have to store that in my *I don't know what happened box.* More info needed. That experience does remind me of one thing though. Something Tina and I both share: night terrors. It wasn't long before I started having them myself, then it dawned on me Tina was having immense night terrors last year. Some of them were so intense that it woke me up. Imagine being awakened by your baby's bad dream. Night terrors are just that, night terrors. Your body rocking back in forth. You're semi-talking to yourself and there are tears involved. That how it was for me. I've never had dreams like this in my life. Not until the fall of 2014. All I see our shadows. Shadows and family members are what star in my bad dreams.

It's like something is downloading my memories in the middle of me sleeping. It's like they're rummaging through areas of my past that were the darkest for me—the saddest parts of my life. I'm talking about things I forgot about. Things I've regretted, ignored, and utterly can't stand. That's what my night terrors are about now. It's ugly; it's really, ugly. You wake up shivering. You wake up in a cold sweat. Hell, you wake up crying, and I did. I've woken myself up a few times. I'm awake with tears in my eyes (that never happened before). How long are the dreams? I don't know. But that's how real the dream is. They're very personal. No one has permission to play my past back to me. The stuff I regret. The stuff I've seen. The people I've lost or let down. I'm asking myself, who hit the rewind button? Who checked out a box of microfilm titled: The Life of Keith Linder? That's what being played when I'm asleep at night. Not every night. Thank God, I don't think I could survive it if it were every night. I mean Tina's night terrors last year, last two months. Mine has just started. I get them once a week now. They will increase as we get closer to the darker chapters.

A few days had passed since the bed incident. Nothing but baseline activity. Pops, thuds, pacing, occasional pitter-patter noise, and the continuous off and on of our bedroom lights. Still no word from the bishop that Tina spoke to. If I didn't know any better, I'd say the house was in some sort of holding pattern; we're waiting for the next outbreak Tina and me. That's a bad position to be in. Instead of just waiting for the next attack, I decided to increase our search radius. I decided to email paranormal teams in other cities. Cities like Portland, Vancouver; Spokane.

Let me tell you as an IT professional; the internet is one the greatest utilities ever to be invented. One of the easiest utilities to ever be invented. There's no excuse for abysmal websites. Zero contact info. I don't know which is worst, the local priest not calling Tina back or undeliverable emails we got back whenever we contacted paranormal teams via their web page. I don't care if your organization has two people in it or twenty people. You need an IT person. Someone has to manage the technology side of the organization—I'm talking about the customer-facing side. If your connection to the outside world is still the twentieth century, then what the hell are you doing this for? Why are you trying to help people? You can't be an effective researcher if you don't know about the specimens in the world. The house itself is a specimen. That's all it is. One giant 2,300 square foot specimen. Tina and I are trying to tell people about it, and all we're getting is voicemail and undeliverable emails.

Time to head back to Spokane—Tina and Kim decided to do something different this time. Instead of Tina spending the night with Kim, Kim's going to spend the night with Tina. I'm thinking to myself, why would Kim want to do that? Our house is the Bothell Hell House. None of our friends have volunteered to spend the night with us after learning about what takes place. Then I remembered something. This is Kim we're talking about. Kim was the one who held up her iPhone after the plant incident. She had first row seats to an object being thrown. This might be interesting. Tina and Kim staying alone in the house.

We have to set some ground rules before you ladies stay here by yourself. Our communication is going to have to be spot on. We've had our issues in the communication department Tina and me. Some of it's our fault, and some of it is the spirit's fault. We can't control what the spirit does with our communication which makes me nervous about them staying in the house. But Kim wanted to stay with Tina, and Tina loved that idea so guess what? Let's do it.

Here are the ground rules. Tina's to call me before going to bed, and she's to call me when she wakes up. I mean, we're talking about her safety and Kim's safety. If we follow the protocol we set forth, everyone will be OK. Nothing was unique about Spokane trip. I go there every ninety days to work out of our sister office. We're talking about a twenty-minute flight from SeaTac. I'm probably the only person you'll ever meet that treats a business trip like a vacation. I mean, I'm no longer in the Bothell Hell House—*I'm free.* I might get eight hours sleep while here. I've forgotten what that feels like. *No more sleeping on eggshells. Hurray!!*

The week went by and the house appeared to be fine. Tina and I were talking every night. She spoke of an occasional bang here and there. I know I'm not going to get much more information than that based on the fact that Tina and Kim are like sorority sisters whenever they're together. There are as a merry as can be. And that's perfectly fine. No one deserves a good time more than Tina and me. Hopefully, the spirits will be contained due to the ladies' merriness. Ah, my business trip. Hurray!

The Davenport Hotel is where I stay when visiting Spokane. It's become a prescription sort of speak. A touch-stone if there ever is one. You know you're being tormented when you unknowingly prefer a cramped hotel room over your master bedroom. But that's exactly what this is now. Any hotel I stay when I travel on business trips has become my safe house. My place of refuge. My place of Zen. That would soon change.

It happened on the third night of me staying at the hotel. I was asleep as I should be. No woman in my bed, just me—*jokingly.* I'm in a deep sleep, probably snoring my ass off when all of a sudden, the comforter gets yanked off me. I wake up immediately and see the sheets that were once on me are now lying on the floor some few feet away. The room is pitch black. Was someone in the room with me? Of course not. I'm in a hotel room in downtown Spokane. *Time to analyze the situation.* Was I dreaming? Was I having a night terror? A night terror so extreme that maybe, just maybe, I threw my sheets off me? The answer I'm left with is no. *This wasn't a dream.* I wanted to call Tina so bad but thought to myself that calling her this late in the morning might terrify her. If she's asleep, let her stay that way. I'm sketchy on what I did afterward. I probably went back to sleep, although not immediately.

I woke up around 7 am the next day and saw that my cell phone was off. Fully charged, but off. I didn't turn it off before I went to bed. That would defeat the purpose. *Tina can't reach me if my phone is off, dammit!* After the phone powered up, all these text messages came pouring in. The first text message, at 2 am, read—*the door just slammed in the room Kim is in—Kim didn't hear it, it didn't even wake her up. Call me! No answer.* Minutes later another text message—*loud banging coming from the hallway, loud banging coming from the guest bedroom—I keep calling Kim, she won't answer.* Tina was telling me in her text the house was making noise. She can hear it. But Kim can't—Kim's not responding. *I'm thinking, where in the hell is Kim? Oh, Kim's in the guest bedroom, the room by my office.*

Had my phone not been off, my response to Tina would have been: check on her. Tina didn't. The fact that she didn't let me how scared she was. We never discussed them sleeping in different rooms. Why they chose to sleep in separate rooms is beyond me. I comb through the other missed text messages and see some more missed messages. This one came in a few minutes ago. Loud bangs, *loud bangs, Kim was taking a shower, and the door slammed shut on her, we're leaving!*

I got Tina's voicemail every time I called. Her last text message came just minutes ago. She'd said they were leaving the house. It sounds like they were being run out of the house. I finally got a hold of Tina after about the tenth time trying. Tina was on her way to work when she answered. Surprisingly she wasn't hysterical.

She didn't appear to be mad at me, whew! The last thing I needed from her was some false accusation as to why I didn't answer my phone. That would just piss me off. Neither one of us needed to be pissed off right now. So, what happened? A series of bangs and door slams. Kim's bedroom door slammed shut. The noise didn't wake Kim. Then the lights in the hall flickered off and on, followed by more bangs. The bangs kept going throughout the night. The bangs and thuds finally woke up Kim, and she walked to Tina's room; they both agreed that since the banging was happening, they might as well stay up. Morning came and Kim left to take a shower. The bathroom door slammed on her within seconds of her taking a shower. The incident startled them so much they said, "Screw it. Let's just get dressed and get the hell out of here." Both ladies were pretty much running for the door. Tina even told me the last banging noise they heard was right when they reached the garage door to leave the house. Kim says to Tina (and I quote): "I'm never coming to your crazy house again."

What spirit can haunt two places at once? *Talk to me, Mr. Paranormal researcher?* I don't think a poltergeist can, could, or would haunt two places at once. This confirms one of my biggest fears. Being followed.

What spirit can follow people? No way are we dealing with one spirit here. Jane Doe said her son still see's shadows from time to time. She used the word "shadows" not shadow. It wouldn't surprise me if we had multiple spirits attacking us. I mean, look how long we've been here. Every infestation, be it real or paranormal, seems to follow the same logic. Where one exists, others will surely follow. Don't solve that rodent or cockroach problem right away, soon you're going to have multiple rodents and cockroaches. Your problem increases ten-fold with each passing day.

Tina and I had dinner together that night when I got back in town. Away from the house. Time to compare notes. What scared Tina that night were the loud banging noises. Rapping's coming from the walls and ceiling near the hallway. Kim was dead serious when she said she was never coming back to our house. Not after what she experienced. I told Tina about the sheets being yanked off me while I slept. I told her about the poking and prodding I feel when lying in our bed. She looked at me with the widest eyes ever. There we were huddled in a booth inside Tom Douglas restaurant among other couples, talking about stuff that would terrify the average homeowner.

No one knows what we know. No one knows the problem we're having. There's no logical explanation for a bed sheet being yanked off you while sleeping. Nothing can explain that. Nothing except, I have a demon on my ass. I would gladly tell the local priest these things if he'd just return our phone calls. I'd tell him and his bishop. Neither one of them has called us back. I'm trying very hard not to indict organized religion. But what choice are you giving me when you won't call us back?

Chapter 27
The White Lady

Early October. There's not a day that goes that I don't think about the Gray Lady. Why did she reveal herself to me and not Tina? The books I've read online say apparition sightings are extremely rare. Not unheard of but rare. The apparition I saw (as it's defined) was somewhat interactive. She looked tired and confused. Above all else she looked conniving—she looked sneaky. Maybe she's the one trying to set me up? As you can probably tell, I'm about to see her again, except she's not gray anymore. That matte color gray has now become one hundred percent white.

It was a great night to be in the Pacific Northwest. I mean it must be mid-sixty degrees outside. The weather was normally a little colder outside but not tonight. The activity inside our house was showing no signs of tapering off. My office and my side of the bed had become ground zero for some of the most malicious attacks. The bed shakes whenever I lay down. I'm constantly being poked when trying to sleep. Pause your reading for now! I want you to try an experiment for me. I want you to poke the person sitting next to you. Poke them in the rib cage area. Poke them in their kidneys. Make sure you do it repeatedly, so they spin around and look at you like you're crazy. Keep poking them till they tell you to STOP! That's how it feels. It's very annoying. That's what was happening to me now. I was being poked and jabbed, and there's nothing I can do about it. Tina was sound asleep beside me—they don't even care that she's next to me. It's like she not even here. The only thing Tina hears while sleeping is the loud bangs. You can't help but get accustomed to them based on how often they happen. She was asleep. I'm not

Which brings me to a conclusion I was hoping to avoid. *I feel like I'm the only one doing stuff.* The only one following the steps the priest gave us. Whether the priest helps us or not, the advice he gave is still sound. We should still follow it. I mean it's all we got. No one's jabbing Tina in her rib cage. She would have told me if that was the case. She was sleeping soundly right now. I know because I'm looking dead at her.

So, I'm a little wired. I'm a little cranky. What the priest warned us about seems to be coming true. It looks like the spirits are focusing on me. They're bombarding Tina with female trinkets, which makes her more withdrawn. Makes her more upset. At the same time, they're messing with me. I can't help but be irritated. Why am I the only one smudging? Why am I the only one leaving music on when we leave the house? The only one reciting prayers? Lighting candles? Remember the chef's knife that was thrown at me? It's been thrown at me again. Tina seemed detached from it all. She seemed detached from a lot of things of late. How do I know?

I know because I had confiscated her entire kitchen knife collection. I'd taken them all, some thirty of them and hid them in my car. The knives I confiscated are the ones being thrown. No one was throwing knives at Tina. The knives had been in the trunk of my car for several weeks, and Tina was not even aware of it. Not once had she asked me where her knives went. Meanwhile, I'm getting candles thrown at me while trying to smudge the hallway. Last week I had a smudge tray thrown within inches of me. The thing was a missile. Have you ever had an ashtray fly at you like a bullet? How about one logged in a wall?

Fig 27.1 Smudge tray thrown seconds after I completed smudging. Misses me by inches. Leaves a golfball size hole in the wall.

We're back to the accusation of a woman being in the house while she was gone. Tina doesn't have to preach it to me. I know the signs. *Tina, the priest said we should take turn smudging; we have to do it together*. Her response would be a "sigh" and the rolling of the eyes. Granted neither one of us was operating under normal hours of sleep. Nor were we aware of how much we're being manipulated. These abrupt move swings are being inserted into both of us. We're not aware of it at the time, but that's what's happening. I mean we didn't even know the house was humming until Jennifer told us. There's an unseen presence that's altering the mood of both of us. Could that explain why the apparition was gray two years ago and is white today? Is our weakness making her stronger?

I was trying to do everything I can in lessening the negative energy around us. A few our friends suggested that we went out and bought salt rocks. "Get two of them. Place one upstairs and one downstairs." The reason for these salt rocks is simple: to increase positive energy levels. "Try to offset the baseline of the house right now?" Maybe the salt rocks can offset that? Maybe that'll lessen the bed activity. If it engages Tina more, I'm all for it. Let me do my homework (before we go out and buy them). The advice from our friends seemed credible. The recommendation came from a sincere place—Tina's friends. So, we went out and bought them, together with Tina. *Wow, they're huge. Should we be putting rocks this big for our house?* God help us if one of these rocks decides to go airborne. But hey we have to try, right? It can never be said that we didn't try anything and everything.

A few weeks after we bought the salt rocks was when Tina and I had our next argument. I should be more conservative with that word argument. This was more like a disagreement. The outcome was still the same though. A malevolent spirit never lets a good opportunity go by. Spirits can do a lot with just one disagreement. Especially a disagreement about them. Who's turn is it to smudge? Who's not smudging enough? That night Tina didn't want to. Fine, I'll smudge by myself and go back to my office when done. No need to make this bigger than what it was. A shouting match is only going to put this house at greater risk of exploding. So, we squashed the argument quickly which is to say we went our separate ways. Time to give each other the cold shoulder. I could feel the atmosphere changing in the house again.

How did I know that? I knew that because the lights in my office started going off and on. The room never lost power which does happen, but today, the lights just flickered off and on. Minutes later, the hallway light began to flicker off and on to. Until finally, all the upstairs lights just went off together.

Fig. 27.2 One of the most extraordinary paranormal attacks in the Bothell home. a.) power goes off upstairs(only) b.) objects thrown c.) 2nd appearance of female apparition—resembles someone I know?

Knowing that she was in the kitchen cleaning up, I decided to head back to my office. The lights in my room went off within seconds of me sitting in my chair. Now my heart was beating fast. I'm sitting in the dark, ladies and gentlemen. I'm scared. Knives have been thrown at me at this point. I'm talking about chef knives. Let me tell you something. You don't know what fear is until you have a chef knife thrown at you in pitch blackness. There's a snap, crackle, pop sound and then suddenly a loud *BOOM*! Something's hit something. Lights flicker on and there it is in the hallway. Right outside your office door—a kitchen chef knife. Tonight, it was a little different.

I rose and walked over the light switches. Something inside me told me something important was about to happen. *Keith, you should get your cell phone out.* I figured the lights were going to be going off again real soon. Let me try to catch it on my cell phone. If I can catch my lights going off and on by themselves, surely a paranormal team will see that and say, OK, we have to help this guy. That's what I thought. I reached into my pocket and pull out my cell phone and aimed it towards the ceiling in my office when suddenly I heard crashing sounds.

The noise was coming from the hallway. Something was being thrown towards my bookshelf. It sounded like the broken bottle cap convention had arrived in town. But no, it's not bottled. It's candles. Luckily, I had my cell out already. Lucky, I hit the record button and began recording. The attack was over within seconds. That's how unpredictable the attacks can be. They happen very fast. Blink your eye or turn away and you've missed it. But I saw it as clear as day. Two or three objects flew towards my bookshelf. They hit it and *BOOM*, such a loud noise. It's like the hallway had turned into pool hall all of a sudden. Ricochet after ricochet until an abrupt stop. That's it? It's over.

I stepped into the hallway and saw broken glass everywhere. I'm still recording. If you've looked at the pictures of my bookshelf, you know how thick the two shelves are. They're sizeable. The lower shelf has a new nick in it. We now have a new hole in the wall the size of a tennis ball. There was broken glass everywhere. Including the shelves. Hold up, I know these candles. I know where they came from. They came from our bedroom; from our night-stands. I reviewed my video footage within minutes of the attack and learned that it was three that had been thrown. Three loud thuds. I purposely went to our bedroom a few minutes after the attack, to confirm which candles had been thrown. I was right. The candles that the priest gave us are gone. All three of them. Link https://youtu.be/PFBtpo9OOU8

https://youtu.be/PFBtpo9OOU8

Fig 27.3 Flying candles. Part 2 and 3 are in the back of the book.

I went back to recording this event on my cell phone, narrating as I went from room to room. I stepped into the bedroom, and the light went off. I stepped out of our bedroom; the light turned back on. I do this over and over just to see if I was imagining things. I'm not. This was happening. The only thing I can now before cleaning up the damage is to upload the video to YouTube.

FYI: YouTube's my primary back up mechanism now. I've lost too many hard drives. Too many video cameras with the SD card inside. If the spirit can steal the internet, then it deserves to have any video it wants. *Let these captures live on YouTube forever is my thinking.* Of course, the more I share, the more vulnerable I am to ridicule.

The comment I get the most from skeptics as it relates to this video is: *why are you acting so calm? Why aren't you fearful or panicking?* Followed by: *why are you holding the phone in such a way to avoid seeing the objects flying? There's someone on the other side of that wall throwing candles at the bookshelf.* I can understand someone asking that question; it's a fair question to ask. What most people don't understand (about this video is) this isn't the first time we've had objects thrown. It's not even the tenth time. It's not even the twentieth time. We're past the stage of how many objects are being thrown. If you were to ask me that question over Titos cranberry, my response would pick a category. Small, medium, and large. How many small objects have been thrown? How many medium objects have been thrown? How many large-size objects? How many sharp objects? How many objects were thrown at us while we were sleeping? How many objects were thrown while we were awake? I could go and on about the various categories these attacks fall into where thrown objects are concerned. To answers the skeptic's question (the person who refuses to believe no matter what). The reason you don't see me shit my pants when the candles start to fly because objects this size have been flying for the last two years.

I will admit I have no idea what's about to happen. I don't. Only the poltergeist knows that. All I know is seconds before the candles got thrown massive electrical issues broke out. Lights went off in my office, in the hallway, and the bedrooms. There was a period where everything went off upstairs—at the same time. All the power downstairs was on. Not so much as a flicker. The objects I'm witnessing are flying at incredible speeds. So much force and precision were involved. You would not want to be on the receiving end of those candles when they were being thrown. So, it was a spectacular moment. A moment I believe a researcher would appreciate witnessing. These candles being thrown are not even in the top five of all objects thrown around the house. They're not even in the top twenty. The reader needs to understand that. Considerable damage was done to the hall and bookshelf. Watch the three videos in the order of which they occurred. Maximize your computer screen. Hit the slow-motion button on YouTube. Wear headsets when watching. There's so much there. I dare not spoil for it for you. There's so much there.

Fig 27.4 Hallway attack – 3 candles encased in glass go flying through the hall. This is the wall impact from one of them.

Tina never responded to the attack. I'm not even sure she heard it. I didn't tell her about it either. She did come up the hall a few minutes later and saw me vacuuming up glass and candle debris. She stepped right over me without asking one single question. I thought she would since it was her candles that got thrown. But she didn't. I picked up two severely damaged candles off the floor that night. I have no idea where the third one went. To my knowledge, it has never reappeared.

Now I know Tina is detached. I can always tell how mad she is by her level of housecleaning. She's cleaning downstairs, not upstairs. *Remember, we're keeping our distance from one another.*

The second time Tina came upstairs, it was to clean up the bedroom. *After the candle incident, mind you.* She makes up the bedroom, and within minutes heads back downstairs. It wasn't long before I heard our garage door open. I heard her SUV engine and I'm thinking: where is she going? But no, Tina's not going anywhere; Tina's backing her SUV out the garage. As I said, I know she's mad because she's doing mass house cleaning. I soon heard the vacuum cleaner come on and thought, *ah ha, she's pissed. No one vacuums their car at night.* Throughout the night I heard Tina go in and out of the house. ADT system: *Garage door open, garage door open.* Which is a good thing because I know where Tina is. I can hear her from my office window, and I can hear her from whenever the alarm door chimes —*Garage door open, garage door open.*

And now for the white lady. I'm pretty sure I was watching the video of my candles being thrown. I must have watched it over and over that night—up until the time where I heard new noises coming from the hallway. Not a loud bang. Not the sound of footsteps. This noise was brand new. What I heard now I'd never heard before. And that's when my brain kicked in, *Keith, there shouldn't be any noise coming from the hallway; Tina's outside, she's in the driveway vacuuming her car, look up from the keyboard. Look up from the keyboard you idiot someone's coming down the hallway.* My brain was right. Someone was coming down the hallway. Who in the hell is coming down the hallway?

I turned from my computer to face the doorway. I could see the bookshelf. I could see the guest bathroom. I'm looking dead center at the hallway. I know pacing noise when I hear it. This was not pacing noise. It sounded like rustling leaves or rustling paper. It sounded like my hallway had suddenly become a paper mill, or better yet like someone was gathering a pile of fall leaves with both their arms. It sounded like something rustling. The noise was very distinct. And it was growing louder, which suggested whatever it was, was coming my way.

I couldn't get on the phone. It was happening too fast. This time I just had to look. As soon as I turned towards the hallway, there she was. A woman looking almost identical to the Gray Lady, with one exception: she's white. Last time I saw the Gray Lady she wasn't holding anything. The lady I saw in 2012 looked worn out. She looked tired and confused. She looked furtive. This time she looks different. Same woman, but now she's white, all white. And she's holding something. Her hands are full: *what the hell is she holding?* It was like she was holding a load of clothing. Except it was not clothing. At least not based on the sound I was hearing. Imagine you're a paper collector. You collect bucket loads of paper, so you can recycle it later. The act of emptying whatever receptacle you keep the paper requires you grabbing loads of paper with both arms. That's what I heard. The sound of someone carrying loads of paper; or a trash bag full of leaves.

The woman I'm looking at walks past my door and enters the room to the right of me. Something told me not to look her in the eye. Not that she was looking at me. But what if she did? What then? What do I do if she turns and looks at me? What if she starts screaming, "Why don't you get of my house already?!" I tell you what I would do. I'd piss the carpet if that happened.

Thank God she never looked at me. She kept looking dead ahead, looking straight into the room she walked in. It was like I was watching a movie play out. A movie of woman walking through the hallway. Not hologram. She was fully white. No transparency whatsoever. Just like the Gray Lady two years ago. She walked into the guest bedroom—the room next to me. That's when I said OK. I can move now, she gone let me see what's in the room next to me. Naturally, when I arrived in the room, nothing was there. I have no clue as to what I would have done had there been. Be sure to review the reenactment video below. At the tail end of writing this book I decided to something I don't think has ever been done: I decided to locate a computer animator. Words can only describe so much. Pictures can only describe so much. The video is a good reenactment of what happened that night. Thank you, Fiverr.com CGI animator, for recreating the woman based on my description.

Video https://youtu.be/urjrfaWj8mk

Fig 27.5 October 2014 – The White Lady. Completely opaque as The Gray Lady before her.

What a difference two year makes. I didn't go looking, Tina, like I did last time. I didn't want to. Screw it; if she's mad at me, then she doesn't need to know. I told you resentment was going to set in. As was isolation. I believe I told you at the beginning of this book that one of the reasons for Tina and me moving in together was to work on our relationship. How are we doing?

We've changed tremendously. We don't know it yet, but we have. The house might as well had been a rainbow the day we got the keys to it. Now it's a mushroom cloud. We're stuck. We're stuck because of the baggage we brought into the house when we arrived and because of the invisible force sitting between us both right now. If you think about it, there's no wrong or right here. Just "Geist." Shit doesn't happen here. "Geist" happens here. I can't be plainer than that. Tina's not my enemy. I'm not her enemy. What's happening to us could happen to ninety-nine percent of the world population. "Geist" happens.

Back to the apparition. Where does it fit in all of this? I have no stinking idea where she fits in all of this. All I know is she looked vaguely familiar. I've seen two apparitions in roughly the same place. I have the Gray Lady, and I have the white lady. *I should probably reveal to the reader my artistic background. Drawing has been a hobby of mine since I was a little kid. If I can see it, I can draw it. The key to drawing what you see is remembering.* I'm ninety-nine percent sure what I saw that night was the Gray Lady. Why is she white?

Both apparitions were identical in size. Very thin, very petite, and frail looking. I can describe each woman's hair for days. Straight and frizzy looking—thin as spaghetti angel hair. The Gray Lady looked lost and confused. Extremely timid and tired. Not the white lady. No, the white lady looked more trance-like. She looked like she was doing something. She had a monotone aura about her. What the hell was she holding? I've seen that face before. That mannerism, I know it. Who is she?

I don't think it was the white lady who threw the candles. I'm almost sure of it. I'm forever revising my theory about more than one spirit being in this house. I'm pretty sure we have more than two attacking us. More than five attacking us. That's what my gut is telling me. How involved the Gray Lady and white lady are with the danger happening around us remains to be seen (no pun intended).

Chapter 28
Halloween 2014

"This year Halloween fell on a weekend."
Geto Boys

The following Monday Tina and I woke up one day and noticed that both our phone chargers were missing. Tina had hers on her lampstand, as did I. Tina woke up before me and noticed her cord was gone. Her cell phone had little juice in it, so she asked if she could borrow my charger. I said yes, and that's when I realized mine was gone as well. Both of our phones had about fifty-percent of battery life left in them. I call this the *incommode phenomenon*—the art of being inconvenienced. The spirit takes these things to slow you down. They do it with the hopes of creating angst. The minute I knew my cell phone charger was gone I looked at Tina and said, don't even bother looking for yours. We'll never see those cords again, and I was right. They never resurfaced. So, what is *incommode phenomenon?*

The *incommode phenomenon* is quite simple. The spirit takes your stuff and then watches you search for it. There are certain things in the house that you noticed within minutes of it being gone: mom's coffee cup, toothpaste, toothbrush, hairbrush, your favorite CD, cash, watch, car keys, and so forth. Some of these items that go missing create a level of angst when you begin searching for them. That's why they stole it—to make me and Tina upset.

Now the story I'm about to tell you is extremely bizarre. Even for me. It's a strong contender for winning the 'weirdest shit of the week' award. You would think I would have learned my lesson by now; which is, I should leave when Tina leaves. Based on the poster experience, and a few other experiences that took place immediately upon Tina's departure, I should have been out of the house already.

I was about to leave the house that morning, thirty minutes or so after Tina. I walked downstairs and grabbed my laptop bag. The only thing I had to do now was to turn on the ADT security system and walk out of the house. When I got to my front door, I noticed something very weird. Three buttons are missing from the middle of my short sleeve shirt—all in a row.

Fig 28.1 Three buttons mysteriously disappear off my shirt.

There's no way I would have put this shirt on had I seen three buttons missing. That's not something I would do. It can't all be ghost related, right? The only thing I can do is put on another shirt. That's what I did. I went upstairs. I ironed another shirt, put it on and walked out of the house. What did it cost me? Cost me thirty minutes which is a long time when you're trying to beat the morning traffic.

A similar story would emerge the next day. Tina left the house again before I did. There I was again getting dressed. This time I was wearing one of my long sleeve button-down shirts. I came downstairs a half an hour after Tina's left and began locking up the house. I walked towards the TV in the den, turn it on to the Gospel channel. Goodbye, bitches! I made my way to the front door and all of a sudden, my shirt flied open. *What the hell*? I looked down at my shirt wondering what just happened and I got my answer right away. Every button on my shirt was gone. I kid you not. Now, I'm not suggesting that my shirt came unfastened, meaning the buttons are still there. No: I'm saying my shirt came unfastened because the buttons are gone. Vanished, disappeared—gone entirely. This is what happened yesterday with my three missing buttons. We went from three buttons to nine missing buttons. In the blink of an eye, mind you.

I don't know about you, but to me, that sounds very up close and personal. How could a spirit do that? I mean, I took a shower and got dressed. I buttoned my shirt before I walked out of our bedroom. I went downstairs and turned on the TV to the Gospel music channel. I grabbed my laptop bag. I turned on the ADT alarm system. My shirt is still intact. I get to the front door, and my shirt becomes unfastened. The buttons were nowhere to be found.

Now this thing with my buttons is not dangerous. That's not the message the spirits were trying to send. No, they were trying to convey something else. The message I got from this event was 'we're here.' I never felt a tug or tear. I didn't feel anything. My shirt is still in good shape—minus the missing buttons, of course. This reminded me of the envelopes disappearing off my keyboard. A similar instance of now you see it, now you don't.

It's like the episode of *I Dream of Jeannie*, where the beautiful Barbara Eden does that famous nod, and all of sudden nine buttons disappear. That's the only way all of this could have happened. I got dressed. That much we know. Minutes later all the buttons are gone. I would be late for work again, and that's why they did it, they did it to inconvenience me. I'm thinking to myself: *what's preventing it from taking the buttons off the next shirt, I put on?* Nothing. I mean, it could if it wanted to. Lucky for me it didn't. Remember: they're in control right now. They take what they want when they want. There's nothing Tina, and I can do about it. I've included more asport, apport experiences at the very end of this book. There's so much you should know about in regards to what Tina and I witnessed. Be sure to check that appendix out.

In the interim, the cameras I positioned throughout the house are not even my cameras anymore. I configured them and within minutes they were showing me rooms that they were not supposed to. That's when the problem begins. That's when my IT side kicks in and tries to problem solve. I'm constantly rebooting cameras. Constantly reconfiguring my cameras to the point of it becoming frustrating. Both Foscam and Trendnet help desks are at their wits end about what's going on with the cameras in my house. Speaking of my house.

There's something new to see every night now. The couch and love seat are rearranged in such a way to where Tina and I are just dumbfounded. Items we owned for years are just being manipulated at will. What do we do with these items once the activity stops? If the activity stops? Do we throw them away? Do we burn them? Definitely can't donate them to the Salvation Army or Goodwill. What's to become of them? I'm clueless as to what to do.

It seems that if you keep emailing enough paranormal teams, sooner or later someone is going to respond. A few finally did. A team from Spokane, Washington, and a team right here in Seattle. The methodology and preliminary analysis from both teams were as different as night and day. The team in Seattle leaped to the conclusion very early on that Tina and I were facing something demonic. How do reach a conclusion like that without even investigating? That should have been the first red flag Tina and I should have caught. But we didn't. We just wanted help. See what happens when the local priests ignore you? We found ourselves wandering endlessly Tina and I did. If you were receptive to our pleas, odds are you got into our house. Now don't get me wrong. Tina and I know we have something nasty on our hands. I'm hearing grunts and growls when I'm in my office working from home. I see shadows and black figures out the corner of my eye whenever I turn my back to do something. I'm coming back to rooms where the light is off when I'm a hundred percent sure I left it on. Is that a demon doing that? Or a poltergeist? I want to believe it's a poltergeist so bad, at least that tells me this is going to wear off eventually. But who's the agent? No agent, no poltergeist, right?

Now the Seattle team upon their first visit did witness some usual activity— they saw one of Tina's candle rod slide across the kitchen floor. This seemed to be a night where the entities wanted to show off their apporting capabilities. I mean, seriously, here we are—all of us gathered in the master bedroom. The leader of their group is speaking to us about the cross that reappeared in the washing machine (See Appendix B: Disappearing Cross) Tina and I are giving them that rundown when all of a sudden, one of Tina's two feet step ladder appears.

Tina keeps two step ladders in the house. She keeps one in the living room closet and the other in the guest bedroom closet. Neither ladder was in our bedroom when we all walked in. We've assembled in our bedroom for quite some time. The paranormal team is talking to Tina and me near the foot of the bed when out of nowhere appears this step ladder.

Who noticed it first? We all did. Ladders don't appear out of thin air, right? *Well, in our house they do.* The ladder had previously been in the kitchen—it's the kitchen step ladder.

So that was a big deal. I mean, it blows you away to see something like this. "Welcome to our world," Tina said. Now you've seen an object appear, what can you do to make it stop? That's my number one question for every team that's been to see us. Now, remember what I just said. This team believes we have a demon in our house. I've sensed learned that paranormal teams love to throw the word demon around, without doing the homework first. Evidently, it's en vogue to use the word demon now, due to certain TV shows. Another reason why it's en vogue is that the person making the declaration is interestingly positioned themselves as being the "demon remover?" Anyone with the ability to declare a demon is present, conveniently can remove it.

Tina and I know we have something or something nasty living with us. We know that better than anybody stepping foot into our house. You don't have to twist my arm to convince me that there are demonic forces at play here. These spirits are leaving female jewelry in and around the house for Tina to find as a means of oppression. You don't have to convince me; I get it. What I don't get is you telling me that you're going to perform a ritual in which all the demons in this house are going "to stop what it is they're doing, and suddenly leap into your body and possess you" as a result of you being a badass. That's how badass you are. You're like Yoda absorbing force electricity. "Very few investigators can do what it is you're about to do." This is what we were told when the team came by the third and fourth time. They give us the "kids don't try this at home" speech.

Now Tina and I have been through a lot at this point. We've seen a lot. We've heard a lot. Regardless of our disagreements. Regardless of what we might think of ourselves as a couple, we know snake oil when we see it. We know when someone's fake. Don't confuse us still living here with being born yesterday. Nothing irks me more than having my intelligence insulted. It ranks high in my book, and it ranks high in Tina's. It's equal to wasting my time. I hate when my time is wasted. Tina does too. The Seattle team came back a few days later and announced that they have a game plan. They've thought this over, and the decision they've agreed is "simple." The leader of the group is going to summon the demon to come out. He's going to command that it jump in his body. Once the demon does that, the leader and the group that came with him will then walk out of the house together. He'll go to war with it internally and release what's left of it somewhere else. I know my mom and dad raised me right because a part of me wanted to dropkick him so bad. Dropkick him to the point of him (the group leader) flying out one of our windows. Tina saw the look on my face and knew exactly what I was thinking. She gave me a *Keith don't you dare do it* look.

I know now based on my reading that the mere suggestion of performing some New Age exorcism was, in fact, putting Tina in greater harm's way. Spirits that are currently oblivious to this house and its occupants can come running. Tina and I watched the joke ceremony in frustration. We were angry and upset. We thought the team was going to return with another priest or something. Return with a shaman possibly. Matter of fact the lead team member said he was "shaman." He's a priest; he's a shaman, he's the team administrator, he's the jack of all trades evidently. He's malfeasance. That's what he was.

That was the last time that team came to our house. I mean, it takes three months to find help, or what we thought was help. I had to find out the hard way: all help is not good help. There's not a paranormal team on this planet that doesn't want to see something like this. But wanting to see and being qualified to see are two different things. Tina and I are in desperate need of someone who's qualified; someone's who skilled and patient. This team witnessed a lot of stuff when they visited us. But it soon became apparent that witnessing was all they were doing. Yes, furniture moving about, and growls being heard from different parts of the room does give off the appearance that our house is a circus. But that's not why you're here. You're not here to enjoy the circus. You're here to put the circus out of business. Next!

Spokane WA—all-female team. Tina and I identified with them within minutes of talking to them on the phone. Yes, Christians! What they lacked in experience or expertise, they made up for in empathy. Empathy (not sympathy) wins every time with Tina and me. It gets you through the door.

You see, Tina and I are lonely at this phase. We're isolated. We're cut off. There are just a handful of people that know exactly what it is we're going through. We no longer tell our families what's going on. They've stopped asking. Everyone's reached the bottom of their idea-bucket in regard to what to do next about our situation. Since no one can come up with a solution, they just stop asking for updates. That's what Tina's family did. That's what my family did. Our friends are the same way. Everyone was at their wit's end now.

The good thing about all of this is we've not slowed down our social appearance. Tina does her thing. I do my thing. Occasionally when we're not at odds with one another, we do things together.

When the Spokane team reached out to us, they were pretty much reaching out to us on someone else's behalf. That someone else being a priest of sorts. The initial emails are always the same. The questions centered around who I am? Who is Tina? How long have we been in the house? When did the activity begin? What are you experiencing? Tina and I know these questions all too well. The back in forth emails is pretty consistent at this stage—up until the time of "what type of activity are you experiencing?" This is where Tina and I pause. We pause because we know communication usually stops at this stage. You ask us a question; we're going to give you an answer; an honest answer. Now you might like it. Doesn't mean the answer isn't true just because you find it unbelievable. You asked for honesty; we're giving you honesty. Take it or leave it. Most teams leave it. Most priests leave it. Those who don't leave it still don't believe it—they, in my opinion, do something worse. They start asking us stupid questions.

Tina and I have never been allergic to questions. We understand the importance of asking questions. Her jobs require it as does mine. We're getting oppressed now. The activity is forcing us to sleep in different bedrooms now. Sheets have been yanked off both of while sleeping in our bedroom. The bedroom door slams extremely loud whenever we forget to prop it with a pillow. I'm irritated. Tina's irritated. We're pointing at each other whenever one of us realizes the other person forgot to smudge. The other person forgot to leave the gospel music on when leaving for work in the morning. If you're going to ask us questions, make sure you make those questions count. Tina and I are in a storm now. Understand we're in the middle of a storm. Asinine questions only make a situation worse.

A few days later after my initial email exchange with the team in Spokane, I get a series of emails from Father John Ashcraft's assistant (the organization mentoring the Spokane team). The emails explained that before John Ashcraft could take on this investigation, there's a series of things he wants me to do.

Fr. John Ashcraft would like you to insert cameras in the house "without telling Tina?" Put some cameras under the couch, put some under the love seat, put them in the air ducts and air vents. Leave them on at all times. This came from his assistant. Ashcraft has been copied on the email but for some odd reason never comments—he remains silent throughout the entire exchange.

The exchange, as you'd expect, becomes heated. Are you asking me to install cameras without my girlfriend's knowledge? That's not going to happen. I'm not hiding anything from Tina. Tina's not throwing armoires across the room. Tina's not lighting Bibles on fire. Tina's not writing six-six-six and upside-down man symbols in my office. She's not lighting posters on fire, and she's certainly not bringing woman's jewelry in the house for the purpose of falsely accusing me. Tina and I are being told that Fr. John Ashcraft can't help us until he sees some real activity taking place. No phone screens. No video chats. No interview whatsoever. They want to see a video of us being oppressed. They want me to install cameras and "not tell Tina."

There's never been doubt in her mind or my mind about the culpability of the other person. Can you imagine Tina's reaction if I did this? Can you imagine the spirit's reaction? Yes, the spirit's going to react to the addition of new cameras, it's going to react to Tina being upset. And Tina has a right to be upset—her boyfriend has just labeled her a suspect. Recall, too, that Tina was never a fan of the cameras. She found the cameras an invasion of our privacy. And she was right. The cameras are an invasion of our privacy. That's a fact that Tina and I agreed to early on. But hiding a camera from your girlfriend as a means of convincing a priest? That and the "I'm going to summon all the demons in yourself into my person and walk them out of the house" were no doubt the stupidest things we've heard since living in this house. I want to be blunt as possible when I say this. If your primary concern is being taken advantage of by hoaxers, then you're in the wrong field. That cannot be your number one concern as a researcher, as an investigator, as a seeker of truth. That lets me know how fake you are.

The Spokane team's founder and I continued our conversation without Fr. Ashcraft's involvement. She heard the loud bangs. She heard the ruckus and commotion that was going on—all while she was on the phone with me. But even her ears and her gut instincts were not enough to change Fr. Ashcraft's mind. A few days after our heated email exchange I got a phone call from the Spokane team. Through their deliberation, they'd reached a conclusion: "we're going to help you guys; we're coming to Seattle." I told Tina the next day over dinner about the Spokane team's decision. She, like me, was very reluctant, due to the debacle we had with the last team. We're tired of subjecting ourselves to foolishness. Bad help is worse than no help, ladies and gentlemen, it is. I assured Tina that would not be the case with this team. This team seems to have their heart in the right place.

One of the questions I began asking myself was why does the spirit wait for us to leave before attacking the house? Granted it's attacked us when we were home, but those are different types of attacks. The attacks we have while at home are more like explosions. The attacks that take place while we're at work seem to suggest mass chaos while at the same time suggests mass order. The pictures you see (below) suggest that the spirits intentionally wait for us to leave the house before performing some of its most secretive feats. Why is that?

Fig 28.2 Kitchen camera and den camera capture after the fact house attack. Cameras went through a series of reboots which suggests power loss.

This attack (Fig 28.2) happened early in the day. I remember it vividly. Both motion and sound detection emails filled up both our inboxes. We're talking about a hundred emails within the course of a few hours. Of course, the cameras go offline which prevents me from seeing anything. This is what we see hours later. Cameras inexplicably come back online after the attack has ended. I keep coming back to the notion of them not wanting to be observed. I can't understand why though. Is this scientific or is this their demented way of toying with us? Are they trying to make prisoners in our own home?

It hasn't worked. Tina and I are keeping our schedules. We're performing at work, and we're keeping our friends. The only thing I can see that's suffering right now is our relationship. We're not the same people anymore. I can feel us slowly slipping away, and I feel no need to put a stop to it. It's weird; it's so damn weird. A perfect example of us needing time away from each other was Halloween night.

October 31st—we decided to do our own thing. Tina decided to go out with her friends, and I was going to go out with mine. That would have been unheard of this time last year. Last year Tina baked chocolate chip cookies for the trick-or-treaters. Last year we took turns handing out candy. What a difference a year makes, right?

Not only did we need a break from the house, but it seems like we needed a break from each other. Tonight, we need to be with our friends. Tonight, it's all about letting lose—forget the Bothell hell house even exists. Be with your friends, Tina, and I'll be with mine. But! Text me before you come home. Do not walk in the house by yourself. Thank God, Tina didn't get home before me tonight. I arrived back at the house after 2 am Halloween night, walked in through the front door, and knew something was wrong. The house was just too serene. It was as if I'd walked in while a burglary was taking place— like I was interrupting something. I got to the kitchen and saw the rearrangement of the kitchen chairs. There on the floor was my cross (the gift from my cousin), next to it was something I've never seen before: a puddle of water. *That's got to be paranormal because there was no known water source.* The drops began and ended between my kitchen chair, cross, and wine rack. That's what made me grab my cell phone. I began videotaping it all. Now keep in mind, I just came from a Halloween party clear across town. I'm tired and a little dazed. This is the first time this house has been in disarray this late in the day. In keeping with the theme of something new always being added, we now water puddles. Tina was not here, so I'm going to say it for her. That's different.

I had to go upstairs and see if our upstairs was still there. And it was. It is still there but, wow: no way could I have imagined what I was about to see. Every wall in my office (including the ceiling) had writings on it. Writings and drawings. Three crosses in the room were turned upside down. Everything had been rearranged. The upside-down man was drawn multiple times, as was the numbers 666. Two things caught my attention that night: The puddle of water downstairs and the seemingly unfinished marking in the hallway. There have been multiple wall markings in my office throughout this year. This is the first time in the history of living here has there been markings on the wall in the hallway. It seemed incomplete though. Look closely at Fig 28.9; you'll see how incomplete it looks.

That in addition to concussion-like atmosphere forced me to believe that the spirits weren't done. The house seemed to have a pissed off vibe right now. Reminiscent of the Katie Perry weekend? It felt like they weren't done. I mean how long does it take for droplets to dry on a wooden floor? That puddle of water had to have recently been put there. It was like I interrupted them.

Enough with the cell phone I'm holding. It's time to pull out the video camera. Which is exactly what I did. I needed to send tonight's attack to Jennifer, to the team in Spokane, and to the local priest. Tina was going to be shocked when she got home.

Ten minutes later. I videotaped the kitchen, the den, and the messed-up office upstairs. Fifteen minutes of video footage, not counting what I got my cell phone. My protocol for videotaping anything was to back it up into the cloud, i.e. YouTube, or my DropBox account. That's what I normally do with my so-called after-the-fact footage. That night I didn't do it. I was tired. Hungry, buzzing, and tired. I remember lying on the couch (after cleaning up the mess) and going to sleep. I remember where I put the video before falling asleep. I sat on the arm of the love seat—right in front of me. It was maybe four feet away by the time I closed my eyes.

Twenty minutes later—Tina arrives. My eyes dart open within seconds of her walking through the door. Her reaction was the same as mine. Disbelief, disgust, helplessness, and frustration. Tina glanced at me for one second and took off upstairs. That was my cue to get up. I followed Tina upstairs, forgetting something very important. *The video camera.* Six hours later, I wake up and go back downstairs to finish what I started. Time to back up the video footage. I get downstairs and notice the video camera is gone. That was the last video camera I owned.

Halloween Night: 2014
https://www.youtube.com/watch?v=Pow8xFUDWW4

Fig. 28.3 Kitchen chairs are aligned in a weird way. Bedroom cross is lying on the floor. November 1st, 2014.

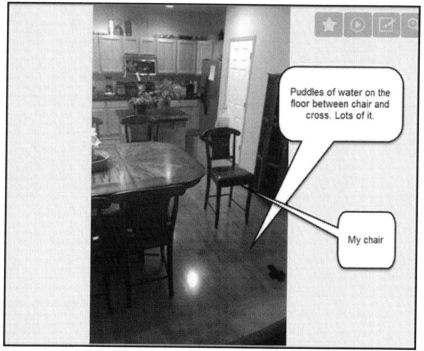

Fig 28.4 Different angle.

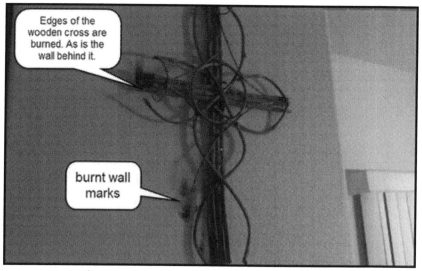

Fig 28.5 The edges have been burned on this cross.

Fig 28.6 Office – New unknown substance.

Fig 28.7 New upside-down man symbol.

Fig 28.8 666 closet door/wall writing.

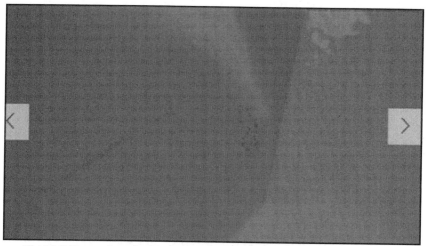

Fig 28.9 Never shared with the public till now. Mysterious pattern on the hallway wall.

Fig 28.10 2nd upside down man symbol. Look closely and you'll see marking goes behind the TV screen. Both TV and entertainment center were not moved.

Chapter 29
Ghost Adventures I

How did *Ghost Adventures* find out about our house in the first place? Two words: Elisa Jaffe. Who is Elisa Jaffe? Elisa Jaffe is the Seattle KOMO CBS news reporter who got wind of our situation upon receiving a series of emails. My next-door neighbor (a Catholic as well) upon learning of our problem with the local priest told us we should reach out to the local news. News outlets have an inordinate amount of resources. They know people in just about every space imaginable. Perhaps they know of other churches in the area—other churches that would be eager to help. Maybe they know of research teams, of paranormal teams. It's worth a shot, right?

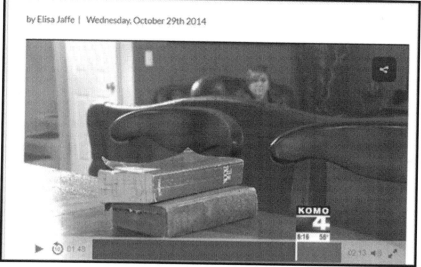

Fig 29.1 KOMO House visit
http://komonews.com/news/local/bothell-man-claims-his-house-is-haunted-this-is-no-casper

Fig 29.2 Tweet: ## crucifix not enough to keep me feeling safe. Freaked by the boom during Interview at haunted house. Oct 29th, 2014 ~ Elisa Jaffe

Rewind. Elisa Jaffe and her cameraman arrived at our house October 29th, to see if there was truth to what I was saying. STOP! Do you know how rare it is for a third party to arrive in a haunted environment and witness something themselves? Set aside the paranormal teams that have come in. Yeah, they've all witnessed events themselves. This is different. I mean KOMO news spent about an hour in my home and during that hour heard one of the most common wonders associated with a poltergeist. Rapping. *Elissa's and her producer's account are in the link above.* That's what I needed. I needed our claims substantiated. And there's no better way to do that other than inviting the public in. A day later I got a call from Dave Schrader—Darkness radio chief researcher for *Ghost Adventures* television show.

He talked to me for about fifteen minutes. That was it. I guess the loud bang left an impact on Elisa because Dave's questions were short and basic. He told me his crew *Ghost Adventures* would like to investigate the activity; they wanted to help. His last comment to me was we need home owner's approval. Can you get your landlord to approve our visit? My reply to him was yes. I think my landlord would be relieved to know a bona fide investigative team was going to come to research our problem. *By all means, research the problem.* Research the problem, don't investigate the problem—there is a difference.

I mean a team affiliated with the Travel Channel has to have resources out the ying-yang, right? I mean the world over? They just have to? We'll see. I mean the onus was on me now. The moment had now presented itself. It's time for me to let the landlord know what's been going on. It's time for him to know that his house is haunted. And maybe he already knows—*after all he's not living here.*

So how do you tell your landlord that his house is haunted? How's he going to react to Bibles catching fire? To posters igniting? How he's going to react when I show him the multiple holes in the wall? The wall writings. The wall scratch marks? What's his response going to be? Is he going to kick Tina and me out? Is he going to call us crazy? Are we going to lose our three-thousand-dollar deposit? Every one of those scenarios is a possibility. Time to email him.

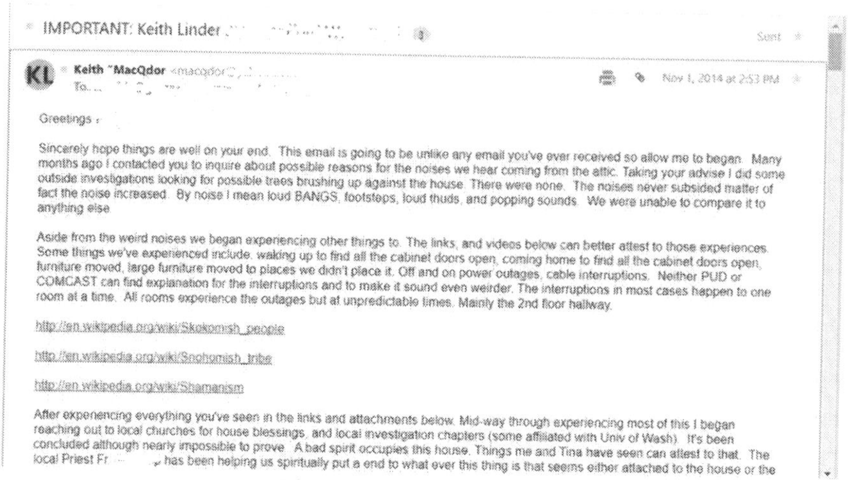

IMPORTANT: Keith Linder

Sent

Keith "MacQdor

To...

Nov 1, 2014 at 2:53 PM

Greetings ,

Sincerely hope things are well on your end. This email is going to be unlike any email you've ever received so allow me to began. Many months ago I contacted you to inquire about possible reasons for the noises we hear coming from the attic. Taking your advise I did some outside investigations looking for possible trees brushing up against the house. There were none. The noises never subsided matter of fact the noise increased. By noise I mean loud BANGS, footsteps, loud thuds, and popping sounds. We were unable to compare it to anything else

Aside from the weird noises we began experiencing other things to. The links, and videos below can better attest to those experiences. Some things we've experienced include, waking up to find all the cabinet doors open, coming home to find all the cabinet doors open, furniture moved, large furniture moved to places we didn't place it. Off and on power outages, cable interruptions. Neither PUD or COMCAST can find explanation for the interruptions and to make it sound even weirder. The interruptions in most cases happen to one room at a time. All rooms experience the outages but at unpredictable times. Mainly the 2nd floor hallway.

http://en.wikipedia.org/wiki/Skokomish_people

http://en.wikipedia.org/wiki/Snohomish_tribe

http://en.wikipedia.org/wiki/Shamanism

After experiencing everything you've seen in the links and attachments below. Mid-way through experiencing most of this I began reaching out to local churches for house blessings, and local investigation chapters (some affiliated with Univ of Wash). It's been concluded although nearly impossible to prove. A bad spirit occupies this house. Things me and Tina have seen can attest to that. The local Priest Fr. has been helping us spiritually put a end to what ever this thing is that seems either attached to the house or the

Fig 29.3 Email to landlord

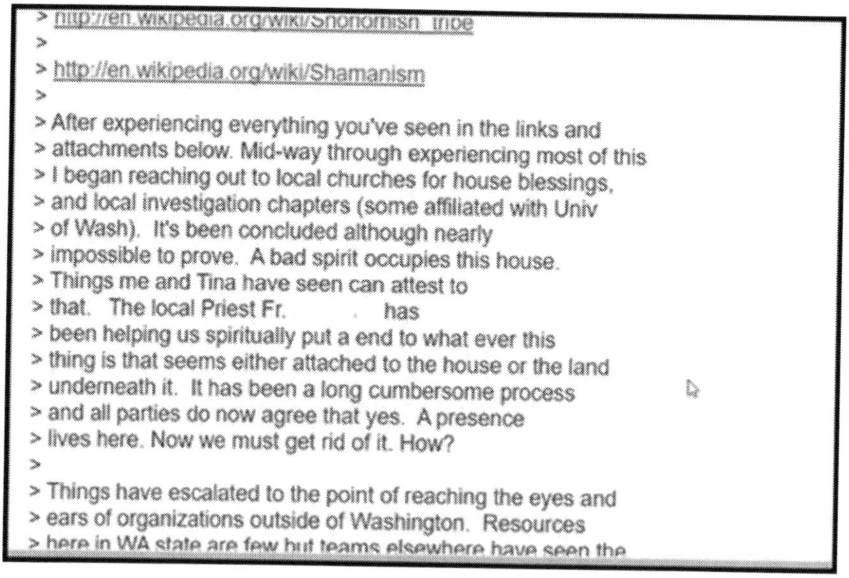

> http://en.wikipedia.org/wiki/Snohomish_tribe
>
> http://en.wikipedia.org/wiki/Shamanism
>
> After experiencing everything you've seen in the links and
> attachments below. Mid-way through experiencing most of this
> I began reaching out to local churches for house blessings,
> and local investigation chapters (some affiliated with Univ
> of Wash). It's been concluded although nearly
> impossible to prove. A bad spirit occupies this house.
> Things me and Tina have seen can attest to
> that. The local Priest Fr. has
> been helping us spiritually put a end to what ever this
> thing is that seems either attached to the house or the land
> underneath it. It has been a long cumbersome process
> and all parties do now agree that yes. A presence
> lives here. Now we must get rid of it. How?
>
> Things have escalated to the point of reaching the eyes and
> ears of organizations outside of Washington. Resources
> here in WA state are few but teams elsewhere have seen the

Fig 29.4 Email to landlord. Continued

← Back ◀ ◀◀ ➡   📧 Archive   🏠 Move   ⏸ Delete   ✖ Spam

>
> This team. (Ghost Adventures) has reviewed all the videos and has
> offered to help us. To get to the root cause.
> They've asked me for your contact info in order to gain
> approval. The theory this is a native
> American spirit tied to the house or land, we think the land
> based on research we uncovered that points to the Skykomish
> and Snohomish tribes once occupying these areas in the 1800
> and 1900's.
>
> I would like to give them your email and phone number and
> have them contact you to go over specifics. I think I
> told you before before moving here my goal as a tenant will
> be protecting, and preserving what I view as a nice home.
> Beautiful home. And beautiful neighborhood. I like to view
> myself as probably being the best renter you've had with
> never a late payment. And reaching out to you only when a
> situation warrants it.
>
> I have no ill will. I've seen and experienced a lot in
> this house and still have NO desire to move. It's
> important that you know that. My intentions after exhaustive
> research and data compiling is to find to right people and

Fig 29.5 Email to landlord. Continued

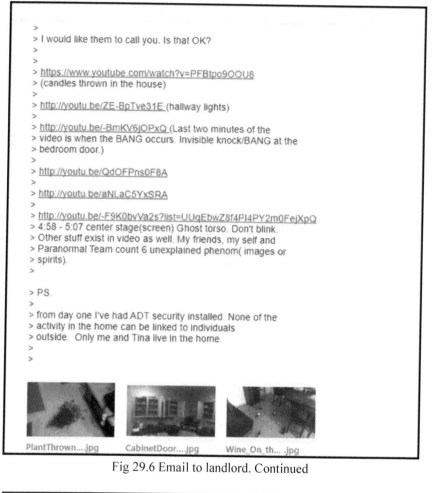

> \
> I would like them to call you. Is that OK?
> \
> \
> https://www.youtube.com/watch?v=PFBtpo9OOU8
> (candles thrown in the house)
> \
> http://youtu.be/ZE-BpTve31E (hallway lights)
> \
> http://youtu.be/-BmKV6jOPxQ (Last two minutes of the
> video is when the BANG occurs. Invisible knock/BANG at the
> bedroom door.)
> \
> http://youtu.be/QdOFPns0F8A
> \
> http://youtu.be/aNLaC5YxSRA
> \
> http://youtu.be/-F9K0bvVa2s?list=UUqEbwZ8f4PI4PY2m0FejXpQ
> 4:58 - 5:07 center stage(screen) Ghost torso. Don't blink.
> Other stuff exist in video as well. My friends, my self and
> Paranormal Team count 6 unexplained phenom(images or
> spirits).
> \
> \
> PS.
> \
> from day one I've had ADT security installed. None of the
> activity in the home can be linked to individuals
> outside. Only me and Tina live in the home.
> \
> \

PlantThrown....jpg   CabinetDoor....jpg   Wine_On_th....jpg

Fig 29.6 Email to landlord. Continued

Nov 2, 2014 at 9:41 AM

[I'm happy to support whatever you need so please go ahead and give my contact info to the investigation team to formalize permission. ....

I will let you know after I hear from them and next steps. I do believe this is fixable and thanks for hanging in there so far. Hopefully the spirits are just throwing tantrums and not trying to hurt anyone.]

Thanks

Home Owner Response

Fig 29.7 Home Owner's Response

Home Owner Response – "Hopefully the spirits are just throwing tantrums and not trying to hurt anyone."

The letter you just read "Home Owner's Response" is what I received. Maybe three or four lines. That's it. Let's forget about my calmness for now and analyze the home owner's calmness. I just sent him a huge email filled with pictures and videos of the destruction—activity taken place in his home. His house was recently on Seattle KOMO news, the news reporter who came to the house pretty much ran out of the house when the interview was over.

The landlord's initial response was not what I was expecting. It came too quickly. He was calm. Calmer than I expected. Our landlord wrote, "Hopefully the spirits are just throwing tantrums and not trying to hurt anyone." Let's see: the ambulance has been to my house. The fire department has been here. A poster caught fire. My computers caught fire. Objects large and small are flying north, south, east, and west.

It took me four hours to write that letter. I debated myself about sending it— *meaning I debated the contents of it.* I asked myself, what do I include in the letter? What do I leave out? Do I show him the wall markings? Do I show him the burnt computer monitors? Do I let him know how many times the fire departments been by? Do I mention the water puddles? The holes in the wall? Do I mention any of that stuff? What would I do if I got a letter like that? What would my response be? Mind you; the house was attacked again less than a few hours ago.

I was expecting an angry response, an email saying I'm suing you, I'm serving you papers! I want you and Tina and out my house. That's what I was expecting. I was so expecting to be put on the defensive. Screw the skeptics. Screw the cynics. If there's anyone who deserves to be a skeptic about the activity taking place, it's the homeowner. Never did he accuse Tina and me of doing this stuff ourselves. Never did he accuse me of attention seeking. Never did he ask us if he could stop and see for himself. He never served us with papers or anything. Quite the opposite. I can prove it. The letter you just read came from him. That was his response after he got my email. Three to four sentences. That's it. I was shocked. Tina was shocked. His answer, in a nutshell, was yes have the house investigated, get those temper tantrum spirits out and send *Ghost Adventures* my contact info.

I can't prove it, but I'm willing to bet Dave Schrader was shocked. Shocked by the quick response from the owner of the house. One of the last things Dave said to me was "you're going to have to get the homeowner's approval, we can't help unless he approves. Can you get that?" I said yes, I believe I can. I could hear a little doubt in the back of Dave's mind when I said that. He must have thought there's no way Keith was going to get a homeowner to approve. We've called his bluff. That's the vibe I got towards the end of our conversation. Well, guess what? The homeowner called everyone's bluff, including mine. He agreed to have his house investigated. I'll answer the question on your mind and perhaps on other people's mind. Do I think the landlord knew the house was haunted before we moved in?

I've wrestled with that question numerous times. The answer I keep coming up with is I don't know. A part of me says yes, he knew and a part of me says no he did not. Usually, it's action that arouse suspicion, in this case, it's more like inaction. The homeowner never asked me if he could come inspect the place. Not once did he ask could he visit the house to see if we were telling the truth. We could have been meth heads for all he knew?

Had he asked to visit the house, had he asked to inspect the room where there two fires I would have obliged. I was so expecting a back in forth between him and I when I emailed him the first time. It never came. Instead, he said "yes." No one with half a mind would make something like this up. That's the notion the home owner is operating from. I vehemently disagree with the notion adopted by a majority paranormal groups and organizations. That notion is that people make stuff up. No, they don't. Most people don't.

I was glad the landlord said yes. I mean I had positioned myself on a limb all by myself. All by myself. KOMO TV has just told the Pacific Northwest how haunted my house was. The only person more shocked about the homeowner saying yes was Tina.

The fact that the homeowner said yes and so quickly caught her by surprise. Tina was cold to the idea of having another team coming in—so far everyone's told us what we already know. No one's solving the problem. We know our house is haunted. Our house is crazy; we know that. That's not why we invite you. We invite into your home, hoping you can make our house un-haunted. If an armoire can fly across the room on its own, I don't care what anybody says; your house is haunted. What we want to know is can you deal with these spirits to where armoires stop flying across the room? Can you stop that from happening? So far no one could. So far all we get is empty promises. So far all we get are thrill-seekers. That's what Tina was tired of. She was tired of the inconsistency.

No one makes their word bond anymore. No one does what they say they're going to do. No one calls us back after the first visit. They say they will, but they don't. I can't tell you how many teams have promised Tina and me a concise written report within weeks of leaving the house. These are people who have seen stuff. What are you, snake oil salesmen? You talk a good game before coming and vanish after investigating. Where's the report they promised me? They never send it.

Look at what the local priest did. Look at what the bishop did. So yes, Tina was well within her rights to be reluctant. My opinion of *Ghost Adventures* then was them having resources—resources the world over. I mean they're on the Travel Channel, they tour the world. They have to have come in contact with reliable clergy, reliable researchers, reliable investigators who just maybe, might have seen this before. Remember, our motive for staying in the home has pivoted somewhat. There's no way I can leave now for fear of something following me, and there's no way I can leave this house without first making this house somewhat livable.

What happened to Jane Doe's family could happen to the next family who moves in after us. Obviously, the homeowner is thinking the same—he wouldn't have said yes had he thought his house was not haunted. He obviously believes me.

Maybe *Ghost Adventures* will be able to tap into their vast worldly resources and solve this thing. Talk about naivety. I can tell you my naivety began to evaporate within seconds of learning the *Ghost Adventures*—investigative schedule. Here it is.

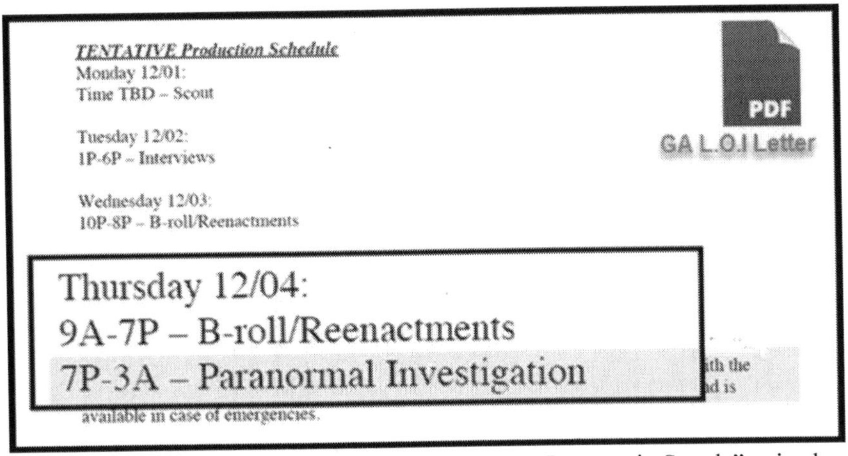

TENTATIVE Production Schedule
Monday 12/01:
Time TBD – Scout

Tuesday 12/02:
1P-6P – Interviews

Wednesday 12/03:
10P-8P – B-roll/Reenactments

PDF

GA L.O.I Letter

Thursday 12/04:
9A-7P – B-roll/Reenactments
7P-3A – Paranormal Investigation

th the
d is

available in case of emergencies.

Fig 29.8 Tentative Schedule – *Ghost Adventures* "Demons in Seattle" episode
12/03 is a GA typo. Should be 10 am to 8 pm – B Roll/Reenactments

I'm asking myself how successful will they be based on the schedule they have outlined? When I say successful, I mean how much activity will they capture? After the Halloween attack, the house went dead quiet. We went from level four activity to no activity in forty-eight hours. The letter above arrived on November 18th, 2014—the house was very quiet then. Even the baseline noise—the taping, banging, the sound of footsteps, and the occasional pacing back in forth had all but subsided.

So, I read the schedule, and I thought, well, they have the photos I sent them. They have the videos of objects moving. They have the video of the female apparition, and they have the pictures of the destruction that took place between 2012 and 2014. They have the timeline (my Excel spreadsheet) that shows when the house is most active. They have all of that and more; maybe they'll alter the schedule based on what I gave them. I was wrong; they didn't alter it. They stuck to their schedule religiously and as you can see above only one day was carved out for a full-blown investigation. Eight hours. That's it? And don't mistake the eight hours for being the length of time they spent investigating. That number is more like five hours. Why do I say five hours?

I've supervised an enormous number of projects over the years. The word we use often is lead time and lag time. Lead time is the latency between two phases. Lag time is a period between two related actions (such as a cause and its effect).

Ghost Adventures' lag time would be the period between arrival/meet and greet and equipment setup. I can tell you because I was there; it took the production crew two to three hours to get situated. Nothing starts until the producer says OK. They have to set up first, and that's understandable. It makes perfect sense for that happen. What didn't make sense to me was why are you only giving yourself a short time window to conduct an investigation? Five hours investigating something is nothing. Even I know that. I mean, we're talking about a very powerful spirit here. An evasive spirit?

In going back to the lead and lag time thingy—you have to understand that if it takes two and half hours to set up something, it's also going to take two hours (a little bit less) to disassemble everything. Then you got a pack up. I saw the B-roll teamwork for three days. Three days before the investigation even began. Both crews run a tight schedule. 3 am means we stop at 3 am. I became worried before they even arrived as to how successful they would be in catching something—especially with the time constraint, and especially with the activity dying down. A researcher with a lot of poltergeist experience will tell you that's not unusual. Activity dying down before a team arrives.

The second to the last blow to my naivety came at the arrival of the investigative team. I see the familiar faces. I see Dave Schrader, and I see the GA guys. The people I don't see are priests or mediums. Why didn't a priest accompany you? Why not a medium? Neither was present on the day of the lockdown. The good feeling, I had had finally evaporated.

The house has been filled with B-roll production crews for three days. I mean a mass amount of people traffic ensued as a result of the filming. And that's understandable, once again I get that. Did it ever dawn on anybody that the immense coming and goings of people, i.e., staff, reenactment actors/actresses, production crew, pizza guy, etc. would impact your evidence gathering efforts? Did it ever occur to Zak and Dave, that all the commotion before the investigation itself might have impacted their ability to find anything? I'll reveal towards the end of this book the level of difficulty one has when investigating poltergeist phenomenon. There are so many variables at play that are worth considering. Most of those variables are unknown to the average researcher. As *Ghost Adventures* eloquently demonstrated, the constraints are a bitch to manage but not impossible to manage if you have proper planning and convey a sincere interest.

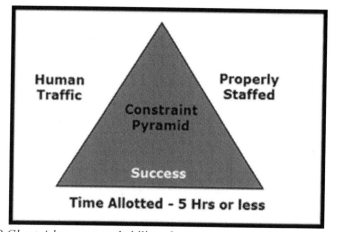

Fig 29.9 *Ghost Adventures* probability of success was greatly impacted by three Fundamental constraints 1.) Human Traffic 2.) Not properly staffed and the most important constraint of all: Time. All a spirit has to do is wait.

Sent: Wednesday, November 19, 2014 11:33 AM
To: Jeff P
Subject: RE: Ghost Adventures
Importance: High

Hi Jeff

Tina informed me we have contractors coming in this weekend to fix up the damage done to hallway, bedroom and office. The cosmetic and damage done by fires and objects thrown will be repaired, painted over and fixed. Is this OK?

Does your team need any of this stuff to stay as is? Or are we OK to begin repairing?

Fig 29.10 Email exchange

From: Jeff Bc   ̈[mailto:jeff@ _____ m]
Sent: Wednesday, November 19, 2014 1:26 PM
To: Keith Linder
Subject: RE: Ghost Adventures

Keith,

Is there any way to schedule the repairs until after the filming?

Also, could you put me in contact with that previous tenant you spoke with?

Regards,

-Jeff B
Ghost Adventures

Fig 29.11 Email exchange / *Ghost Adventures* producers

Chapter 30
Die KL

Here on out, no more Bibles will be catching fire. No more banging noise from the ceiling or behind the walls. No more large objects being thrown, no more office fires, no more emails informing me that an invisible attacker is ransacking the house. No more visits from the fire department. No more water puddles, (which is a huge relief), and lastly no more doors being slammed while we're asleep. The Spokane team has come and gone. The *Ghost Adventures* team has come and gone. You would think all this 'no more' stuff would be a good thing, right? It probably is a good thing. I mean, the armoire in the guest bedroom could tip over at any moment. Not from a "Geist" attack, just from how badly damaged it is. So, yes, it's a good thing the violence has stopped. I mean it sort of stopped.

Notice I said, sort of? If there ever was a moment where the spirits began telegraphing everything it would have to be Thanksgiving Day. Two things made that day interesting. Number one, it snowed. It rarely snows in Seattle, let alone Bothell, let alone in November. Tina had invited her oldest son and his girlfriend over for Thanksgiving dinner. Her son knew of our ghost problem, which is to say he knew nothing. His eyes almost popped out of his head after I showed him the wall writings——yes, the markings from Halloween night were still present. Holding one of the burnt Bibles in your hand forces you to reevaluate what your definition of what a haunted house is. Tina's son held the burnt Bibles in his hand and was so taken aback. I'm telling you it moved him internally.

I've always believed in God. I believed in Him before I moved into this house, and I will believe in Him after I move out. But my belief has been altered somewhat. I would like to think I'm a much stronger man now, compared to what I was on April 30th, 2012. This experience has moved me internally. It's moved Tina internally, and from the reaction of Tina's son, it would appear it's now in the process of changing him internally. There's no way you could be the same person after living through something like this. No way could we be the same people after seeing what we've seen. Seeing a plant rise off the ground and spin three hundred and sixty degrees and then fall back down, forces you to re-evaluate everything, and I do mean *everything*. Tina's son got a glimpse of that tonight the minute I placed one of the burnt Bibles in his hand.

I'll never forget how he placed the Bible back down on the table, walked over to me, and gave me a big hug. He let go of me and immediately grabbed his mom, giving her the biggest hug of all. It was an emotional moment. After a few more hugs, Tina's son, finally decided it was time for him and his girlfriend to go home. Not without an inordinate amount of food. A mom's gotta do what moms gotta do—by giving her son a majority of the Thanksgiving leftovers. We did the kiss, the hug, and handshake thing while walking them to their car outside. I'm thinking, *wow, tonight was powerful, I can't believe how emotionally drained I am right now.*

Five minutes later, knock-knock-knock. *Someone's at the door.* It was Tina's son. Something outside has caught his attention: weird writings on our lawn. I'm looking at him and thinking to myself, *what writing?* He ushered me outside and pointed to an area on the ground where there was a word or two written in the snow. It looks like the word "Dick."

The letters had begun to melt, but it looks like there are two lines. Line 1 carved into the snow says what looks like "Dick." The second word on line 2 was unintelligible—smudged due to the melting of the snow. Tina's son chuckled, and said it looked like someone wrote the word "dick." The second word began with the letter K, but that's all you could make out of that word. Whatever it was, it had been here awhile.

I asked myself the question, *who'd write this on our lawn? On Thanksgiving of all days? What asshole does this?* I mean, we're already walking on eggshells. Yeah, we've had ghost vans parked in front of the house. We had the Travel Channel here for a week, and true, they turned our house into a production studio. We've had the fire department here. We've had ambulances here. Is this someone's passive-aggressive way of saying, "We don't appreciate what you're doing to our neighborhood"? Is that what this about? Is someone trying to send us a message? Why would you write the word "Dick" on someone's grass? That's what I was thinking. That's what it appeared to look like. It looked like "Dick K —" After a few minutes of looking at the writing, Tina's son finally said goodbye to me again. This and what he saw inside was just becoming too much. I couldn't disagree with him. This didn't make sense. I went back into the house to let Tina know her son had come back. I told her what we saw written on the lawn. She shook her head, as did I. People are idiots.

A few hours later I stepped out of my office and saw something I've never seen before. I saw my Seahawk football jersey lying on the hallway floor. Not only was my jersey lying on the floor—so was my favorite pair of blue jeans. Allow me to describe to you how they were laying. Let's go back to the upside-down Native American symbol: remember how that looked? It's a stick figure of a man. It's an upside-down man—meaning, "a man has died, or a man is about to die." That's not my interpretation. That's the interpretation from various internet sites. Well, guess what? That's how my clothes were laid out. That's the position they were in. The manner in which they were laid out was quite troubling. Both shirt and pants were aligned and positioned on the ground to where you would think I was lying on the ground, spread eagle style, except I'm not. But my clothes are. Facing upside down.

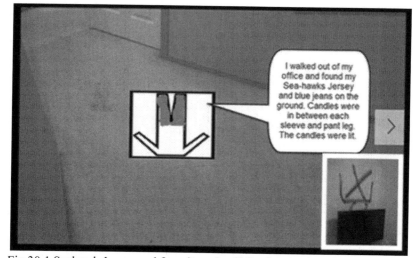

Fig 30.1 Seahawk Jersey and favorite pair of blue jeans were found laid out in the hallway. Upside down with three white candles between sleeve armpit and both legs.

One thing which was especially troubling was the uncanny precision. I couldn't help but notice the neatness of it all. I mean, I could not have done it any better. Shirt and pants were so well aligned. And that's not all. What's up with lighted candles resting underneath each arm and pant leg? Why are these candles lit? What does it mean? These items were originally hanging in my closet. How did they get here? Tina! I'm thinking; Tina needs to see this. We've never seen this type of activity before. The candles came from our bedroom lamp tables. Now they're sitting on the floor next to my shirt and pants. Tina looked at me, and I looked at her. Neither one of us could figure this out. Google wasn't much help either. Why are lit candles positioned under the arms and legs of my clothing? Someone tell me please.

Pop quiz time. What was the first item I noticed missing from our house? Answer: my spare car key. Remember we moved into the house in May 2012. A year or so later, I began asking myself the question, why is my trunk light always on? Why is it always open, i.e., unlocked, before I get into it each morning? What's going on? My first assumption was: I must be fat-fingering my car fob when I hit the unlock button. I've mentioned several instances in this book of me walking out my front door; Tina kisses me goodbye and closes the door behind me. I get to my car, climb into my seat, and there on my dashboard is the trunk light. It's lit.

Nothing weird about that if it happens once. Nothing weird about that if it happens several times through the course of your lifetime. It's been happening to me three or four times a week for over a year. I feel stupid for not realizing it sooner. The spirits have been using my extra set of car keys against me. They've been hitting "unlock trunk" button on the key fob. They've been doing this within seconds of me walking out the door. Up until now, I thought I was somehow fat-fingering my key fob when unlocking my car. I was wrong. How do I know I was wrong? How do I know it was them doing this? Well, they made a mistake, which is extremely rare. Minions rarely make mistakes.

I left for work one morning like I always do. I get all the way to the car door, and then realize I don't have my keys on me. I left them in the house. But guess what? I'm standing at my car door. I can see my dashboard. Why is my trunk light lit? How can my trunk light be on when I don't even have my keys on me? Son of a bitch! That's when I realized. I haven't been fat-fingering my car fob at all. It would seem I ignored my intuition a year or so ago when I asked the rhetorical question: how I am always doing this, given the location of the trunk button? It was located in a way which made an accidental hit unlikely. One's finger would deliberately have to go out of its way to touch the 'trunk unlock' button. Not only that, but you also have to hold it down considerably to activate it.

The spirits must have gotten a huge laugh out of me. They must have been very proud of themselves. So, what happens now? What can I do about it? Honestly? Nothing. There's nothing I can do about it. That's the reality of living with asshole spirits. They control everything. They're pranksters. They're bullies. They're liars. They're manipulative. They've perfected the art of being coy. This prank of unlocking my car trunk within seconds of me getting in my car would go on for several more weeks. But with a difference. See, now they know that I know they're doing it. You would think they would stop; maybe it's time to move on to other things. No, they did the opposite. They started popping my car trunk when I left work. They started popping my car trunk when I left the movie theatre. They started popping my car trunk after I've had dinner in downtown Seattle.

Keep in mind, while all of this is happening I'm still being poked and prodded when sleeping. Our bed sheets are still being pulled and yanked in the middle of the night. My side especially. No one's heard from *Ghost Adventures*. Not me. Not the homeowner. No word as to what they found. I'm still sending them pictures and videos of what's happening as a way of keeping them updated. Everybody gets the same information. Everybody gets blind copied (bcc'd) on the same email. Jennifer, the local priest, the Spokane team, and now *Ghost Adventures*. The only people I hear back from are Jennifer (No Bull Paranormal) and the Spokane team. They're the only ones checking in on us. They're the only ones dishing out a great deal of empathy. The only ones advising Tina that she can't let me do everything. I can't be the only one smudging. The only one reading from the paper the priest gave us. I can't be the only one looking for help.

What people don't know is, Tina and I are basically done at this point. We're hardly talking to each other. Yeah, we get along. Yeah, we're still having dinner together. But we're not a couple now. We're roommates. Roommates who share the same bed. Sharing the same bathroom. Some days we fall back into that loving couple mode. But that's happening less and less now. A dark cloud has taken root above our house. Above and below our house—we can't see it. Half the time we can't even feel it. But it's there, and it's getting bigger. How do I know it's getting bigger? I know because I left the house one morning and there on our front lawn was another writing.

December 2014. It snows again in the Pacific Northwest. *Uh oh, one of our neighbors is being an asshole again.* The writing looks similar to the markings Tina's son and I saw a few weeks back. This time the condition of the writings is a little bit better than what we saw on Thanksgiving. There's that letter "D" again. The letters that come afterward resemble an "E" or an "I." It's hard to make out what the remainder of the first is, or if there is even anything after that. The second word seems to have the letter "K," followed by another letter that I can't make out. Both words are huddled together. We're talking about two lines – what it says exactly I don't know.

It's hard to make out exactly what it says due to the melting snow. The ground is above thirty-two degrees, even when the atmosphere is not. So yes, it's snowing, but it's not staying around long. Pacific Northwest snow rarely does. That's why I can't understand the writing entirely. It looks like somebody wrote the word "Dick K" on my front lawn again. But the snow is melting, so there's no way to be sure.

I have an entity inside my house that's depriving me of sleep. My girlfriend is pissed at me. *Ghost Adventures* left without telling us anything. The local priest is MIA, as is the shaman that Jennifer mentioned. That's all I need to worry about, is some neighborhood prankster. Nothing to do now except get rid of it. And that's what I did: I got rid of it the writing by stomping my feet over the letters written in the snow. That was easy, now please, no kid pranks. My memory of the prank writing had evaporated by the time I got to work. Other things are in front of that. Being attacked in bed is one of them. The spirits are not harassing Tina as much as they are harassing me. And that's good. I don't want my girlfriend being harassed. But I can't forget what the priest told us. I can't forget what Jennifer told us. "Don't let them silo you two, don't let them divide and conquer."

How does a spirit divide and conquer? We're in the initial stages of it now. Remember, the house is not being attacked, we are. Myself more than Tina. It's quite simple to figure out, hindsight being twenty-twenty and all. Name one paranormal incident in this house that Tina noticed before me. Where did the poster catch fire? Where are the wall writings located? Who fell down the stairs? Who saw the Gray Lady? Who saw the white lady? Whose key went missing? Whose trunk keeps getting popped open when they leave the house? Whose Bibles got burned? And we're only two years in. Imagine seeing an upside-down cross written on your side of the bathroom mirror. Imagine seeing that within seconds of stepping out the shower. Imagine 666 writings on your side of the bathroom mirror—Tina's not even in the house.

Imagine the bathroom lights going off while you're taking a shower. Or the door slamming while you're in the shower. Imagine that the clothes you laid out to wear are now nailed to the wall or the ceiling. I'm talking about the clothes I just ironed. I come back from taking a shower, and those clothes are gone. They're hanging from the wall inside the bedroom with nails in them. I can't help but mention me not hearing so much as a thud while taking a shower. No noise what-so-ever. Just clothes hanging on a wall with the help of nails.

By the time December 15th rolled around, Tina and I were pretty much living separate lives. The only interaction we had now was when we passed each other in the hallway. We've essentially become a bell curve as far as relationships go.

There are good days, and there are bad days. The bad days are easy to describe. Zero communication and zero interaction. I would still call Tina whenever there were new events taking place. But even that's dwindling. Tina no longer wakes up to flying ironing boards. She sleeps through it. A can of starch flying above our heads at night does not affect her. Never before have these items landed near me. Now they are. Now they're landing within inches of me. I'm woken to crashing objects. I turned and looked at Tina. Tina? She's sound asleep. I think it's safe to say, Tina and I are on the outs.

All of this became vividly clear the day of my birthday, December 15th. I got up that morning and began prepping the house for my birthday party. Wow, what a difference two years makes. Up until now, every house party Tina and I had, we always worked as a team. "Geist" be damned, nothing's going to stop us from entertaining our guests with good music, tasty food, and good drinks. I was in charge of the booze and the meats. Tina was in charge of the side dishes and dessert. I've never seen Tina stay in bed past 10 am. Not till now. Not until the day of my birthday. She knew today was my birthday. She knew what had to be done. I'm not implying that she was asleep. Far from it. Tina was on the phone while watching TV.

Instead of antagonizing Tina by asking, shouldn't you be getting ready? Shouldn't you be helping me with getting the house ready for our friends? I decided just to ignore her. Triple my things-to-do list. Combine her tasks with mine. Our friends would arrive at 5 pm. That's when the party starts. And guess what? It did. Only it was way past 5 pm when Tina decided to join us. I'm not going to lie. I was pissed. It was my birthday. But why should I be pissed? I mean, look where we're at now? Look at the downslide things have taken. Is the spirit doing this? You're damn right it's doing this. Jane Doe said the house was "a living hell" for them. She said it was "the beginning of the end in that place." I'm slowly beginning to understand what she meant. I'm not quite there yet, but I'm close.

I said to myself before my friends arrived, I know what my reaction is going to be should I decide to postpone this party. I've seen this movie before. Today reminds me of how I felt after seeing the scratches on my car. The scratches that I thought Tina had made. If I postpone this party now, due to Tina still being in her pajamas, that's going to escalate the tension. We're going to argue. There's no avoiding it. And that's what the spirit wants. It wants one of us to get angry beyond measure. It wants one of us to explode. An explosion of that degree would not have been good. No, the party must go on.

Did anything weird happen? Yeah, one of Tina's work notebooks appeared out of nowhere during the middle of my friends Barbara Karaoke song. Yes, a notebook. It just came out of nowhere. No one could remember where it came from. No one knows how it got on the floor. It just appeared, and we all noticed it. Tina didn't even know that it was missing. Not until it appeared she didn't. It's here now. It's here in the middle of my birthday party, and we're asking ourselves, where did it come from? Unexplainable. But the night's not over yet. My friend Jose, inexplicable problems with the Wi-Fi. We're talking about delay after delay after delay. All my guy friends work in the IT field. We're talking Microsoft, Amazon, and Boeing. They're all network engineers with over twenty-five of experience—we know Wi-Fi (them especially). Jose even asked me "Man, what's up with your Wi-Fi? Something's going on?" When it came time for him and family to leave another inexplicable moment happened—his car battery died. Coincidence? Maybe. An inconvenience to him and his family? Definitely.

But that's how it always happens. Someone's always being picked on more than anyone else. My friend was the one that provided the music, the one that arrived with all this electronic music equipment; it makes sense to pick on him. He and I talked about the intermittent Wi-Fi issue. Why is he the only one having problems when it comes to using the house Wi-Fi? He's the DJ of the party. The one in charge of playing loud music.

The next morning, I went through the house picking up all the left-over beer bottles. Minus the tension between Tina and me, the party was a success. My friends and I share a key trait; we're all observant. Everyone could tell something was up with Tina and me. It was very noticeable. I can't remember one conversation Tina, and I had that night while entertaining guests. It was like we had previously agreed to stay away from each other. Not one interaction whatsoever.

I decided to go into my office when I finished cleaning. Time to watch one of my favorite western movies, *The Man Who Shot Liberty Valance.* Hangover or not. I'm watching my John Wayne movie. Movies are what keep me sane. They're what keep me grounded. My recommendation for those dealing with something similar to this is knowing your Zen. Know what makes you happy. Old-fashioned movies make me happy. Watching sci-fi movies makes me happy. Wine tasting makes me happy. Being among friends and family makes me happy. Happy hours in downtown Bellevue make me extremely happy. Not even a "Geist" can destroy that. They try, oh you best believe they try. I wasn't in my office long when suddenly a loud noise came flying in. I thought *please, please not right now, ghost, not right now. I have a hangover and I'm tired. Please don't attack me today.* But it's too late; something flew into the room. I mean that's what it sounded like.

It was loud whatever it was. It even caught Tina's attention. That's how loud it was. I got up from my chair and began looking around. I saw nothing. Tina walked in a few seconds later and asked, "What was that?" I looked at her and said something just flew in my room. She was looking at me funny because there was nothing out of order in my office. We started searching the room together— I was giving the room a complete look at when my eyes suddenly reached the wall by the window. I saw a new hole in the wall, right by the window. Damn, the last thing I need is another hole in the wall—why the office of all places? I could tell something round was thrown based on the crescent-shaped hole. Something did fly in here. So where in the hell is it? Tina and I looked the room over, and we found nothing. I think we searched for about five minutes. Whatever was thrown in here, was gone now. But, not so fast. I came back to my room thirty minutes later and find a beer bottle lying in the middle of the floor. Aha, that's what got thrown, a freaking beer bottle.

As I'm picking up the bottle, I see what looks to be a white powdery substance—drywall powder? This had to have come from the wall. I called Tina back into the room to confirm what was going on. We laid the nose of the bottle next to the new hole in the wall and got a perfect match. I'll be damned. This spirit threw a beer bottle at me? It's not the scariest thing I've had thrown at me. I mean, the chef's knife was pretty scary. This, however, comes close. I mean, it's a glass bottle, a *Pacifico beer bottle*. All I saw was a blur when it came flying in. I saw it zip by out of the corner of my eye. But that happened thirty minutes ago—where did the bottle come from? No way could we have missed this. Tina would have found it before I or I would have found it before her.

This beer bottle incident reminds me of the three round holes we found on Tina's side of the bed earlier this year. We heard the knocks first, three loud bangs. There were no holes in the wall when we got up that morning. They'd be impossible to miss. No, they showed up later. In each case, there is a weird delay.

Imagine a piano falling or a giant dresser drawer being flung across the room. The noise is so loud, so distinct you have no choice but to investigate. And when we do, we come up empty-handed. I might have mentioned this earlier that sometimes we hear the noise way before the object appears—the damaged object. Why? That's poltergeist physics, ladies, and gentlemen.

The last thing Tina said before walking out of my office was, "That's different." When and where this bottle was taken is anybody's guess. The spirit could have taken this bottle last night. It could have taken it after we went to bed. Heck, it could have taken it today. There was no way of knowing. I remember tossing the bottle in our recycle bin outside and returning to my office—hopefully I can finish watching my movie. An hour or so later I get the urge to go back upstairs—I'm about to approach my office door when something comes flying through. Whatever it was it missed me by a few inches. This time the object ricochets off the door and bounces back into the hallway. Lying on the floor in front of me is another beer bottle. I pick it up and see the same white residue. I'll be damned. This is the same bottle as before? The same drywall residue as the other bottle. But is it? No way this can be the same bottle. I have to confirm my suspicion. Yes, ladies and gentlemen, I marched all the way back to the trash receptacle. I emptied the recycle bin of everything. The bottle I just put in here can't be far. It has to be on top of the other trash items. Nothing else had been added to the can. I looked and looked, but I never find it. You know why? Because I'm holding it right now, it's the same bottle that was thrown earlier.

I name this chapter Die KL because I wanted you to get a sense of how long it takes for me and Tina to grasp certain events happening around us. This and my car key disappearing when we moved in are perfect examples of that. I'm almost embarrassed to admit that it took me over a year to realize my getting into my car and see the trunk light on had nothing to do with me fat-fingering my key fob. I was not unlocking my trunk at all. The spirits were. If that doesn't prove how much spirits monitor people, I don't know what does. They're monitoring me very closely. Imagine the level of observation being applied here? Supreme dedication. No boredom whatsoever. I know me; I would get bored real fast. But they don't, and that's very telling. It's more than telling; it's downright scary.

Now, it was only three weeks ago that Tina's son rang our doorbell, informing us of those weird writings on our lawn. The words were impossible to make out, due to them being written in the snow. That's why it took it me awhile to know what it meant. The other reason? One word. Inconceivable.

For some reason or another, I had adopted the mindset that anything worse was inconceivable. I mean, it's unthinkable thinking this is happening. My brain simply views this revelation as being a bridge too far. No way would I have deciphered that on my own—not without the help of the poltergeist. And boy did it help me.

That following Monday I woke up with only one thing on my mind. Get to my doctor's office—it was time for my yearly physical. All I have to do is walk into my office, unlock the safe, and grab my wallet and car keys. How hard can that be right?

I walked into my office (Tina had left for work already), I opened the safe, using the combination which only I knew. I opened the safe door—and low and behold—my wallet's gone. That's right, Keith Linder's wallet is gone, ladies and gentlemen, as are a few extra wooden crosses that I put in the safe as a means of protection.

For some odd reason, the spirit chose not to take my car keys. I'm thankful for that (it costs $400 dollars to replace a car key). Do you see how weird it's become? The spirit has just robbed me of my wallet. It's robbed me of my credit cards, my debit cards, my social security number, my personal information, business cards, driver's license, and a host of other stuff.

So here I am standing in my office. I took the morning off so that I could go to my doctor's appointment. I can't do that now. The only option for me to take is the one that the "Geist" created. Ask yourself the question: who's controlling who now? Whose plans just got changed? Mine did. Instead of going to the doctor's office, I now have to go to the bank. I now have to go to the driver's license office. I have to cancel my credit cards. I have to call my boss. I have to let him know I'm going to be arriving in the office later than expected. I'm not telling him that a poltergeist took my wallet. No way am I going to tell him about demons breaking through safes. If the "Geist" won't tell him, neither will I. But do you see the inconvenience taking place? Do you see the out of pocket expense? The wallet is nowhere to be found. I'm going to have to begin a search for my birth certificate—I can't get a driver's license without it. I don't know where my birth certificate is. I haven't had any need for it since I moved here. Well, I'm going to need it now. I left the house an hour or so later – off to the driver's license office I go. There first, and then the bank.

I'm not sure what made me go back home after leaving the bank that morning. I must have thought, with it being after 12 pm, there was no reason to go into the office. I might as well work from home. The second I walked through my front door I could tell something was wrong. Pop quiz: what's the quickest way to confirm if something's wrong in this house? Answer: go to Keith's office. If something's wrong, that's where it will be. Correctamundo! A lot was wrong in my office; a lot was wrong upstairs. Ladies and gentlemen, you could come home and see your house upside-down ten million times and still not be used to it. The amount of times this has happened doesn't soften you. It's still raw and unnerving each time you see it. That's exactly how it was right now. And it's especially unnerving, due to some new elements being added. The kitchen bar stool is sitting in my office chair. That's new. Why is our bar stool in my office? The spirits always add something new to the destruction. The most unnerving thing today was the writings, Die KL. It's on every wall in my office—including the ceiling.

Fig 30.2 "Die KL" is written all over my office. Including the ceiling (not shown here). Kitchen stool and more 666 propaganda. Scissor dead center of stickman skull.

I'm thinking about what I saw on Thanksgiving. It all made sense now. I was not reading the word, Dick. I was reading the words Die KL. That's what it was. There's no way of knowing how long Die KL was written on our lawn. I mean, Tina's son found it after leaving our house. It must have been put there earlier that day. No way was I thinking that was Die KL back then. But I know it's Die KL now. I know that because it's written on my wall. It's written on a solid wall versus melting snow.

I can see the words loud and clear. You spirits have been busy while I was at the driver's license office. What else is new here? Time to analyze everything else. The cross that was nailed to the wall downstairs by Tina and me as a means of keeping spirits at bay is now nailed to the wall in my office. Upside down of course.

We have the familiar 666's written everywhere again. We have the upside-down man stick figure—again. That correlates well with the Die KL. Heck, who am I fooling, it correlates with the upside-down cross also? I've seen plenty of 666 wall writings, plenty of upside-down man figures in this house. What else is new besides the Die KL? Every cross we own, gifts from the priest and a few we bought online, are all neatly assembled underneath my television, leaning against the entertainment center. They're all turned upside-down. I've seen that before.

The Bible is on the floor, there's a wooden cross lying on the pages, and its upside-down—that's new. 666 is written on the closet door—not new. 666 is written behind the office door as is another upside-down cross—not new. There's another Die KL written on my computer desk. I almost didn't see it. Brand new.

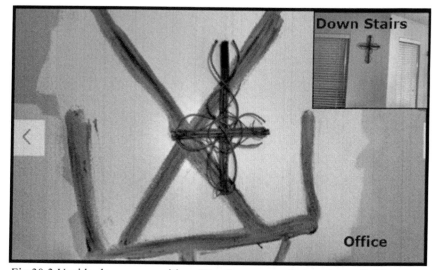

Fig 30.3 Upside-down man writing. Wooden cross nailed on the wall. The cross was downstairs when I left. December 2014

If it weren't for the Die KL writings, the most unusual thing in my office would have been the weird-looking paw marks going across the walls. I have to think the demon who did this, who did all of this—made those paw marks as a means of trying to fuck with me. *It's fucking with me, right? It has to be.* I mean there are three paw marks—not dog, not a cat, not anything I can imagine. Just three of them, which suggests whoever did this only has three legs. *They're fucking with me. Right?*

They're trying to get me unglued. Let me go back to the hallway—there's crazy stuff in there I've yet to acknowledge. The hallway was littered with upside-down crosses, crosses that we bought, crosses that the Spokane team left us. But that's not what's weird about the hallway. What makes the hallway weird is all the toy spiders lying around. Where did these toy spiders come from? Plastic spiders—small, medium, and large ones. What's that all about? Why are they sitting next to my crosses? Next to the spiders is the picture I bought from Amazon of Michael the Archangel, the famous picture of him standing on Lucifer's head. Where was that picture before today? Oh, it was resting on top of the new Bible I bought. I left both of them on the hallway bookshelf. The Bible's in my office—several crosses are laying on it (all of them upside down). The picture has been altered, the same way the pictures of me were altered. Michael's face is gone. It's been burnt off.

Fig 30.4 Michael the Archangel's face is scorched. Same thing was done to photos of me.

Fig 30.5 Ceiling paw prints

If you ignore the fact that most of the crosses in the hallway were taken from my side of the bed and that the bar stool sitting in my office was taken from the kitchen, the final assessment of today's attack is that no other room was touched. Everything the spirit touched belonged to me. Everything but those plastic spiders. I don't know where they came from. What reason would they have for placing spiders around my religious items? I have no idea why they would do that. The only question I have is: what time does Tina get home? Wait till she sees this. Wait till she sees the Die KL writings. Link: https://youtu.be/Q3meCW-YznM

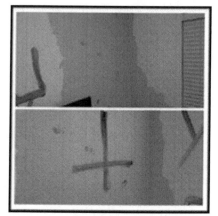

Fig 30.6 Paw prints.

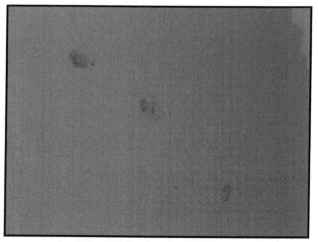

Fig 30.7 Paw prints. Close up.

https://youtu.be/Q3meCW-YznM

Fig 30.8 House attack video

Link: https://youtu.be/Q3meCW-YznM

Did you notice the words "Die KL" on the book cover?

Chapter 31
Keith

You can probably guess what this chapter is going to be about based on the title. I think we all can agree they've been focusing their attention on me for quite some time; it's time the spirits go all out. I hope I can get it all in one chapter. There's just so much to share. So much to mention. How are you doing? Are you still hanging in there? It's going to be a loopy ride so get ready. The last chapter you read contained a lot of info. Here come's some more. Just in case you haven't noticed, these spirits don't believe in ambiguity. The Die KL proved that. Reminder: All I've been doing throughout this book is describing what my girlfriend and I went through. No more, no less. Do you remember how all of this started? It started with the 'kid's cough.'

May 1st, 2012. Tina and I were sitting on the living room floor. We were proud. We were excited. Christmas 2014. For whatever reason, Tina and I had chosen not to go out of town. The Die KL ended up being a real game changer for me. It cannot be ignored. We were warned not to get to this stage. The priest warned us. Jennifer warned us. The paranormal team from Spokane warned us. Look where we're at right now. Look what's happening. I have to say this because it's the feeling I had after seeing the words Die KL. I've seen the laws of physics compromised in this house. I've seen objects on fire. I've seen objects thrown. I've seen doors slam in the dead of night when there was no window open. I've seen front doors open and close. I've been locked out of the house. I've been poked and prodded. I've had sheets yanked off me in hotel room four hundred miles away from ground zero. All of that pales in comparison to what I've just described in the previous chapter. That attack got to me. It got to me because of the words Die KL. These spirits know my freaking name? And why wouldn't they? You see the Die KL words brings all the horror's we've experienced into focus. It adds dimensions to what already happened. Example one: the fall downstairs. Example two: my burnt face in all my family pictures.

There never was a moment where I had a greater urge to get out of this house than right now. Sure, I've wanted to run away plenty of times. There's been plenty of moments like that. The poster catching fire was one of them. Seeing the words, Die KL beats all of that. Let me put it like this. When a spirit starts writing your name on the wall, that might be the time to call it quits.

We're talking about the unimaginable. Those who follow the show *Ghost Adventures* religiously might have incorrectly assumed that the 666 stuff is what terrified Keith and Tina. It didn't. The spirits didn't write that to scare us. They wrote that so Tina and me wouldn't be taken seriously. That wasn't a scare tactic. That was a misdirect. Obviously, it worked (as you will soon see in the next chapter). But the words, Die KL? That's a whole different situation.

Like I said, I shouldn't be shocked that the spirits know my name. We've been living here for two years. Tina calls me Keith, as do my friends when they arrive. My name is Keith Linder. My mail comes here. Several things in this house have my name on it. My wallet that went missing has my name on it, as does my driver's license, as does my credit cards, as does my business cards, as does my social security number. The spirits knew my name the second I moved in. Hell, my name is on the lease agreement. They know Tina's name. Hell, they probably know the names of everyone who walked through our front door. It wouldn't surprise me if they knew the names of everyone who's ever lived here.

I'm the only person who had his initials written on a wall. The only one whose initials have been written outside in the snow. If that's not proof of the spirits focusing on me and only me, then I don't know what is. Tina came home that day and was surprised to see me sitting at the kitchen table. There I was working. She walked up and asked, "Why are you home so early?" I couldn't even tell her why. How does one utter the words, the ghost wrote Die KL on the office wall? That's how shook up I was. All I could do was look up and say, look at my office. Tina saw the expression on my face and immediately knew something new had happened. She turned away and walked upstairs. It had been quiet for five minutes, ten minutes, fifteen minutes. I haven't heard Tina scream yet. I haven't heard her run down the hallway. I haven't heard anything. I best go upstairs and see what she's doing. I didn't have to travel very far; Tina was in our bedroom. She was crying.

There's an uncomfortable feeling I get when seeing a woman cry. I compare it to someone accidentally knocking a lollipop out of a baby's hand (which I've never done, but if I did this is how I would feel). Even though you didn't do it on purpose, you feel bad regardless. It's gut-wrenching. I mean, what do you do? You don't have another lollipop. What do you do? I know what I do; I just stand there and feel remorseful. And then I do something else. I freeze. I clam up. I don't try to console my girlfriend while she's crying. I just stand there. I hover, and I go silent. It's like all of a sudden; I become inept as to what to do next. It's a character flaw I'm not proud of. My girlfriend's crying her eyes out; she's weeping. Why is she crying? She's crying because she thinks the demons are after me. She's crying because deep down she knows, despite our problems, despite her trust issues, we are still together. We might be alone. We might be the stupidest people in the world—her friends think she's the stupidest girlfriend in the world, and my friends think I'm the stupidest boyfriend in the world. All of them are probably right. But right or not, we still have each other. And that alone means no ill will should come to me. Yes, we're mad at each other, most of the time. So are a lot of other couples. Do they have a poltergeist writing stuff on their wall? No, they don't. The devil has no right doing this to us. That's why she's crying. And look at me. I just stand there.

Don't get me wrong; I'm not inconsiderate—I'm just inept, I'm short on emotional genes (when it comes to situations like this). I'd rather drive Tina to Nordstrom's and hand her my credit card and say buy something. I don't possess that instinct that says, Keith, sit down by your girlfriend, put your arms around her and tell her we're getting out tonight. Just say that, Keith. That's all you have to do. None of this is worth it. Leave tonight. Leave now.

So, what do I do? I lower myself down on the bed. I sit next to my girlfriend. I take her hand, and I say we'll get through this. We have to be strong. We have to be vigilant. We'll get through this, is what I kept saying. This would be the first time since living in this house where I began to doubt everything I was saying. I was telling Tina one thing and thinking to myself; we're not going to win this. To win now would require us doing something drastic. I'm beginning to believe drastic wants nothing to do with this house? To turn the tide now would require some sort of divine intervention. How do you scare away the vultures that are circling above our house? How do you prevent them from diving in? I can't help but envision a Hollywood scenario of—the shaman that Jennifer was looking for suddenly ringing our doorbell. He rings it right now.

The local priest is pulling up to the house behind him. Zak Bagan is suddenly texting my phone—he's found a rabbi in the alleyway of Israel who's dealt with something like this before. The Travel Channel has chartered him a flight, so he can get here within the hour. That's what would have to happen for us to move the ball off our one-yard line. That would put us back in the game. Did any of that happen? Of course, not—this isn't Hollywood, this is real life. The spirits are not even close to being done with their Die KL campaign. Talk about homing in on someone—here goes.

I walked into the Christian bookstore a week after the first Die KL incident shaking like a leaf. Call me a dead man walking. That's how out of it I was. Earlier that morning I'd left the house to go to the grocery store—Tina asked that I pick up some eggs and milk. I left the house through the front door like I always do. I opened my car door and there it was again the words Die KL. It's written on *all of the upholstery*. Including the car ceiling. How could this happen? My car was locked. What the hell is this oily like substance?

Tina can't see this. If Tina sees this, she's going to freak the fuck out. I mean, I'm trying hard not to wig out. She can't see this. Whatever I have to do to prevent her from seeing this, I better do it quick. Tina is expecting me to come back soon. This doesn't look like soon to me. This looks complicated. I can't walk back in the house and say; can I use your car. That'll raise suspicion. But I can't sit on this shit either; the words Die KL and numbers 666 is written everywhere. No way am I driving off with this stuff in my car.

I decided to act quickly as I could without drawing Tina's suspicion. I backed the car into the garage and prayed we had some cleaning stuff somewhere. Lucky for me there was some Oxy clean on the garage counter. Lucky for me the substance hadn't yet dried, and lucky for me I was able to get most of it off my upholstery. And last but not least, lucky for me, Tina didn't come outside during the middle of me cleaning the insides of my car. Who scrubs their car clean before going to the grocery store?

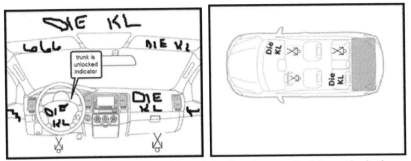

Fig 31.1 Die KL, 666 written with weird oily substance inside my locked car.

Suffice to say; I got it done. I cleaned the car that a demon just wrote in. I never said a word to Tina about the car during breakfast. Not one word. The only thing I said was, "I'm going to the Christian bookstore after I finish breakfast." Her reply was, "OK." That's it, nothing else.

So here I am standing in the checkout line, dazed as to what just happened. I'm so out of it that I can't see the woman standing beside me. She's trying to tell me something, but I'm not paying attention. All I hear is: *Keith, your car had Die KL written in it. Keith, your car had Die KL written in it.* That's all I hear. I'm stuck in my own world. What am I thinking about? I'm thinking about the 666 written on my dashboard. I'm thinking about the upside-down man drawn on the floor on the passenger's side. I'm thinking about the Die KL written on my car seat. I'm thinking about the Die KL written above my seat, the Die KL wrote on the dashboard next to my steering wheel.

I finally snap out of it and realize I'm in the Christian bookstore. I was standing in line here because of what happened earlier. I have to buy more Christian paraphernalia. Will it work? I doubt it. It hasn't worked yet. Then I hear something. "Excuse me, sir; excuse me, sir." I'm thinking, *who's talking to me?* I turn around, and this old lady is standing behind me. She hands me a card and says, "It sure looks like you need this." I look down at the card she handed me; it's basically a card with the Lord's Prayer written on it. This lady had to have been in her eighties. She looked so nice. I had no choice but to smile. That's how heavenly she looked. And then she said, "Take this card, young man, it looks like you need it, remember Jesus loves you, He protects all of his children." She walked off. I turned back around and faced the register. The lady behind the register looked at me and shrugged; she heard everything, as did I. I'm not going to lie; the minute I got to the parking lot, I began looking around. I was hoping to God that I would bump into this lady again. I didn't. The card she gave me was no bigger than an index card. One side of it had the Lord's Prayer written on it; the other side had a giant cross symbol. The terror in me was gone. I know exactly where this card is going. It's going in my office.

A few days later: Christmas Day

https://youtu.be/rX5PKCPhsck

Fig. 31.2 The demons in my home took the card the lady gave me. It disappears/reappears With the words Die KL. Same substance as the car and office on my birthday.

That card you see above (Fig 31.2) is the card the lady gave me. What's on the left of it is a Native American protection necklace. A co-worker brought it back from a Native American store in Arizona while on vacation. Card and necklace were on my computer keyboard, or at least I thought they were. The writing reads Die KL; same substance as before. This was 9 pm, Christmas day.

The vultures aren't diving anymore; they've landed. How do I know they've landed? Well, let's go back to the poking and prodding. Nowadays, something starts poking me within seconds of me getting in the bed. What used to be a once in a while thing has now turned into every night thing. It's every night in the house, and it's every night when I travel on business. It gets worse. I'm now being poked the second I hit the couch. I'm being prodded at when I lay on the couch. How does it feel? Well, you're watching TV, flipping channels with the TV remote when all of sudden you get jabbed in the rib cage. Not once but many times. You feel a tug on your feet, a tug at your socks. This is not a ten-minute thing; this is a couple of hours thing. It's like now that we've woken you, let's throw something across the room type of thing. And that's exactly what happens. An iron or a can of starch gets thrown across the bedroom; always landing on my side of the bed.

Now, we have three bedrooms upstairs. Sometimes the activity gets too hot for us to sleep in one; sometimes we leave and go into another room. Some nights I'm sleeping by myself. Those are usually the nights when Tina falls asleep on the couch downstairs. Nothing's happening downstairs as a result of her sleeping alone. That's not where the activity is. The activity is happening in whatever room I'm in. The spirits are smart; they know I have to sleep. One night I was in bed asleep. Tina was downstairs. It was very late, had to have been past midnight. I woke up suddenly because of a presence I felt in the room.

It felt like all eyes are on me. There I was circling the room with my eyes. I couldn't see anything. But it doesn't take me long to realize where the heaviness was coming from. It was coming directly from my left. As soon as I turned towards my lampshade, I felt something warm graze my chin. Something went by me and hit the lamp head on, knocking it off the drawer. Now the room is pitch black – it's impossible to see what just happened. I'm out of bed, pretty much flying towards the light switch. Something just glazed me. My heart was beating fast at this stage because I know whatever it was that barely missed me had to have been caused by the "Geist." Evil is in the room with me right now. I feel it looking at me.

Since I'm still alive still, I might as well walk over to the other side of my bed and see what it was that was thrown. Well, I'll be damned. A candle, that's what was thrown at me—one of the missing candles. The night the white lady appeared was when this candle went missing. It's back. It barely misses me and instead takes out the lamp. This candle I'm talking about is your typical size candle. There's nothing special about it except to say that it's encased in glass. Weighs twelve ounces. Now, the heat that I felt had to have come from the candle; it was warm, noticeably hot. And that's not because the candle was lit. It was a different type of warmth. It felt like it traveled a great distance. I'm talking about being thrown from outside our house.

By the time I picked it up, there was nothing, no heat whatsoever. Then I noticed something. I'm still being watched; I can still feel the heaviness in the room. It's time to get out of here. No way am I sleeping in this room by myself. I have to go downstairs; I have to find Tina.

And that's pretty much what I did. I mean, you have to learn from your experiences, right? The words Die KL were heavy on my mind at that time. Not only am I walking on eggshells now, I'm pretty much sleeping on them at this stage. Countless possibilities are running through my head right now. Countless thoughts. One thought, in particular: there's safety in numbers.

The spirits are not going to attack me if Tina is in the room. That's been the pattern as of late. They torment me when I'm in my office. Torment me when Tina's in the shower. Torment me when Tina leaves for work. Torment me when I'm sleeping in the room by myself. I'm only attacked when I'm by myself. When I got downstairs, I found Tina sound asleep. The commotion upstairs didn't even stir her. At least one of us is getting some sleep.

Why are the spirits focused on me and not Tina? Is it because they hate me and not her? No, not at all. The spirits don't like either of us. What's happening now has nothing to do with who the spirits like or who they dislike. The ultimate goal is to divide and conquer. For whatever reason, they have decided to make this house a living hell for both of us, surpassing what they did to Jane Doe and her family. Tina's living hell is different than my living hell. The fact that Tina and I are sleeping in separate rooms two to three nights a week means the spirit's strategy is working. Right now, the mood is dark and gloomy. It was gloomy that night, and it was gloomy come morning. Tina never asked me why I was sleeping on the floor. She never asked about the noise coming from upstairs. She was gone within an hour of waking up. I have thirty minutes to get out of the house. That's usually when stuff happens.

Stuff like:

Light flickering off and on while I'm ironing clothes
Ironing board being thrown (if I'm still in bed)
Lamps thrown
Iron and can of starch thrown (if I'm still in bed)
Toothpaste/toothbrush disappearing—reappearing in the kitchen or guest bathroom
Plants thrown
Plants disappearing from the staircase/reappearing in the bathroom doorway (where I'm taking a shower)
Power cuts in the entire house
Loss of power in the room I'm in
Door slams (while I'm taking a shower)
Bible laid on the floor of the bathroom and water puddles all over it
Bible thrown at me (while I'm taking a shower).

Everything I've just listed above are deliberate attacks. There's nothing coincidental about lights going off within seconds of me entering a room. They come back on again when I step out of that room, and I mean, they immediately come back on. As they come back, other lights go off (always the current room I'm in). Upstairs or downstairs, it doesn't matter. That's happened more than once. It only happens when Tina leaves the house. Everything I've listed has happened more than once. I wouldn't mention it otherwise. The one I'm going to expand on now is the instance that involved my last remaining Bible—the one I bought from the Christian bookstore. That Bible was thrown at me one day while I was taking a shower.

There's nothing like having an object thrown at you while your back is turned. Try to think about all the moments in your house where you are most vulnerable. We're vulnerable when we're asleep, right? I think that's the number one vulnerability for anyone living in a home. What comes to mind after that? If you're like me, you'll say bath or shower. That would be number two, at least it is for me. One of the terrifying experiences (and I've had a lot) for me took place while I was taking a shower. What makes that moment unnerving is how it was carried out. Remember, it was only eight months ago when I was in the shower and a poster caught fire. I'm not going to say this was worse than that—but see for yourself.

I jumped into the shower within minutes of Tina leaving for work. I can't remember how long I was in the shower when all hell broke loose. It must have happened within minutes of me lathering up. All of a sudden there was a loud noise—not a bang, just a loud noise. I turned around and looked towards the direction of the noise and saw the bathroom door slam shut. *I'm having a tough time remembering which came first; the door slam or the lights going off.* To the best of my knowledge, I believe the lights went off first, and the door slammed shut soon after. It felt like less than a second between the two.

There I was in the shower with the lights off. It was pitch black. I can't see a thing. Someone threw something at me. My heart was racing. Tina was gone, it was just me in the house, and look where I'm located? I was in the smallest room of the house with no exit. The only exit for me was the door that was just slammed shut. It's best to die fighting, right? Why not fight and see what happens? *Well, if I'm going to fight it can't be here, it can't be in a bathroom, screw it!*

The first thing I did was dart out of the bathtub. I was now feeling my way towards the light switch. I was thinking, *oh, death by electrocution, that's an effective way to go, reaching for the light switch while soaking wet—excellent job, Keith.* As soon as I'd turned on the light switch, I yanked open the bathroom door and darted into the hallway. *Pause—let's take it all in, Keith, don't overreact, don't underreact, you're in the hallway now, nothing on fire, nothing looks out of order. What happens next is up to them, you're still alive.* And that's what I did, ladies and gentlemen. I had to take several assessments. One assessment involved ruling out Tina. Another assessment involved potential danger in the hallway, danger in the rooms next to me. My brain had to answer those questions before I even thought about going back into the bathroom. Lucky for me it answered those questions quickly. It seems whatever these minions were doing, they were done with it. They'd achieved their primary objective, which was invoking fear. I turned around (heart still racing) and walked back into the bathroom in search of whatever it was that flew at me. Found it.

There in the corner of the bathroom near the bathtub was my Bible. Where was the Bible at before I took a shower? The hallway bookshelf. I dried it off and put it back there. It disappeared a few weeks later and has never resurfaced.

Fig 31.3 This Bible has been thrown at me while taking a shower. It later appeared in the doorway of the master bedroom with puddles of water all over it. 2X

It made no sense for me to tell Tina about what had happened. I doubt she's going to change her departure time in the morning on account of me. There was once a time where coordinated our departures. That time has long since passed. The only way for me to mitigate these morning attacks is to get up when she gets up; leave when she leaves. That's exactly what I did. And it worked, no more morning attacks. But what about attacks elsewhere?

What about paranormal activity happening elsewhere? Well, the activity that happened elsewhere include:

Spokane WA
Sheets yanked off the bed while sleeping
Poking and prodding
Sacramento, CA
Sheets yanked off the bed while sleeping
Poking and prodding
Place of employment
Downtown Seattle
The hotel (which *Ghost Adventures* put us in)

One event that isn't hard to prove is the moment I was almost knocked out of my seat at work—something I refer to as the shoulder check.

Shoulder check: *The act of intentionally bumping another person's shoulder with your shoulder as you walk past them. It is meant as a display of open aggression or simple disrespect, depending on how roughly the shoulder check is performed* (Urban Dictionary).

I was sitting at my desk one morning when suddenly something bumps me on my right shoulder. The bump was so significant that it almost spun me around in my chair. I hate the phrase "I was taken aback," but that's exactly how I felt when it happened. I mean, it humbles you to know that some invisible force—something you can't see—is lurking in and around you. What sort of ability does a spirit need to have to follow someone? To cause someone to move inches out of their chair? What are these things?

I had to go back to Jane Doe. I need more information. We have rapport now to where I feel comfortable asking her more questions. Our conversations are not one-sided either. Jane Doe emails me occasionally on Facebook asking how things are holding up. My answer was always: we're taking it one day at a time. Some days are better than others; some days are harder to get through than others. I'm lying to her, to avoid burdening her with our horror stories.

The last thing I want is contamination of her family. I wouldn't know what to do if I got an email from Jane Doe one day saying activity has surfaced at their current location. I mean, when you escape something like this you hope it never finds you again.

So yes, Jane Doe and I became good friends. And with that friendship came something else, something unexpected. The interesting thing about our chat sessions is we see each other's face every time. We soon migrated to video chat which is when you someone's face in real time. That's when it hit me. The gray and white look like Jane Doe. The look on Jane Does face is the look of someone tired and worn out. That's exactly how the lady looked when I saw her. She looked tired, worn out, and yet conniving. The gray and white lady were the same height. Same hair length and hair type. Jane Doe is the same size. All three women have the same mannerism.

If I had to compare all three ladies: Jane Doe, Gray Lady, and White Lady to a female actress it would have to be Carmen Diaz. Jane Doe after experiencing some of what we experience in addition to her son's illness, in addition to turmoil in her marriage, among other things looks way older. Speaking of the Gray Lady—she's come back.

It was January 2015 now. The office was pretty much off limits, which means I'm now doing everything from the kitchen table. The portable terabyte hard drive that I bought to replace the other portable hard drive is gone. The Bible that was thrown at me while I was taking a shower is gone. The attacks I was dealing with now happen while traveling on business or while trying to sleep. My thirty-minute window of leaving the house after Tina leaves is gone. Objects are being thrown at me while Tina is backing out the driveway. To go into my office would be like walking into a lion's den with a big steak wrapped around my neck. That's how frequent the attacks come when I'm in the office.

Occasionally I'll get something thrown at me while working at the kitchen table. Today I didn't. Today I got something better—today I got to see the Gray Lady again. Tina had not yet come from work. I was working from home that day at the kitchen table. I had my back to the sliding door. This allows me to see the entire house. It's the only way I can have some peace of mind. I was doing work on my laptop when the feeling of being watched occurs.

I mean, how can you not know this feeling by now? I know it, and I hate it. Things go quiet all of a sudden—and that's even with the TV on. I looked up from my keyboard. And there she was, looking dead at me: The Gray Lady. There she is poking around the corner of the staircase wall. Our eyes deadlocked on each other. That stare felt like an eternity, but it probably, in reality, lasted no more than five seconds. Five seconds is all you need to take an apparition in—to store whatever it is you think you see in your psyche. I stored the Gray Lady's face in my psyche and thought immediately about Jane Doe.

I didn't get goosebumps; I didn't have the hairs stand up on my arm. What happened instead was her pulling back from the wall and disappearing. And I don't mean disappearing like some ghost. She didn't fade away. She moved back gradually from the wall to where I couldn't see her anymore. But I could still hear her. What I heard were footsteps. The kind of footsteps you hear when someone goes upstairs. I was able to follow the noise from the staircase to the hallway. Then from the hallway to our bedroom, which is right above my head. But the footsteps don't stop there. No, they continue all the way into our bathroom. Once they got there, they stopped.

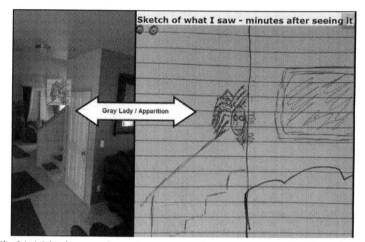

Fig 31.4 I look up and see a woman staring at me. It was the Gray Lady.

Jane Doe and I had a chat a few days later. I'm surer now than ever as what it is I'm seeing. The face staring at me confirmed it for the most part. I mean it had to be her, the mannerisms, the look, the height, width, hair type, and hair length were all there. Jane Doe's hair and eyes and the Gray Lady's hair and eyes. Both of them had the look of being tired and worn out.

I have nowhere to go with this. I mean, where do you go with this kind of information? Who's equipped to handle it? The priest? Jennifer? The team in Spokane? Tina? What does it mean when an apparition takes on the appearance of a former tenant? The first apparition happened before Jane Doe, and I met, years before. That makes me think this is not some fucking-with-Keith moment. There was no way I was going upstairs after seeing what I saw. I mean, I could have given chase, but I didn't. I chose not to. What I saw was good enough for me. I decided to sit still. No sense chasing what can't be seen.

One thing for certain, the Gray Lady and the shadowy figures I'm seeing are two different things. She's not what shoulder checked me at work. Whoever is doing that is running the show here. How many spirits are poking me? Between five and eleven. That's my conservative estimate. Multiple jabs while sleeping. They all happen at the same time, in various parts of my body. Whoever is poking my rib cage is not poking my chin, my ankle, my neck, and face. It's all happening at the same time or one after the other.

Allow me to introduce a new element to that level of violation: the feeling of helplessness. It's irritating when I'm trying to sleep and irritating when I'm sitting on the couch. I can't imagine Tina is experiencing anything close to this. I mean, I would know if she was. The signs I see in myself I'm not seeing in her. The signs of fatigue, restlessness, anxiety, angst, sleep deprivation, almost falling asleep while behind the wheel, at traffic lights and stop signs. That's every day now—it's been like that for two months. This is not sustainable in the long term. No way am I going to survive another month of this. No way is Tina going to survive another month of thinking I'm cheating on her. The spirits seem to be working both sides perfectly. They seem to be in control, and we seem to be unwilling participants in whatever it is they're conspiring to do.

One thing they're doing, as I've said, is jabbing me from all sides. Well, now that I go back to read Jane Doe's original email, I can't help comparing what her son said he saw while living in the house to what I'm now feeling as I sit on my couch. Imagine you're sitting on the couch and all of a sudden someone drops an invisible pound of sugar next to you? That's what I feel when I'm sitting on the couch. Something invisible has just landed on the couch with me. It doesn't stop there. Whatever flopped on the couch is now making its way towards me. The indentations on the couch cushion feel like the ones on the mattress; they curve towards you. Jabbing, poking, combing, stabbing, and just outright invasion.

No human can deal with this long term. I know I can't. Their ability to keep me up at night speaks to their level of tormenting—and make no mistake about it, that's exactly what they're doing. I'm being sleep deprived to where I'm nodding off while being stuck in traffic. Falling asleep at the wheel is something I never imagined myself doing. But here I am doing it. I never imagined I would see shadowy figures out of the corner of my eye—figures with heads, arms, and legs. Some are furry. Some are scaly. All of them get on your nerves. They're all pestering you at the same time. To the point where you just can't take it anymore. To the point of just acting out.

Fig 31.5 Shadowy images in corners of the room. Couch, love seat, bed.

Take for example, the morning I went out of town for business. Had to have been late summer or early fall 2014. Tina and I were sleeping in the same bed when all of a sudden, the lamp on my side of the bed just raised on its own and flew across the room. You know you've reached new depths when you crave the seats at SeaTac airport more than you crave your bed. That's where I'm at now—screw sleeping on this king size mattress. I'm going to SeaTac to get some sleep. I'm angry at two things right now. One, the lamp flying across the room while I was half asleep, and, two: I'm angry at Tina for not waking up.

When activity of this magnitude happens, Tina and I are usually in lockstep together. She gets up, and I get up. We get up and leap into our clothes. We're running out the door. I've lost count as to how many times we've done that. That didn't happen that day. The only person who leaped out of bed was me. It's not like Tina didn't hear it. She did—I know she heard it because she raised her head and looked around. I told her the lamp on my side of the bed was just thrown. She didn't utter one word; she didn't get out of bed. Not even an inch. Instead, she went back to sleep. This attack didn't faze Tina at all. Normally she's out the bed and out the door in less than thirty minutes. Granted, we had argued the night before—about her not leaving the music on when she leaves the house as we agreed to do.

Tina's very smart and very observant. Every day she comes home and finds a new hole in the wall—usually in whatever room I'm in. Every day she comes home and sees a house in disarray. Every day she comes home and finds one of her plants lying on the floor—usually near me. She comes home and sees me cleaning up stuff that the poltergeist threw. She doesn't ask a question. You know why? She's become jaded to the fact that we're not getting resolution. We're not hearing from *Ghost Adventures*, the priest or anyone else for that matter. Combine that with the fact that our relationship is deteriorating then what do you have? You have a mindset of just being done. Tina's done mentally. The attacks are only happening around me now.

This is where we're at in January, 2015. Neither one of us wants to call it quits. Neither one of us wants to be the first to say goodbye. We're not even making eye contact anymore. We're not doing a lot of things anymore. Remember those pillow talks we had? Gone. Dinner together? Not anymore. Joint social outings? Gone.

I delay coming home now. Who wants to come home to a spirit that centers on them? No more, honey, I'm home! Those days are gone. I walk through my door, and the lights flicker. The chair that I sit in when eating dinner is now in my office, with a note of course. Another note that says Die KL, that's meant for me. Who wants to come to a home that? This is a daily activity, ladies and gentlemen. Tina doesn't see any of this. The stuff I do tell her about just goes through one ear and out the other. Her reaction is now "oh."

I share this with you because I want you to understand the next actions I'm about to take. It's an action I'm not proud of. Under normal circumstances, I never would have left the house with Tina still sleeping in the bed. I would have demanded that she get up. I wouldn't have to. Tina would have gotten up on her own. She doesn't have to hear the noise to know it's time to go. She wakes up, takes a shower, grabs her things and darts out the door and heads to work. She does this because I ask her to. She does this because the armoire is lying upside down in the room next to us. Tina will not stay in the house alone, at all. She's always driven me to the airport when I go out of town. That's been our routine for two years. Not anymore. The morning the lamp got thrown was the morning where I drove myself to the airport. Tina didn't move a muscle.

So, I got up within seconds of the lamp being thrown. I was angry, scared, and frustrated—which leads to bad decision making. Hopefully, I'll get some sleep at the airport. *Hopefully, I'll get some sleep while in Spokane.*

I was gathering my things together in my office some thirty minutes later. It was near time to go, which means load up the car, Keith, let's get the hell out of here. Not once did I ask Tina to get up. Not once did she ask me, why was I leaving so early. She knew the lamp had gotten knocked over. I told her that. It was her lamp after all. But she remained asleep. I resented that. So, I was eager to get out of the house. I feel like I'm being watched and guess what? I am.

There's something about the feeling of being watched, some sort of instinct that's embedded in human beings. Be it an inner sense (spider sense, if you will), or better still a disturbance in the Force—you feel it and when you feel you know it's true. You know something's trying to tell you something. Could this instinct have carried over from our more primitive days as a species? I don't know.

All I know right now is this instinct deserves to be paid attention to. Ignore it at your own peril. Not me. Not today. I've made multiple trips from my office to my car. I was loading up my belongings in the trunk of my car when something tells me to turn around. *Turn around, Keith Linder, something's looking at you. Something's pissed that you're leaving. Turn around right now, look up at your office window, look up right now.* I looked up and guess what I saw? My inner voice was correct. The light in my office was off. It shouldn't be. I just walked out of that room twenty seconds ago. It was early in the morning. There was no reason for that light to be off—I was coming back to that room to get some more things. Wait a minute? Someone is in my room. The venetian blind is pierced open—like someone was peeking through. It lowers within seconds of me looking at it. Right there in front of me.

Fig 31.6 My rendition of what I saw that morning.

Fig 31.7 The venetian blind. Actually lowers while I'm looking at it. Fig 31.6 shows were I was standing when the a part of the blind went down.

What do you do when you see something like this, ladies and gentlemen? Something just lowered the blind in my office. Could that be the Gray Lady? Was this a minion? It has to be the spirit that threw the lamp off the drawer. Why else would it be watching me? I'm thinking; I *should just leap in my car and drive off. Drive, Keith, get to SeaTac, get to Spokane, get to your hotel, and go to sleep.* Those are but a few of the questions running through my head as I stand outside in my driveway.

I can't leave right now. Tina's inside the house. So, I run back into the house, passing our bedroom, and reach my office. It would have pleased me beyond measure to see Tina walking out of my room. That's what I was hoping for. I was hoping she had woken up and in doing so thought I had left without saying goodbye. But I was wrong. Tina's not in the hallway. I didn't catch her leaving my room. She was where I left her. Sound asleep.

I told Tina what I saw and how I saw it. I was hoping that would wake her up to the point of leaving the house. I mean, the lamp flying across the room should have been enough. The old Tina would have leaped up, taken a shower, gotten dressed, and beat me to the front door. Not anymore though. Tina after hearing the lamp commotion simply rolled over and went back to sleep. I told her about the venetian blind, and all I got was something dismissive.

I left the house ten minutes later. The old Keith would have never done that. If it causes an argument so be it. "I'm in the right. Tina get your butt up; pack your stuff and stay at Kim's house. I'm not leaving this house until you leave with me." I only advised Tina one time. The old Keith would have advised her twenty million times. The old Keith would have forced her to leave. We stick to the protocol—the one we created when we weren't mad at each other. I didn't do that. I was angry and resentful. It hurt me to see Tina not react to me being attacked. To the point of just walking out.

Chapter 32
Ghost Adventures II

February 28th, 2015—if you told me in advance that the takeaway message from the "Demons in Seattle" episode was going to be: "Keith and Tina are hoaxers," I would never have believed you. If you told me that the second conclusion from the episode was going to be, "Tina is some demon lady," I really wouldn't have believed you. I would've thought you were nuts. How do you go from a team not finding anything, to "Keith and Tina were lying about the whole thing"? That's an awesome leap, even for a skeptic. Surprisingly that's what some took away from the episode titled "Demons in Seattle."

I've been conducting cause analysis at some of the biggest companies in the world. I'm talking, Dell, Microsoft, Philips, McKesson Healthcare, and Abbott Laboratories. Every problem has an elusive component to it: that's why it's called a problem. The only way to solve a problem permanently is to go after its cause. I've never encountered a unit or a field which would give up so easily for want of evidence until I met *Ghost Adventures.* Where I come from the belief is: the more elusive the problem, the greater the learning experience. That doesn't seem to be the mindset within the paranormal community—at least not with the majority of people I've come across.

In the period between *Ghost Adventures'* visit and the screening of the actual episode, Tina and I were left in the dark as to what the investigators found (or didn't find). So was the homeowner. We both asked the Travel Channel the same question, what did you find? The answer we got was, "You'll know when the episode airs on TV." That should have been our first indication of Tina and I not being put in a positive light.

Tina and I woke up on Saturday, February 28th, 2015 ready to watch the episode amongst our closest friends. Friends who've seen and heard things when visiting our house. These are our core friends. These are the people who love us. Some have advised us to move. Some have advised us to stay—defend your home. Some have sought assistance on our behalf. So, Tina and I wake up that Saturday around 10 am, and immediately begin preparing for our midday departure. No way are we going to watch the episode at ground zero. More like a hotel suite. I wasn't in fear of something happening while my friends were here, I was more fearful of something happening within minutes of them leaving. Fear of something happening to me. The activity around the house has settled down. The activity on me has not.

February 28th, 1 pm. Tina walked up to me and let me know that her car keys were missing. I asked her when she last saw them. Her reply, "They were in my purse." I went and looked for my keys the minute she told me her keys were missing. I remember when the spirits took my second car key. Five hundred bucks, that's about how much it cost to replace keys nowadays. Tina was not happy—she remembers what I spent to get mine replaced. So, I told her, let's just go, let's leave now before my keys go missing, we'll sort this out later.

Fig 32.1 10pm PST – episode ends

I can still remember how our friends' faces looked as soon the episode went off. Someone blurted out: "is there a part two? Was that it?" The men were pissed, and the women dumbfounded. Everyone was taken aback. I was especially. I took a sip of my Tito's cranberry and thought, *this is not going to be good.* I wasn't thinking about Tina and me (that would come later). No, this is going to be controversial with *Ghost Adventures'* fanbase and the paranormal community in general. Reason being? Its abrupt ending. I mean, no one who was in the hotel with us knew what was going on. "What did we just watch?" became the repeated question. Kim looked at me and then looked Tina, who was visibly upset, and says: "wow, they made you two looks like you didn't know what you talking about? Kim wasn't lying. The show's portrayal of us was very negative.

I saw how upset Tina was, and said to myself: *the owner is going to evict us tomorrow if he believes what he just saw on TV. I know I would if I was him. Tina's instinct was right, and my instinct was wrong—they messed over us.*

My thoughts got interrupted by the sound of immense sobbing. It was Tina. She was crying her eyes out. Why? The show before going off the air through the use good post-production editing mischaracterized an event in the house that put Tina in a negative light. The suggestion that she might be responsible for what had taken place. I mean, if that's the chief investigator's theory so be it. I can't fault you for having a theory. But what are you basing your theory on? Prior to *Ghost Adventures'* arrival, I took it upon myself to email them some stuff. We're talking about mass amounts of data. None of which made it on the show. The show doesn't even mention previous tenant's testimony. That's something the audience might want to know about. A fellow researcher would want to know about that. No video of the female apparition. No loud bang footage, no video of lights going off and on. I'm thinking, *there has to be a part two somewhere. A continuation. No way is this it?* That's the prevailing wisdom in the room right now.

Everyone's asking me: "are they coming back? Are they bringing more people next time? Are they going to stay longer?" These are excellent questions my friends are asking. Unfortunately, I have no answers for them. Neither did Tina. What you saw just now is what we saw just now—first time around. We had no preview showing, no heads up, no email alert saying what the synopsis of the show was going to be. I'm trying hard not to turn blue because I have a strong feeling I'm going to get a phone call tomorrow, asking Tina and me to get the hell out of the house. I have a strong feeling the landlord is going to want to evict us based on this ill-portrayal. By "ill-portrayal" I mean this: if a majority of what you just saw is incorrect or didn't happen that way, that to me is an ill-portrayal. I can't tell you how many letters, emails, tweets, and instant messages I got from people we knew who, after watching the episode, was like "what happened? They made you and Tina look bad. It's almost like they thought you two were faking everything, or that Tina was behind it all." Those are not my conclusions. Those are the conclusions from people that we know who watched the episode.

And the irony of it all is that our friends (who know nothing about the paranormal, who knew nothing about *Ghost Adventures*) have come to a different conclusion as fans of the show and members of the paranormal community. All our friends believe we were poorly portrayed, including family members. Fans of the show felt otherwise. Their response, "You and Tina are hoaxers, how dare you waste *Ghost Adventures'* time."

If you asked me what I knew about *Ghost Adventures* before May 2012, my answer would be very little. I knew there was a reality show on cable TV that goes around investigating haunted locations—it seems like they've been around awhile. That's all I knew. The fact that it was on the Travel Channel led me to believe the show was on the up and up. I mean, it's the Travel Channel. If these guys are investigating haunted locations the world over, here's a case in their backyard that will spark their interest. Maybe they'll be able to see the wall markings in our home and be able to connect them to another case somewhere else. Maybe they've seen similar markings in Scotland, in Ireland, in other parts of the world? Maybe they've heard similar tales in Arizona, in Pennsylvania? I mean, why would a Travel Channel network have a paranormal show if it isn't going to tour the world and get some global comparisons? That's my only reason for having them in here. That's the only reason the homeowner allowed them in.

When Elissa Jaffe told me, she knew of a team that might be in a position to help, that's where my mind went. A team that's in a position to help, versus exploit. Don't make us look like we don't know what we're talking about, as a result of you leaving empty-handed. And just to be clear, the word "hoax" is never mentioned in the episode. The accusation of Tina and me faking something is never explicitly uttered or even discussed. It doesn't have to be. Any producer or director can get the audience to believe what they want them to believe, through a process called post-editing.

I can't fault a team that comes in and after giving it all they got; still, leave empty-handed. I mean, look at what we're chasing? We're chasing energy for Pete's sake? That energy chooses who it wants to interact with and when. It's called the paranormal for a reason.

I've lost over twenty cameras as a result of chasing these things. Two portable drives and two video cameras—all gone. What did you think your percentage of success would be based on five hours of investigating?

247

Everyone that was in that hotel room with Tina and me made their opinions known as to how bad the episode was. What a wasted opportunity. There's so much there—it's impossible to get it all at once. Maybe the team should have lived in the house with Tina and me. Maybe the environment was too sterile? Meaning full of equipment, personalities, gadgets, and void of Keith and Tina. That's what my friends and I talked about within minutes of the episode being over.

What do we do now? "Let's go have dinner, let's go dancing." That's what our friends said. We're already in downtown Seattle. Might as well enjoy it. That's exactly what we did.

I pulled Tina aside and said, "You're not the woman they portrayed on TV. Let's have fun with our friends—they're here to celebrate with us, regardless of what the show aired." And it was true. Our friends, hers and mine, were awesome. They've been supportive throughout the whole ordeal and even more so now. Kim walked in on our conversation and resumed where I left off. "Let's go drink and have fun!" The girls alert the men that they need a few minutes to get to freshen up. Ten minutes later we're all walking out of the hotel room when suddenly one of Tina's friends begins yelling that she can't get out of the bathroom. All the ladies stop in their tracks. Where are the guys? We're all waiting for the elevator.

We all heard the rattling of the bathroom door where we were standing. I was standing closest to the elevator, pressing the down button when all of a sudden, I saw Tina dart back into the room. Kim was right behind her. That was when someone blurted out, "Tina's friend is stuck in the bathroom." *Is someone stuck in the bathroom?* My first thought was, someone's having way too much fun, right? Someone's tipsy. So tipsy to where they forgot how to open a door. It happens. I left the elevator and headed towards the bathroom. I saw Tina and Kim fiddling with the door. I stepped next to Tina and asked her what was going on. She was as clueless as the woman inside. And that's when someone blurted out: "I was just in that bathroom, it has no lock!" We confirmed this five minutes later. That's how long Tina's friend was stuck in the bathroom.

Tina and I made eye contact with each other and answered each other's question—*that door wasn't jammed. It wasn't stuck.* I immediately recalled last summer's incident of what the two church ladies went through when they came to bless our house. They had a similar problem with the front door; it wouldn't open. It embarrassed Tina and me greatly because we had to let them in through the garage. Kind of cheapened the moment, them coming through the garage versus coming through the front door. Those ladies came to bless our house and the only door we could let them use is the garage door. This bathroom door was behaving the same way. It doesn't have a lock. What gives? Five minutes later the door popped open. Seriously, it popped open as if to say, 'I'm done now, I've inconvenienced you all long enough.' We all left right away. The women were laughing at the whole ordeal, and the men were scratching their heads as to how that was even possible. Tina walked up to me and shook her head in disbelief. We both knew what had happened. Our friends, bless their hearts, were none the wiser. The most they could say was, "That was weird, that's never happened to me before." I thought, *that won't happen to you again, trust me.*

As weird as that was, it would not win the Weirdness of the Night award. That award goes to my friend, Joe. Four hours later, we all returned to the hotel after a night of partying. Some of our friends had driven home; some opted to get their own rooms. My friend Joe walked up to me and asked if he could "crash on the couch" versus driving home. I said yes because we had a two-bedroom suite. *Kim has the other bedroom; you can have the living room. Thanks for supporting Tina and me. It's been a long, disappointing day, at least from the episode standpoint.*

That's what friends do; they stand by you through thick and thin. A majority of our friends can't quite put their finger on what's going on in our house. Some describe it as strange; others describe it as remarkable. No one and I mean no one (Tina and I have a lot of friends) have ever thought for a second that we are making things up. Our friends believe us more than some family members. Simply because they live here. Everybody came to the same conclusion after the watching the "Demons in Seattle" episode, which is we were portrayed poorly. As I laid in bed that night, I was thinking *what the fallout from this is*? I have to say, I was worried.

Will the landlord share the same sentiment of those who watched the show? Throughout the night I would occasionally log into Twitter, onto Facebook—I wanted to see what sort of reaction was taking place through social media. My worst fears had come true. The sentiment on social media was that the house occupants are at fault because of what *Ghost Adventures* couldn't find. Can you believe that? It was our fault? Talk about blaming the patient. *Oh, it was bad.* Some of the comments coming in were mean-spirited, some outright racist. Ignorant stuff was being said about the both us—Tina especially.

No way was I going to tell Tina what was being said online about her. That was not going to happen right now. Let's just go to sleep. I'll deal with the heat tomorrow—*I hope to God the owner of the home does not believe what's being written about us.* That was the last thing I thought about before going to sleep. What would be the landlord's response?

7 am the next morning; I heard a knock on our bedroom door. Tina and I both darted our eyes open—a *force of habit*. I was thinking: why is my friend knocking on the door so early in the morning? Maybe he wants to say goodbye or something? I get to the door and open it, and sure enough, there's Joe. He's standing there with a puzzled look on his face. *What's up, Joe?*

"Bro, sorry to wake you up, I was about to leave, but I noticed all this blood on my t-shirt. I went to the bathroom to try to rinse it out, and I look in the mirror and see all these scratches on my face." I was still half asleep until I heard Joe say the word "scratches." That and the word "blood" made my eyes light up. And he wasn't lying either. His t-shirt was covered in streaks of blood. The blood had to have come from his face. Razor-thin scratches. The one that stood out the most was the scratch going across the bridge of his nose. Very noticeable.

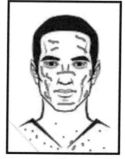

Fig 32.2 Friend, Joe R. wakes up with mysterious scratches His T-shirt is spotted with blood.

Tina comes over to the doorway and throws her hands up to her face and says, "Oh my God, what happened to you?" My friend can't explain it. This is beyond weird. I mean, how do you explain it? My friend has multiple scratches on his face. I'm not talking about one scratch. I'm not talking about two or three scratches. I'm talking about multiple scratches. Razor-thin scratches. These scratches are freshly made. Tina asked him to raise his hands up, to show us your nails—maybe he scratched himself while he was sleeping. My friend raises his hands and reveals to us that he has no long nails. There was no skin under his nails. No blood whatsoever. Nobody could scratch their face the way my friend's face was scratched and sleep through it. You would wake up first. It looked like he got into a fight with a cat while he was sleeping. Like a cat mistook his face for a nail post.

And then he said something I knew all too well. His biggest worry was not the scratches on his face. It wasn't the blood-stained t-shirt. His biggest fear was: what would his girlfriend say? His girlfriend hadn't come to the hotel. She didn't watch the episode with us. She knew he went out partying with us after the episode aired. What will she say when he gets home? How will she react? How would any one of us react if our significant other came home the next day with scratches all over his or her face? A lot of women would assume you got into a fight with a woman somewhere. A lot of women would think your mistress scratched you. I knew exactly how my friend was feeling. I knew exactly why he was worried. I thought to myself: *I hope you don't have a woman's ring in your pocket. Might want to check your pockets before walking in your house.* I wanted to say that so bad with Tina standing there. But I didn't. The reason he knocked on our door was that he wanted permission to use our bath towels. He wanted to clean his face. His fear was we'd wake up, find him gone, and there on the floor of our bathroom are these blood-stained towels. He woke me up to give me the heads up. I'm glad he did. His face scratched up was a crazy discovery.

Tina and I knew who the perpetrator was (we didn't tell him that, even though he knew). If a spirit can yank off my bedsheet in hotel four hundred miles away, it can follow Tina and me to a hotel twenty minutes away from our house. No one ever called us to see how we were doing. No one ever called us to ask: have you been followed? No one ever called to see if we were experiencing any activity. The answer would have been yes. The lights in our room flickered off and on throughout the night—exactly like they do in our house. They flickered off and on in the hotel bathroom. The hotel staff could not get our door keys to work. We couldn't get into our room for the first thirty minutes of us being there. A true researcher would have anticipated this. The *Ghost Adventures* crew did not.

Meanwhile, on this latest weekend, the weird came in sets of three: Tina's missing car keys was the first event. Tina's friend getting locked in the bathroom was the second event. The third event (probably in the early hours of the following morning) was the scratches on my friend's face. They're all related. This morning's event and yesterday's events combined were the preludes to a bigger punishment. *This wasn't over*. Not by a long shot. The official breakup of Keith and Tina was imminent. I have to admit; Michael Corleone could not have orchestrated a better takeover of our home than the event that was about to happen.

Tina and I got home after 3 pm that Sunday. You could almost taste the fallout that was about to happen. Family member fallout. Tina's cell was ringing as was mine. I knew who was calling me. My mom and my brother. My mom's reaction was one of confusion. She couldn't quite figure out why Tina was ill-portrayed. Everyone, including my mom, knows of the Native American history in and around Bothell. I mean, that's public knowledge. You don't have to outsource that. It's in the textbooks here. She found that omission interesting, as did I. My brother, on the other hand, thought the whole thing was premature. If they didn't have evidence, why air their visit at all? Why promote it in such a way that implies something was found? Their narration just didn't make sense to him. The abrupt ending didn't make sense either. There's so much that could have been done that wasn't, and my brother couldn't understand why. Why didn't they take samples from the door? Why not take pieces of the wall with them? I'm talking about the markings themselves. Why do a piss poor job at investigating something? What hoaxer would allow you access to his house while they slept elsewhere? Who does that?

When I got to work that Monday, my co-workers were like: "what the heck happened? How come *Ghost Adventures* didn't find anything? How's Tina doing?" Some of my coworkers, the ones who'd never known the story, were in complete shock. The cat was out of the bag now. I know there was a fallout brewing. Tina doesn't, but I do. I'm afraid of what her reaction will be once she finds out. Most of the negative comments online were aimed at her. People with no evidence whatsoever were accusing Tina of being the demon. They think she was the poltergeist.

What makes them think that? I mean, how could you think that if the show ended with zero evidence found? Ask the lead investigator. Ask for the unedited footage. Ask for the frames that sit on the cutting room floor. That, ladies and gentlemen, is what's fueling the fallout. If you leave your audience with nothing but fill-in-the-blanks, some are bound to make up their own ending. And you've provided them a lot of fill-in-the-blank material. Now, you don't have to take my word for it. After all, I could just be having sour grapes. I'm not, but you don't know that. By all means, feel free to comb through the paranormal blogs dating back to February 2015. Comb through the message boards and message forums. Comb through the Twitter feeds of those who were at the house. See what their fans got from the episode. I guarantee you it will match what I've been stating in this chapter.

Later that day I got an instant message from one of my coworkers who worked out of our Spokane office. He, like many, had watched the episode this past weekend, not knowing it was my house that was being featured. It was a shock to him, the claims we were stating. He told me his father is a priest. I think I responded with, huh? How can your father be a priest? I wasn't sure how that concept worked. And he replied again, his father was a priest within the Episcopal Church. He'd been one for over forty years. He didn't know it, but my eyes lit up while my fingers typed on Google search the words, Episcopal priests. I was not familiar with that denomination. I already had great rapport with this colleague, even before the episode had aired. He had my attention when he said his father, through the course of his priesthood, had cleaned homes of demonic activity. He'd battled forces before, him and his bishop together. He might be able to help Tina and me.

This was great news. Though I didn't yet want to get too excited about this new revelation. There were a lot of unknowns still. Number one: would his father help us? Number two: could his father help us? I mean, everyone's who's walked through our front door has told us, "We are the ones who can help, we are the real deal." Each one of them brought about a level of disappointment. The biggest disappointment of all came from the team who left without finding anything—the *Ghost Adventures* team. Tina and I were tired of being burned. We were tired of being taken advantage of. We were tired of dealing with thrill-seekers. Our goal—and I've said this numerous time already—is to make this house livable. We're not going always to live here. But I can't make the mistakes that others made. I can't leave the house like it is right now. Whoever comes after me, will know how haunted it was. Notice I used the word "was."

Who out there is in a position to help us? Who out there can problem solve? Who wants to see it through with Tina and me? I have to assume it's not *Ghost Adventures* based on how they twisted the truth. Maybe it's my co-worker's dad. Nothing's set in stone yet. My colleague has to first ask his dad if he wants to get involved. He has to confirm if his dad is still physically able. I found it to be good news nonetheless. I know my co-worker. He's a good sound man. I've worked with him on various projects; he wouldn't have stepped forward had he thought there was little chance of his father getting involved.

Later that day I got a text message from Tina. She was sending me screenshots of *Ghost Adventures'* Twitter and Facebook page. *Dammit, she knows now.* Everyone was ridiculing Tina. I mean, the comments were downright ugly. Everyone was calling her the "demon woman," the "crazy bitch." Some were even suggesting that "the demons are inside Tina." A lot of people wanted Zak to investigate Tina: "the demons are in her, Zak, please go back and investigate Tina." I already knew what Tina was showing me. I'd known it since Saturday night. I hoped that Tina, not being as internet savvy as me, might not know how to retrieve such information. It never dawned on me that Tina's friends and family would be sending her this stuff. And that's exactly what some were doing. So much for weathering the storm. The text messages keep coming. So much that I finally had to call her, which didn't do much good. What could we do? These are people who don't know us. These are people behind a computer screen. Majority of them are kids. Majority of them are infatuated fans of Zak Bagan's. One thing I knew that Tina didn't was the internet gives everyone the right to be an asshole. These people couldn't survive one night in our house. They'd shit their pants if they saw what we saw. No one has to tell me that. I know that about people already. Tina didn't, though. Had she known we wouldn't be dealing with what we're about to deal with.

Let's not forget us being blindsided. Obviously, the show is yours, so that means you can do whatever it is you want with it. Surely someone with a heart, someone with a Christian background, would have thought, or better yet suggested—let's give the homeowner and house occupants some warning. What are we giving away by informing them of our investigation? An investigation that we conducted based on them giving us access. That would've helped me and Tina deal with the fallout. Of course, that heads-up never came, and now my girlfriend's blowing up my cell phone angry by what strangers are saying.

Nobody with a decent job, or with day-to-day responsibilities, is going to go out of their way to write such vile words, especially about people they don't even know. Nobody but internet trolls. Tina didn't like that explanation at all. It wasn't so much the comments that angered Tina; it was the percentage of comments that were aimed at her. And why were they aimed at her? They were aimed at her due to the innuendo by the show's lead investigator. That's all a troll needs to form a lynch mob. And they got it with the loosely-based narrative. If the investigators have little knowledge about investigating this type of activity what makes you think their fans don't either?

It riddles me, how some of these opinions get formed. The only thing I could say was: these people don't know us. They'll never step foot in the Bothell house, and that's a good thing. They wouldn't last a second if they did. Is what I'm saying to Tina working? Heck, no! She's pissed. She's angry. Whatever her family sends her, she forwards to me. I'm like, why would your family do this? Why are they fanning the flames? I know there are negative comments about me online; I've read all of them. The only people I'm responding to are those being empathetic to our situation. Fuck the rest. *Ghost Adventures* told a story. Allow me to tell you the real story. That's what I wanted Tina to understand.

When I walked in the house that night, I found Tina in a heated debate with one of her family members. Her family was not happy about how she was made to look. Which I agree with one hundred percent, my question to them would be: what problem are you solving right now? The episode has aired. It's over; it's done. It was a mistake. We learn from it, and we move on. Nothing's being done when two people are screaming. Tina did nothing wrong. She wasn't in the editing room. She nor I are executive producers of the show. Lastly, remember you're arguing with Tina (when she's at home). Guess who's home with us?

I looked at Tina and gave her the look of "just hang up on them." That's what I did with my brother's months back. I hung up on them. It's easy to armchair quarterback something from the comfort of your own house. Do me and Tina and favor: buy a plane ticket and see for yourself. Your comments mean nothing to me until you do.

Yes, I'm upset about how we were portrayed. I'm pissed. What does being pissed get us at this moment? It gives us nothing. We can fret and argue over matters we can't control, or we can try to unite and look for the silver lining in all of this. *Ghost Adventures* had their chance, and they blew it. Trust me, they're not the first team to blow an investigation of a lifetime, and they won't be the last. The spirits played them, played us all, played us perfectly. Zak and the crew's mindset were that of playing checkers, while the spirit's mindset was 'no baby, the game is chess'. Who won? Well, that's on them. If you want to help us solve this problem, then buy a plane ticket and move in with us. If not, shut the fuck up. I told Tina to tell her family that—because that's what I told my family.

My brother tried to chastise me about the episode. He was the one saying to fill the house up with cameras. "Put cameras everywhere." I did. That made the activity worse. Did I call him back saying, saying your idea sucked! Your idea made matters worse! No, I did not. I figured his heart was in the right place. Up till now, everyone's been making it up as they go, paranormal investigators especially. You try one thing, that doesn't work. You stop trying it and move on to something else. It's that simple. The only thing being created right now is angst. Angst leads to frustration. Frustration leads to anger, and anger leads to a couch being thrown.

Tina turned her anger and frustration towards me within seconds of being off the phone. *Let the finger pointing begin.* That's what our first Monday was like, the first Monday after the show aired. My response to Tina's finger pointing was that we can't let that bullshit get to us. We can't afford that now; the minions are listening. That didn't work. Tina kept going and going to the point of me just walking away. Normally I'd go to my office to get away, but that's not going to happen today. Stuff starts flying when I go into the office. That's how thick the tension is right now; we're talking Katie Perry weekend levels. You see, Tina and I agreed three weeks ago that we wouldn't argue in the house anymore. Arguing causes objects to fall out of thin air, so why argue? It results in me getting attacked. I can't sleep when I'm being attacked. I'm averaging four hours as it is. I can't afford to lose anymore.

So: where do I go if I can't go to my office? I drive up the street and park my car in the parking lot of Fred Meyer and wait it out. My advice to Tina before leaving the house was to stay off the media websites. Ignore the bullshit! If your family calls, let it go to voicemail. Ignore them! This will blow over in a few days!

Did Tina heed my warnings? Of course not. I came home an hour later and found my girlfriend doing exactly what I advised her not to. I found her glued to her phone—she's on *Ghost Adventures'* Twitter and Facebook pages. It was like she had become entranced with the phone all of a sudden. I wish to God she didn't; those comments about us were horrible. You would think someone at *Ghost Adventures* would have come to our defense. I mean, the invite to appear on Travel Channels *Aftershocks* came around this time. You would think someone would go online, one of the investigators and say, hey gals, guys: cut it out; we didn't find anything, that doesn't mean Keith and Tina are liars. Certainly, doesn't mean Tina is a demon lady. I'm not saying that tweet doesn't exist; I just never found it— and trust me, I looked. I looked all night for it.

Tina was quickly out the door the next morning. Usually, I'm up when she's up, *same protocol as before: leave when she leaves*. But I was tired. That's what happens when you're averaging four hours sleep. You don't hear when your girlfriend wakes up in the morning.

I leaped out of bed the second I heard the garage door go up—Tina leaving. Her SUV wasn't even halfway down the driveway when all of a sudden, the lights went off in the room. *Keith, hurry up and get out of the house.* Lucky for me I had some clothes already ironed. I left the house that morning twenty minutes after Tina. The lights in the bedroom went off and on the entire time.

Chapter 33
The Break Up

When the devil has you in his sights, every day becomes a Monday. Nothing's going right. I go for a walk on my lunch break, and lo and behold, crows start diving at me from above for about fifty yards or so. Five of them, relentless and unforgiven these crows are—for reasons I can't explain. They're loud too, so loud my co-worker Anong, observing from far behind, utters "crows diving at a person while they're walking is an omen of some kind." I looked at her and thought to myself, *tell me about it.* But it was weird the way these crows were attacking. They weren't diving at anyone else that walked by, just me. I know, because I watched. I went to my car and watched while eating my lunch—hoping these black birds would attack someone else. Hundreds of people walked by. No one got attacked. When it came time for me to walk that same sidewalk again, here they come. Five blackbirds diving and nicking at my head. What's that about? I can't think of a lower time in my life than right now. With that in mind, let me continue.

I got three more stories to tell you before I explain Tina and I's breakup. The first story involves Tina—remember what I said earlier about spirits not liking anyone? Just because they're attacking me all the time, doesn't mean they've forgotten about Tina.

I hope Tina never thought that. If she did, she got a rude awakening one morning. She woke up with scratches all over her body. Extensive and noticeable scratches on her left and right arm. I was watching TV downstairs when all of a sudden Tina came running downstairs towards me. She was frantic and fidgety. I could tell by the look on her face that something was wrong. Tina threw her arms up, and I saw it for myself. There were a series of scratches on both of her upper arms.

Save for my friend Joe; no one's ever been scratched till now. The next morning Tina comes running at me again. She's dripping wet having just got out of the shower. This time I can see the scratches without her pointing them out. Scratches on both arms and both legs. I mean, it looked like she had just walked through a rose bush. This was a new type of activity—a dangerous one at that. I pleaded with Tina to stay with Kim until we got this figured out. She refused. The word coming from Jennifer was the spirits might be pivoting, this speaks to it being demonic. She would try to call her priest and the shaman she knew one more time. The Spokane team tried contact Fr. Ashcraft again and got the same response. "Send me a video of you and Tina being attacked."

I'm not sure what category this next event falls into because it happened outside the house. Is it still considered paranormal if it involves my 2008 Hyundai Sonata? I already told you about the trunk incidents involving my key fob. What I'm about to share with you now is crazier than that. I mean, it's insane to even to think something like this could happen. But it did happen, and it happened more than once—which means I have to share it with you.

One morning Tina and I got a doorbell ring. It must have been 5 am or so. I remember it being on a weekday because it was close to getting up time. Now, who in the world would ring a doorbell at 5 am in the morning? I know I wouldn't. I know Tina wouldn't. I think we all can agree that there's bad news on the other side of that door.

Tina and I rose out of bed at the same time and looked at each other, asking ourselves: did we hear that? The doorbell decided to answer our question for us by ringing again. I walked downstairs very hesitant, thinking, *this is not going to be good. If it's a phantom doorbell ring, I'm going to be pissed.* I opened the door, and lo and behold; it was my next-door neighbor. *What the heck is he doing here?* He had his car parked in our driveway, and he was shivering in front of me. I asked him what was going on, and he replied: "I was leaving for work and couldn't help but notice that your car doors are open." *My car doors are open?* He then stepped aside so that I had a full view of my car and sure enough, there it was my Hyundai Sonata. All of my car doors were open, and my trunk too. Tina strolled down the stairs in her night robe and uttered something to the effect of: "what the hell?" "Doesn't look like it was broken into. I looked it over as I was pulling up into your driveway, and it doesn't look like it's a burglary. It's weird— I stopped to see if you guys were OK." I turned and looked back at Tina, and said, "Yeah, we're OK, thanks for letting me know."

Tina and I inspected the car. There was nothing wrong with it. Nothing missing. But all the doors were wide open. Now, I wouldn't even be sharing this incident if it just happened once. But it didn't happen once—it happened three times. Three mornings in a row. My neighbor rang our doorbell three days in a row. Tina and I finally came to the decision that we needed to keep my car parked in the garage. The spirits were doing whatever they wanted, whenever they wanted, with my car being parked on the curb. If you think the incident was resolved, guess what? It wasn't.

This is a textbook definition of what it means to be oppressed. The fact that my car is now parked in the garage doesn't mean anything. I've mitigated nothing by doing that. The next day it happened again. And the day after that, and the day after that. Now comes the moment where the spirits say: 'we own you.'

https://youtu.be/c3iD366V1hU
(Reader should type the URL above as I'm about to explain it)

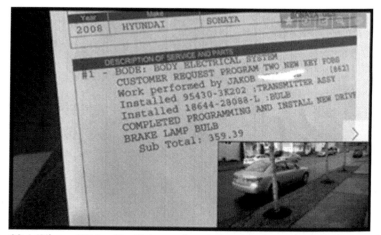

Fig 33.1 Winter 2015 – Car lights and car horn sounds uncontrollably. To the point of putting it in the garage, but that doesn't solve anything.

As kids growing up, we were instructed to never play with our food. That's a no-no when sitting at the dinner table. The cat I had as a kid was great at it. I mean, she'd catch a mouse and toy with it for hours. You almost feel sorry for the mouse, that's how bad it got. That's what it felt like a week after the "Demons in Seattle" episode. It felt like we were being abused to the point of just saying, just get it over with. I know that's how I was feeling. The torment of Keith Linder is pretty much in full effect come March of 2015. If ever there was an example of the spirits bullying people, this would have to be it. Tina and I had just come back from the movies. I parked the car right in front of the house like I always do. Tina walked into the house. Me? Well, I'm making my way towards the mailbox.

I was heading back from the mailbox when suddenly I saw my car lights flashing off and on. I wish I knew Morse code because the lights were flashing like they were trying to say something. Either that or they're just fucking with me—which is a strong possibility. I mean, my car lights are going off and on for a considerable amount of time. Long enough for me to yell: Tina, come here! This off and on thing went on for about twenty minutes. Tina and I finally decided we just needed to go into the house, don't give them the attention they seek. Ignore them. That was a big mistake.

It would seem the spirits were not done with their show of 'how to annoy Bothell tenants,' because once the sun went down, that's when the action started. Tina and I had been home for a while now. I was sitting at the kitchen table, and she was upstairs watching TV. All of a sudden, we heard a car horn go off. My car horn was going ballistic. I was thinking, *did I hit my key fob by mistake? Did I activate something? Of course not, your keys are in the safe, Keith Linder, you put them there hours ago.*

Tina came rushing out the bedroom and met me downstairs. "Is that your car going off?" I opened the front door and walked outside and... suddenly the car horn stops. Dead silence! *Please, please, please God, please don't make this a night where I'm tormented beyond belief, please don't.* That's what I said as I closed the front door. And, soon as the door closed, the horn goes off again. Soon as I open the door, the horn stops. Close the door—the horns begin screaming again. This happened so much that finally, people were beginning to come outside their houses. My neighbor (the one who told me that all my car doors were open one morning) came outside. "Are you guys OK?"

One neighbor, who I never met before came outside, and even asked us if everything was alright. I turned and looked at Tina and said, we got to park my car in the garage. And that's exactly what we did—we moved her SUV out of the garage, and we moved my car in. *Keith, that's not going to solve anything*—oh, you have been paying attention, good for you. Two hours later the car horn began screaming again. Lucky for us it was in the garage now—but being in the garage doesn't solve anything. The noise is still irritating. Tina comes running down the stairs again and says: "is your car still doing that?" The only thing I could do was shrug. The spirits must be extremely restless because this is the longest they've ever tormented us—I mean actual activity. The noise stopped as soon as I opened the garage door. As soon as I closed the door, it began again. It's irritating me to the point of becoming angry—and I know what that gives me. If I succumb to anger, I'm through; you might as well call the coroner at that point. The horn is beeping, beeping, beeping, beeping, beeping—and you know the car lights are going off and on too, because cars nowadays do that. Tina looks at me, and I look at her—we're powerless, we can't stop this. Or can we?

Maybe I can locate the fuse box. Maybe I can disconnect the fuse that controls the alarm system? Maybe I can deactivate the car horn? *It's worth a try, right*? I grabbed the owner's manual out of the glove box and realized within minutes that the car alarm was a computerized system. There was no fuse to remove. Keep in mind, while I was doing this the car horn was still going off. My car lights were still flashing off and on. Suddenly the doorbell decides to get in on the fray.

The doorbell starts ringing on its own. *How can a doorbell ring when no one is at the door*? An hour had now passed, and we've not moved the needle in solving this thing. I was trying my best not to get upset. I was trying my best not to get angry. Neighbors were still walking up to our driveway, asking us if everything is alright. Tina gives them an innocent assurance that yes, "everything is OK." Later that night the word Google crosses my mind. Ah, Google! The internet has the answer to everything. *A problem solvers cheat sheet.* I walked up to my office (car manual under my arm) with the aim of Google searching 'how to disconnect your car alarm system.' My car horn had been going off and on intermittently for several hours now. It's been an irritant for a majority of the evening. How do I turn it off permanently? *Come on, Google, don't let me down.*

I'm sad to inform you that I never got to Google—not at first, anyway. Every time my fingers touched the keyboard—and I mean touched the keyboard—the car horn would get even more. As soon as I raised my fingers from the typing position, the noise stopped. As soon as I walked out of the office, as a result of the noise stopping—the noise resumed. Once I stepped back into the office, the noise stopped. As soon as I sat down at my desk and began typing—the noise resumed. This is what I mean when I say playing with your food. I'm damned if do, damned if I don't. The electrical abuse that started at 4 pm that day would finally come to an end some six hours later. I was beaten and exhausted. I'm pretty sure the Homeowners association is going to send a letter to my landlord about the noise from tonight. I'm pretty sure our neighbors hate us by now. I informed my job that I would be late coming in that following Monday. I needed to go to the Hyundai dealership to get new key fobs. Maybe that'll stop the car alarm from going off. And it did. It really did. No more waking up to open car doors. No more alarms going off. No more trunk door being raised. No more walking to my car in an underground car garage and finding every door open—including the trunk. Can you imagine that feeling? It's a dark feeling. An oppressive feeling. Buying a new car fob put an end to so many things. So many things related to my car. No more Die KL stuff appearing in both the car and the office.

A few weeks before Tina and I broke up, I told her we can't afford to have arguments in the house. No disagreement what-so-ever. If we disagree, let's go to the coffee shop. Let's go to an open cornfield or something. Arguments will get us killed. Will get me killed. I can't sleep in the house anymore. I'm getting more sleep at a red light than I do at home. More sleep in the grocery aisle. I'm not saying Tina, and I can't have disagreements. All I'm saying is, we can't have them in the house. The house is alive. It's occupied by spirits and trust me; they are out to get both of us. We had this discussion at Tully's coffee shop—a few miles from where we lived. Tina agreed. I'm proud to say that it appeared to be working for a while. Then came the "Demons in Seattle" episode, i.e., the visceral attacks against Tina. I'm still waiting for *Ghost Adventures* to defend us? One tweet to your fans is all we need. Can you tell your fans to stop attacking Tina? Stop calling her the demon lady. Nothing, not one word of defense. No callback whatsoever.

I take that back. We made a phone call. We got a phone call asking if we'd be interested in appearing on their show *Aftershocks*. What's *Aftershocks*? *Aftershocks* is a program where Zak invites the most memorable characters from the series back onto the set, to update viewers on how their lives have fared since the *Ghost Adventures* crew paid them a visit.' The format is simple: Zak interviews you (me and Tina) for an update. It's like a question and answers session. They asked us to appear. Obviously, the answer was no. Short answer: "Fool me once, shame on you; fool me twice, shame on me."

March 6th. I can't lay my favorite shirt out on my bed and go jump in the shower. I can't do that anymore. I mean I could. I could lay it out on my bed. But there's a downside to that. The downside being, I come back in and find that shirt nailed to a wall. It's now missing somehow. The only way to mitigate that is dropping my clothes off at the cleaners. Which was fine. I love taking my dress shirts to the cleaners. Not every week, though. Especially not this week. This morning I went to go pick up a series of shirts, my favorite Tommy Bahama shirts. *Damn, I love these shirts.*

I walked into the cleaners that day—it's a husband and wife establishment. Normally when I walk in, it's the wife that greets me. She's the one behind the register. Today, I walked in and gave her my ticket, and within seconds I sensed something was wrong. She took my ticket and looked over her shoulder—signaling for her husband to come over. Her husband was in the back doing something. He saw me and began making his way up front. As soon as he got to the front, she reached under the counter and brought up a bundle of clothes—my clothes. I was now baffled. I can tell my clothes haven't been dry-cleaned, they look exactly how I left them. *Or so I thought.* The wife began raising up the shirts one by one, explaining to me the shirts' condition. All the shirts were shredded, almost to the point of confetti. The husband grabbed one shirt and held it up to the light and began explaining how a shirt like this "can't be dry cleaned."

It can't be sewed or repaired. Now mind you, I dropped these clothes off two days ago. I didn't bring them in to have them sewed. I bought them in to have them dry-cleaned. They were not in this condition when I bought them in. As soon as the husband opened up one of the shirts, that's when I knew what had happened. The cuts I saw looked exactly like the cuts our bed sheets had that morning when Tina and I woke up. We're talking about seven shirts.

Was I mad? Of course not. Who could be mad, knowing what I know? The look on the husband and wife's faces said it all. They were dumbfounded. They could not explain how seven shirts got cut up so bad. These shirts never went through the dry-cleaning process. That much we know. The husband was very apologetic, as was the wife. And guess what? They didn't have to be. The problem wasn't theirs. The problem was mine. I know that based on what I've seen. That's not the first time I had my shirts cut up that way. They've been cut up that way at the house. But I know I didn't bring them to the cleaners that way. I know that because the wife always counts the shirts before printing the receipt. She dangles the shirts in front of me, and she counts them. She then tallies them on the register and prints me a pick-up receipt. The receipt lists how many shirts I dropped off. Had these shirts been in the condition they were in when I dropped them off, the wife and I would have caught it. No sense in arguing about the supernatural—especially to those out of the loop. The best thing I can do is grab the shirts, apologize for the inconvenience, and go home. And that's exactly what I did.

I walked through the front door and saw Tina sitting on the couch. She had her cell phone up close to her face, which wasn't good. She had become addicted to the negative comments being said about both of us, her especially. I knew from my observation that the reviews of that episode were still trending on *Ghost Adventures'* Facebook and Twitter pages. It was slowly becoming one of their most controversial episodes, and at the beginning, I couldn't understand why. To this day I still can't quite understand why that episode lit the fire among so many people. Both skeptics and followers of the show had pretty much united against us. The fans thought we wasted the investigators' precious time. The skeptics, who never believe in anything, including paranormal TV shows, were all of a sudden praising the show's lead investigator. Did people think they were going to witness a Bible catching fire? Is that how uneducated the paranormal audience is? *You, investigators on TV have not been educating your audience. Shame on you.*

The next day I was walking around the house, not too long home from work. I saw my girlfriend curled up on the bed. She wasn't watching TV, even though the TV was on. She was watching in real-time the various negative comments, various negative tweets coming in from around the world—about her especially. Something told me I had to intervene; I might lose Tina completely if I didn't. The comments about her were extremely harsh—therefore, why read them? In my mind, the only thing that can offset bad news (i.e., bad reviews) is good news. And I had some, or at least I hoped I did.

I stopped at the foot of the bed and looked at Tina. "Hey, I have some good news. There might be a silver lining to this after all. A co-worker of mine, his father, is a priest." (I was hoping me mentioning the word priest would cause Tina to look up from her phone. I was wrong; she didn't.) "My friend at work believes his father might be able to help us with our situation, he's an Episcopal priest, and according to my friend he's dealt with issues like this before. He's going to ask his father on our behalf. Progress!"

Tina looked up at me and said, "Oh really?" She said it in a sarcastic voice, and that's understandable. I get it. She has the right to be sarcastic. She has a right to fold her arms and look at me strangely. But at least she's not looking at her phone anymore. At least she's not reading what's being said about her on some social website. I sat on the bed next to my girlfriend. I told her what my friend was going to do. Now, it's not guaranteed, his father might be retired. He might not want to deal with this—and who can blame him?

I felt I had made a dent in our communication problem. I felt I made progress. Tina and I had hardly spoken since the episode aired. Both our families were upset about our ill-portrayal. Our friends were upset as well. Never in my wildest dreams could I have imagined such negative fallout. Words can't describe how bad we were being beaten up online. Which is why my next suggestion is going to sound shocking. I looked at Tina, and I said, "We should watch the episode again. We should watch it together, right now, just you and me. On the couch, you and me right now." Now, I know what you're thinking. Why would I suggest something like that? What's my aim? In case you didn't know it by now, I'm a cup-is-half-full kind of guy. I always see the light within the darkest of situations. I'm a firm believer in the phrase "life is what you make it." Yeah, it sucks how we were portrayed on TV. It sucks that we have to pay the price for them leaving with zero evidence. There's no need to argue about that. No one knows better than us how bad that sucks. But guess what? We're still here. Guess what? We're still alive. A wise man once said, "When life gives you lemons, you make lemonade." Let's make some lemonade right now. Let's watch this episode together. We'll sit on our couch, screw the "Geist"; this is still our home regardless of who found what or not, this is still our home. Let's watch the episode, Tina. You and me, let's laugh at ourselves.

Let's use this moment as means of getting reacquainted. My dad taught me always to take the negative and turn it into a positive. Grab that bull by the horns. Ride that boy back into the stall where it came from. We've been through a lot. We've seen a lot. We can afford to laugh at ourselves—I think we've earned it. Hell, we can even laugh at *Ghost Adventures*. Let's laugh at them. Those internet trolls weren't here to see the investigation. We were. We know where they went wrong. We know how they fucked up. Let's laugh at that. Tina looked at me and began to chuckle. I think *God is great!* Tina smiled and laughed. I hadn't seen my baby smile in months. *Please say yes, please say yes.* Tina looked at me and said, "OK, let's watch it." But first, she wanted to go put on her pajamas. I looked at her and said, fine, go put on your pajamas, I'm going to go downstairs and pull up the episode from our cable box. I'm going to make me a cocktail; I'll meet you downstairs. So that's where I went—I headed downstairs and went straight towards the kitchen. I was thinking to myself: this is all therapeutic, Tina and I watching this episode together is therapeutic. I'll make sure to laugh at myself throughout the episode. I have to melt the ice between us. I know what jokes to say. I know how to make my baby laugh. I'll ridicule myself. I'll ridicule Zak Bagan. I'll ridicule their asinine questions, and I'll poke fun at her as well. I'll poke fun at Tina. Tonight's mission: to laugh at ourselves. Create some levity. This is positive reinforcement, right? What I'm suggesting is a good thing? I can't remember the last time Tina, and I watched TV together. Nowadays we usually watch TV in different rooms. If we could just resume doing that together—then it might have all been worth it.

I have Tito's cranberry in my left hand and the remote control in my right hand. All I had to do is hit play, and the episode will begin. The only person I was waiting on is Tina. She was upstairs getting comfortable—changing into her pajamas. Or so I thought. Remember that dark cloud that was hovering above our house? Well, it finally threw a lightning bolt, and that lightning bolt hit me dead on. Zeus couldn't have thrown a better one. I had just swallowed my first sip of vodka cranberry when I heard a stomping come from upstairs. There are two types of stomping in this house. The one the "Geist" makes, and the one Tina makes.

As God is my witness, I so wanted that stomping to be the "Geist" and not Tina. If the demon was coming to get me finally, I would not change a word of what I just said. I would say, take me. I would rather be taken by the minions themselves than accept the realization of Tina stomping through the house. I know what her stomping means. It means she's coming towards me. It means she's pissed, and I have no clue as to why.

Tina stomped her way downstairs, and sure enough, she was coming to see me. She had her cellphone in her hand, and she was waving it around. She was screaming! She was pissed. She shoved her cellphone right up in my face. The first thing she uttered was: "You tweeted to someone you loved them?" My response was: huh? What are you talking about? Tina then shoved her phone back in my face. "You tweeted some girl you loved her?" Keep in mind she's waving her phone at me the while and screaming something to the effect, "you tweeted to someone that you loved them!" She swings her phone towards me again and holds it still. I see what looks like a Twitter page. But I can't make out what she's showing me because she was throwing it in my face only for only a second and then yanking it back to read it herself. She was leaving me no choice but to ask, what are you talking about? What tweet? What tweet about I love you, I love who?

Now she's pacing back and forth. She's screaming louder now. "I'm tired of all this shit! I'm tired of *Ghost Adventures;* I'm tired of this house. I'm tired of you. I'm tired of everything." I'm still not up to speed on what she's talking about. All I can ascertain at this point is that something on my Twitter page upset her. So, while she was screaming and wailing, I reached into my pocket and pull out my cell phone. Let me see what's on my Twitter page? Let me see what has her riled up. I log into my Twitter and what I see are nothing but comments from other people about the "Demons in Seattle" episode.

"Tina, what are you talking about? What tweet? I see no tweet on my phone!" Tina suddenly blurted out: "February 28th you sent a tweet out on February 28th, saying I love you. In my mind I'm thinking, *February 28th, February 28th - that's the day the episode originally aired. That's the day we were in downtown Seattle. We were with friends—yours and mine. How hard can it be for me to go to my sent messages, my February 28th sent messages and see what (if anything) she's talking about.* Shouldn't be hard at all. I've sent very few messages during this time period. *If you're accusing me of sending something, then I should be able to see it to.* But I can't see it. Not at this very moment, because Tina is screaming at me. She's shoving her phone in my face, saying, "Look at this, look at this, it's right here, it's right here." I still can't see what she's referring to. She storms off and within seconds starts tossing things. She comes back and starts tossing more things.

The first thing she tosses in the air is my gallon of Tito's vodka. Everything was flying in the air now. Everything that I own. This is not the "Geist" throwing stuff; no, this is Tina throwing stuff. I suddenly realize something. *Our agreement of having no more arguments in the house was now null and void.* I don't know what I'm going to do; whatever I do it'd better be fast. I've seen armoires fly across the room based on the level of anger this house now has. I'm going to have to calm Tina down; she's on the warpath... and that's when it then dawned on me. That's when I thought; something's afoot here. It was hard to concentrate with Tina going off the way she was. She had gone from Cool-Hand Luke to Hurricane Sandy in a matter of minutes.

My girlfriend was all over the place. Innuendos and accusations were coming at me left and right. The one that got her up in arms, the one I could not quite figure out was the tweet she said I sent on February 28th. I tried to remind Tina about the rule we created. The rule we created when we were calm, cool, and collected. The rule we made for ourselves in the hope of protecting ourselves. The rule doesn't stop us from arguing. It postpones us from arguing. If Tina has an ax to grind, so be it. Let's argue somewhere, let's argue at a place we agreed we would go to in the event of an argument. She and I came up with this rule several weeks ago. A hundred percent agreement from a meeting I initiated. Tina has seen our arguments take on a life of their own by the spike in activity happening around us. So far, the activity has never broken right in the middle of us arguing. It takes a while, a short while, to blow up. It usually happens when we're about to simmer down, when we reach a stalemate. We go our separate ways. But Tina is so pissed; I'm fearful of our refrigerator being tossed. That's never happened BTW. It might today though.

This is huge. What Tina is accusing me of is huge. I've never seen her this angry. If the spirits were to act on Tina's anger right now (or act on it later), I have no reason to doubt I'm in big trouble. We've got to get out of this house. We've got to leave right now. We can sort this out somewhere else. Let's get to our safe zone. Tina was livid. She was pacing back and forth while pointing her fingers at me. "How could you? How could you?" I turned from her and noticed that the bottle of vodka she threw landed upside-down in the kitchen sink. I reached in and set the bottle up. Tina came immediately behind me. She yanked the bottle from my hand and threw it back in the sink. I turned to face her and said, "If we're going to argue we need to leave the house, we need to leave the house now. There's no upside to us arguing inside the home. We're being watched right now. We need to leave."

No way would Tina be this unruly in public, and that's another reason for why we need to leave. Cooler heads must prevail. My biggest fear at the moment was the large amounts of furniture being tossed around. Last time I saw Tina she was in the bathroom getting dressed. I finally got her to smile. I finally got her to laugh. We agreed to watch *Ghost Adventures* together. We agreed to laugh at ourselves. So much for that moment of levity. I will say this right now. I never tweeted anyone that I loved them on Twitter.

Who's behind this? Who's orchestrating this? There have been a number of female jewelry items popping up in convenient locations over the past few months. Tina has been finding most of them. I have no doubt the spirits put those items in Tina's path deliberately. I have no doubt they wanted her to find them. They wanted her to confront me about them. Could this be something like that? If you think that's far-fetched and too fantastic to be true, then you haven't been understanding fully everything I've shared. You haven't been understanding my conversations with the cable company. My conversations with the utility company. If you think that's a bridge too far, then you haven't been understanding lights going off in the rooms that I immediately step into. You haven't been understanding fires starting on their own with zero explanation, so says the Bothell fire department. Malevolent spirits have been infiltrating communications for some time, the world over. In the nineteenth century they loved to ring servants' bells—sometimes even after all the bell wires were cut. In the twentieth they could dial the speaking clock.[1]

Looks like we're just the latest update. If this is a demon, then nothing I've described or told you is too unbelievable. Tina won't let me look at her phone, so I can't see what she's seeing. I want to see what she's seeing. She won't let me. She's too angry. She waves the phone around while at the same time accusing me of something unthinkable. She's accusing me of something horrible. I find it odd that this would happen now, minutes after us reaching some form of ceasefire. But why should it be odd? Why should it be impossible? The spirits have been trying to get me to fight since day one. They've been trying to get us at each other's throats for quite some time. They did the same thing with Jane Doe. Her marriage ended in this house. Call it a demon. Call it a poltergeist. Call it whatever you want. The word means very little to me. It's the actions that should be studied. It's the invisible hand that controls things. That controls moods. The hand that is carefully manipulating Tina and me. That's all a demon is. Study the actions, not the words.

I need for Tina to see what I see. I need her to stop yelling. I screamed at her to stop yelling. Who can concentrate when all this screaming and yelling is going on? Calm the fuck down. Show me this suspected tweet. Screen capture it and email it to me. The fact that it took place on February 28th the day the show originally aired—is highly suspect. If what you say is true, then why hasn't a

[1]   See http://coolinterestingstuff.com/the-german-poltergeist-who-dialed-the-speaking-clock

group of internet trolls exploited it? Who do I say I love? These are the questions I'm asking myself while Tina's yelling at me. The house looks like a tornado has just run through it. Tina's going through everything.

Tina never showed me the message entirely. I couldn't find anything on my Twitter that would help me understand what she was talking about. No, I love you whatsoever. I don't doubt for a second what she thinks she sees. I just think she's misinterpreting it. I think someone is manipulating her. No arguing in the house. That's easier said than done when you're angry. I understand that. But guess who doesn't?

The best thing we can do now is leave the house. I'm getting aggravated due to Tina's constant finger pointing—her sticking her fingers in my face. That's when I knew the time had come for me just to walkway. *Just go to another room, Keith. Get away from Tina. Let her calm down.* You can't reason with someone when they're bloodthirsty—and Tina was way past bloodthirsty. Everything was coming out now. All of her pent-up feelings. All of her pent-up emotions. They were all coming out; I'm talking about in droves. If I become angry, we're done. That's all the spirits in this house need, is for the both of us to get angry. They're not going to get that. No way, no how. If Tina wants to argue, then she's going to have to argue by herself. I'm out of here.

The best way to deal with Tina when she's mad is to ignore her simply. Let her anger die down—even if that means she leaves the house to stay with friends. That's all I have up my sleeve right now, the ability to walk away. But no, Tina's pissed. She's pissed. She knows I always walk away. Today, Tina's going to follow me. She's going to follow me and still thump her fingers at me. Now she's in my office. Now she's tossing everything in my office. She's suddenly doing what the spirits have been doing for two years. She's destroying my stuff. That's unacceptable. No one has the right to destroy another's person property. Be mad all you want, go outside and bite a tree, why don't you? Don't destroy the stuff I work hard for. This goes on for about an hour or so. It felt like an eternity.

With no end in sight, I finally took it upon myself to just leave. Tina can maintain her rant for hours. I know it, I've seen it. She's so mad right now that she might be intimidating the spirits her damn self. I wouldn't doubt it. That's how mad she was right now. That was why I'm leaving. It's only a matter of time before her anger begets my anger. This house won't survive that. So, I left. No way was I coming back to the house that night. I'll spend the night somewhere else. When I got home the next day, Tina was gone.

Chapter 34
T.W.K.D.T & T.W.T.D.K

"Those who know don't talk. Those who talk don't know."
~ Lao Tzu

A couple finds a house online that they love. One of them emails the landlord, who responds with "yes, the house is still available; would you like to see it?" Girlfriend and boyfriend see the house and fall in love with it immediately. The day of the lease signing, they hear a kid 'cough.' It all goes downhill from there— within two years. That's what you're reading in a nutshell: that slow downhill decline of Tina and me. I don't know if that's a love story or not. The only thing I know is, it's the truth. Most love stories have happy endings. The couple, regardless of their differences, has to find their way back to each other towards the end of the third act, or all is lost. In the end, they ride off into the sunset together and live happily ever after.

In Hollywood, the spirit that lurks behind the scenes gets called out. It gets dealt with by a priest that's semi-retired. A huge spiritual battle ensues, the priest ultimately wins by banishing the evil spirits, everyone goes home. End of story. This story is not going to end that way. A malevolent spirit lurks within the walls of our house. It's inflicted pain and torment. It has beaten a previous family into submission, to the point of them moving out. Add what they went through to what we've been through, and you're forced to agree that we're not dealing with something that can be cajoled into some sort of light. The first thing that came to my mind after Tina moved out was Jane Doe. She said it went downhill for them within days of moving into the house. Now I'm alone. I now have to deal with something I was hoping I didn't have to deal with. I have to deal with a breakup. Tina and I are no longer together. She's taken all of her things, and she's gone. What does that mean to a malevolent spirit? Did they want Tina to leave? Do they approve of her leaving? Will they follow her? Do the spirits view her leaving as a setback? Do they view it as mission accomplished? These are the questions running through my head right now. Am I more vulnerable now? Am I exposed?

With Tina gone, I have to be mindful of not falling into some form of depression. I can't despair. Whatever talons are in me now will deepen if I get too depressed. We all know breakups suck. We all know the pain that comes with losing someone. Regardless of our problems, there was a time (not too long ago) where Tina and I were madly in love with each other. There once was a time when I looked into her eyes, all I could see was the history of the universe. In her arms is where I wanted to die. Those days are gone, which raises the question. How do I mourn her loss and mine? A man should be allowed to cry in his own house, right? What's the consequence if I do? You know the spirits are hovering by. You know they're throwing suggestions my way on how to feel sorry for myself. That's what I have to be mindful of. I have to make sure their suggestions are not filtering into mine. Which, ladies and gentlemen, is very hard to do.

So, what's the house like now with just one person living in it? Well, the pitter-patter footsteps haven't subsided. What I like to refer to as being the baseline noise, i.e., the knocks and tapping noise, is now easier to hear due to one person living in the house now. I never knew how much noise could be made in a house with two people living in it until after Tina moved out. Now it's just me. *I need to decide within a few days as to whether or not I'm going to stay. Something happens now, who's going to know about it? Matter of fact, I might as well turn the living room into my bedroom until I figure out what plan B is. No way am I sleeping in the bedroom now.*

I received an email from my co-worker the next day. His father, the Episcopal priest, wanted to know what Tina and I were experiencing. He wanted to review the material: the notes, the pictures, the videos, and the answers to the questions he gave me. I sent Fr. Roy Sr. the same information I send to everyone who's had an interest in the case. At the time I thought, what are the odds another priest helping me? The local priest was out of the picture now. Not one follows up as to how Tina and I were doing. His bishop never called us back after promising he would. So, when my co-worker asked me for more info, I was shocked. The reaction my co-workers had after watching the "Demons in Seattle" was different than the reaction I got from members of the paranormal community. I mean, fans of the show were still trolling Tina and me. We're taking it on the chin big time! Here's my co-worker on the other end of that spectrum. Not once did he ask me, were we on the up and up? He never put me on the defensive. He never said, "Everything is happening off camera."

The only thing he said was, "My father is an Episcopal priest, he's dealt with hauntings like this before—maybe he can help you." I bring this up as a means of showing the contrast between those with spiritual beliefs and those without. Those with a degree of faith seem to the empathetic to me and Tina's suffering. Those who do not, have been brutal and mean-spirited. I have to be honest about that.

So, I emailed Fr. Roy Sr. the videos and pictures that he requested. Now the wait begins. What will his decision be? Can he help me? Will he help me? Will his help be long term? Will it be organized and structured? *Well, there wasn't a long wait.* I would get an email from Fr. Roy Sr. a few days later informing me of his interest. His bishop said OK. My co-worker told me his dad, Fr. Roy Sr., was in his eighties. He's blind; he's basing everything off the eyes and ears of his wife and the bishop. If the videos and pictures are true, and he believes that they are— then our house is the most active house they've ever come across. The next day Fr. Roy Sr. called me to confirm his church's involvement. It didn't shock him to learn about the other priest's disappearance. It didn't shock him to learn about my break up with Tina. You see, Fr. Roy has been doing this for over forty years. He understands there's a physical component and a psychological component. No one (*Ghost Adventures*) included, ever thought to ask Tina and me, the most fundamental question of all: How has this thing affected your relationship? Fr. Roy Sr. knew to ask that question. "It's a wonder we lasted this long as a couple," the priest said. "It's not uncommon to be at each other's throats." I knew right then that Fr. Roy has been around the block with these sorts of things. He's conducted house cleansing throughout the Puget Sound. Through the use of scripture and other church ceremonials, he's created a sort of house exorcism doctrine. A procedural on "how to remove unclean spirits" if you will. It meets the Episcopal church's definition of house exorcism.

It shocked me to learn that a majority of his house cleansings (those that involved unclean spirits) involved members of his congregation. You see, Fr. Roy Sr. and his bishop have dealt with a lot of stuff in the Puget Sound. They've responded to outbreaks on Indian reservations and in homes through the Pacific Northwest. "New housing developments have the potential for increasing activity. The earth has been turned upside down, and new development units typically anger wandering spirits." That's one assessment. Per Fr. Roy Sr. that still leaves an unresolved question: why our house? Why not the neighbor's house?

I told Fr. Roy Sr. what Jane Doe told me. I told him what Jennifer told me. I told him what the Spokane team told me. I shared everything. Since we're in the fact-gathering stage, I felt it important that he know everything. His reply to all of that was to keep the information coming. He and his bishop will need a few weeks to comb over everything. A few weeks to prepare mentally and spiritually. They would need to incorporate the help of a shaman in addition to the house cleansing. Now, I'm familiar with the shaman concept because Jennifer has mentioned it to me a few times. The upside-down man wall markings seemed to interest Fr. Roy Sr. and his bishop. Why would a spirit draw a Native American symbol on the wall like that? *A shaman would know probably. A shaman will know things that Fr. Roy Sr. wouldn't know.* It might be a while before we get to the bottom of this, is what Fr. Roy Sr. said when talking to me on the phone. House infestations are difficult to remove. There are too many unknown variables. If what Jane Doe says is true, then we have our work cut out for us. I like the use of the word "we" versus them or me. I so like their humble, we-gotta-proceed-with-caution approach.

This house might be made livable after all. Is that possible? I'm back to my original plan. The plan that Tina and I had, which was to leave the house in better condition than when we found it. Leaving abruptly only postpones the problem. It doesn't solve it. You're leaving the problem for someone else to deal with. Why blindside the person moving in after you? Who does that? Not me. Tina and I had always wanted to do our part. Just tell us what that part is, and we'll do our best. I'd like to think Tina, and I could have been stronger (perhaps even still be together) had we had a support system in place. I'm talking about the spiritual and paranormal community.

Fr. Roy Sr. was able to give me a clear overview of what his plan was. I always bond with people who think as I think. People who problem solve. Fr. Roy was approaching this as a problem solver. Way back, I had thought other teams in the area had their plans. I thought the local priest had a plan. I thought *Ghost Adventures* had a plan. So many teams have come into this house uttering the words "we have a plan," when in reality they didn't. In reality, they just wanted to see Caspar throw something across the room. In reality, they just wanted to be wowed and awe-inspired. That's not a plan. That's gross negligence. That's putting the house occupants at risk. Those people are thrill seekers. As of right

269

now, only two teams have had their heart in the right place when coming here: those were Jennifer and the ladies from Spokane.

My decision to stay was on more solid ground after my hour-long conversation with Fr. Roy Sr. There's something to be said about the word of God and the motivation that comes from hearing it. Am I scared? Damn, right I'm scared. I'm terrified. Being terrified is OK. Being scared is OK. The thing I have to keep reminding myself about (especially before going to sleep) is: if these spirits wanted to kill me, they would have done it already. Lord knows they've had plenty of opportunities. Maybe they're here to torment people. Maybe they're here to cause trouble. I don't know, anything's possible. I'm basing my assumptions on what Jane Doe told me and one what I've seen and lived through.

There's no telling what these spirits are going to do as a result of the church's official involvement. If it's a poltergeist that we're dealing with here, then it's a rare form of poltergeist. Just to be clear all "Geist" are rare forms of poltergeist—each is uniquely different. It would appear this "Geist" doesn't need adolescent children, or a troubled teen, as some so-called experts like to say. This poltergeist, according to Fr. Roy Sr. might have mastered the art of self-sustaining. It can go dormant, and it can lash out when it wants to. If I didn't know any better, I would have to say Fr. Roy Sr. was more confident about dealing with a demon than dealing with a poltergeist. I always felt a demon was worse to deal with. According to Fr. Roy, not necessarily. Demons are thought to flee and flee quickly from the word of God. They're fallen angels, which means they know the power of the word, they know its origin. Demons are in a sense cowards. They exploit weakness but vanish immediately when truth arrives. Their biggest defense on Judgement Day is simply, "we didn't tell them to do anything, we just suggested it." That's how cowardly they are.

Poltergeists, meanwhile, are just nasty and vindictive. They seem to have some sense of entitlement. 'How dare you try to eject me? That's a no-no. Do so at your own peril.' Exhibit A? Keith Linder.

That's the mindset I'm getting about poltergeists. They could very well be demons themselves. Who knows? Wouldn't surprise me if they were some higher form, some more nasty type. In any event, we have to follow protocol. The church's protocol of first removing unclean spirits, who could have come here as a result of a poltergeist. One could have summoned the other. We don't know. Fr. Roy Sr. tells me, "We'll know a lot more after we complete the cleansing."

Eradication will be very difficult. It's very important that I understand the risks. Our conversations are not in a secured room. The spirits are hearing everything. They know I've found a new priest. They know Tina and I are no longer together. They know I'm still hurting. I'd be lying if I said I didn't want to cry as a result of losing Tina. I'd be lying if I said I didn't miss her. You can't just erase four years. Four years is four years. Tina was my girlfriend. She was my best friend. She put up with my foolishness, and I put up with her foolishness. Some things we did well and some things we didn't.

I compare our break up to death in a family. Especially with everything we've been through. There's only one person on this planet that understands what I've been through, and that's Tina. There were times when we could finish each other's sentence speaking about our house.

I'd get winded, and Tina would leap in and begin where I left off. Not missing one element of detail. People ask me "where's Tina?" Oh, we broke up, we're no longer together. Their immediate response is, "Oh, I'm so sorry, you two looked so good together." It's hard to respond to comments like that because the breakup is still brand new.

How many of us can relate to losing someone over something you didn't do? How many of us have lost someone due to a demon, "Geist," or both working overtime? The only person who knows what I'm feeling is Jane Doe. Their marriage dissolved in this house. The first couple of weeks are the hardest. I so wanted to lay down in a ball and just forget about it. I wanted to cry so badly. But I can't. I'm afraid to. They're watching. You think I got problems now? You think I got minions poking me in my sleep right now? Well, wait till I start crying. Wait I start downing a bottle of Jack Daniels, a bottle of vodka. Wait till I stop shaving. Wait till I start missing work. Wait till I start losing weight. Wait till I stop taking a bath. Wait till I become a hermit. I can fall into a whole lot negative stuff if I'm not careful. If I don't remain grounded in the way I was raised, I can be undone in seconds. I can't become suicidal and let me tell you, that's easier said than done. Remember: as I'm offering myself suggestions on how to stay strong, the spirits in this house are offering suggestions on how to just quit. 'Just lie down and quit, Keith, we got you.'

And they've got some pretty good suggestions. I'm a single man now. I'm free of Tina. She's gone, hallelujah! I'm making great money. I'm traveling. I'm excelling in my profession. I have a big house. What's to stop me from becoming a playboy? What's to stop me from having a different woman in my bed every night? What's to stop me from making this a bachelor paradise? I mean, Tina's always thought I was bringing women in here behind her back, and look what that got me? If my punishment is losing her, then I might as well do the crime? That's fair, right? Well, I'm single now—I can be with whomever I want, sleep with whomever I want, and not feel guilty. Right now, I couldn't find a female earring if my life depended on it.

Those wonders ceased to happen the minute Tina moved out. These suggestions and more are what I have to be mindful of. These spirits would love nothing better than to see my fall from grace. It took me ten years to get to this point. It could be gone in a day if I'm not careful. I cannot afford to let my guard down or fall into some sort debauchery. It's just me now. Me and the assholes that live here. *Don't become bitter, Keith. Don't let disappointment turn into anger. Don't despair.* That's what I include in my prayers now; the words *don't despair*.

Jane Doe told me on more than one occasion that she tried to commit suicide three times in this house. Each time the paramedics saved her. That's how dark her life got while living here. The same cloud that hung over her family, that dissolved her marriage, was still here. Her family's ordeal combined with mine speaks volumes about the clandestine acts being carried out here.

Chapter 35
Poking and Prodding

The first time I was poked and prodded I was in bed with Tina. What I hoped would be a one-time thing slowly turned into a nightly occurrence. It's one of the simplest yet most aggravating occurrences I've experienced while living in this house. Let me describe it again to those who lack familiarity. Think of a child poking you in your rib cage or your kidney area. There's no mistaking that feeling. I mean, how can you deny something as obvious as that? I've tried: trust me. I'm unable to pierce this poking and prodding. I don't know what it means. I don't know where it leads, and I don't know how to make it stop. If something's close enough to poke you, then they're close enough to do just about anything else. The first few times I was poked, I assumed it was a defect in the mattress. Maybe it's time to flip the mattress. And we did, Tina and me. That didn't stop it. We tried moving into another bedroom. That didn't work.

Is it hard to comprehend that a mattress can pulsate? That it can throb? It's almost impossible to describe—let alone explain. It's happening more and more, which makes me think they're getting bolder. At first, it was the kidney and rib cage area. Now it's everywhere. That started about the same time as Tina leaving. Have you ever tried to sleep while someone is pulling on you? It's intensely frustrating. I call it the ultimate Catch 22. If I rise from the bed and scream, leave me the hell alone! Guess what happens? It intensifies—naturally. I've just told them what they're doing is getting to me. If I just lay there in silence, I get more of the same. We've tried different remedies, Tina and I, when all this started. We've bought brand new beds. We've smudged. We've laid salt underneath the mattress. Salt underneath the bed. We've recited the Saint Benedict prayer, and we've used holy water. Nothing works.

Now, there's another bed activity which overlaps with the poking and prodding. I'm not quite sure which is worse. This next one feels like something leaping into the bed. This leap into bed feeling started way before the prodding. If you recall, this started when I was recuperating from my knee surgery. I compare it to a cat leaping in the bed with you while you're trying to sleep. What makes this phenomenon scary is that it happens before, during and after the prodding. They're happening simultaneously now. But, one interesting distinction. I already told you about the poking and prodding taking place when I'm in hotel rooms. I've yet to experience the leaping into the bed, the indentation in the mattress, while away from home. That should be significant to any researchers reading this. I mean, there has to be reason for that, right? Like I said before, it's concerning and alarming these instances where the mattress indents. First the approach, the depression in the mattress. And then something goes through you. Is it a spirit? A minion? Is it energy? The closest thing I can compare it to is those electrical cow fences back home in Texas. There's a buzz feeling first, not a shock. Too euphoric-like to be a shock. It freezes you still whatever it is. That's the passing through phase. The euphoric feeling, I speak about. Something in me is trying to fight it off. I can feel the conflict sort of speak. They keep coming back no matter what I do. It's like open season on Keith.

Hopefully I've described some real and tripped out things to you. Hopefully I've given you a glimpse into my world at night. Who do I think is behind this? Well, I call them minions. And I'm not talking about the movie *Despicable Me.* What's a minion?

Minion – a servile follower or subordinate of a person in power. A minor official. Yeah, they're spirits, but they're a different kind of spirit. What's a poltergeist? A "noisy spirit?" What does a poltergeist do? They raise hell and create turmoil? When I think of poltergeist, I think of energy. Pure havoc-raising energy. These spirits (the ones poking me) are either byproducts of the poltergeist or byproducts of something else. I've seen them out the corner of my eyes throughout the house. Someone's guiding them. I can't explain it, except to say, it's what my gut instincts tell me. Always trust your gut instincts.

If I add what Jane Doe's son saw with what I see and throw in for good measure the shadowy images that Microsoft saw when they were here. What are we left with? We're left with shadowy figures roaming around this house. It's impossible to think otherwise. Now the interesting thing about my chat with the previous tenant is this: I never told her about what I saw. I don't volunteer that information to anyone. Jane Doe doesn't know about the Xbox One testing Microsoft did at my house. She doesn't know about the weird black lava-like images the Microsoft guys picked up on their monitoring devices. She only knows what her son told her. That was four years before Tina, and I moved in. I believe he was six years old when he began seeing this stuff. The majority of these figures, I would say, are six inches tall. The others, about one foot or more.

Seeing the Die KL markings on my lawn and in my car educated me on their ability to leave the house. Go back to the Die KL markings: look at the pictures in this book and look at the video on YouTube. Ask yourself the question: aren't the patterns the same? Isn't the signature and liquid sort of the same? The Die KL is nearly identical in all three places. Whatever substance they used to write Die KL in my office, is the same substance they used to write Die KL in my car.

One of the interesting things about these shadows is their movement. They seem to move with the same freedom as we do—with one crucial difference: they can become invisible. And how, precisely, do they move? My experience teaches me that they cannot step towards you directly. More like indirectly. By indirectly, I mean when your back is turned. They love appearing while you're preoccupied. Right when you're about to close your eyes and fall asleep, the indentations begin. The mattress starts pulsating and throbbing. I can't tell you how many times my motion cameras would send me an email saying motion detected, motion detected. I get five snapshots per email when that happens. One or two of the snapshots appear normal. Two out of the five appear to show black blobs, black shadows in and around the corners of the room. The last snapshot to arrive via email shows the room back to normal again—the black shadow(s) are gone.

I'm not sure where Jane Doe's son was when he saw the shadows. She never told me that. I know where I see them. I see them outside my office. I see them when I'm sitting at the kitchen table—when I'm working from home. I see them when I'm sitting on the couch. I'm watching TV like anyone else, except I see movement out of the corner of my eye. Always near the staircase. At the foot of it. If I try to look at it directly, the figure recedes backward. It doesn't vanish or goes poof! No, it just steps back behind the wall. Two things happen after that: pitter-patter footsteps which go from the direction of the landing area (top of the stairs) to one of the three bedrooms. Utter silence after that.

Does any of this dissipate as a result of Tina leaving? No, ladies and gentlemen, it does not. It picks up. If I had to narrow it down as to what nights were worse, I would have to say Sunday. Now relate that to my work schedule, which is Monday through Friday, and you'll see why this is happening. If you want to make someone tired and irritable what better night than Sunday? Send them to work with just four hours sleep. Let them deal with sleep interruption for five days. The more tired they get, the less likely they want to smudge, fast, and pray.

Now, I know what you're thinking: dude, there's no way I would stay in that house. I'd be so long gone. And guess what? You're absolutely right. But try to look it at from another angle. Try to get acquainted with Keith Linder for a second. Try to understand who I am. Try to understand what it is I'm trying to do. We'll agree later that I failed miserably, sure, but for now, try to walk in my shoes.

Think back to the time when I fell down the stairs – January 2nd, 2014. I tore my right patella tendon. I delayed surgery for six days so that I can keep my job interview. Tina took me to the job interview; I arrived on crutches, in pain, leg straight as an iron board—zero pain meds. Where's my kneecap? Oh, it's up inside my thigh muscle. How long was I there? Six hours.

Now, I'm not trying to make myself into some Billy-bad-ass person. That's not why I'm telling this story. I'm telling this story about my fall and what happened days after with the hopes that you might understand what lengths I will go through with the hopes of reaching a positive outcome.

Our reason for staying was simple: we were trying to get a positive outcome. We know what the current state looks like. Current state looks like hell. Two couples have been torn apart. One couple (Jane Doe's family) has just gotten back together. One family's son became terminally ill. One family woke up and found kitchen cabinet doors open. One couple comes home and finds kitchen cabinet doors open. One family experienced suicide attempts. One couple is at each other's throats. One family went through so much shit through their short period that they just picked up and left. And one couple, six years later decides to stay. Can you imagine that?

I'm getting sheets yanked off me at the Davenport Hotel—in downtown Spokane. I'm getting poked and prodded at 35,000 feet? While traveling to my final destination which happens to be Spokane, WA or Sacramento, California. What's the positive outcome from moving? Strong possibility—another family moves in—with infant children. What happens to them? What happens to any child conceived in that house? What are the spirits doing while the man makes love to his wife? Are they watching? Are they manipulating? Remember the things Tina and I have seen pales in comparison to the things we can't see, let alone hear. That feeling of being watched is called that for a reason. You're being watched when you're sleeping. You're being watched when you're awake. Tina and I were lying on our backs when the bedroom door slammed. They slammed because we were laughing. How do they know they we were laughing? They know because they were watching us. How do they know to leap on the bed within seconds of me lying down? They know because they're watching me. How do they know where Tina keeps her truck keys when she's not using them? They know because they watch her. Who thinks that's going to stop the second I move from this house? It doesn't stop. It keeps going—for whoever moves in here next. Might not be the family right after me. Doesn't have to be. Could be some family five years from now. Ten years from now. Who knows? Several years exist between Jane Doe's family and Tina and me. We still don't know if the families in between both of us experienced anything. If they didn't, why not? If they did, what was it?

If Jane Doe tried to kill herself several times in this house, what chance does a mother who's about to give birth have? Think about the amount of mood swings a woman goes through when pregnant. The amount of hormonal changes. Do you want that woman living in this house? The positive outcome I got for postponing my surgery was me working for a company that I always wanted to work for. It's why I moved here in the first place. I was trying to make this house livable. That's the positive outcome I'm trying to get. I'm trying not to have a knee-jerk reaction. I'm trying not to cut and run. It's my house, dammit. I worked hard to get here. Why should I run? Shouldn't the negative spirits be running and not us humans?

One the biggest problems Tina and I faced was the inconsistency among the people we dealt with. Why are we chasing priests down? Shouldn't it be the other way around? Why are paranormal teams incompetent? Tina and I will own our part, we played a role—but we're house occupants, we're naive and clueless. What's their excuse? Why would you bring your ego here instead of a solution? Why would you put Tina and me on the defensive? By defensive, I mean offering theories and conjectures that are more outlandish than the activity being reported. Waiting for the positive outcome is frustrating. The spirits are winning big time. Tina's moved out. If Zak thinks his near headbutt with Tina during their roam the kitchen scene was off-putting, try to imagine it from Tina's point of view. In that (carefully edited scene) Tina's trying to home in on what she says was "burnt sage smell." She smells it in the kitchen—she just doesn't know where it's coming from. The room is pitch black. The audience doesn't know the dialogue being discussed because the scene was edited. There's a sage stick resting on the kitchen table, right underneath Tina and Zak. That sage stick was used to create a reenactment scene. Someone placed it on the kitchen table after they got done with it. Anyone who's handled sage stick knows the smell of burnt sage can linger for quite some time.

The smell of burnt sage might not mean much to an average person. It means everything to Tina and me. It means trouble is coming. Tina wasn't following Zak. She wasn't hovering around him (not on purpose). Neither one can see each other, at least not until they're right up close. And that's only because Tina homing in on where the smell is coming from. The production crew saw the whole thing; obviously. That moment of levity when Tina blurts out "Zak stop acting like a pussy." Tina said that. You see Zak jumped when he came head to head with Tina (in the dark). The audience (that being you if you watched that episode) don't see that. You saw a different version, a version that brought about the trolling of Keith and Tina; Tina especially. The spirits in our home seized upon that angst and the rest is history; my girlfriend moved out.

So, I've talked about the shadowy figures. I've told you where I've seen them. I'd be doing the reader a disservice if I didn't describe how they look like. Just saying there's a shadow here and there doesn't do them justice. The minions would be nothing if they on occasion didn't reveal themselves. Are you ready?

So, you know they're short. Short and stout looking. They have two legs. Leg's sort of like an alligator or bullfrog. Matter of fact a bullfrog is the overall size of most of them. Reptilian texture but hairy. Very tile like skin. Color? Try charcoal black dipped in black tar. That's how dark they are. They're mean, tough and nasty. The ones I see outside my office door are always moving very stealth like. There always creeping about. I don't know if they know that I see them, all I know is I see glimpses of them. I'm pretty sure they're the ones poking me. I bet my life on it.

The question that I wrestle though, the one I can't make sense of is their ability to go stealth while I'm sleeping. There's no way I would be laying in a bed and there coming towards me is some six-inch black critter like figure. I feel the bed indent. I feel the tapping and the pulsating. I never see what's heading towards me.

They have mass. I know that by the way, the mattress feels. You can't help but hear the pitter-patter noise in the house. The scurrying noise when you come home from work. Now imagine sleeping at night—you're sound asleep when all of a sudden something starts making its way towards you from within the mattress. Not on top of the mattress, we've talked about that enough already. I'm talking about from inside the mattress.

You're lying on your back and all of a sudden you feel something inside the mattress scurrying underneath you. I'm not talking about under the bed or the mattress. I'm talking about inside the mattress. Directly under you. It's like they want to align with you specifically, for what I don't know. Imagine a pulsating knot forming underneath your person in the middle of the night. You move that knot moves.

You wake up and switch sides, and that knot underneath switches sides. The first time I felt that I was like WTF? I've pushed my hand down on what I thought was a knot. My hand doesn't feel the knot, my body does. My hand feels something worse. It feels the pulsating—the throbbing knot underneath me. Tina and I were looking and feeling this together. Now she's gone, and I'm feeling this by myself. Not only in the bed, but on the couch and love seat. Like I said some days are worse than others. What started out as a onetime instance slowly becomes multiple instances. This knot thing is no exception. It wasn't long before I was waking up and finding myself in even a weirder and scarier situation.

The knots are now under my pillow. The knots are now on top of the pillow. They've positioned themselves on top of my shin and ankle. Each knot is pulsating. Of course, nothing visible to the naked eye. But there's mass though, there's weight. It feels like a one-pound sandbag resting on you. Like someone filled a tube sock up with sand and laid across your ankle, shin, elbow, and arm while you were sleeping. Each one is now pulsating on top of you. They're assembling on you like pigeons do a powerline. Everything dissipates when you wake up, not entirely though. The weigh you felt returns back to the knot you felt before going to sleep or the pulsating you felt within seconds of climbing into bed. This is nuts, ladies and gentlemen. It's weird, and it has yet to stop. Stop this Fr. Roy Sr. Stop this whomever. The spirits have not rested since Tina left. They've done the opposite. They've come closer in.

Now imagine what would happen if I was a drug addict. Imagine what would happen if I was an alcoholic. And I don't mean I became one after moving in. Imagine if I was addicted to barbiturates before moving in this house? Imagine if I was addicted to painkillers? If I was addicted to porn or addicted to methamphetamine? Do you know what would happen if that was the case? The spirits would be all over that.

If you're depressed, guess what? They're going to make you more depressed. If you're a recluse, they're going to make you become a hermit. If there's anything about you that makes you self-destruct, they're going exploit it. I've woken up and found knots under me, over me, and next to me. Sometimes it's night terrors that wake me. Didn't know what that was till I moved here.

Not until the attacks escalated that I began to experience these unspeakable— almost non-mentionable bad dreams. I mean you haven't experience torment till you've experienced it while being sleep deprived. I would say the sleep deprivation; I'm talking about the stuff that is happening in the bed. The poking and prodding. The sheets yanked down to your ankles or just yanked off the bed outright. That's become the status quo. That's what I'm hoping Fr. Roy Sr. can address.

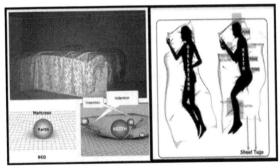

Fig 35.1 Pulsating mattresses, moving indentions, are at the root of my sleep deprivation. (M) Minions.

Fig 35.2 Minions

Chapter 36
House Exorcism

Remember what I said earlier how when it came to helping Tina and me, human beings, not spirits would be the ones getting in the way of us achieving a positive outcome. Now ask yourself the question: what should the mission be? Should the goal be to fix Keith and Tina's problem, i.e., make the house livable? Or should the goal be my team and my team alone can fix this? Therefore, no other team is needed. When did getting credit for being involved become more important than fixing the problem? Someone forgot to tell people in the business of removing unclean spirits that ego is a sin.

We were now two months into Fr. Roy's preparation for conducting a house exorcism. A duality as emerged—readiness versus availability. We've already encountered one major setback, that setback being the bishop. The bishop has informed Fr. Roy Sr. that he cannot assist him in carrying out of the house exorcism. It's a major setback based on the fact that the bishop and the Fr. Roy Sr. has performed countless exorcisms together throughout their priesthood. We're talking about thirty or more.

Both men have been combing through the evidence for weeks. They've been re-familiarizing themselves with the city of Bothell; the history of the Pacific Northwest in its ill-treatment to Native Americans. The upside-down man symbol which means "a man has died" or is "about to die" has both men behaving cautiously. Fr. Roy Sr. is blind; therefore, he has to rely on the sight of others; mainly his wife and the bishop. Both have been by Fr. Roy's side for quite some time. They've never seen so much evidence come from one house before. You, the reader, should know a little bit about what it is they're feeling. Both men sense multiple spirits are living here. "These are some ugly sons of bitches," the men said. And by sons of bitches, I mean demons.

The bishop cited personal reasons. Reasons stemming from his negative involvement in the Vietnam War. Actions he took against the Vietnamese people that he's yet to ask forgiveness for. When Fr. Roy Sr. first told me that I must admit I was taken aback. I was like, *come on, man, not now, please don't chicken out now, I can't deal with another back peddler*. But I thought it about it long and hard and realized, that was the first time since No Bull's involvement that someone had come to me and said their "continued involvement might make the situation worse than what it is now." No one on Keith's team should want that, right?

A thrill seeker would never say that. An investigator-driven by ego and TV ratings would never say that, right? No, they wouldn't. Now Fr. Roy Sr. is eighty-something years old. He's blind, and he's frail. We've not yet met face to face. Our communication has strictly been email, and telephone. I can assess from my conversations with him on the phone that mobility and strength are not his strong suit, at least not physically. My question to Fr. Roy Sr. upon learning that his bishop was not going to help us, brought about another question; why don't I ask the Spokane team to help us? Their case was officially still open. They can assist Fr. Roy in whatever he needs to do, and while at the same time, capture any activity should there be any.

Fr. Roy Sr. thought it was a great idea. He wanted the ceremony tapped anyways as did I. I presented my idea to the Spokane team, and the answer they gave me was yes. Then came the conference call, i.e., the strategy meeting which involved me, Fr. Roy, and a local shaman. Not the shaman Fr. Roy had reached out to, that shaman, unfortunately, remained unreachable. I, being the facilitator of the meeting, immediately began witnessing the jockeying for power of certain individuals within minutes of the conference call. Everyone was trying to tell Fr. Roy what they wanted him to do. Someone even blurted out that they got their demonologist certificate by taking one of Fr. Jack Ashcraft's online classes. This certificate makes them more qualified to handle house exorcisms. Therefore, it might be best if Fr. Roy Sr. backs them up. Talk about the ultimate facepalm. I was so embarrassed.

Then it dawned it on me. The house occupant is the final decision maker. Nothing gets executed unless I'm OK with it. I mean, that's what every paranormal investigator told me before taking our case. Whatever Tina and I don't feel comfortable with we don't have to do, we can say no. Every paranormal team that's come here regardless of their approach has made that statement. Now seemed like the perfect time to interject me in this back in forth conversation of who's in charge. It was time for me to inform everyone how I want the investigation to be conducted. And that's exactly what I did. I said, "Fr. Roy is performing The Holy Eucharist with Rite of Exorcism, the landlord and I have permitted him to do that. He's asked that you ladies assist him. All of us will be serving as his assistant." Nothing else. Mind you I'm not trying to diminish their previous involvement or current contribution. We all can agree, we have a hard job ahead of us. The last thing we need to do is have a 'mine is bigger than yours' debate. This exorcism is over before it even started if that's the case.

So, I gave Fr. Roy the reins and the room went dead silent. You could almost feel everyone's interests diminish within seconds of me saying that, everyone except Fr. Roy. I know that's true because of a few weeks later when it came time to perform the exorcism, nobody showed up. It was either a no call, no show or an email saying after careful advisement we have decided to not assist Fr. Roy in performing a house exorcism. Mind you, Fr. Roy Sr. is the only tenured exorcists on the conference call. He's been a priest for over forty-five years. His experience is older than some people on the phone. His bona fides didn't come from a virtual class on exorcisms. He's not a demonologist, whatever that means? Why wouldn't you want to partner with him? That's what I mean when I say people have prevented a positive outcome more so than the spirits.

We were down to five people: Fr. Roy Sr., his wife, myself, my friend Laura, and her husband. I had no clue on what to expect. All I know is what I want to accomplish. All I know is I want peace. I was shocked by the shamans no call, no show. Fr. Roy Sr. said at the first meeting that a shaman is probably where this thing is going to end up. If the house is built on Native American land, which is all of America for that matter, then having a shaman is a must. I can respect a phone call saying, "Keith, I can't be involved, or Keith can you reschedule, something happened to where I can't come." That's called communication. But to outright say you're going to come and don't. No phone calls. No email. No text whatsoever. Who does that after seeing what goes on here?

I had no clue on what to expect, on the day Fr. Roy Sr. decided to conduct the exorcism. What I know of exorcisms I learned from Hollywood. I'm not going to lie. I had high hopes for some activity breaking out as a result of Fr. Roy's house visit. I mean who doesn't want to see a chair fly across the room as a result of Fr. Roy Sr. tossing holy water around?

But then I thought about it, these spirits have never been the type of spirits to give the people what they wanted. They know how to avoid being detected. I know that. They know that. And the priest knows that. If there's one thing, I love more than progress is executing a plan that comes before it. Fr. Roy Sr. and I had been communicating for quite some time now. We'd talked this through countless times. Now we're executing. We're taking the fight to them.

What does a house exorcism look like? What does it include? Well, it includes ingredients, and it includes tools. Tools the priest will use to conduct this ceremony. Tools like.

Fig 36.1 Items Fr. Roy requested be on hand when he arrived. A.) Pita bread B.) Gallon of water C.) Salt D.) Wooden crosses E.) Video cameras F.) Italian red wine

And the ceremony is pretty straightforward from there. Fr. Roy and his wife arrived on time, congrats to them for being on-time. We're talking about over an hour drive from where they lived and where I lived. A husband and wife are traveling that far in their eighties to conduct something as momentous as this will always have a special place in my heart.

Laura and her husband arrived as well, and that was it. I told Fr. Roy that the team that agreed to help us backed out at the last minute. I didn't tell him why.

No need to get negative. He asked where the shaman was, and I said he must be running late or something, which was a fair assessment because he never called. The time had come to move on without him. Time to begin the ceremony.

The evening pretty much belonged to Fr. Roy Sr. We were here to assist him in any way we can, my friends and me. He told me weeks prior that this would be a three to four-hour ceremony. He was right. It was. I thought the communion the local priest did last year was long. Fr. Roy Sr. ended up being way longer than the local Catholic service—I base that more on his age than anything else. To their credit, both men were extremely thorough. I mean extremely thorough. I would like to think I would have been able to sense both men cutting corners. The service Fr. Roy Sr. was conducting is called "The Holy Eucharist Rite of Exorcism." Wiki defines it as—a Christian rite that is considered a sacrament in most churches and an ordinance in others. The word Eucharist means "Thanksgiving." Unfortunately, I don't have a soft copy—if I did, I would have included it here. The pamphlet below is what Fr. Roy read from:

THE HOLY EUCHARIST

with

A RITE OF EXORCISM

Fig 36.2 This 19-page pamphlet is what Fr. Roy read from primarily. It's my understanding that he and his bishop authored this years ago—to assist them when performing house exorcisms in and around the Puget Sound.

I've concluded that Hollywood has it wrong and that the local priest and Fr. Roy Sr. have it right. Cleansing, house blessing, communion, and now this exorcism all have one thing in common. They're boring. From a ceremonial point of view of course. And that's probably how it should be. Less theatrics and more thoroughness. Fr. Roy's goal when coming to my house was, in layman terms, to remove the home of unclean spirits. Fr. Roy Sr. rarely used the term demon or devil. Fr. Roy after reviewing the evidence and after conversing with his bishop concluded that multiple spirits were residing here. Not all of them can necessarily be classified as demons. It's much easier to go at them by calling them unclean spirits, meaning use term they're familiar with. Call them what Jesus called them.

Fr. Roy Sr. made it very clear he was here to remove those that were here to do the devil's bidding. The spirit that put the earring in our bed for Tina to question me. That was an unclean spirit. The spirit that keyed my car with hopes that I marched back into my house and escalated a fight with Tina was an unclean spirit. The spirit that caused my poster to catch fire on its own could be an unclean spirit, or it could be a pissed off Native American spirit. Pissed off at Tina and me for smudging the house or for decorating the house with Christian themes. The same themes and symbols that brought smallpox to him and his people. Or it could be a poltergeist. According to Fr. Roy, poltergeist hate being expelled more than demons do.

The ceremony was going to tackle many facets of this case. The one we knew we had little power and control over was the poltergeist. But first things first. Let's deal with what we know is here which is unclean spirits. Unclean spirits can create negativity, and they can feed off negativity, as can a poltergeist. Based on what Jane Doe told me and based on the arguments Tina and I had, which include weird mood swings, I have no doubt unclean spirits are what's at the root of what plagues this house.

There's an old proverb that says 'it takes two to tango.' It also takes two to argue. The entities in this home know that. Tina and I have seen activity spike and by spike, I mean, large objects were thrown across the room within minutes of our heated debates. Objects have been thrown during a house full of laughter also, countless times. I would have to say the ones thrown during or after our argument is far the more terrifying. So, the ceremony is progressing nicely. Everything Fr. Roy Sr. said he would do; he was doing. We're an hour or so into the ceremony and guess what?

The walls didn't shake. The house didn't vibrate. Nothing flew out of the kitchen cupboards. The front door didn't open and slam on its own, but stuff was happening. Noticeable stuff. Even my friends began to notice. The rapping's started within hours of the ceremony. I know when the atmosphere in the house begins to change. The house was quiet the majority of the day. Then came the ceremony. My friend Laura looked at the ceiling—towards the direction of the pitter patter. Towards the knocks bangs and wall taps. Not loud, but noticeable.

Me? I was not trying to focus on the noise around us because I wanted to dedicate my energy to walking these spirits out the door. Fr. Roy Sr. told us to expect this stuff. I mean the spirits know why he's here. They know what's going on and they know where we were doing. We were in the kitchen right now and boy let me tell, you the banging, the pops, pings, snaps, cracks, and taps are very noticeable. Laura tugged on my shirt and said, "Wow, I can hear them, you have a lot of spirits living here, darling." That's the baseline noise—it's what Tina and I always heard. It's what Laura's is hearing right now. The day that baseline activity goes away is the day this house becomes spirit free.

Fr. Roy Sr. advised everyone to not stand in the doorway of whatever room we were in. Do not block the walkways or stand in front of a window. A malevolent spirit fleeing God's word will have no regret tossing one of us aside when fleeing the house. It could also possess us if we're blocking its exit. We don't want that. And for the record, the ceremony Fr. Roy Sr. conducted did call for an exorcism being done on me. You can't say you were thorough if you ignore the house occupant. Remember those pokes and prods? Remember that swoosh feeling of something rushing through me while I was sleeping? Fr. Roy Sr. will attempt to address those as well.

The last portion of Fr. Roy's ceremony involved what I would call the offering. Time to appease the Native American spirits residing here. This is where the shaman would have been useful. I bet my neighbors must think I'm weird or I'm crazy. We've had paranormal vans parked in front of our house. We've had *Ghost Adventures* here and all that they bring with them. And look at what we have today? Today we have Fr. Roy Sr. outside in full priest garb, being led by his lovely wife with a cross and a gallon of holy water. He's sanctifying the lawn, the plumbing, drainage system, certain areas of the house and certain areas of the sidewalk. In short, he's laying down boundaries. How do you appease the Native spirits?

By digging into the earth—burying salmon, fruit, tobacco, and whiskey. We bow our heads and ask for forgiveness. "Forgive us for what the settlers did. Forgive us for what the white man did in the name of Christianity. Forgive us for their persecution of you, and for them introducing small-pox. Forgive us for them stealing your land." We did that for about an hour, ladies and gentlemen, and that in a nutshell is what Fr. Roy Sr. did. Now, remember Rome was not built in a day. These spirits who occupy this house didn't all show up in a day. If they increased over time, it's probably safe to say they're going to decrease over time too.

Fr. Roy reminded me of an important fact. You can't kill spirits. You can only expel them. Any person who tells they can kill spirits is lying. "Flee from them immediately." They're lying.

"We can rejoice in the fact that we expelled some spirits today." We didn't expel all of them. Expelling every spirit that lived here was never the plan the first time around. A house this active can't be rid of spirits in one clean swoop. We'll see what happens next. The house felt way lighter than it ever did before. I attribute that to one person living in the house versus two. No more tension. No more sleeping in separate rooms. I can tell the exorcism made a difference in removing some spirits. The baseline I spoke about earlier is still here. Laura can attest to that. It's slowed down somewhat. But it's not gone entirely, and neither was the poking and prodding.

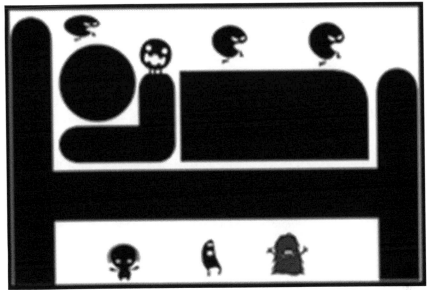

Fig 36.3 Minions.

Chapter 37
Anonymous

I'm trying to learn everything I can about poltergeist activity. What is it exactly? How does it start? How can it end? How can you prevent it? I've covered these grounds before. Now it's time to dive deeper. My dad always said, "The more you know in life, the less likely you are to be taken advantage of." I'm going to apply that logic to the phenomenon known as a poltergeist. Not at home though. I will not be exercising this quest when I'm at home. I'm too scared to do that. I'm going to conduct my research during lunch breaks at work. I'm going to conduct my research from the parking lot of Fred Meyer grocery store (two miles from my house). My computer at work and my smartphone will help me sort this out. Fr. Roy Sr. said some interesting things about poltergeist that I need to get a better understanding on. He said, "Poltergeists have been known to resent exorcisms." Poltergeists hate being told what to do. Well, guess what? We've been doing that for the last three years—Tina and me. We've been telling them that they need to leave. It didn't work. They got crazier and crazier.

That's just one theory out of countless others—that I believe needs to be analyzed. I figured the best time to learn more poltergeist and malevolent spirits for that matter is during the "Geist" downtime. The house was very quiet now. We're talking about level one type activity. If it wasn't for the poking and prodding, and the movement I hear while watching TV, I would say this house was semi-livable. How long will that last? How long before it goes active again? We're back to what we had in 2013? Knocks, tapping sounds, an occasional shadow here and there and the stuff I named above. What happens if I fall again? Those are just some of the questions I have right now, and I begin my quest to learn more about poltergeists. It's not good to live one's life walking on eggshells. I've done that for three years—time to turn the tide.

Time to get empowered by learning what these bastards are. It's easier said than done, trust me. I mean, look where I'm sitting? I'm sitting in my car in a giant parking lot, two miles from my house. I don't want the poltergeist in my home to know I'm researching them for fear of reprisal.

That Die KL is still on my mind. Is that a bounty to passerby demons? Do "Geist" issue out bench-warrants? Some of you might think that is a foolish question. Hold that thought until we get to the end of the book.

Now I've gotten plenty of emails from people who say Tina and I were hoaxers. I can't even begin to count them all. I always say this when asked. A demon has no choice but to be a demon. That's its lot in life. A "Geist" has the same fate. It has no choice but to be an asshole. What's people's excuse? Why are there so many assholes in the world? I mean out of all the things you can be in life. Why be an internet troll? Why be a cynic? Tina and I are the bad guys because *Ghost Adventures* didn't find anything (due to their ill-investigative methods). That's how you know the world is upside down. Remember the spirits that gave me and Tina hell are the only Rolo Tomassi's here. They've been fooling everyone for God knows how long. To the extent of some thinking, all this was faked. That's what fills my inbox now. Hate emails.

Now and then a word of encouragement would seep into my inbox. A silver lining if you will. Sort of like the lady in the Christian bookstore last Christmas. These people I can deal with. These people have empathy and understanding. It's for that very reason and that reason alone that I decided to open a particular email one day. An email from a young woman. We'll give her a fictitious name (because she prefers to remain anonymous). We'll call her Mary.

There's one thing I want you to know before I begin telling the story about Mary. Something I want to call attention to. Remote home monitoring—it's when monitoring a house remotely to catch evidence—well, here it was. Think of it as virtual house sitting. The concept will become clear to you in the coming chapters. I opened Mary's email and oh boy!

Hi thanks for getting in touch with me. The reason I added you to my paranormal circle was because I co-host a internet radio show called My Paranormal Experience and I am always looking for interesting guests to have on and share their experiences. I do my show with Niki Paranormal have you heard of her?
I was wondering if you would be open to doing a pre-interview via skype and then maybe coming on our show in the future. We are on liveparanormal.com on Sunday nights at 10PM EST to 11PM EST

Fig 37.1 "… I co-host an internet radio show called *My Paranormal Experience*
and I am always looking for interesting guests to have on and share their
experiences. I was wondering if you would be open to doing a pre-interview via
Skype and then maybe coming on our show in the future…"

My first reaction to the invite was: *oh man, do I want to go down this road again? Can I tolerate the questions and accusations coming my way? Why do these people want to interview me?* Do they want to ridicule me? What's the motive here? You'd be surprised how much hate mail I got from fans of the show. Wherever Tina is at right now, I hope she's learned to walk away from these negative tweets and email responses. They've not let up one bit. But this email seems different—the person who wrote this seems calm, cool, and collective. So, I said yes.

I mean, there were so many mistruths out there about this case, about Tina and me. The thing I kept hearing over and over from multiple sources was: "extraordinary claims require extraordinary evidence." Well, that might be true, but guess what? The evidence has to be compiled by competent people, and the investigation shown on TV was not competent. Not even close. So, my answer to Mary was yes.

Mary and Niki would first conduct their phone screen. You know, make sure I'm not some nut or crazy person. It was then that I discovered that there was a community out there that believed Tina and me. We had a following. Interesting enough our followers were mostly people who at some point in their life had gone through something similar. Those followers wanted answers to their questions. The consensus I kept running into as a result of talking to Mary and Niki was the "Demons in Seattle" left many people high and dry. The abrupt ending alone seemed to rub many people the wrong way. These are the people that Mary wanted me to talk to.

Instead of looking at this ordeal as a cup being half empty, maybe I should start looking at it as a cup half full? *Don't be a cynic, Keith. Don't turn into what you despise. Think of it as telling your story. You got questions? Guess what? I got answers. Lots and lots of answers.*

The format for the radio interview was simple. Arrive on their show via Skype and provide a narrative of what happened before, during, and after the "Demons in Seattle" episode. Talk about what you and Tina experienced. Tell the audience what you saw and what you heard. How did the experience impact you? What did the show get right and what did the show get wrong?

Tonight, it's all about being open-minded. It's about listening to what you have to say. Each listener can make up his or her own mind after hearing everything that what was said. "Just be yourself," is what Mary told me. That's a fair assessment. I can live with rules like that. All I can hope for is for people to be open-minded. I decided to send Mary and Niki videos and pictures of what took place in our house. They needed to see some of the hell that we experienced. Both ladies' minds were blown as to the level of detail within each photograph and video.

The interview went off with no glitches whatsoever. Total success! This was the first time since the airing of the *Ghost Adventures* episode that the case was talked about publicly. It was like a coming out moment. Bear in mind: the KOMO interview in October 2014, followed by *Ghost Adventures*, February 2015, were the only times where the world knew what was taking place in our house. This new radio audience had watched the episode, and they had questions about what was shown and not shown during the show.

One question put in front me was: why weren't any samples taken from the wall itself? My answer: I don't know. It shocked me to learn that *Ghost Adventures* didn't take any samples of the 666 wall writings. To be honest, I thought they would. The second question was probably the most talked about question of all: the burning Bibles. How were they burned? How many got burned? And once again, why didn't *Ghost Adventures* take one with them for analysis? Excellent questions, mind you. I don't know why *Ghost Adventures* chose not to take any wall samples. I don't know why Zak and crew didn't ask to take a Bible with them. They could have taken a burnt page while Tina and me where at the hotel and I never would have known it. They had the opportunity. No one asked.

This LiveParanormal interview took place in the spring of 2015. It needed to happen. There was so much misinformation out there about Tina and me. So much misinformation about the case in general. And you know what? We're never going to be able to squash all of that disinformation. That's just the nature of the world we live in. The paranormal community didn't invent cynicism. That's always been around. Everybody's a cynic. Everybody's a critic, and everybody wants to second guess the house occupant. People go by what they see on TV, that's unfortunate. That forty-five-minute episode only shows you a second of what happened.

If you listened to that interview that night, you probably left with a better understanding of who Keith and Tina are. A better understanding of what we went through. And most importantly, a better understanding of how the episode portrayed us. Niki said something during the interview that I thought was very important. "99.99 percent of all investigations end with zero evidence." That's just a fact. Doesn't mean there's nothing there. "These paranormal shows on TV have created a false narrative because they make investigations look easy. They've made it out to be so routine when in truth, it isn't. Just because you don't get evidence, doesn't mean something never happened."

She's right. And you know how I know she's right? I went to the Seattle public library a few days after the radio interview. I wanted to see what the library had on poltergeists. Don't laugh. But, I haven't been inside a library in over twenty years. Now I'm in one. I was in the biggest library in Seattle—the Seattle Central Library. I was searching for any book I could find that'll educate me on what poltergeists are. Two hours into my search I finally found a book to my liking. It was written by a parapsychology organization. *That's an interesting word,* I thought. What's a parapsychologist?

One of the chapters in the book was titled "poltergeists". Here I was sitting between two bookshelves on the fourth floor of the Seattle public library. I was absorbing everything there is to absorb about poltergeists when suddenly I came across something rather interesting. This book in particular says that "despite the popular depiction of these events, poltergeist activity is elusive and typically difficult to observe. [2](Carrington & Fodor, 1951)" The key word here is "difficult". This literature and the literature I have listed in the back of the book together state that poltergeist by design are purposely evasive. No one's ever told me that before till now. Except Fr. Roy. Why didn't Dave Schrader and Zak mention this in their forty-five-minute episode I wonder?

As proud and relieved as I was about doing the Mary and Niki interview, I was nowhere near dispelling the mistruths about our ordeal. Not even close. Mark Twain put it best when he said, "A lie can travel halfway around the world while the truth is putting on its shoes." This one interview was nothing compared to the lie that went viral on February 28th, 2015. But it felt good anyway. It felt good talking about what happened. It felt good answering questions. As I sat in my car at Fred Meyer, I thought to myself, *all you did today, Keith, was put one shoe string through one loop in a large boot.*

Now, did you catch the part where I said I was sitting in the Fred Meyer parking lot? I'm pretty sure Niki and Mary were in their respective homes while conducting the show. Not me. I was sitting at Fred Meyers parking lot, interviewing via smartphone. I don't even utter the word poltergeist when I'm home. I don't conduct research there. I don't read the negative comments, and I don't read the positive comments. I don't do anything when I'm at the house. I'm trying to conquer my fear of talking about demons while at home. I'm not there yet. Who's going to help me up if I fall down those same stairs again? The

---

[2] Hereward Carrington, Nandor Fodor "Haunted People: Story of the Poltergeist Down the Centuries" – 1951

minions are not going to help me up. They're the ones that pushed me. Tina's not going to help me up. She's gone.

Do you remember what Jane Doe told me when I first asked her about the house? Do you remember what her response was? She said she needed to get her thoughts together before she could tell me. Remember how long it took for her to get her thoughts together? Do you know why it took her that long to respond? She was scared of the activity resurfacing. I mean, imagine if the activity had resurfaced for her. Imagine the bad timing. She and her husband had just gotten back together. Here comes this stranger. A stranger who's living in the same house they lived in previously. I now understand what she felt like. I understand that feeling perfectly—it helps to be still living here.

The house has become a demilitarized zone. I'm assuming the spirits won't attack if I don't talk about them. If I don't start lighting sage sticks. It's an unspoken rule. Now, mind you, they still get to poke and shake my bed when I'm trying to sleep. They still get to pace the hallway right outside my bedroom door. They can still do the banging. The taps and thuds from the behind the headboard, they can still do all of that.

We were at a stalemate. Fr. Roy Sr. was able to eject a few unclean spirits when he conducted his house exorcism. How many? We don't know. I have to believe he ejected a few; there comes a time where you have to rely on the power of the word. There's more work to be done though. I know because Fr. Roy Sr. told me he would be back.

I'm embarrassed to say this but it's true, it's the lesser of two evils right now. If you had a choice, what would you rather live with? Level one activity, which is pretty much what I already mentioned, or level five activity? At least with a level one I know I'm not going to be sweeping up debris anytime soon.

This level of activity means I can finally get around to doing some house repairs. I can begin fixing up the walls in the hallway. I can begin repairing the carpet. I can begin replacing the light fixtures. Heck, I can even begin painting over the wall writings.

That's what malevolent DMZ (demilitarized zone) is like. It's the unspoken agreement. This is my definition of ideal living conditions. That's how beaten down I am. I can't tell you how many times I've sat in my car while having conversations about the house. Or how many times I've slept on the couch or floor since Tina moved out.

My ten-minute showers are now two-minute showers. When I come home from work, the first thing I do when I walk through the door is turn on every light. Sometimes the light is off in the room I was just in. If the light goes off, I turn it back on. If it goes off a second time, I walk away and leave it as it is.

I'm scared to light sage right now. I'm scared because it's just me living here. I have to let my guard down sometimes—after all, I have to sleep sooner or later. I'm averaging five hours of sleep as it is. And it's sad, it is. It's sad because I've accepted it. I don't remember accepting the status quo as being the long-term solution. But for some odd reason, it's become that. But we're not done.

Bothell home – Types of Activity

Level One Activity
Feeling of being watched
Unexplained noises
Footsteps
Tapping
Rapping
Poking and prodding
Pacing back and forth

Table 37.1 Where things are right now

Level Two Activity
Moving shadows
Loud bangs
Asport/apport/teleport
Door slams
Flying pottery
Objects appearing that no one owns
Electrical issues

Table 37.2 I don't want to go back to this level.

Level Three Activity
Repeated loud bangs
Repeated door slams
Phantom noises
Cabinet doors opening
Apparition appearance

Table 37.3 I don't want to go back to this level.

Level Four Activity
Humongous objects thrown
Wall writings
Water puddles
Mist coming from the floor
Humming
Physical attacks, e.g. scratches
Grunts and growls

Table 37.4 I don't want to go back to this level.

Level Five Activity
Level one activity
Level two activity
Level three activity
Level four activity
Spontaneous fires
Bites
Dangerous activity
Animal appearances
Flies
Unimaginable things

Table 37.5 The wrath of Satan

Chapter 38
House Monitoring

Mary came to me a few weeks after the *LiveParanormal* interview and asked me if I'd be interested in letting her and Niki monitor the house. I have to say I was quite shocked. Have you ladies not heard what I've been saying? I tried to chase these things down using CCTV cameras for over a year. The community you belong to told me to put cameras in every room. Individuals representing Fr. Jack Ashcraft and a few others said the same thing. "Hide the cameras inside your plants. Hide them under the couch and love seat. Don't tell your girlfriend." Even my brother suggested that.

It never occurred to me that the activity was going to intensify as a result of me buying cameras. But that's exactly what happened. The more cameras I put up, the more active the house got. Talk about a futile quest. Imagine doing something over and over expecting the same results? I'm not talking about Captain Ahab obsession. I'm talking the Coyote chasing the Road-runner obsession. Tina could only feel sorry for me, that was how bad it got.

But as you have read throughout this book, my motive and the spirit's motive are two separate things. Remote viewing means putting a camera in every room of the house. You're waiting for lightning to strike. What are we trying to achieve here? You're asking me to re-open an investigation, one where I inherit all the risks. Let me be clear. I never got the impression that Mary or Niki didn't care about my experience. Quite the contrary. They were simply what they have always been: truth seekers. I reminded myself of what they told me when I they approached online. "There's way more to this story."

The epitaph for this case in the eyes of many now reads: "A team came in to investigate Keith and Tina's claims. They found nothing, the way it was revealed on TV made it look it look like Keith and Tina exaggerated for attention-seeking purposes or was completely made up, i.e., a hoax. "There's nothing to see here. Move along, move along." Mary never had to tell me that. I knew it already. I read the comments online, and I read the emails I got from just about every continent you can imagine. A portion of the paranormal community seems to follow a doctrine that nothing is real until an investigator says it's real.

Mary was very descriptive about what their investigation would entail. Her aims were simple:

The house will be under twenty-four surveillance. Seven days a week. Three individuals will be monitoring the house.

No one is under the illusion that this will lead to spontaneous fires being captured on video. Which is the mistake most teams make.

No one believes this will lead to us capturing flying candles on video.

The goal: to try to capture what I'm currently experiencing.

Try to capture the bangs, the footstep noise, the knocking, and the loud thuds. The pacing back and forth. Try to capture weird light anomalies. Try to capture the noise the house makes when I'm home and when I'm at work. Use the evidence that they gather to substantiate my claims about weird noises, weird sounds, thuds, phantom footsteps, etc. Make the argument based on the data from this investigation that house occupants are often telling the truth. Activity usually subsides by the time the researcher arrives.

Para Unity: share the evidence with the overall community so all can understand the true nature of investigations and the true nature of poltergeists. TV paints an inaccurate picture of what that's like.

The overall response from their radio listeners was positive. Many people, after hearing me talk, changed their minds about this case. Now the real question comes. What do we do now? One thing I wasn't a hundred percent aware of when *Ghost Adventures* arrived that I'm totally aware of now is the level of infighting taking place within the paranormal community. Go figure? The community is very segmented. The left-hand refuses to talk to the right hand. No one shares anything. Seriously!

You'd be surprised how many well-known individuals stopped sending me emails based on the fact that *Ghost Adventures* found nothing. A new meaning to folding up your tent and going home. That to me was insane. This is the storm Tina and I landed in when we decided to go public with our claims. This disunity hit us like a bag of bricks.

At the time of this writing, paranormal teams were more interested in debunking their colleague's work than investigating. It's like a bunch of crabs stuck in a barrel: the one on top is constantly being pulled down by the ones on the bottom. No evidence sharing whatsoever. Can you imagine Albert Einstein being obnoxious about Niels Bohr's findings via Twitter, via Facebook? Can you imagine Roger Penrose and Stephen Hawking doing what many in the paranormal community are doing? Can you imagine them taking sides? A part of me understood what Mary was saying. If there's evidence to be gathered here, then that evidence needs to be shared. Tina and I have experienced quite an ordeal. Too much to just sweep it under the rug. Too much to say, "That's all, folks."

So, we're talking about rehabilitation. The rehabilitation of our claims. Going back to my DMZ analogy: what will the spirits do as a result of cameras being reintroduced? How will they react? Will they get hostile? Or will they stay dormant? Dormant I can deal with. Hostile? No way is this house going to withstand another hostile attack. It couldn't, and I couldn't. No way, no how. Next steps? Talk to Fr. Roy Sr. I need to get his input before making a decision. The ladies just want to put cameras up, that's it. No "do this, do that" whatsoever. Just put cameras in the rooms where you hear the most activity. That seems simple, that seems doable. But the only way to be sure is to ask Fr. Roy Sr.

I emailed Fr. Roy the next day to update him on what was happening with the house. It so happened that he had an update for me. His "bad back condition" had taken a turn for the worse; he needed surgery. This was a big deal. Surgery, no matter what age you are, is always serious. It's even more serious if you're an older adult. I remember the condition he was in when he came to my house. Full of spirit, full of vigor; yet at the same time full of fatigue. No excuse needed, ladies and gentlemen, Fr. Roy is eighty plus years old. He's going to be incapacitated for a while: we're talking about three months if not more.

That left me with two decisions to make: Move out now. *Move now while the getting is good, you gave it your best, and the timing just wasn't there.* Option two: do what Mary and Niki had suggested. Rehabilitate this case. If the house is active as you say it is, even with a level one rating, you still have more activity than the average infested home. If it's as active as you say it is, then you have to let a team investigate. House occupants will never go public with their claims again if you bow out now. Remember: a portion of the paranormal community believe this case was either faked, hoaxed or exaggerated. *Ghost Adventures* was wrong to suggest zero evidence means zero haunting. "That's not how the paranormal works," said Niki.

I remember what my grandmother said back when I was a child. She said, "You should never try to appease Satan." She often quoted Ephesians 6:12: "For our struggle is not against flesh and blood, but against the rulers, against the authorities, against the powers of this dark world and the spiritual forces of evil in the heavenly realms." I heard that from her a lot. I know what spiritual wickedness is. I've seen it. I've felt it. It crawls up my leg every night. These bastards love framing people. They love to hide when teams come around— making you look like an idiot.

They can put a child on his deathbed. They can make a woman suicidal. These are just minimal examples of what they can do. That might be a tough pill for some people swallow, but it doesn't make it any less true. Malevolent spirits are malevolent for a reason; they want to end you.

I would be fooling myself if I thought for a second the level one activity I'm now experiencing is the result of some peace agreement. Demilitarized zone my ass. That's not why this house is quiet. The house is quiet because the tension Tina and I created is no longer here. You can't orchestrate an argument with just one person in the house. Who am I going to argue with, the refrigerator? You can hide my toothbrush all you want; I'm still never going to argue with it. Put a piece of jewelry in the bed now and see what happens. Nothing, absolutely nothing. And the spirits know this. They know with Tina gone, the level of what they can inflict has been significantly diminished. They've become a level one hurricane with no land to hit. All they can do now is just churn in the middle of the ocean. They hope somebody moves in with me. My grandmother was right. There's no appeasing spirits. No peace treaty whatsoever. Since they're here, we might as well expose them. We might as well learn from them. I had a lot on my mind when I left work that day. The paranormal community, through fault of their own, have left a bitter taste in my mouth. Why am I contemplating a refill? Where's Tina when I need her? Ah, Tina?

I miss bouncing ideas off her. I miss our pillow talks. How many did we have in 2014? Too many to count. She and I are salty right now. She thinks I'm a cheat, and I think she's uncomprehending. Uncomprehending of what went down that day.

If ever there'd been a time not to let your emotions get the best of you, that time was when we lived in the house in Bothell. She never understood that. She never entertained the thought that she was being played.

So: where am I now? I was sitting in the Fred Meyer parking lot again. I had a composed email pulled up on my cell phone. It was addressed to Mary and Niki. Should I send it? *I can still make out the words Die KL when I look up at my car ceiling.* Just barely visible now. *You spirits have had more than a thousand opportunities to kill me. Why haven't you? Why am I still here? Maybe you were just scaring me? Maybe you were sure that I'd run. That I'd move out. Maybe you'll show up at my next place of residence and wreak havoc?* As God as my witness, I looked down from the car ceiling and opened up my Gmail again. My thumb hit the send button, and the email was gone. The email to Mary and Niki read, let's do this!

What did I just agree to? I'll tell you what I agreed to. I agreed to best practice. I agreed to me becoming a project manager. I'm no longer taking the back seat in what's happening around me. If we're going to be successful, then we have to agree to run this investigation with some methodology. There are no Big I's and little U's on this team. We're all equal, with one minor exception: I'm the house occupant. I have value. Don't relegate me to a corner somewhere. That's a no-no. The day of the house occupant not having any value is over. When it comes to the activity taking place here, I'm the subject matter expert. I know what rooms are most active and I know which rooms are not active.

What excited me about Niki and Mary was their will. These are intelligent women. Strong women. Niki is her own team. She has no official affiliation with any group or organization. Both ladies are lone wolves in a field dominated by men. The scope of this investigation is simple. "Monitor the house 24/7. Let the evidence guide us, not our own opinions."

Chapter 39
The Washington State Poltergeist Case

The Washington State Poltergeist case officially began in the summer of 2015: a year after some of the most violent activity ever to be talked about within the paranormal community. The case went active the moment I turned on the first CCTV camera. I put one camera in the office and one camera in the hallway, as requested. Everyone has his or her login for house monitoring—the same set up I gave Tina when I wanted her to listen in. Mary chose the day shift; Niki chose the night shift. Both ladies are free to impede the other person's shift. They will. What's my role in all of this? I'm the IT helpdesk. The system administrator. The one who dishes out permissions and sets up login accounts. I promised the ladies I would respond right away (even if I'm at work) to any technical issue they encounter. I have the technology and internet capability in my house to make this as seamless as possible.

As much as I had tried to monitor the house back in 2014, I was always faced with the constraint of having a life. I had a day job. I had commitments that I had to keep. Meetings I had to attend. I had a social calendar. I had friends to see and a life to maintain. But now Mary and Niki have agreed to stake out my house for a considerable amount of time. I don't know if this has ever been done before. I mean, they're on the East Coast, three thousand plus miles away. What they're doing I couldn't do. Which is watch the house twenty-four seven.

I was at work the day Mary heard the child's "scream" coming from outside my office door. We know that because the camera began sending out sound alert emails around the same time that Mary began pinging the group chat. Her original thought was, *maybe it's coming from outside? Maybe it's a group of children walking home from school?* But this is not a playful scream, at least not according to Mary. And it's summertime. School is out.

I got a text from Mary, asking me if I ever heard children playing or children screaming at this time of day while working from home. Not to my knowledge. I've worked from home a lot of days—winter, spring, summer, and fall. I can't think of any day where I was working from home and in doing so heard children playing outside—let alone screaming. But there's a first time for everything, right? Certainly. Mary reviewed her notes with Niki: children playing in the middle of the day seemed reasonable. It's not far-fetched to think that could happen. Odds are it probably is happening. The two ladies decided to make a note of it in their log. Document the day it occurred, and the time. Let's see if this happens tomorrow specifically at the same time. Did it? It most certainly did. The scream they heard resurfaces. At the same time *as theorized*. What are the odds of that? Now, the noise Mary heard was coming from the hallway. The camera she was listening through was on the bookshelf, which as you know is in the middle of the hallway. If you can hear kids' noises in the hallway, then you should be able to hear those same kids' noises from the office camera, which faces the street.

Shouldn't the kid's scream be louder from the office camera? Let's find out. In an attempt to debunk what they thought was children, the two ladies decided to log into the office camera. They can still hear the child scream from the hallway camera. Sound is not prejudice, therefore, the ladies should hear the same noise within seconds of accessing the office camera. But they don't. They hear nothing. Virtual silence from the office area. Which sort of makes sense because the hallway camera was sending everyone sound detected emails and the office camera was not. Why is that?

Well, maybe the noise is coming from the backyard? If true, that would put the noise closer to the hallway camera. Maybe that's why the office is not hearing anything? Maybe the scream is coming from someone's backyard? Two things worth noting here. None of my neighbors have children. Neither do their neighbors. That's about two to three houses on each side. What about the houses behind me? Well, there's a wetland creek sitting behind my house. On the other side of that is a neighborhood. Maybe the sound is coming from that neighborhood? Maybe the sound Mary is hearing is coming from a few houses down? Maybe the sound is bouncing off the water in the creek. We know sound can sometimes travel great distances with the help of moving water. Highly unlikely, but plausible. The assignment given to me by the ladies upon arriving home was verifying how much water was in that creek.

So, I checked the creek, and just as I thought, it was as dry as a bone. I mean, it was summer, zero water runs through that creek during the summer. We were back to where we started. No big deal: we'll classify this as noise contamination for now. But note in the record, why is one room picking up the sounds of children screaming and not the other? Just when we were about to forget that event ever taking place something unique happened. Mary sent out a high alert Skype message. A high alert (via Skype) message means: please stop what it is you're doing, log in, and help confirm what it is I'm hearing. Once again, I was at work, my response time can't always be right away when it comes to logging in. But Niki can. Niki and her associate, Dominick Valerio, were online and did just that. They logged in to see what Mary was talking about. Mary has just typed into the chat box that she heard a child and a woman screaming. They were screaming at each other. Niki logged into the office camera; she can't hear anything. She then logged into the hallway, and sure enough, two people were arguing. A mother and her young child. We're not talking whispers; we're not talking distant. It's where it was before, right outside the doorway of the office—which once again begs the question, why can't we hear it from the office camera?

The next day the mother and child (girl) screaming returned, just about the same time as before. Mary was remoted in, as was Niki. The sounds were identical. Mom and daughter were arguing about something. I was free at the time, so I logged in to help confirm what everyone was hearing. Sure enough, there it was. It's a weird feeling to hear something of this magnitude coming from your house when you're not at home. I mean, I live alone now. There is no easy explanation to what I'm hearing right now.

The three of us were discussing what we just heard when Niki decided to ping one of her consultants. This is one of our rules. When the evidence is borderline inconclusive, consult an independent third party. The people Niki would rely on had no vested interests in the case. Nine times out of ten they were in the middle of something, which means they would have to get back to her. Some of them are driving home from work. Some are doing other things. All of sudden they get a message from Niki to look at something. Niki sent them the file and waited for their response. Their response to this particular activity was: "this is weird. This doesn't make sense." Children talking, laughing, playing, etc. can be explained. It's summer. We get that; there are children outside somewhere. We can't see them, but we can hear them. Keith's confirmation that children never play outside during the middle of the day is noted, but little credence can be given to it. The fact that two houses on both sides of my house have no children was also noted. We'll note the wetlands behind the house. We'll note the dry creek. Even with all that being noted, we still must lean on the side that this can be explained somehow. If it had not been for the screams being captured on video and audio, that's how that week would have been summarized. A rule we created and agreed to follow was that the consensus must be a hundred percent. For something to be considered evidence, we all must be in a one hundred percent agreement. If we can't all agree, then we drop it and move on.

The noise that sounded like children screaming could not get us to one hundred percent consensus. Not by itself, it couldn't. What made us reach the hundred percent agreement threshold was the daughter and mother screams. Two days in a row, at about the same time—and the same scream, mind you. It's rational to think kids could be playing outside. It's highly unlikely they're playing outside, making the same screams, for several days and at the same time each day. Still: as near impossible as that would seem, it still would not push everyone to conclude a paranormal origin. What did it for everyone, including the consultants, was this: the screams could not be heard on nearby cameras.

The question Niki and her team are asking themselves now is: how is it possible to hear noise from one room and not the other? Who argues about the same thing two days in a row, at the same time, using the same loud words? Mother and her young daughter in a huge back and forth row? Who can explain that? Both cameras were operative. Both cameras were behaving and functioning normally. The hallway camera was sending sound alerts. The office camera was sitting on top of my entertainment center. No sound detection emails whatsoever.

The garbage truck picks up trash every Thursday in my neighborhood. Both cameras can hear that. But that's not happening when it comes to the screams we're hearing. The screams are limited to just the hallway. Let's try something else. Let's rotate the cameras. "Keith, can you put the hallway camera in the office and put the office camera in the hallway?" Sure, I can. Guess what? Nothing's changed. The scream is only being heard in the hallway. Changing the camera does nothing.

This should not be a shock to you. You've heard me speak of this before. You remember the summer of last year? Remember the dragging furniture sounds? One camera hears it. The other camera doesn't. It happened then, and it's happening now. It pleased me to see how dumbfounded these ladies were. It's cool to see them go through their thought process and then blurt out: "this is nuts!" They couldn't explain it. And they should be able to. It doesn't take a rocket scientist to understand how sound works. Sound travels three hundred and forty-three meters per second. Even with doors and walls present, the office should still hear something. Doesn't have to be the same decibel level. But it should be something. The ladies heard nothing. Conclusion: paranormal.

This was just week one. We still had five months to go. That's how long phase one was. Later that week, when I arrived home, I saw that Mary and Niki were both online. Both ladies heard me walk into the house. I know this because in their case diary it reads: *5:52 pm, Keith arrives home.* Now, this is where the set up pretty much resembles that popular CBS TV show, *Big Brother.* The cameras the ladies are logged into are upstairs. The ladies have just heard my arrival through the cameras, and they've just read it through the group chat. My presence should not be viewed as contaminating the investigation, quite the contrary, it enhances it.

I bring this up now because I'd just got home from work. I was moving through the house, going about my daily routine. Everything I do can be heard through the cameras upstairs. Remember, the ladies aren't monitoring me, they're monitoring the house (upstairs only). Some might say this is the time where the observation should be suspended? There's too much going on. My presence is contaminating the home monitoring. You're making the same mistake *Ghost Adventures* did if you believe that. Have you ever thought about a location being too sterile, too clean, and neat to where it suppresses everything? Scientists, when they go out into the forest, out into the jungle: what's their number one mission? Impact the environment as little as possible. My presence is the most important ingredient of this investigation. I'm the house occupant, as was Tina when she lived here. The odds of something happening should increase with me being home.

So, the sun was setting now. Shift change: Niki (who is a night owl) was very anxious to begin her night monitoring. The last few days had been awesome for her, in the sense of trying to understand what it is I'm going through when trying to sleep. Describing the loud bangs is hard. You have to hear these for yourself to appreciate the level of consistency. One of the things that always angered Tina and me were skeptics telling us: the noise you're hearing is house noise. Which sort of insults our intelligence. We know what house noise sounds like. Ask Elisa Jaffe: was the noise she heard house noise? Ask the investigators that came here last year if what they heard was house noise. Ask the married medium couple Dennis and Alice Jackson if what they heard while here was house noise. Everyone who lives in a house knows what house noise sounds like. It's not a sudden bang. It's not a loud thud. If house noises throughout the world resembled anything close to poltergeist rapping, well, trust me—they'd be a lot of empty homes throughout the world.

Poltergeists don't want the noise they make getting confused with house noise. Poltergeists make the noise they make as a means of getting your attention; they want to evoke fear. The first time Niki heard the loud banging noise was when she was monitoring the hallway. I had not too long since gone to sleep. There was a loud bang (something I'm all too familiar with) that I heard while sleeping. I try to sleep through them now; that's how used to them I've gotten. But I remember hearing the noise; it was very loud. I get to work the next day, and there in the chat box is a conversation Niki had with one of her team members. The question she asked the group was: "What the hell was that? Did anyone hear that?" Her team members responded, "Yes, we heard it, wow!" From Niki's point of view, the noise sounded like it came from the hallway. That's the camera she was observing the house from. Niki sends me an instant message that morning, asking me did I hear it. I said yeah, I heard it. She immediately understood what it means when I say the noise just comes from out of nowhere. There's no precursor or anything. All of a sudden you hear it, and when you hear it you're like, what the fuck was that? This has been going on since 2012.

Poltergeist Bed Time Knockings
https://youtu.be/k0mV6vZWYHs

The consensus among everybody right now is that the "scream" and the temper tantrum are between mother and daughter. Which is what Jane Doe said. Their home was dark and stressful. Conflict after conflict would ensue over a variety of things. Things demons love to exploit. So: is this a residual haunting? Investigator Dave Juliano (his writings) describes a residual haunting as being "a playback of a past event. The apparitions involved are not spirits, they are recordings." Recordings of a previous event? Could be a past event, e.g., great battle, great fire, massacre, small box outbreak whatever. It could also be a past traumatic event, e.g., murder, holocaust, domestic abuse, etc. How plausible is that? No one knows for sure, I mean, the theory sounds very close to something else I found online. Something called stone tape theory. Both theories emphasized placement. Placement, as in something specific taking place either in the house (likely) or before the house was built (likely). What if something took place in the house itself? What about a traumatic event? That's where the Gray Lady and Jane Doe come in.

I've yet to tell anyone about the apparitions I've seen resembling Jane Doe. The similarities are striking. Jane Doe doesn't know, and neither do Niki and Mary. This is the first time I ever felt comfortable talking about it. Jane Doe and I have had numerous conversations already. She'd told me numerous times some of the horrors that went on there. Not all of it was paranormal.

Some of what she experienced was human-made; we're talking traumatic stuff. I have to accept what she told me as being the truth. A mother and daughter screaming at each other near my office door could be a ghostly like a record playing over and over. Jane Doe has told me over, and over that, she wants no involvement with the case. No involvement whatsoever. It's not like I can send her an audio-visual file and say, please listen to this. Does this sound like you and your daughter? If I did, I'd be violating the agreement we made. No in-depth discussions about the house. All she's told me so far is what I've told you. Minus the redactions of course.

I never got the impression that the Gray Lady was a recorded event. I saw her clear as day. She purposely turned off my office light and stood there puzzled as fuck. She decided to disappear into the washroom, can't, turns tail, and takes off near running (fast walking pace). I got the sense she knew what she was doing up until the moment she turned off the light. Why would you manually turn off a light? Our lights go off and on all the time. The power gets cut all the time. Why do it manually? No, the Gray Lady did what she did because she *wanted me* to see her. I'm sure of it now. More now, than when it happened. I heard the click sound. That was no accident.

The white lady is a different story. What I saw that night could be interpreted as being recorded. The lady walked by my office, coming from the direction of the landing area. We never made eye contact. What I heard before her walking by is astounding. I heard the sound of rustling paper. A rustling noise. The noise was what made me turn toward the door. I thought, *who's in the hallway? I can hear Tina; I know where she's at. Who's walking through the hallway?* Sure enough, here she comes, the white lady. Her hands were full of something. It was hard to make out what she was holding because everything was white. It looked like I saw a movie. Now that was a dangerous night.

Tina and I had heard plenty of voices while living here. But we'd never heard a mother and daughter exchange. What Mary found is new. Mother and daughter are screaming, especially the mom. What pisses us off is that we can't quite make out the conversation. We can't quite tell what the argument is about. It's extremely loud. It's happening close to the Foscam. That much is certain. But we can't make head or tails of what's being said. You'd think we'd be able to, given that we can tell it's a mother and child.

It's important to note that residual hauntings don't burn Bibles. Residual hauntings don't steal coffee cups, jewelry, silverware, cameras, and car keys. Residual hauntings are just that: residual. Passive. Nothing malevolent about them whatsoever. Therein lies the question. Residual haunting or poltergeist? What's going on here? That's what Niki and Mary are discussing right now.

After about the fourth week, Mary and Niki approached me with the idea of adding more cameras. How about the kitchen? There was also the request to switch cameras around, permanently. *Let's put the hallway camera in the office, and you reconfigure it. Let's put the office camera in the hallway, leave it there after you reconfigure it.*

The rationale for having a camera in my bedroom was simple. "We need video footage of you sleeping while the noise is happening elsewhere. We need to show you sleeping. We need to show the world you've gone to bed. We need to show the world you've been asleep for a considerable amount of time before the loud bangs start happening." No one doubts what we had at the time wasn't good. Quite the opposite, it was fantastic. But now we needed to go a step beyond what we'd done already. Everyone was of the same mindset, which is: we're going to be as thorough as we possibly can. It's impossible to sway every skeptic. We know there will forever be internet trolls who say, 'all of this was staged; Mary and Niki are in on it too.' *They're trying to advance their agenda by substantiating Keith Linder's clams.* That's what the trolls are going to say. We can't control who chooses to remain a skeptic, and who doesn't. But we can limit the number of skeptic responses if this information goes public.

It didn't take long before Niki began picking up the loud bangs within my room (see link above). Or what we thought was my room. Some nights the motion camera in the bedroom would send sound alert emails notifying us that sound was detected. These emails were in sync with the loud bangs. Not always, though. Some of the loudest banging noises went undetected by the motion cameras. It would seem the cameras had a hard time pinning down the location of the noise as we did. Some of the loud bangs seemed to come from the attic. Some seemed to come from the hallway. Matter of fact, most of them seemed to come from the hallway.

One-night Niki had the house all to herself. I was in my bed, snoring my ass off. All of a sudden, she heard a loud noise. It came through the hallway camera, but the noise wasn't in the hallway. The sound she was hearing was the sound of the cabinet doors opening and closing. Or maybe not. I went downstairs the next morning, and nothing was out of order. This happened more than once. I'm talking about four times a week during the time of their investigation.

Perhaps the doors had opened and closed, hence, no sign in the morning. But one thing we had to remind ourselves constantly was this: just because we hear a noise, a noise that sets off a sound detected email, doesn't necessarily mean that noise is physical. That noise could have been artificially created. The perfect example of this was back when Tina would sometimes come and say, "What do you want?" I'd look at her and say, "I don't want anything, what are you talking about?" She'd be pissed because she could have sworn she heard me call her name. Similarly, I could have sworn I heard Tina call my name numerous times, though she swore she hadn't. I'd bet my retirement money on it. Same went for Jane Doe. She and her nanny on occasion would hear what sounded like cabinet doors being closed. One night the nanny heard it and chose not to respond. The next day she came downstairs and discovered "every kitchen cabinet door open." Jane Doe had that happen to her numerous times.

I can't remember who made the assertion first, but someone finally uttered the word "poltergeist." I didn't want to put the idea in their head, but that's what my brain had been entertaining for quite some time now. That and demon are at the top of my list. The interesting thing about those two types of hauntings is that their manifestations and actions are almost the same. I'd been reading about what a poltergeist is for several months now. I'd ordered books from Amazon, and I'd checked out books in the library. Every chapter I read about poltergeist forces me to set the book down and ask the silly question: Why were Tina and I given so much grief about the claims we were making? Most of what we'd been reporting has happened elsewhere, and I mean multiple times elsewhere. Would it shock you to know that there are reports throughout history of Bibles being burned? Of wall writings? Of objects being thrown? Of kitchen cabinets being opened? Of water puddles? Of families being at each other's throats? A majority of these cases start off the same. Soft and subtle, and then *BOOM!* Mass destruction. You'd think Tina and I were introducing something into the paranormal field based on the negative treatment we got.

August 18th, 2015, the camera in the hallway detected sound six times. That's six emails to everyone's inbox. The noise Mary heard were thuds and knocking sounds. We compared it to two wood planks being banged together—or, as one person put it after watching the video, a set of billiard balls being broken up. The noise campaign that day lasted ten hours (that is not a typo).

On August 24th, Niki and Mary decided to monitor the hallway together. Here are their notes.

Date: 8/24/2015
Area: Hallway
Remote Camera notes
Investigator (s): Mary/Niki
Jenna(Consultant)
Day

3:47PM EST Bang loud & close by
3:48PM EST Thud
3:49PM EST Mic disturbance – Long
3:50PM EST Mic disturbance
3:51PM EST Mic disturbance – Long
3:52PM EST Bang/mic disturbance 2x
3:54PM EST Mic disturbance
3:55PM EST Mic disturbance
4:56PM EST Mic disturbance
4:57PM EST Thump/footsteps
4:59PM EST Movement then bang
5:00PM EST Mic disturbance, click
5:01PM EST Distant noise/ mic disturbance
5:02PM EST Mic disturbance
5:03PM EST Mic disturbance/movement
5:05PM EST Mic disturbance

Notes were sporadic as a lot was going on in the house that day, and I wanted to video and focus on what was happening. Also, Niki took her own notes as well.

Morning notes
Investigator: Jenna (Consultant)
Attic Cam/Hallway camera simultaneous listening

9:49AM EST Sounds like a rock hit something in the attic
9:54AM EST Knock on wood 2X
9:55AM EST Knock on wood 2X
9:59AM EST Knock on wood – Attic/Bang – House
10:03AM EST Wooden bang in the attic 2X
10:06AM EST Wooden bang in the attic

10:07AM EST Bang – House
10:08AM EST Wooden bang - attic
10:13AM EST Wooden bang – attic
10:18AM EST Bang - House
10:19AM EST Loud bang – house
10:21AM EST Knock on wood – attic
10:21AM EST Bang – House
10:23AM EST Wooden bang 2X – attic
10:24AM EST Large bang - House
10:25AM EST Bang - Attic
10:25AM EST Bang - House
10:28AM EST Wooden bang – Attic 2X
12:08AM EST Knock – Attic

The noise Mary and Niki are picking up is a poltergeist activity known as rapping. Not to be confused with rapping, as in Jay Z or Snoop Dog. What we're getting is a continuous knocking noise. Out of all the activity taking place in this house, out of everything we've seen and heard this rapping has been the most constant. Think of it as your heartbeat. Pause from reading right now, place your forefinger on your wrist for a second. You feel your pulse? That's what my house is like. A continuous knocking. It's heard throughout the house. Now it can get faint and hard to hear sometimes, or it can be loud. Today it's loud. Loud and repetitive. The ladies took exceptional notes that day—and for quite some time.

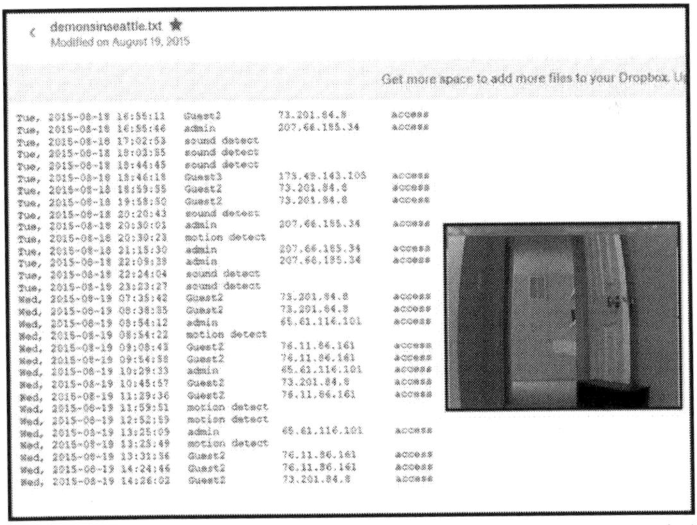
demonsinseattle.txt
Modified on August 19, 2015

Get more space to add more files to your Dropbox. U

Tue,	2015-08-18	16:55:11	Guest2	73.201.84.8	access
Tue,	2015-08-18	16:55:46	admin	207.66.185.34	access
Tue,	2015-08-18	17:02:53	sound detect		
Tue,	2015-08-18	18:03:55	sound detect		
Tue,	2015-08-18	18:44:45	sound detect		
Tue,	2015-08-18	18:46:18	Guest3	173.49.143.105	access
Tue,	2015-08-18	18:59:55	Guest2	73.201.84.8	access
Tue,	2015-08-18	19:58:50	Guest2	73.201.84.8	access
Tue,	2015-08-18	20:20:43	sound detect		
Tue,	2015-08-18	20:30:01	admin	207.66.185.34	access
Tue,	2015-08-18	20:30:23	motion detect		
Tue,	2015-08-18	21:15:30	admin	207.66.185.34	access
Tue,	2015-08-18	22:09:39	admin	207.66.185.34	access
Tue,	2015-08-18	22:24:04	sound detect		
Tue,	2015-08-18	23:23:27	sound detect		
Wed,	2015-08-19	07:35:42	Guest2	73.201.84.8	access
Wed,	2015-08-19	08:38:55	Guest2	73.201.84.8	access
Wed,	2015-08-19	08:54:12	admin	65.61.116.101	access
Wed,	2015-08-19	08:54:22	motion detect		
Wed,	2015-08-19	09:08:43	Guest2	76.11.86.161	access
Wed,	2015-08-19	09:54:58	Guest2	76.11.86.161	access
Wed,	2015-08-19	10:29:33	admin	65.61.116.101	access
Wed,	2015-08-19	10:45:57	Guest2	73.201.84.8	access
Wed,	2015-08-19	11:29:36	Guest2	76.11.86.161	access
Wed,	2015-08-19	11:59:51	motion detect		
Wed,	2015-08-19	12:52:59	motion detect		
Wed,	2015-08-19	13:25:09	admin	65.61.116.101	access
Wed,	2015-08-19	13:25:49	motion detect		
Wed,	2015-08-19	13:31:56	Guest2	76.11.86.161	access
Wed,	2015-08-19	14:24:46	Guest2	76.11.86.161	access
Wed,	2015-08-19	14:26:02	Guest2	73.201.84.8	access

Fig 39.1 Foscam motion/sound detection log / House is empty or is it?

Fig 39.2 Files on the harddrive and Cloud dropbox accounts fill up quickly with 24/7 home monitoring

Chapter 40
The Design

Some words are going to be used in the coming chapters that reader might not quite understand if it was not for this chapter. Try to think of this chapter as being the owner's manual, i.e. project plan of the investigation that Niki is about to lead.

None of us thought when we started that this would end up becoming one of the most documented poltergeist cases of all time. That wasn't at the forefront of everyone's mind right now. Mary and Niki wanted to shine a light on the case (in the event of evidence being obtained). Every paranormal organization that's contacted me after the airing of the "Demons in Seattle" episode seemed to understand when conducting an investigation, (paranormal is no exception), nothing is guaranteed. Tools, gadgets, handheld devices are cool things to have around when entering a home—they look cool on TV, but that's about it. They're just cool things.

The only thing you can have to rely on are your instincts, your gut feeling, and the person next to you. The spirits are not under any obligation to give you anything. If you can understand that, if you can understand what it is I'm about to tell you then get ready for some compelling piece of evidence. Finally!

But first things first. Let's look at the team, the core team as we call it. The setup we agreed on that made this evidence-gathering mission possible. This chapter talks about the structure. It talks about the people involved. It talks about the technical setup that made remote house monitoring possible.

Core Team

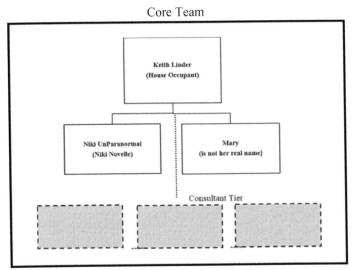

Fig 40.1 The core team

The only people involved in this case right now were Niki and Mary. Niki has been in the paranormal field for quite some time—having met tons of investigators through her private research and her radio show, had a list a people she could reach out to in the event she and Mary found something. Project scope—monitor the house—constantly. Let the activity (if any) dictate what happens next. We're not chasing burning Bibles or burning crosses. Expectations are zero; we get what we get when we get it.

The ladies want to substantiate what I'm currently experiencing. The baseline activity, if you will. If the spirits want to provide more data, i.e., we'll take it. Mary and Niki live three thousand miles away. Therefore, this has to be a remote investigation. That's what the investigation consists of; this will be a surveillance exercise.

So, when I say Niki, Mary will be investigating remotely I mean in the technical sense. They will be house monitoring by using existing hardware and software. Items I already own.

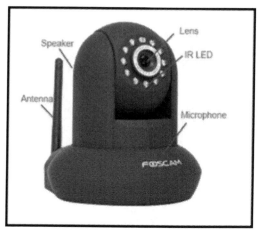

Fig. 40.2 Foscam Motion/Sound IR detection camera.

Features of the camera that pertain to the investigation include:

300-degree pan and 120-degree tilt
Supports IE/Firefox/Google/Safari browser or any other standard browsers
Supports WEP, WPA, and WPA2 Encryption (**enabled**)
Supports image snapshot
Supports dual-stream
Embedded FOSCAM DDNS (dynamic domain name service) Service
Supports two-way audio / remote viewing & record from anywhere anytime
Multi-level user's management with password protection
Motion detection alert via email or upload image to FTP
Supporting Third Party Domain Name Service

Supports multiple network protocols: HTTP /TCP /IP /UDP /FTP /DHCP /DDNS / UPNP

How do the Mail Settings work?

"If you want the camera to send emails when motion/sound has been detected. Configure Mail Setting to receive email alerts."

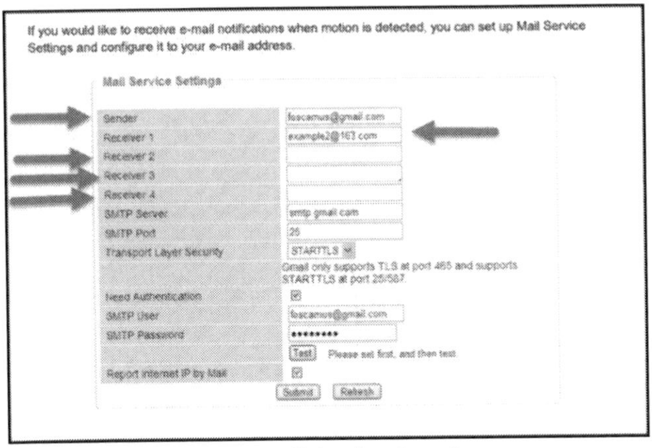

Fig 40.3 Mail Setting Interface.

User Account Set Up

Here I can create users and set privilege e.g. visitor, operator or administrator. The default user accounts are admin, operator, and visitor, with a blank password.

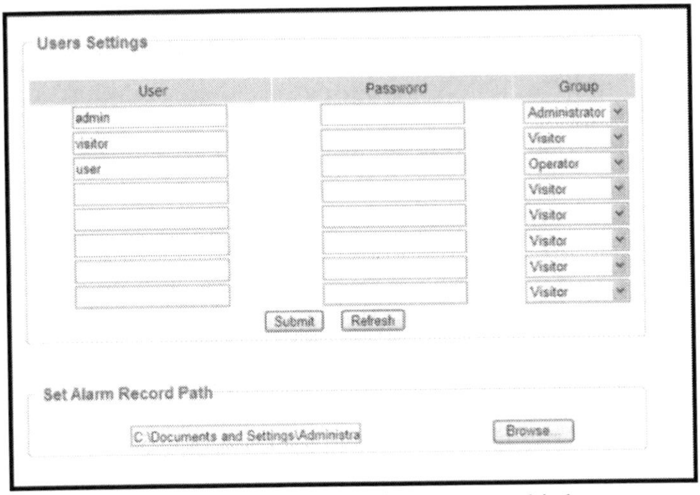

Fig 40.4 User Setting: No one has access to this but me.

Visitor Access –It's what we call "read-only" access in the IT world. Mary and Niki can log in, based on the username and password I give them. This allows them to view the room the camera is in. They cannot tilt, pivot, pan left or pan right the camera's lens. Only the administrator can do that. That would be me. Now, let's say Mary hears something that she wants Niki to verify. All she has to do is ping Niki on Skype. If Niki is available, all she has to do is log in with her credentials and access the camera Mary wants her to access. If what she wants her to see or hear is still going on, Niki will see it. The camera takes a series of snapshots should motion or sound be detected. Everyone listed as Receiver (Fig 40.3) will receive that snapshot. But there's a back up to the snapshot feature. Something the ladies thought of that I found to be outstanding. They introduced me to LiteCam. https://www.litecam.net/en/

"LiteCam - HD is the easiest-to-use computer screen recorder for Windows users that helps create professional-looking HD videos in no time! Simply record anything on your PC screen with video, audio to teach, demonstrate, present, and create video tutorials and much more. It's easy and powerful interface makes for quick recording. Amazing tool.

Sometimes we all can't login quick enough. Sometimes we're just out of reach. If Niki or Mary hear a sound they believe might be related to the case the first thing they must do is execute the LiteCam. All the LiteCam does is record (makes a video) what's being shown on your desktop. That would be the Foscam dashboard in this case. You can save stuff instantly with this tool. What gets saved, gets reviewed. What's agreed upon is sent to the cloud, i.e., Google Drive, Dropbox, etc.

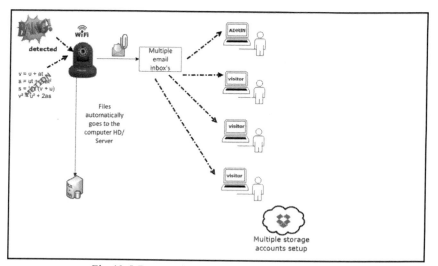

Fig 40.5 Remote house monitoring architecture.

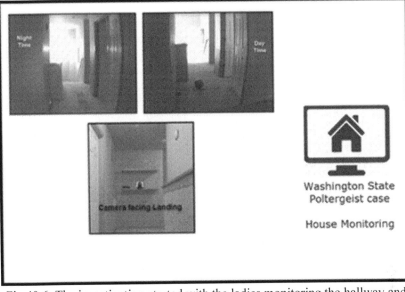

Fig 40.6 The investigation started with the ladies monitoring the hallway and office.

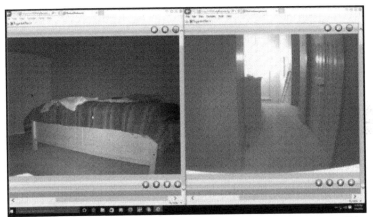

Fig 40.7 Left - Master bedroom. Right - Hallway - Foscam View, Niki and Mary's view.

I'll explain more about the camera as the investigation unfolds. Understand these cameras have Wi-Fi and LAN capabilities. Encryption has been enabled to prevent hacking. When the camera sends an email, it goes to everyone's inbox. I get an email, Niki gets an email, as does Mary. But that's not all. A snapshot and video of whatever the email is gets sent to my back up hard-drive. This feature of everyone receiving the same email at the same time shields us from evidence tampering.

Niki can't walk up to me and say "look what we found, an apparition, looks good, huh? I found it last night while you were asleep." The first thing I would do, the first thing Mary would do, and Niki to if the tides were reversed was, let's compare it to the snapshot I got. Remember, we all get notified whenever motion or sound is detected. There's no such thing as an independent discovery. I mean you can witness activity by yourself, but you can't vet it by yourself.

The process keeps everyone honest. This is not a blue ribbons contest. Now the Foscam is one of the top surveillance cameras on the market when it comes to home monitoring. The cameras come with mobile apps for both the iPhone and the Android—we're talking real-time viewing. I used this feature a lot in 2014. I think we all can agree the camera as good as they are they were never intended to go after a poltergeist. These cameras that I own have been called motion cameras, home surveillance cameras, infrared cameras and motion-sound detection cameras built with infrared technology. Call them whatever you want they still fall into the category of an electronic device. And you know what spirits do with electronic devices?

Chapter 41
Equipment Malfunction

It's hard to know exactly when the spirits became aware that someone else monitoring the house and not me. The ladies had been monitoring for two months now, the possibility of them experiencing technical difficulties was bound to happen. I just didn't know when. It was September now. I bet the spirits were saying, 'oh, Keith is doing this again? Hasn't he learned his lesson? Haven't we destroyed enough of his cameras already?' Prepare yourself for what I'm about to share, I'm sure you'll agree, this was not computer error. No, this was someone purposely sabotaging something.

Niki and Mary were monitoring both the master bedroom and hallway when suddenly Niki's camera went offline. She can't see into the bed anymore. But Mary can. I got a Skype message within seconds of Niki's camera going offline. That's never happened before, them losing access. Lucky for them I wasn't doing anything serious at work, so I launched my browser and logged into the Foscam dashboard. I looked at Niki's profile, and it looked fine. I looked at Mary's profile, and it too looked fine. Now, I can be anyone I want to when I'm logged in. I'm the administrator of everyone's account. The first thing I did after logging in, was access the bedroom camera using Niki's username and password. I got in instantly. I tried Mary's username and password and got in just as fast.

I asked Niki to retry, and the same thing happened. Nothing. She can't see into the bedroom. Her hallway access is fine, for now. But her bedroom access isn't, at least not when she tries. I can get in with permissions and see everything. Now, this isn't new to me. I had this problem before when it was just me monitoring back in the summer and fall of last year. The solution at first is simple. "Niki, can you please close your browser and relaunch it?" And she does, but the problem's still there. Niki, can you please close everything? Can you reboot your machine? And she does, and sure enough, the problem is fixed. For now.

When I got home from work that night, I received another Skype message from Niki. She was now having problems with both cameras: now she can't see either room. Her problem presented me with two choices. I could crack open my laptop and troubleshoot the problem at my kitchen table, otherwise, or I won't be able to help until I'm back in the office tomorrow morning. Both ladies know I'm not comfortable talking about the case while at home. Both ladies know I'm not comfortable talking about what happened to Tina and me while I'm home by myself. Yes, I've reinstalled the cameras. Yes, the case is actively open. And yes, I'm contradicting myself. And yes, it doesn't make any sense. But you see, that's one definition of a poltergeist. What it does makes no sense. What I do makes no sense. Emotionally, I'm still walking on eggshells. When I come home from work each day, the first thing I hear when I open the front door is the sound of someone running upstairs. When I go at night, the last thing I hear before falling asleep is the sound of a cabinet door opening and closing. As soon as I hear it my eyes pop back open. That keeps me up another hour or so. That's why Niki and Mary are here. They're here to catch that stuff.

It was Niki's shift now; her assistant had gone to bed. If I tell her she has to wait until tomorrow, we might lose valuable evidence. The spirit has sabotaged her account that could mean they want to be active tonight. I'm starting to understand how paranormal research works. It reminds me of fishing. You have to fish when the time is right. And by right, I mean when the odds of catching something are high. Tonight, seemed to be one of those nights. The only solace I have right now is knowing should the spirits decide to attack me; Niki and Mary may be around to capture it.

Suffice to say; I decided to help Niki. I decided to troubleshoot her problem at home versus at work. *It took me three hours to fix her account.* We're chatting back and forth, Niki and I, when she finally gets in. We typed the words hurray! Hurray! in our group chat. She can see both rooms now. But, not so fast, Keith and Niki. Niki's cameras go offline again within minutes. "Keith, the problem is happening again, both cameras just went black" is what Niki told me. I wasn't even logged out of my computer yet when she told me this. Next, Niki's browser done something totally unexpected. It refreshes itself and then, voila! She can see the hallway. I would be fine with that if it weren't for one slight problem. The camera she was logged into is labeled 'master bedroom.' Why would a camera in the bedroom suddenly show the hallway? Of course, my question's purely rhetorical because I've seen this happen before. I've lost count how many times this has happened to me. It's very frustrating. It took me three hours to get her account working. Three hours to fix one camera. And keep in mind, the problem is not the camera. I can see the room's fine, for now. If the camera were at fault, then I would be having the same problem. Mary would be having the same problem. I logged into the bedroom camera, praying I run into the same problem. I didn't. I could see my bedroom easily. Let me log in as Niki. Once again, no problem. I can see the bedroom with my account, with Niki's account, and with Mary's account.

And then it hit me. The entities had finally figured it out: it wasn't me that was monitoring them. The fact that they restricted Niki's view and not mine (at least not yet) told me they knew something was going on. *I've learned a lot by watching these bastards. They're extremely smart. Very elusive.* One of the things *Ghost Adventures* failed to call attention to when they were at my house was the constant equipment malfunction they kept experiencing. Their infrared cameras kept going offline. I'm talking about immediate battery drainage. Why they chose to gloss over that is beyond me. I mean they've called attention to lesser things on other episodes.

The cameras Niki are Mary are using are very similar to the cameras *Ghost Adventures* used. Similar technology. I would never call attention to an anomaly such as this had it happened just the one time. I would never call attention to it had it happened five times. I'm only calling attention to it because it happened hundreds of times. I just shared the first time it happened. It's going to happen every day now. You may already have noticed that things tend to start small and ramp up into the heavy phase. There was a ramp up to the loud bangs. A ramp up to the door slams. A ramp up to the flower pots being thrown. A ramp up to objects being thrown. A ramp up with the electrical issues. Niki and Mary's technical difficulties are no exception.

So: when it came to accessing the bedroom, Niki had the most problems. When it came to monitoring the hallway, Mary had the most problems. It took me a while to figure out why that was the case, but I finally got it. The poltergeist was sabotaging whatever room the ladies liked the most. The hallway was Mary's favorite room to monitor. She was supposed to monitor both rooms during the day. And she did. But the room she was always looking at is the hallway. Mary's reason for loving the hallway is obvious. It's been the most active room throughout the whole ordeal. The thoroughfare for just about everything that's taken place. Niki's favorite room is the bedroom. My poking and prodding intrigued her. The fact that I'm hearing loud bangs, loud footsteps, and knocks above my head was just unbelievable to her.

So, the spirits messed with each woman's favorite camera, to frustrate them. And it worked. That's what a malevolent spirit does; they create frustration.

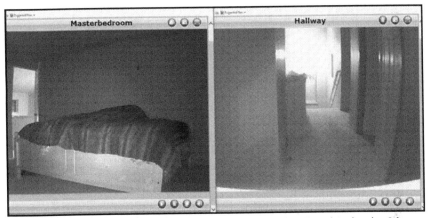

Fig 41.1 Summer 2015. Niki and team watch the room I'm sleeping in. 8 hrs. that night. They're recording the series of bangs.

They take what you like or love and turn it against you. Trust me; we'll come back to this interesting tactic soon enough.

Allow me to share with you the next leg of this investigation. That being my homework assignment. Mary and Niki have taken a lot of notes over the last few weeks. They've recorded screams, conversations, temper tantrums, pacing back and forth, footsteps, inexplicable noises, bangs, door closures, and just recently the camera malfunctions. Now they want to see if they can get some interaction.

Can they insert something into the house? Something the spirit will interact with? Can they get this interaction on camera? I've been told that I need to go out and buy something. "Go buy a plastic ball, a stuffed animal, and a touch-activated light, the kind that turns on by touch."

These spirits know we're here. They know they're being watched and studied. They know it's not the same as before. Keith has enlisted some outside help. The spirits must know by now that the help I got is three thousand miles away. The question now is: what are they going to do? Niki has an inclination that there are multiple spirits are living here. Some are evil. Some are mean. Some are nasty, and some are lost. Maybe we can interact with the ones Niki believes are lost. Will they interact with an object we've placed? Will they manipulate something as obvious as a red beach ball?

Mary's and Niki's thought experiment.

- Experiment number one – place the touch-activated light device on the wall – facing the master bedroom. In clear view of the hallway camera.
- Experiment number two – place a teddy bear on the landing banister, facing the master bedroom.
- Experiment number four – place the beach ball on the floor dead center of the hallway. In clear view of the camera.
- Experiment number five – place a butterfly wind chime in the middle of the hallway (the wind chime would hang from a coat rack.) Clear view of the camera.

Mary wanted these items in the hallway. I must admit I wasn't too impressed with the setup at first. It had a goofy element about it, I thought. Why would a spirit move a beach ball on the floor? What could it possibly do with a teddy bear? As you can see, I still had much to learn about what spirits chose to do and what they chose not to do.

Spirits do things because they can; it's that simple. There's no predicting when they will interact, no timetable to speak of. All we could do was to wait. Wait and hope they move one of these objects. Hopefully, the cameras will catch something like that. And the ladies didn't have to wait long either. Interactions began to happen within days of the props being added. I'm glad to admit I was proven wrong. Good idea, Mary, very good idea.

Fig 41.2 Experiment number five – place a wind chime in the middle of the hallway.

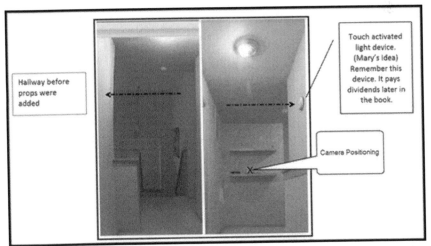

Fig 41.3 Hallway camera position

September – October. Niki and her team have amassed a lot of evidence thus far. Their curiosity has now been taken, hostage. The conclusion they've reached about the noise being heard is that it's not house noise. Niki admitted to me that she knew very little about poltergeist activity, but what she knew applies to what she believes is happening here. That would be the constant tapping sounds. The pacing back and forth. The ladies essentially hear noise where there shouldn't be any. They know I'm at work. So, it's not me. The noises they are hearing, suggest someone's home. But that's just it; no one is—that's the weird thing about it. Why do they hear cabinet doors opening and closing when the house is empty? Each discovery creates twenty new questions. It's impossible not to get obsessed. And they're not even visited the house yet. This is what they gathered by observing from the comforts of their own home. Wait till they arrive on the scene.

Three Dropbox accounts, two Google Drive accounts, and one box account was all full of video and audio footage. Much of that had yet to be reviewed. This portion of the investigation is where I believe teams often lack discipline: in the act of reviewing what you find, and quickly. I can't tell you how many times Tina and I had paranormal teams come to our house, set up equipment, gather evidence, leave, and never give that evidence to us. No Bull Paranormal team caught a mist coming from the hallway floor. They caught it on video. We all watched it. Did they give us a copy? Of course not. Does it exist today? Who knows? Should it be accessible to the paranormal community? Yes, it should. No one's more upset about the paranormal community kidnapping our evidence than Tina and me. That midst coming from the floor in the hallway should be in the hands of everyone. It's not. And that's sad.

No way is the evidence from this case going to end up that way. Granted there's a lot to sift through. We all can agree, reviewing video and audio files is boring. It's tedious work, and no one likes to do it. You're looking for a needle in a haystack. So, Niki, Mary, and I agreed we have to be more proactive in the evidence review department. Missing something of consequence is a detriment to the case. It's a detriment to the truth. The ladies know better than me how the skeptic community views negligence. These people seize upon it right away.

We need research consultants. Fortunately, Niki knows a lot of them. We'll have them review the data. If they find something, inform Niki. Niki will inform the team. The hundred percent agreement rule is still in effect. Nothing goes into the evidence folder unless it's been vetted. All of us have to agree. I wish the reader could see some of the debates we've had. These are not heated debates. No, these debates are purely intellectual. To use a bad analogy, we poke and prod everything that we encounter.

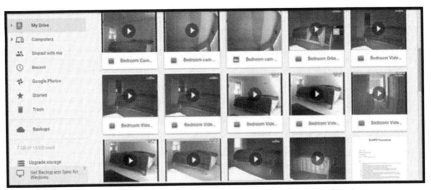

Fig 41.4 Libraries are filling up fast. When to review?

Which leads to our next discovery. Investigations have three components to them. There's the investigation side—the phase we're currently in now. The second phase I call the why phase. Be it paranormal or non-paranormal: the question we have to ask ourselves is why is it happening? Somewhere during the investigation, the researcher is supposed to provide the house occupant with answers. I would like to know what's causing all this activity. Why this house? Why the previous tenant and me? Why aren't the other houses in the area being affected? You can't make something stop if you don't know what the cause is. The third phase, should one reach it, is the resolution phase. I can tell you right now, out of all the three phases I've just listed, phase three is the phase Tina, and I had the most problem with. No one has been able to provide us with a solution. Should the activity stop and never happened again, the question remains? Why did it happen? Niki felt it was time to introduce mediums into the equation. Individuals with the ability to see and feel things. Those individuals were Karissa Fleck and Vanessa Hogle. Their involvement couldn't have come a moment too soon. Well, I'll be damned: The Gray Lady is back.

Chapter 42
The Gray Lady Returns

I woke up one morning to my Skype ringing off the hook—Niki was blowing up my Skype account with incoming messages. I know what that means; it means she'd found something new. I looked at my phone, and there was her message: "look at this and tell me what you think?" I think, *Wow, this is a big photo that she sent me.* No way am I going to look at that with my cell phone; let me walk into my office and view it there. As I'm heading towards the office I'm thinking; *maybe she's sending me a weird light anomaly?* Maybe the teddy bear finally moved? I had no clue it would the Gray Lady?

So, I'm sitting at my desk now. I click the file Niki sent me and scream, wow, that's the Gray Lady, that's her, that's the woman who turned off my office light. That's the female apparition. Niki replies, saying the picture does appear to show something. This is a huge finding, as stated by those who've seen the photo. According to the time stamp, the appearance of the apparition took place while I was downstairs painting my living room. That was yesterday. It was during that time that I decided to turn on the record feature of the Foscam. When you activate the record feature of the device, you turn your Foscam into a video recorder. The hallway and bedroom Foscam were taping that day at the same time; that's how we were able to get it. It would never have occurred that a snapshot of an apparition would come from the bedroom door. But then again, I'm not surprised. That door has been on the receiving end of some violent house attacks. It has been slammed shut so many times. Objects have ricocheted off it so many times and now, a gray apparition. I was excited, as was Niki. Let the vetting process begin, I said, while knowing deep down that this was a darn good find.

Fig 42.1 Master-bedroom door.

The kid's 'cough' and the Gray Lady are equally as important to this case as are the burnt Bibles. The same with the wall markings. They sit above all the other unexplained events taking place within this house. I will never forget that day when Tina and I heard the kid 'cough.' I'll never forget where I was when my office lights went off. That clicking sound. That sound was what made me turn toward the doorway. And there she was: The Gray Lady. This picture would stand side by side with the video apparition I caught back in July of 2014. Nothing strengthens credibility more than collaboration. I'm talking about similar sightings being picked up on different types of technology. In various rooms of the house.

I couldn't help but send a series of thank you emails to Mary, Jen, and Niki, to everyone. For their challenging work thus far. For their commitment to the plan. If you looked at Fig 40.5 closely, you'd know the way I set everything up makes evidence tampering virtually impossible. Niki and Mary were three thousand miles away. They've yet to set foot in the house. They were using my cameras. The video and audio files they combed came from my cameras. Try not to think of this as your normal paranormal investigation. Most paranormal investigators arrive at your home with their equipment. They set up and monitor your house for a few hours and then leave. It takes days, sometimes weeks before you hear back from them. The reason it takes that long is because they have to review everything. And by review, I mean listen to the audio files. Hopefully, they come back to you with what they found. Hopefully.

Now Niki and Mary are on the East Coast. They don't have the luxury of bringing in their camera equipment or any other device for that matter. All they have is their eyes and ears—and the Foscam lens of course

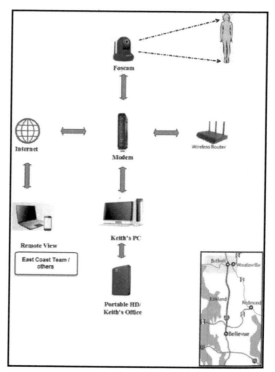

Fig 42.2 How information is shared – Internet / Email

Someone else on our team would have found the Gray Lady photo, based on the fact that it was in the cloud, i.e., the internet (see Fig 40.5, 42.2). Remember, everybody gets the same photo if and when motion or sound is detected. Niki's, Mary's, and now Karissa Fleck's emails are configured into the Foscam, as is my email address. They have visitor permission, i.e., read-only access. They can view the house to their heart's content. But that's all they can do. No one, and I mean no one, can sneak in something that the camera didn't detect.

Still though, we have collective information sharing, and collective vetting, it was Mary who'd said "put a camera in the bedroom. Leave it on constantly and maybe we'll get lucky." And she was right. We got lucky. And then it was Niki—just coming off her graveyard shift—who found the photo.

So, we're back to the question of why this house? Why not my neighbor's house? This phase of the investigation is less technical. It involves looking up a lot of things, beginning with the house itself. Records show no one's died in the home, that's good. We're all aware how long it takes to research something. Niki asked one of her consultants to get right on it—find whatever you can about the house. About the city. About the neighborhood and about the Native Americans that once lived here. Why would a poltergeist go out of its way to draw an upside-down man? I can't find any case where that's happened before. The search for what's causing this continues.

Chapter 43
"Geist"

The day I heard the sound of an attic door lowering will be forever in my memory. How can I forget? My grandmother in Houston had an attic like that when we were growing up—the metal springs are what I remember the most about it. The sound is very distinct; you only hear it when the ladder unfolds. These types of attic ladders, the ones with the pull-down string, are extremely heavy and extremely dangerous if not handled correctly. Our elders told us to stay away from them. "Don't pull that string."

The second thing I remember is those old storage chests. We used to call them giant suitcases. My grandparents had plenty of them in their house when we were growing up. They sat at the foot of every bed. One per bedroom. You knew how good one was by how much it weighed.

My grandmother would occasionally ask my brother and me to move one from one side of the room to the other. Being that they were heavy, brother and I decided just to drag them—grab onto the side latches and pull it across the room. And that's when you heard another distinctive sound. The latches are swinging up/down or left/right against the chest itself. Creating its unique noise. Damn, those things were heavy.

I spoke about these noises earlier in the book. It's what I heard when I was monitoring the house myself last year. I even told you how they start off gradual, and then build up to what I can only describe as unbelievable. I know these sounds are real because the hallway Foscam would all of a sudden send sound-detected email alerts. The sound is its mystery. It's impossible to define, except to say that it's real. I've sat and listened to the noise several times, so will you in a few seconds. Now, the second part of the riddle is almost as weird as the first part, maybe weirder. It's weird because it defies logic—it literary throws into question what we know about the laws of physics. The laws of sound.

Imagine you're home by yourself. You hear a loud crash. Something big has just hit something. That how loud it was. You turn towards the direction of the sound and see nothing. Thirty minutes later you walk by the area you recently searched and see a new hole in the wall. Debris is everywhere. It could be a flower pot, a vase, a sage tray, a candle, a bowl, or whatever.

The reason we're talking about this again is that Mary and Niki are about to experience what I just mentioned. They're about to experience one of the weirdest events in our house. The furniture being dragged wonder— sound which no one is making; the sounds of furniture being dragged around, or an attic ladder coming down. Except that my house doesn't have an attic ladder, and I don't have storage

323

chests. Watch all my videos, and you'll see there's nothing in our house that will even come close to explaining what it is you're about to hear.

The day Niki and Mary heard that was the day they both were monitoring the hallway. I got an instant message through Skype that something was going on at the house. I thought they were having technical difficulties, but it turns out they weren't. What got everyone excited was the number of emails coming in—sound has been detected—hallway camera. The ladies heard the noise within seconds of logging in. Our chief consultant Dominick was logged in as well. He heard everything. And let me tell you the noise became so rampant, so obvious that I too had to log in. Everybody's Skype was blowing up. And it sounds exactly how I described it. An attic ladder lowering, somewhat incorrectly, because of the loud boom. This lasted for a while. The sound of something being dragged around, e.g., a storage chest, happens a few minutes later. It's like someone opened up their attic, by lowering the ladder. Now they're moving something, something heavy. Think of it as drag, drag, drag, latch swinging back and forth, latch swinging back and forth, drag, drag, latches swinging back and forth, thud, thud, attic ladder moving up and down, the metal springs contracting or expanding. That's my narration of the sound. Niki and Mary spent days on this.

House Activity (best with headsets)	Live Sounds: Rapping's, Thuds, Snaps, ladder door, and furniture moving sound.
https://www.youtube.com/watch?v=y9SuwZcXddM	Time Stamps 1:10, 12:09, 3:18, 3:52, 5:14,5:55, 6:26, choppiness, 6:57, 7:00, 7:33, 11:18,16:55, 19:11, 19:26, 20:08, 21:49, 21:55, 22:00, **22:28, 24:28,** choppiness sounds return, knocks, **24:55, 25:58,** 27:04, subtle noises, taps near the camera or mic, continuous low sound, timid taps, tapping **25:00 - 28:00, 30:00, 30:50,** 30:56, 31:40, taps, movement, noises, taps, 32:08, 33:01, 36:50, 38:26, subtle taps, faint taps, faint taps close to camera or mic, static, interference, 39:00, **39:20, 39:27,** new noise, **40:00, 40:58,** tap, tap, tap, cont.....
https://www.youtube.com/watch?v=r5nkckHHCa4	**4:00** Major noise. **4:26** Sound triggers Foscam (beep alert, sound has been detected). **5:08, 6:14** loud noise triggers another FOSCAM alert. Skype chatter can be heard as all team members are notified and are observing the room LIVE. 6:54, 7:18,
https://www.youtube.com/watch?v=ngBtcaRFsjw&t=420s	4:52, 5:42, 6:51, 9:43,

Table 43.1 Furniture being dragged sounds.

Hopefully, you were able to listen to all of those through headphones. It's the best way to appreciate this stuff. Remember, I was not at home. You're hearing what Niki and Mary heard that day while monitoring the house. I mean we're a team, so when someone hears it, they immediately notify somebody else. If you listened to every video (from start to finish, before cutting to just the time-stamps provided) you'll be able to see just how abrupt the sounds are. They come without warning. Those are just snippets of what Tina and I heard. The fact that Niki and Mary are hearing this live, with me not being home is remarkable. This "Geist" is carrying out activity without anybody being home. How is that possible? What's good about this phenomenon is the ladies are hearing what I described a year ago. It's in my notes. It's on various paranormal websites. They're now hearing it live.

The ladies ended up compiling over six hours of footage that week. All of it relates to the events I've just described. That wonder more than others I've witnessed has gotten to me. I mean there's a lot of stuff in this house that keeps me up at night. This isn't one of them. I wish I could show you a lamp flying across the room. I wish I could show you an armoire being swung from one side of the room to the other. I can't; the paranormal doesn't work like that. The spirit owns the right to those violent acts. This is different. We recorded this, and to a degree were able to predict when it would occur again. It happened a few days in a row. It lasted a lot longer than an object flying across the room. That has to mean something, right?

The reader should take it upon themselves to google the term "furniture being dragged." Add the words *poltergeist* or *paranormal* and see what results you get. You'll find what I've been reporting has been previously reported in other poltergeist-like cases. A paranormal researcher would do his/herself credit if they chose to invest in studying this phenomenon versus chasing orbs. There's something about these sounds that's off-putting. They seem to not belong in our time period. They seem manufactured, i.e. orchestrated in a way that goes far beyond the word paranormal. Might not be as sexy as listening to voice boxes but trust me, there's a lot of there, there. These files are available to anyone who wants them. Dissect them as much as you want. Get back to me. Get back to the paranormal community.

When I got home that night, I decided to do something I haven't done in a while. I decided to not worry about what would happen to me if I began researching at home. No more sleeping on the living floor. No more sleeping on the couch. I mean, lately, the only time I slept in my bed was when Niki was monitoring me. That was the only time you found me sleeping in my bed.

That had to change. I had to take control of my house. I have to start going into every room again, including my office. I have to stay there longer than two minutes. I have to stop sleeping with every light on in the house. I have to stop doing a lot of things that in my opinion are not only feeding my fears but also feeding my ignorance. The spirits in this house feed on fear and ignorance. I have to stop being an enabler. Niki and Mary had walked me back from the ledge of constantly looking over my shoulder. Their professionalism and consistency removed some of the eggshells that formed around me. I have to remove the rest. There's only one name on the lease agreement now. I'm the only person who has a legal right to be here. It's time to learn who these squatters are. It's time to learn everything there is to know about the phenomenon known as poltergeists.

I walked into my office that night and sat down at my computer desk and did something I haven't done in months. I booted up my laptop and began searching on Amazon for books about poltergeists. The first book to catch my eye was titled "The Poltergeist Phenomenon: An In-depth Investigation into Floating Beds, Smashing Glass, and Other Unexplained Disturbances" by Michael Clarkson. I thought to myself, *wow, this guy must have lived in my house before. His title matches what we've witnessed and experienced over the last three years.* I ordered his book and finished reading it in a matter of days. It left quite an impression on me. I mean, here's a guy who's done his research.

According to Michael, this phenomenon takes place more often than people realize. It's under-reported, or better yet, it's mischaracterized. Clarkson tells us: "the first poltergeist was reported as early as 858 BC in a farmhouse in Rhine, Germany, where an unseen force reportedly threw stones, shook walls, moved objects, and produced loud banging noises." Click or type the link below for a quick understanding of what a poltergeist is.

http://web.newworldencyclopedia.org/entry/Poltergeist

Michael's book provided me with a detailed listing of multiple cases throughout history. I mean, we're talking 1st- century stuff. B.C., A.D you name it, there's a reported case in every calendar month, one on nearly every continent from 800 B.C to today. Every one of them resembles mine and Tina's situation. *I'll be damned; King Solomon was right. There isn't anything new under the sun.* The more I read, the more my fear began to subside. I was telling myself over and over, knowledge is power, knowledge is power, knowledge is power—and I'm starting to believe it. My dad told me a long time ago that "Knowledge is power." The more you know about something, the less inclined you are to fear it. Not only am I gaining insight into the phenomenon known as a poltergeist. I'm also gaining insight into the people who experienced it. What they experienced and what we experienced can be summed up in two words: Pure hell.

One word comes to mind as to what the book is doing. Empowerment. The book is telling me it's OK to ask questions. It's OK to be frightened. Priests have been frightened. Rabbis and monks have been frightened. Police, firefighters, and others who descend on the homes that are infested with poltergeist have been frightened. *Now, take that fear and turn it upside down.* Try to ascertain what is happening, in addition to ascertaining why it's happening. There's not a case in Michael Clarkston's book that I can't relate to.

Of course, theory is one thing; reality is another. Don't get me wrong: to not fear these things is easier said than done. They've become masters at unpredictability. I mean, what's more terrifying, a fire in your office or an invisible force running past you after the fire has started? What's more terrifying, a flying ironing board or a flying bar stool? If those things were to happen right now, I would be terrified. The book can't solve that problem. The book gave me something I had not yet had. Intelligence. Intelligence about the events Tina and

I had experienced. Certain names were popping up in my research—ones that I'd been oblivious to, until now. Certain titles and certain professions. The discipline I kept coming across was that of a parapsychologist. This community above any other seems to understand the existence of poltergeists. I mean, the jury is still out as to what causes this. Multiple theories are being floated about. That's fine; I can deal with that. Every case has its similarities and every case its differentiator. It's hard to nail down cause when the differentiator varies from outbreak to outbreak.

Now Michael Clarkston didn't write the book by himself; he had to go out and find the information. And it's not readily available. News clippings aside, where else can you find historical data about the phenomenon known as poltergeists? He had to have reached out to a group of people, an organization who through their research kept an up to date repository. If an organization like that exists (*and I hope to God one does*), that to me would be the closest thing to evidence retention. Every investigator that's come to my house has come with the intention of gathering evidence. Very few have possessed the mindset of retaining that evidence. You keep it, so it can be studied later. Paranormal evidence should be shared not quarantined; not lost. There's nothing more embarrassing than me (the house occupant) getting an email from a paranormal researcher asking for a file they sent me days ago. They've lost there's so they're asking for mine again. Or worse I'm asking for a file I was promised and given the runaround.

I'm very proud of Niki and Mary. I'm proud they felt a need to contact me. I'm proud they felt a need to get the true story. Mary knew immediately after the airing of the "Demons in Seattle" episode that there was more to this case than meets the eye. I like to think we've proven that by now. We have a lot of data. But we haven't even scratched the surface. We still have substance on the wall that has yet to be analyzed. Measurements of the holes in the wall still need to be taken. Electromagnetic field readings of the hallway. EMF readings of the bed I'm sleeping in. None of that's been done yet. Loads and loads of files that we have yet to analyze for possible electronic voice phenomenon. But that only explains one half of the retention side. The other half involves saving the data for future technologies. Future analysis. Is there an organization out there doing that? Is there a group of people out there who've adopted best practices when it comes to "Geist" phenomenon? The author must have interviewed a lot of people when writing his book. I need to speak to one of those people. What better place to look than to the resources in the back pages of his book?

One of the names that kept coming up throughout Michael's book was the name, UK Steve Mera. The Scientific Establishment of Parapsychology or MAPIT as it's called. This organization is led by parapsychologists Steve Mera supposedly has cataloged an inordinate amount of poltergeist cases the world over. And I'm not talking about just the Enfield case, (which I noticed seems to be the only case people want to talk about.)

One case, in particular, sparked my curiosity the most, probably because of the events that family experienced, was the one that involved Maria José Ferreira. Who is Maria José Ferreira? She's one of the women I dedicate this book too. December 1965, in Jabuticabal, 220 miles from São Paulo, Brazil, a respectable Catholic family became the center of malicious and violent poltergeist activity. Their hell began when pieces of brick began falling inside the house, seemingly from nowhere. A local priest attempted an exorcism, but this only made things worse. Sound familiar? The attacks seemed to center on the young daughter, Maria. She seemed to be the so-called "agent"—the cause as to why the events are even happening. One of the things she experienced that I could relate to was her clothes catching fire. The eerie thing about that event, besides the actual clothes catching fire, is the cigar burn marks on her clothing. Tina can attest that I had similar burn marks on my clothing weeks before *Ghost Adventures* arrived. I don't know what I would have done had my clothes ignited. Maria's did, unfortunately, and that ladies and gentlemen, are what makes living through a "Geist" attack so horrifying. Maria's clothes caught fire while at school. Mine semi-ignited while standing in my hallway.

Let Maria José Ferreira's story be an example of what hell feels like. Imagine having zero options. No one knows what to do. You pay the price for those around you not having the ability to diagnose you correctly. The demon attacks you more versus attacking those trying to help. Death feels better than living.

The Maria José Ferreira - Poltergeist Case
http://istina.rin.ru/cgi-bin/eng/print.pl?sait=1&id=311

I couldn't even begin to imagine what I would have done had I been a teenager living through this. Our ridicule, isolation, and feeling of helplessness pales in comparison to Maria's. Compare 1965 to 2015. How far have we come in understanding the poltergeist? What are they? Who are they and I know it doesn't make much sense, but I have to say it anyways—why are they? Why Maria José Ferreira? Why Jane Doe's family? Why Tina? Why me? Why countless other people? My question to the organizations that study this. Why no advancement in the study? I'm talking to you, Mr. and Mrs. Paranormal Researcher. Mr. and Mrs. Parapsychologist. Let me contact Steve's organization. Let's see what they know.

Chapter 44
Psi

Ψ

It shocked me to get an email from Steve Mera—we're talking about an email all the way from the United Kingdom. I'd been emailing parapsychology organizations for weeks now. I'm talking about undeliverable email, after undeliverable email from multiple websites that say, 'contact us if you need help.' It's hard to contact you if your website doesn't work.

Why am I emailing parapsychology organizations? Short answer: My garage door raises by itself when I leave the house in the morning. I hear it going up as I'm coming downstairs for the first time. Most people hit that panel before getting into their car. The door raises, you back out and stop at the driveway. You then hit the garage fob on your sun visor and watch the door lower—you drive off. That's what I used to do. My garage door raises on its own now. It's like it knows when I'm about to leave the house. There have been mornings where it's already up. And these are not one-time instances. Nor are they garage door malfunctions. That's just one phenomenon out of many that I believe the parapsychology community might be interested in knowing about.

Steve Mera's response to me was short and cordial. He had videos and pictures of everything you've already read about. His reply to me was he would evaluate it; he and his team would get back in touch with me. Now Steve lives in the UK; that's where his organization is. If his response is anything like the response I got from US teams, then I'm pretty sure I won't be hearing from him again. Every time I send somebody an email about what Tina and I been through I can almost hear them say, "This is too good to be true, therefore, it must be a hoax. No way could a person survive something like this; oh, and that 666-writing stuff, that proves it's fake."

That's been the response from many teams, including parapsychologists. To use a bad expression, *what do I have to lose*? I have to keep casting my stone. Someone, upon seeing this stuff, is going to fall out of their chair and say, this is an unusual type of poltergeist. And guess what? Someone finally did. Two people: Steve Mera and his chief researcher, Don Philips.

I got another email from Steve a few days later asking me if I would agree to an interview. My response to him was, sure I'll be interviewed. In response, Steve explained that the interview wouldn't be with him, but with his colleague, Don Philips. Though I hadn't come across Don Philips yet, it was clear that Steve valued his opinion. It didn't take me long to realize that Steve Mera is a man of few words. He keeps his correspondence down to just one sentence. It irritated at me first, because I'm like, "Dude, my garage door goes up and down by itself. My toothbrush is never in the same spot when I get up in the morning. Neither are my car keys. Lights go off and on by themselves throughout the house. And all you got for me are these one-line sentences?"

We have a saying in Texas: "this is not my first rodeo." Everything I've sent Steve, he's probably seen or heard before. He's a parapsychologist; he's an analytical thinker. He's shrewd, and he's cautious. No way is he going to book a plane ticket without first running me through a few filters. Every investigator I've come in contact with, with the exception of Jennifer, Niki, and Mary have viewed our claims as being suspicious at first. It's like you're a hoax until proven otherwise. Steve's short email replies are going to have to do for now.

Don Philips is the total opposite. I mean, the men are different as night and day. Steve reminds me of Spock, and Don reminds me of Captain Kirk. One is very procedural, keeps everything close to his vest, and the other is very charismatic, authoritative, very easy going. I remember how my first Skype conversation went with Don. It went smooth. I knew why Steve had chosen him within seconds of us chatting.

You see, Don was a spiritual man; his persona was multi-dimensional, connected, and very down to earth. I couldn't help but think he's connected to something. And by connected, I mean dialed in. I'm not sure what it is, but if I had to guess I would have to say he's less instrumental and more spiritual when it comes to evidence gathering. I went to bed that night thinking to myself, *Keith, you have to be out of your mind; you're trying to invite a scientific organization into your home? These spirits made you and Tina look like a fool in front of Ghost Adventures. Imagine what they'll do with a parapsychology team. These guys are going to have you committed. I mean, the bar is extremely high where parapsychologists are concerned.*

Still: even with level one activity I was experiencing, Niki's team was still capturing a lot of data—the house is still being monitored. And we have a backlog now. The ladies cup runneth over in regard to the evidence they were gathering. And that's just from them monitoring a house that by all definition is simply a level one home—a low level one at that. Don Philips told me during our conversation that he and Steve were currently reviewing the evidence I sent them. It'll never be said that I wasn't a good record keeper. Thanks, Dad. Thanks, ITIL. Thanks, PMI. I'm beginning to feel blessed in knowing what my role is through all of this.

My role as house occupant is to answer questions. I have to make myself available to you and your organization when the need arises. That's my role. Some of you have made that nearly impossible based on how disorganized you are. Based on your in-fighting and siloed mentality. The homeowner has already given me permission to seek help. He wants answers as much as I do. There's a lot going on here, which I believe deserves the attention of the parapsychology community (if that community even exists).

I went to bed that night with Niki and Mary watching me. I'm thinking to myself, if Steve and Don are who I think they are, then they have their work cut out for them. And you know what? That's a good thing. What I've learned about parapsychologists so far makes me believe they're a little more disciplined than your average paranormal team. A little more meticulous. A little more conservative. Whether that's a strength or a weakness with this case remains to be seen. I hope they say yes, I really do. Niki and her team have been spot on so far. Whatever they find combined with whatever Steve and Don find should keep the paranormal community busy for quite some time. The question both sides will have to answer, i.e., reconcile with is, how has the "Geist" been able to sustain itself?

November 2015. The Washington State Poltergeist case was well into its fifth month. I think now would be a good time to give everyone a shore leave. The timing was perfect. One team member was beginning to show signs of irritation, becoming irritable as a result of the cameras constantly malfunctioning. You see, that's how it starts. It starts with the little things. Those little things eventually become bigger things. I know all too well how irritating it can be when you're trying to view something and all of a sudden, Bam! You've lost visibility. There's a reason for that; it's called manipulation. Mary's favorite room for home monitoring has always been the hallway. Niki's favorite room has always been the bedroom. Both ladies were having problems getting into the room they loved the most. Not the other rooms. Just the rooms they were particularly interested in. The hallway and office were my favorite rooms to monitor when I was doing this a year ago. It irritated me that they could erase my config within seconds of me setting my cameras up. Both ladies are living witnesses as to how that feels. It sucks.

We've gotten multiple bangs on video. Multiple sounds of furniture being dragged around. We've captured voices, and we've captured screams. Not to be overlooked is my bedroom. Niki has been monitoring my sleep for two months now. She's captured the rapping, the knocks, and the loud thuds. She can't capture the poking and prodding stuff. But she can see how much I'm tossing and turning at night. She can see my sheets moving while I sleep. She can see me sort of fight something off? She can see the night terrors and the bad dreams. She can hear something tapping on the headboard, and she can hear the loud boom! That and more is on video. It's on audio, and it's on digital.

There's one thing I have to stay on top of. One thing I can't afford to be caught flat-footed on. That's bad energy. Activity spiking in and around the house as a result of people getting frustrated with their camera equipment. The spirit that wrote Die KL is still here aka the minions. I noticed Mary's fuse was getting shorter every time her favorite camera went offline. The spirits began to notice as well. Heck, they were the ones causing it. So, on that note: shore leave for everyone. Let's pause the monitoring for now. I mean we have enough data we still haven't reviewed. A backlog if you can believe that. Let's focus on that as a means of keeping the tensions down. I can't afford to have my armoire go flying across the room again. Not if I can help it.

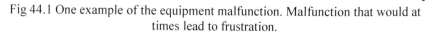

Friday, September 04, 2015

weird — 3:20 PM

I give up honestly — 3:21 PM
I should just go up and go to bed

other cams work, just sound... — 3:21 PM
and it might come back
just have to keep trying intermittantly
we're dealing with extreme intelligence and its putting up road blocks
none of this is new to me

the fav cams r being messed with, im looking for the url for the kitchen, one i gave — 3:24 PM
is internal

Yeah and I can't pull it up — 3:25 PM

Fig 44.1 One example of the equipment malfunction. Malfunction that would at times lead to frustration.

December 2015: I received another email from Steve Mera. The Scientific Establishment of Parapsychology wants to investigate my house. Their reasoning being, if what I'm saying is true, this could potentially be the most active poltergeist house in the history of poltergeist.

There's enough data to support my claim that something is going on. They can't say for sure what it is until they arrive. I've not told them about the investigation that's been going on. It's none of their business—not right now it isn't. I've been around enough teams to know neither puts much stock in the other team's findings.

Steve and Don don't need to know right now what Niki and her team have found. The only thing Steve and Don need to know right now is that they have their work cut for them. Steve informed me via email that it would be him and Don coming. "Can we live in the house for a few days?" My answer to them was a yes. You most certainly can; how soon will you guys be here? Steve's answer was: January. "We'll be there at the end of January."

How many teams have I tried to get over here in the past six months? Lots! How many parapsychology organizations? Lots! How many "we're too busy" emails did I receive? Lots! How many "Seattle is too far away," emails did I receive? Lots! My response to emails where geography was an excuse for not investigating the house is sharp and blunt—you've picked the wrong field.

Steve and Don's involvement was good news. This house deserved scrutiny from the parapsychology discipline. I mean, we can go all the way back to the humming noise. We can go all the way back to the Katie Perry weekend. We can't forget the exploding light fixtures. We can't forget the wall writings, the puddles of water, the spontaneous fires, and the one that's forever bothering me: the poking and prodding I feel while sleeping.

Niki's team had done a tremendous job in how they conducted the home monitoring. I mean, you heard the loud bangs? Those bangs came from the ceiling above me. There's no confusion whatsoever as to if I'm asleep or awake. I'm asleep, and I've been asleep a while. The bangs jolt me awake. That is just a glimpse of what Tina and lived through. I hoped to God, Steve and Don can get to the bottom of this. I hoped they can substantiate my claims. I wanted them to do the same thing that Niki and her team were doing. I wanted them to help the world understand that Tina was never the agent, as *Ghost Adventures* tried to imply. Zak Bagan's accusation was not scientific; it's innuendo. Zak knows that, his audience doesn't. I wanted Don and Steve to gather enough evidence that it becomes crystal clear: just because one team doesn't find anything, doesn't mean the house occupants are liars.

You can't say we were lying when you wrote the words "No Evidence" towards the end of the show. Leaving empty handed means leaves empty handed, doesn't prove fraud, not one bit.

Substantiating our claims and hopefully coming up with a cause as to why all this stuff is happening is my only reasons for doing this. Thank you, Michael Clarkson! Knowledge is power. The parapsychology discipline is coming to the Bothell Hell House.

Chapter 45
Attachments

Jane Doe told me her relationship with her husband had taken a turn for the worse again. Things seemed to be spiraling out of control where they lived. Not in a paranormal sense. In a domestic sense. I didn't have the heart to tell her that Tina and I had broken up. No sense pouring bad news on top of bad news. Jane Doe had become distraught and depressed over her family's current domestic situation—to the point of maybe moving back to Seattle. It was during that time that the question arose of her and me meeting face to face. That's how often we talked at the beginning of our friendship. She was going to be in Seattle soon— "let's meet for coffee?" I was nervous about that. My biggest fear was whatever attachment I might have would begin seeping into Jane Doe's current home situation. Malevolent spirits are opportunists—whatever problems Jane Doe was having at home the spirits will latch unto. The chance of any of that returning to where she is now lived is what keeps from arranging a face to face meeting.

But man, did we talk and laugh a lot, in spite of what we both were going through currently. Jane Doe felt Tina and I were achieving what her family couldn't, which was: don't run, stay in the house and fight these bastards. I wanted to tell her so badly how Tina and I failed as well. How nothing seemed to work. But I didn't. I want to be clear about something else. Jane Doe had labeled the house "the house from hell." Jane Doe never uttered the word Poltergeist, she never saw a gray lady (she's the Gray Lady), and most importantly they never saw a need to bring a paranormal team in. They did what other would do. They moved. Her words of "the house was a living hell" for me, and my family strengthens my belief that something was there with them. Her son had admitted such when he mentioned dark shadowy figures lurking near him. I didn't have to pry that out of Jane Doe; she volunteered the info. Just like she volunteered the sliding door locking her out of the house—to the point of her breaking the glass in a means of getting back in. Never forget that.

Niki and Mary asked me repeatedly, could they interview Tina. My answer was no. Tina doesn't want to get pulled into anything. She's lost faith in the paranormal discipline. Whatever rehabilitation or fact-finding mission you guys decide to take on, it will not involve Tina. I don't care if Tina and I reconciled today, she's not to be messed with. Tina wants nothing to do with paranormal teams and rightfully so.

One of the things Jane Doe and I never talked about (and I guess that's because she and her family weren't experiencing anything paranormal at the time), was the issue of attachments. Paranormal activity happening beyond the Bothell house. I mean, she said her son, the one who almost died when living here, "still sees shadows out the corner of his eye." Keyword being "still-sees." I didn't know what she meant until I began seeing them myself. The generic definition of an attachment is something that follows you from place to place. Are we talking spiritually? Or are we talking physically?

If I have a sheet yanked off me in the middle of the night while I'm in a hotel room, I guess that means I have an attachment. Is it an attachment or is it just me being followed? A lot of people at my job know of my ghost problem. It's kind of hard to keep that a secret. But they don't know everything. No one looked at me weird after I spun around in my chair by an invisible shoulder check assailant. They weren't aware that I sometimes came into the office on the weekends in order to get a few hours' sleep. One of the questions I planned to ask Steve and Don when they get here is: what can haunt two places at once? I'm talking about the same time. Niki and Mary had heard footsteps at my house when I'm out of town. They've heard loud bangs, and they've seen lights go off and on by themselves. Some of the cameras they're viewing from have moved or shut down by themselves. I'm on the other side of the country, on business. And you know what that means? Bed shakes, sheet tugs, sheets pulled down to the ankles and of course, the poking and the prodding. What type of spirit does that?

I'd read a lot of books over the last few months. Books that the parapsychology community respects. Names like Colin Wilson, William G. Roll, and Dr. A.R.G Owens' book, *Can We Explain the Poltergeist?* I know these men are on to something because I've lived it for three years. I've not yet found in their writings something that speaks to "Geist" being in two places at one time.

One night I got a phone call from my attorney (this was during in the middle of one our house attacks – Summer 2014). Tina and I were barely speaking to each other at the time. The house was extremely active that night. The lights are going off and on in every room upstairs. I was capturing this light show with my Foscams, and suddenly my cell phone rang. It was my attorney. She was freaking out tremendously. I mean big time. I asked her what's going on and she told me the lights in her house were going off and on like crazy.

Poltergeist – Light activity
https://www.youtube.com/watch?v=3_I2mfhJnDY

Fig 45.1 Off/On – Off/On

Now, before you leap to the conclusion and say oh that could be anything, remember what my prerequisite is for sharing information. If I'm telling you something happened, that means I've already ruled out the obvious. I'm ninety-nine percent sure it's paranormal, given what she told me previously. My attorney was unloading her groceries one day. She made back and forth trips from the car to the kitchen. She returned to the kitchen a few minutes later and discovered half of her groceries gone. She should have five bags on the table. Instead, she had three.

Now, Tina and I have never experienced disappearing grocery bags. But we have experienced disappearing food. One night we were watching a movie together. I believe it was Tina who, before the movie started, decided to go into the freezer and pull out a frozen chicken for us to eat that night. She set it on the counter, so it could thaw out. An hour or so later I got up to get a refill of wine or something (you know me and my refills). I walked into the kitchen and noticed that the frozen chicken was gone. I asked Tina what happened to it, and she replied, "I set it on the counter." I told her, it's not there anymore; where did you set it?" Tina leaped up from the couch and joined me in the kitchen with a look of "what do you mean it's not in the kitchen, I set it right here?" She pointed to where she set it and guess what? It wasn't there. Now we found the frozen chicken, but you're not going to believe where we found it. We found it under the toaster—literally under the toaster (toaster is sitting on top of a frozen piece of chicken), located on the other side of the kitchen. Now think hard and try to picture what it is I'm describing. I couldn't sit a toaster on a frozen piece of anything (let alone a piece of chicken) if my life depended on it. It would slide off (making a considerable amount of noise). We heard nothing, not such as a twitch coming from the kitchen. I think Tina ended up throwing that frozen bird away after learning that it had been teleported.

Other friends have called me reporting similar instances—unexplained events happening in either their car or their house. It's always the ones that have gone out of their way to mock what Tina and I were going through. To be precise, my friends were not mocking Tina and me. They were mocking the spirits. They were challenging them whenever they came by and visited. One person stopped by my house while on their way to the airport. I warned him not to make fun of the spirits, and he ignored me. Two hours later I got a phone call from him: he can't find his passport. Talk about being inconvenienced. He had to miss his flight because he had no other ID on him. That's what I wanted to ask Steve and Don about. If it's not a "Geist" at work here, then it has to be a minion, and by a minion, I mean a demon. But let's get back to this attachment thing.

My conversations with Jane Doe, combined with what I'm experiencing when not in the home, gave me cause for concern should I finally decide to move out of this house. Jane Doe's son did take his illness with him when they moved. The mysterious meningitis illness. That and the shadowy figures too. The books I mentioned above speak of people who've been followed from point A to point B. And by follow, I mean the violent stuff still happens. It's gotten worse in some cases. Imagine moving to a new location, and the events happening around you is worse than the previous place you lived in. It's almost like they're punishing you or something. Will that happen to me?

The poking and prodding, ladies and gentlemen, is relentless. It's worse this year than it was last year. What proactive measures have I taken to lessen it? Well, Fr. Roy's Sr. house cleansing involved cleansing me too. It slowed the prodding for a few days. Fr. Roy Sr. had agreed to do more until he was told he needed back surgery. What else have I done? Let's see. I've visited shamans. I've been prayed over, danced over, and laid hands on. I've signed up and attended multiple attachment ceremonies. The times vary as to how long they last. I know for a fact that I've done five of those. I guess I won't know until I finally move out of the house, whether I have attachments or not.

Late December 2015. Shore leave is now over. Two months without home monitoring did everybody some good, especially Mary. I could tell she needed it. She had sort of become like me when it came time to watching the house via Foscam. You get addicted. I mean, I totally get it. Not too many people have witnessed what they've witnessed.

You kind of don't want it to end; the house has slowly become the gift that keeps on giving where activity is concerned. Two months of shore leave had meant two months of evidence to review. It was time to discuss what the next steps would look like. What success looks like? It was time to discuss phase two. Everyone agreed that phase one had been a success. There was enough data here to substantiate my claims in regard to the rapping's, weird sounds, light anomalies, apparition sightings, and screams.

So, what is phase two? Phase two involved the ladies coming here. That's right, they were coming here. It was always planned that way. The community these ladies belong to is not going to take these findings seriously if all we have are pictures from CCTV cameras. Don't get me wrong. We've done pretty well so far. Who else out there have videos of furniture moving sounds? Who out there has screams, conversations, lights acting weird, cameras moving by themselves, and apparitions on a wall on multiple hard drives? If anyone else has, they're not sharing the data. Well, guess what? I am. I'm sharing everything.

We reached a decision that night on who was coming. Niki Novelle (Niki), and medium Karissa Fleck. It was discussed early on, that if phase one were to give rise to phase two, that phase two would involve Karissa Fleck coming to Bothell. She would stay for three and a half weeks. Mary and Niki excel in the monitoring department, They're very technical, and they're very protocol oriented. Karissa is a medium; she senses stuff, and she attracts stuff. She's sort of like a spirit agitator. Spirits seem to run to her, for reasons I can't yet explain. It's like she has a Pied Piper effect on them or something. That's my understanding about Karissa. A young woman with unbelievable insight. That's been my perception of her as of late

Niki's going to stay a week in the house. She will rendezvous with Karissa on week two. She and Karissa will be working non-stop for the duration of her trip. Mary and Dominic will be backing them up remotely. That means they'll be monitoring the house while all of us are here. One guy and two ladies living in the Bothell Hell House—you know that's going to trigger something. Let's review what's about to take place. Steve and Don are going to arrive from the United Kingdom at the end of January, 2016. They're going to stay a week. Karissa will be arriving a week after them. So, they'll be a little bit of an overlap. Niki will arrive two weeks later.

The goal is for her and Karissa to conduct round the clock investigations. Niki will be here six days. When she leaves, that'll leave just me and Karissa. One last week of investigating.

I knew what rooms Niki wanted to investigate when she got to my house. The living and bedroom. Karissa wanted to investigate the hallway and guest bedroom. Why the guest bedroom? I have no idea. That's what she wants, and that's what she's going to get. No one had any objections to Steve and Don coming. No one cared. I mean, everyone felt good about the evidence already captured. Now it was time for phase two. Everyone, and I do mean everyone, will be basically tracing over *Ghost Adventures'* footsteps. Both teams are doing something that Zak Bagan's and his crew should have done, which was to live in the house. If you want extraordinary evidence, then you got to be prepared to do extraordinary things.

Can you imagine the evidence *Ghost Adventures* would have gotten had they lived in the house? Not alone, but with Tina and me. If that proof of concept is still foreign to you—wait till you see the evidence both teams are about to uncover.

Chapter 46
Case Ref: 26411

Steve Mera and Don Philips arrived on January 21st, 2016. I decided to go to Hawaii for a well-deserved vacation before both team's arrival. That was my shore leave. I sent an email to both Fr. Roy Sr. and the landlord, letting them know who was coming. The house was going to be empty for eight days. That's how long I was gone. Interesting I had no sheets yanked off my bed when I was Oahu. I wish I could say the same about the poking and prodding. That and the bed vibrations continued, but hey, you got to take what you can get, right?

To accommodate Don and Steve meant I had to be at home for the duration of their investigation. That meant I had to work from home. Six days, that's how long the UK guys would be here. Was I nervous about Steve and Don coming here? Damn, right I was nervous. I'd gone on an eight-day vacation before their arrival. I arrived home two days before they got here. If the house is empty, it usually takes three days—if not more—for the spirits to begin acting up again. Three days after I've arrived back in town. I knew this, and I went out of town anyways. I kept reminding myself over and over; the burden is not on me; the burden is on Steve and Don. I know what my house is capable of. It's capable of a great many things, and those things may or may not present themselves to a parapsychologist and his chief researcher. But I'm optimistic. Niki and her team were very successful. I'm hoping Steve and Don will be also.

So, I was at home waiting for them to arrive at the airport. Steve informed me early on that they had already secured transportation. Their friend, Patty, would be picking them up from SeaTac. *That was a relief.* That gave me time to prepare. Prepare myself mentally for what might happen. The house was ready as can be for both gentlemen. I came home early from work, that day and tidied up everything. All I needed to do now was welcome them in.

It must have been after 8 pm when Steve and Don finally arrived. Their arrival felt like it had been planned for years. I went to open the front door after hearing it ring: there were Steve and Don. I was surprised to get a hug from Steve; our email communications were always short and to the point. Nowhere near as personable as me and Don's. I had the strangest feeling I was on the BBC channel I mean, both men had strong British accents. Now you might be asking yourself why a team would fly all the way from the UK to investigate a house that had been labeled a hoax. Short answer: they found me credible. Steve and Don had screened me for three months before booking their trip. They'd been evaluating me for quite some time, and now here they were. Shorter answer: they know a good case when they see one.

I have to admit I was excited to meet Don. He and I had been having ongoing conversations for weeks now. I turned from Steve, and there was Don. He extended his hand towards me and said, "We're here to find answers; we're here to get to the bottom of this." All I could say at that time was OK. Every team that's come to my house has uttered those words. *Ghost Adventures* said they "wouldn't leave until they got to the bottom of this," and we all know how that turned out. What Don said felt different. It felt sincere. I was beginning to think Don and Karissa might be ahead of the game in the way they view the paranormal. It was important for Don to know as much as possible about me before arriving. I think we chatted every day on Skype up until the time he arrived.

Our conversations were about paranormal stuff and personal stuff. Don never asked me the same question twice; he paid attention. Sixty years of experience had just walked in my door—and with it came loads of equipment. They brought a lot of stuff. It took us three trips to the car and back just to get it all in. *How and the world did you get all this stuff through customs?* The time had finally arrived. The Scientific Establishment of Parapsychology had entered the building. Time to give both men a tour of the house.

I showed Don, Steve, and their friend Patty every room upstairs—even the infamous office. Steve was fascinated with the holes in the hallway. The hallway was still littered with holes. Some I'd patched up, some I hadn't. The wall writings were still bleeding through the primer paint for Steve to see. Leftover ash was still on the floor from the poster fire. Burn marks on the carpet from the countless times Tina and I had smudged. There was a lot for them to see. Imagine two matadors walking into a bull arena. The bulls are nowhere in sight. It's just the two matadors that are present right now. They're surveying the establishment. One of them kneels down and grabs a fist full of dirt. The other matador walks towards the stands and looks around. This is what they live and die for. Somewhere in this stadium, in a corral perhaps, is a bull. A bull that if provoked the scientific way will have no choice but to charge out of the stall and reveal all its feats and tricks. That's how I would describe Steve and Don's tour of the house.

As they looked around, I couldn't help but think, *I wish Tina were here. I wish Tina could have met Don.* These guys are way more receptive than the previous investigators that came here. Don and Steve are not compromising anything by being empathetic, they're not drinking the Kool-Aid, and they're not acting like assholes while being here. Study everybody's body language from the "Demons in Seattle" episode. Study the GAC crew's body language in conjunction with Tina and me. It's obvious we're not on the same team.

Later that night. I decided to show Steve and Don their bedrooms. I'm not sure how the rooms got chosen, but Steve ended up getting the room closest to my office. The room the white lady darted into. Don got the room where the armoire was. That's the room Karissa will be in when she arrives.

So, we were back downstairs now. Patty said her goodbyes and departed. Don and Steve then realize they didn't bring any personal effects. "Would it be OK if we all ran to the store really quick?" I'm like, sure, let's go. So, we're off to the neighborhood grocery store to pick up some personal effects for the men.

An hour later we were heading back from the store. Whatever anxiety I had about these men finding evidence was about to disappear as I drove up to my street. I pulled up the driveway, and Steve says, "the front door is open." Whatever small talk we had while driving home was suddenly put on the back burner. Everyone was looking at the front door. And it was open alright. I mean we were gone no more than an hour.

Now, I've seen this movie before. Coming home and finding my front door open is nothing new. Just to be clear, the front door wasn't open the entire time that we were gone. Oh no, the spirits are smart; they would never expose my house like that. No, the front door was opened tonight within seconds of us pulling up to the driveway. It had happened to me before. This wasn't a coincidence; I'm a hundred percent sure of it. Remember that morning when my neighbor knocked on my door to tell my car doors were open? The 5 am knock on my door that woke up Tina and me. Take note. The contents of my trunk that morning was warm, not cold. Dry, not wet. It had rained that night, and my trunk was wide open. But everything was dry inside, which makes me believe the spirit did that within a few minutes of us waking up. Same thing with the garage door going up in the morning. Something I encountered before Tina moving out.

Narration: I'm grabbing my laptop, turning on the ADT security system. I open the door that leads to my garage and guess what I see? The garage door is open. But it gets weirder than that. I'm coming home from work. I reach the street I live on and drive up towards my house. Before I can even lower my sun visor to access my garage door opener, I see my garage door go up on its own. I mean, it's literally going up on its own, no help from me. It's almost as if they were welcoming me back home. Or better yet, that they were expecting me. So, I knew what this meant when I saw the front door open as Steve, Don and I pulled up to the house. This was the spirits' way of welcoming Don and Steve. Their way of saying *come on in, gentlemen, we've already rummaged through your crates of goodies, let's get this party started.*

I knew then and there that these men were in for the investigation of their lives. "Welcome to Wonderland," gentlemen, and remember, you're no longer in Kansas. As we walked in the house, Steve asked me if this had happened before. I could only smirk at him and say, "Oh, this is nothing." Steve must have found it interesting because I saw him do something I've never seen another investigator do (when inside my house). I saw him write something down. I thought to myself, *wow, an actual investigator taking notes while on an investigation—who would have thought?*

The investigation of my home had officially begun. The entities in the home were on their game; it was time for Steve and Don to get on theirs. Don and Steve began unpacking their stuff. It took them awhile, before realizing how late it was. These men had just flown from the UK. It was best to rest now; hit the ground tomorrow. There'd be no letting up once they got up in that morning.

I have to admit; it felt good to have somebody in the house with me. I was in my room, and they were in theirs, goodnight world. Around 5 am, I heard a door slam that sounded like it came from the hallway. I learned later that morning that Steve was lying in his bed taking notes when the sound occurred. I rose up a few hours later and saw Steve sitting downstairs at his computer downloading stuff. I asked him, "Did you hear that noise?" He replied, "Yeah" and acknowledged that everyone's door was closed when it occurred. I saw Steve write that event down on his notepad. I'm thinking to myself, *hmmm how astute of Steve to have heard that noise—to have written it down.*

The men haven't even been in the house twelve hours yet and have already experienced a front door open by itself. Steve heard a loud door slam, and knew it wasn't me. Their next encounter would be absolutely mind-blowing—even for me. Time to get the coffee going.

Time to set up my workspace at the kitchen table. That's my spot for the duration of their investigation. I'm sitting here on purpose (at the kitchen table) so they know where I'm at all times.

Fig 46.1 I purposely went out of my way to make myself visible at all times during the course of their investigation.

When Don Philips woke up that morning his mission seemed somewhat different than Steve's. I attribute that to both men having different strengths. Picture Spock investigating my house; that's who Steve reminds me of. Picture Captain Kirk beaming into the middle of my living room—that's how Don is. Both men seemed to know when to partner up and when to separate, each one owning his facet of the investigation. They tag team a lot (instigated by Don), and they break apart.

A few hours later Don came walking up to me and requested something I wasn't expecting. He asked to see the burnt Bibles. I was taken aback. No one's ever asked for the Bibles before. I'm not talking about asking for them to hold them. No one's ever asked to study them—to analyze them up close and personal.

So, I marched upstairs to my office, unlocked the safe, and grabbed the three Bibles. I came back down and set them on the kitchen table. Both men began looking them over. I thought to myself; *no other team has asked me specifically for these Bibles*, let alone inspect them in the manner in which Don and Steve did. I mean, let's talk it about it for a second. These Bibles in one sense have been a curse for Tina and me. We introduced them to the paranormal community with the hopes of the community knowing what to do with them. No paranormal organization has yet to exercise their intellectual curiosity by studying the Bibles. You can tell by looking at them that each Bible has been burnt differently; there has to be a reason for that? I mean, they were taken differently, and they were burnt differently—does anyone care why and how? Apparently, Steve and Don do.

The first thing Steve and Don did when viewing the Bibles was inspect the pages. We're talking about pages within each book that were severely burned. What was interesting about them is the manner in which they were burned. The burn marks on each page seemed oddly confined. Confined in a way that suggests an inordinate amount of focus. Extreme intent. Don picked up one of the Bibles and did something that almost made me throw up my coffee. He began tearing out pages. Don was ripping out pages from the Bible—while fumbling for his cigarette lighter. Steve was standing right next to him. Both men looked at me and asked, "Is it OK if we go outside on your patio? We'd like to test something." That's what Steve says.

I was shocked at the question. It never occurred to me that someone would do what Steve and Don were requesting to do. I paused for a second.

I wasn't sure if I should say yes. I mean I'm a southern boy; my grandfather was a Baptist minister—are you going to burn these Bibles? *Calm down, Keith, calm down; this is a scientific experiment, Quantico would be doing the same thing if these Bibles were in their possession.* Then it hit me. These men traveled across the Atlantic Ocean to get to the bottom of things. There comes a moment in one's life where you have to recognize the now. The only thing you're required to do when now arrives is get out of its way. Don't interfere; just get out of the way. Don't even try to understand it. That's exactly what I did. My reply to Steve and Don was, "Yes. you want to go outside to the patio? Be my guest. I'm going to make some more coffee."

The men spent a lot of time on the Bibles. The conversation they were having as they walked back into the house was, "It would be hard for a human to do this." Not to burn a Bible (of course not) No, it would be hard for a human being to burn these Bibles in the manner in which these were burned. Especially the last two. It then dawned on me that this might be the perfect time to remind Steve to where the third Bible was found. I mean, if the Bible is worth looking at, then it's worth looking at where Tina and I found it. Hallway bookshelf. Follow me, gentlemen; we're going upstairs.

Fig 46.2 The two Bibles that were of interest to Steve and Don. The manner in which they were burned is interesting.

So, I show Steve and Don where the third Bible was when it got burned. *This is the Bible I came home to and discovered after a series of motion detected email alerts.* Now, the walls around the bookshelf have suffered heavy casualties over the years. Candles have hit them, as well as other projectiles. The bookshelf, saving a nick or two, is relatively unscathed. There are no burn marks, no scorch marks or anything. Nothing that would suggest a book caught fire here. Remember, we were not home when this Bible was burned.

The question I had for Steve and Don was: the area around the Bible is clean as a whistle. How is that possible? I'm pretty sure the book hadn't been moved when it burned. But that begs the question: How did the spirits burn it? There's no damage whatsoever to the bookshelf that the Bible rests on) nor to the shelf above or the wall behind it. No smoke damage, no fire damage. Not one jot of ash was on the carpet when I got home. Judge for yourself from this video (below).

May 18th, 2014 – 3rd Bible Burning
https://youtu.be/CjkYw2kleBU

I'm hoping Steve and Don can provide some answers as to what is going on, while at the same time appreciate the ground, they're walking on. Science should have an explanation as to how a book can get burned like this. Everything you saw in that video happened while Tina and I were gone. What does that mean? Where is the "Geist" getting its energy from? Is it a "Geist?" Steve and Don were in awe at the mere mechanics of it. Welcome to my world. I've been in awe at the mechanics of it for over three years.

So, we're back downstairs now. I was back on my laptop. Don was messing with cameras and Steve was listening to last night's audio files. An hour later Steve spun around on the stool and instructed Don and me to come over. He was grinning. "I've got something." I have no clue what he's talking about, but somewhere during our dialogue, I must have approved him putting headphones on my ears. He wants me to hear something. I hear silence at first, and then suddenly the words: 'removed our pillow.' A female whisper? I look at Steve, who right now has a giddy grin on his face. What was the heck that? I ask. "That's them," Steve replied. I was thinking to myself *what do you mean, that's them? What's them? Who is them!* Steve plays it for me again in loop fashion. Who stole what pillow? I asked. Steve looked at me and Don shrugged. "Someone removed someone's pillow" (see fig 47.1). Steve took the headphones from me and put them on Don's head, hitting play again. Don says something to the effect of "wow," and begins laughing. Steve and I are asking ourselves the question, when did EVPs become so hysterically funny? Evidently, Don thinks this one is. Don finally got control of his laughing and asked Steve to play the recording again. Steve does; and once again, Don smirked and laughed. Steve said, "that's a good EVP, that's super clear; that's a clear audible."

Finally, Don placed the headphone on the kitchen counter and began clueing us in as to why he was laughing. I mean, he was busting a gut. Turns out, sometime during the night, when we all were sleeping, Don says that he, being somewhat of a two-pillow guy, decided to take it upon himself to sneak into Steve's room. He steals a pillow off Steve's bed. Steve was asleep and didn't notice.

I was immediately impressed. Impressed by the swiftness of their equipment set up—just in, straight off the plane. Steve and Don had set up listening surveillance throughout the house. They did this before they went to bed. The last paranormal team that slept at my house had left nothing on when they went to sleep. And they got nothing as a result. But not Steve Mera. Steve laid down voice recorders before going to go bed. I mean, they were all over the place. I'd never noticed them until now.

I know what an EVP is. I've come across it in my paranormal studies. But this was the first EVP ever to be captured in my house. The first electronic voice phenomenon. It sure wouldn't be the last. It would appear that whatever voice was on Steve's audio was, in fact, observing Steve and Don. Think about it. This is what I've been saying all along: they're always observing. All those people who suggested we hide cameras in the vents. Hide cameras in the pottery and in the air ducts. Heck, hide them underneath your couch and love seat—the ghosts can't see them. Listen and learn. You don't know what it is you're talking about. If a spirit can comment on Don stealing Steve Mera's pillow, then it can comment and interfere with me hiding a camera in the air duct.

I can vouch for Don's need for a pillow. I'm the one that arranged each of their rooms. I found myself short one pillow when it came time to make up their beds. Three pillows for two men. How's that going to work? One of them was going to have to make do with one pillow. I remember taking one of the pillows out of Don's room and throwing it into the room by my office. As I was doing this, I thought to myself, *I sincerely hope one of them can make do with one pillow.* I guess I was wrong. Steve then put the EVP on speaker for all of us to hear. I think we must have listened to it five more times before Steve looked at Don and uttered something to the effect of, "this is a clear voice." Now I wouldn't be doing my job in calling out the obvious. The voice that ended up on Steve's computer (which shouldn't be there BTW – only us three are here) said 'removed our pillow.' Can be described as a pronoun—a form of the possessive case of we used as an attributive adjective—according to your nearest dictionary. Who is we in the EVP that Steve that Steve just discovered? You shall soon see.

Don would approach me later that day to reiterate his reason for being here; which was to provide me with answers—to substantiate my claims that something was here. Don reiterated the obvious; he and Steve had "only begun our investigation; all of this equipment we've bought should be a testimony to our level of seriousness." Steve walked by Don and uttered something in his ear: "there's more on there, more voices." Don looked back at me. "You're in good hands, Keith, I promised you we would provide you answers. Now I'm going to go outside and have a smoke." Both men headed outside, as professional and as sure of themselves as can be. Me? I wanted to cry, right then and there. This has been an extremely long journey for me. Extremely long. Matter of fact the word journey doesn't even explain it entirely. But this was good. Both men then decided to go outside and smoke a cigarette. I knew what that meant. It means they needed to talk about this case. I'm an IT professional. I've seen projects run correctly, and I've seen projects run incorrectly. It's like poetry, it really is, those projects that get run correctly. This is the first investigation to reach my doorstep where I can say, without a shadow of a doubt, it was being run correctly. Affirmation is probably the second most important thing an investigator can provide to a client. Empathy being the first. Remember, the answer won't always be that something paranormal lives here. The answer just needs to be the truth.

If a raccoon is causing all the havoc, then introduce the house occupants to the raccoon creating all the havoc. Don't just guess and say that there is. Show it! If it's paranormal, provide that too. Tina and I are not crazy; we're far from crazy. Some of you reading this might shrug and say, a voice captured on a voice recorder doesn't equate to burnt Bibles or burnt crosses. It most certainly does—if you understand the nature of the poltergeist.

When both men entered the house again, they went in two directions. Steve walked back to his bar stool and returned to what he was doing earlier, which was reviewing last night's audio. If there ever were confirmation that Keith doesn't live by himself, it would be the second EVP Don captured that said: "this is the spirits." Don captured this while standing between Steve and me. The voice was female, same as the pillow EVP. I've heard several EVPs now. Both of them speak in the plural sense—suggesting that there's more than one spirit here. Which doesn't shock me.

I've always thought multiple spirits lived here. It just kind of felt that way. I mean, this was nuts. If misery indeed loves company, then this would be a scenario of company causing misery. Misery for Tina and me. Misery for Jane Doe and her family (when they lived here). Is one of these voices the Gray Lady? There's no way of knowing. What we do know, me especially, is that the voices Don is picking up sound very similar to the voices me and Tina heard while going about our daily business.

There have been moments where Tina's doing something, or I'm doing something, and out of the blue, we hear each other's names called. This happened so many times I lost count. One-time Tina came to me, shaking like a leaf. I asked her what was wrong, and her reply was something to the effect of, "someone just whispered in my ear." My eyes got big when she said that. I mean, Tina was taking a nap at the time. She was on the couch. I believed her one hundred percent because I've heard phantom voices too. Never like that though. Not yet!

More EVPs are being discovered as a result of Don's Q&A EVP session. Let me explain. This is a live review session. Don will ask a question while he records. Pause. Then play back what he asked. In real time, all you hear is his question and then a 'voice.' It's quite trippy. I mean, the voices are clear. It might as well be you and me talking. That's how clear it is. Both men then run the audio loop through several audio devices for further analysis.

It's time-consuming, but it works. Steve then backs the audio up on his hard drive, memory stick, and internet. With all the baseline analysis pretty much out of the way, Don and Steve began combing the house with listening devices. Time to investigate the upstairs area. Where, unbeknown to them, were my cameras. I don't know what made me think of it, but before both men arriving, I decided to set up my cameras again. I had one on the hallway bookshelf and a few in the living room. I don't know what prompted me to put cameras in the corner of the living room. I've never done before, den yes. Living room no. But I'm glad I did. Forget about the door opening by itself for a moment. Forget for a second that it was Steve Mera who first saw the door was open. Forget about the EVPs; we'll come back to them, trust me. What's about to happen next is pretty much what made Steve Mera a staunch believer in all of my claims.

A few weeks before the men arrived I'd gone online and ordered some new cameras. Instead of buying the usual Foscam, I switched up and bought CCTV Trendnet cameras. I wanted to use 1080p cameras this time versus the 720p cameras I already had. The mechanics of the Trendnet and Foscam are pretty much the same. But there is one basic difference: I can maneuver the Foscams remotely. They have a built-in tilt feature that was highly valuable. I mean who wants to get up and move a camera when you're trying to look at something? You can't remote tilt the Trendnet camera. Once you set that camera down, it's down. To move it just a little requires you getting up and manually moving it yourself. I wasn't aware of that when I bought it. But the cameras were here now, so I gotta use them. One was in the hallway, and one was sitting in the living room—the room Tina and I were sitting in when we heard the kid 'cough.'

So, I was sitting at the kitchen table working from my laptop; Steve and Don were in the kitchen reviewing evidence and configuring equipment. We were all accounted for. All of a sudden, the Trendnet dashboard on my laptop began beeping. It was telling me that motion has been detected—in the living room. Steve and Don are still doing their thing. They haven't asked me about my cameras yet. That's about to change. They're both about to appreciate the proactive step I took, because I believe it was this event and this event alone that made them believe without a doubt, Keith is not only sincere, but we may have underestimated some of the things he's been telling us.

Cynics, skeptics, and researchers have been throwing back in my face as a means of debunking my claims, the question: "why does everything always happen off camera? Why can't we see it when it's happening?" My response to them has always been, your guess is as good as mine; you tell me. You're the researcher. Your average skeptic will think all of this fake, based on the fact that it wasn't caught on video. It riddles me why a field such as the paranormal would put much stock in a belief system that says: nothing is real until you capture it on camera. That mindset has got Tina and me in so much trouble. You're calling us liars. You're saying: the art of capturing poltergeist **phenomenon** is relatively simple. Grab a video camera, throw an SD card in it, and aim it towards the direction you think the activity is going to spring from. If the entity messes with that camera, go out and buy more cameras. Have cameras watching cameras. It's not real until you capture it on video. If you can't get a Bible burning on video or something invisible writing on the wall, then it never happened. Nice try—next!

We've heard it all. Now, let me be clear: Steve and Don never gave me the impression they felt like that. Both men with thirty years of experience know "Geist" chasing is not a one method fits all type of thing. The camera going off in the living room is about to confirm that.

Steve and Don have not yet broken away from what they're doing. The beeping is loud enough for them to hear, but they're engulfed right now in the EVPs Don has found. I finally said, "Guys, motion is being detected in the living room." I can tell you, motion being detected was music to Steve's ears. Steve spun around and looked at me. "How so?" I pointed in the direction of the living room without looking up from my screen. Don then lifted his video camera and began walking towards me. Everyone can hear the series of beeps coming from my laptop. I looked at Steve and Don and said, "I've got an email, I'm logging into my account now to look at it." Whatever motion is taking place, we can't see it.

If it's motion going on in the living room that means the entity's messing with the camera. I know it all too well. It's messing with the camera. Steve and Don walk over and stand behind my shoulder as I get into my inbox. There at the top of my inbox is the email alert message. I open the attachment and there it is, plain as day: a picture of a wall. Steve looked at Don; Don looked at Steve. Everyone was looking kind of puzzled. The camera was facing the door; there was a previous snapshot of the camera facing the door. It was now facing the wall.

The camera's been turned around a hundred and eighty degrees. Don said something to the effect of, "it's backward." Steve replied, "Let's go see." We all walked over together. I'm talking about a few feet at best. Now we're in the living room now, and sure enough there it is, plain as day. The camera I left facing the front door is now turned around. It's facing the wall.

That's what triggered the motion alert. The minute Steve and Don saw what had happened they immediately knew what was going on. Steve said a word I never heard before, not from paranormal investigators. Steve said, "It's elusive." Both men inspected the camera and verbally admitted out loud that 1.) "Keith has been with us the whole time" 2.) This camera being turned around, and the act of sending an email seems to support the argument that we are dealing with a spirit that doesn't want to be detected." Steve and Don were thinking out loud, and I loved every minute of it. To purposely avoid detection is a conscious act. You don't have to be a parapsychologist to know that. We all head back into the kitchen and continue our discussion.

Steve updated his notebook on what just happened. Don walked back to my laptop to inspect the email again. The time stamp on the email fits with the time frame of the beeps going off. Steve turned from his note taking and looked at me: "can you send me that email? That's good evidence; we'll need that." It goes without saying that a capture like this is extremely rare. You can be an investigator your whole life and not witness a wonder such as this. Some will say this is why they do what they do; finds like this are why people become paranormal researchers. Science can frown on this field all it wants: you have no choice but to believe something paranormal has just taken place when you have three men situated in a room. All men are accounted for when the beeps go off. Don and Steve saw the camera facing the door due to their multiple trips outside. They saw the camera facing the door when they came back in. Don even asked the question, "Keith, what's that in the corner?" To which I replied, "One of my motion cams." As I said, this Trendnet cannot be turned remotely. It doesn't have that capability. You have to move it manually if you want it facing something. No vibration, no earthquake, no fakery, no hoaxing: zero. Nothing could have turned that camera around manually except the entities living in my home.

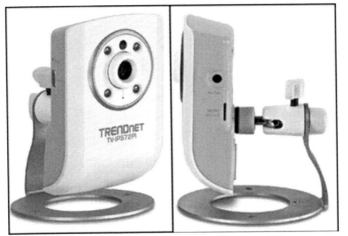

Fig 46.3 Trendnet Camera: I had two when Steve and Don were here.

Don after leaving my computer walks over to Steve. "So, this explains everything in the past happening off camera. This man has gotten so much stick, so much heat from *Ghost Adventures* about stuff always happening away from the camera; you and I have just seen why." Things were happening off camera because the spirits were orchestrating everything.

Steve nodded and agreed. "It's very elusive; it wants to avoid detection." I could tell both men were relieved. They've seen with their own eyes a spirit manipulating cameras to avoid detection. The jury has come back with its verdict. Keith has been telling the truth. It's been Keith versus the spirits ever since this whole thing started. Don and Steve were pleased with this discovery. I could tell by the look on their faces that they were pleased; they needed to go back outside to have a cigarette.

Fig 46.4 Ex. living room corner setup / Steve and Don arrival. Cameras are mine. Both men acknowledge camera was turned 360 degrees on its own.

Chapter 47
Evasive

"What the heck is going on in Keith's house?" That was the scribble writing on Steve Mera's notepad on day two and day three of his and Don's investigation. I can't overstate how significant the camera movement was to them. What a huge revelation this is. Not only is Keith Linder telling the truth. He's telling the truth about a very important activity. Remember all those cameras I owned that went missing? Steve and Don know why now. They know a lot of things because of it happening to them. I've told that story to so many people—the story of cameras being turned around, some upside down. Tons of people in the paranormal community know this story. The response from skeptics has always been "buy more cameras. Hook your cameras up to a backup battery—so they'll keep running when the power goes out. We need to see activity in real-time, or we won't come out and help you."

Steve Mera's notebook was filling up fast with information. I never knew till now how much the house was laced with listening devices. Neither men have set up a camera yet. They've yet to ask me for permission on setting up cameras. And you know what? They never did. Both men seemed more interested in setting up listening devices.

The Trendnet moving by itself forced Steve and Don to re-evaluate their tactics. Whatever plan they had before landing in the United States would have to be set aside. Most parapsychologists will tell you, investigating a poltergeist is extremely difficult. Your odds have greatly diminished the minute you throw in the word elusive. Investigating a poltergeist that is purposely elusive is nearly impossible. Tactics would need to be changed.

Fig 47.1 Parapsychologist Steve Mera was a meticulous notetaker at my house.

Both men were gathering more and more evidence that day. What am I doing? Nothing, absolutely nothing. My goal is to stay out there way. Both men will tell you; my role was simple and plain. Answer questions. If needed, reiterate something I've already told them. I'm not looking over their shoulder, except when asked to. Steve is doing his thing, and Don is doing his thing. I found out later on that Steve had discovered more voices on his audio equipment. I mean, we're talking about conversations between one spirit and another.

Don was immersed in a few experiments of his own. The ambient voices he was able to pull out of the air with me and Steve standing in front of him, helped me understand what Don Philips was. A channel. He can summon spirits to him by simply asking a question. Steve had headphones on. He was reviewing audio from the previous night and writing down EVPs in the process. Don was standing near both of us, asking a basic question while holding his Olympus voice recorder. He was getting responses in real-time. Clear responses, mind you.

The more I observed Don, the more I began to understand the level of spirit activity taking place in this house. It's weird how we've become so accustomed to only focusing on the most tantalizing stuff; we often forget there's more happening around us that we can't see or hear. I mean, if a spirit can watch Don steal a pillow out of Steve's bedroom, imagine what it's been doing with Tina and me. Do I need to go there? I guess I have to. I mean, Tina and I were a couple.

There have been times when we've been intimate. We've woken up in the spoon position. We've cuddled tremendously, and all the other physical forms of affection. We've done it all. I wonder what the spirits are saying to themselves when they see that. I wonder what they're saying when Tina undresses and gets in the shower. Do they see us twenty-four seven? Do they even want to? Remember where I was when the poster caught fire. I was taking a shower. Tina had just left. I wonder if they said, *don't start the fire until she leaves*? I would love to know the conversation before and after they placed female items in our bedroom. I'm dying to know that. The answers to those questions are equally important to me as the chair levitating. Equally important to me as the wall writing and Bible catching fire. Imagine the conversations that took place before those events. I can't even begin to fathom it.

One of the most startling EVPs caught in my house was the unexplained voice saying, 'I hear springs.' A female voice. I mean, the pure clarity of it, is what moved me. 'I hear springs'—what does that even mean? When Steve found it, we were all like, what the heck? It was a strong ambient voice. As I hear it over and over, I was thinking to myself, who was (or is) this woman? She sounds beautiful. Angelic, if that makes any sense. The reader deserves a listen.

Ambient Voice – Unexplained Voice phenomenon – Keith's House	https://soundcloud.com/user-423872078/evp-raw-i-hear-springsmp3	00:04 from the Scientific Establishment of Parapsychology

Table 47.1 EVP "I Hear Springs"

Is there a connection between "I hear springs" and the creek that flows behind my house? And what's up with the accent? Every piece of evidence brings about new questions. I was raising a lot of questions with Steve and Don. Can you men please explain to me what these voices mean? The short answer is: no one knows. The accent is interesting, Steve said. That could be a clue as to what was here before this house was built. "We could be dealing with multiple events taking place. A house built on a previous settlement, a previous landmark of some sort could explain some of the residual events being captured. That's one theory," Steve said.

Poltergeist infestations vary. Regardless of what you hear people say the evidence as to what causes isn't as conclusive as some researchers will allow you to think. The outbreak, i.e., the violent stuff, is just one aspect of what's going on. As an IT person, I can honestly say I love it when Steve and Don think out loud. I love it when they spitball ideas off each other. Steve is walking back and forth with his pipe in his hand – comparing this case to the others he's worked on. He refers back to the Enfield case from time to time and even mentions the Bell Witch case. All of them had similarities, and all of them had unique differences. The good thing about the evidence being captured now is that it's going to get analyzed even more once they get back to the UK. No one doubts that the 'I hear springs' is an EVP. Class A EVP, to be exact. Steve told me there were other voices on the audio, other conversations that needed to be sorted out. That's where the Scientific Establishment comes in. Other individuals at S.E.P and even some third-party individuals will need to be called in to view and substantiate Steve and Don's findings. And that's exactly what I wanted to be done. That's exactly what I hoped got done. The keyword here is hope.

The activity taking place in this house needs to be studied. I hope the data is analyzed and studied for years to come. I hope they share it with their colleagues. I hope they share it with other parapsychology organizations. I hope they share it with the science community, and yes, even the skeptic community. The data being captured needs to survive everyone who was involved. It needs to be stored somewhere, cataloged correctly, and made available for future access. This is what I envisioned the whole time while living here. Achieving a positive outcome that includes collaboration beyond measure.

Consider this, for example. I asked Steve, "How do we know the 'I hear springs…' is brand new?" He looked at me sort of puzzled and said, "Huh?" So, I said, "We're all in agreement that the 'I hear springs' is a high-quality EVP. There's no disputing that. I saw you write it down as such. My question is, how do we know that phrase 'I hear springs' has never been uttered before? Shouldn't there be some database where we can throw it in, to see if it was ever captured somewhere else? Wouldn't it be good to know if another team caught that very same voice pattern elsewhere in the world?" Steve was still puzzled. I decided to help him by pulling out my cell phone.

I launch the app called Shazam. If you have a smartphone, you'll know what Shazam is. I showed Steve my app and said, "I launch this app whenever I want to know the name of a song. I could be anywhere on this planet (as long as I have cell phone service). It's a basic interface. You launch it by simply clicking it. All the app has to do is hear the song. It just needs to listen to ten seconds of a song— it takes what it heard and begins searching its database. I'll know the artist name, song title and where I can buy it in less than two seconds. Why doesn't the paranormal community have something like that? Why isn't there a database for all electronic voice captures, Class B and above? Those that have been thoroughly vetted are entered, and researchers throughout the globe can access for analysis or for comparison." I could see the wheels turning in Steve's head. He finally understood where I was coming from. His reply, "I don't know why we don't have anything like that."

Where are my things? was the next question I had. Where's my missing Bible? Who stole Tina's iPad? Who pushed me down the stairs? Was I pushed down the stairs? And the biggest unanswered question of all. What do they want?

It would seem the task of learning why these beings were here would fall more on Don's shoulders than on Steve's. And that kind of makes sense, based on what I observed about Don. When Don interviewed me a few months ago, he asked me for a list of names. He wanted to know who had worked on the case previously. I gave him Fr. Roy's name and I gave him Jennifer's name. Jennifer's testimony was crucial. Remember she was the only first responder ever to visit the house when the activity was at its highest. She heard the humming noises, and she saw the mist coming from the hallway floor. Fr. Roy was the last person to visit the house. His role is significant because of his background. He's handled demonic infestations before. He has opinions about this house that I think Steve and Don should know about. I can't wait for the three men to get together. Time to visit Fr. Roy. Sr. Steve and Don had expressed an interest in meeting. It was now time.

There was more paranormal activity, even before we left the house. You see, Don was filming his and Steve's involvement with the case. Prior to us going to Fr. Roy's house, Don blurted out he needed footage of us all leaving the house. We have to show that the house was vacant for a few hours, in case something happens.

Well, something happened that I'm sure Don didn't quite expect. Don had a video tripod set up outside my house. It would inexplicably turn off the second Don walked away from it. I mean, it became a point of amusement, this back and forth between Don and this unknown entity. I'm not talking about battery drainage, which we know has happened here before. I'm talking about something hitting the off switch the minute Don's back was turned. I have to admit I was amused. I mean, welcome to my world. I have had cameras turned upside within seconds of walking away. I have had cameras turn off within seconds of me walking away. This was proof once more of what I've repeatedly been saying. The spirits have a fixation when it comes to cameras. If you still doubt that, wait till you see what happens tonight.

Fig 47.2 Trip to Kent, WA to meet Fr. Roy Sr.

When I say, the guys were non-stop while here I mean exactly that. We're talking about eighteen to nineteen hours a day of investigative work. No one's asked me to leave yet. No one said "we need you out of the house in order to continue our investigation." I've been here the whole time. Where am I at? In the kitchen, in plain view of both gentlemen. I have my work laptop in front of me. I cook breakfast, lunch, and dinner. Steve and Don work through all of that. Our drink of choice—Seattle's Best coffee. What's on the dinner menu? Hamburger helper and pizza from Pizza Hut. But I can do better, than right? Why come to the Pacific Northwest if you're not going to get what the Pacific Northwest is known for? King salmon. I'll cook Steve and Don a salmon dinner for their last night here. I promised both men that verbally. Remember that.

Both men got what they wanted from Fr. Roy Sr. which was his take on the overall situation. What did Fr. Roy think of the activity? What did he think of the claims being reported? More importantly, what did he think was causing it? The same conclusion once again was multiple spirits are living here. Mean sons of bitches. The Native American component shouldn't be overlooked Fr. Roy says. The upside-down man calligraphy has never been seen before in "Geist" related cases. That has to mean something. What's the ink made out of is another question. Suffice to say the three men had an interesting conversation about the house I live in. I was glad to set it up.

Back at my house— Steve decides to open up one of his crates. The elusiveness of the spirits had finally gotten to the best of him. It was time to introduce a new device inside the Keith Linder home. Is it time we set up tripwires? I've seen paranormal teams walk into my house with a lot of devices. Never has a team entered my house with tripwires. I asked Steve what it was, and he told me. It's a motion detection device that utilizes passive infrared technology (PIR). Steve will lace the hallway upstairs with several of these devices. The hallway has been declared off-limits.

So, Steve came back downstairs after successfully lacing the hallway with tripwires. He was walking towards his laptop downstairs, when all of a sudden, we heard a series of beeps. The tripwires were going off: The beeping seemed to catch everyone off guard. I mean Steve had not too long come from upstairs. No one thought the alarms would go off so soon. Even I didn't, and I live here. Steve darted upstairs right away, with Don behind him. Me? I'm staying put. Remember, my goal is always to be visibly accounted for whenever activity breaks out. These tripwires belonged to Steve. He set them up, not me. The fact that they're going off by themselves suggest the spirits were extremely curious.

Steve and Don came back downstairs a few minutes later. Discovery number one: The tripwires went off. Discovery number two: Steve and Don heard pitter-patter footsteps. The sounds of someone running away—apparently due to Steve and Don arriving on the landing. It must have been a noticeable pitter-patter of footsteps because Steve Mera ran downstairs, grabbed his notepad, and jotted down the manner in which events occurred. Don came down right behind him; the two begin discussing the footsteps they just heard. The look on their faces says it all. "Unbelievable." That's how Steve described what they just witnessed.

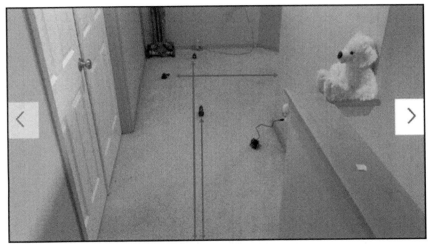

Fig 47.3 Example of a tripwire setup. Not Steve's exact setup, but close.

It's not often you see a parapsychologist openly admit that what they just heard was indeed footsteps. The sound of someone running away from Steve and Don as they made their way up the landing area. You see, the spirits were trying to approach Steve's tripwire setup. They accidentally set off the tripwires in an attempt to understand what Steve had just set down. I've never used tripwires in my house. No other team has used them either. Not even *Ghost Adventures*.

Imagine the spirits coming in for a closer look, not knowing that they are now entangled in invisible infrared beams. Those beams if broken are going to sound off, and they did. This was a successful experiment. It substantiated an important claim that I had been making. Two claims. A.) The hallway is very active; it's a thoroughfare for spirits. They come and go at will B.) Unexplained footsteps are a constant in the house. It's always been that way.

Let's recap what has happened so far. Day one of their arrival, both men noticed the front door was open upon our return from the grocery store. We all went to sleep that night. Steve heard a sound that resembles a door slam. He verified that it wasn't Don or me. He noted the door slam as being unexplained.

Both men have picked up voices on their recording devices. One in particular talks about Don sneaking into Steve's room while Steve is asleep and taking one his pillows. The spirits watch the thievery unfold and openly discuss it. The investigation takes a huge leap forward when the guys see something they never expected. One of my cameras gets turned around. Emails are sent confirming motion was detected during the maneuver of it. Those are just some of the highlights of what they've encountered so far.

The next morning, I woke up and found Steve Mera reviewing audio. I'm thinking to myself, *does this guy ever sleep?* I look to my right and see Don knocked out on the couch. I could tell it was a long night for both men. On the kitchen counter were empty coffee cups, empty bags of Doritos, and empty bags of cookies. I might have to run to the store; these guys have a sweet tooth that rivals my own.

I was making my way to my laptop, when Steve motioned to me to come here. *Uh oh, good news, Steve has found something.* The last time Steve motioned me to his laptop with this much excitement was when he discovered the first EVP. And that's exactly what I asked him. "Steve, did you find another voice?" Steve smiled and said, "Come look at this." I'm thinking, *oh, he's found something super interesting. He's got video.* Steve placed the headset on my head and clicked the play button.

It showed Steve and Don entering the hallway. They were setting up equipment in the landing area. Steve mentioned for me to listen to the video, not watch. The video he wanted me to see (listen to) showed both men attempting to set up listening devices in the landing area. As I'm listening to their conversation, I suddenly hear whispering voices. Someone's talking. It's not Steve and Don.

Fig 47.4 Location: Hallway landing area.

Keith's House – Hallway Landing Area	https://youtu.be/0O_1_vEomBk Listen 1:11, 1:14, 1:23, 1:25,
It's a Camera - Nite Cam EVP - Bothell House	https://youtu.be/OTWVDkIIS04 analysis version

Table 47.2 - Hall Landing Area / EVPs discovered

Two voices are whispering: 'it's a camera, it's a camera...tat tat tat... pause night cam.' I looked at Steve. *Did I just hear what I think I heard?* Steve with a smug grin on his face chuckled and said "yes." I'm thinking to myself, *are they discussing what I think they're discussing?* I'm going to go out on a limb and just say one could be in this field for twenty years and never hear the stuff these men are capturing. This is up there with what Niki and Mary had captured. The clarity is remarkable. What Steve just showed me, just confirmed another one of my hunches.

There's more than one spirit here. More than two, more than three, heck more than five or six. They've been playing me all along. They've been watching me. They've been watching Tina. They've probably watched every person that's lived in this house. Not only are they watching, but they're talking. They're trying to figure out what Steve and Don are doing. Who's investigating who I wonder?

358

Steve replayed this video for me over and over. I needed to watch it a few times to take it all in. You can see how engaged Don is, how procedural Steve is in the video. Neither men can hear the voices underneath them. The voices say, 'it's a camera, it's a camera, tat tat tat' pause; and then 'night cam.'

What's up with the words 'night cam'? You probably are already aware, but every camera I've brought into the house for the purpose of catching something has been a night vision camera. Steve and Don were setting up a Tascam DR-60DmkII 4-Channel Portable Audio Recorder. They were following protocol by videotaping themselves. Steve and Don can't even hear the words being said. That's how remarkable this is.

Steve saw Don waking up and motioned for him to come over. Don put on the headphones and within seconds hears what Steve and I had just heard. Now, he's been in this field for thirty years. Don's reaction was priceless. "Wow!" This was huge even by Don's standards. The men would review that video and other audio capture for the remainder of the morning.

Chapter 48
Interview

"Any case that turns current beliefs upside down while creating new ones is without a doubt a good case."
Keith Linder

The evidence captured so far has, for the most part, matches what I've been saying for quite some time now. The spirits here are intelligent and elusive. Those are not the top five words you hear when describing poltergeist, regrettably. I mean, there's more to a poltergeist than the throwing of objects. There's more to them than loud bangs. Steve has heard a few rapping's. He has heard a few knocks, pings, and thuds. That's standard poltergeist behavior. It would be easy to classify this house as your typical poltergeist-infested home if that's all that was happening here. But it's not. The men have picked up multiple unexplained voice phenomena's, a majority of them have Irish accents. What's up with that? What's up with spirits talking to each other? What truth is there to Fr. Roy's Sr. claim that this part of Bothell (where I'm sitting right now) was once a hotbed for settler and Native American uprisings.

Steve and Don have to compare the evidence they've compiled with the events I've reported. They've analyzed the Bibles. They've analyzed the wall writings. Paint experts have gone on record to say, "No human could have done this." Steve looked at my medical report which shows when I had a fall. He stood on the steps where I fell. He slept in the room where objects were thrown. There's so much to take in. So much to decipher.

Jennifer of *No Bull Paranormal* talked to them about her involvement with the case. She told them how she was pulled into the picture. That frantic email and phone calls when the house was being attacked. She went on record about the sage stick catching on fire. The one she was holding right before doing her house cleansing. She explained to Don how this area was once Native American land. She shared with them some stories of how certain tribes were treated. How smallpox was spread. How mass graves were dug and how land was taken. She explained that my house is the most active house she's ever seen. She's been doing this close to thirty years.

She's seen angry spirits invade houses before. Some have been linked to angry Native American spirits. The wall writings suggest that might be what's happening here.

Interview Names	Status
Keith Linder	Completed
Fr. Roy Sr.	Completed
Jennifer	Completed
Jane Doe	Ultimately Obtainable
Elissa Jaffe	Declined
Next door neighbors	Completed

Table 48.1 S.E.P Interview List

Fig 48.1 Woodinville Reporter

http://nwnews.com/index.php/news-features/features/12586-the-haunting-in-bothell-paranormal-researchers-from-uk-investigate-infamous-house

"These are human vocal replies," Philips said, "as clear as I'm talking to you."

Don Philips

One of the things I wanted to do when Steve and Don got here was make them available to the local media. When KOMO news ran a story about this house, last year's news traveled fast about a haunted house in Bothell. Bibles burning at will and unexplained wall writings were intriguing everyone—including the media. The first person to get an invite was KOMO news reporter, Elissa Jaffe. She was the one that heard the loud bang, and the one who referred our ordeal to Dave Schrader. Occasionally I would get an email from other news outlets about the status of the house. It was during this time that I told them I had a parapsychology organization coming from the United Kingdom. They were excited to know that. No one ever comes to the Pacific Northwest. They know that, and I know that. Seattle's too far to come. So, suffice to say, FOX news was interested, as was the local newspaper—The Woodinville Weekly.

Some may frown at the idea that the media was involved. But I don't. No, the media has a very important role to play. One of the things I learned while reading Michael Clarkson's book, *The Poltergeist Phenomenon*, is that journalists are typically one of the first agencies called by people dealing with a "Geist" infestation. Occupants are at their wits' end as to what to do. Local authorities are called in to assist with an extreme domestic disturbance. Police officers and firemen arrive on the scene, and they too are at their wits' end. Police are not trained in how to deal with a poltergeist. They're civilians like you and me when it comes to witnessing an outbreak. Firemen are no exception; they too are ill-equipped. The media is invaluable in my opinion. Every book I read about poltergeists pretty much got their information from newspaper clippings. I'm talking about clippings from all over the world. This case is no exception.

In my opinion, the media is a neutral party. They're extremely valuable because the only thing they're after is a good story. That's their only vested interest. A hoax is just as interesting to them as a true bona fide case. Let's deal with the elephant in the room for a second. *Ghost Adventures* came in a little over a year ago and found nothing. Some thought that was a done deal. There's nothing here to see. Next story, please.

But no, we can't move on. At least not me. The fact that they found nothing doesn't solve our problem. Doesn't solve my landlord's problem. Now, what's up with this UK team? What the hell is a parapsychologist, and why would a parapsychologist's organization fly all the way from England to investigate a case that a TV show suggested was hoaxed? Why would they do that? What's the matter with them? Do they want to get egg on their face? *Ghost Adventures* said nothing was there. And they're correct. Nothing was here, caveat being—while they were conducting their investigation. I'm pretty sure some of Steve and Don's colleagues probably asked them 'why in the world do you want to involve yourself in a case like this? You'd be legitimizing a TV show by involving yourself, especially if you find nothing. 'Geist cases are the hardest cases to investigate; it's quite possible the activity has simply receded.' I'm pretty sure Steve and Don were told this before their departure.

There was a risk for them. The risk that this might be a hoax. There was a risk that they might have been duped. So, their reputation was on the line. But their risk pales in comparison to my risk. No one was risking more than me. I've come back to the roulette table with the same amount of chips I had before. I've come back with the same mindset. The strategy is pretty much identical to what it was before. If Steve and Don leave empty handed, that will be the end of me from a paranormal-problem reporting point of view.

Steve and Don made it clear to me before arriving that they are going to investigate my house to the best of their ability. They're going to be thorough, and they're going, being frank. They will be reporting what they find. That includes nothing—if "nothing" is what they find. Lucky for me that won't be the case. Just like and Niki and Mary their cup now runneth over to.

So, you see, the media has to be here. They have to be here to record if my claim was false. If it was exaggerated. If it was hoaxed or if it was me simply being deranged and delusional. The researchers entering the home are not the subject-matter experts. If there's to be a subject matter expert here, it has to be the house occupant. I live here. Tina lived here. We're the only two people that know the entirety of what happened. We're the only two people that know exactly when stuff happened. Forget all the handheld devices. Forget the items you checked in through customs. Forget your EMF machine. Forget those devices even exist. Ultimately, the best tool you have for figuring stuff out is right in front of you. It's the people that lived there. It's Tina and me.

362

How seriously have past teams taken us as an evidence resource? Well, my phone interview with Dave Schrader was less than thirty minutes. It's the only interview I had before *Ghost Adventures* showed up. Tina was interviewed just the once when *Ghost Adventures* showed up. Steve and Don interviewed me over and over for more than three months. I even asked myself the question one day when driving home from work: I wish these guys would cease with the questions. Just get here already. The answers you seek are right here in this house. I later found out that their reason for questioning me was scientific. I was being scored. I was being weighed. The men found zero contradictions after interviewing me. My story hadn't changed one bit. Think about it; it was 2016. This hell started in 2012. Not one atom changed within my story. As frustrating as it was to be interviewed, I get it now. I respect Steve and Don's method for getting at the truth.

I was hoping Don would interview Jane Doe. She and I had talked a lot before Steve and Don's arrival. Her relationship with her husband had taken a turn for the worse, so she told me she didn't know how readily available she could be. The outcome of this case was not her concern; it was mine. No way was I going to add more stress to what she had going on. I mentioned to her early on that Steve and Don were coming. I told her Don would like to talk to you. She said she would think about it. A few days later she came back and said "yes."

When it came time for her to be interviewed, she'd disappeared. I knew what that meant. That means things at her house have gotten significantly worse. I told myself Steve and Don were just going to have to settle for the Facebook conversation between Jane and me. Let that be entered into the record, and the reader can make of it what they will. The evidence you have, and the evidence Niki and Mary have is going to blow this case out the water anyways. So, the last people to be interviewed turned out to be Don and Steve. FOX news came to the house with the hope of learning two things: Is there any truth to what Keith is claiming? True or false, repercussions are guaranteed either way. Secondly, if true, why is it happening? That's all the media wants. What's happening and why?

Fig 48.2 Fox news descend on the Bothell home.

"…a team of scientists from England is at his home. They brought an arsenal of ghost hunting gadgets and will collect a lot of data during a weeklong stay."

Q13FOC - UK Parapsychologists Team descend on Bothell WA

There are two things I want to share before closing out Steve and Don's investigation. One involves the touch light thingy Mary (the woman who wants to remain anonymous) asked me to buy months ago. Remember the grocery list she gave me? Well, the spirits finally decided to do something with it.

Don, Steve, Patty, and myself were downstairs in the kitchen discussing the FOX interview when all of sudden we heard a loud bang. I looked at Don and Steve and told them point-blank (because I've lived this so many times), something was just thrown. Steve looked at Don. "Sounds like it came from upstairs." I agreed and looked at Don. "Yeah, that came from upstairs, I know that sound all too well; something was just thrown up there." Don picked up his video camera and motioned for us to follow him. The loud thud sounded like it came from the hallway.

[See Chapter 41] Experiment number one – place the touch-activated light device on the wall – facing the master bedroom. In clear view of the hallway camera.

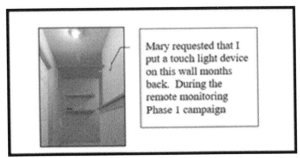

Mary requested that I put a touch light device on this wall months back. During the remote monitoring Phase 1 campaign

Fig 48.3 Item was found on the floor after a loud thud.

We found the touch-activated light device sitting on the floor. It's been five months if not more when Mary came up with the idea of placing it on the wall. Niki's team wanted to see if it would light up by itself. Now it's on the floor.

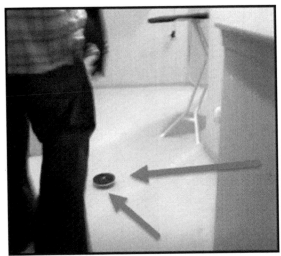

Fig 48.4 Object on the floor.

What happened?

Fox team leaves.
Minutes later LOUD THUD
(everyone was in the kitchen)
We all go upstairs together and see the touch
light device resting on the floor.

Fig 48.5 Parapsychologist narrates what just happened
with the touch light device.

No way a small touch light would generate the sound we heard by just falling from the wall. *Why did it fall off the wall in the first place?* Both men proceeded to knock it off the wall again in an attempt to measure the noise level. Nothing came close to what we heard when we were downstairs. Even when they threw it down forcibly, the sound still wasn't the same. Unfortunately, we had no camera upstairs that had been running—I doubt it would have fallen had there been one. I mean, we're talking about my house here. Since it was Mary's idea to put this object on the wall, I'm giving credit to her for this one. We'd got good data from it—albeit months later. Thank you, Mary. A great idea.

Fox aired their interview with Don and Steve a few days later and in doing so reignited a question within the paranormal community of "isn't that the house *Ghost Adventures* went to and found nothing?" Those were the type of comments being left on Fox News Facebook page, as well on *Ghost Adventures* Facebook page. A rather large percentage of individuals believed zero evidence equated to "you guys were making it all up." That was the teachable the moment *Ghost Adventures* failed to take advantage of, once the episode aired. Steve and Don flew all the way from the UK with no idea on what to expect. Niki and Karissa were doing the same thing. Steve and Don walked through the same front door that Zak and crew walked through. Karissa and Niki the same way. All the teams before them, all the priests, all the clergy, and all our friends and family entered through the front door. Every team that's come here has left with something. Has seen something. Every team except *Ghost Adventures*. Why is that?

Don made a point to tell me before his arrival that he and Steve would conduct their investigation in a matter of six days. They were not interested in seeing Pike Place market, or Starbucks headquarters. They wanted to know what's going on in this house. Why this house? Why not the house next door? Why not a house in Kirkland? What makes this house so special? That's what Steve wanted to know. Their level of effort can ascertain by their desire to know what's going on.

It's day four now, and the investigation was nearing an end. They say, "Time flies when you're having fun"; it must also fly while gathering evidence. Don was playing back some of the voices that he and Steve had captured. Steve turned from Don and jotted down notes on his computer. The men spend hours uploading files to flash drives. It's very meticulous this process that Steve and Don are engaged in. Far from exciting but necessary.

I can't tell you how many times I've heard Don say, "Steve, come here. We've got something." That "something" will later turn out to be unexplained voice phenomenon, also known as an EVP. Where am I during all of this? Sitting at the kitchen table, in plain view. Unlike the "Geist" living here, I for one want to be seen at all times. I already know what the skeptics are going to say. "Where was Keith through all of this?" The answer I want Steve and Don to give is "he was sitting at the kitchen table. He was in plain sight, always right in front of us."

You would want to be taken seriously to if you saw an object fly across the room. There's a psychological component that goes hand in hand with the need to be taken seriously. It's called affirmation. One of the biggest headaches Tina and I experienced while living here that didn't come from the poltergeist. It came from the people we dealt with. It came from the hurdles many paranormal investigators had us go through in order to be believed. It came from lack of empathy. Or an overabundance of innuendos, based on the fact that we couldn't get a video of a Bible catching fire. We tried. My God, we tried, almost to the detriment of our lives. Certainly, to the detriment of our relationship. You see, the more headaches we get from people, the more energy the malevolent spirits get.

The spirits have been busy as bees ever since Steve and Don got here. What will the spirits do when Niki and Karissa arrive? Talk about pivoting. Two men being replaced by two women. I could not have planned this more perfectly—two teams unknowingly passing the baton to each other. They may have a policy about not working together, guess what Scientific Establishment of Parapsychology, you're working together.

Karissa arrives tomorrow night. Her arrival's bound to add a dynamic to the house. I'm hoping it does—for obvious reasons. I've not had a woman in the house since Tina left. That has to mean something to a spirit. What will the Gray Lady do? What will the white lady do? How will the apparition react to a woman being in the house? How will it react to two women being in the house? Will it view them as trespassers? Oh, ladies and gentlemen, the investigation is just getting started.

Day five—One of the last things Steve and Don wanted to do before leaving the U.S was to take a field trip. Not a field trip through wine country, no a field trip to downtown Bothell. What information can we get about the house from the city record's office? I'm thinking to myself, sure, why not? The sixty-four-thousand-dollar question remains unscathed. Why is Keith Linder's house haunted? They want to know that. You want to know it. My landlord wants to know it. Jane Doe wants to know. My neighbors want to know, as do my friends and family. And you know I want to know it.

I had five theories in the back of my head right now—none of them were right. We were probably all wrong—and that's not a bad thing. I mean, look at what we're chasing. We still don't know what we don't know. It's called paranormal for a reason. EVPs with Irish accents. What does that mean? Was there a mass exodus of Irish settlers back when Bothell was founded? Maybe, we don't know yet. That's what Don wants to find out. What about the Native American wall symbols in my office? What about the "longhouse" EVP Don captured downstairs? Maybe the city record's office knows something we don't. Don says to me "we need to get as much information as we can about the city, and land underneath this house. Keith, can you take us to downtown Bothell?"

So, we spent a few hours at the Bothell City Hall that day, and that was it. Don and Steve asked a few questions when they went inside. It seems the records they wanted would take a few weeks to compile. So, I now have a homework assignment. The records we need exist at the Snohomish County office. That's thirty minutes from where I live. I told Steve and Don I would make it a personal mission of mine to get down to the Snohomish County office in the next few days. If I found something of value, I would let them know. Let's do a quick rundown of the recent EVPs that Don has captured. They are as follows.

(These EVP have been accepted as being authentic by the S.E.P)
"I want more"
"Who are you?"
Question – Are there any Irish here? Answer – "Yes"
Question - "Can you confirm that there's nothing negative? Nothing to harm Keith Linder?" Answer – "I confirm."
"Hello?"
"Longhouse."

Fig 48.6 Bothell City Hall	Fig 48.7 Snohomish County Records Office – Everett WA

You remember the dinner that I promised to cook for Steve and Don on their last night at the house? Tonight, was the night. Later that day, Don's friend Patty arrived. It was time for their well-deserved shore leave. Neither man had ever been to Seattle before. Never had a Starbucks coffee; never seen the Space Needle; and (it saddens me to say), never ate King Salmon. King Salmon, I can handle; that's what's for dinner tonight. Patty (Don's friend) decided to handle the rest— time to take these men into downtown Seattle. They won't get the fully-fledged tour, but hey, they can always come back, right? The men have been working non-stop since they got here. The last night of their stay involves feasting on some Pacific Northwest cuisine—King Salmon—grilled asparagus, and wild rice.

Now, you know the reason I'm telling you this story is because something is about to happen. Instead of saying shit happens, I say "Geist" happens. We all know what shit happens means, right? It means bad luck. "Geist" happens means someone's about to be inconvenienced. Big time. A malevolent spirit will always try something when you least expect it. The three of them were on their way back from downtown Seattle when the oven decided to explode. Seriously! Sparks started flying from behind the stove. Allow me to explain to you how this all transpired. As soon as the guys left, I began prepping for dinner. I went all out. I ran up to Safeway, grabbed the ingredients for our meal, arrived home, and began cooking dinner. Or, I tried to. I asked Patty to text me an hour before they arrived, so I could prep the salmon right. I went into full cook mode after getting Patty's text. I seasoned the salmon like I always do, and then I put it in the oven. As soon as I turned around POP POP POP POP BOOM BOOM BOOM POP POP!

I spun around, and all I saw were sparks flying. The sparks were not coming from the range or the oven. No, the sparks were coming from behind the stove—damn, it's coming from the electrical socket. The electrical socket! There comes a time when a knee-jerk reaction is appropriate. This is one of those times. I did what my mind told me to do. I pulled out the stove, lightning fast, and grabbed hold of the thick power cord and yanked it from the wall. Sparks and flames were gone now.

Attempts to revive the stove were futile. It was deader than a doornail. The outlet still functions, but the stove does not. There are no coincidences in Keith Linder's house. No coincidences whatsoever. Pop quiz: do you remember where Steve, Don, and myself were standing when I promised them a salmon dinner? Answer: We were standing in the kitchen. Has that not been the spirits' number one characteristic? Their number one trait is the ability to eavesdrop. How far do you want to go back? May 1st, 2012? That's when the landlord gave us the keys to the house. How about the housewarming party? My mom's coffee cup? How many conversations have they listened in on when Tina or I was on the phone? The door slamming during the middle of me and Tina's pillow talk. They've been listening in since day one. Occasionally they'll intervene as a result of listening in. Occasionally they'll manipulate something with the hopes of altering a specific outcome. Another woman's jewelry in the bedroom, scratches on my car within minutes of Tina and me arguing. The attack on Tina when she was home alone, my cell phone not getting any sort of phone call from her.

I could go on and on. I've listed them all in this book. This oven shooting sparks is no different from the rest. This was a big inconvenience. I'm not going to be able to cook the men dinner now. I told Steve and Don what happened within seconds of them walking through the door. Both men had a peculiar response. Why would an outlet shoot sparks on tonight of all nights?

Fig 48.8 Pic of stove minutes after sparks flew from behind it.

Later that night, Steve approaches me in the kitchen to go over next steps of their involvement. He assured me that the Scientific Establishment would have my back from here on out. Consider this phase one of an on-going investigation. The easy part has been done already. Now the hard part begins. The hard part being what to make of the evidence they'd compiled. The men had audio devices running non-stop since being here. Devices they've yet to analyze. Hopefully, they'll be more stuff on their equipment when they get back home. Steve and the organization he belongs to will analyze the data in the UK and get back to me when done. That's what he said. That's what I'm expecting.

One thing he said that caught my attention more than anything else was a comprehensive report that he and S.E.P would be compiling. The report is broken down by everything they've found here. It'll contain what found after returning to the UK. A majority of the data has yet to be reviewed. So, you see the process is just getting started. I hope I get this report. If I get it, you get it. It belongs to the paranormal community.

SEP Investigation Ref: 26411

Evidence	Information	Location
Female Voice "On Three"	Video / Audio	https://youtu.be/WyRll8gIFEY
"It's a camera, It's a camera*	Video / Audio	https://youtu.be/8M6UPUPKMF0

Table 48.2 EVPs

Fig 48.9 Steve discusses next steps with me. Analysis of the evidence gathered, interview, and the soon to be released comprehensive report – detailing him and Don's findings.

Chapter 49
Phase 2

January 28th, 2016. I had arranged for Karissa to arrive at the house via a cab ride from SeaTac airport. And it soon became clear that I was not the only one aware of her arrival. Karissa arrived a few hours before Steve and Don's departure. I wanted them to overlap each other. How often do you see US and UK teams descending on a house such as this? I would have to say not often.

Karissa Fleck was in the house now and the spirits know it. I know this because of the event that took place within minutes of her arrival. Steve, Don, and I had just finished up a radio interview—announcing a few of their findings when all of a sudden Karissa's cell phone flips into the air. It had been resting on the arm of the love seat. Seriously! It does a cartwheel and falls back down—reminiscent of the levitating plant Tina and I saw back in 2012. Now, Steve's and Don's backs were turned to Karissa, so they couldn't see it. But I saw it. I was looking dead at her when it happened. It was a weird launch I might add. Very spur of the moment. How far did it travel in the air? Pretty damn far. Karissa's reaction? Pure shock.

I love it when researchers see what Tina and I have seen; it's priceless because half of them think it's me over exaggerating. I'm not. I mean coins go up in the air and never come down in this house. Throw rugs levitate, float, and spin like they were in a *Sinbad* movie. The same thing happens with our silverware and the TV remote control. Where do they go? Someone tell me.

I had an inclination that the spirits were going to do something within minutes of Karissa's arriving. Sort of like the open front door that Steve and Don witnessed. The door opening on its own is the spirits' way of saying, 'welcome home, gentleman, welcome to Keith's house. We've been waiting for you.' That's what I got from that incident. Karissa's incident was very telling in its way. You see, Karissa walked into my house with just one suitcase. Suitcase and a laptop bag. That's about it. No rigs, no crates, nothing else. Suitcase, laptop bag, and cell phone were what she came through the door with. The woman lives and breathes through her cell phone, and the spirits know that. That's why they flipped it up in the air. They weren't done with it either. Not by a long shot. Wait till Karissa gets acclimated. Watch what happens then.

So that was the first event for our phase two investigation. Don and Steve can't comment on it because they didn't see it. I did. I can now breathe a sigh of relief as a result of her arrival. Her investigation would be different from Don and Steve's. Far less technical. Karissa was here to experience the living conditions. The conditions I've been talking about for quite some time now. Those conditions include rapping noises, footsteps, pacing back and forth, wall taps, and electrical issues. That's why she was here. Her, Niki, and Mary were going to pick up where Don and Steve left off. The house monitoring, they did last year was back in effect. Substantiate Keith and Tina's claims by documenting whatever transpires.

That's our charter. That's our mission. Mary said it best: "it's time for everyone to reassemble again; it's time to monitor Keith and Karissa." So, I pulled out the cameras again. The same cameras as before—they proved useful over the summer and hopefully will be useful again. Everyone was setting was the same as before. The only difference now was that we had one of the team members living with me. The house was hers for a majority of the day. Unlike Steve and Don, where I was home during their entire stay, I would not be working from home while Karissa was here. She was here for three and a half weeks. The idea of her being home alone was golden. The house makes different noises during the day compared to the night. The wall tapings are different. Lots and lots of footsteps—especially in the hallway. Sounds of doors opening. Doors closing are possibilities that Karissa might experience as a result of being home alone. Karissa's not alone. Niki and Mary are watching the house through the cameras I set up.

The house now belongs to Karissa Fleck. The refrigerator was stocked with food, although no means to cook it. The oven was inoperable, remember? My mission that day was to contact the landlord. Let him know that the oven had copped out. And I didn't lie about the event. I told the truth. I gave him the full narrative of what had happened. He seemed cool with it. I mean, he's always been cool and receptive to everything I've said. Not once did he make me feel defensive about the damage being done to his house. Never questioned me about the writings, the fires, the equipment and appliance malfunctions. We're talking about a considerable amount of money here. A new stove costs about five hundred dollars. He was paying for it, not me. The response I got from the landlord was: he would have a brand-new oven delivered to the house in a few days. And he did.

The spirits must be asking themselves the question: who is this person living with us? Why is she here? Where are her cameras? Where are her tools and gadgets? These questions and more had to be running through the spirits' minds. I mean, a few days ago this house was occupied by two grown men. Men in their forties. Karissa is twenty years younger than the men who just left. That's a totally different mindset in comparison to Steve and Don. And to me as well. I'm Steve and Don's age. Now, try to imagine this from a "Geist's" perspective. This house hasn't had a female occupant in over a year. The generational gap between Karissa and me, between Karissa and Steve and Don, is twenty plus years. That's got to mean something to a "Geist." I can't wait to find out.

Later that day I got a Skype message from Karissa. She was still getting acclimated to the house. Still sort of chilling (as she calls it), when suddenly she admitted to hearing pitter-patter footsteps, thuds, and other inexplicable sounds. Mary and Niki were monitoring from the CCTV cameras. They can hear everything. Both ladies would occasionally hear a loud bang coming from one of the rooms upstairs. I know Steve found these noises interesting because he was always writing them down within seconds of hearing them.

The ladies knew the noise didn't come from Karissa. They can see her as plain as day. One camera was on her (no fakery going on), and the other cameras were where I left them: bedrooms, office, hallway, and kitchen. Where am I? I'm exactly where I want to be when activity breaks out. I'm at work in downtown Seattle.

By the time I got home that night, the team had already documented the daytime occurrences. I got the sense from Karissa that she was not much of a TV watcher. I walked in and not one TV was on. The house as quiet as a mouse. What I did hear was Niki, Mary, and Karissa all chatting via Skype. Which kind of made sense. After all, it must have been a paranormal investigator's wet dream to investigate a house like this. One of my dreams as an IT professional is to manage a project that involves working with Bill Gates. For him to be a sponsor of a project I'm working on would be a dream come true. I hope that's what Karissa, Niki, and Mary were feeling right now. I hope that's what Steve and Don felt while here. I mean, this is the profession you chose. Forget why you chose it. The question now is: what you are going to do as a result of being here? I've watched many teams come in. A majority of them expose their inexperience within seconds of being in the house: *Ghost Adventures* included. One thing this house is good at is exposing people's credentials. The spirits seem to relish their role in determining who is real and who is fake when it comes to studying the paranormal. No one takes the paranormal more seriously than spirits. The question for the researcher should be: how serious are you? How dedicated are you to the science?

It pleased me to see the ladies immersed in discussion about what to do next. Three ladies, mind you. Not egotistical men. Three ladies, executing a plan of action that was agreed upon before Karissa's involvement. I tried to stay out of their way as much as possible. I'll come running if you need me. And trust me, they'll call me if they need me. Karissa will make sure of that. It's steady as she goes right now. The next morning Karissa decided to text everyone—she wanted everyone to know she was about to walk into the office to conduct an EVP session. I had to pause and think for a second. *Oh wow, you're going to the office?* Are you sure you want to do that? That's what I asked her. Her reply was basically, "We go big, or we go home." No team has ever done an EVP session in the office? Karissa would be the first. Steve and Don had other fish to fry while here—they simply ran out of time. Not Karissa, she was determined to take the bull by the horns sort of speak. She made it her number mission of conducting an EVP session in the most dangerous room in the house.

Who am I to stop her? I mean, I'm at work. The whole point of her coming here was to experience what I've been seeing. To hear what I've been hearing. That includes voices. That includes asking certain questions. I got home from work a few hours later. Perfect timing too, because Karissa had just gotten done with the office. She was on her way to her bedroom to review the audio with Mary and Niki. I went downstairs to do whatever it is I was doing until I'm called for. And guess what? I was called for. The ladies found something they wanted me to hear. Karissa struck gold while in the office. She got several vocal responses. One which confirmed what I already knew. She got a "yes."

Question	Answer
"Did you write on this office wall?"	'Yes' 00:14
"Do you need help?"	'Just look at it' 00:27

Table 49.1 EVP – Keith's office

Karissa Fleck - EVP Session /Office
Question: Did you write on this office wall?
Answer: 'Yes'

Fig 49.1 Karissa conducted a stellar EVP session in the office. First investigator to ever do so.

Karissa Fleck's EVP capture
https://youtu.be/gLFvlEl9GTc

I'm not sure which response is more startling: the 'yes' that Karissa was able to obtain or the whisper after it that said, 'just look at it.' What do you mean 'just look at it'? If I didn't know any better, I would say the spirit was sort of taking pride it what it had done or what another spirit had done. That's the impression I got after hearing Karissa's question and answer session. What does the spirit want us to look at? I mean the 666 and upside-down man are still there. I've been unable to paint over the writings entirely, the wall writings for reasons I can't explain keep bleeding through the paint and primer that I lay down.

When Karissa told me that's the room she wanted to conduct her first EVP session in, I was like: really? I mean, as hard as Steve and Don worked while here neither of them spent a lot of time in my office. I don't know if that was by design or if it was outright forgetfulness. Well, Karissa didn't forget anything. That was one of the first rooms she ventured into, and lucky she did. Her "did you write on the office wall?" conjured up a very definite response, which was 'yes.' They didn't pause either which suggests the spirit was comfortable admitting its culpability.

This confession to the wall writing goes hand in hand with the EVP Don had captured a few days ago. A voice that said: 'pushed Keith downstairs.' They didn't say 'pushed him downstairs.' They said, 'pushed Keith downstairs.' They specifically said 'Keith.' Remember the Die KL, writings on the lawn? The writings on my office wall? One revelation being formed as a result of Don's and

Karissa's EVP is the spirits know who I am. They know my name, and they know my office. We can't forget about my kitchen chair, how it was possibly asported into my office. We can't forget about the burnt photographs. Every photo of me (photos I didn't even know I had) scorched. Just my face, no one else's. We can't forget about the car trunk incident, which went on for over a year.

We can't forget about the poster fire. That one still rocks me a little bit. We can't forget about the poking and the prodding. The bed shakes. The sheet tugs and all the other stuff I mentioned through the course of this book. Fr. Roy was right "there is an inordinate amount of spirits living here."

Fig 49.2 1.) Die KL – 2014, 2.) My face burned off the family photo 3.) Ransacked office 4.) The chair I sit in the kitchen – mysteriously pulled out (several times) teleported to the office.

It didn't take me long to appreciate Karissa Fleck's method for investigating a residential home. I mean, every team is different. We all play to our strengths, right? I do when I'm at work, and I'm sure you, the reader, do as well. Karissa's strength is doing nothing. The first few days I was like, what the hell? I mean I'm Daniel Son, and she's Mr. Miyagi. That's how we looked on the surface. Every morning I'd get up for work and walk by the room Karissa is sleeping in. She's sound asleep. I'm thinking to myself, *shouldn't you be up by now?* Steve and Don worked eighteen hours straight. Matter of fact I can't remember Steve Mera falling asleep ever. The man was a walking, living, breathing data center. I'm talking about a full day. Karissa is the total opposite. She has to sleep first.

Then it dawned on me. She has something Steve and Don didn't have. She has birds in the sky. That's what we called it. The format for Karissa Fleck's investigation is the total opposite of Don and Steve's. Steve and Don, with thirty years of investigative experience, went looking for the truth. Karissa Fleck performs under a different operating system. She doesn't need to go looking for the truth. The truth, i.e., the spirits go looking for her. Niki and Mary were observing it all from carefully positioned CCTV cameras.

So, I get to work each morning, and nothing's happening. At least that's what I'm thinking. 11 am rolls around, and all of sudden Skype blows up. It's Karissa—she's awake now. Karissa goes into detail about how much she was being poked at and jabbed while trying to fall asleep. She describes them as being relentless, persistent. She's right. They're a damn nuisance. Niki and Mary have been watching Karissa sleep and have written down in their notes her constant tossing and turning, her fighting off something while trying to sleep. No camera in the world can capture poking and prodding. That's not going to happen. So, let's toss that expectation out the window. But what the ladies witness is useful. It adds weight to my complaint of constantly being bombarded while trying to sleep. Karissa wakes up, and she hardly has to mention the type of night she had, because the ladies already know it. They've just seen the type of night she had. What they see how she was tossing and turning. They see a woman at war with her bed pillows. They see a woman talking in her sleep. Occasionally they'll see a corner of the sheet rise on its own. They don't know if it's Karissa's ankle, foot, or another part of her leg. All they know is that it looks weird and downright uncomfortable. I don't want to use the word contorted because that sounds downright scary but that's exactly how they say describe it.

This is what they're writing down in their notes. Everyone in the chat room agrees that Karissa had a tough time sleeping last night. We got it on video, and we got Karissa being vocal about what she experienced. Karissa finally felt the time was right for clueing me in as to how she conducts her investigations. Her method involves chilling around the house. She has to get acclimated to the environment first before carrying out her investigation. It's important that the spirits see her as not being a threat. That they see her as being laid back. She wants the spirits thinking that she's in over her head; total naivety. Be as off-putting as possible. That lures them in. *Ghost Adventures* thought they could come here with all their expensive gear and that alone will get the spirits shaking in their boots. They were wrong. Like I said earlier, when Karissa walked through my door, all she had was a suitcase and laptop bag.

So, we're all in agreement: Keith is getting beat up tremendously when he sleeps. Niki and Mary are interviewing Karissa—they're documenting her experience and comparing it to mine. The question everyone's asking themselves now is: how do we make it stop? No one is under the impression that moving out of this house is going to solve the problem of sheets being yanked off the bed when trying to sleep. "If you have paranormal occurrences outside of the home, then odds are you're going to have paranormal occurrences in your new place of residence." That's what Karissa said, and that's what Niki said. Moving solves nothing.

Fig 49.2 24/7 Monitoring

Fig 49.3 Guest bedroom – Karissa's room for one month.

Chapter 50
A Child's Voice

One of the benefits of being monitored twenty-four seven is that you can go to bed and not worry about anything. The birds in the sky 'Niki and Mary' are always watching. The ladies don't need me anymore—I'm just the tech guy now. Their goal is to monitor Karissa's movements; monitor her interactions with the spirits in the house. So far so good. The house belongs to the three ladies the minute I go to bed. Karissa retires to the guest bedroom to conduct several EVP sessions within minutes of us saying goodnight to each other.

Later that night I heard something that I haven't heard in a while. Rustling noises. *It's 3 am, and I'm exhausted.* This noise I was hearing has been going on for quite some time now. The rustling sound was going back and forth as if someone was pacing the hallway. In my half-asleep state I did something I'm not overly proud of—I did nothing. Yep, that's right: I did nothing. I mean, protocol dictates that I leap out of bed and start running to the door. But I don't, and I can't for the life of me figure out why. I was more concerned with going back to sleep versus investigating what the noise was. I was tired, but it was a weird sort of tiredness. It was an energy drained type of tiredness. I was mentally slothful if that makes any sense. To justify my slothful tiredness, I said to myself: *Karissa must be going to the bathroom.* That has to be her making that noise.

This rustling sound went on for an hour or so. I could see shadows pacing back and forth through the cracks of my bedroom door. Reminiscent of mine and Tina's encounter two years ago. I'd bet my last dollar it was the Gray Lady traveling back and forth from the guest bedroom by my office to the hallway landing area. I bet that's what she was doing. I wonder if Karissa's presence (the fact that she's a female) somehow conjured up the Gray Lady, aka the Jane Doe lookalike?

I asked Karissa that morning if she was roaming around in the hallway last night. She replied "no, she wasn't." I asked her did she hear it, and she replied back with an enthusiastic "yes!"

I asked her why she didn't get up and investigate, and her reply was, she was uncharacteristically tired. She felt drained. Almost to the point of not wanting to move. And I'm like, so was I. I felt slothful and lazy. The last time I felt like that was when I felt those footsteps approach me in the bed. That was back in 2014. Instead of leaping out of bed like I normally do, I just acquiesced. Total submission almost—and that's when I felt the swoosh feeling. Last night's fatigue was like that. We both heard the rustling noise, and we both felt too weak to get up. So: what did Niki and Mary get? Sadly, they got nothing. The ladies were monitoring Karissa the entire night. It appears that the noise we heard was limited to just us. But that's not even the scary part. If I had to guess how many people were in the hallway last night, based on the noise level I heard, I would have to say no less than four individuals. That's how many spirits I believed were in the hallway. So, the Gray Lady wasn't alone.

When it came time to review the hallway footage the only thing worth noting was a few taps, pops, springs, and pings. The hallway camera picked up some minor rapping sounds but nothing close to what Karissa and I were describing. Karissa and I both slept with our doors closed. The ladies know how to call us should something go down. That night nothing did. The all too familiar rustling sound. I know it was the Gray Lady; my instincts tell it was her. She was roaming the house last night, and if I had to guess, I'd say it was because Karissa was here. So now I'm thinking: what's going to happen once Niki gets here? Two women and one guy? How are the spirits going to react then? Damn, I wish I'd leaped out of bed and opened the damn bedroom door. I wonder what I would have found. Nothing, probably. Everything stops the second you open the door. Everything vanishes. Sort of reminds me of the Schrödinger's Cat - Copenhagen interpretation theory. The theory states *that a quantum system remained in this superposition until it interacted with, or was observed by, the external world, at which time the superposition collapses into one or another of the possible definite states.* It's the observer effect all over again.

We talked about that rustling sound for a while that day. But forget about that story for now. Remember the kid 'cough'? Well, he's back. Only this time, he doesn't cough. He speaks. I'm talking about a kid electronic voice phenomenon. That's what Karissa's going to get next.

As I said earlier, the ladies don't need me anymore. All Karissa does is raise her voice recorder. She could be in her room, in the kitchen, in the office, or in the hallway. She was always kneeling somewhere. Always conducting an EVP session. That night she decided to do something different. She walked up to me and said, "I'm going to sit outside on your backyard patio; I'm going to see if I can get some spirits to talk to me." Very nonchalant like. She and Don gave me goosebumps every time they said that. I mean, who wants to talk to spirits? I don't. Not after what Tina and I tried in summer 2014.

Washington State Poltergeist "Three" EVP
https://youtu.be/IJdqk8xPKVE

Karissa: "Are there shadow people out here?"
Karissa: "How many"
Answer: "Three"

Fig 50.1 "Three"

Top: My hand sketch drawings of shadow figures I've seen.
Left: Night? House attack. Three chairs were pulled away from the table – Triangle?
Right: Day – house attack.
Three chairs again. Same chairs. Almost identical. Occurrences were months apart.

I think we all can agree that the voice you just heard is a child's voice. A male child. Now it's impossible to know if the kid 'cough' Tina and I heard and the 'three' that Karissa captured on her voice recorder is the same spirit. We'll never know that. No one has ever captured a child EVP in this house before. This being one of the best EVPs ever to be captured at Bothell home.

There are several things about this child EVP that haunt me. Karissa got this off the backyard patio in the dead of night. You can hear the wind whistling in the background, as well as trees rustling, cars driving by. Now some people think the boy said 'tree.' I believe he said 'three,' based on the fact that Karissa asked him a direct question: "are there shadow people out here? How many?" Pause. 'Three/Tree.'

I truly believe it's 'three' and not 'tree.' There's a lisp in the response that might confuse some in thinking the kid said 'tree,' it cements the notion that this is a child responding. Please listen to it again with headphones and tell me it sort of feels like the child is everywhere and nowhere at the same time. It not like 'three' came from beyond the backyard fence line. It's not like it was distant or far away. I don't know who uttered the word 'three' when asked a question. All I know is it responded to a question about shadow people, which leads me to my next weird thing. When the ladies analyzed the 'three' the next day, everyone agreed that this was to be documented as Class A EVP. But no one was thinking

381

what I was thinking, which was: this thing just admitted to three shadow people being nearby. Over the last few years, that's all I've seen walk by my office—shadowy figures. Those paw prints on my office wall, the ones that appeared in the December attack. They came in sets of three—single file. All three sets of them.

I can't tell you how many times Tina and I walked through the front door of our house and saw three kitchen chairs pulled out to form what looks like a triangle (See Fig 50.1). The chairs were arranged in such a way as to suggest there had been a meeting of some sort? Speculation or not this happened several times in 2014. It went on for months. Always three chairs. No more, no less—always triangle shaped. That's where my mind went after hearing the cryptic 'three' response.

Are you still with me? We're almost at the end, ladies and gentlemen. I promise you we're going to go out with a bang (no pun intended). Niki Novell (Niki) hasn't even arrived yet. If you think Steve Mera never sleeps, wait till you see how Niki conducts her investigations. It makes sense for her to be in the house—she's been the team leader since this project began. Bird in the sky Mary is her investigative assistant—the one that made all of this possible.

You have to live in this house if you're an investigator if you're to have any chance of understanding what goes on here. Be a squatter for a week or two. Or three like Karissa did. S.E.P knew that. As did Niki, as did Karissa. Colin Wilson and Harry Price would be so proud of these ladies right now. But we're not done. I made a promise at the very beginning of this book that I wasn't going to pull punches. The facts you seek about what Tina and I went through are in these pages, nowhere else. I only share what's relevant, no more, no less. The events Tina and I experienced are connected to everything the previous tenant experienced. I'm talking about Jane Doe and her beloved family. I've not been able to reach any of the other previous tenants. I haven't given up trying, no way no how.

Chapter 51
The Moment of Truth

If there were one investigator I was most excited about arriving, it would have to be Niki Novelle. None of this would be happening if it wasn't for her and Mary inviting me on their radio show. They were closer to the paranormal community than any team thus far. The first to believe our claims post "Demons in Seattle" episode. Things were sort of taking off again due to the lady's involvement— word was getting around that this case was open again. 'I wonder why that house is still being investigated? And by who? I thought *Ghost Adventures* reached the conclusion nothing was there?' One of the first things Niki told me when she decided to help me was: "anything we find will be given to you first. You decide what the world sees." Even the Scientific Establishment of Parapsychology never told me that. The only thing Niki wanted to do was capture it, and analyze what they've caught, show me the results if I say yes, it goes out to her paranormal colleagues. Colleagues after colleagues will see the evidence in doing so come to the conclusion that there was more to this case than *Ghost Adventures* realized. No paranormal team should ever position themselves as being the ultimate thumbs up, thumbs down on what's paranormal and what's not.

Remember: absence of evidence, does not mean evidence is absent. https://en.wikipedia.org/wiki/Evidence_of_absence

February, 2016—Karissa and I were picking Niki up from the airport. The second part of phase two is about to begin. Remember how I described Karissa's arrival? What she brought when she came here? What Steve and Don brought? Well, Niki brought multiple suitcases. Three in all. Each one was packed to the hilt with paranormal gear. I'm talking handheld devices. The same type of equipment that Steve and Don used when they were here. This was going to be fun. Something tells me they were going to uncover something that no one else has ever seen. *The apparition standing near my bedroom door notwithstanding.*

Now there were certain aspects of this case that interests people more than other aspects. For example, one of the first things Steve and Don asked for when they got here was the burnt Bibles. They ran their fingers up and down the pages. Tore a few pages out and tried to replicate the pages being burned. They couldn't. One of the first things Mary did when the cameras were set up in my house last summer was monitor the hallway. The hallway was her favorite room to monitor. Why? Because I said, it was the most active room in the house. Niki's favorite room when it came to house monitoring was the master bedroom. The events coming out of that room are some of the most profound claims the paranormal community has ever heard. My claim of being poked and prodded when sleeping. To prevent someone from getting a good night's sleep is one of the most extreme forms of torment.

How does one investigate torment? How do you analyze someone being poked and prodded? I'm not even sure you can. Niki wasn't either. But she has to investigate it, and that's what she'd been doing prior to arriving. Monitoring the bedroom for weeks and months with the hopes of catching some of what I've been reporting. And she did. She captured the loud noises. The thuds. The knocking. She got all of that. I've made that available in this book and on my YouTube channel. But the ultimate claim of all is the poking and prodding. You can't approach that from CCTV. I'm not sure you can even get that while being here on site. But we're going to try, ladies and gentlemen. The Washington State Poltergeist team is going to try.

The four of us talked about a lot of things that night. Niki, Karissa, Mary (via CCTV camera) and myself. We've just completed week one of their three-week investigation. Karissa has captured some amazing EVPs. She's logged in her video diary the weird noises she's heard. Now she and Niki must team up and go after some other stuff. Interactive stuff, if you will. Let's see what these spirits can do when everyone's back is turned. Niki has a lot she wants to do in the five days that's she's here.

Niki went upstairs after our conference call, and it wasn't long before she called us up there. While we were downstairs talking, the spirits were upstairs doing their thing. Niki walked into her guest bedroom and immediately noticed that all her equipment had been rearranged. One of the first things Niki did when arriving at my house was go upstairs to her room. She spent the first hour or so unpacking everything. Imagine coming back later and finding all your equipment rearranged in a way you know you didn't do. It would appear her equipment had been rummaged through. By who? We don't know. If I had to guess I would say it was the same spirits that uttered 'It's a camera, it's a camera,' they seem to have an interest in electronic devices. That's what Niki had on her bed.

Recap: Steve and Don experienced the front door being opened when they arrived. Karissa's iPhone done a cartwheel in the air within minutes of her arriving. Niki has just had her equipment rearranged. Go back to the video where Steve and Don are in the hallway setting up stuff (see below). On the playback of that moment, voices can be heard around them: 'it's a camera, it's a camera... Nite cam.' Same kind of curiosity with Niki's equipment—only more hands-on. You know an investigation is off to a good start when the lead investigator equipment gets rearranged.

Refresher (best with headsets on)	https://youtu.be/0O_1_vEomBk	Listen at 1:11, 1:14, 1:23, 1:25

Table 51.1

I remember saying to myself before as I lay in bed that I can't wait for Niki and Karissa to be alone in this house. Two weeks ago, it was Steve and Don. Last week it was just Karissa and me. This week it's Karissa and Niki. All of this has to mean something to an entity. Be it negative or positive; it has to mean something to the "Geist" living here. I've seen the energy level change in our house numerous times with just me and Tina living here. I've seen the energy change when we've had a house full of friends and family. The activity tends to change when different individuals come and go. The entities must be enjoying all this attention. Their curiosity must be at an all-time high.

I went to work the next morning knowing that I now had two women in my house. Two diverse backgrounds. Two different walks of life. The house is yours. Remember, I'm only a Skype call away, should you ladies need anything. It wasn't long before Niki began to appreciate what was taking place. One of the drawbacks of monitoring the house last summer was not knowing what to expect. It's hard to discern what something is and isn't when you're three-thousand miles away. Niki could now hear the rapping's from the rooms she was sitting in. I can't state this too strongly. There's a case to be made about sleeping in an infested house. A case to be made about a researcher taking a shower in an active house. About a researcher going to the bathroom. To the kitchen. Doing stuff that Tina and I did. A case can be made about a lot of things. Everything helps.

The anomalies taking place around Niki and Karissa were similar to the anomalies taking place around Tina and me. Around Steve and Don, and around all the other investigators that came here.

Poltergeists are notorious for draining electronics and battery powered items. A device that's been recently charged should not go from 100% to 0% in a matter of seconds. This happens multiple times on multiple devices. It pisses you off when it does—at least it did for me. It takes about an hour or so to charge stuff. You're ready to go the minute an item is done charging. But the entity has other plans. It knows what you're trying to do. It knows you need that device in order to detect it. So, it steals it from you—it drains your power pack. That device is suddenly useless. Karissa and Niki had their battery drainage issues within days of being in the home. But that's not all.

They begin to understand my claim of voices appearing out of thin air. I'm talking about EMF fluctuations throughout the day, especially around the door area of both the master and guest bedrooms. The readings would vary. Why does a doorway have high EMF, when an office with tons of electronic gear does not? Why does a headboard have a higher EMF reading than the television (when it's on)? The fluctuations come and go. The reading of the office is normal (for a room with electronic gear in it), whereas the readings from in and around the hallway are not. Readings vary from day to day.

Now, the voice captures are interesting. We've now switched from disembodied male voices to primarily female disembodied voices. I was getting texted at work via Skype that a new EVP was found. A female voice. Niki got on her device, and Karissa got it on hers. Mary being the virtual person on the scene can vouch as well. The majority of the EVP sessions were being conducted in and around the cameras. I've included the videos of some of those disembodied voices. Evidence captured by Niki, Karissa, Steve, Don, and others is in the back of this book. This chart below summarizes what Niki witnessed and experienced for her one week stay.

Week 2 Niki and Karissa	Events Witnessed
Day 1	Equipment on bed re-arranged. Electronic interference. Vibration
Day 2	Equipment drainage, EVPs, knocking, phantom footsteps.
Day 3	Pulsating mattress e.g. heart beating bed, EMF fluctuations and anomalies, footsteps, vibrations.
Day 4	EMF fluctuations and anomalies, footsteps, vibrations.
Day 5	Knocks, footsteps, vibrations.
Day 6	Baby doll experiment, Tripwire, EVPs, knocks, Bible turning pages, EVP bible reading

Table 51.2 Events Niki / Karissa witnessed during Niki's one week stay

If there was one thing that was worth the price of admission for Steve and Don it had to be the day when both men were close to me, and the camera moved on its own. That incident set the bar for the remainder of their investigation. It told Steve and Don what they were up against. Niki and Karissa were about to experience a similar moment—their moment of truth.

Day 3. I asked the ladies what they needed (if anything) when I come home from work each day. They usually told me "no, they've got everything they need." Day 3 was different—they needed personal effects and supplies. So, we went out for supplies. We were back home an hour later. Karissa and Niki immediately began setting up their equipment for tonight. Normally, the Curious George in me would pull up a chair to watch or listen in. I mean, some of the investigative work is fascinating. Not today, though. I was tired. I needed a power nap. The only way I can be productive later is if I can get an hour's nap in. So, I told the ladies I was going upstairs to take a nap. I'll close my bedroom door and let them do what they need to do. Minutes later, I'm lying in bed, about to fall asleep when all of a sudden, I felt what I normally feel. *I feel the minions approaching.* The ones responsible for my sleep deprivation. The ones that carry out the poking and prodding.

The minions weren't doing anything new. The same bombardment as before, the same molestation. I just wanted to watch TV and hopefully dose off. *Uh, uh not going to happen, Keith Linder. Here we come.* They arrived at the foot of the bed. I could feel the mattress indenting at the foot of the bed. They're very subtle. Almost like ants responding to a dropped candy cane. One by one they come, until all of a sudden there were several of them around. We've all seen the Disney *Dalmatians* movie? Imagine ten puppy Dalmatians leaping onto the bed with you. The minute you lay down, here they come. It's like they've been waiting all day for you. You're finally coming to bed. *Daddy's home!* Is the only way I can describe it? My bedroom, guest bedroom, or hotel room, doesn't matter—the experience is the same. I can't tell why it's happening. I can't even tell you what is happening. All I can tell you is: it's happening, and it's real. I know it's real by the pressure in the mattress. I know it's real by the pokes in my rib cage. I know it's real by the pulsating coming from inside the mattress. Some mornings I wake up with a headache. Like I've been partying all night. That's how bad it becomes. Some mornings I wake up feeling fine. Most of the time I'm just tired. I leave my house or hotel and go about my business. It's not fun.

So, I began to feel another unnerving activity, one I know all too well. The pulsating from within the mattress. Best way to understand this? Think about a real human pulse. Place your forefinger on your wrist or neck. Locate your pulse and hold your finger there for a moment. Feel your heartbeat? Well, guess what? That's what my bed is doing right now. Not the entire mattress—particular sections only, the areas where the indentations occurred. Some nights the pulsating is normal speed—the same as your pulse when the body is at rest. Some nights it's rapid, so pitter-patter that you think these things must have been running a marathon to get here. Now understand me when I say this. Just as each bed indentation is different (suggesting they're different sizes), the throbbing and pulsating varies too. I have had heavy bed indentations. I compare it to a bowling ball being placed on a bed. It falls on the bed and rolls toward what's heavier than it; me. Those are rare occurrences though. Thank God! No, what I felt was more similar to billiard balls being placed on the bed. A better example of that is the cat or small analogy. The weight? It varies.

We've all driven on the highway and seen those small sandbags lying across the legs of those detour or road construction signs? That's the perfect example of what these minions do. They drape themselves across my extremities: ankles, inner knee, elbow, and feet. Extremities and pillow are where you'll find them. They usually come after 3 am or so. The fact they're descending on me now is not troubling; it's happened many times before—coming when I'm trying to take a nap.

Now, so that you know that I'm not imagining things: I finally worked up the nerve to do something. Something I've never done before. I decided to remove my leg from the area where the throbbing was. I wanted to confirm if the pulse was there before calling Niki. I knew it was, but I just wanted to be sure. When I placed my finger on the spot of the bed where the throbbing was, I felt it ten times better. The pulse is rapid, consistent, as in repetitive. It's strong. I got no sense that it was about to dissipate as a result of my hand being over it. And that's when I screamed out, "Niki and Karissa, come up here right now!"

It didn't take long for them to arrive. The first thing I told Niki was, "Put your hand right there." I lifted up my hand and made way for Niki's. It didn't take her long to feel what I was feeling. The first words out of her mouth were, "oh my God."

Neither lady had ever experienced anything like this. The looks on their faces were priceless. Whatever plane ticket they bought to get here had to have been sizable. Its pittance compared to what they've just now seen. There are things you can't understand. And there are things you can't explain even if you understand them. This is one of those things. Bed mattresses don't have heartbeats, ladies and gentlemen. Heartbeats do not come from inanimate objects. But here's a section of the mattress beating as if it was a heart, Niki and Karissa can feel it with their own hands and fingers.

Steve and Don's moment of truth was the camera incident. They heard the beep from my laptop indicating motion had been detected. They saw the email that came in showing nothing but a white wall (with the camera facing backward). Karissa and Niki's moment of truth came the minute they felt the pulse coming from within the mattress. This has been going on for over three years now. That's when the night terrors began. The weird dreams. Both teams were aware of my claims before taking my case. If you google the words Keith Linder Forum, you'll find communities online where I've mentioned both instances. Years before I knew Steve Mera even existed. Years before I knew Niki or Karissa existed.

The repeated feedback from most has been: can you take a picture of it? Which, as you know, is ludicrous. How do you photograph a pulse? You can't. I've seen a lot of equipment come through the front door of my house. There's not been a paranormal team yet that's walked into my house with equipment capable of capturing what I just described. Do you know why? Because it's unimaginable. It's a whole new paradigm. Niki feeling my mattress pulsate is better than all the evidence combined. The pulsating doesn't last long either. It's momentary. It's exactly how I described it. Unnerving.

Washington State Poltergeist
Case Timeline

- Phase I – Constant house monitoring by US Teams (Niki and Mary). Summer – Fall 2015
- Phase II – Enacted if Phase I was successful. Involves Niki Novelle and Karissa Fleck living in the home for a considerable amount of time. 3 ½ weeks total.

The Scientific Establishment of Parapyschology and Don Philips were contacted without the consent or knowledge of the US Team. Reason #1: Both investiagtions needed to be conducted without the other team's knowledge. The activity Tina and I endured warrants more involvement from the paranormal community. It deserved the attention from a Parapsychcologists organization. Many were contacted. A few responded saying, "Seattle was too far from them to travel. Seriously?"

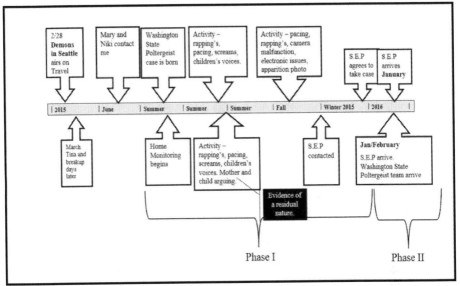

Fig 51.1 Washington State Poltergeist case timeline

Chapter 52
The Doll Experiment

One of the first things Niki wanted to do once she arrived was come up with an experiment which, if successful, would blow the minds of those in the paranormal community. We know there are spirits here. We know they can manipulate our electronic devices. We know they love to get close to just about everyone who's come to the house. We know they can rearrange objects. We know a lot of things. We don't know what they'll do when we're not around. Can we get them to interact with a foreign object? We're all in agreement you can never have too much evidence. It's time to spread the evidence cache out a little bit. We've got voices. We've got rapping's. We've got pulsating mattresses, and we've got devices that lose power inexplicably. Steve and Don were up to their necks in evidence just a few weeks ago. According to the email Steve sent me last night, they were somewhat overwhelmed by the quantity of information they've brought back home. They were working feverishly as we speak. But you can always get more, right? I mean, we're talking about the paranormal here. We're talking about a poltergeist. A "Geist" with the ability to go dormant, resurface, and go dormant again. A "Geist" with enough energy to haunt Jane Doe's family eight years ago. That's how long the "Geist" has been here—that we know of. It could be longer; we just don't know.

We know there's more information to be had. Niki knows this. Her experience has taught her always to go up and beyond. If you have an idea, run with it. And that's exactly what the Washington State Poltergeist team was going to do. I think it was two days before Niki's departure that she introduced to me and Karissa to her shadow baby doll. What the hell is a shadow baby doll? That's exactly what I said when Niki revealed it. This doll is no ordinary doll. It's not a child's toy. This doll is a shadow detection doll.

The experiment Niki wanted to conduct was relatively simple. We were going to place this shadow doll in the house somewhere, surround it with cameras, and hopefully get some response. The doll will send a signal if and when it detects a moving shadow. Understand me perfectly. Movement alone won't do it. It has to be a shadow. This is different from my Foscam cameras. This is different from the infrared tripwires Steve Mera used.

But that's not all. Once we get the doll propped up somewhere with several cameras trained on it, the situation calls for voice recorders as well. Why voice recorders? Well, we want to see if there are conversations taking place while we're away from the house. You see, we're leaving the house. After Niki and Karissa set up everything, we're leaving. This experiment is useless if one of is here. The cameras are going to be our eyes, and the voice recorder is going to be our ears. Plus, Mary, our virtual bird in the sky, has agreed to be on standby. She'll be monitoring all the rooms upstairs. The cameras she's logged into are close enough to hear the sound the doll makes if and when it goes off.

The doll is Niki's experiment. It's her brainchild. But why stop there? That's what my thinking was when Niki informed everybody about her idea. She wants to put her doll on the couch. She needs for it to be out in the open—in plain view. We'll have multiple cameras on it and a few voice recorders. And we're bouncing. We're leaving the house for three hours. Now, there are risks to this experiment. The spirits here know our limitations. They know all they can do to render this experiment failure is just zap the battery life out of every electronic device. They can cut the power to the house. Hell, they can even take the doll or the cameras for that matter. They've done that to me plenty of times. We're talking about four hundred dollars' worth of equipment gone in the blink of an eye. That's nothing to them. I think Niki paid two hundred dollars for that doll. We were going to be gone for three hours. The spirits don't need three hours. They don't need ten seconds. When stuff disappears, it disappears within the blink of an eye. That's happened to me standing right next to something. Imagine setting your iPhone down on the table. You turn for a second and turn back. That iPhone's gone. That's the risk I'm talking about. Still, remember Niki's response to risks: "we go big, or we go home."

I decided to build on Niki's idea. If we're going do this "Gangnam style," then I need to lace the house with tripwires. We'll have cameras on the doll downstairs and cameras on the tripwires upstairs. It'll be like Fort Knox in here.

We all made a point of baselining everything before leaving. Remove any potential false-positives. All devices were fully charged. System check: passed. Soundcheck and person check. Mary had access to every camera upstairs. The doll was good to go, as were my tripwires. Now, where are we going to go for three hours? Kurt Cobain's house, that's where the ladies wanted to go. That's been on their bucket list for as long as they can remember. And that's where we went. The information below describes what happened within minutes of us leaving.

Please watch the video before proceeding further -
https://youtu.be/_xt7GiGhlrs

Fig 52.1 bought off eBay

Paranormal Ghost Hunting Equipment Trigger Object with Shadow
Detection Alarm

Unexplainable events happened when the house was empty	Responsible for the Evidence being captured	Details	Technology
Shadow Baby Activation	Niki Novell	Doll goes off less than ten minutes after leaving. Doll vibrates and gives off a creepy laugh when it detects a shadow. Happened several times.	Shadow Detector – Toy baby doll. $260
Footsteps, lights going off in master bedroom room, Talking	Karissa Fleck	Karissa placed several GoPros in the hallway. Camera detected movement, captured lights going off in bedroom. Voices are heard, footsteps, rapping's, and shadows.	Several GoPros, Several voice recorders.
Trigger Alarms going off	Keith Linder	After seeing the success Steve Mera had with tripwire trigger alarms, I bought and setup through the hallway devices with invisible red beams. They send out an alarm when tripped.	Trigger alert – Motion beam detectors.

Table 52.1 Mary observed the house while we were gone; we call her our bird in
the sky.

Evidence	Information	Location
Demons in Seattle - Doll Video	Camera 1. 3:49 1st Baby laughter; Camera 3 at 5:20 Karissa's cameras at 14:28 Upstairs baby laughter POV (Point of View); Tripwires go off at 31:58 Tripwires get Activated; again at 32:32 Tripwires get taken over. Again at 33:12 lasts over 10 minutes. 39:33 Loud bang/Movement in the house. Sounds like something fell over? Tripwires finally stop at 39:44; [house goes quiet] 1:12:55 Final baby laughter.	https://youtu.be/_xt7GiGhlrs

Table 52.2 Demons in Seattle - Doll Video

All three of us have left the house. We were all in my car, heading to Seattle when Mary sends us all a Skype message. The shadow baby has just gone off. She heard it from the camera she was listening through upstairs. We weren't even gone ten minutes, and the trigger doll had been stimulated. So, let's check that off. Niki had three cameras pointed at the shadow baby. Camera 1 is what you saw first. We don't have footage of camera two because its battery died. We're not sure when, but it was drained completely by the time we got home. We have to think it drained within minutes of us leaving because the other camera caught footage of the shadow baby going off. Camera three was located upstairs. It was perched on the upstairs landing area, looking down.

The tripwires that I ordered off Amazon started going off thirty minutes later. Three of them all together. Make sure you go to 33:12 (table 52.2) it's very important. Here you see the tripwires going off for a considerable amount of time. Almost ten minutes, I believe. Mary was observing all of this from the hallway camera. She was keeping all of us up-to-date via Skype. Did we feel the urge to make a U-turn in the car and go back to the house? Of course, we did. I know I did. I thought for sure hell was about to break out. I'm glad we didn't though. The experiment was underway. We would have contaminated our experiment had we rushed back home. The tripwires were ringing non-stop for nearly ten minutes. That's a fantastic amount of time.

Then came the loud bang at 39:33. It's easy to hear, and it sounds like it came from the hallway. The noise finally stops at 39:44, and the cameras keep rolling as you can see. Thirty-odd minutes later, the shadow baby goes off again at

1:12:53 that same creepy cry indicating a shadow is nearby. Not us, we're downtown Seattle. It's been dark outside for quite some time, ladies and gentlemen. No outside atmospheric condition is causing that shadow baby to go off. Three things have taken place simultaneously A.) Shadow baby going off B.) Tripwires being activated (something broke the invisible red beam) and C.) The loud thud sounds. Watch the videos of me sleeping again, and you'll see the noise is eerily similar.

This was compelling evidence. We had three devices, all independent of each other, informing us that something was happening. The doll was downstairs, and the tripwires were upstairs. There's so much going on in the hour and a half video. Think shadow baby is going off. Think rapping's, wall taps, pacing back and forth noises, and multiple UVPs. Please watch the video again, on a large screen (preferably your computer monitor). Don't watch it on a handheld device. Think IMAX experience. I want you to watch the video again because there's something you might have missed—something extremely important.

Maximize your computer browser and go to 3:49 (loop it on YouTube). Don't blink. You'll notice the entire house flickers, almost like an eye blink, seconds before the shadow baby laughs. The room blinks. The sun doesn't do that when passing through clouds. It's weird. That energy loss or energy flux (before an event taking place), is what I've been trying to tell people for many years. It's what Tina tried to tell people. I'm talking about the level of energy. How can a TV come in if it's not plugged in? What can drain a handheld device within seconds? Niki and Karissa were able to see this with their own eyes. Neither could explain how that happened. Then you have the tripwires going off upstairs some thirty minutes later. Who's in the house? No one is. That's what's makes this good evidence.

So, where do we go with this? What do you do with a mattress that pulsates? Who out there can explain why my bed has a heartbeat of its own? Several heartbeats of its own. This is the second bed, third mattress I've had. Same thing. Pulsating and beating. I was beginning to realize, as were Niki and Karissa, it's no wonder we can't get rid of these spirits. It's no mystery why others have failed. Look at the activity taking place. Look how powerful they are. I mean, think about it. It shouldn't be a mystery anymore as to why the Bibles caught fire. Or why Tina and I had such a tough time. Everything Niki, Mary, Karissa, and the Scientific Establishment have uncovered speaks to the capability these spirits have. Every experiment Steve and Don conducted that Niki and Karissa conducted deserves its own book. When I say book, I mean the amount of information in need of being deconstructed. *But what do I know? I'm just the house occupant.* Parapsychologists and researchers the world over should be conferencing amongst themselves as to what's taking place here. No adolescent child is living here. Not now and not in 2014, when the activity seemed to reach its apex. Just Keith and Tina. It's always been just us.

Niki had several things she wanted to do before she headed back to the East Coast. Several more experiments to conduct that prove how active this house is. I would say the spirits were enjoying everything. I mean, look at the attention they've been given. Not only by Niki and Karissa but by Steve and Don. Look at the amount of equipment that's been brought in. The spirits have not been shy whatsoever. Multiple battery loss, multiple equipment failures, equipment misplacement, and rearranging of items.

The first thing Niki did after we came back from the Kurt Cobain trip was check her equipment. We noticed several devices had lost power. No surprises there. Some of Niki's stuff and some of Karissa's stuff had mysteriously died, after being fully charged. Once again, not surprising. The most important thing to do now was to back up everything we'd got. We'll review it later. We know we caught something, given what Mary told us. We also know that spirits can and will steal SD cards. We know they can erase data from a hard drive. That's happened many times already. Niki and Karissa worked feverishly to get their stuff copied and backed up.

Before Niki embarked on her next experiment, it was time to do something she had promised. It was time to inform the paranormal community that the secret investigation that she had been involved with was, in fact, the "Demons in Seattle" house.

Evidence	Location
Full Shadow Baby Video	https://youtu.be/_xt7GiGhlrs
Audio Shadow Baby*	https://youtu.be/AOvnyqIFgN0
"Shit" Voice 00:24*	https://youtu.be/vE-tbI438Vs

Table 52.3 * Voice recorder left on when Karissa, Niki and I vacated the house.

Deserves a full listen as there are unexplained voices on it.

A decision was reached before both ladies arriving that, should they find convincing evidence, evidence that coincides with what they got last summer, here is where they would make it known. Time to move on from all the misinformation after *Ghost Adventures*. Time to inform the paranormal community on what was found. Niki and Karissa officially said that something weird is going on here. They are now officially Keith and Tina are Telling the Truth club members. As far as they're concerned, everything we've stated is real.

But the question remains. How do we solve Keith's problem? How do we solve the landlord's problem? One fear being discussed is that this problem may not be solvable. Not in keeping with the happy endings of Hollywood movies. Remember what I said at the beginning of the book about know and don't know constantly being at odds with each other. Well, guess what? Solutions is not required to make an entrance just because we say 'solution, make an entrance.' It takes time. Every poltergeist book I've read describes the specter quite accurately. Poltergeists are home disrupters. They're a bull in a china store. You wouldn't wish one on your worst enemy; I know I wouldn't. The consensus among many is that poltergeists are the byproduct of troubled teenagers, particularly females. Activity is centered on an agent—a house occupant who seems to supply the poltergeist with energy. And all the books I've read ask the question that I'm asking now. How do you get rid of a poltergeist? The short answer is you can't. "Geists" typically get rid of themselves. They dissipate or fade out themselves over a period of time. Without as much as a goodbye, sorry for the hell we caused. We're assuming that's what poltergeist do. No one knows for sure. But there's more here than just a poltergeist. I mean, who is yanking sheets off my bed when I'm in Spokane? Who's doing that to me and at the same time attacking Tina? What about the shadowy figures Jane Doe's son still sees? What about the attacks my attorney endured at three of her houses? Three of her houses! What about the electrical problems she had in conjunction with mine? Can one poltergeist do all of that? I doubt it. I've not yet found a case that resembles my own when it comes to attacks happening at multiple places at the same time. Who's poking and jabbing me in my sleep, while at the same time scaring the crap out of Kim and Tina? The only thing I can think of is the word minions. Specters, demons, unclean spirits, as Fr. Roy Sr. liked to describe them. They're the ones causing some of the underlying trouble. The ones feeding the poltergeist. How can this house ever be a hundred percent safe with those bastards lurking around? I call them Trouble. Trouble can go dormant for a while, but it always resurfaces. What happens then? That question keeps me up at night. That and the possibility that I might be followed. Do I have attachments as a result of living in this house? No one knows the answer to that question—save maybe the spirits themselves. And they're not telling.

The agreement between Niki and her team was the house has a lot of activity associated with it. Something happened here that no one is aware of. Something that we may never get to the bottom of. One of the reasons for going public is to see if maybe someone knows more than we do. Someone whose input can help us ascertain the cause. Better than that. Maybe someone will know how to make this house habitable.

I was on the way to the county records office in downtown Everett the minute Niki heads back home. I have to complete my homework assignment that Steve and Don gave me. They'd asked me to retrieve any information I could get about the land underneath the house. Anything about the city of Bothell. What was Bothell, Washington before it was Bothell, Washington? Was there a Native American settlement within yards of this house? We already know the strong presence natives had in and around Bothell. This area and the entire Pacific Northwest were once fertile with Native settlements.

So, the substantiation of our claims would take place on Niki's radio show: *Niki UnParanormal.* Remember how this investigation started? It started with a simple email. A simple inquiry. That seems like ages ago. This whole experience seems like it began ages ago. I'm thinking, *wow, who would have ever imagined two teams coming here within days of one another? and leaving with so much material?* I remember how reluctant I was to even talk to Niki and Mary. How timid I was to even utter the word 'haunting' within the confines of my house. I didn't want to talk about it. I wasn't comfortable, especially under my roof. But the truth needed to get out. No way was *Ghost Adventures* going to get the last word about what happens inside this house. They're not worthy of defining this case. Only Tina and I are. We lived it. We fought against it, and we know it backward and forwards. That's why I was reluctant when Mary first approached me.

I remember how the first interview went. Niki and Mary were in their respective homes, and I was sitting in a grocery store parking lot. Wow, we've come a long way since then. There once was a time when you couldn't pay me to say the word 'spirit.' I mean, I was terrified after Tina left. I was alone. Who's calling 911 if I'm pushed down the stairs again? Who's going to miss me if I don't come home from work one day? Those questions and more were at the top of my mind after Tina moved out. Sure, we had major differences, Tina and me. But regardless of our differences, we had each other's backs in that house. At least at the very beginning, we did.

So, yeah, I was terrified. I was scared. Scared to where I was sleeping on the couch for weeks on out. I mean, there I was sitting in my car in the Fred Meyer parking lot. Talking to Niki and Mary. I remember one time I saw the street sweeper machine come out and clean the entire parking lot. That's how late it got.

I bet the employees were wondering who I was. Asking themselves, 'why is he just sitting here?' 'Doesn't he have a home to go to?' Yeah, I have a home alright. It's called The Bothell Hell house.

Niki's last night in the house—in keeping with the "strike while the iron is hot" metaphor, Niki had a few more experiments she wanted to carry out. I would not know until tomorrow morning how prophetic that statement actually was—the iron was extremely hot still. The shadow baby experiment is about to be outdone by something more profound, more compelling—something very controversial.

I decided to go upstairs for a few hours. Let the ladies have the downstairs to themselves. They were backing stuff onto the cloud and prepping for Niki's show. I needed to get some things done on my end. The first thing I needed to do was email Jane Doe. Niki and Karissa wanted to talk to her while here. I don't think that's going to happen, based on what I knew about Jane Doe's current situation. I emailed her on Facebook, hoping to get some response. Nothing. I decided to email Fr. Roy Sr, let him know what was going on. I told him and Jennifer, from *No Bull Paranormal,* about what the ladies had found, and that was that.

Now, the new oven arrived a few days ago. The replacement for the one that exploded during Steve and Don's visit (their last night in the home). I told the Sears guys what happened with the current oven and I got a funny look. Neither men had seen an oven shoot sparks from behind before. They delivered and replaced defunct ovens through the Puget Sound; reasons vary as to why an oven would go on the fritz. Exploding from the power-outlet is not one of them

I'm mentioning this now because I emailed the landlord that night. I gave him the latest update on the US and UK team as well as informing him that the new oven was working fine. The last thing I did before departing my office was to back up my video and audio. My shadow baby evidence data. I came back downstairs and found Niki and Karissa live on air.

The response from Niki's audience was good. I was surprised by the level of interest. A few weeks ago, when Karissa and Niki announced online that they were heading to Seattle to investigate a possible poltergeist, the immediate response was: "isn't that the house that *Ghost Adventures* went to? I thought it was proven it was a fake?"

Niki and Karissa's official on-air response: "it's not a fake; we've been monitoring the house for nearly eight months. We've been on site for a total of three and a half weeks." How quickly the response turned to, "Oh, I thought something real might be going on, they seemed like a nice couple. Good luck, Niki and Karissa." The ladies would talk about the house and all therein for the next two-plus hours. I left them to do what they do best. Investigate. I went to bed.

Niki and Karissa – LIVE stream	https://youtu.be/IaDDePbEqIo

Table 52.4 Niki announces her findings to her radio audience.

I woke up the next morning and found Karissa and Niki huddled over a new video they had put together. "Keith! Come here." This felt reminiscent of the time when Steve called me over—the day he and Don discovered the hallway EVP: "it's a camera, it's a camera." On one of the ladies' laptop was a video of them performing an EVP session over one of the burnt Bibles—a question and answer session. The video shows the Bible resting on the couch, with the two of them standing over it. This had to have happened when I went to bed. Now I must admit I was shocked. Why had no other team ever attempted to do what Karissa and Niki were doing? Which was perform a voice session over the burnt Bibles?

One of the things that made this case so hard to believe for some people was our claims of three Bibles catching fire. Talk about creating angst within the paranormal community. You, the reader, should understand now why a majority of that angst was misplaced. There are over ten-thousand documented poltergeist cases throughout the world. A percentage of those cases involve Bibles catching fire. Our Bibles caught fire because we put them out for display. Poltergeist love when you do that. Of course, we didn't know that at the time. Our mistake should have been the scientific community's moment of opportunity. Brace yourselves because I'm about to say it—each burnt Bible deserves a book written about it. The science of how they caught fire, how they disappeared just riddles the mind. Tina and I were called some of the worst names imaginable for coming forward with that information. I mean, a person has to be lower than low to burn a Bible, let alone three Bibles. Who does that? Not Tina and me. The fact that *Ghost Adventures* found nothing while here sort of increased the name calling. Once again, a wasted opportunity on *Ghost Adventures* part because had they asked, they could have taken one of the Bibles with them for testing and analysis.

I asked Niki and Karissa what kind of experiment they'd conducted. They replied, "We opened up one of the burnt Bibles and started asking questions. We recorded the whole thing."

"Oh shit, are you fucking for real?" That's what I said. The ladies wanted to find out if the spirits who burnt the Bibles still were still here. It would appear that the answer is yes.

EVP Session: Karissa and Niki	Evidence
YouTube	https://www.youtube.com/watch?v=_pJLbMwP1w4
Bang heard in the background	First bang at 3:22
Ping "Noise"	3:35
Female voice	3:55 'Show Me How To'
2nd Bang	4:00
Female voice	4:19 'Coming for You'
Question: "can you flip the page…" Female says	4:49 'Yes'

Table 52.5 Niki and Karissa Bible experiment

The ladies got some interesting responses to their EVP session. I mean 'show me how to,' 'coming for you' and 'yes.' Niki and Karissa couldn't hear the words while they're being spoken—not in real time. They found those voices while analyzing the video. Sound familiar? Don and Steve captured similar activity when they were here a little over a week ago. That, combined with the pages turning by themselves, would end up being the highlight of Niki's investigation. Combine that with the shadow baby doll incident and Niki's testimony of her equipment being rearranged on the bed, and you're left believing this investigation was a success. We're not done, though. Niki had to go back home today and review the other audio files. One and half weeks was what we have left. What can we find next?

Karissa Fleck	Description	Activity Type
Week 3	Locked out of the house	Torment
Week 3	Missing phone – 18 Hrs.	Apport
Week 3	Poking and prodding	Torment

Table 52.6 experiences Karissa had while living in the house. Highlights.

Chapter 53
Rich Schleifer

Karissa Fleck, Week 3—If there ever was a good example of one going from disbeliever (based off of what GA didn't find) to believing, that person would have to be Rich Schleifer. When I say, disbeliever, I mean to the point of writing unflattering comments about Tina and me after the airing of our house on the Travel Channel. A chorus had formed on the *Ghost Adventures* Facebook page hours after the episode had ended. The consensus there was Keith and Tina are the biggest fakers in paranormal history. Hang them by their toenails for wasting Zak Bagan's time. So who is Rich Schleifer? He was my neighbor. Actually, he lived a few houses down from mine. About a block over. We met the week of the *Ghost Adventures* investigation. Our garage door was open before the infamous lockdown investigation, which as you can imagine was attracting a lot of neighborhood attention. Lots of stuff going on. Well, Rich Schleifer is a video hobbyist. Not only that, he's a paranormal enthusiast's video hobbyist. He conducts paranormal investigations in and around the neighboring states. That's what he told me when we first met and how did we meet? We met on the sidewalk right outside my house (the night Zak and crew were at the house).

I could immediately tell from the look on his face that he was a big fan of Zak and his crew. There he was standing there with his lovely daughter. They watched the guys work for quite some time.

I wouldn't see Rich again until a few weeks later. He lived on his side of the street, and I lived on mine. Now and then he would approach Tina or me asking if we knew when the episode was going to air. I kept brushing him off at first because I didn't know. It was not like *Ghost Adventures* were contacting me all the time, they weren't. Not until a week or two before the airing of the episode did I hear back from them and when I did, I told Rich. The guy was ecstatic to know that our house would be on *Ghost Adventures*. He met them. He watched their show numerous times, and he's paranormal enthusiast. Why wouldn't I tell him?

I can't say it was a mistake to tell him when our house was going to be aired because Rich and I are good friends now. There are but a few silver linings to this story—Rich Schleifer is one of them. But it wasn't always like that. Not at first.

I spoke previously about Tina logging onto the social media sites and reading the comments people were saying about her. Tina read a lot of stuff. But nowhere near as much as me. Tina was never a social media person—that came after the airing of the show. And that was because her family members (who are into social media) were texting the comments of what people were saying. That prompted Tina to get online. Something I wish she never did. I can't remember if it was Tina who found Rich's comments online or if it was me. I think Tina saw it and sent to me. She knew who Rich Schleifer was. So, I was reading these negative comments on Facebook, and I got to Rich Schleifer comments—what Tina texted me.

I was immediately shocked. It hurt to see him say that we did this for attention-seeking purposes. That we probably made it up. Oh my God that stung. And let me tell you why it stung. The opinions people were giving about me and Tina never stuck to me, because guess what? It was coming from strangers. It was coming from people who have no idea what it's like living in a home occupied by an evil spirit. They have no idea whatsoever. No one, and I mean no one, has met Tina and me. We're strangers to them, and they're certainly strangers to us. Rich Schleifer is different. I met Rich Schleifer. He lives a few houses down from me. Rich and I have had numerous conversations before. I knew he was a fan of the show and I knew he was a paranormal hobbyist – researcher. I never got a bad vibe from him while talking to him.

To see his comments embedded with all the other vile comments (even saying that he lived a few houses down from us) and to his knowledge no previous tenant ever expressed to him that the house was haunted. Tina was hurt over those comments as was I. I mean, think about it. This was the end of February, 2015. Tina and I were a few days from breaking up. The vile comments had consumed her in such way that it might be a good idea just to write everybody off. Seeing Rich's comments (the one Tina sent to me) was like a Jenga block on an already unstable woodpile. It didn't help the situation. And my thinking has always been regardless of whatever situation may be transpiring. It's a code I try to live by. We've all been in that situation where the solution to a problem can't always come from us. But the code should still hold true, and that code is: if you can't be a part of the solution, at the very least don't become a part of the problem. And Rich's comments albeit minuscule was like a log being placed an existing fire. He was not aware of it at the time, but he should have been—he's a paranormal investigator.

I didn't speak to him till about eight months or so after the episode had aired. Not because I was pissed. I mean I was, my not speaking to Rich was more to do with our competing work schedules. We probably would have never met had it not been for *Ghost Adventures* showing up at my house.

So, what got us talking again? It was Steve and Don's visit. Up to now, I'm thinking Rich still doesn't believe our house is haunted. I'm not even sure he's aware that Tina left me. I saw him walking up the street one day and decided now was the perfect time for him to stop by. He needed to see what Steve and Don were finding. He and I were talking on the patio about the EVPs Don and Steve were finding. I uttered the word parapsychologists, and Rich's eyes lit up. Somewhere during our conversation, Rich does something I wasn't expecting. He apologized. He admitted to me how wrong he was about the comments he made online, about what we were going through. I asked him how did he come to this conclusion and it was pretty much along the lines of he talked to a friend, a more knowledgeable paranormal researcher who had the opposite view of what he had. That view being that it's wasn't Tina's fault or my fault that *Ghost Adventures* didn't find anything. This woman gave him the infamous Gandalf and Frodo speech about dishing out "judgment." Ninety-nine percent of those comments online came from people who know nothing about paranormal research. What they learn, they get from TV. There more curious about the personalities on TV than they are about the subject matter. What's worse is the TV personalities aren't educating anybody. That "Demons in Seattle" episode was a teachable moment that *Ghost Adventures* failed to take advantage of.

Rich's apology meant a lot to me (meant a lot to Tina), and she wasn't here. So, I did something unexpected. I invited him into my house. I wanted him to see how parapsychologists conduct investigations and just like a true enthusiast Rich responded with a quick "yes, he would love to talk to the guys" but not before grabbing some of his gear.

So, Rich got to meet Steve and Don while they were here, and he did observe the men in action. It was on that note that I thought of something else. In the interests of Para-unity (the campaign) that many in the paranormal community had adopted as of late. I asked Rich would he like to investigate with Karissa, Niki, Mary and myself.

This was the last week Karissa was here. Niki was back on the east-coast. The conclusion we've all come to is we need one more investigation. One that encompasses everyone and everything. The phrase "go big or go home" was uttered again by Niki and Mary. If we're going to research, then let's research goddamnit. And that's exactly what we did. I want to use this part of the book to thank Rich Schleifer. Thank you for the equipment you bought over to my house—Rich's comments are below. The video below is the investigation he conducted.

Ghosts of Bothell: The Demons in Seattle House by Rich Schleifer
https://www.youtube.com/watch?v=b9pVNMyUG58&t=76s

"...I saw the Ghost Adventures episode that was filmed at this location and I even had a chance to talk to a member of the GAC as well as some of the production staff. It was great seeing people from one of my favorite shows in person! After the episode aired in which no evidence was found, I kind of wrote the house off and didn't think much about it. It wasn't until a local news channel came out and aired a piece on the house in February that got me thinking about the house. It turns out that Keith, the resident of this house, had a couple paranormal investigators come out from the UK (Steve Mera and Don Philips) to spend a week at the house and conduct an investigation during that time frame. That got me thinking that something must really be going on there if people are coming over from England and staying there for a week to study and investigate the house. Then I found out that he was going to have another investigator stay there (Karissa from the East Coast) and have her paranormal team conduct a continuous investigation through cameras, audio recorders and other devices over the web. Being that I do some paranormal investigations as well, I got back in contact with Keith and asked if he needed any help. He invited me over to help document the setup of some laser "tripwires" to see if they can catch any movement. I accepted the offer and joined Keith and Karissa. What you see here is a collection of evidence that I recorded from two separate nights of investigations with Keith and Karissa. This is an evidence review video since I didn't produce it and edit it like one of my full "Ghosts of" shows. In this video,

you can see that we get the tripwires being set off and some EVPs. In fact, the first EVP that I present in this video is one of the best EVPs that I have ever recorded. After seeing some evidence that Karissa, the investigators from England captures, as well what I have here to show, I am confident that there is something paranormal going on in Keith's house. Sure, I didn't capture an apparition drawing symbols on the wall, kitchen drawers opening on their own, candle sticks crashing into the wall or Bibles and posters bursting into flames. Now those would be really cool to see and capture on video to make the skeptical side of me become more convinced that this is a "demon" situation. Right now, I think there is a paranormal presence there that is bothering Keith. What is this spirit's (or spirits) goal? I am not sure. All I know is that there's activity there that needs to be explored a bit more so we can hopefully find out its origin and purpose." ~ Rich Schleifer

Fig 53.1 San Diego Con 2010

I was very impressed with Rich Schleifers attention to detail when it came time to conduct our last investigation. I can't tell you how much a relief it is to have someone be more serious about documentation than myself. Here is the link to the video spreadsheet he gave me within days of his investigation. One should view it while watching the video above. All you have to do is email me if you would like the individual files. The evidence Rich gathered while here sits comfortably with everyone else's. Amazing.

Rich Schleifer's Evidence Chart (detailed noted taking)
https://macqdor.box.com/s/1k4z7qffyghclysb79ealkjrb9br755t

	Sony CX-900 Portable	Sony XR-520 Stationary	Sony SR85 Stationary	Zoom HI	Others
8:14 PM		201440- 00:04:18 Time Check	203016- 01:12:12 Time Check		
8:17:00 PM EVP	045: 44:00 EVP: "Slow"	201440- 3:31:02 EVP: "Slow"	203016- 04:38:23 EVP: "Slow"		
8:21 PM Time Check	046: 01:38:15 Time Check			Z22 0:09:080 Time Check	
8:21:00 PM EVP	046: 01:59:08 Possible EVP	201936- 02:18:05 Possible EVP	203016- 08:20:25 Debunked	Z22 0:31:014 Possible EVP	It's Keith!
8:31:00 PM EVP	046: 12:02:14 Possible Female EVP (TV??)	201936- 12:20:29 Not Caught	203016- 18:24:10 Possible EVP	Z22 10:35:050 Possible Female EVP	
20:35	046: 16:14:01 Time Check	201936- 16:30:28 Time Check	203016- 22:34:16 Time Check	Z22- 14:45:432 Time Check	
8:36	046: 17:59:13 Sensors Go Off	201936- 18:09:13 Sensors Go Off	203016- 24:12:03 Sensors go off		
20:38	046: 19:08:12 Time Check	201936- 19:26:16 Time Check	203016- 25:29:21 Time Check		
8:52 PM	049: 00:13:23 Time Check	201936- 32:46:08 Time Check	203016- 38:46:06 Time Check		
8:54 PM		201936- 35:18:11 Time Check	203016- 41:20:19 Time Check		
8:55 PM Banging/Thumping	049: 01:47:09 Banging/Thumping on wall				Wind
9:02 PM Time Check	049: 10:21:18 Time Check	201936- 42:50:25 Time Check	203016- 48:53:10 Time Check	Z23- 5:15:246 Time Check	

Fig 53.2 Notes after investigating my house.

					9:38 Possible Motion Pic Upstairs 9:44 Motion Alert Hallw
9:45 PM Time Check	053: 00:03:21 Time Check	212650- 19:20:13 Time Check	212651- 19:02:13 Time Check		
9:48 PM Thumping	053: 03:58:06 Thumping				
9:49 PM 2 Thumps	053: 04:25:07 2 Thumps				
9:54 PM EVP (?)	053: 09:02:16 EVP (?)	212650- 28:20:03 Not Caught			
9:54 PM 2 Thumps	053: 09:55:08 2 Thumps				
9:57 PM Time Check	053: 11:41:05 Time Check	212650- 30:55:25 Time Check	212651- 30:38:18 Time Check	Z24- 11:22:321 Time Check	
10:05 PM EVP	053: 19:08:21 EVP Whispering... Moving camera gear	212650- 38:30:09 Not Caught. Debunked		Z24- 18:50:731 EVP Debunk	
10:10 PM EVP Vocalization	053: 24:47:16 EVP Vocalization			Z24- 24:30:21 EVP	
10:12 PM Time Check	053: 26:59:15 Time Check	212650- 46:15:15 Time Check	212651- 45:58:04 Time Check	Z24- 26:42:358 Time Check	
10:14 PM Time Check	054: 00:14:13 Time Check	212650- 47:48:27 Time Check	212651- 47:30:25 Time Check	Z25- 0:09:447 Time Check	
10:17 PM Possible EVP	054 03:39:20 Possible EVP	212650- 51:15:21 10:17 PM Possible EVP	212651- 50:57:17		Person Karissa is talking
10:18 PM EVP Laughing (?)	054: 06:00:08 EVP Laughing (?)	221854- 01:34:07 EVP Laughing (?)	221932- 00:39:29 EVP Laughing	Z25- 05:55:18 EVP Laughing (?)	
10:19 PM EVP Laughing (?)	054: 06:17:19 EVP Laughing (?)	221854- 01:51:20 EVP Laughing (?)	221932- 00:56:25 EVP Laughing	Z25- 06:12:29 EVP Laughing (?)	
10:20 PM EVP "Go"	054: 06:49:08 EVP "Go"	221854- 02:23:03 EVP "Go"	221932- 01:28:18 EVP "Go"	Z25- 6:44:783 EVP "Go"	
10:23 PM EVP Vocalization	054: 09:40:08 EVP Vocalization	221854_ 05:14:03 Not Caught	221932- 04:19:01 EVP	Z25- 9:35:587 Not Caught	Possible movement
10:29 PM Time Check				Z25- 15:00:425 Time Check	
10:37 PM EVP	055: 01:56:17 Possible EVP after wind gust			Z26- 0:29:784 Not Caught	
10:39 Time Check	055: 03:26:17 Time Check			Z26- 1:57:703 Time Check	
10:45 PM Time Check	056: 00:03:13 Time Check				
10:46 PM Time Check					

Fig 53.3 Notes after investigating my house.
https://macqdor.box.com/s/1k4z7qffyghclysb79ealkjrb9br755t
download here

Chapter 54
The Landlord

For we wrestle not against flesh and blood, but against principalities, against powers, against the rulers of the darkness of this world, against spiritual wickedness in high places.
Ephesians 6:12

There's no way I can close this book without making mention of the homeowner. Let's recap. I'm the renter. Tina and I began our search for a home around March or April of 2012. I had recently got a new job that allowed me to afford a house like the one I moved in. I asked my girlfriend Tina to move in with me—take our relationship to the next level if you will. Tina and I had a few back and forth emails with the landlord before finally securing the house on May 1st, 2012. The rest, they say, is history.

I want to go back to a question that I'm often asked which is "why we stayed so long?" Especially me after Tina left. "Why did I stay so long?" There are multiple answers to that question—the answer I want to give now sort of centers around the movie *Saving Private Ryan*.

There's a scene at the beginning of the movie where Capt. Miller (Tom Hank's) character and his men are walking through an open field. They've discovered a Nazi bunker in the far distance. They can see the Nazi's hunkered down, but the Nazi's can't see them. The consensus among the Tom Hanks men is we should go around. This is a fight we don't need. Why sustain casualties if we don't have to? Let's go around (add a few more miles to our hike) and avoid this conflict. No one will ever know we were here. Do you remember that scene in the movie? Do you remember Capt Miller's response? We all know Tina and I could have moved out. We all know that's the easiest thing to do. There's little consequence in doing that. Well, maybe one consequence. Someone else has to move in. A husband and a wife. A husband and wife and kids. Do you remember what Capt. Miller told his men? I'll paraphrase. "Yeah, we can hike around this Nazi bunker. We can go undetected, and no harm will be done.

But what happens when another group of soldiers comes walking through? Our soldiers, our allied soldiers? What if they don't see what we see? Odds are they're going to get mowed down. Our job as soldiers is to confront the enemy on the battlefield. Make him see the error of his ways. All we're doing by sidestepping this bunker is leaving a problem for someone else to deal with." That's all Tina and I would be doing if we just upped and left. In summary (and this is me talking now) the reaction can no longer be just up and leave. Now each incident should be viewed independently, and no situation is exactly the same. I mean there are a few things to consider like children. Our decision was somewhat easier to make. Tina and I had neither. The crux of our decision (especially mine) was I can't just up and leave. I can't leave the house is worse condition than when

I found it. There are an inordinate amount of spirits living here. Majority of them are evil. That's my assessment. Science can disagree all they want. They're not living in the house, which means they're not privy to what goes on here.

I don't care what atheists say. I don't care what agnostic people say. I don't care what religious people say. Evil spirits are living in this house. Their actions speak louder than words. They admitted to Don via voice recorder that it was them that pushed me downstairs. I wasn't smudging. I wasn't doing anything challenging. I was going downstairs for a glass of water. The next thing I know I had a torn patella tendon. When Jane Doe me told what happened to them, that solidified my stance about not leaving. If I'm going to leave, then it has to be on my terms, not the minions' terms. Not the poltergeist's terms. My terms.

Now there's a footnote to everything I've just said, and that footnote is: there have been times where we came close to leaving. I mean we're human beings. Those thoughts entered my mind every day. As did the question: are we doing the right thing? Am I doing the right thing? Who should I be more concerned about? My girlfriend or the people moving in after us.

My biggest fear is watching television one night, from a new address, and all a sudden I see this house. I see it burning down to the ground (individuals inside). No one knows the real reason why. All they know is weird things were happening around them, and things got out of hand. Domestic squabbles ran amok. Suicidal tendencies were the prelude to the house finally burning down to the ground. That's in back of mind when I think about just up and leaving. I think about Jane Doe's son still seeing shadowy figures. I know he sees them because I see them. I know the spirits had a hand in Jane Doe's marriage falling apart because look what happened to Tina and me. I know a lot of things. I've seen a lot of things. I've shared most of it but some I can never share. Certain things I have yet to make sense of.

I remember when Tina called the power company to get the utility switched over in her name. One of the first things they told her was that the house had had multiple tenants. Names keep getting switched over. This happened the first week of May, 2012. One of our neighbors walked across the street one day to introduce himself. He said the house we were now moving into always seemed to have people moving in and moving out. He hopes we stick around longer than the previous tenants. He's not talking about Jane Doe. She lived in the house years ago. He's talking about the people before us.

When I told the landlord that *Ghost Adventures* wanted to research the house I was shocked by his quick response. I was shocked that he said yes. Tina was extremely shocked. I went back to read the email I sent him, and my shock quickly subsided. There in black and white were the sincerest words imaginable. I was frank, timid, and very honest with him. I thought he would think I was nuts. I mean, I sent him some horrible pictures. The damage the "Geist" was doing to his house, not mine. I thought for sure he was going to kick Tina and me out. I thought for sure he was going to sue us for the damage being done to his property. Three thousand dollars gone—non-refundable deposit, is what I thought.

This house needs to be investigated, and it needs to be investigated thoroughly. Do I have your permission to pursue investigative avenues? The landlord's response was "yes." That response alone should tell you a lot about him and a lot about our relationship. The landlord never visited us. Even after I told him his house was haunted. Not once did he ask to come by. Not even when Fr. Roy was over. Not even when *Ghost Adventures* were over did he stop by. Not even when the UK team was here did the landlord asks to come by.

The homeowner is the only one who's within his rights to question our motives. Tina and I are living in a five-hundred-thousand-dollar house. We're reporting fires, noises, objects thrown, wall writings, puddles of water, and an occasional scratch or two. If anyone wants to doubt our claims with prejudice, it's the landlord. He never did. Not even after *Ghost Adventures* aired the "Demons in Seattle" episode, pitching the landlord's home onto international television, with the conclusion "no evidence." Did the owner come running? Nope, he did not.

He never accused us of making stuff up. You know why? The landlord knows we didn't make stuff up. Do I think the landlord knew the house was haunted before we moved in? It's impossible to know if he knew or not. Washington State is not a disclose state. Meaning the homeowner does not have to disclose to the new tenants that their house is haunted. Some states you have to disclose, not Washington. So, I can't tell if he knew or not. It would be hypocritical of me to accuse him of knowing without ample evidence. I'd be doing exactly what the trolls, cynics, and skeptics were doing with Tina and me.

The reader will have to make up his or her mind about what the owner knew and didn't know. All I'm saying is he permitted me to have the house investigated. Permission to have teams in and permission to have an exorcism done. Jane Doe said they just picked up and left. They didn't tell the homeowner anything. That's not unusual. Most people pick up and leave at the first sign of activity. I know that because that's what people told us. That's what our friends told us. That's what our family told us. Co-workers, you name it. Tina and I were told this. You would not be reading this book had Tina, and I left after the first plant got thrown. Imagine that scenario? They'd be no true story to tell.

Tina and are not asking for accolades for staying in a hell house. We stayed (with the hopes of this house being correctly investigated). That word correctly is relative and elusive. More elusive than the spirits living here if we're going, to be frank about it.

Conclusion

Do a quick mental inventory of your wrongs, your rights, your regrets, your demons, your charity, your love—and lastly, your fears. Multiply each of them all by a million. Whatever your total is, whatever you can accumulate—determines who you are. Those things I've just mentioned are what fuel a poltergeist. When Tina and I got the keys to the house from the landlord, one of the first things I said to her was, this house will either make us or break us. I said that within seconds of the landlord leaving. I remember Tina looking at me with somewhat of a puzzled look. I knew from the expression on her face that she had a question. I knew what she was about to ask me, so I decided to respond before she could ask a question.

I told her moving in together is a major step, I don't know if this is a good idea or if it's a bad idea. People typically get married before they move into together, that's how I was raised. Something about the commitment that comes with being married sort of puts a shield around you. I said, let's be real, we have an enormous set of problems. I know I can be set in my ways at times. The last relationship I was in with this type of significance was eighteen years ago. You've just come out a marriage. This is the conversation we're having. Let's agree to some ground rules. Let's give each other one hundred percent. Let's make this beautiful house our home. Let's let bygones be bygones. I'm up for it if you are? I then uttered something to the effect of our failures (if any) won't be minor. Same for our success. If we succeed, we will forever have a story to tell. Here is a couple who, despite whatever problems they had when they moved in, came out on top. This all took place within three minutes of being in the Bothell home. It never dawned on me that we were being eavesdropped on. Then we heard the kid 'cough.'

I hope I've altered your thinking about haunted houses. Hopefully, I've sparked your interests in poltergeists. About demons and apparitions. Want some advice? Forget what you see on television. The only people worth paying attention to are the ones who lived through such a thing. They're the subject matter experts. Now I said subject matter expert, not paranormal expert. There's no such thing.

Ask yourself this question: If you have cancer, or better yet if you have a desire to know everything there is to know about cancer, who do you want to talk first: the patient or the doctor supervising the patient? Who's the expert on what it feels like to have cancer? Cancer survivor or the doctor? A person diagnosed with cancer feels cancer from the inside. The same thing can be said about those who experienced unexplained events. I've tried to the best of my ability to relate to you the reader, the things we've seen and heard while living in the Bothell house. Allow me to share a few more things in the spirit of leaving no stone unturned.

When I stepped out of my bedroom that morning, talking about the day the poster caught fire. I felt a force run pass me on the hallway landing. I felt it. How do I know something ran past me? I know because of the force I felt. Something went stomping past me. The front door of the house opened soon after and then slammed shut.

Note: Which shows you that the door was always working—no reason for being it jammed when I got there, two seconds later.

I wish I could assemble all the world's paranormal researchers, past and present, a few skeptics, a few astrophysics, and one internet troll—I'd put them all on that landing that day. Paranormal TV personalities are to be positioned on the front row. If all of you were there that morning, the day something ran past me, ninety-nine percent of you would stop saying "come out, come out wherever you are," when entering a home believed to be "Geist" infested. You wouldn't ask stupid questions like, "Why are you here? What do you want? Please throw something, show me what you got." I wish you could hear what the spirits say and do when you ask questions like that. I'm talking about the malevolent ones. They laugh and they snicker.

But that's not why you'd cease asking stupid questions. Oh no, the spirits commentary wouldn't do it. Something else would. If you stood on my landing that day, you would say, "What the hell was that? What ran past me just now?" You would have to open up another paranormal case right then and there. You see the question you just asked yourself didn't come from your brain. Oh no, dear researcher, it came from your feet. Your heart is already pounding by the time those questions reaches your brain. Hold onto your feet because they're about to leave you. You suddenly realize you are not the expert on anything. You suddenly realize that soul inside you, the one you hold dear reigns at the bottom of the food chain.

You see it wasn't me that recognized something had run past me. My ears heard it. My soul felt it. I knew right then and there that I was not the sharpest tool in the tool shed. Whatever ran past me on that landing: if it wanted to, if it was so inclined, could have snapped my neck like a twig. How much strength does it take to launch an armoire in mid-air? Multiple times? How many men would it take to launch something that size? Hurl it as if it was a nerf football. Oh no, you wouldn't be saying "light this sage stick" if you were there that day. You wouldn't be handing out demonologists certificates online. Not if you if you lived in my house. One of the questions I keep asking myself is: What if I had stepped out the room sooner? What if I had impeded its pathway? I hate imagining what would have happened.

I'm forced to believe based on what I've heard and seen — "Geist" and minion are the same. Two sides of the same coin. Whenever you hear me say the word minion, understand that I'm referring to a lower form of demon. A low-ranking demon. But don't confuse low rank with lack of power. Don't make that mistake. Now I'd be derelict in my duty if I didn't conclude the book with some parting advice. If you should ever (and I hope you don't), live in a house occupied by a poltergeist, here are some tips that will help you.

Tip number one: all "Geist" outbreaks are not created equal, same for paranormal teams. It's hard to vet a paranormal team when you have furniture flying in your house but try. Do the best you can. Most of the teams that came to our house were piss poor at documenting. Lack of documentation usually means lack of verifiable references. I doubt that means lack of casework. Be mindful of those who utter, "Nothing is real until we (the team) says it's real." That's ego talking. Any researcher worth his/her weight in gold will vet you before taking a case. There's no reason for them to take your case if they don't believe you. And yes, you can be objective and still believe everything the occupant is saying. If you understand poltergeist behavior, you should.

Tip number two: be honest and upfront with an investigator/researcher. Tell them everything. The quicker you establish a trust and believability factor the better. Watch the "Demons in Seattle" episode again. Compare it to Steve and Don's investigation, to Niki and Karissa's. Look at the *Ghost Adventures* crew's body language when standing next to Tina and me, look at their attitude. You'll clearly see everyone had different objectives. The ultimate responsibility of an investigator is getting to the root of something. Not being accusatory or inventing innuendos as a means of covering up their ineptness.

Tip number three: document religiously. You can never have too much documentation. One of the first jobs I had out of college was working in an IT helpdesk. One of the things we learned in IT was that you document everything. When people call the helpdesk to submit an incident—it was my role as helpdesk agent to be as descriptive as possible. Capture the voice and frustration of the customer. In this particular moment, the situation calls for you to write, not think. There's no such thing as too much information. That belief underlines every segment of IT, be it hardware or software. Believe it or not but documenting what's going on adds credibility to your story. You'll need that. The more work you put around the activity you are experiencing, the better. Hoaxers, those who fake paranormal for the sake of attention, make life extremely hard for those who have something. There's no way of getting around that. You can mitigate it, though. By documenting. Anything and everything. Be as descriptive as possible. If you hear a strange noise, write down when that occurred. What time of day it was. What time of night it was. What day of the week it was. What were you doing when you heard it? Was there any appliance on at the time? Were you alone? Who else heard it? What were the weather conditions outside? Document, document, and when you're done documenting, document some more. Remember, we're dealing with the paranormal—there's no such thing as too much information. An experienced researcher will be able to filter the noise from the detail. All "Geist" cases are different. But the fundamentals are still the same, those being the loud bangs, objects moving, objects being thrown, doors slamming, cabinet doors wide open, rocks falling, electronic issues, items missing, items appearing that neither of you owns, etc.

Your house will have a unique signature. Ours was the upside-down man (strange how no team took a wall sample of that stuff), but that was our unique signature. That's where the documentation comes in. You might be experiencing something brand new, something unheard of. The average hoaxer is not going to know about that. The average hoaxer will focus on mimicking the common stuff being reported online. Stuff like flying books, swinging cabinet doors, fake apparition photos, etc. Our case is similar to a lot of historical poltergeist cases. But we have differences too. That's where the meticulous note taking comes in.

I had a lot of famous parapsychologists tell me "no" via email, and their excuse was they're too busy. Or worse than that, "Seattle's too far away." That's the most idiotic thing I've heard. What do you have an ankle bracelet? Whatever happened to follow the outbreak? How can investigators afford to cherry-pick cases based on geography and zip code when they openly admit such occurrences are extremely rare?

Tip number four: if hell breaks out, leave. Even if you have to leave for a few days or a few weeks, don't be afraid. Just do it. Orchestrate a safe zone. Preferably a hotel. Remember the "Geist" wants to haunt you without attracting too much outside attention. I would avoid staying with a relative or friend. Choose a hotel. "Geist" are about isolating you from the outside world; from your significant other. Trust your instincts: that's why you have them. The minute you feel things heating up, leave. Get to your safe zone. Have a backup safe zone as well.

Tip number five is primarily for couples: If there's a "Geist" in the home, odds are one of you is going to be attacked more than the other person. Don't get too comfortable if you're not the one being attacked. The tides can switch in an instant. Understand that. Do yourself a favor, form ranks and watch each other carefully. Don't fall for the earring in the bedroom technique. "Geist" are manipulative. They are the masters at creating division. Yield them an inch, and they'll create a mile. The quicker you understand that, the better.

Always trust your instincts. Always trust your gut. Disavowing things is easy. It's easy to listen to our friends, our family, paranormal teams, skeptics, and cynics and walk away thinking, maybe they're right? Well, guess what? You, the victim, are right. If you and your significant other saw something together, then you're both right. Lean on each other. Remember the "Geist" is going to take whatever insecurities you have and multiply it by two hundred.

Whatever demons you brought into the house, be it drugs, alcoholism, domestic abuse, substance abuse, infidelity, pride, pre-existing health condition, unknown health condition, unemployment, gambling addiction, sex addiction, tax evasion or whatever: becomes tools for the demons living in your home. No one is off limits. Please take this to heart. No one is off limits where poltergeists are concerned.

And lastly: know when to leave, and by leave, I mean move out. Yep, that's right. Know when to leave the premises; leave for good. I see no difference between renting a home and owning a home where poltergeists are concerned. To me "home is where the heart is" a place becomes my home the minute the paperwork is signed. This house was personal to me, as was the idea of just cutting and running. One doesn't spend ten years acquiring the skills for which to afford a house like this, only to throw it away due to a few bumps in the night. Granted we had a whole lot of bumps in the night. But that's just part of it. The other part I already mentioned: it would haunt me forever knowing I left this house in worse condition than I found it.

But this, in the end, is a personal decision—your decision. Poltergeists are extremely powerful. They're not to be taken lightly. And every encounter is different. The only thing I'm a subject matter expert on is the events Tina and I witnessed. You can waterboard the hell out of me, and my story will still be the same. I'm not altering one aspect of it. Everything you read in this book happened the way I say it did, give or take a week or two. If you have a "Geist" infestation, you have to stay cognizant of that fact. You have to know when to leave. Every circumstance is different. Trust me, there's no wrong or right here. There's only you. There's only you and your partner. What's your breaking point? What's your tolerance level look like? What's your baseline? For me, my baseline was leaving on my terms. I did not want to get run out of my own house. My first house. If they can punk me out of this house, then they can punk me out of every other house I ever live in.

A person who runs has to forever look over their shoulder. I didn't want to do that. I can't do that. I can't live like that. I'm a chill guy. I'm laid back. I moved to the Pacific Northwest to live, not look over my shoulder. Staying cost, me a hell of a lot. It cost me the woman I loved. It subjected me to ridicule and scorn. Even by people in my own family. Probably cost me things I still don't know about. Who knows what the future holds? My dad said a "man who plans for the future will never have to face uncertainty." Since I believe that wholeheartedly I know I could never leave my house running. I didn't run when I moved to Seattle. So why am I running now? "The lord is my shepherd…

I received an email from Steve and Don two weeks after they left. The men were letting me know they were about to go public with their findings, as well send me information about what it is they'd found. So, I'm being bombarded with Steve's good news, as well as Karissa and Niki's good news. At the same time. It could've been planned more perfectly. We're talking about a year of work here. Niki and Mary approaching me with an idea and Steve and Don flying across the Atlantic Ocean after receiving an email from me. A cry for help if you will. And it started with a book on poltergeists: *The Poltergeist Phenomenon* by Michael Clarkson. That and the trip to the Seattle public library are what led to me contacting parapsychologists. Many were contacted. Only one responded. Don informed me that FOX news would be calling me back real soon. The Scientific Establishment of Parapsychology was sending them their initial report. Not the comprehensive report, just the initial report.

And Don was right. Fox did call me. They called me that same week, requesting an update on Steve and Don's investigation. *Perfect timing,* I thought. Steve and Don had just made it official in the UK, throughout their respective parapsychology communities that, "Yes, Keith's house is in fact haunted, there are unexplained events taking place." Those were the words of Steve Mera and Don Philips. Then came the email from David Rose of Fox News Seattle—the station had kept an interest in the case from the beginning of both teams' arrival. David wanted to know what both teams had found. Instead of telling David what both teams found, I decided just to email him. Don and Steve can send the write-up. I'll send Dave the evidence that Steve and Don left me.

Seventeen million people saw David Rose report about the house. Emails were piling in from Louisiana, Florida, Spain, Australia, Italy, and California. The old narrative of a couple exaggerating or outright lying was finally being contradicted. Contradicted by something scientific. I mean, which makes more sense? Researchers, who live in the house for one week to four weeks or a team that investigates it for a few hours? *Ghost Adventure* said they're found no Native

American history in the area anyone with a mouse and keyboard can contradict that assessment.

But it doesn't stop here, ladies and gentlemen. Please, please, don't take my word for it. Review the evidence. All of it. It's my gift to you. The letters, the email exchange between a multitude of individuals, the reports, the x-rays, the photos, the videos, the audio, the statements from witnesses, previous tenants are all for you.

Announcement	FOX News
The Scientific Establish of Parapsychology	http://q13fox.com/2016/02/15/bothell-home-haunted-by-poltergeists-parapsychologists-have-proven-it-resident-says/

Conclusion 1.1

Jane Doe – Update

I was wrong when I said earlier that there was only one person in the world who knows what I've been through. There are actually two people: Tina and Jane Doe.

It saddens me to say that Jane did not live to see the publication of this book. Rhonda Lee Jimenez aka Jane Doe, passed away August 16, 2016. Rhonda Lee Jimenez ended her life by standing in front of a moving train near Bonner, Montana. I learned of her passing when attempting to reach her. Our last conversations were about Tina and me. We talked about the house over-all, our experiences—we talked about a lot of things. Things I mentioned earlier about your demons possibly getting the best of you—began surfacing for Rhonda while I was writing this book. She tried so desperately to break out of it but unfortunately could not. I will take to my grave some of the horrible things she's seen and went through while living in this house.

The world should know that Rhonda loved her family very much. She loved freedom. She loved the outdoors, and yes, she even loved life. I'll always remember how timid and scared she was in going against her husband's wishes when it came time to tell me about their experience in the house. She felt it was her Christian duty. She and Maria José Ferreira deserve to have a book like this dedicated to them. Rhonda never saw herself as a poltergeist survivor, but she was. More than she'll ever know. The reader will do themselves a favor. Learn who Maria José Ferreira is. You won't have a problem understanding her story. Both women, unfortunately, succumbed to events that were beyond their control. They didn't ask too to be afflicted. No one does. Go to God, Rhonda Lee Jimenez. Be at peace, finally. Jesus is watching over your children. They are in our hearts. I miss you. Amen.

http://www.kpax.com/story/32772848/pedestrian-killed-by-train-in-bonner-idd
Pedestrian killed by train in Bonner has been identified.

SEP

The Scientific Establishment of Parapsychology
Investigative Measures & Analytical Research
Case Ref: 26411

CLEARED FOR RELEASE

CONFIDENTIAL

SEP have attended a location in Seattle and carried out a two stage active investigation using rig 2 and rig 4 equipment for the duration of 6 days in an attempt to obtain credible and authentic evidence in support of reported paranormal disturbances by the house owner (Keith Linder). All preliminary test procedures and analytical questions were carried out prior to SEP arrival on January 21st 2016. Satisfactory preliminary results were obtained leading to active investigation. Occurrences logged and post analytic evidence produced...

Logged incidents:

1. Three noted accounts of physical phenomena, ie physical manipulation, one account provides a digital log of the event at a time no human agencies were present in the incident location. Details of time stamp and incident recorded within the official completed documentation.

2. Three accounts of in air audible phenomena noted and heard by multiple witnesses at the time of the incidents. No rational explanations were discovered. Failed replications and incidents noted within the official completed documentation.

3. A large amount of unknown audible phenomena captured on digital recording devices and digital professional cameras during active investigation over the period of 6 days. 93% of audible incidents demonstrate possible vocal recordings. Electronic Voice Phenomena (EVP) obtained 427 recordings, 318 of those have now been categorised as Class B, 81 have been categorised as Class A and 28 have been categorised as Actual Voice Phenomena (AVP). Those vocal recordings in direct response to questions or current environmental undertakings. Three vocal in air audibles were also logged as noted in section 2. Many recordings demonstrate Irish Accents.

4. Research carried out to date: Environmental perimeters, geological and aerial survey, geomagnetic and electromagnetic measurements, magnetometer and radiation tests. Temperature and humidity analysis, electrical leakage survey, site maps and pre-build surveys (currently on-going). Stray reflective light conditions, psychoanalytic surveys and questionnaires completed. Interviews carried out with client and visiting priest.

Current diagnostic due to conclusive evidence: LIH
Localised Interactive Phenomena: Often referred to as an Intelligent Haunting.
Diminishing Possibilities: Evidence supports land locked phenomena with possible subtle decreasing incidents and passive physical occurrences continuing at low frequency/severity.

Dated: February 6th 2016.
Case Ref: 26411

Mr. Stephen Mera: SEP Director
BSc,Dip,fS,Dip,FPsy

CLEARED FOR RELEASE

Order Date	Item went Missing	Items I bought to mitigate our ghost problem	Quantity	Price
11/19/2012		Night Vision Spy Cam	1	$59.97
3/6/2014		Security Safe	1	$105.00
3/6/2014		Electronic Digital Safe	1	$98.90
3/24/2014	YES	Holy Water, Oil, candle - Jerusalem	1	$9.90
3/24/2014		Holy Water - Jordan River - 120ml 4.2 fl oz.	1	$13.99
5/21/2014	YES	Trendnet Wireless N Network Cloud Surveillance Camera	2	$149.99
5/24/2014		White Sage Incense, 120-Sticks	1	$8.50
5/24/2014		White Sage Incense 20 sticks	1	$11.99
6/25/2014	YES	Sony DCR-SX45 Camcorder	1	$198.00
8/6/2014		DC Power Adaptor 12 V DC 2.1MM	2	$1.99
8/6/2014		48-LED CCTV IR Infrared Night Vision Illuminator Light	1	$46.00
8/6/2014		CM Vision Wide Angle IR Illuminator	1	$8.99
9/18/2014		LE 20.0 M Pixel USB 6 LED Webcam Mic PC Laptop Camera	4	$3.93
10/15/2014		White Sage Jumbo Smudge Stick - 8-9 in.	2	$6.33
10/15/2014		JBJ Sac White Sage Incense, 120-Sticks	1	$5.25
10/15/2014		Dragons Blood - 120 Sticks Box - HEM Incense	1	$5.99
10/15/2014	YES	Olive Wood Catholic Crosses (4 Inches)	2	$6.99

Order Date	Item went Missing	Title	Quantity	Price
10/15/2014		White Sage 100 Incense Sticks (5 x 20 stick packs)	1	$6.99
10/20/2014	YES	316L Stainless Steel Pendant Necklace Silver Black Jesus Christ Crucifix Cross Vintage-with 23-inch Chain	1	$6.99
10/20/2014		Bell 22-1-33653-8 Cargo Net	2	$11.84
10/24/2014	YES	4.13 Inch Archangel - Saint Michael Standing on Demon's Head	1	$32.99
10/24/2014	Burned	Saint Michael and the Demon Old Masters Holy Card	4	$0.69
11/15/2014	YES	Men's Black Stainless-Steel Rosary Necklace with Cross 32" Strong 8mm	1	$22.95
11/19/2014	YES	The Ghost Meter EMF Sensor	1	$49.99
11/19/2014		Foscam FHC51 Hidden Clock Radio Mini Camera & DVR	1	$75.95
12/16/2014	YES	Olive Wood Catholic Crosses (4 Inches)	2	$7.99
12/23/2014		Palo Santo Holy Wood Incense Sticks 25 Pcs	1	$6.92
1/5/2015	YES	SanDisk 16GB Micro SDHC Memory Card with SD Adapter	5	$62.99

Ref Table: Items I bought from Amazon to mitigate the poltergeist activity.

PHOTOS FROM WITHIN THE BOTHELL HOME

Spring, 2014 – Exploding light fixtures.

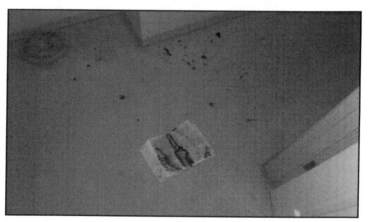

Spring, 2014 – 1st Bible Fire

This used to sit in the hallway. Was thrown at least eight more times. Took three men to carry it upstairs when we moved in

2nd Bible went missing. Returned a few hours later in the kitchen in this condition. Disembodied voice was later discovered. The voice utters 'Jesus Christ'

Summer 2014 - Master bedroom - One camera out of many.

Summer, 2014 – Office attack

Keith's office –Summer, 2014

Camera takes a series of snapshots (motion detected) the monitor no doubt. Folders and files being moved around. This camera went missing a few days later. Summer, 2014

Keith's face burned out. Pictures were packed away.

8:29:26 AM 3/3/2016

VALUATION

ACRES OR LOT NUMBER	LAND	BLDG	INITIAL	DATE

Previous house – I discovered this during a field trip to the county records office. Still trying to locate the tenants of this house.

Bothell, WA -- https://en.wikipedia.org/wiki/Bothell,_Washington Prior to European settlement, the Sammamish River Valley from Lake Washington to Issaquah Creek south and upstream of Lake Sammamish was inhabited by a population of as many as 200 Native Americans known as the Sammamish. The Sammamish were relocated after the Puget Sound War in 1856 to reservations and non-reservation lands.

Sammamish Tribe - https://en.wikipedia.org/wiki/Sammamish_people the largest Sammamish village was tlah-WAH-dees at the mouth of the Sammamish River, which at the time was between present-day Kenmore and Bothell. *History contradicts Ghost Adventures assessment of Native Americans living in the area.*

Recommended Reading

An Introduction to Parapsychology 5th Edition, Harvey J Irwin and Caroline A Watt
A.R.G Owen. Can We Explain the Poltergeist? 1964, Garrett Publications
Claude LeCouteux. The Secret History of Poltergeists and Haunted Houses, 2012, Inner Traditions
Michael Goss. Poltergeists an Annotated Bibliography of Works in English, circa 1880 – 1975 1979, the Scarecrow Press Inc.

Washington State Poltergeist Case – Keith Linder
https://www.facebook.com/Washington-State-Poltergiest-House-705963559540294/?ref=bookmarks
https://youtu.be/ZE-BpTve31E
The Beginning – Hallway 2012

https://youtu.be/uVZVtcjZzgo
2nd Bible Burning EVP at 2:08
"Jesus Christ"

https://youtu.be/AQpnnsvU5ws
House Attack, 2014

https://youtu.be/56vzeJFj6Zg
House Attack – Summer, 2014

https://youtu.be/AQpnnsvU5ws
House Attack – Summer, 2014

https://youtu.be/cMflNdqHayo
House and Office Attack

Evidence and Interviews

https://youtu.be/zhA-tqf19Es
Don Philips
January, 2016

https://youtu.be/YnEjPKWdca0
Zoho har Stargate TV

https://youtu.be/c3iD366V1hU
Car phenomenon
Winter, 2015

United States – Washington State Poltergeist

https://youtu.be/_pJLbMwP1w4
Karissa Fleck and Niki Novelle – Moving Bible pages

https://youtu.be/_xt7GiGhlrs
Doll video

Karissa Fleck Channel
https://www.youtube.com/channel/UCUNmdQbvf0ZRzsWf1GO64og/featur
ed

Niki Novelle Channel
https://www.youtube.com/channel/UCwjLfdpvYNulGGBz6L0p2AA

https://www.youtube.com/watch?v=PfH6mlKg63E
Keith Linder & Karissa Fleck interview
Paranormal Zone TV

https://youtu.be/_rlldSmE5T4
In-Depth Interview 2015
Washington State Poltergeist Team

http://supernaturalmagazine.com/articles/living-with-a-poltergeist-an-
interview-with-keith-linder
Living with a Poltergeist

https://www.youtube.com/watch?v=dRetk4MaDvI&t=2178s
Episode 22: Washington State Poltergeist [Keith Linder Interview] (Secret
Transmission Podcast)

http://www.coasttocoastam.com/pages/parapsychologists-declare-home-has-
poltergeist/
2016 Parapsychologists Declare Home Has Poltergeist

http://komonews.com/news/local/bothell-man-claims-his-house-is-haunted-
this-is-no-casper
2014 Bothell man claims his house is haunted: 'This is no Casper'.

https://www.youtube.com/watch?v=aPpPDAG-WFc&feature=youtu.be
KOFY Episode 6 Keith Linder Interview
https://www.youtube.com/watch?v=HBXCL81h3jI&t=19s
KOFY Episode 5 Keith Linder Interview

https://paranormalheraldmagazine.com/2016/01/10/the-two-leading-ladies-of-the-paranormal-tackle-the-demons-in-seattle-case-niki-paraunnormal-and-karissa-fleck-2/

Niki *ParaUnNormal* and Karissa Fleck tackle The Demons in Seattle case,

http://jimharold.com/tag/keith-linder/

Guests: Keith Linder, Don Philips, Steve Mera

http://www.americas-most-haunted.com/2016/03/18/washington-poltergeist-case-psychic-attorney-mark-anthony-hours-amamericas-haunted-radio/

Washington Poltergeist Case on After Hours AM/America's Most Haunted Radio

https://www.youtube.com/watch?v=VzB-i2V9y70&t=8s

Demons in Seattle with Keith Linder Part 1 - December 10, 2016

Appendix A:
Flies November 2014

Flies began appearing the week of November 17th, 2014. One fly would appear for three days straight. The interesting thing about these flies was their size. They were the size of a US nickel. The first fly to appear was in the hallway. Very close to where the Die KL writing was that appeared on Christmas Day. I killed this fly within seconds of seeing it—twenty-four hours later another fly appeared this time in my office. I killed that fly very quickly and soon noticed something. Why are these flies easy to kill? I never saw the flies fly or land somewhere; there was no buzzing or humming sound. They just appeared out of nowhere—they appeared motionless. When I killed the second fly I thought to myself, *it didn't move a muscle while I searched for something to kill it with. It just sat still like the one in the hallway above our bedroom door.* Day three another fly appeared. If I didn't know any better, I'd say that it was the same fly. They acted the same: motionless. The third fly to appear (day 3) landed in the area where the first Bible was taken. The same table, same spot.

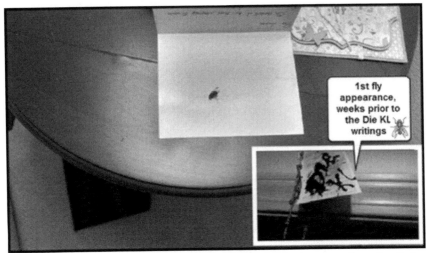

1st fly appearance, weeks prior to the Die KL writings

Fig A-1 3rd siting - Living room lap table. Fly was in the spot where the first Bible went missing. These flies are fearless. They didn't act like typical flies which is fly off when you try to kill them. They appeared when we had snow on the ground.

Appendix B:
The Disappearing Cross

Fig B-1 Unimaginable asportation story

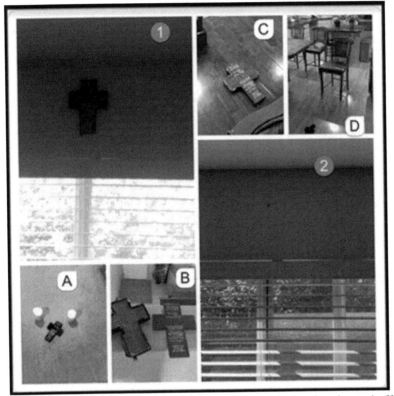

Fig B-2 Multiple instances where the cross was mysteriously relocated off bedroom wall A.) Hallway, surrounded by candles B.) Washing machine C.) Kitchen table D.) Kitchen floor

Appendix C:
Foul Stench Smell

I vividly remember five instances of foul smell. In the location (see below) where the dent in the floor is: from spring, summer, fall, winter, 2014. A smell that brings you to your knees almost. Very localized. I'm talking about being confined to a small area (see below). Move an inch, and the smell is gone. Return where you were before, the smell is there. The smell would appear a few times when entering the master bedroom. Imagine every septic tank on your block for twenty-plus houses all backing up. That's how bad the odor was. The stench appeared abruptly and vanished abruptly. An important thing to remember about this smell is it smelled like rotten flesh, mixed with bowel. It lasted about three to five minutes. Then *POOF!* It's gone.

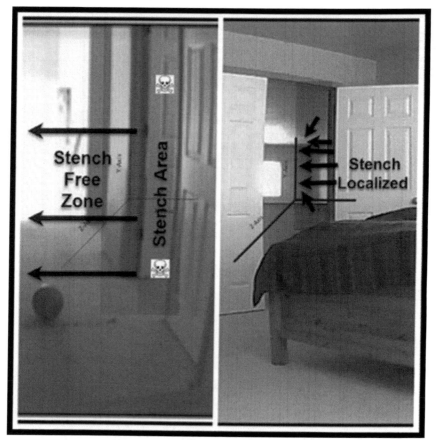

Fig C-1 Foul stench smell – Localized

Authors Afterword

If any of my family members had warned me to stay away from haunted houses before moving to Seattle, I would have looked at them and said, what are you talking about? I would have laughed while uttering that's never going to happen. The Pacific Northwest is known for a lot of remarkable things. Haunted houses are not one of them. NOTE: another reason why we weren't taken seriously.

That's unfortunate because there's a lot of stuff going on up here that the paranormal community should pay attention to. A lot of history is being ignored based on Seattle's geographic location. I'm talking about the history between settlers and Native Americans. Why ignore it? I mean how many times can you investigate Gettysburg? How many articles must be written about Enfield, about Amityville, before realizing there's more to poltergeists than those two cases. Way more. The Pacific Northwest is one of those places. Want to advance the subject matter? Visit the Pacific Northwest.

The high-level assessment given to me by The Scientific Establishment of Parapsychology classifies our house an intelligent haunting, aka LIH - Localized Intelligent Haunting. I wasn't surprised to see the word intelligent listed. I mean the evidence alone supports that conclusion. What Tina and I have been battling for the last four years has been nothing short of the word intelligent. Nothing short of deliberate.

Speaking of Tina, what's our status? At the time this book was completed, we were amicable friends. That friendship has since evaporated. Tina wants nothing to do with the memory of that house. Nothing to do with the findings of both UK and US teams. I shared it with her. I had to. Of course, she pushed it away. And that's fine. Most people do. In Chapter Seven I said different people respond to the paranormal differently, Tina is no exception. She and I still have a bond, regardless of how she feels. We've been "Geist" baptized. Four years, ladies and gentlemen. Four years living with a poltergeist. Not too many people can say that. We can.

So, what happens now? What are our options? The only thing left now is to live with it. Sounds cheapish to say, but it's true. The only I can do now is doing what I was doing before May 1st, 2012, which is live my life, the best way I can. There's just one small little detail worth mentioning. There's no going back to the status quo after seeing what I've seen. It changed me tremendously. Now I have to wait. I have to wait for the complete report that Steve Mera and his organization promised me.

The question both men were asking while here was, where are these unexplained voices coming from? We're talking about an inordinate number of EVPs. Why this house? Jennifer and Fr. Roy Sr. spoke of a smallpox outbreak in the mid-1800's that decimated hundreds of people living in the area. We're talking Native American and settlers. Could the voices be from them? But that begs the question, why this house? No one knows the answer to that, and guess what? That's OK. If you hit a brick wall, you just hit a brick wall. But you don't quit.

Leonardo da Vinci said that it best when he said, "Works of art are never finished only abandoned." Not only is that true in art, but it's also true in paranormal research. Horror aside, there's so much going on in this house, that deserves attention. I'm talking about constant attention. How can you research something if you're financially and logistically challenged? I'm aiming that question directly at the paranormal / parapsychology community. So, let's see what The Scientific Establishment of Parapsychology can come up with. Let's see what report gets handed to me. I've been promised one. Let's see if it gets delivered. If I have it, you'll have it. I promise.

I'll end by giving thanks. First, thank you goes out to Mary (that's not her real name). Thank you for finding me online, for encouraging me to re-opening this case. What an awesome snowball effect. Thank you, Fr. Roy Sr. You and your wife were an immense help to me. Thank you for the humor and the knowledge. The next thank you goes to a book I read titled *The Poltergeist Phenomenon* written by Michael Clarkston. That book opened up a whole new world for me. If you want a crash course in poltergeist, start there.

Jeremy Scott, Jim Harold, and Norene Sampiere Balovich—all three of you deserve a tremendous thank you. You knew there was more to this case than what originally reported on Travel Channel's *Ghost Adventures.* You gave me a forum. Thanks.

I can't forget to thank my friends in the Pacific Northwest. Thanks for sticking with me when things got dark. When things got bleak. Special thanks to Jackie, Justin, Laura, Barbara, Erlinda, Jose, Tony, and Joe for coming to our house even after learning of our situation.

Thank you, Vanessa, Jenn, and Dominic, you all were great consultants on the case. Thank you, Rick Hale. My fellow Star Wars fan. Thank you, kind sir. Thank you, Steve and Don. Kudos for being risk takers. The world awaits your official report. I'm pretty sure some of your UK colleagues doubted the validity of this case. Who's doubting now?

Lastly, thank you Niki Novelle, Karissa Fleck, Jennifer (*No Bull Paranormal*), and my friend Patty. Thank you, Niki, for your challenging work and dedication. I'm glad you witnessed the loud bangs and pulsating mattress. You forever have a story to tell. Karissa, you lived in the house for almost a month. That has to mean something—it does mean something. It means the paranormal community should mimic you versus what they see on television. Thank you, Jennifer, for hanging in there all the way, for responding quickly, and for hugging Tina. Thank you, Patty. I'm so glad we've maintained a friendship after our first encounter. God bless you and your wonderful family.

Postscript

I invited Steve and Don back to Bothell April of 2016. *Three months after their first visit.* Activity that had went dormant in 2014 were showing signs of resurfacing. New wall markings began to appear. This time downstairs. The men decided to bring a second organization this time—the SSPR (Scottish Society for Psychical Research), researcher Nick Kyle. This time they stayed eight days. I moved out of the house two weeks later. May 8th, 2016.

Fig. Oct 31st / Nov 1st Office attack wall markings

Analysis of the wall from the October 31st, 2014 wall markings consisted of tricalcium phosphate (or hydroxylapatite) high concentrate, calcium carbonate and carbon. 100% organic. The final verdict from multiple paint stores and galleries. Bone Black / Bone Char (cow bones, bison bones). The lab department at my place of employment conducted the 1st analysis. NOTE: no team has ever asked for a sample of the wall or door to conduct an analysis themselves. Including the Travel Channel's *Ghost Adventures* team.

Lights .s.

4402 . SW

, WA

February 23, 2017

Re: 4434   h 1

Leak from Ceiling in

On approximately Tuesday May 10 ... ith reported that he had dripping coming out of his ceiling.

Zack went into P1 and discovered dripp... ming ... t of the ceiling hallway outside of the kitchen. Found damp carpet, no water on the lam...ate. He ...ocked upstairs to see what had occurred above to cause this. They looked at all the suspect p... der the kitchen sink, bathroom sink and dishwasher and there was no obvious cause. Per P7 nothing h... ...d to their knowledge! After Keith's report, he cleaned up the water and there were no further o...ur ...ces.

Very Truly Yours,

An

Property Manager

May 10th, 2016. 2nd new place of residence. Unexplained water puddles. Zach - building maintenance. Who responded to my call of unexplained water drippings? This case remains open.

Front Cover Design by: Kevin Cassidy

https://qxigears.deviantart.com/

Back Cover Design by Keith Linder

Made in the USA
San Bernardino, CA
17 July 2018